The Fall

Dispensational Truth

or

God's Plan and Purpose in the Ages

By

Clarence Larkin

Author of a Work on
The Book of Revelation, and a Pamphlet on
The Second Coming of Christ

Copyright © 2015 Merchant Books

ISBN 978-1-60386-705-4

DIGITALIZED BY
WATCHMAKER PUBLISHING
ALL RIGHTS RESERVED

Dispensational Truth

or

God's Plan and Purpose in the Ages

By

Clarence Larkin

Author of a Work on
The Book of Revelation, and a Pamphlet on
The Second Coming of Christ

For Sale by the Publishers
Rev. Clarence Larkin Est.

This Book is
DEDICATED
to the
LORD JESUS CHRIST
who, through the Holy Spirit, has imparted to me the knowledge
and mechanical skill to construct these Charts.

Table of Contents

CHAPTERS

#	Title	Page
1.	The Prophetic Word	2
2.	Pre-Millennialism	4
3.	Mountain Peaks of Prophecy	6
4.	The Second Coming of Christ	8
5.	Rightly Dividing the Word	19
6.	The Present Evil World	44
7.	The Dispensational Work of Christ	46
8.	The Dispensational Work of the Holy Spirit	53
9.	The Jews	59
10.	The Gentiles	67
11.	The Church	74
12.	The King	82
13.	The Kingdom	85
14.	The Spirit World	96
15.	Spiritualism	100
16.	The Resurrections	103
17.	The Judgments	107
18.	Satan	111
19.	Antichrist	115
20.	The Satanic Trinity	123
21.	The Four Gospels	126
22.	The Seven Churches	128
23.	The Tribulation	133
24.	Babylon the Great	140
25.	Renovation of the Earth	144
26.	The Covenants	149
27.	The Mysteries	151
28.	Types and Antitypes	153
29.	The 3 Trees to Which Israel is Compared in Scripture	156
30.	The Feasts of the Lord	159
31.	The Offerings	161
32.	The Dispensational Teaching of the Great Pyramid	164
33.	Scripture Numerics	171
34.	The Signs of the Times	173

CHARTS

#	Title	Page
1.	The Ages As Viewed From Different Standpoints	3½
2.	The Mountain Peaks of Prophecy	5½
3.	The Perspective of Prophecy	7½
4.	The Two Comings	8
5.	The Two Stages of the Coming	12
6.	Time Element of the Comings	14
7.	7000 Years of Human History	16
8.	Rightly Dividing the Word	17½
9.	Relation of Jew, Gentile and Church to Each Other	19½
10.	The Times and Seasons	20
11.	The Creation of the Earth	21½
12.	Generation	23
13.	Six Days of Re-creation	23½
14.	First Day (Cosmic Light)	25
15.	Second Day (Firmament Formed)	25
16.	Third Day (Land and Vegetation)	26
17.	Fourth Day (Solar Light Restored)	27
18.	Fifth Day (Fish and Fowl)	27
19.	Sixth Day (Animals and Man)	28
20.	Diagram of the Eight Works of the Six Days	30
21.	The Seven Cosmic Phases of the Earth	30
22.	Degeneration	31½
23.	Edenic Dispensation	32
24.	Book of Genesis	33½
25.	Antediluvian Dispensation	35
26.	Post-Diluvian Dispensation	37
27.	Patriarchal Dispensation	38
28.	Legal Dispensation	38
29.	Ecclesiastical Dispensation	39

CHARTS

		PAGE
30.	The Tribulation	40
31.	Dispensation of Judgment	41
32.	Regeneration	42
33.	Messianic Dispensation	43
34.	Perfect Dispensation	43
35.	The World's 7 Great Crises	43½
36.	The Prophetic Days of Scripture	43¾
37.	Greater Life and Work of Christ	46
38.	The Heavenly Tabernacle	52
39.	The Jews	59½
40.	Book of Exodus	60½
41.	The Royal Grant to Abraham	66
42.	Book of Daniel	67½
43.	Prophetical Chronology	71½
44.	Daniel's Seventy Weeks	72
45.	Map of Old Roman Empire	73
46.	The Gentile Nations	73½
47.	The Church	74½
48.	Failure of Christianity	77½
49.	God's Eternal Purpose As to the Earth	81½
50.	The King	82½
51.	Book of Matthew	84½
52.	Kingdom of God Vs. Kingdom of Heaven	85
53.	The Kingdom	85½
54.	The Church Vs. the Kingdom	86½
55.	Kingdom of Heaven Parables	87½
56.	The Millennial Land	93½
57.	Book of Ezekiel	95½
58.	The Spirit World	96½
59.	Threefold Nature of Man	99
60.	The Three Tabernacles	100
61.	The Resurrections	105
62.	First and Second Resurrection	106
63.	Resurrections and Judgments	107½
64.	Judgment of Reward	110
65.	Satan	111½
66.	Antichrist and Times of the Gentiles	115½
67.	The Four Gospels	126
68.	When the New Testament Books Were Written	127
69.	Book of Revelation	127½
70.	Messages to the 7 Churches	128½
71.	The 7 Churches	129
72.	Messages to the 7 Churches	129
73.	Daniel's Seventieth Week	133½
74.	Daniel and Revelation Compared	139½
75.	The 3 Stages of the Earth	144
76.	Renovation of the Earth	145
77.	The Holy City—New Jerusalem	148
78.	The Covenants	149½
79.	The Mysteries	151½
80.	Five Fingers Pointing to Christ	153
81.	Types and Antitypes	153½
82.	"As" and "So"	154
83.	The Feasts of the Lord	159½
84.	The Tabernacle	160½
85.	Book of Leviticus	161½
86.	Great Pyramid (Diagram A)	165
87.	Vertical Section of Great Pyramid	166
88.	Christ and the Saints Compared to the Heavenly Bodies	170½
89.	The Weeks of Scripture	171½
90.	The Signs of the Times	174

CUTS

		PAGE
1.	The Passover	58
2.	Michael and the Dragon	114
3.	The White Horse Rider	115
4.	Daniel's Fourth Wild Beast	116
5.	Ram and He Goat	117
6.	Four Horned Ram	117
7.	Paul's Man of Sin	119
8.	John's Beast	120
9.	The Scarlet Woman	122
10.	The False Prophet	123
11.	Image of the Beast	125
12.	The Sun Clothed Woman	133
13.	The Vine	155
14.	The Fig-Tree	156
15.	The Olive	157

FOREWORD

The preparation and publication of this book is a wonderful story of Divine leading. The Author by profession was a Mechanical Engineer and Architect. When he entered the Gospel Ministry direct from business and without any previous theological training, at the age of 34, he believed that he would have no further use for his skill as a draughtsman and sold all his professional books and appliances except his drawing instruments. His first charge was in a small town, where he remained fifteen years. He was not premillennialist at the time of his ordination, but his study of the Scriptures, aided by some books that fell into his hands, led him to adopt that view. He began to make large colored wall charts on "Gospel Truth" for use in the pulpit. This led to his being invited to teach, in connection with his pastoral work, in two Bible Institutes. During this time he published a number of "Prophetical Charts" which had a wide circulation. These led to the request that he publish a book, illustrated with charts, on "Prophetic Truth." But it was not until the spring of 1915 that the Lord laid it upon his heart to prepare a work on

"DISPENSATIONAL TRUTH"
or
"GOD'S PLAN AND PURPOSE IN THE AGES"

illustrated with charts. The designing and drawing of the charts and the writing of the descriptive matter took over three years. The book therefore has not been hastily gotten up. It is the outcome of over 30 years of careful and patient study of the Prophetic Scriptures, and aims to give not the opinions of men, but the teaching of the Word of God. The writer's purpose has been to prepare a standard work on "Dispensational Truth." That such a work was greatly longed for is evidenced by the reception the book has had. In ten months the first edition was exhausted and was widely circulated all over the world. The first edition was a "feeler" to see whether such a book would be in demand, and so was printed and circulated in the cheapest form. When the Author awoke to the fact that the book was what the "Students of Prophecy" were looking for, he decided to revise and enlarge the book and put it out in a more substantial and usable form, but before he could do this, a second edition was called for and had to be printed in the old form.

This, the Third Edition, has been revised and enlarged by the addition of twice as many charts and twice as much descriptive matter as the previous editions, and the charts are now inserted in the descriptive matter where they belong. The book has also been printed in Atlas form, 11 inches square, and bound in cloth, making it more convenient to handle and carry about. The large charts of the earlier editions have not been reduced in size or form, but are printed from the old plates, and when the book is open, spread across two pages. This method and manner of printing the book adds greatly to its cost, but the buyer gets far more than the additional cost in the increased value of the contents of the book, which contains twice as much as the previous edition. There are 170 double pages of descriptive matter in the book, or 340 single pages, and as each page contains one-half more matter than the page of an ordinary book, there are the equivalent of 500 pages of an ordinary book.

If the Author had had to employ a skilled draughtsman to draw the charts the cost of the book would have been prohibitive. In fact, the charts could not have been drawn that way, for the draughtsman would have had to have had the Scriptural knowledge of the Author; for the charts had to be thought out and developed under the direction and guidance of the Holy Spirit. In this the Holy Spirit did not confuse the Author by suggesting all the charts at one time. When one was completed another was suggested. And upon more than one occasion when a problem arose the answer was given in the night or at awakening in the morning.

The Author does not claim infallibility for the charts, but having drawn the main chart, "Rightly Dividing the Word of Truth," it stands to reason that in developing the "Sectional" or "Topical" Charts, if he had made an error in the main chart it would have been detected in the "Sectional" or "Topical" Charts. It is this agreement in the study of the "Sectional" or "Topical" charts with the main chart, that confirms the Author in his belief that the charts are scripturally correct.

The Author has always deplored the tendency of writers on "Dispensational Truth" to say uncharitable things of each other, and to unfairly present the side of their opponent; he has therefore earnestly and prayerfully sought to avoid any such criticisms and to simply expound the Word of God as the Holy Spirit opened it up to him. He has sought not to be influenced by any religious or doctrinal bias, and with "open mind" to follow the leading of the Holy Spirit, and let the Scriptures say what they want to say. His writings therefore must be judged by their agreement or disagreement with the Holy Scriptures.

With profound gratitude and thankfulness for the blessing of his Heavenly Father upon the previous editions of this work, the Author sends forth this Third Revised and Enlarged Edition, earnestly praying that it may be of untold blessing to thousands of God's dear children who love the Lord's Appearing, and be an instrument in the hands of the Holy Spirit for the conversion of the unsaved, and of those who "deceitfully handle" the Word of God.

THE AUTHOR.

CLARENCE LARKIN,
"Sunnyside," Fox Chase, Philadelphia, Pa.
March 25, 1920.

I
THE PROPHETIC WORD

The Bible is not a systematic treatise on Theology, or Morals, or History, or Science, or any other topic. It is a REVELATION of God, of the Fall of Man, the Way of Salvation, and of God's "Plan and Purpose in the Ages." It treats of—

1. **Four Persons**—God the Father, God the Son, God the Holy Spirit, and Satan.
2. **Three Places**—Heaven, Earth and Hell.
3. **Three Classes of People**—The Jew, the Gentile, and the Church of God.

The Scriptures were given to us piece-meal, "at sundry times and in divers manners." Holy men of God spake as they were moved by the Holy Spirit, during a period of 1600 years, extending from B. C. 1492 to A. D. 100. The Bible consists of 66 separate books; 39 in the Old Testament, and 27 in the New Testament. These books were written by about 40 different authors. By kings such as David and Solomon; by statesmen, as Daniel and Nehemiah; by priests, as Ezra; by men learned in the wisdom of Egypt, as Moses; by men learned in Jewish law, as Paul. By a herdsman, Amos; a tax-gatherer, Matthew; fishermen, as Peter, James and John, who were "unlearned and ignorant" men; a physician, Luke; and such mighty "seers" as Isaiah, Ezekiel and Zechariah.

It is not an Asiatic book, though it was written in that part of the world. Its pages were penned in the **Wilderness** of Sinai, the cliffs of Arabia, the hills and towns of Palestine, the courts of the Temple, the schools of the prophets at Bethel and Jericho, in the palace of Shushan in Persia, on the banks of the river Chebar in Babylonia, in the dungeons of Rome, and on the lonely Island of Patmos, in the Aegean Sea.

Imagine another book compiled in a similar manner. Suppose, for illustration, that we take 66 medical books written by 40 different physicians and surgeons during a period of 1600 years, of various schools of medicine, as Allopathy, Homeopathy, Hydropathy, Osteopathy, etc., and bind them all together, and then undertake to doctor a man according to that book, what success would we expect to have, and what accord would there be in such a medical work.

While the Bible has been compiled in the manner described, it is not a "heterogeneous jumble" of ancient history, myths, legends, religious speculations and superstitions. There is a progress of revelation and doctrine in it. The Judges knew more than the Patriarchs, the Prophets than the Judges, the Apostles than the Prophets. The Old and New Testaments are not separate and distinct books, the New taking the place of the Old, they are the two halves of a whole. The New is "enfolded" in the Old, and the Old is "unfolded" in the New. You cannot understand Leviticus without Hebrews, or Daniel without Revelation, or the Passover or Isaiah 53 without the gospels of Matthew, Mark, Luke and John.

While the Bible is a revelation from God, it is not written in a superhuman or celestial language. If it were we could not understand it. Its supernatural origin however is seen in the fact that it can be translated into any language and not lose its virility or spiritual life giving power, and when translated into any language it fixes that language in its purest form.

The language however of the Bible is of three kinds. **Figurative, Symbolical and Literal.** Such expressions as "Harden not your heart," "Let the dead bury their dead," are figurative, and their meaning is made clear by the context.

Symbolic language, like the description of Nebuchadnezzar's "Colossus," Daniel's "Four Wild Beasts," or Christ in the midst of the "Seven Candlesticks," is explained, either in the same chapter, or somewhere else in the Bible.

The rest of the language of the Bible is to be interpreted according to the customary rules of grammar and rhetoric. That is, we are to read the Bible as we would read any other book, letting it say what it wants to say, and not allegorize or spiritualize its meaning. It is this false method of interpreting Scripture that has led to the origin of so many religious sects and denominations. There are three things that we must avoid in the handling of God's Word.

1. The **Misinterpretation** of Scripture.
2. The **Misapplication** of Scripture.
3. The **Dislocation** of Scripture.

The trouble is men are not willing to let the Scriptures say what they want to say. This is largely due to their training, environment, prejudice, or desire to make the Scriptures teach some favorite doctrine.

Then again we must not overlook the **"Parabolic Method"** of imparting truth. Jesus did not invent it, though He largely used it, it was employed by the Old Testament prophets. In the New Testament it is used as a **"Mystery Form"** of imparting truth. Matt. 13:10-17. A mystery is not something that cannot be known, but something that for the time being is hidden. I hand you a sealed letter. What it contains is a mystery to you. Break the seal and read the letter and it ceases to be a mystery. But you may not be able to read the letter, because it is written in a language with which you are not familiar. Learn the language and the mystery ceases. But perhaps the letter contains technical terms which you do not understand, learn their meaning and all will be plain. That is the way with the Mysteries of the Scriptures, learn to read them by the help of their author, the Holy Spirit, and they will no longer be mysteries.

This brings us to the great question—

Is The Bible God's Book Or Man's Book?

That is, did God write it, or is it simply a collection of the writings of men? If it is simply a collection of the writings of men, without any divine guidance, then it is no more reliable than are the writings of men; but if God wrote it, then it must be true, and we can depend upon its statements. It is clear from the character of the Bible that it is not the work of man, for man could not have written it if he would, and would not have written it if he could.

It details with scathing and unsparing severity the sins of its greatest men, as Abraham, Jacob, Moses, David and Solomon, charging them with falsehood, treachery, pride, adultery, cowardice, murder and gross licentiousness, and presents the history of the Children of Israel as a humiliating record of ingratitude, idolatry, unbelief and rebellion, and it is safe to say, that the Jews, unguided and undirected by the Holy Spirit, would never have chronicled the sinful history of their nation.

How then was the Bible written? The Bible itself gives the answer.

"ALL Scripture Is Given By INSPIRATION OF GOD." II Timothy 3:16.

I. **What Are We To Understand By the "INSPIRATION" of the Scriptures?**

We are to understand that God directed men, chosen by Himself, to put into writing such messages, laws, doctrines, historical facts, and revelations, as He wished men to know.

All Scripture (the **Graphe** writing), is given by **inspiration** (The-op-neu-stos), that is, is—

GOD BREATHED.

That is, God Himself or through the Holy Spirit told holy men of old just what to write. The Bible, then, IS the Word of God, and does not simply here and there contain it. God is a **Person** and can both **Write and Speak.** He wrote the two "Tables of Testimony" on stone. Ex. 31:18; 32:16, and on the wall of Belshazzar's Palace. Dan. 5:5, 24-28. He talked with **Moses** on the Mount when He gave him the Specifications for the Tabernacle and its furnishings, and all the Levitical Law and order of service. **He spoke** at the Baptism of Jesus (Matt. 3:17), and on the Mount of Transfiguration. Matt. 17:5, and one day when Jesus was talking to the multitude. John 12:27-30. But God not only spoke directly to men, He spoke to them in the person of Jesus, for Jesus was **God Manifest In The Flesh.** John 1:1-5, 14. I Tim. 3:16. Matthew and John's Gospels contain 49 chapters, 1950 **verses,** 1140 of which, almost three-fifths, were spoken by Jesus, and He claimed that what He spake, He spake not of Himself, but that the Father which sent Him, gave Him commandment **What He Should Speak.** John 12:49, 50. We see then that God can both write and speak, and therefore can tell others what to write and speak.

II. Does the Inspiration of the Bible Extend to Every Part?

Yes. From the dry lists in Chronicles to the very words of God in Exodus, and through Christ. And more, it extends to every **sentence, word, mark, point, jot and tittle in the original parchments.** When Jesus said in Matt. 5:17, 18, That not one "jot" or "tittle" should pass from the Law until all be fulfilled, he referred to the smallest letter (jot) and the smallest mark (tittle), of the Hebrew language, thus indicating that even they were inspired, and were necessary for a complete understanding of God's meaning in His Word.

But how about the words of Satan, and wicked and uninspired men, the genealogical tables, and the account of the Fall of Man, the Flood and other historical portions of the Bible. They were inspired of **Record.** That is, the inspired penman or historian was told what historical facts to record and what to omit. To one who has read the Old Testament, and also profane history covering the same period, with its legends and traditions, and detailed descriptions, it is very clear that the writers of the Old Testament were divinely inspired to record only those things that would throw light on God's Plan and Purpose in the Ages.

III. HOW Were These Men Inspired to Write the Scriptures?

Were they simply thrown into a kind of "spell," or "ecstasy," or "trance," and wrote under its influence whatever came into their mind, or did God through the Holy Spirit, **dictate to them the exact words to use?**

We know that thought can only be expressed in words and those words must express the **exact thought** of the speaker or writer, otherwise his exact thought is not expressed. We see then that inerrancy demands that the sacred writer be simply an amanuensis. This we see is what the Scriptures claim for themselves. In II Pet. 1:20, 21, we read that—"No prophecy of the Scripture is of any **private interpretation.**" That is, no man has a right to say what the Scriptures, according to his opinion, means. Why? Because—

"The Prophecy came not in old time by the **will of man,** but holy men of God spake as they were **Moved by the HOLY GHOST.**"

And this is confirmed by the fact that much that the Old Testament Prophets wrote they did not themselves understand. I Pet. 1: 10, 11. They must then have been mere amanuenses, recording words that needed an interpreter. That they were mere instruments is shown by the fact that not all of them were good or holy men, as Balaam (Num. 22:38; 23:26), King Saul (I Sam. 10:10-12; 19:20-24), the Prophet of Bethel (I Kings 13:7-10; 20:22; 26), and **Caiaphas,** John 11:49-52.

That the Old Testament writers spake and wrote the exact words that God gave to them is clear from their own statements. Moses declares that the Lord said unto him—"Now therefore go, and I will be with thy mouth, and **teach thee what thou shalt say.**" Ex. 4:10-12. The Prophet Jeremiah says—

"Then the Lord put forth His hand, and touched my mouth, And the Lord said unto me, Behold, I have put **My Words In Thy Mouth.**" Jer. 1:6-9.

Ezekiel, Daniel, and all the prophets make the same claim. The expressions—"**The Lord Said,**" "**The Lord Spake Saying,**" "**Thus Saith the Lord,**" etc., etc., occur 560 times in the Pentateuch, 300 times in the Historical and Prophetical books, 1200 times in the Prophets (24 times in Malachi alone), in all over 2000 times in the Old Testament, thus proving the statement of Peter, that Holy men of God spake **as they were moved by the Holy Ghost.**

But you say—"If this be true how do you account for the difference of style of the writers; for Isaiah's style is different from Ezekiel's or Daniel's, and Peter's from that of John or Paul?" This is easily explained. On the principle that when we wish a legal document written we choose a lawyer, or a poetical article a poet; so God when He wanted to speak in symbols chose an Ezekiel, a Daniel, a John, or in poetry a David.

How are we to explain the fact that sometimes a New Testament writer in quoting from the Old Testament, instead of quoting literally paraphrases the quotation? For instance in Amos 9:11 we read:

"In that day will I raise up the Tabernacle of David that is fallen, and close up the breaches thereof; and I will raise up his ruins, and I will build it as in the days of old."

But when the Apostle James, in the First Church Council at Jerusalem, quotes this passage, he paraphrases it, saying—

"After this I will return, and will build again the Tabernacle of David, which is fallen down; and I will build again the ruins thereof, and I will set it up." Acts 15:16.

Why the change in the wording? Simply because the author of both passages was not Amos or James, but the Holy Spirit, and an author has a perfect right to change the phraseology of a statement he may make in the first chapter of his book, in the tenth chapter, if by so doing, without contradicting himself, he can make his meaning clearer.

That is an illuminating statement in I Pet. 1:11, where the Apostle tells us that it was the "**Spirit of Christ**" that testified through the Prophets of His "**Sufferings.**" That is, the "**Spirit of Christ**" took possession of the Prophets and through them forecast or prophecied His "Sufferings" on the Cross, as in Isa. 53:1-12.

The question is often asked, "Is there any difference between Bible Inspiration and the so-called 'inspiration' of Poets, Orators, Preachers, and Writers of today?" In answering the question we must distinguish between "Inspiration," "Revelation," and "Illumination."

As we have seen "Bible Inspiration" is something totally different and unique from the inspiration of Poets, Writers and Public Speakers. It is an inspiration in which the **Exact Words of God Are Imparted to the Speaker or Writer by the Holy Spirit.**

The "Ages" As Viewed From Different Standpoints

As The Jew

As Post-Millenni...

As Pre-Millenni...

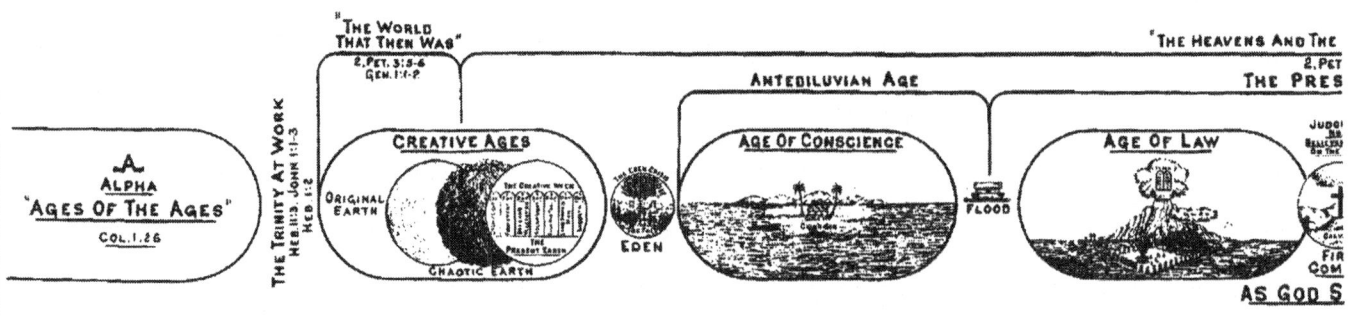

As God S...

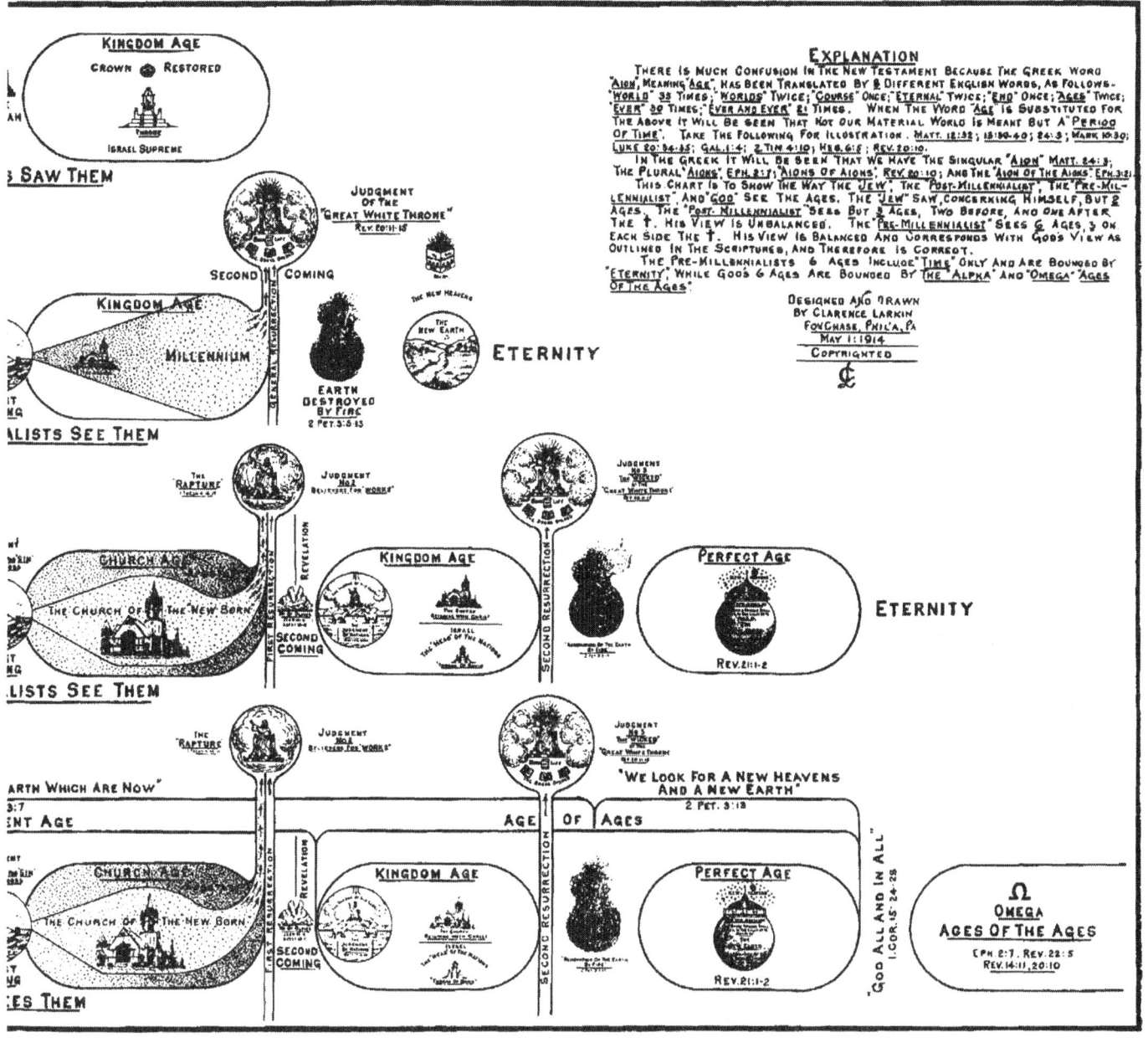

"Bible Revelation" is the disclosure to men of things that they otherwise could never know. Things hidden in the mind of God, such as His "Plan and Purpose in the Ages."

"Bible Revelation" ceased with the Book of Revelation. There has been no new revelation from God since then. When men today claim that they have received some new revelation they must be classed as imposters.

"Spiritual Illumination" is different from either Bible Inspiration or Revelation. It is the **Work of the Holy Spirit** in the Believer, by which he has his "Spiritual Understanding" opened to understand the Scriptures. John 16: 12-15. The "Natural Man" cannot receive the things of the "Spirit of God," neither can he know them, because they are **Spiritually Discerned.** I Cor. 2: 11-14. The work then of the Holy Spirit in these days is not to impart some new revelation to men, or to inspire them to write or speak as the Prophets and Apostles of old, but to so illuminate men's minds and open up their understanding of the Scriptures that their heart will burn within them as they compare Scripture with Scripture, and have revealed to them God's Plan and Purpose in the Ages as disclosed in His Holy Word.

II
PRE-MILLENNIALISM

The time of the Second Coming of Christ is the key that unlocks all "Dispensational Truth." The vast majority of Christians believe in the personal return of the Lord, but they differ as to the time. They are divided into two schools, the "Pre-Millennialists" and the "Post-Millennialists." The "Pre-Millennialists" believe that Christ will return before the Millennium, the "Post Millennialists" that He will not come until after. By the "Millennium" is meant the period of 1000 years mentioned in Rev. 20: 1-7. It is a common, but wholly erroneous impression, that Pre-Millennialists base their belief mainly, if not solely, on this passage in the Apocalypse. The fact is, the question of whether Christ's return will precede or follow the Millennium antedates the Apocalypse. The Old Testament prophets in plain language, and in glowing terms, foretold an era or age of universal righteousness and peace on this earth, under the reign of "Messiah the Prince." That the disciples were not mistaken in their belief in such an "Earthly Kingdom," ruled over by their promised Messiah, is evident from the fact that Jesus never reproved them for holding such a belief. And after His resurrection, and previous to His Ascension, when they asked Him if He would "at that time restore the Kingdom to Israel" (Acts 1: 6). He did not say—"You are mistaken in your idea of an 'Earthly Kingdom,' the **Kingdom** I came to set up, and that was meant by the prophets, is a 'Spiritual Kingdom,'" but He said—"It is not for you to know the 'Times' and 'Seasons.'" That is, when it shall be set up.

The whole teaching of the Old Testament as to the "Coming of the Messiah" is Pre-Millennial. The only use that Premillennialites have for the "Thousand Year" passage in Rev. 20: 1-7 is to fix the length of that "Age of Righteousness and Peace." In fact Jewish tradition, based on the "Sabbatic Rest" of Gen. 2: 1-3, taught that the "Seventh Thousand Years" from Creation was to be a period of "Sabbatic Rest," or what we call the Millennium. The passage in Revelation simply confirms this tradition. Expunge the passage and you do not weaken the argument; you only leave as uncertain **the length of** time that Age shall last.

The Apostolic Church was Pre-Millennial, and for over 200 years no other view was entertained. The writings of the "Church Fathers" abound in evidence of the fact. But about A. D. 250, Origen, one of the Church Fathers, conceived the idea that the words of scripture were but the "husk" in which was hid the "kernel" of scripture truth. At once he began to "Allegorize" and "Spiritualize" the Scriptures, and thus founded that school of "Allegorizing" and "Spiritualizing" interpreters of Scripture, from which the Church and the Bible have suffered so much. The result was that the Church largely ceased to look for the Lord to return and set up an earthly kingdom.

When Constantine became sole Emperor of Rome in A. D. 323, being favorable to Christianity, he united Church and State. A new difficulty now arose in the interpretation of scripture. If, as was at that time believed, Rome was to be the seat of Antichrist, the question arose, or rather was suspiciously whispered—"Is Constantine the Antichrist?" Such a notion was unpalatable to the Roman Emperor, and so a convenient explanation was discovered and adopted, that Antichrist was "Pagan Rome," and that the Millennium commenced when Constantine ascended the throne. This was given color by the great gifts and privileges bestowed on the Church by Constantine, and led to the claim that the Millennial blessings of the Old Testament had been transferred from the Jews to the Christian Church.

But the claim that the "Papal Church" was the Antichrist would not down. When it was found impossible to expunge the Book of Revelation from the sacred canon, it was decided to lock up the Scriptures, and the Bible became a sealed book, and the gloom of night settled down upon all Christendom. The result was the "Dark Ages." But amid the gloom God was not without witnesses to the truth. The Paulicians, Albigeneses, Waldenses, and other sects, bore testimony to the Premillennial return of the Lord.

But the darkness was not eternal. When the fulness of time was come the "Morning Star" of the Reformation, John Wycliffe, arose, and was soon followed by the "Sun," Martin Luther, the brightness of whose light dispelled the darkness. The doctrine of the Premillennial Return of the Lord was revived, but the Reformers did not go far enough. The period was one of religious strife and the formation of new religious sects. The result was an ebb of Spirituality and the growth of Rationalism, which refused to believe that the world was fast ripening for judgment, and a new interpretation of the Millennial Reign of Christ was demanded. This interpretation was furnished by the Rev. Daniel Whitby (1638-1726), a clergyman of the Church of England, who claimed that in reading the promises made to the Jews in the Old Testament of their restoration as a nation, and the re-establishment of the Throne of David, he was led to see that these promises were spiritual and applied to the Church. This view he called a "New Hypothesis."

He claimed that Israel and Mount Zion represented the Church. That the promised submission of the Gentiles to the Jews was simply prophetic of the conversion of the Gentiles and their entrance into the Church. That the lying down of the lion and the lamb together typified the reconciliation of the Old and New natures, and that the establishment of an outward and visible kingdom at Jerusalem, over which Christ and the saints should reign, was gross and carnal, and contrary to reason, as it implied the mingling together of human and spiritual beings on the earth.

His "New Hypothesis" was that by the preaching of the Gospel Mohammedanism would be overthrown, the Jews converted, the Papal Church with the Pope (Antichrist) would be destroyed, and there would follow a 1000 years of righteousness and peace known as the Millennium; at the close of which there would be a short period of Apostasy, ending in the return of Christ. There would then be a general resurrection of the dead, followed by a general judgment, the earth would be destroyed by fire and eternity would begin.

The times were favorable for the "New Theory." A reaction had set in from the open infidelity of those days. All England was in a religious fervor. The "Great Awakening" followed under Whitefield and Wesley, and it looked, as Whitby claimed, that the Millennium was about to be ushered in. That he was mistaken the events of history since that time have shown. It is evident that we are not in the Millennium now.

Nevertheless his "Theory" was favorably received everywhere, and spread with great rapidity and became an established doctrine of the Church, and is what is known today as the "Post-Millennial" view of the Second Coming of Christ, and supposed to be the orthodox faith of the Church. In short, "Post-Millennialism," as advocated in our day, is barely 200 years old, while "Pre-Millennialism" dates back to the days of Isaiah and Daniel.

The sad thing is that this "false doctrine" of Post-Millennialism is taught in our Bibles by the headings of the chapters in the Old Testament. For illustration the headings of chapters forty-three and four of Isaiah read—"The Lord comforteth The Church with His promises," whereas the chapters are not addressed to the Church at all, but to Jacob and Israel, as we see by reading them. The ordinary reader overlooks the fact that the chapter headings of the Bible are put there by the publisher and should be omitted, as they are misleading, as for illustration the title to the Book of Revelation, which is called—

"The Revelation of St. John the Divine," whereas it should be called—

"THE REVELATION OF JESUS CHRIST."
Rev. 1:1.

Premillennialists are divided into three different "Schools of Interpretation," which are fundamentally antagonistic, known as the "Preterist," "Historical" and "Futurist" Schools.

The "Preterist School" originated with the Jesuit Alcazar. His view was first put forth as a complete scheme in his work on the Apocalypse, published in A. D. 1614. It limits the scope of the Apocalypse to the events of the Apostle John's life, and affirms that the whole prophecy was fulfilled in the destruction of Jerusalem by Titus, and the subsequent fall of the persecuting Roman Empire, thus making the Emperor Nero the "Antichrist." The purpose of the scheme was transparent, it was to relieve the Papal Church from the stigma of being called the "Harlot Church" and the Pope from being called the "Antichrist." It is a view that is now but little advocated.

The "Historical School," sometimes spoken of as the "Presentist" scheme, interprets the Apocalypse as a series of prophecies predicting the events that were to happen in the world and in the Church from John's day to the end of time. The advocates of this School interpret the symbols of the Book of Revelation as referring to certain historical events that have and are happening in the world. They claim that "Antichrist" is a "System" rather than a "Person," and is represented by the Harlot Church of Rome. They interpret the "Time Element" in the Book on the "Year Day Scale." This School has had some very able and ingenious advocates. This view, like the preceding was unknown to the early church. It appeared about the middle of the Twelfth Century, and was systematized in the beginning of the Thirteenth Century by the Abbot Joachim. Subsequently it was adopted and applied to the Pope by the forerunners and leaders of the Reformation, and may be said to have reached its zenith in Mr. Ellicott's "Horae Apocalypticae." It is frequently called the Protestant interpretation because it regards Popery as exhausting all that has been predicted of the Antichristian power. It was a powerful and formidable weapon in the hands of the leaders of the Reformation, and the conviction of its truthfulness nerved them to "love not their lives unto the death." It was the secret of the martyr heroism of the Sixteenth Century.

The "Futurist School" interprets the language of the Apocalypse "literally," except such symbols as are named as such, and holds that the whole of the Book, from the end of the third chapter, is yet "future" and unfulfilled, and that the greater part of the Book, from the beginning of chapter six to the end of chapter nineteen, describes what shall come to pass during the last week of "Daniel's Seventy Weeks." This view, while it dates in modern times only from the close of the Sixteenth Century, is really the most ancient of the three. It was held in many of its prominent features by the primitive Fathers of the Church, and is one of the early interpretations of scripture truth that sunk into oblivion with the growth of Papacy, and that has been restored to the Church in these last times. In its present form it may be said to have originated at the end of the Sixteenth Century, with the Jesuit Ribera, who, actuated by the same motive as the Jesuit Alcazar, sought to rid the Papacy of the stigma of being called the "Antichrist," and so referred the prophecies of the Apocalypse to the distant future. This view was accepted by the Roman Catholic Church and was for a long time confined to it, but, strange to say, it has wonderfully revived since the beginning of the Nineteenth Century, and that among Protestants. It is the most largely accepted of the three views. It has been charged with ignoring the Papal and Mohammedan systems, but this is far from the truth, for it looks upon them as foreshadowed in the scriptures, and sees in them the "Type" of those great "Anti-Types" yet future, the "Beast" and the "False Prophet." The "Futurist" interpretation of scripture is the one employed in this book.

The Second and Premillennial Coming of Christ is the "Key" to the Scriptures. All of the prophetical writings make it their terminal end. This is a dark world and the "Sure Word of Prophecy" is given as a light to show us the way over the stormy sea of time. 2 Pet. 1:19. Prophecy is not a haphazard guess, like our weather probabilities, it is

History Written in Advance.

The moment we grasp this idea of prophecy and clearly see the relation of Christ's Premillennial Coming to scripture truth, the Bible becomes a new book, and doctrinal and prophetical truths at once fall into their proper place, and our theological system is no longer a chaos but an orderly plan.

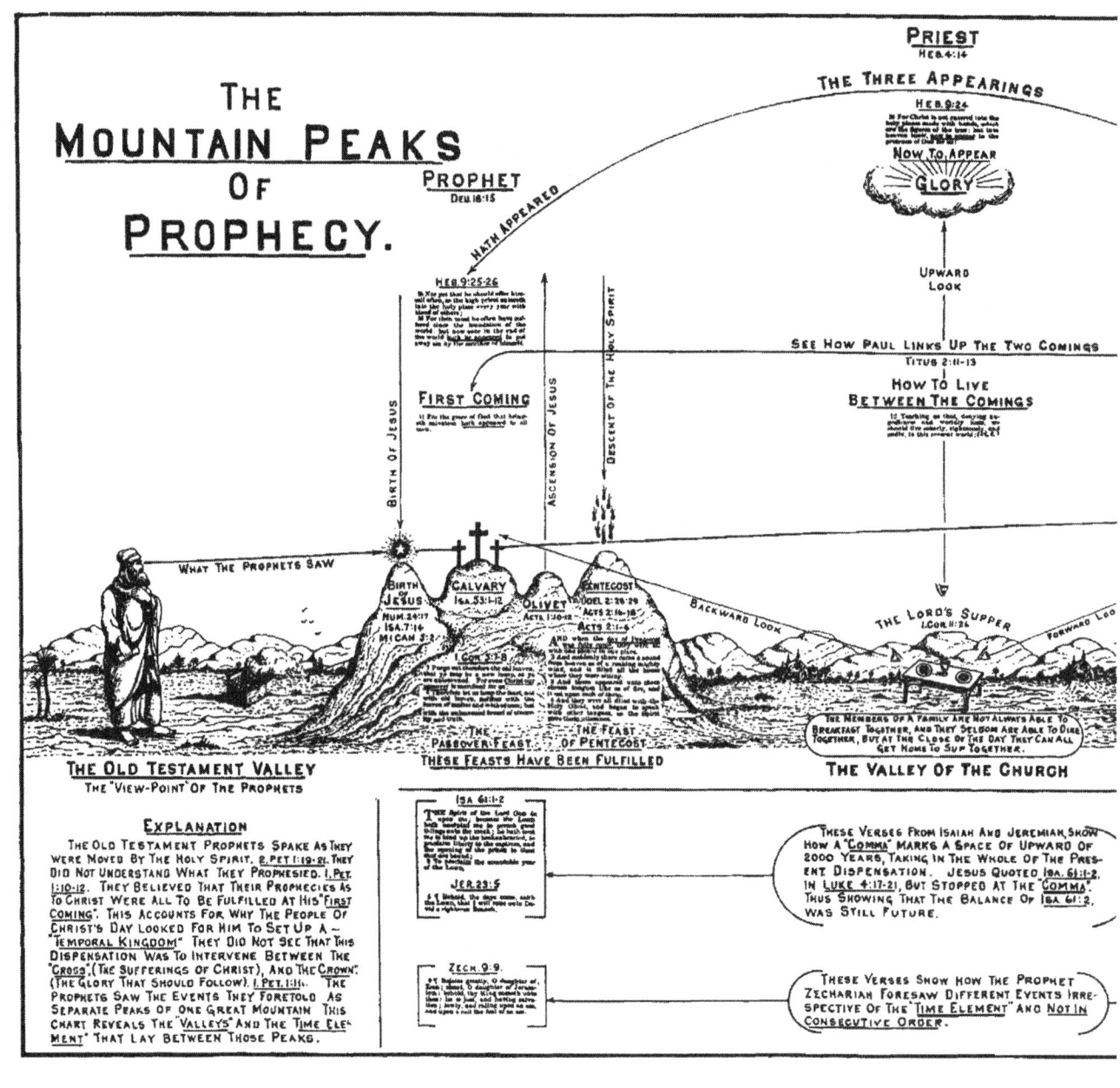

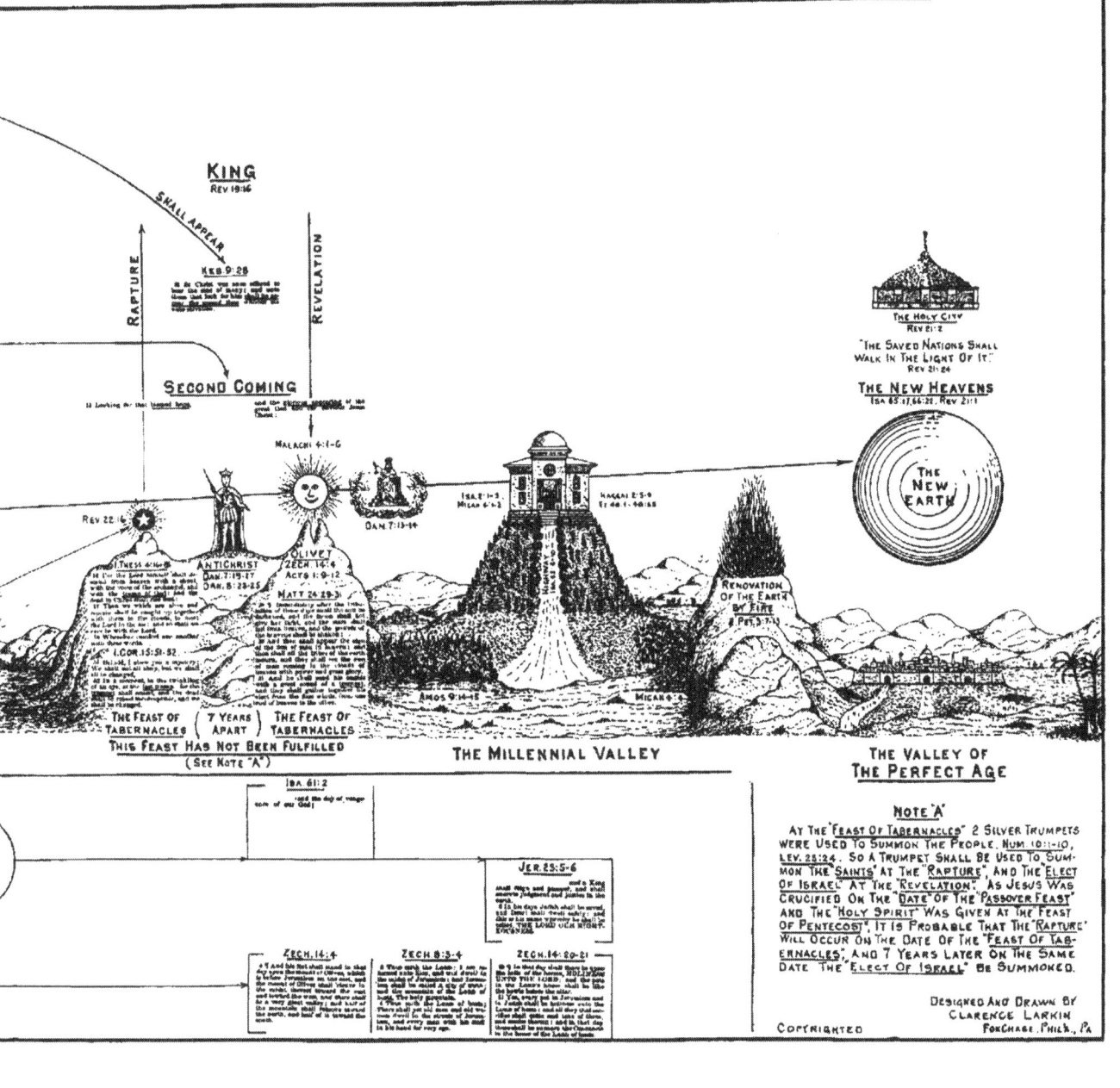

III
MOUNTAIN PEAKS OF PROPHECY

The Bible is unlike all other "sacred books" in that it bases its "Authenticity" and "Authority" on **PROPHECY.** All other "sacred books" contain no predictions as to the future. If their authors had attempted to foretell future events, their non-fulfilment would, long ere this, have discredited their writings. Fulfilled prophecy is stronger evidence for the "Inspiration" and "Authenticity" of the Scriptures than miracles. Prophecy is not a "haphazard guess," nor a "probability" made up on uncertain data like our "Weather Probabilities." Prophecy is

"HISTORY WRITTEN IN ADVANCE,"

or, as another has said—"Prophecy is the **MOLD OF HISTORY.**"

The importance of the study of the Prophetic Scriptures is seen when we recall that two-thirds of the Scriptures are Prophetic, either in type, symbol, or direct statement; and more than one-half of the Old Testament prophecies, and nearly all of the New Testament, point to events yet future. Then this is a "Dark World," and men need the **"SURE WORD OF PROPHECY"** to **LIGHT** them over the stormy "Sea of Time." 2 Pet. 1:19. When men see that God has a "Plan and Purpose" in the "Ages" they take heart, and have something to pin their faith to. It was because the religious leaders of Christ's day were not students of the Prophetic Scriptures that they failed to recognize Him when He came, and if the religious leaders of our day despise and reject the study of Prophecy, they will not be ready for Christ's Second Coming.

There are "Four Prophetic Periods" clearly outlined in the Scriptures.

1. **PATRIARCHAL**—B. C. 1921-1491
2. **MOSAIC**— B. C. 1491-1370
3. **JEWISH**—Post-Exilic—B. C. 500-400
    Exilic—   B. C. 600-500
    Pre-Exilic— B. C. 900-600
    (400 Years of Silence)
4. **APOSTOLIC**—A. D. 27-100

These Prophecies divide themselves into three grand divisions:

1. **PAST**—Fulfilled Prophecy.
2. **PRESENT**—Fulfilling Prophecy.

These are the prophecies that refer to the Jews, the Nations, and the moral and religious character of the times.

3. **FUTURE**—Unfulfilled Prophecy.

The "Requirements" of a Genuine Prediction are five in number:

1. It must have been made known **PRIOR** to its fulfilment.
2. It must be beyond all **HUMAN FORESIGHT.**
3. It must give **DETAILS.**
4. **A SUFFICIENT TIME MUST ELAPSE BETWEEN ITS PUBLICATION AND FULFILMENT TO EXCLUDE THE PROPHET, OR ANY INTERESTED PARTY, FROM FULFILLING IT.**
5. There must be a **CLEAR AND EVIDENT FULFILMENT OF THE PROPHECY.**

The value of the argument for the "Inspiration of the Scriptures" from Prophecy is evident when we study the Law of

"COMPOUND PROBABILITIES."

If I were to predict an earthquake in Philadelphia next year the chance would be 1 in 2 that it would occur. If I should add another prediction, that it would be on the Fourth of July, the chance is decreased to 1 in 4. And if I add another detail, that it will be in the daytime, the chance then becomes 1 in 8. And if I should add a fourth detail the chance would be 1 in 32. And if the details were 10 in number, the chance would be 1 in 1024.

Now there were 25 specific predictions made by the Old Testament Prophets bearing on the betrayal, trial, death and burial of Jesus. These were uttered by different prophets during the period from B. C. 1000 to B. C. 500, yet they were all literally fulfilled in 24 hours in one person. According to the Law of "Compound Probabilities" there was one chance in 33,554,432 that these 25 predictions would be fulfilled as prophesied. If one prophet should make several predictions as to some one event, he might by collusion with others bring it to pass, but when a number of prophets, distributed over several centuries, give detailed and specific predictions as to some event, the charge of collusion cannot be sustained. It is a fact that there were 109 predictions literally fulfilled at Christ's First Advent in the flesh. Apply the Law of "Compound Probabilities" to this number, and the chance was only one in **BILLIONS** that they would be fulfilled in one person.

The argument that Jesus employed to convince those two mourning disciples walking to Emmaus that He was "The Messiah," was the appeal to "Prophecy." "And beginning at Moses and **ALL THE PROPHETS,** He expounded unto them in **ALL THE SCRIPTURES** (O. T. Scriptures), the things concerning Himself." Luke 24:27. It would be intensely interesting reading, and amazingly helpful, if we only had in Luke's Gospel a full report of that afternoon's conversation. The two disciples were familiar with the things that had occurred the previous week at the arrest, trial, crucifixion and burial of Jesus, as well as the rumors of His resurrection. It was not difficult therefore for Jesus to take those things and by quoting from the Old Testament Scriptures show that they were just what the prophets had foretold would happen to the Messiah when He came. He reminded them that the prophet had said that the Messiah should be sold for 30 pieces of silver (Zech. 11:12), be betrayed by a friend (Psa. 41:9), forsaken by His disciples (Zech. 13:7), accused by false witnesses (Psa. 35:11), be dumb before His accusers (Isa. 53:7), be scourged (Isa. 50:6), His garments parted (Psa. 22:18), mocked by His enemies (Psa. 22:7-8), be given gall and vinegar to drink (Psa. 69:21), not a bone of His body broken (Psa. 34:20), die with malefactors (Isa. 53:12), that the price of His betrayal should be used to purchase a "Potter's Field" (Zech. 11:13), and that He should be buried in a rich man's tomb. Isa. 53:9.

But Jesus doubtless did not stop with simply proving that the crucified Christ fulfilled all the requirements of prophecy. It was a long walk they had. Jesus doubtless joined them soon after they left Jerusalem for Emmaus, which was some 6 miles away, and so had ample time in which to outline the "Prophetic Portrait" of the Messiah. Turning to Gen. 22:7-8, He pictured Isaac as a "Type" of Christ, and that God spared Abraham's son, but did not spare His own Son. He then called attention to the institution of "The Passover," and recalled the fact that in preparing the lamb for roasting, two spits were used, one thrust lengthwise through the body for support over the fire, and the other across the shoulders for turning, thus symbolizing the Cross on which the Lamb of God was suspended. He then reminded them that Jesus had said in one of His discourses—"And I, if I be **LIFTED UP**, will draw all men unto me." John 12:32. And having thus refreshed their memory, He took them back to that incident in the history of the Children of Israel of "The Brazen Serpent," and pointed out that that was a type of how men are bitten with the serpents of sin, and need a Saviour, and how Jesus by being lifted up took the place of the "Brazen Serpent," and that all that look to Him in faith shall be delivered from the results of sin. Then Jesus spoke of the Prophet Jonah, and what befell him, and recalled His own prophecy, which doubtless they had heard but had forgotten, that—"As Jonah was three days and three nights in the whale's belly, so shall the Son of Man be three days and three nights in the heart of the earth" (Matt. 12:40), thus showing them that they should not have been surprised at the report they had heard that morning, that Jesus had **RISEN FROM THE DEAD**.

Is it any wonder that as Jesus thus went on outlining the "Prophetic Christ" and comparing Him with the "Historic Christ" they had known and loved, that their heart **"BURNED WITHIN THEM"** as He talked with them by the way, and opened up to them **the Scriptures**. Luke 24:32. How easy a conundrum seems when we know the answer, and how simple the Scriptures become when we see Christ in them, for "the **TESTIMONY OF JESUS**" is the **"SPIRIT OF PROPHECY."** Rev. 19:10. That is, the Spirit and purpose of all Prophecy is to **testify of Jesus**. How important then is the study of Prophecy.

Now we have seen that there were **109** predictions of the Old Testament Prophets literally fulfilled at Christ's First Advent, but there are **845** quotations from the Old Testament in the New Testament, and **333** of these refer to Christ. They vary from types and figures, that seem meaningless unless you place Christ in them, to exact predictions that at times descend to the minutest details. The only books of the Old Testament not quoted in the New Testament are Ruth, Ezra, Nehemiah, Songs of Solomon and Obadiah.

The Old Testament Scriptures bear a **"double witness"** to Jesus. They point out both His **"FIRST"** and **"SECOND"** Comings. And the same Prophet in referring to the "Two Comings" did not always name them in the proper order. This was confusing to the Bible students and religious leaders of Christ's day. In fact they did not know that there were to be "Two Comings." Therefore they are not to be too harshly judged because they rejected Christ, because He did not at once set up an "Earthly Kingdom." They did not separate the prophecies that foretold His **"SUFFERINGS"** from the prophecies that foretold His **"GLORY."** 1 Pet. 1:10-12. They believed that all the prophecies that referred to the Messiah (Christ) were to be fulfilled at His First Coming. This accounts for why the people of Christ's day looked for Him to set up an Earthly Kingdom. They did not see that this "Present Dispensation," or **"CHURCH AGE,"** was to intervene between the **SUFFERINGS** (the **CROSS**) and the **"GLORY"** (the **CROWN**). But we stand on this side of Calvary and can readily separate the **fulfilled** prophecies of the "First Advent" from the **unfulfilled** prophecies of the "Second Advent." This is clearly brought out on the Chart of the "Mountain Peaks of Prophecy."

The Old Testament prophet saw the future as separate peaks of **one mountain**. He did not see that these peaks assembled themselves in groups, with a valley, the **"VALLEY OF THE CHURCH,"** between. In the first group is the "Birth of Jesus," "Calvary," and "Pentecost." In the second group is "Antichrist," the "Revelation of Christ," and the "Kingship of Christ." The Prophet Isaiah (Isa. 61:1-2) did not see that **"comma"** in the second verse, that separated between the statements—**"THE ACCEPTABLE YEAR OF THE LORD,"** and **"THE DAY OF VENGEANCE OF OUR GOD,"** was to span a period covering the whole of this "Present Dispensation," and already over 1900 years long. Likewise the Prophet Jeremiah (Jer. 23:5-6) separates with a **"comma"** the First and Second Advents, or between **"THE RIGHTEOUS BRANCH,"** and the **"KING WHO SHALL REIGN AND PROSPER."** The Prophets saw the **"Prophetic"** and **"Kingly"** work of Christ, but they did not see the **"PRIESTLY."** They saw the **"Altar"** (Sacrificial), and the **"Throne,"** but they did not see the **"TABLE"** (the Lord's Table) that was to come in between.

As shown on the Chart the Prophet saw in a direct line along the "Peaks of Prophecy," and did not see the **"valley"** of "The Church" in between. Our viewpoint is from the side. We face the "Valley" with the "First Advent" (the **CROSS**) to our left, and the "Second Advent" (the **CROWN**) to our right. All we have to do is to separate the prophecies of the "First Advent" from the prophetic references to Christ in the Old Testament, and apply the balance to His "Second Advent." This simplifies the study of Prophecy.

Isaiah's prophecies have mainly to do with the **Messiah and Israel**. Jeremiah is the Prophet of **Israel's return to their own land**. Ezekiel has to do with the **Restoration of Israel** to their own land, and with the **Millennial Land, Restored Temple,** and the **form of Worship**. Daniel is the Prophet of the **Gentiles** and their final great Leader—**ANTICHRIST**. Zechariah is most concerned about the events that shall happen at the Second Coming of Christ, as—

1. **ANTICHRIST** (the Idol Shepherd). Zech. 11:15-17.
2. **ARMAGEDDON** Zech. 14:1-3.
3. **CONVERSION OF ISRAEL.** Zech. 12:9-14.
4. **CHRIST'S RETURN TO OLIVET.** Zech. 14:4-11.
5. **OLD AGE IN JERUSALEM.** Zech. 8:3-8.
6. **FEAST OF TABERNACLES.** Zech. 14:16-21.

Notice that Zechariah does not see these events in their chronological order. All the Major Prophets, and 9 of the Minor Prophets, emphasize the **"Kingship of Christ,"** and it was this that confused the Religious Leaders of Christ's day.

THE PERSPECTIVE OF PROPHECY

The Chart on "The Perspective of Prophecy" shows what each of the prophets foresaw of future events from the Birth of Christ on down to the New Heavens and the New Earth. A careful study of the Chart will show that the Prophet Nahum saw nothing beyond his time, while the Prophet Isaiah saw more and the farthest of all the prophets.

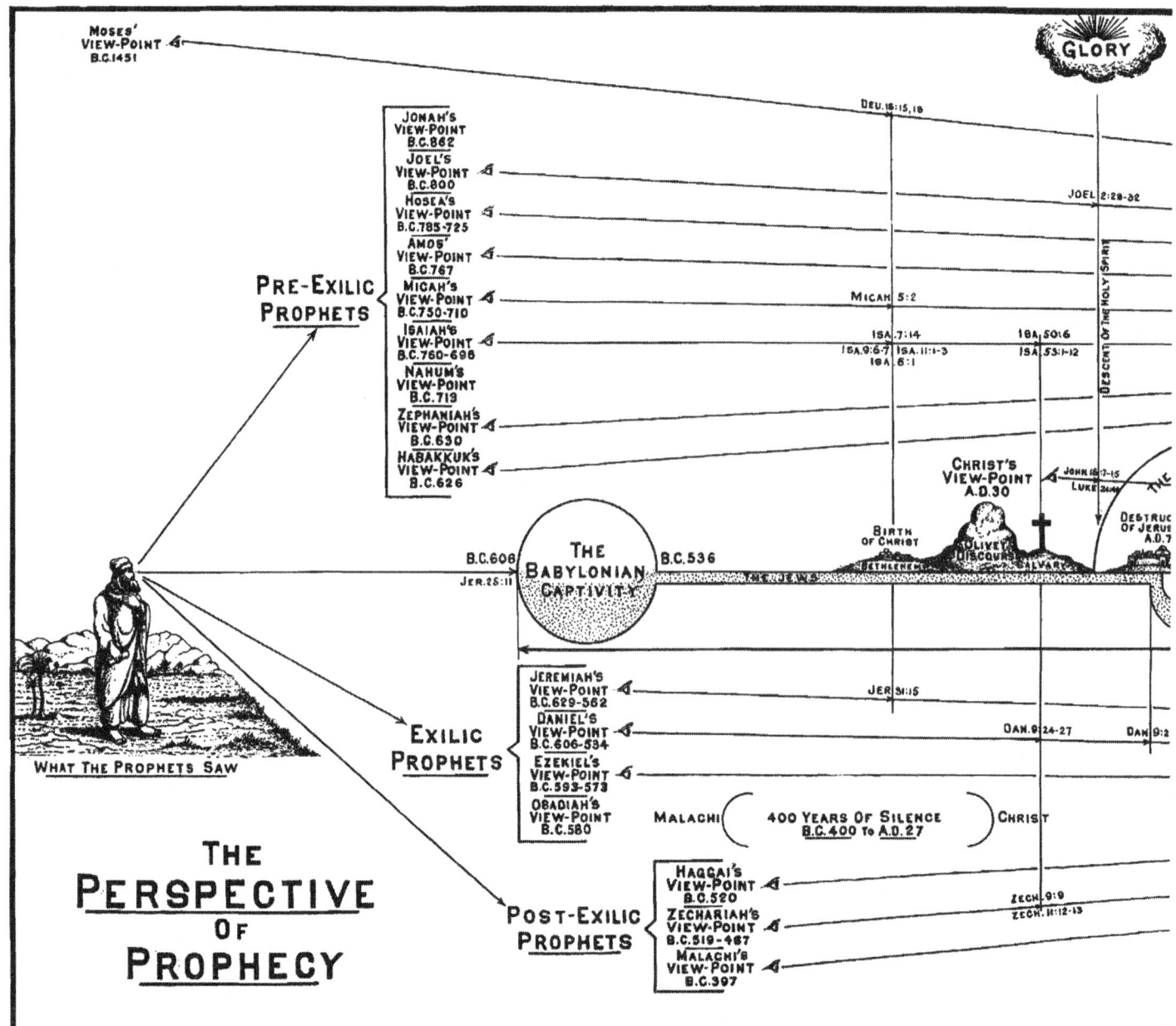

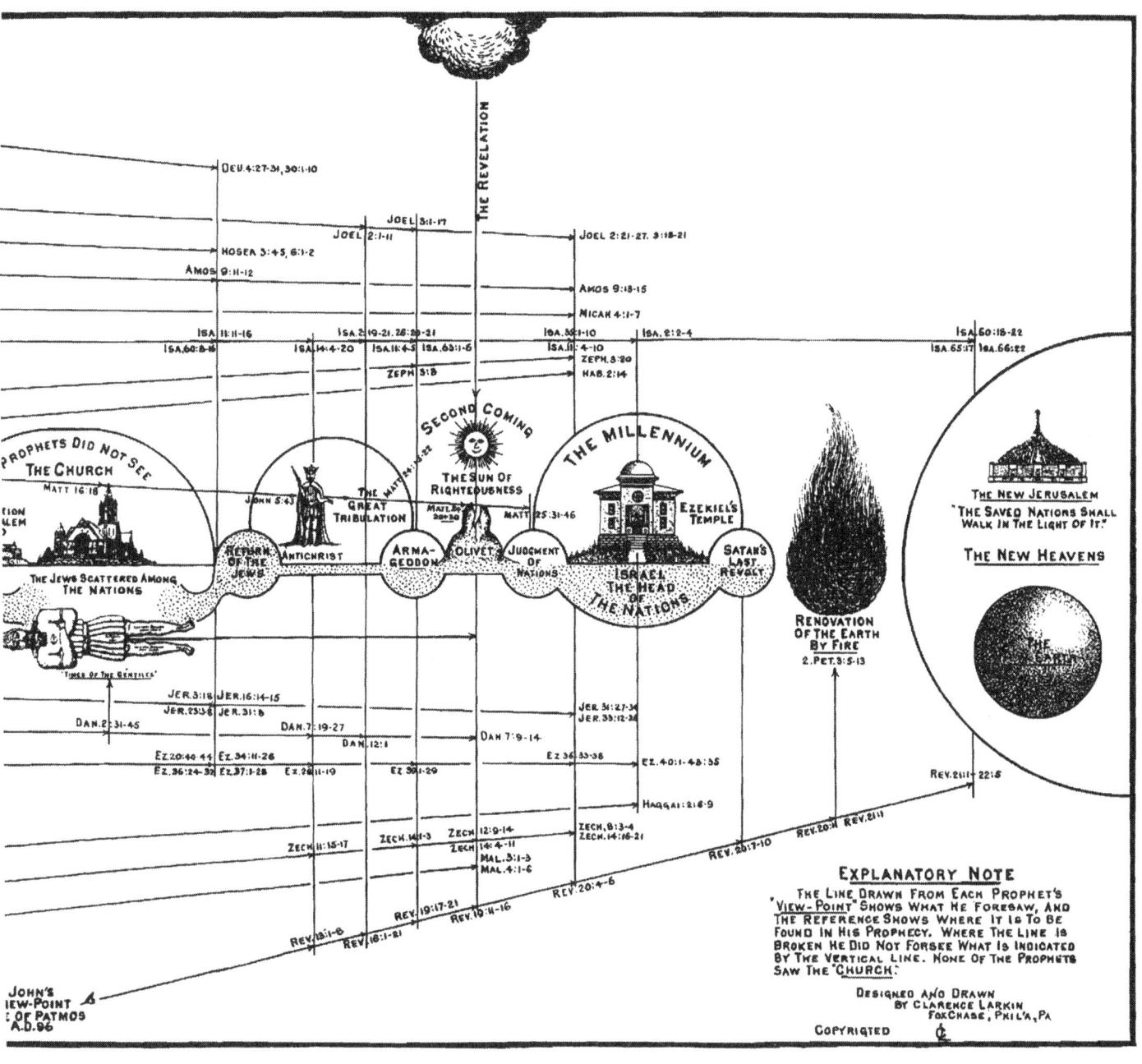

IV
THE SECOND COMING OF CHRIST

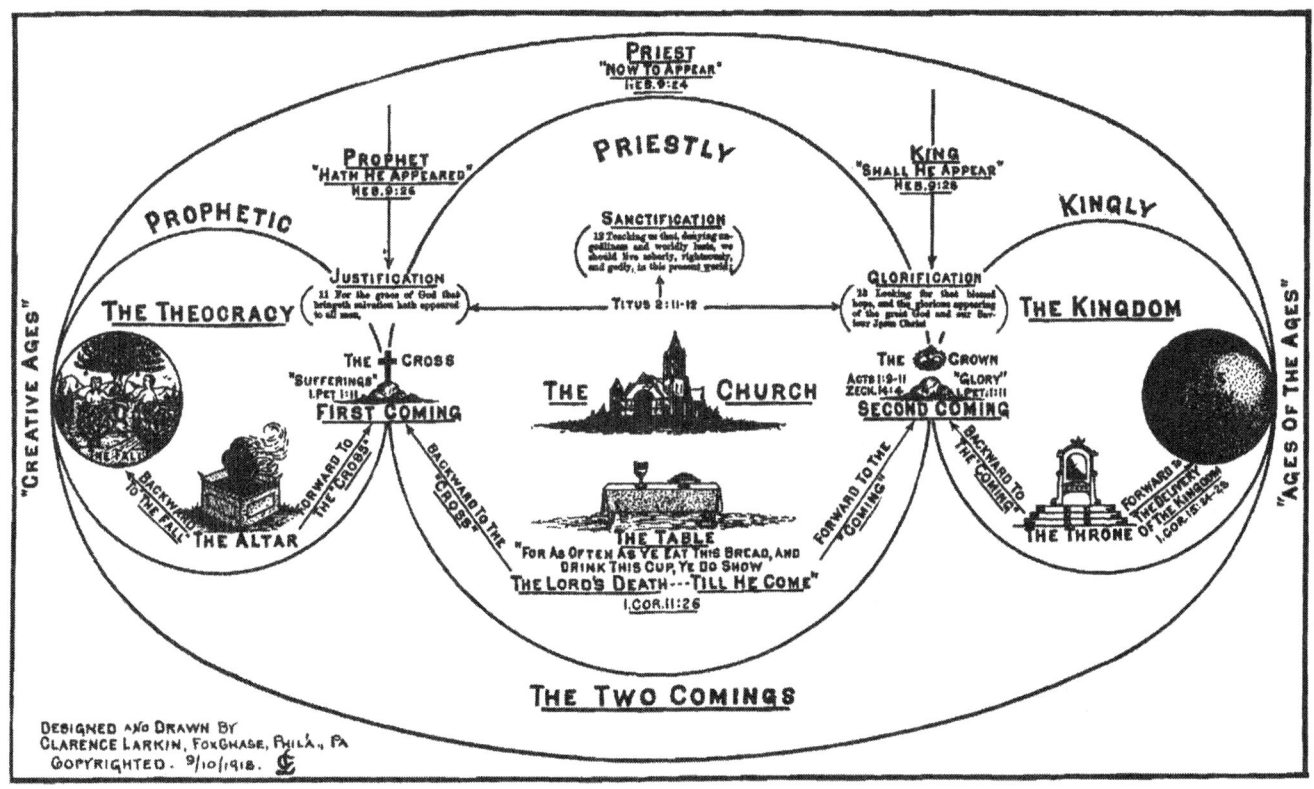

There is no fact in history more clearly established than the fact of the "First Coming" of Christ. But as His "First Coming" did not fulfill all the prophecies associated with His "Coming," it is evident that there must be another "Coming" to completely fulfill them. It was because the religious leaders of Christ's day failed to distinguish between the prophecies that related to His "First Coming," and those that related to His "Second Coming" that they rejected Him. Peter tells us (1 Pet. 1: 10-11) that the prophets themselves did not clearly perceive the difference between the **"Sufferings"** and **"Glory"** of Christ. That is, they did not see that there was a **"TIME SPACE"** between the **"Cross"** and the **"Crown,"** and that the "Cross" would precede the "Crown." But we have no such excuse. We live on this side of the "Cross," and we can readily pick out all the prophecies that were fulfilled at Christ's "First Coming" and apply the remainder to His "Second Coming." It is clear then that Christ's "First Coming," important as it was, is not the "doctrinal centre" of the Scriptures, that is, Christ's First Coming was not the centre of a circle that contains all doctrine, but was one of the foci of an ellipse of which the other is the **"SECOND COMING."**

This is shown on the above Chart on "The Two Comings." The chart takes in the whole Mediatorial Work of Christ, Prophetic, Priestly and Kingly. This is included in an ellipse, the foci of which are the "First" and "Second" Comings of Christ. The "Cross" represents His "First Coming" and the "Crown" His "Second Coming." Between the "Fall" and the "First Coming" we have the **"ALTAR,"** which points backward to the "Fall" and forward to the "Cross." Between the "Comings" we have the **"TABLE"** which points backward to the "Cross" and forward to the "Second Coming." Between the "Second Coming" and the surrender of the "Kingdom" we have the **"THRONE,"** which points backward to the "Second Coming" and forward to the surrendering of the "Kingdom." The Apostle Paul in his epistles clearly distinguishes between the "Comings" and

8

their doctrinal significance. In his letter to the Hebrew's he classifies Christ's "appearings" as "Hath He appeared" (Heb. 9:26), "Now to appear" (Heb. 9:24), "Shall He appear" (Heb. 9:28). In his letter to Titus (Titus 2:11-12), he brings out the doctrinal significance of these "appearings." As a Prophet He died for our "JUSTIFICATION," as a Priest He lives at the right hand of God not only as our Advocate, but our "SANCTIFIER," and when He comes again as a King it will be for our "GLORIFICATION."

While the First and Second Comings of Christ are separated by this Dispensation they are nevertheless not complete in themselves, the Second necessitated the First, and the First demands the Second. They are both necessary to complete the Plan of Salvation. The First Coming was for the salvation of my "SOUL;" the Second is for the salvation of my "BODY," for there can be no resurrection of the body until Christ comes back.

THE SECOND COMING

I. AS TO THE FACT

1. THE TESTIMONY OF JESUS HIMSELF.

Matt 16:27. "For the Son of Man shall come in the glory of his Father, with his angels, and then he shall reward every man according to his works."

Matt. 25:31-32. "When the Son of Man shall come in his glory, and all the holy angels with him, then shall he sit upon the 'Throne of His Glory;' and before him shall be gathered all nations; and he shall separate them one from another, as a shepherd divideth his sheep from the goats."

John 14:2-3. "In my father's house are many mansions; if it were not so I would have told you. I go to prepare a place for you. And if I go and prepare a place for you I will come again, and receive you unto myself; that where I am, there ye may be also."

John 21:22. "If I will that he tarry till I come what is that to thee? Follow thou me."

2. THE TESTIMONY OF HEAVENLY BEINGS.

Acts 1:10-11. "And while they looked steadfastly toward heaven as he went up, behold, two men stood by them in white apparel; which also said, Ye men of Galilee, why stand ye gazing up into heaven? This **SAME JESUS**, which is taken up from you into heaven, shall so come **IN LIKE MANNER** as ye have seen him go into heaven."

This passage declares that the **SAME JESUS** shall return **IN LIKE MANNER** as He went, that is, that His return will be **visible** and **personal**. The two "men" that "stood by" were probably Moses and Elijah. They appeared with Jesus on the Mount of Transfiguration. They were doubtless the "two men" who testified to the women at the tomb that Jesus had risen (Luke 24:4-5), and they will be the "Two Witnesses" that shall testify during the Tribulation. Rev. 11:3-12.

3. THE TESTIMONY OF THE APOSTLES

PAUL—"For our conversation is in heaven; from whence also we look for the Saviour, the Lord Jesus Christ: who shall change our vile body, that it may be fashioned like unto his glorious body, according to the working whereby he is able even to subdue all things unto himself." Phil. 3:20-21.

"Looking for that 'Blessed Hope' and the 'Glorious Appearing' of the great God and our Saviour Jesus Christ." Titus 2:13.

"So Christ was once offered to bear the sins of many; and unto them that look for him shall he appear the 'Second Time' without sin unto salvation." Heb. 9:28.

JAMES—"Be patient therefore, brethren, unto the coming of the Lord." James 5:7.

PETER—"For we have not followed cunningly devised fables when we made known unto you the power and coming of our Lord Jesus Christ, but were eye-witnesses of his majesty." 2 Pet. 1:16.

Peter here refers to the Transfiguration of Christ on the Mount (Matt. 17:1-5), which was a type of His Second Coming. Moses was a type of the "resurrection saints," and Elijah of those who shall be translated without dying. Peter, James and John were a type of the Jewish Remnant that shall see Him when He comes, and the remaining disciples at the foot of the mount, unable to cast the demon out of the boy, of those professed followers of Jesus who shall be left behind at the Rapture, and who shall be powerless to cast the demons out of the demon-possessed people of that period.

JUDE—"And Enoch also, the seventh from Adam, prophesied of these, saying, Behold, the Lord cometh with ten thousand of his saints, to execute judgment upon all, and to convince all that are ungodly among them of all their ungodly deeds which they have ungodly committed, and of all their hard speeches which ungodly sinners have spoke against him." Jude 14-15.

JOHN—"And now, little children, abide in him; that, when he shall appear, we may have confidence, and not be ashamed before him at his coming." 1 John 2:28.

"Behold, he cometh with clouds; and every eye shall see him, and they also which pierced him: and all kindreds of the earth shall wail because of him. Even so, Amen." Rev. 1:7.

4. THE TESTIMONY OF THE LORD'S SUPPER.

"For as often as ye eat this bread, and drink this cup, ye do show the Lord's death till He come." 1 Cor. 11:26.

The Lord's Supper is not a permanent ordinance. It will be discontinued when the Lord returns. It is a Memorial Feast. It looks back to the "Cross" and forward to the "Coming." An engagement ring is not intended to be permanent. It is simply a pledge of mutual love and loyalty, and gives place to the wedding ring. So the Lord's Table may be looked upon as a betrothal pledge left to the Church during the absence of her betrothed.

Paul in all his epistles refers but 13 times to Baptism, while he speaks of the Lord's return 50 times. One verse in every 30 in the New Testament refers to Christ's Second Coming. There are 20 times as many references in the Old Testament to Christ's Second Coming as to His First Coming.

THE FIVE THEORIES

While the majority of professing Christians admit the fact of the Second Coming of Christ, they are not agreed as to the "manner" or "time." There are five theories as to the Second Coming.

1. That His Coming Again Is "SPIRITUAL" and Was Fulfilled at Pentecost.

It was not Christ but the Holy Spirit that came at Pentecost, and his coming was conditioned on Christ's absence, for Jesus said, "It is expedient for you that I go away; for if I go not away, the Comforter (H. S.) will not come unto you; but if I **DEPART**, I will **SEND HIM UNTO YOU**." John 16:7. If the Holy Spirit is only another manifestation of Christ, then they are identical, and that **NULLIFIES**

THE TRINITY. The fact is, the whole New Testament was written after Pentecost, and declares over 150 times that the Second Coming of Christ was still **future**. And more, none of the events predicted as accompanying the Second Coming occurred at Pentecost, such as the **Resurrection of the "Dead in Christ,"** the Translation of the **"Living Saints,"** the **"Binding of Satan,"** etc.

2. That the "CONVERSION OF THE SINNER" is the Coming of the Lord.

This cannot be, for at conversion the sinner comes to Christ, not Christ to the sinner; and the sinner's conversion is the work of the Holy Spirit, and not the work of Christ. It is true that there is such a thing as the spiritual **indwelling of Christ** in the believer, but His Second Coming, like His First Coming is to be an **outward, visible, personal coming**.

3. That "DEATH" is the Coming of the Lord.

The text that is used more than any other for funeral sermons is —"Watch, therefore; for ye know neither the day nor the hour wherein the Son of Man cometh." Matt. 25:13. The context shows that this refers to a future coming of Christ. Christ could not come to the earth every time a person dies for two reasons—

(1) A soul passes into eternity every second, and this would necessitate Christ's remaining continuously on the earth.

(2) Christ is engaged in His High Priestly functions in the Heavenlies, and could not leave them to come to the earth for the souls of the dying.

The fact is, that at death the believer goes to Christ. Christ does not come for him. Death is always spoken of as a departure. "Absent from the body, **present** (at home) with the Lord." 2 Cor. 5:6-8.

If Jesus had meant by His Second Coming **"Death,"** he would have said to His Disciples—"If I go and prepare a place for you, I will send 'Death' to bring you to myself," but He did not. He said—"**I will come again** and receive you unto myself." The last chapter of John's Gospel settles the matter. Peter said to Jesus—"Lord, and what shall this man (referring to John) do? Jesus saith unto him, If I will that he tarry till I come, what is that to thee? Follow thou me. Then went this saying abroad among the brethren, that that disciple (John) **should not DIE.**" John 21:21-23. We see from this that the Disciples did not think that the "Coming of the Lord" meant "death." There was a great difference between these two things in their mind. Death is an enemy (1 Cor. 15:26, 55), it holds us in the grave, it robs the body of its attractiveness, it is the "Wages of Sin" (Rom. 6:23), and the result of God's wrath, while the Second Coming of Christ is a manifestation of His love. Christ is the "Prince of Life." There can be no death where He is. Death flees at His coming. When He was on earth nothing could remain dead in His presence. His coming is not death but resurrection. He is the **"Resurrection"** and the **"Life,"** and when He Comes, He will change our **vile body**, that it may be fashioned like unto His "Glorious Body." Phil. 3:20-21.

4. That the "DESTRUCTION OF JERUSALEM" in A. D. 70 by the Romans Was the Second Coming of the Lord.

The Lord was not present at the destruction of Jerusalem. It was destroyed by Roman soldiers, and none of the things that are to occur at the "Second Coming" occurred at the destruction of Jerusalem, such as the resurrection of the dead, the translation of living saints, and the physical changes that are to occur at Jerusalem and in the land of Palestine at Christ's coming. Zech. 14:4-11. Ez. 47:1-12. Christ's purpose in coming back is not to **destroy** Jerusalem, but to RESTORE it. It must be trodden down of the Gentiles until the "Times of the Gentiles" are fulfilled, "**then shall they see the Son of Man coming in a cloud with power and great glory.**" Luke 21:24-28. The Book of Revelation, **written 26 years after the destruction of Jerusalem**, speaks of the Second Coming of Christ as still **future**.

5. That the "DIFFUSION OF CHRISTIANITY" is the Second Coming of the Lord.

This cannot be true, for the "Diffusion of Christianity" is gradual whereas the Scriptures declare that the "Return of the Lord" shall be **SUDDEN** and **UNEXPECTED**, as a "Thief in the Night." Matt. 24:27, 36, 42, 44. 1 Thess. 5:2. Rev. 3:3. Again the "Diffusion of Christianity" is a **process**, while the Scriptures invariably speak of the "Return of the Lord" as an **EVENT**. The diffusion of Christianity brings **Salvation** to the wicked, whereas the "Return of the Lord" is said to bring not salvation but **SUDDEN DESTRUCTION**. 1 Thess. 5:2-3; 2 Thess. 1:7-10.

II. AS TO THE TIME

Of the exact time we cannot be certain. When Jesus was on the earth He said—"But of that day and that hour knoweth no man, no, not the angels which are in heaven, neither (not yet) the Son, but the Father." Mark 13:32. After His Resurrection and before His Ascension, He refused to satisfy the curiosity of His Disciples, saying to them—"It is not for you to know the '**times**' or the '**seasons**' which the Father hath put in his own power." Acts 1:7. Jesus knew of Daniel's prophecy of the "Seventy Weeks" (Dan. 9:20-27), but He fixed no dates for their fulfillment. The student of prophecy is not to be a "date-setter," but he is to **watch**. "Signs" are for the Jew. There is nothing to prevent Christ coming for His Church at any time.

While we do not know the day or the hour of Christ's Coming we know that it will be

PRE-MILLENNIAL.

By Pre-Millennial we mean before the Millennium. That is, before the period of a "**Thousand Years**" spoken of in Rev. 20:1-6. This period is spoken of in other scriptures as "The Kingdom," and is described in glowing terms by the prophets as a time when the earth shall be blessed with a universal rule of righteousness. The passage in Rev. 20:1-6 simply tells us that the length of the period shall be 1000 years.

The very structure of the New Testament demands that Christ shall return **before** the Millennium. Here are a few reasons.

1. When Christ comes He will **RAISE THE DEAD**, but the Righteous dead are to be raised **BEFORE** the Millennium, that they may reign with Christ during the 1000 years, hence there can be no Millennium before Christ comes. Rev. 20:5.

2. When Christ comes He will **SEPARATE THE "TARES" FROM THE "WHEAT,"** but as the Millennium is a period of **UNIVERSAL RIGHTEOUSNESS** the separation of the "Tares" and "Wheat" must take place **BEFORE** the Millennium, therefore there can be no Millennium before Christ comes. Matt. 13:40-43.

3. When Christ comes Satan **SHALL BE BOUND**, but as Satan is to be bound **during** the Millennium, there can be no Millennium until Christ comes. Rev. 20:1-3.

4. When Christ comes Antichrist is to be **DESTROYED**, but as Antichrist is to be destroyed **before** the Millennium there can be no Millennium until Christ comes. 2 Thess. 2:8; Rev. 19:20.

5. When Christ comes the Jews are to be **RESTORED TO THEIR OWN LAND**, but as they are to be restored to their own land **BEFORE** the Millennium, there can be no Millennium before Christ comes. Ez. 36:24-28; Rev. 1:7; Zech. 12:10.

6. When Christ comes it will be **unexpectedly**, and we are commanded to watch lest He take us **unawares**. Now if He is not coming until **AFTER** the Millennium, and the Millennium is not yet here, why command us to watch for an event that is over 1000 years off?

III. AS TO THE MANNER

He will return in the **SAME MANNER** as He went. **Acts 1:11.** He went up **BODILY** and **VISIBLY** and He shall come in like manner. He went in a cloud, and He will return in a cloud. "Behold, He cometh with the **clouds**; and **every eye shall see Him**, and they also which pierced Him; and all kindreds of the earth shall wail **because of Him.**" Rev. 1:7. The only difference will be that He went up **alone**, He will return as a King (Luke 19:12), followed by a retinue of the angelic hosts. "For the Son of Man shall come in the glory of His Father **with his angels**; and then He shall reward every man according to his works." Matt. 16:27. His "Return" however will be in

TWO STAGES.

He will come first into the region of our atmosphere, and the "**dead in Christ**," and the "**living saints**" shall be "**caught up**" to meet Him "**IN THE AIR**." Then after the risen and translated saints have been judged and rewarded for their works, and they, as the Church, the Bride of Christ, have been married to Him, He will come **with them** to the earth and land on the Mount of Olives, the place from whence He ascended. "And His feet shall stand in that day upon the Mount of Olives, which is before Jerusalem on the east, and the Mount of Olives shall cleave in the midst thereof toward the east and toward the west, and there shall be a very great valley; and half of the mountain shall remove toward the north, and half of it toward the south." Zech. 14:4.

The First Stage of His Return is called "**THE RAPTURE**;" the Second Stage—"**THE REVELATION**." The time between the two Stages is not less than seven years, and is occupied in the heavens by the "**JUDGMENT OF BELIEVERS FOR WORKS**," and on the earth by "**THE GREAT TRIBULATION**." See Chart that follows, marked Chart No. 3.

FIRST STAGE—THE RAPTURE

The Rapture is described in 1 Thess. 4:15-17. "For this we say unto you by the word of the Lord, that we which are alive and remain unto the coming of the Lord shall not prevent them which are asleep. For the Lord **HIMSELF** shall descend from heaven with a **shout**, with the **voice of the Archangel** (Michael) and with the **trump of God**; and the **DEAD IN CHRIST shall rise first**; then we which are **ALIVE AND REMAIN** (saints only) shall be caught up together with them in the clouds, to meet the Lord **IN THE AIR**, and so shall we ever be with the Lord."

From this we see that "The Rapture" will be twofold.
1. The Resurrection of the "**DEAD IN CHRIST**."
2. The Translation of the "**LIVING SAINTS**."

This twofold character of "The Rapture" Jesus revealed to Martha when He was about to raise her brother Lazarus. He said to her:

"I am the '**Resurrection and the Life**,' he that believeth in **Me, though he were dead yet shall he LIVE** (First Resurrection Saints); and whosoever **LIVETH** (is alive when I come back) and believeth in Me shall **NEVER DIE**." John 11:25-26. This twofold character of The Rapture, Paul emphasizes in his immortal chapter on the resurrection.

"Behold, I show you a **Mystery**, we shall not **all Sleep**, but we shall **All Be Changed**, in a moment, in the twinkling of an eye, at the last trump; for the trumpet shall sound, and the **dead shall be raised**, and **we shall be changed**. For this **Corruptible** (the dead in Christ) must put on **incorruption**, and this **mortal** (the living saints) must put on **immortality**. So when this **corruptible** shall have put on **incorruption**, and this **mortal** shall have put on **immortality**, then shall **be brought to pass the saying that is written, DEATH IS SWALLOWED UP IN VICTORY.**

O DEATH, WHERE IS THY STING?
O GRAVE, WHERE IS THY VICTORY?"
1 Cor. 15:51-57.

The last two lines refer only to those who are "changed without dying," for it is only those who will not die who can shout—

"O Death, Where Is Thy Sting?
O Grave, Where Is Thy Victory?"

In 2 Cor. 5:1-4. Paul expresses his longing, and the longing of the Saints, to be among those who should not be "unclothed" by Death, but who should be "clothed upon" by Immortality "without dying."

"For we know that if our earthly house of this tabernacle (the body) were **dissolved** (that is die), we have a building of God, a house not made with hands, eternal in the heavens. For in this (body) we groan, earnestly desiring to be 'clothed upon' with our house which is from heaven; if so be that being 'clothed' we shall not be found naked. For we that are in this tabernacle (the body) do groan, being burdened; not for that we would be '**unclothed**' (by death), but '**clothed upon**' (by immortality), that 'mortality' might be swallowed up of life."

In his letter to the Philippians, while Paul hopes that—

"If by any means he may attain unto The (out from among the dead) **Resurrection**, yet he pressed toward the mark for the '**prize**' of the High (out and up) **Calling of God** in Christ Jesus." Phil. 3:11-14.

That is, while Paul would esteem it a great thing to "rise from the dead" at the First Resurrection, and be "caught up" with those who should be "changed," yet he would esteem it a "prize" if he could be caught up "without dying," that is, live until Jesus came back.

THE RAPTURE WILL BE A "SURPRISE"

"Watch therefore; for ye know not what hour your Lord doth come. But know this, that if the goodman of the house had known in what watch the thief would come, he would have watched, and would not have suffered his house to be broken up. Therefore be ye also ready; for **in such an hour as ye think not the Son of Man COMETH.**" Matt. 24:42-44. "Behold, I come as a thief. Blessed is he that watcheth, and keepeth his garments, lest he walk naked, and they see his shame." Rev. 16:15. "But of the '**times**' and the '**seasons**,' brethren, ye have no need that I write unto you. For yourselves know perfectly that the 'Day of the Lord' (the day of His Return), so cometh as a **thief in the night**. For when they shall say, '**Peace and Safety**;' then sudden destruction cometh upon them as travail upon a woman with child, and they shall not escape." This refers to the Second Stage of Christ's Coming, the "Revelation," when He shall take vengeance

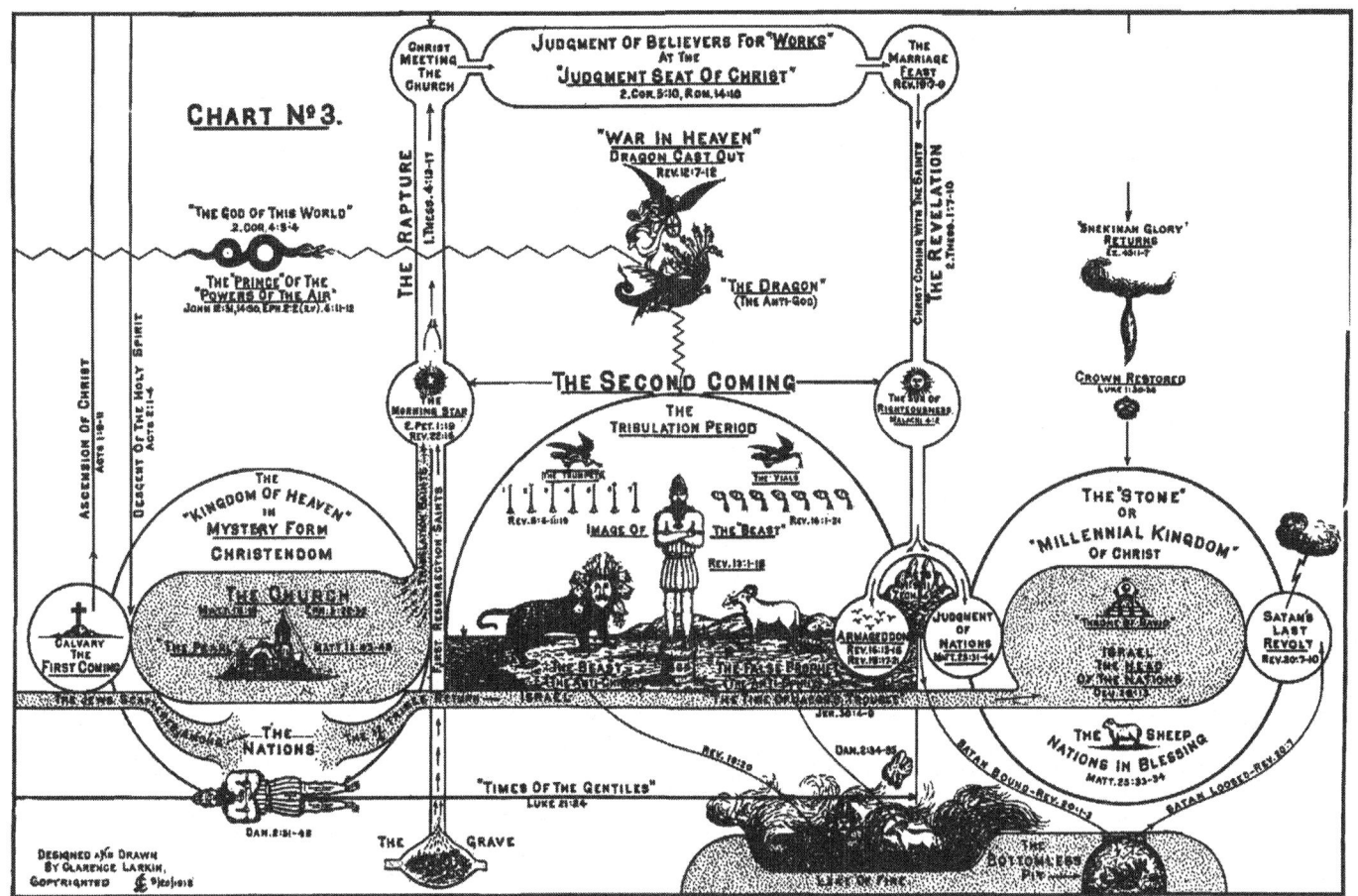

upon His enemies. 2 Thess. 1:7-10. But Paul adds—"But ye, brethren, are not in darkness, that **that day** (the day of His Return) should overtake you as a thief." 1 Thess. 5:1-4.

We see from this that when Christ comes back it will be when we are not expecting Him. He will come as a thief comes. A thief does not announce his coming. He comes for a certain purpose. He does not take everything there is in the house. He takes only the precious things. The jewels, the gold, the silver and fine wearing apparel. He does not come to stay. As soon as he secures what he is after he departs. So Jesus at the Rapture will come and take away the saints only. The thief leaves much more than he takes. He leaves the house and the furniture and the household utensils. So the Lord at the Rapture will leave the wicked and the great mass of the heathen behind, for those who will be taken will be comparatively few.

THE RAPTURE WILL BE "ELECTIVE"

It will not only separate the saints from unbelievers, but it will separate husbands from wives, brothers from sisters, friends from friends.

"I tell you, in that night there shall be two men in one bed; the one shall be taken, and the other shall be left. Two women shall be grinding together; the one shall be taken, and the other left. Two men shall be in the field; the one shall be taken, and the other left." Luke 17:34-36. The words "men" and "women" in this passage are in italics. That means that they are not in the original, and so the passage should read there shall be "two in one bed," husband and wife, or two brothers, or two sisters, or two friends. Two in "bed" indicates night; two grinding at the mill, morning or evening; two in the field mid-noon. This shows that the Rapture will happen all over the earth at the same time or as the Apostle describes it in a **"moment,"** or the "twinkling of an eye." "As the lightning cometh out of the east, and shineth even unto the west; so shall also the coming of the Son of Man Be" (Matt. 24:27) is the way Jesus puts it.

The "Rapture" will be the most startling "event" of this Age and Dispensation. As it is to occur in the "twinkling of an eye" and all over the earth at the same time, that part of the world that is not asleep will witness the event. As to the "Shout of the Lord," the "Voice of the Archangel," and the "Trump of God" we do not know whether their sound will be heard and distinguished by others than the "dead in Christ" and the "living saints." We know that one day the Father spoke to Christ in a voice that He understood, but the people who stood by mistook it for "thunder." John 12:28-29. When the Lord appeared to Saul of Tarsus on the road to Damascus and spoke to him, the men that journeyed with him stood speechless, "hearing a voice," but seeing no man, and not understanding what was said. Acts 9:3-7. We know however that the "dead in Christ" will hear the sound, for it will be "intensely penetrating." There will be no graves so deep, no catacombs so rock covered, no pyramids or mausoleums so thick, but what the sound shall reach their depths and the "dead in Christ" shall hear the cry—"awake ye sleeping saints and arise from the dead, it is MORNING, the morning of the FIRST RESURRECTION."

On the morning of that glorious day the air will be filled with the "spirits" of the "Dead in Christ," come back to earth to get their bodies, raised and glorified. Whether the cemeteries and country church yards will look like ploughed fields, and monuments and grave slabs be overturned and vaults and places of sepulture be shattered by the exodus of those who found their last resting place there, and thus testify to the fact of the literal bodily resurrection of the dead, or whether the sainted dead shall slip out of their sepulchres without disturbing them, as Christ arose and left the tomb without breaking the seal, the angel rolling away the stone simply to show that the tomb was empty, we are not told, only the event itself will disclose the manner of the First Resurrection.

If the dead slip out of their places of sepulture without disturbing them, the First Resurrection will be secret and probably unknown to the world, but it will not be so with the "Living Saints" who are translated. If it is night on our side of the globe when the Rapture occurs the community will wake up in the morning to find all the real Christians gone, disappeared in the night. Many may hear the sound of the "Midnight cry"—

"BEHOLD THE BRIDEGROOM COMETH,"

but thinking it only thunder, will turn over for another nap, but in the morning they will find the bedroom door locked, with the key on the inside, just as they locked it before retiring, and the clothes of the loved one who occupied the room with them lying where they were placed when taken off the night before, but that loved one, who was a Christian, missing. Husbands will wake up to find that Christian wives are gone, and wives will wake up to find Christian husbands gone. Brothers and sisters will be missed, and dear children absent, and not an infant will be left behind. Many faithful servants and employes will not report for duty, and the world will awake to the fact that the Bible is true, and the much despised doctrine of the Pre-Millennial Coming of the Lord to gather out His saints is no fanciful interpretation of Scripture.

If it be day with us when the Rapture occurs, the "EVENT" will be startling. As it was in the days of Noah (Matt. 24:36-39), the people will be eating and drinking, marrying and giving in marriage, buying and selling, planting and building.

If it be at a pleasant time of the year, the boats, and cars, and parks will be filled with pleasure seekers. If it be in the midst of the week, and during the business hours of the day, the shops and stores will be filled with shoppers and the mills with toilers, and the streets of the cities lined with men and women and children on pleasure and business bent. Suddenly a noise from heaven will be heard like a great peal of thunder. The people will rush to doors and windows, and those on the streets and in the fields will look up to see what has happened. To the vast majority it will be but a startling and alarming sound, but to many it will be the

"VOICE OF THE LORD."

But when the people recover from their surprised and affrighted condition they will discover that a great many people are missing, and that the missing were the best people in the community. The large Department Stores, Banking Institutions, Manufacturing Plants, and other places of business will find their working force depleted by the loss of faithful employes. People walking on the streets will find their companions gone, and the street car lines will be blocked because of absent motormen, conductors and teamsters. Railroad and steamboat lines will be crippled, and confusion will reign everywhere. In many homes the servants will be missing and members of the family will come home to find loved ones gone.

At first the whole thing will be a Mystery, until some one who had heard or read about the "Rapture of the Saints," realizing what has happened, will explain the situation.

But one of the surprises of that day will be that so many professing Christians, and among them many ministers and Christian workers, will be left behind, while some who were not known to be Christians will be missing. The next day's papers will be full of what happened the day before, and many of them will be swelled to twice their ordinary size by the pressure on their advertising columns for information as to missing ones, and for help to fill important vacancies and positions of trust. For a few days the excitement will be intense. Then the people will settle down to the inevitable. With the exception of a few who will repent and turn to God, the mass of the people will become more hardened and wicked than before, and some who lost loved ones will be embittered. As the Holy Spirit will have gone back with the "Raptured Ones," and the "Saints," the SALT of the earth, been taken out, there will be nothing to prevent the rapid degeneration and "Moral Putrefaction" of those who are "left," and sin and iniquity and all manner of crime and worldliness will increase and pave the way for the manifestation of Antichrist, under whose administration the world will rapidly ripen for judgment.

WHO ARE TO BE TAKEN

Some claim that "all" the Church are to pass through the Tribulation; others that "all" the Church are to be caught out before the Tribulation, while some claim that only the "Waiting" and "Watching" Saints shall be caught out before the Tribulation, and that the rest must pass through it. The latter base their claim on Heb. 9:28, where it says—"Unto them that look for Him shall He appear the second time without sin unto salvation." While this might apply to the living when He appears, it certainly cannot apply to the dead. There are tens and hundreds of thousands who "fell asleep in Jesus" who never heard of the Premillennial Coming of the Lord, or at least never grasped its meaning, and who therefore never "watched" and "waited" and "looked" for His Appearing. They surely are "In Christ"; and the "Dead in Christ" are to rise at the Rapture. Paul does not say in 1 Thess. 4:16-17, that it will be the "dead" who "watched" and "waited" and "looked," and those who are "alive" and

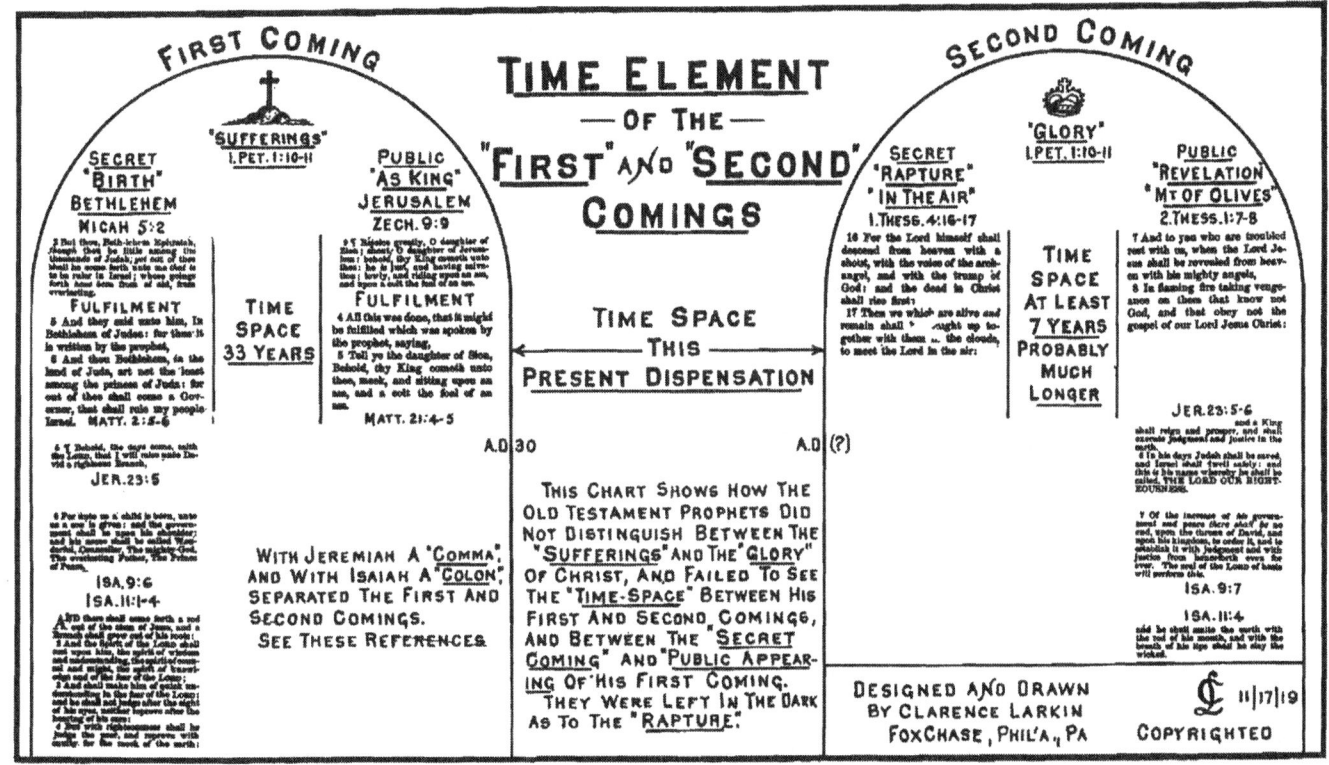

"watch" and "wait" and "look" for His Appearing that shall be "caught out," but the dead **"In Christ,"** and we who **"Are Alive And Remain."**

Then there is another fact that we must not forget, and that is, the Unity of the Church.

"For as the **Body Is One**, and hath many members, and **ALL the Members Of That One Body, Being Many, ARE ONE BODY**; so also is Christ. For by **One Spirit** are we **ALL Baptized Into One Body.**" 1 Cor. 12:12-13.

All then who have been "born again" (John 3:3-7) are part of Christ's "Body," and we cannot conceive of Christ's "Body" being divided; part of it remaining "asleep" in the grave, and part of it "raised in glory;" part of it left to pass through the Tribulation, and part of it "changed" and caught up to meet Him in the air.

If "all" the Church are to pass through the Tribulation, then instead of waiting and watching "for the Lord," we should be waiting and watching "for the Tribulation," which is contrary to the teaching of Christ Himself. Matt. 24:42-44.

The Tribulation is not for the perfecting "of the Saints." It has nothing to do with the Church. It is the time of "Jacob's Trouble" (Jer. 30:7), and is the "Judgment of Israel," and it is God's purpose to keep the Church out of it. Rev. 3:10. The Book of Revelation is written in chronological order. After the fourth chapter the Church is seen no more upon the earth until she appears in the nineteenth chapter coming with the Bridegroom "from" Heaven. The entire time between these two chapters is filled with appalling judgments that fall upon those that "dwell on the earth," and as the Church is not of the earth, but is supposed to " sit together in 'Heavenly Places' in Christ Jesus" (Eph. 2:6), she will not be among those who "dwell on the earth" in those days.

The confusion is largely due to the fact that students of Prophetic Truth do not distinguish between Christ's coming **FOR** His Saints, and **WITH** His Saints. The former is called the "Rapture," the latter the "Revelation."

Numerous passages in scripture speak of Christ coming "with" His Saints (Zech. 14:5, Col. 3:4, 1 Thess. 3:13, 1 Thess. 4:14, Jude 14), but it is evident that they cannot come "with" Him, if they had not been previously caught out "to" Him. All such passages refer therefore to the "Revelation" and not the "Rapture."

The typical teaching of the Scriptures demand that the Church be caught out "before" the Tribulation. Joseph was a type of Christ and he was espoused to, and married Asenath, a Gentile bride, during the time of his "rejection by his brethren," and "before the famine," which typified the Tribulation, because it was the time of "Judgment of his Brethren." This is the time of Christ's rejection by "His Brethren"—the Jews, and to complete the type He must get His Bride—the church, "before" the Tribulation.

Moses, who is also a type of Christ, got his bride, and she a Gentile, "after" his rejection by his brethren, and "before" they passed through the Tribulation under Pharoah. Ex. 2:23-25.

Enoch, a type of the "Translation Saints," was caught out "before" the Flood, and the Flood is a type of the Tribulation, and Noah and his family of the "Jewish Remnant" or 144,000 sealed ones of Rev. 7:1-8, who will be preserved through the Tribulation.

How thrilling the thought that some of us shall not die, that in a moment, in the "twinkling of an eye" without being unclothed by the ghastly hands of Death, and instead of the winding sheet of the grave, we shall be instantly changed and clothed with the glorious garments of immortality. What a transport of joy will fill our being as we suddenly feel the thrill of immortality throbbing through our veins, and find ourselves being transported through the air in the company of fellow Christians and of our loved ones who fell asleep in Jesus. What welcome recognitions and greetings there will be as we journey up with them to the "Bridal Halls of Heaven," where we shall join in the new and triumphal song of Moses and the Lamb. Rev. 5:9-10.

SECOND STAGE—THE REVELATION

At the "Second Stage" of Christ's Second Coming, the "Revelation," we shall behold His "Glory." When Jesus came the first time He was disguised in the flesh. The "Incarnation" was the hiding of His Power, the veiling of His Deity. Now and then gleams of glory shot forth as on the Mt. of Transfiguration; but when He comes the Second Time we shall behold Him clothed with the glory He had with the Father before the world was. The "Revelation" will be as sudden and as unexpected as was the "Rapture." The sun will rise on that day strong and clear. Gentle breezes will waft themselves over the earth. There will be no signs of a storm or of the coming Judgment. The people will be buying and selling, building and planting, eating and drinking, marrying and giving in marriage. The statesmen will be revolving in their minds new plans for the world's betterment. The philanthropic will be devising new ways to help the people. The pleasure-loving will be seeking new sources of pleasure. The wicked will be plotting dark deeds; and the unbelieving will be proving to their own satisfaction that there is no God, no heaven, no hell, no coming judgment, when suddenly there will be a change. In the distant heaven there will appear a

"POINT OF LIGHT,"

outshining the sun. It will be seen descending toward the earth. As it descends it will assume the form of a bright cloud, out of which shall stream dazzling beams of light, and flashes of lightning. It will descend apace as if on wings of the whirlwind, and when it reaches its destination over the brow of the Mt. of Olives it will stop and unfold itself to the terrified and awestricken beholders, and there will be revealed to them Jesus seated on a "White Horse" (Rev. 19:11-16) and accompanied with His Saints and the armies of Heaven. Then shall be fulfilled what Jesus foretold in His Olivet Discourse—"Then shall appear the sign (a cloud) of the Son of Man in heaven; and then shall all the tribes of the earth mourn, and they shall see the Son of Man coming in the clouds of Heaven WITH POWER AND GREAT GLORY." Matt. 24:30.

THE IMMINENCY OF THE SECOND COMING

One of the objections to the Doctrine of the "Second Coming of Christ" is the claim that He may come back at any time. Post-millennialists tell us that the writers of the New Testament looked for Him to come back in their day, and that He did not do so, is proof that they were mistaken, and that Paul in his later writings modified his statements as to the imminency of Christ's return. It is a fact that while Jesus said: "Watch therefore: for ye know not what hour your Lord doth come. . . . Therefore be ye also ready: for in such an hour as ye think not the Son of man cometh" (Matt. 24:42-44), He did not in these passages teach that He would return during the lifetime of those who listened to Him. In fact, in His Parables He intimated that His return would be delayed, as in the Parable of The Talents, where it is said: "After a long time the Lord of those servants cometh." Mat. 25:19. What Jesus wanted to teach was the sudden and unexpected character of His return. As to the Apostles, while they exhorted their followers to be ready, for the "night is far spent, the day is at hand," and the "coming of the Lord draweth nigh," their language simply implied "imminency," but not necessarily "IMMEDIATENESS." And the use of the word "WE" in 1 Cor. 15:51, "WE" shall not all sleep, but WE shall all be changed," is not a declaration that the Lord would return in Paul's day and some would not die but be translated, for the Apostle is talking about the Rapture and he means by "WE" a certain class of persons, the saints that shall be alive when that event occurs, whether in his day or at some later time.

It was clearly known to our Lord that certain events must come to pass before His Return, but to have disclosed that fact would have nullified the command to "Watch," therefore He in "mystery form," as in the seven parables of Matt. 13, hid the fact that His Return would be delayed. It would take time for the "Sowing of the Seed," the growth of the "Wheat" and "Tares," the growth of the "Mustard Tree," and the "Leavening of the Meal." So rapid was the spread of the Gospel in the first century that the followers of Christ were warranted in looking for the speedy Return of the Lord, but it was true then, as in every century since, that we do not know what the extent of the "Harvest" is to be, and when it will be ripe, so the Lord can return. Matt. 13:30. Uncertainty then as to the "time" of the Lord's return is necessary to promote the "watchful" spirit. If the early Church had known that the Lord's Return would have been delayed for 20 centuries, the incentive to watchfulness would have been wanting.

By "Imminency" we mean "may happen at any time." For illustration, you hurry to the railroad station to catch a train. You find the train has not arrived, though it is past the hour. Though it is late it is on the way, and it would not be safe for you to leave the station, for it may arrive any minute, but as a matter of fact, it does not come for half an hour. Now if you had known that it would not arrive for half an hour you would have used the time in some other way than "waiting" and "watching." So we see that "Imminency" does not necessarily imply "IMMEDIATENESS," but does demand "Watchfulness."

It is the firm conviction of the writer that there has been unnecessary delay in the Return of the Lord, caused by the failure of the Church to obey the "Divine Commission" to evangelize the world (Matt. 28:19-20), and it is past the time when He should have returned. Of course, this was foreseen by God, and His foreknowledge has held back the development of the forces of evil, etc., until the "Fulness of the Gentiles" should be gathered in, and the "Harvest" is ripe for the gathering. Rev. 14:14-20. At no time in the history of the Christian Church have the conditions necessary to the Lord's Return been so completely fulfilled as at the present time; therefore, His Coming is IMMINENT, and will not probably be long delayed. Let us be ready and watching.

While the writer, as stated, is disposed to believe that the Return of the Lord is "past due," and while he is no "time setter," yet there is a "theory" that may throw some light on the

IMMINENCY OF HIS RETURN

that it might be well to examine. It is called

THE GREAT WEEK OF HUMAN HISTORY,

and is based on the **"Seven Days"** of the **"Creative Week,"** and the declaration of Scripture (2 Pet. 3:8), "That **one day** is with the **Lord** as a **THOUSAND YEARS**, and a **thousand years** as **ONE DAY**." The Millennium in the Old Testament is described as a "Sabbath Keeping" period of rest, and is referred to as such in Heb. 4:4-11, where it is associated with the **"Seventh Day"** of the **"Creative Week."** Now we know that the length of the Millennium is **1000 YEARS** (Rev. 20:1-9), and if it corresponds with the "Seventh Day" of the "Creative Week," why should not the remaining **six days** be of the same length? If so, and those days correspond with the past of human history, then from the date of the "Creative Week" up to the beginning of the Millennium should be **6000 years** of human history. In confirmation of this we have the **fact** that a careful study of the genealogical tables and history of the Old Testament seem to show that from Adam to Christ was about **4000 years**, or **four days** of a thousand years each, corresponding to the first four days of the "Creative Week," and from Christ down to the present time we have over **1900 years**, or nearly 2 days of **1000 years each**, thus making nearly **6 days** of **1000 years each** of human history, and as Christ is to come back **before** the Millennium, and all signs point to His Speedy return, then the "theory" that the "Seven Days" of the "Creative Week" are typical of Seven "One Thousand Year Periods" is not unwarranted in Scripture.

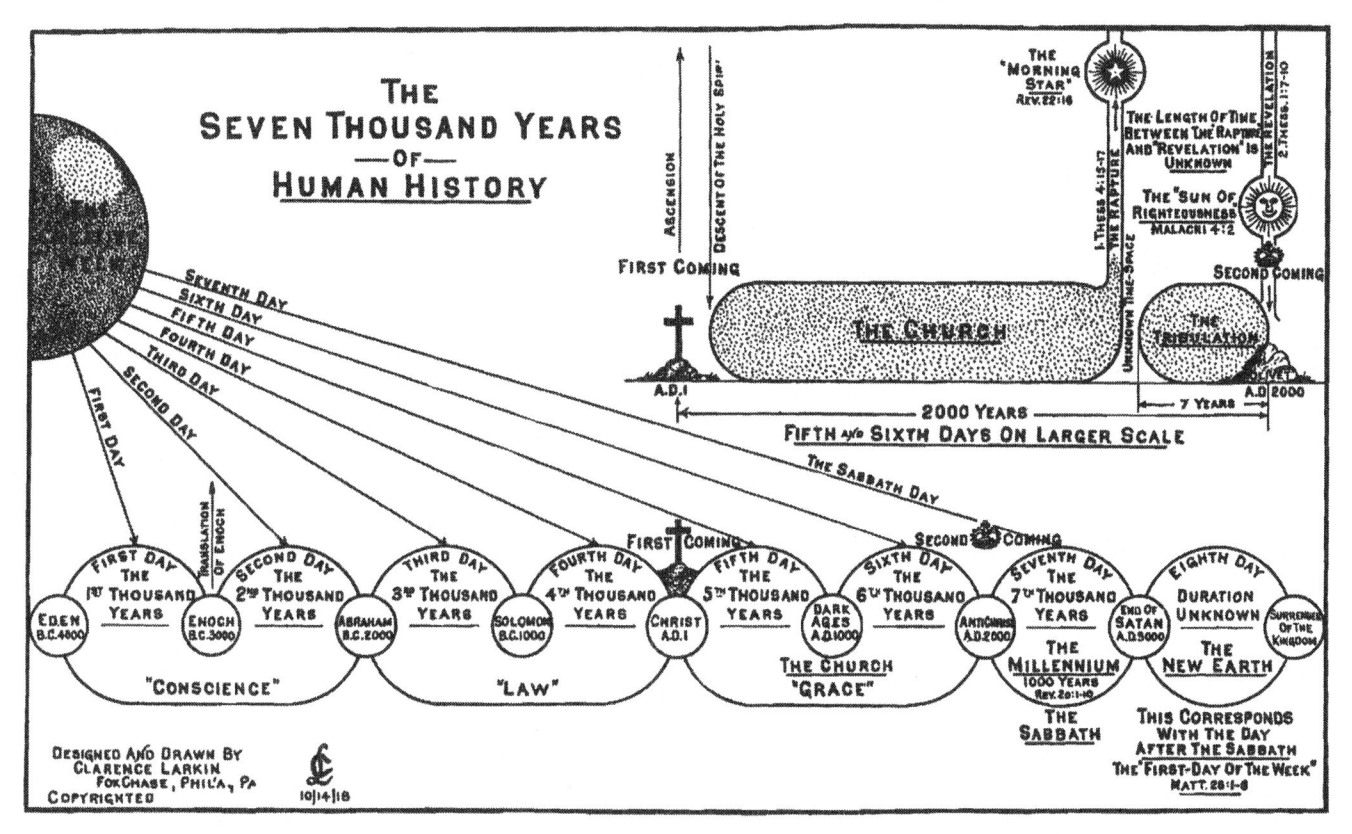

If our inference is correct, then it follows that the Return of the Lord will take place before the close of this present century. How much before is uncertain. If the Millennium is to be ushered in in A.D. 2000, then the "Rapture" must take place **at least 7 years before that.** See Chart below, on "The Seven Thousand Years of Human History." But right here we must sound a note of caution. There is too much confusion in Biblical Chronology to fix any dates with certainty. Doubtless God has ordered it so, so as to keep us in doubt as to the exact date of the Lord's Return. It may have been 4075 years, instead of 4004 (as generally given), from Adam to Christ. In that case we are living in the year 5993 from the creation of Adam, or on the eve of the Rapture. Again we must not forget that God uses in "Prophetical Chronology" the Calendar Year of 360 days to a year, while we use the Julian or Astronomical Year of 365¼ days, and it would be necessary for us to find out what kind of year is used and reduce it to the Calendar year. Thus we might find that we are nearer the end of the six thousandth year than we are aware, and that the Return of the Lord is **IMMINENT**. However, while we may look upon the above theory as suggestive and in a way confirmatory of the near coming of the Lord, it is not conclusive, and we are not warranted in fixing any date based upon it. And further, we must not forget that the "Rapture" may take place **some time** before the "Tribulation Period" begins and Antichrist is revealed. So if we could fix the exact date when this century will close, and count back 7 years, the Rapture might occur 5, 10 or even 25 years before that, so as to give time for the rebuilding of Babylon and other events that are to occur before the Tribulation Period can begin, otherwise the Rapture would not be a surprise. It is not for the Christian to look for "Times" and "Seasons" and "Signs." To do so will put him in the class of those who say: "My Lord **delayeth His Coming**" (Luke 12: 42-48), and he will become preoccupied with other things and neglect to be watchful. Let us live as if we expected the Return of our Lord at any moment.

A PRACTICAL DOCTRINE

But why, you ask, should we put so much emphasis on the "Second Coming of Christ"? Why not talk and preach about the practical affairs of life? About the social and commercial problems of the world and their solution through the Gospel? The answer is that the only way to solve these problems is for Christ to return, and the longer His "Return" is delayed, the longer it will be before these problems are solved.

1. AS TO THE JEWS.

The Jews are a downtrodden people. Their only hope is the Return of the Lord. When He comes back they shall be restored to their own land and become a nation again. "Therefore, behold, the days come, saith the Lord, that it shall no more be said, The Lord liveth, that brought up the Children of Israel out of the Land of Egypt; but the Lord liveth that brought up the Children of Israel **from the land of the NORTH** (Russia) **and from ALL THE LANDS** whither he had driven them; and I will bring them again into their **land that I gave unto their fathers.**" Jer. 16:14-15; Isa. 43:5-7. And they shall never again be dispersed. "For I will set mine eyes upon them for good, and I will bring them again to this land; and I will build them, and **not pull them down**; and I will plant them, and **not pluck them up.**" Jer. 24:6. This has never as yet been fulfilled.

2. AS TO JERUSALEM AND PALESTINE.

"Thus saith the Lord Jehovah; in the day that I will cleanse you from all your iniquities I will cause the cities (of Palestine) to be inhabited, and the waste places shall be builded. And the land that was desolate shall be tilled. . . . And they shall say, this land that was desolate is become like the garden of Eden." Ez. 36:33-35. Joel 3:18. Joel 2:24-26. "Thus saith the Lord of Hosts; there shall yet old men and old women dwell in the streets of Jerusalem, and every man with his staff in his hand for very age. And the streets of the city shall be full of boys and girls playing in the streets thereof." Zech. 8:4-5. Zech. 14:20-21.

3. AS TO THE NATIONS.

When the Lord Jesus Christ returns He will sit upon the "Throne of His Glory" at Jerusalem, and shall separate the "Sheep Nations" from the "Goat Nations," and only the "Sheep Nations" will survive as nations and be permitted to become part of the Millennial Kingdom. Matt. 25:31-40. These nations will become righteous. "And it shall come to pass that every one that is left of all the nations which come against Jerusalem shall even go up from year to year to worship the King, the Lord of Hosts, and to keep the 'Feast of Tabernacles.'" Zech. 14:16. As the result of all this the nations "shall beat their swords into plowshares and their spears into pruning hooks; nation shall not lift up a sword against nation, neither shall they learn war any more. But they shall sit every man under his vine and under his fig tree; and none shall make them afraid." Micah 4:3-4. Isa. 2:4. The only way then to stop wars and labor troubles and all socialistic and anarchistic movements is for Christ to return and set up His Millennial Kingdom.

4. AS TO SATAN.

The only way to get rid of Satan and all his evil influences and powers is for Christ to come back, for when He comes back Satan will be bound and cast into the Bottomless Pit for 1000 years. Rev. 20:1-3.

5. AS TO THE EARTH.

Since the Fall of Man the earth has been cursed with thorns and thistles and all kinds of insect pests and disease germs, and man by the sweat of his face has been compelled to earn his daily bread. Even the brute creation became **carnivorous** and learned to prey upon each other, and the "whole creation groaneth and travaileth in pain together until now." Rom. 8:22. But all this will be changed when Christ comes back, for then "the wilderness and the solitary place shall be glad for them; and the desert shall rejoice and blossom as the rose." Isa. 35:1. "Then shall the earth yield her increase." Psa. 67:6. And the ploughman will "**overtake the reaper,**" and the treader of grapes him that "soweth seed." Amos 9:13.

THE BLESSED HOPE

The Second Coming of Christ is "**The Blessed Hope.**" Writing to Titus Paul said—"Looking for that '**Blessed Hope**,' and the '**Glorious Appearing**' of the Great God and our Saviour Jesus Christ." Titus 2:13. Most Christians when speaking of their "Hope" mean their "Hope of **Salvation**," but we cannot "hope" for a thing we **have** and salvation is a present possession if we are trusting in Christ as our Saviour. The Christian's "Hope" then is the "Return of His Lord." Man is a three-fold being, he has a **body**, a **soul**, and a **spirit**; for him to die is to lose his "body." Now he knows that he cannot get his body back until the Resurrection and he also knows that there can be no Resurrection until Christ comes back. Therefore to him Christ's return is "The Blessed Hope," not only that if he dies he will then be raised, but it is to him the "Hope" that Christ will come back **before he dies** and he shall be "caught up" to meet Him in the air without dying. 1 Thess. 4:13-18.

"The Blessed Hope" is also a "Purifying Hope." "And every man that hath this hope in him PURIFIETH HIMSELF." I John 3:1-3. That is, every one who is looking for the Lord's return will try to keep himself pure. It will make us "**Patient**." "Be patient therefore, brethren, unto the **Coming of the Lord**. . . . Be ye also patient; establish your hearts; for the Coming of the Lord draweth nigh." James 5:7-8. It will make us "**Watchful**." "Watch ye therefore, for ye know not when the Master of the house cometh, at even, or at midnight, or at the cock-crowing, or in the morning; lest coming suddenly he find you sleeping. And what I say unto you I say unto all—**WATCH.**" Mark 13:35-37. If we are watching for the Lord we

"RIGHTLY DIVIDING THE WORD OF T[RUTH]"

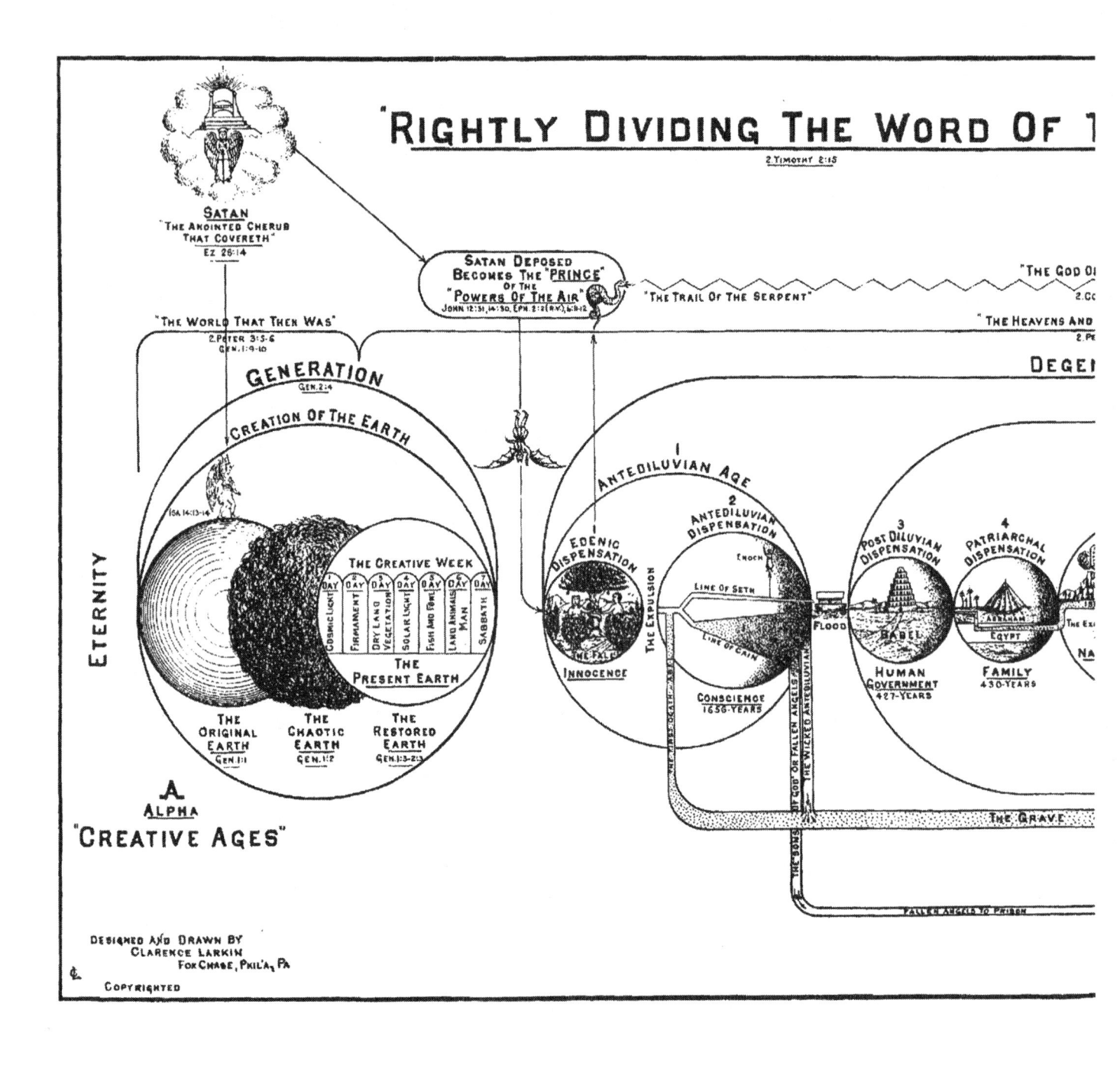

2. Timothy 2:15

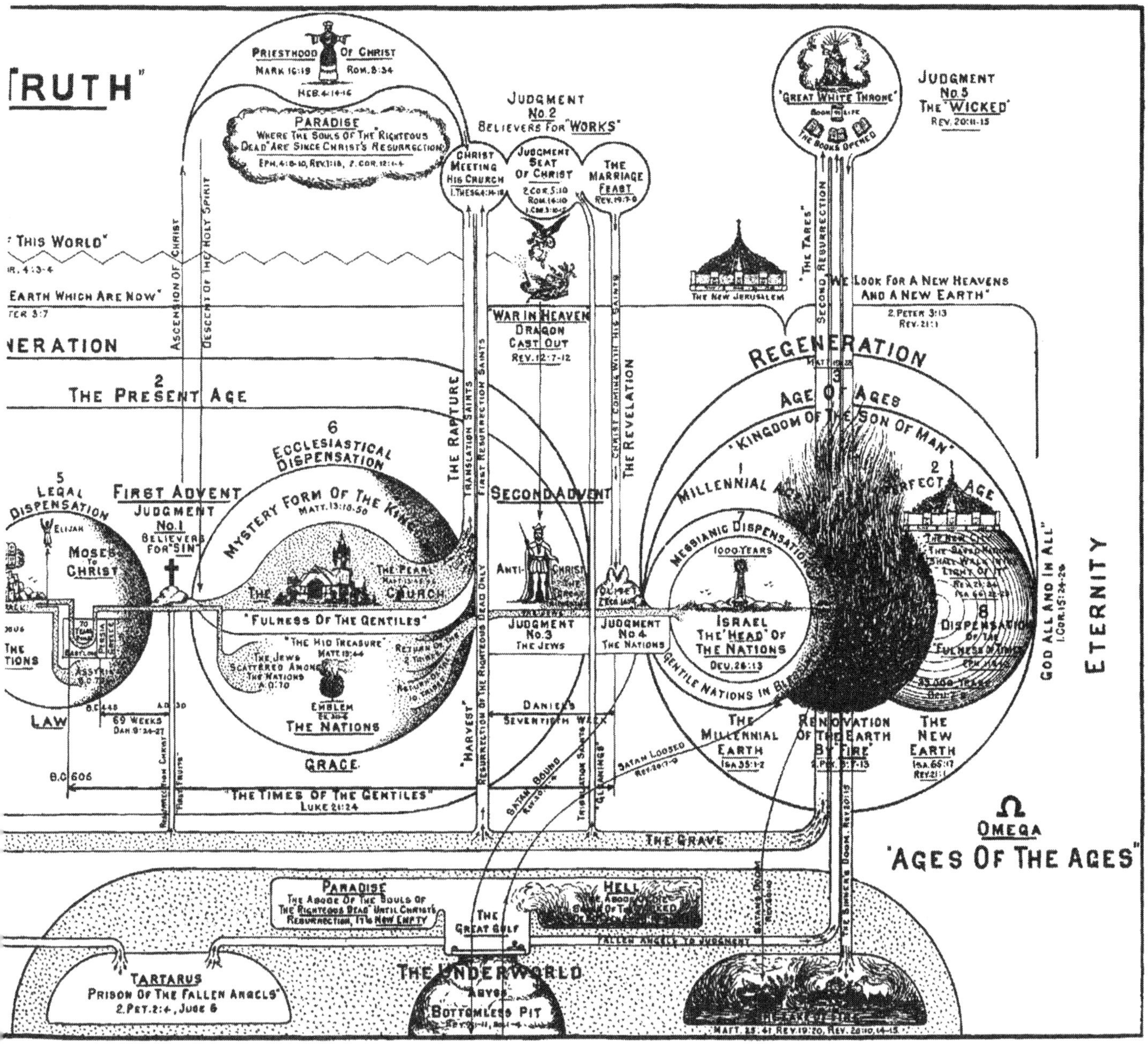

TRUTH"
PRIESTHOOD OF CHRIST
MARK 16:19 ROM. 8:34
HEB. 4:14-16
PARADISE
WHERE THE SOULS OF THE "RIGHTEOUS DEAD" ARE SINCE CHRIST'S RESURRECTION
JUDGMENT No. 2
BELIEVERS FOR "WORKS"
CHRIST MEETING HIS CHURCH
JUDGMENT SEAT OF CHRIST
2 COR. 5:10
ROM. 14:10
THE MARRIAGE FEAST
"GREAT WHITE THRONE"
THE BOOKS OPENED
JUDGMENT No. 5
THE "WICKED"
REV. 20:11-15
THIS WORLD"
EARTH WHICH ARE NOW"
ASCENSION OF CHRIST
DESCENT OF THE HOLY SPIRIT
THE NEW JERUSALEM
"THE TARES"
SECOND RESURRECTION
"WE LOOK FOR A NEW HEAVENS AND A NEW EARTH"
2 PETER 3:13
REV. 21:1
NERATION
WAR IN HEAVEN
DRAGON CAST OUT
REV. 12:7-12
REGENERATION
2
THE PRESENT AGE
THE RAPTURE
TRANSLATION SAINTS
FIRST RESURRECTION SAINTS
CHRIST COMING WITH HIS SAINTS
THE REVELATION
AGE OF AGES
"KINGDOM OF THE SON OF MAN"
6
ECCLESIASTICAL DISPENSATION
MYSTERY FORM OF THE KINGDOM
MATT. 13:18-50
5
LEGAL DISPENSATION
FIRST ADVENT
JUDGMENT No. 1
BELIEVERS FOR "SIN"
ELIJAH
MOSES TO CHRIST
SECOND ADVENT
1
MILLENNIAL AGE
2
PERFECT AGE
7
MESSIANIC DISPENSATION
1000 YEARS
ANTI-CHRIST
THE PEARL
THE CHURCH
"FULNESS OF THE GENTILES"
JUDGMENT No. 3
THE JEWS
JUDGMENT No. 4
THE NATIONS
ISRAEL
THE "HEAD" OF THE NATIONS
DEU. 28:13
8
DISPENSATION OF THE "FULNESS OF TIMES"
"THE HID TREASURE"
MATT. 13:44
THE JEWS SCATTERED AMONG THE NATIONS
A.D. 70
EMBLEM
THE NATIONS
THE NATIONS
LAW
69 WEEKS
DAN. 9:24-27
B.C. 445
A.D. 30
DANIEL'S SEVENTIETH WEEK
GENTILE NATIONS IN BLESSING
THE MILLENNIAL EARTH
ISA. 35:1-2
RENOVATION OF THE EARTH BY FIRE
THE NEW EARTH
ISA. 65:17
REV. 21:1
GOD ALL AND IN ALL"
1 COR. 15:24-28
ETERNITY
GRACE
"HARVEST"
RESURRECTION OF THE RIGHTEOUS DEAD ONLY
SATAN BOUND
SATAN LOOSED
B.C. 606
"THE TIMES OF THE GENTILES"
LUKE 21:24
RESURRECTION CHRIST
FIRST FRUITS
TRIBULATION SAINTS
"GLEANINGS"
Ω
OMEGA
"AGES OF THE AGES"
THE GRAVE
PARADISE
THE ABODE OF THE SOULS OF THE RIGHTEOUS DEAD UNTIL CHRIST'S RESURRECTION, IT'S NOW EMPTY
HELL
THE ABODE OF THE SOULS OF THE WICKED
THE GREAT GULF
FALLEN ANGELS TO JUDGMENT
THE UNDERWORLD
TARTARUS
PRISON OF THE FALLEN ANGELS"
2 PET. 2:4, JUDE 6
ABYSS
BOTTOMLESS PIT
MATT. 25:41 REV. 19:20, REV. 20:10, 14-15

will be careful of our conduct. We will not want Him to come and find us doing questionable things, or in questionable places. We will not want to hoard money, nor spend our money in an extravagant manner, we will want to lay up for ourselves treasures in heaven by contributing to missions. We will see to it that in our homes there is no kind of literature, or art, or pictures, or anything that we would not like His pure eyes to see if He were to be a visitor in our home. In short, "The Blessed Hope" helps us to cling lightly to this world. It will not make us idle and negligent, but will fill us with zeal to be found a faithful servant at His return. For this reason it is a noteworthy fact and a witness to the power of the doctrine, that those who believe it are the most consecrated, unselfish, and strenuous workers in the Master's service.

This "Hope" will also keep us from being **"ASHAMED"** at His Coming. "And now, little children, abide in Him; that when He **shall appear**, we may have confidence, and not be **ASHAMED** before **Him at His Coming."** I John 2:28. If we are watching for Him and our house is in order, and we are ready to give a faithful account of our Stewardship we shall not be ashamed before Him at His coming. Matt. 25:14-30.

The "Hope" of the Lord's Pre-Millennial Return fills the heart of those who believe it with **Joy**. In Luke 24:52 we read that when Jesus was parted from His Disciples and ascended into Heaven, "They returned to Jerusalem with **GREAT JOY**, and were continually in the Temple, **PRAISING** and **BLESSING** God." That seems strange conduct on their part, for naturally we would suppose that His Departure would have filled them with sadness. But when we recall that, when He Ascended, two men stood by in white apparel and told them that Jesus would come back again, we can understand their **joyfulness.** Acts 1:11.

It has often been said in opposition to the doctrine of the Second Coming, "If Christian people believe that Jesus is soon coming back why do they build houses and churches and make investments and plan for the education of their children and so on?" The answer is that Jesus' coming back will not do away with the need for houses and churches and education. The world moved on just as before after His First Coming, and it will do the same after His Second Coming. People will need homes and churches. Business will go on as before, and the unconverted children of Christian believers will be left behind and need homes and education and means to live on. The prosperity of the world will be greater during the Millennium than ever before. So there is no occasion for those who are looking for the Lord's Return to neglect the affairs of this life. What we as Christians hope for is that the Lord will come back and take us out of the world before the awful days of the "Tribulation Period" come, and then when they are over and Jesus comes back to reign we shall come back with Him as glorified beings to rule and reign over the Millennial earth, and probably visit churches where once we worshipped, and institutions that our money built.

The preacher of the Doctrine of the Pre-Millennial Coming of Christ wields a "two-edged sword." The unbeliever when urged to become a Christian may say I am young and there is plenty of time and so may put off the time of decision, but when he is told that it is not a question of time, or the mere salvation of his soul, but that Jesus may be back at any time and it is a question of being ready to meet Him, then he sees the importance of immediate decision.

Dear reader, are you a Christian, and as a Christian are you a believer in the "Blessed Hope," and are you looking for the speedy coming of the Lord, and doing all you can to hasten His Return, and thus bring back **THE KING?** If not, I beseech you to drop everything and settle the question of whether you will be **"caught up"** to meet the Lord in the air when He comes, and thus escape the awful days that are coming on the earth—days in which no one can buy or sell unless he has the "Mark of the Beast," and all those who have that "Mark" are eternally doomed. Rev. 13:15-17.

"WATCH"

By Warren M. Smith.

Oh, the glory fast approaching, of Ascension's happy morn,
When the watchful servants quickly to His bosom shall be borne;
When the dear ones left behind us, shall for us oft seek in vain,
But our spirits shall have risen to the Lamb for sinners slain.

Caught up in the air to meet Him, oh! the heights and depths of joy,
Lengths and breadths of love surpassing, purest bliss without alloy;
Now we see with darkened vision, then we'll see Him face to face,
And we will, through countless ages, sing the glories of His grace.

Two shall at a mill be grinding, one be taken, one be left,
Two shall in a bed be sleeping, one of these shall be bereft;
Oh, what wonder and amazement, shall the ones on earth, possess,
They shall pass through tribulation, pain, and sorrow and distress.

We shall live with Him forever, in the sunshine of His love,
We shall meet to part, no never, with th' angelic host above;
There we'll hear our Father's welcome, as He calls us, one by one,
Saying to each one in person, "Faithful servant, 'tis well done."

Let us, then, our lamps keep burning, and our wedding garments on,
Ready to go forth to meet Him, when we hear Him say, "I come;"
There will be no time to slumber, lest He come whil'st we're asleep,
And the door be shut between us; let us then our vigil keep.

V
RIGHTLY DIVIDING THE WORD

Writing to Timothy, Paul said—

"Study to show thyself approved of God, a workman that needeth not to be ashamed, **Rightly Dividing the Word of Truth.**" 2 Tim. 2:15.

The student of the "Word of God" is here spoken of as a "Workman." A workman cannot intelligently do his work without a plan. He must have drawings and specifications. God said to Moses as to the Tabernacle,

"See that thou make all things according to the 'Pattern' showed to thee in the mount." Heb. 8:5.

The student of God's Word must understand

"God's Plan and Purpose in the Ages,"

or there will be confusion in his work of interpreting the Scriptures.

To this end charts are indispensable. But care must be taken not to depend on them alone. While the drawings and specifications of a building are separate, they must correspond. So a Biblical chart must correspond with the "Word of God," or it may lead to error. The two must be compared.

St. Augustine said—"Distinguish the 'Periods' and the Scriptures will harmonize." After an address by Rev. Dr. A. J. Gordon on "The Plan of the Ages," a gentleman said to him, "Why, Doctor, you have a 'Pigeon Hole' for every text."

We must learn to

"Rightly Divide the Word of Truth."

While the "Word of Truth" is written **FOR all classes of people**, and **FOR our learning**, it is not **addressed** to all peoples in general, but part of it is addressed to the **JEWS**, part to the **GENTILES**, and part to the **CHURCH**. These three constitute the **THREE CLASSES** into which humanity is divided. 1 Cor. 10:32. It follows therefore that while the whole Bible was written for the **INSTRUCTION** of the Church, it is not all written **ABOUT** the Church. The Church is not mentioned in the Old Testament. It was hid from the Old Testament prophets, and was a "Mystery" first revealed to Paul, and disclosed by him in Eph. 3:1-10. The Old Testament is mostly taken up with the history of one nation, that of Israel. In the first five chapters of Genesis we are given the history of Creation, and 1700 years of human history. In the next four chapters we are given the account of the Flood. The tenth and eleventh chapters give the account of 400 more years of human history, and then God singles out one man, Abraham (Gen. 12:1-3), and from there on the whole of the Old Testament centres around the Jewish Race. When we take the Old Testament promises and apply them to the Church we rob the Jew of that which is exclusively his. For illustration, the prophecy of Isaiah is largely applied to the Church, whereas the very first verse declares that it is—"Concerning **JUDAH** and **JERUSALEM.**" Isa. 1:1. In the New Testament the Epistles of Hebrews and James are Jewish. The Epistle of James is addressed, not to the Church, but to the "**TWELVE TRIBES** scattered abroad." James 1:1. Therefore the "Prayer of Faith" (James 5:13-16) for the sick is not primarily a promise to the Church but to Israel, though doubtless it will be answered for all who comply with the conditions. In the Epistle to the Hebrews many Christians stumble at the words "**fall away**" (Heb. 6:4-6), and "**if we sin wilfully.**" Heb. 10:26. But these words do not apply to Christians. They were spoken to apostate Jewish professors of Christianity who had never been born again, and who, if they did not accept Jesus as their Messiah, practically crucified Him again, and were as bad as their brethren who did crucify Him.

Some books are general. As for instance the Epistle to the Romans. No one would apply Romans 8th to the Jews, or Romans 11th to the Church, for in it Paul speaks not only to Israel but also to the Gentiles. Rom. 11:11-13. **ALL** Scripture is profitable for **doctrine**, for **reproof**, for **correction**, for **instruction**, (2 Tim. 3:16), and what happened to Israel was written for our **ENSAMPLE** and **ADMONITION**, (1 Cor. 10:11), but we must not apply to the Church what does not belong to it. We see then that to **misapply** scripture is to not "Rightly Divide the Word" and tends to confusion and error.

In "Rightly Dividing the Word of Truth," we must also distinguish the work of Christ. We are told in the Scriptures that He is a "Prophet," "Priest" and "King." But He does not hold those offices conjointly but successively. From the Fall in Eden to the Cross, He was a "Prophet." He is now a "High Priest" and when He comes again He will be a "King." From Eden to the Cross there was an "Altar," from the Cross to the Crown there is a "Table" (the Lord's Table), and from the Crown to Christ's surrender of the Kingdom there is a "Throne." See the chart on "The Greater Life and Work of Christ."

In Heb. 1:1, we read—God hath spoken "**at SUNDRY TIMES**," as well as "**in DIVERS MANNERS**," and if we are to understand what He has spoken, we must not only distinguish between the class of people He has spoken to, as the Jews, Gentiles or the Church, but we must also note the "**SUNDRY TIMES**" at which He spoke, and the "**DIVERS MANNERS**." We must also distinguish between the "**TIME PAST**" when He spoke by the **Prophets**, and these "**LAST DAYS**" in which He hath spoken to us by His **SON**. Heb. 1:1-2. We must not forget the "**DIVINE CONJUNCTIONS**" and "**DIVINE DISJUNCTIONS**" of the Word of God. We must not separate what God has joined, as the "Word of God" and the "Spirit of God," "Christ and Salvation," "Faith and Works." Neither must we join what God has separated, as "Heaven and Hell," "Baptism and Regeneration," "Natural Heredity" and "Spiritual Heredity," "Standing and State," "the Church and the Kingdom."

We must also distinguish between the "**TIMES**" and "**SEASONS**" of the Scriptures. Daniel said of God—"He changeth the **'TIMES'** and the **'SEASONS'**," (Dan. 2:21), and Jesus said to His Disciples—"It is not for you to know the '**TIMES**' or the '**SEASONS**'." Acts 1:7. Job testified that the "**TIMES** are not hidden from the Almighty." Job 24:1. And of the Children of Issachar it was said that they had "understanding of the **TIMES**." I. Chron. 12:32. By the "**SEASONS**" we are to understand the climatic changes of the earth due to the movements and changing characteristics of the Sun, Moon and Stars, which God ordained to regulate the "Seasons." Gen. 1:14. As to the "**TIMES**" we have them designated as the "**TIMES OF IGNORANCE**," (Acts 17:30); the "**TIMES OF THE GENTILES**," (Luke 21:24); the "**TIMES OF REFRESHING**," (Acts 3:19); the "**TIMES OF RESTITUTION**," (Acts 3:21); and the "Dispensation of the **FULNESS OF TIMES**." Eph. 1:10. See Chart of "The Times and Seasons."

From the statement, "The Times of the **GENTILES**," we see that when the "Gentiles" are in power the "Jews" are not. And as the "Times of the **GENTILES**" is still running, the Church cannot be in this Dispensation a governing or Kingdom power.

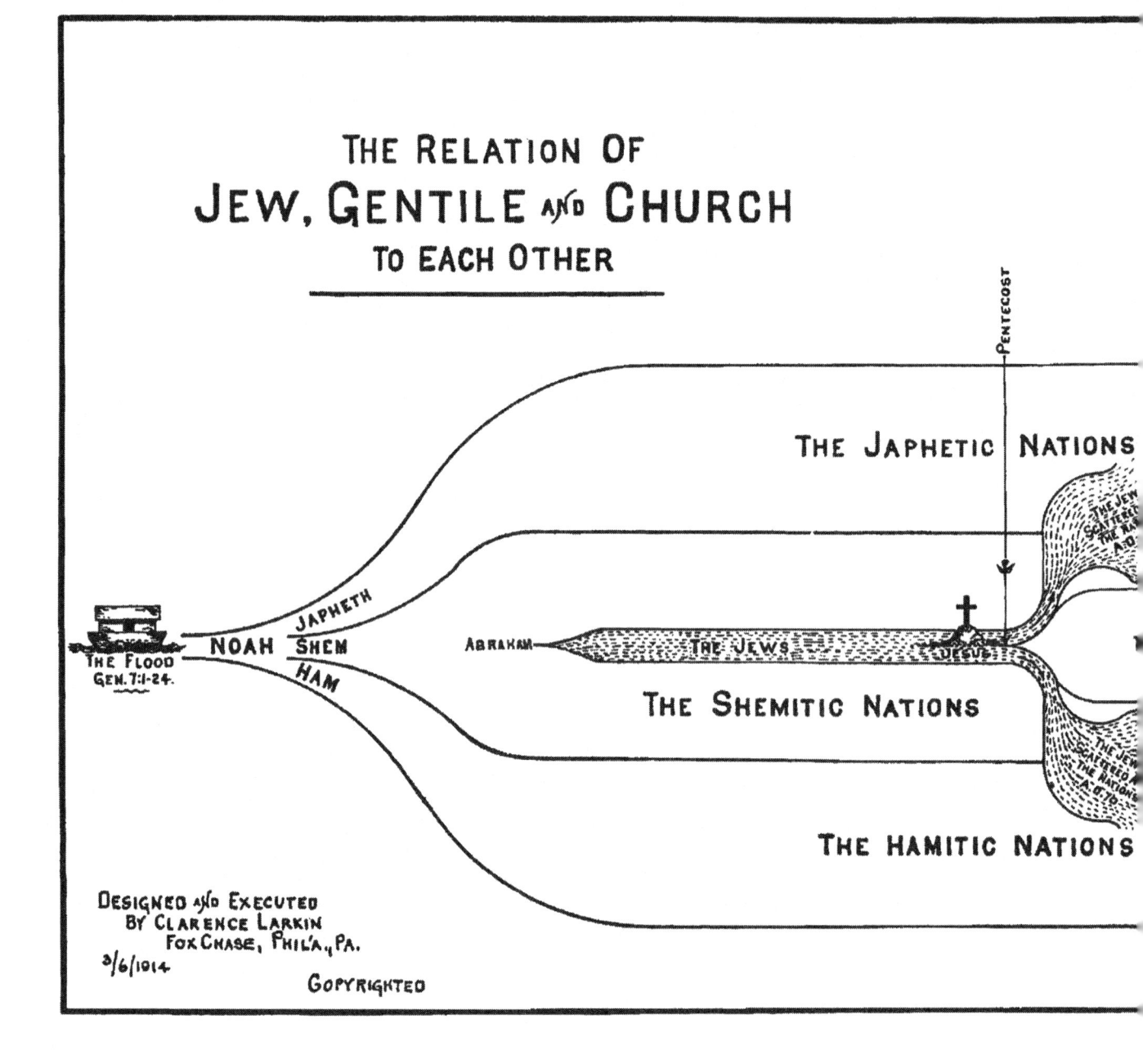

The Relation Of Jew, Gentile and Church To Each Other

THE JAPHETIC NATIONS

PENTECOST

THE FLOOD
GEN. 7:1-24.

NOAH
JAPHETH
SHEM
HAM

ABRAHAM THE JEWS JESUS

THE JEWS SCATTERED AMONG THE NATIONS A.D. 70

THE SHEMITIC NATIONS

THE HAMITIC NATIONS

Designed and Executed
By Clarence Larkin
Fox Chase, Phil'a., Pa.
3/6/1914
Copyrighted

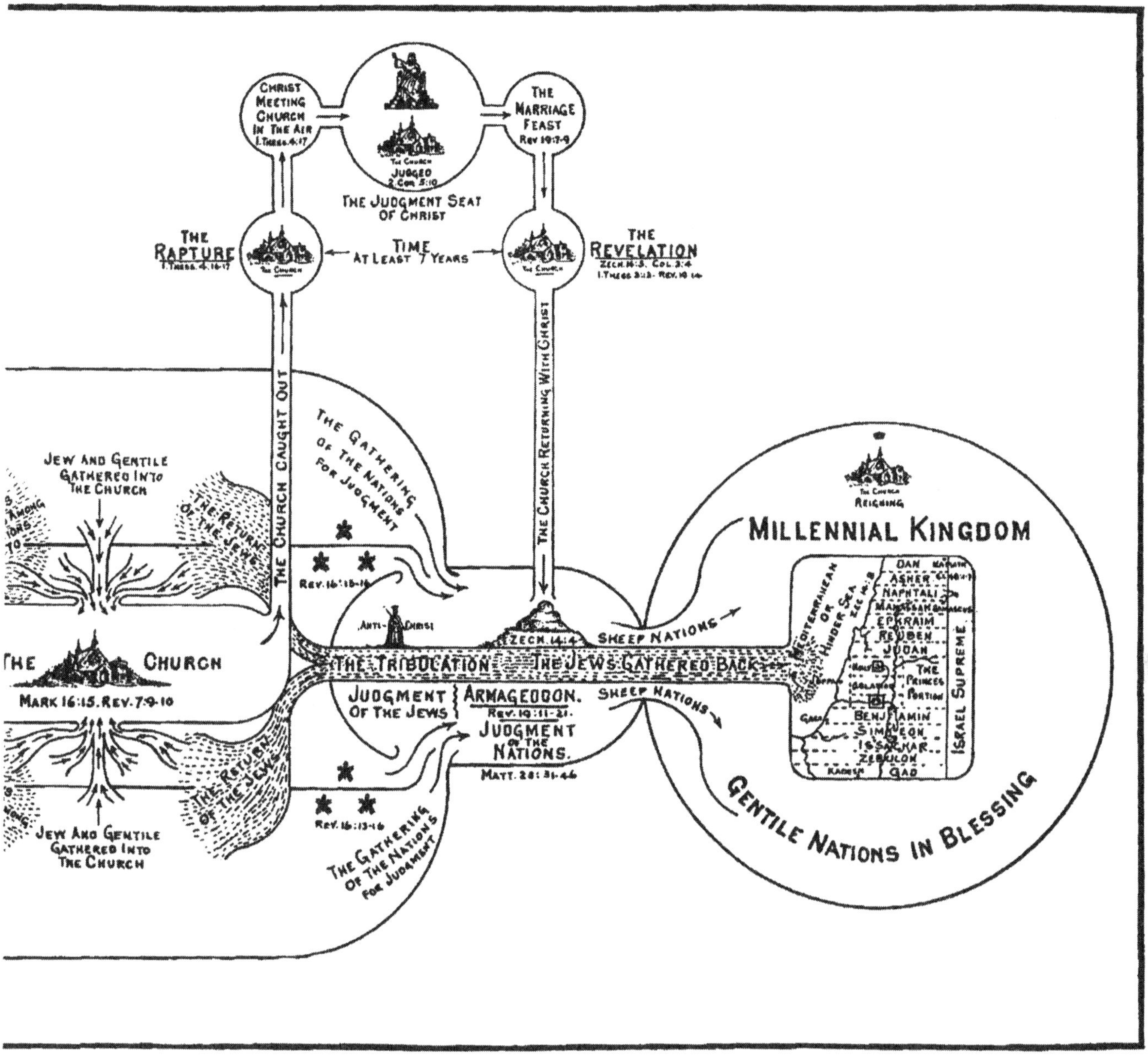
Christ Meeting Church In The Air
I. Thess. 4:17
The Church Judged
2 Cor. 5:10
The Judgment Seat Of Christ
The Marriage Feast
Rev 19:7-9
The Rapture
I. Thess. 4:16-17
The Church
Time
At Least 7 Years
The Revelation
The Church
The Church Caught Out
The Church Returning With Christ
The Gathering Of The Nations For Judgment
Jew And Gentile Gathered Into The Church
The Return Of The Jews
Rev. 16:13-16
The Church
Mark 16:15. Rev. 7:9-10
Anti-Christ
Zech. 14:4
The Tribulation
The Jews Gathered Back
Judgment Of The Jews
Armageddon.
Rev. 19:11-21.
Judgment Of The Nations.
Matt. 25:31-46
Sheep Nations
The Church Reigning
Millennial Kingdom
Mediterranean Or Hinder Sea
Dan
Asher
Naphtali
Ephraim
Reuben
Judah
The Princes Portion
Benjamin
Simeon
Issachar
Zebulon
Gad
Israel Supreme
Gentile Nations In Blessing
Jew And Gentile Gathered Into The Church
The Gathering Of The Nations For Judgment

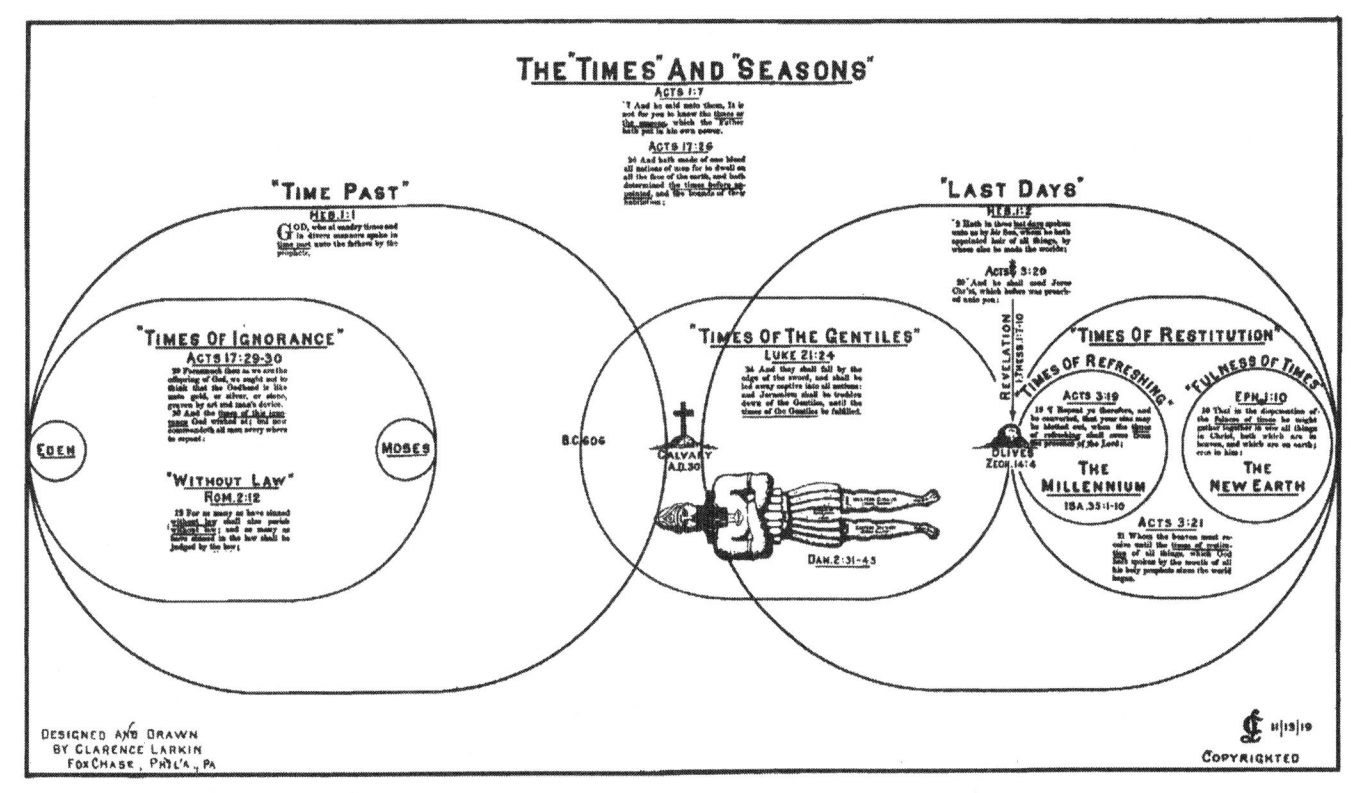

But it is not enough to classify the Scriptures in the manner already mentioned, we must learn to separate the Scriptures as to "TIME" and "ETERNITY" and the different "AGES" and "DISPENSATIONS" of "Time." A reference to the Chart—"RIGHTLY DIVIDING THE WORD" will reveal the fact that outside of "TIME" the Scriptures mention "TWO AGES:" before "Time," the "ALPHA" or "CREATIVE AGES," and after "Time," the "OMEGA" or "AGES OF THE AGES." In "Time" there are three "AGES" and seven "DISPENSATIONS." The three "AGES" are—

1. THE ANTEDILUVIAN AGE.

This extends from the "Fall" to the "Flood."

2. THE PRESENT AGE.

This extends from the "Flood" to the "Second Coming of Christ."

3. THE AGE OF AGES.

This extends from the "Second Coming of Christ" to the "End of Time." This last "Age" is a "Dual Age" composed of—

1. The Millennial Age.
2. The Perfect Age.

The "Millennial Age" is also a "Dispensation" in its relation to the six preceding Dispensations.

An "Age" in Scripture is from one "cataclysmic" or "climatic" change to another in the earth's surface or condition. This corresponds to what is called in Geology an "Age." So we see that Science and the Bible agree as to the meaning of the word "Age."

We know that at the time of the Flood there were great "cataclysmic" and "climatic" changes, for the **fountains of the great deep were broken up.**" Gen. 7:11. That is, there was a subsidence of the land that resulted in great physical changes that affected the climate of the earth, and divested the atmosphere of some of its life-sustaining properties, so that the length of life was reduced from 900 to 100 years, and later to threescore and ten.

At the beginning of the Millennium all this will be reversed, for when Christ comes back—

"His feet shall stand in that day (Millennial Day) upon the Mount of Olives, which is before Jerusalem on the east; and the Mount of Olives shall **cleave in the midst thereof** toward the east and toward the west, and there shall be a very great valley; and **half of the mountain shall remove toward the north and half of it toward the south.**"

"All the land shall be turned as **a plain from Geba to Rimmon south of Jerusalem and it shall be lifted up.**" Zech. 14:4, 10. In verse eight we read—

"Living waters shall go out from Jerusalem; half of them toward the 'former sea' (Red Sea) and half of them toward the 'hinder sea' (Mediterranean)."

That means that the Dead Sea, that is now 1200 feet below the Mediterranean, is to be elevated, and its water flow south to the Red sea, and that it shall lose its saltness and be filled with fish, for we read in Ezekiel 47:1-12, that fishermen shall spread their nets upon its shores.

This great "cataclysmic" change is going to make a great change in the climate and restore the life-sustaining power of the atmosphere like unto that before the Flood, for we read in Isaiah 65:20, that in the Millennial days that are to follow—

"There shall be no more thence an infant of days, nor an old man that hath not filled his days; for the child shall die an hundred years old."

That is, a person a hundred years old shall only be considered a child, which means that men shall live again in the Millennium to the age of Methusaleh.

The Chart is divided into 3 "Ages," corresponding to the Divine number "Three" (Father, Son and Holy Spirit); and into 7 "Dispensations," to correspond to the Perfect number "Seven" composed of the Divine number "Three" and the World number "Four"— Winter. Spring, Summer and Autumn, or the four elements, Earth, Air, Fire and Water.

The difference between an "AGE" and a "DISPENSATION" is that an "AGE" stands for a period between two great physical changes in the earth's surface, while a "DISPENSATION" stands for a "moral" or "probationary" period in the world's history. The form of "Administration" is different in each "Dispensation." For illustration, the Administration of the Jewish Dispensation was that of "LAW," the Administration of the present Dispensation is of "GRACE," and of the one to follow is "RIGHTEOUSNESS."

All the confusion about the "Ages," "Dispensations," and "End of the World" is largely due to the mistranslation of two Greek words in the New Testament.

The first word is "Kosmos." It means the **external arrangement and beauty of the natural world**, and includes the thought of nations, peoples, and worldly possessions, as in Matt. 4:8.

"Again the Devil taketh him up into an exceeding high mountain, and sheweth him all the kingdoms of the world and the glory of them."

Also Matt. 13:38, "The Field is the World." And Luke 11:50, "That the blood of all the prophets, which was shed from the 'foundation of the World,' may be required of this generation." This word "Kosmos" occurs 170 times and is always translated "World."

The second word is "Aion" and means "Age," "Dispensation," "Indefinite Time." It occurs 28 times, and is also translated "World."

To show how misleading this translation is we need only to cite a passage or two. Take Matt. 13:39, 40, 49.

"The enemy that sowed them is the Devil; and the harvest is the **end of the world**."

It should read—the "end of the Age." "Be not conformed to this world (Age)." Rom. 12:2. "In whom the god of this world (Age) hath blinded the minds of them which believe not." 2 Cor. 4:4. "Who gave himself for our sins, that he might deliver us from this present evil world (Age)." Gal. 1:4. "Charge them that are rich in this world (Age)." 1 Tim. 6:17. "Hath in these last days spoken unto us by his Son, whom he hath appointed heir of all things, by whom also he made the worlds (Ages)." Heb. 1:2. "Through faith we understand that the worlds (Ages) were framed by the Word of God (Jesus)." Heb. 11:3. From this we see that Jesus not only made the "earth-worlds," John 1:1-3, but He also made the "time-worlds," that is, He planned the "Ages" and "Dispensations."

Let us now take up the "Ages" and "Dispensations" and study them separately.

I. THE CREATIVE AGES

The Scriptures begin with the sublime declaration—

"In the beginning God 'CREATED' the heaven and the earth." Gen. 1:1.

As the word "heaven" is in the singular it will clarify matters to limit this creative act to our own planet, and the solar system to which it belongs, rather than to the whole of the starry spaces or universe.

1. THE ORIGINAL OR PRE-ADAMITE EARTH

This creation was in the dateless past. It was not at the beginning of the first day as described in Gen. 1:3-5. The six days' work as described in Gen. 1:3-31 was the **restoration of the earth** (not the heavens or starry space), to its original condition before it was made "formless and void," and submerged in water and darkness.

Peter speaks of it as the "World that **then was**, that being **overflowed with water**, perished." 2 Pet. 3:5-7.

The manner of the "creation" of the Pre-Adamite Earth is not revealed in the Scriptures. They simply declare that—"In the BEGINNING GOD CREATED the heaven and the earth." We have to fall back then upon Science. Among the theories advanced for the origin of the Solar System of which our Earth is a part is—

THE NEBULAR HYPOTHESIS

In the year 1796 the astronomer La Place advanced the theory that the sun, planets and moons of our Solar System were once one vast spherical mass of nebulous or gaseous matter, out of which they have developed. He claimed that this mass of nebulous matter coming in contact with the cold of space began to contract, and in contracting a rotary motion was set up around its center, and the more rapidly it cooled the faster it revolved, until it became flattened at the poles and protruded at the equator, until it more resembled two watch crystals placed edge to edge than it did a round ball. As the cooling progressed, and the rapidity of revolution increased, a ring of matter was detached from the edge of the watch-crystal shaped mass, which still continued to revolve around the parent mass, which parent mass as it cooled shrunk away from the ring, and that this process continued until a number of rings were thrown off, all revolving in the same direction within each other and around the central mass. These rings of matter as they separately condensed were broken into fragments, and some of the fragments were retarded and others accelerated until they coalesced and formed a globe which continued to revolve in the same direction, the outermost ring forming the planet Neptune and the innermost Mercury. The central mass of this nebulous matter, after the rings had been separated from the parent mass, is now our sun.

The moons of the planets were formed in the same manner, they having been detached rings of matter circling around their respective planets. As an evidence of this we have the rings of Saturn, that doubtless in time will break up and form moons for that planet.

Between Mars and Jupiter there seems to be a break in the series, which can only be accounted for by supposing that the Asteroids, which appear to be the fragments of a planet, and that all revolve around the sun in the same direction as the other planets, are the fragments of a nebulous ring that would have formed a planet if it had not been for the nearness of the immense planet Jupiter.

If the sun and planets of our Solar System sprang from the same parent mass, they should be composed of the same chemical elements,

CHART OF THE CREATION OF THE EARTH

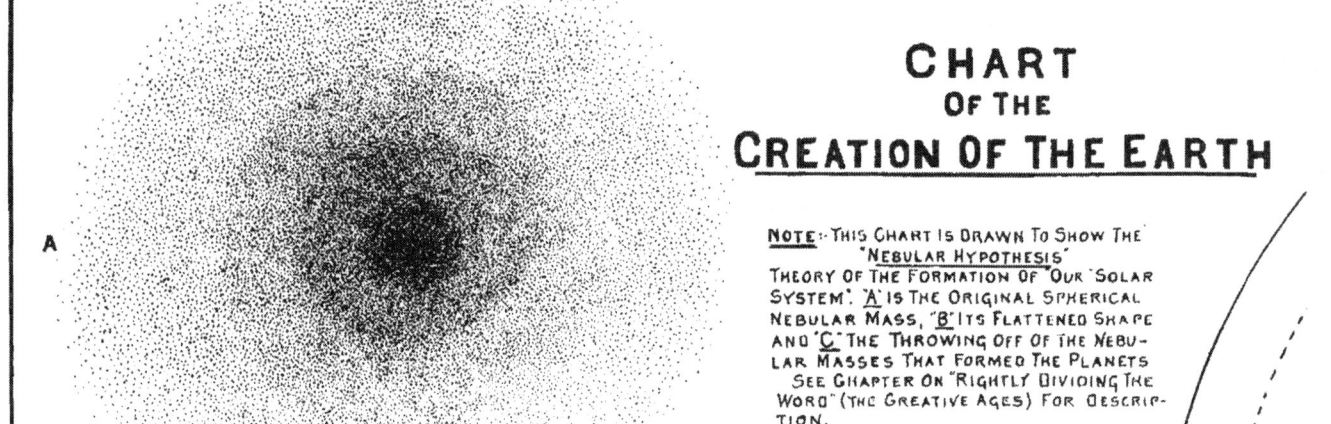

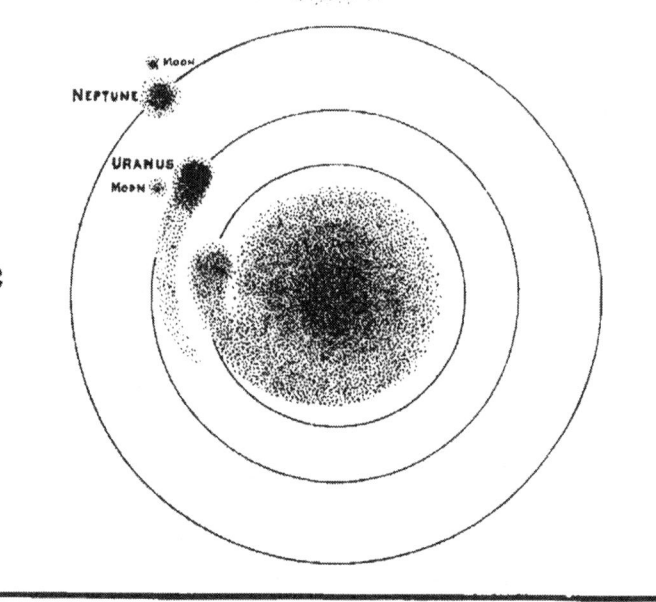

NOTE: This Chart is Drawn To Show The "Nebular Hypothesis" Theory Of The Formation Of "Our Solar System". "A" Is The Original Spherical Nebular Mass, "B" Its Flattened Shape And "C" The Throwing Off Of The Nebular Masses That Formed The Planets. See Chapter On "Rightly Dividing The Word" (The Creative Ages) For Description.

Designed And Drawn By
Clarence Larkin
FoxChase, Phil'a., Pa.
Copyrighted

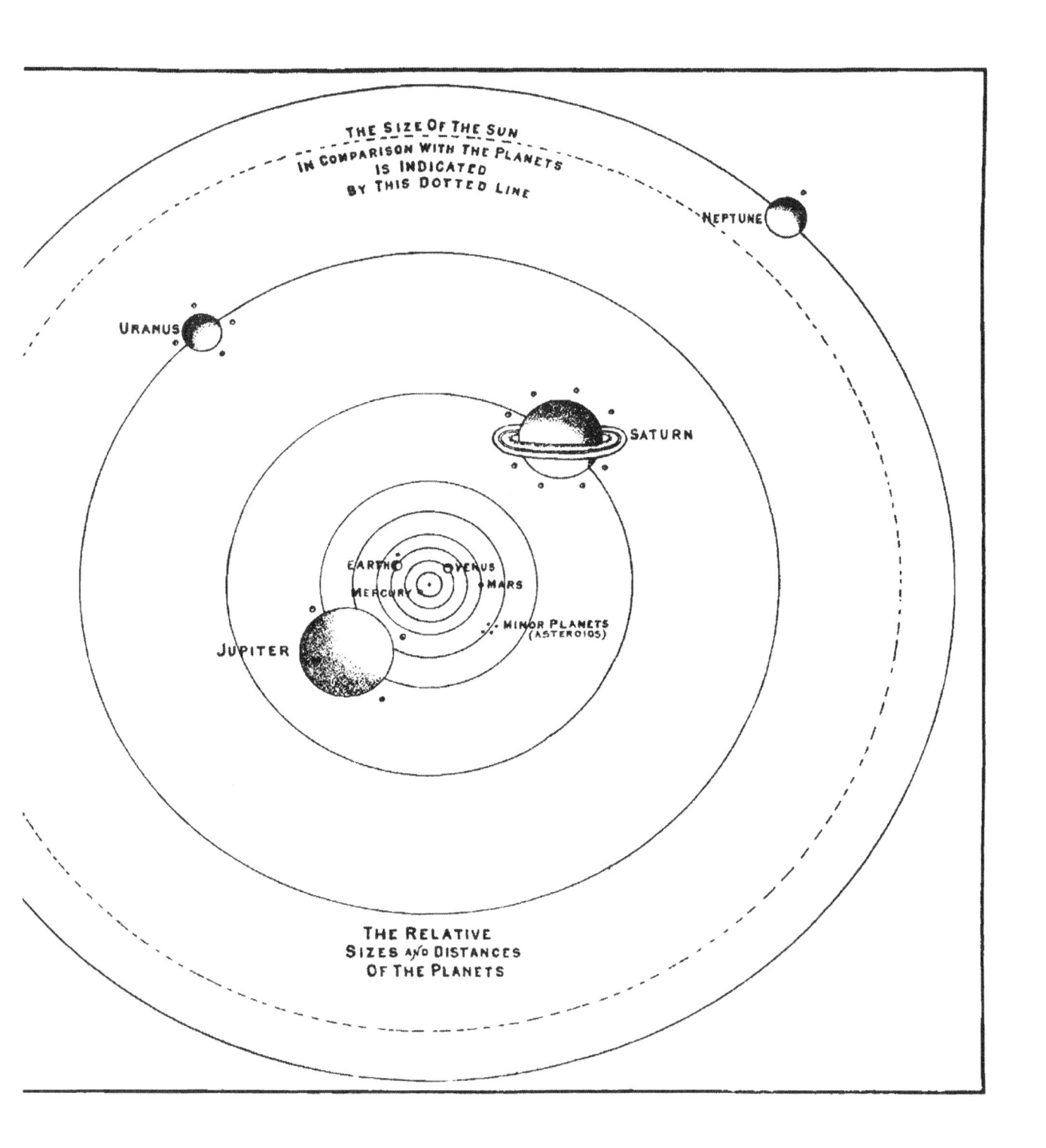

THE SIZE OF THE SUN IN COMPARISON WITH THE PLANETS IS INDICATED BY THIS DOTTED LINE

NEPTUNE

URANUS

SATURN

EARTH VENUS
MERCURY MARS
MINOR PLANETS (ASTEROIDS)

JUPITER

THE RELATIVE SIZES AND DISTANCES OF THE PLANETS

and this has been verified by spectroscopic analysis. Naturally we would suppose that the outermost planets, having been thrown off first, would be in the most advanced stage, but we must not forget that the larger the mass the slower it cools, and therefore, if the Nebular Hypothesis is correct, Jupiter and Saturn must still be very hot, and not as far advanced and fit for habitation as the earth, and this we know to be the fact.

Objection has been raised to the "Nebular Hypothesis" Theory on the basis that a "gaseous" nebula could not exist in the cold of space, and that the nebulous matter of the nebula is not gas, but meteoric luminous matter, made luminous by the collision of meteoric particles, and out of the union of these particles the planets were formed. Another theory is that the planets have been formed by the union of smaller planetary bodies that were welded together by the immense heat generated by their impact upon each other. But each theory has its difficulties.

A survey of the heavens reveals numerous "spiral nebula" that seem to be "Solar Systems" in the process of formation, but the invention of powerful telescopes has revealed that many of these nebula are not gaseous but clusters of stars. Nevertheless it has been shown that many of the nebula are gaseous, but it was not until May, 1914, that Dr. Slipher, of the Flagstaff Observatory, Arizona, by spectograms proved that the nebula in the Constellation of Virgo was revolving, this proving that the Nebular Hypothesis of La Place is not without foundation.

The proofs of the Nebular Hypothesis are—(1) The orbits of the planets are nearly circular. (2) They revolve almost in the same plane as the sun's equator. (3) They all revolve around the sun in the same direction, which is also the direction of the sun's rotation. (4) They rotate on their own axis also, as far as known, in the same direction. (5) Their satellites or moons, with the exception of those of Uranus and Neptune, revolve in the same direction as their planet. (6) The earth is still cooling, as is proved by its outer crust and internal fire that finds vents in volcanoes, for when we examine a hot ball and find it warmer inside than out we know it is cooling off.

The time was then when our earth was a globular mass of molten matter surrounded by an atmosphere of gaseous and metallic vapors. As the globular mass cooled off by radiation a thin crust of rocky formation was formed on its outer surface. This increased slowly in thickness, and as the interior mass shrunk in cooling the outer crust fell in or wrinkled, and was here and there by earthquake and volcanic action tilted out of the horizontal, and thus was formed the diverse stratification of the rocky foundation of the earth's surface. The cooling of the earth's surface and the formation of its rocky crust permitted its gaseous and metallic vaporous atmosphere to cool, and the metallic vapors condensed and were precipitated in the form of metallic rain upon the earth's crust, and, according to their specific gravity, they collected and distributed themselves in pockets and recesses of the earth's crust to be later by upheavals and changes in the earth's crust thrown to the surface for the use of man.

In the course of time—and the formation of our Solar System took thousands upon thousands of years—the earth cooled off sufficiently to permit the oxygen and hydrogen in the atmosphere to form water, that fell in the form of rain on the earth, but like when water falls upon a red-hot plate it is immediately turned into steam, the first rain that fell was vaporized by the heat of the earth's crust, but, continuing to fall, it finally so cooled the earth's surface as to be able to remain and form seas and oceans. As time passed on the rocky surface of the earth was disintegrated and formed soil, and when the soil was fit, vegetation and trees and plant life appeared. Then came the lower orders of marine life, followed by fish and fowl. Then the land animals, and whatever other orders of beings that inhabited the original earth.

That we may have a faint idea of the time it took for the earth to become habitable, we have only to turn to the Carboniferous Period of its history. Coal is formed from vegetable matter. In the Carboniferous Period the atmosphere was full of Carbonic Acid Gas, in which animal life could not exist. The atmosphere was moist and steamy like that of a hothouse, and vegetation was very rank, and ferns and plant life grew to immense proportions. By atmospheric and earthquake action the immense forests of the Carboniferous Period were thrown down and buried under layers of soil and rock, until their vegetable matter was compressed into coal. This was repeated until coal bed after coal bed was formed in overlying seams. The time it took to form these beds of coal is seen when we learn that it would take 1200 years for the most luxuriant vegetation of the present day to form a coal seam 6 inches thick, or 7200 years to form a seam 3 feet thick, the thinnest that can be worked to advantage. In the coal measures of Nova Scotia are 76 seams of coal, of which one is 22 feet thick, and another 37. Thus we see that it took thousands of years to form the coal beds of the earth alone. How many millenniums of years must it not have required then for the earth to pass from a molten state to a habitable condition?

But the "Word of God" and the "Works of God" must harmonize. There can be no conflict between the Bible and Science. Science demands thousands of years for the formation of the earth and all the time it demands is given to it in the sublime words of Gen. 1:1, "In the BEGINNING God created the heaven and the earth." This verse then covers the whole period of the formation of the earth and its preparation for the habitation of man.

The Egyptians, as Plato informs us, taught that the earth and the heavens originated out of a kind of pulp, and that men were generated from the slime of the river Nile. Other sages of Egypt held that the world was hatched from a winged egg. Now as Moses was "learned in all the wisdom of the Egyptians" (Acts 7:22) how is it that he did not say that the heavens originated out of a kind of pulp, and that the world was hatched from a winged egg? Simply because God revealed to him, probably when he was up on the mount with God, just how the world was created.

2. THE CHAOTIC EARTH

The creation of the "Original Earth" was in the dateless past. It was doubtless a most beautiful earth, covered with vegetation and inhabited with fish and fowl and animal life, and probably with human life. How long it continued in this condition we are not told, but an awful catastrophe befell it—it became "FORMLESS AND VOID," and submerged in water and darkness. Gen. 1:2. That it was not originally so we know from Isa. 45:18 (R.V.). "Thus saith the Lord that created the heavens; he is God; that formed the earth and made it; He established it, He created it NOT A WASTE, he formed it to be inhabited."

What caused the earth to become a "Waste" after its original creation is not clearly revealed. It is clear from the account of the Fall of Adam and Eve that sin existed before man was created.

In that remarkable passage in Ez. 28:12-19 there is revealed to us under the title of

"The King of Tyrus,"

a being of surpassing beauty and wisdom, who had been in "Eden," the "Garden of God." Not the Eden of Adam's day, but possibly the Eden of the Earth as it was first created. This being is spoken of as the "Anointed Cherub that Covereth," who "walked upon the 'Holy Mountain of God'," and was "perfect in all his ways from the day that

GENERATION

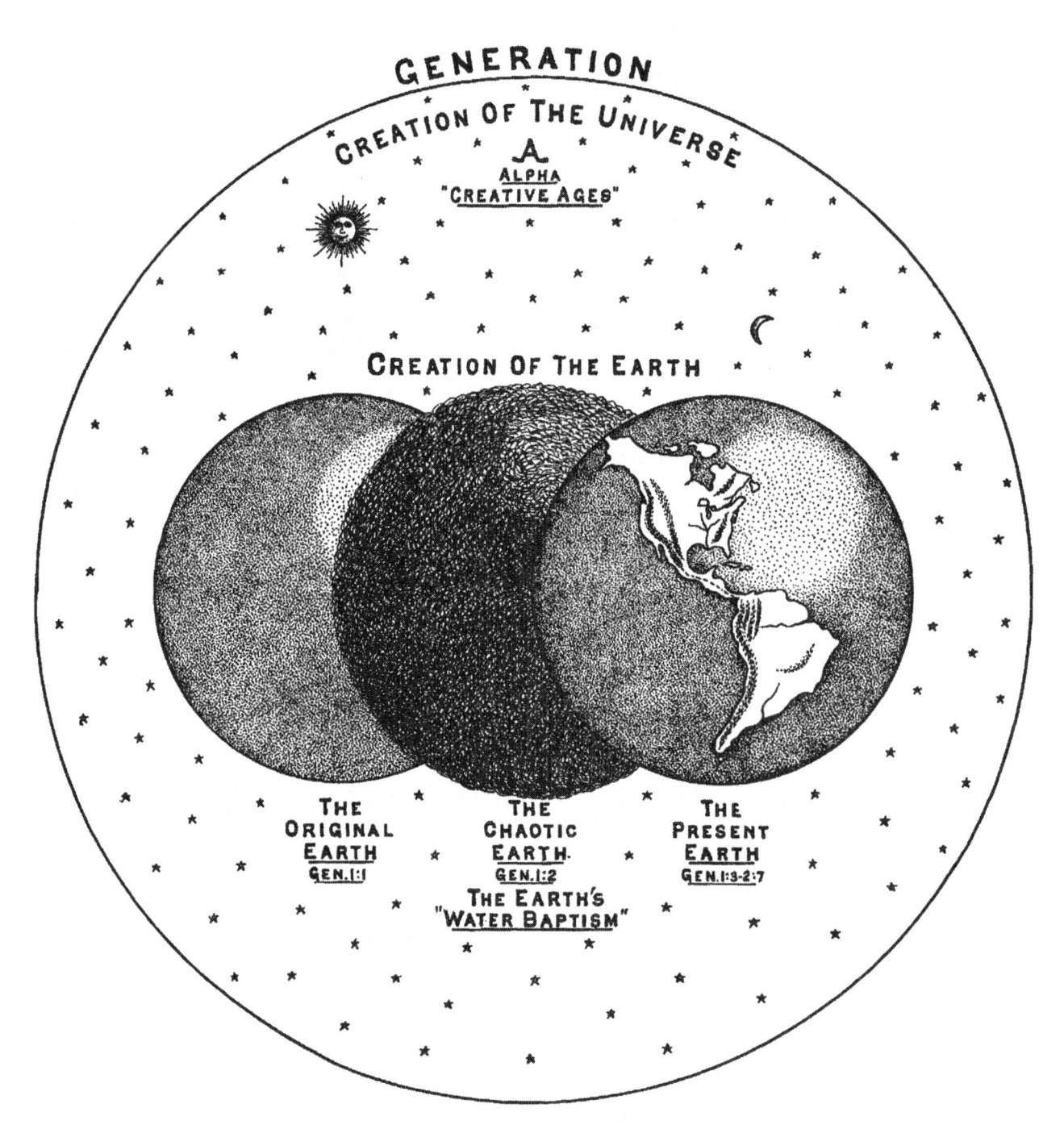

CREATION OF THE UNIVERSE

A
ALPHA
"CREATIVE AGES"

CREATION OF THE EARTH

| THE ORIGINAL EARTH GEN. 1:1 | THE CHAOTIC EARTH GEN. 1:2 | THE PRESENT EARTH GEN. 1:3-2:7 |

THE EARTH'S "WATER BAPTISM"

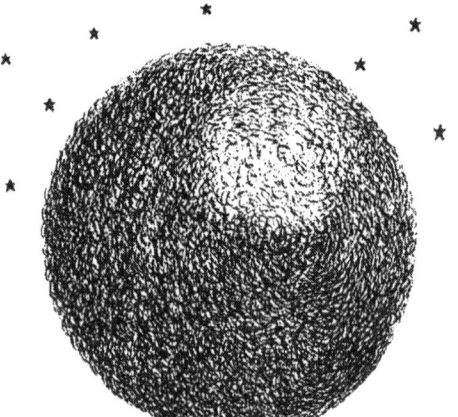

THE SIX DAYS O

FIRST DAY
COSMIC LIGHT

GEN. 1:3-5

3 And God said, Let there be light: and there was light.
4 And God saw the light, that it was good: and God divided the light from the darkness.
5 And God called the light Day, and the darkness he called Night. And the evening and the morning were the first day.

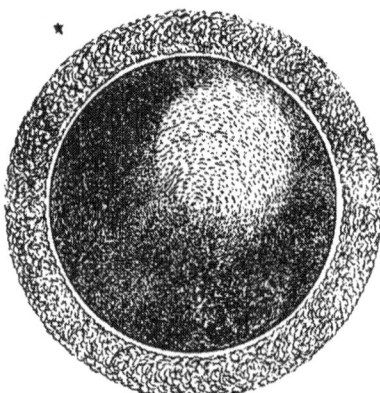

SECOND DAY
FIRMAMENT FORMED

GEN. 1:6-8

6 ¶ And God said, Let there be a firmament in the midst of the waters, and let it divide the waters from the waters.
7 And God made the firmament, and divided the waters which were under the firmament from the waters which were above the firmament: and it was so.
8 And God called the firmament Heaven. And the evening and the morning were the second day.

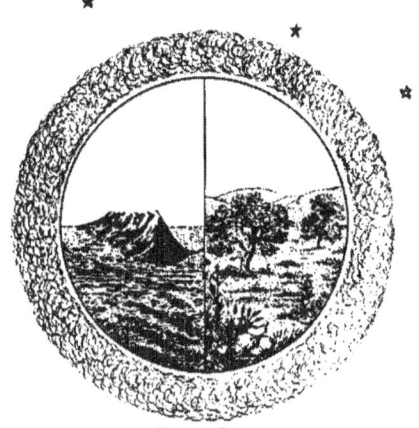

THIRD DAY
TWO WORKS
THE LAND REAPPEARS | VEGETATION REAPPEARS

GEN. 1:9-10
FIRST WORK

9 ¶ And God said, Let the waters under the heaven be gathered together unto one place, and let the dry land appear: and it was so.
10 And God called the dry land Earth; and the gathering together of the waters called he Seas: and God saw that it was good.

GEN. 1:11-13
SECOND WORK

11 And God said, Let the earth bring forth grass, the herb yielding seed, and the fruit tree yielding fruit after his kind, whose seed is in itself, upon the earth: and it was so.
12 And the earth brought forth grass, and herb yielding seed after his kind, and the tree yielding fruit, whose seed was in itself, after his kind: and God saw that it was good.
13 And the evening and the morning were the third day.

DESIGNED AND DRAWN
BY CLARENCE LARKIN
FOXCHASE, PHIL'A., PA
COPYRIGHTED

1/20/1920

F Re-Creation

Fourth Day
Solar Light Restored

GEN. 1:14-19

14 ¶ And God said, Let there be lights in the firmament of the heaven to divide the day from the night; and let them be for signs, and for seasons, and for days, and years:
15 And let them be for lights in the firmament of the heaven to give light upon the earth: and it was so.
16 And God made two great lights; the greater light to rule the day, and the lesser light to rule the night: he made the stars also.
17 And God set them in the firmament of the heaven to give light upon the earth,
18 And to rule over the day and over the night, and to divide the light from the darkness: and God saw that it was good.
19 And the evening and the morning were the fourth day.

Fifth Day
Creation of Fish and Fowl

GEN. 1:20-23

20 And God said, Let the waters bring forth abundantly the moving creature that hath life, and fowl that may fly above the earth in the open firmament of heaven.
21 And God created great whales, and every living creature that moveth, which the waters brought forth abundantly, after their kind, and every winged fowl after his kind: and God saw that it was good.
22 And God blessed them, saying, Be fruitful, and multiply, and fill the waters in the seas, and let fowl multiply in the earth.
23 And the evening and the morning were the fifth day.

Sixth Day
Two Works
Creation of Animals | Creation of Man

GEN. 1:24-25
First Work

24 ¶ And God said, Let the earth bring forth the living creature after his kind, cattle, and creeping thing, and beast of the earth after his kind: and it was so.
25 And God made the beast of the earth after his kind, and cattle after their kind, and every thing that creepeth upon the earth after his kind: and God saw that it was good.

GEN. 1:26-31
Second Work

26 ¶ And God said, Let us make man in our image, after our likeness: and let them have dominion over the fish of the sea, and over the fowl of the air, and over the cattle, and over all the earth, and over every creeping thing that creepeth upon the earth.
27 So God created man in his own image, in the image of God created he him; male and female created he them.
28 And God blessed them, and God said unto them, Be fruitful, and multiply, and replenish the earth, and subdue it: and have dominion over the fish of the sea, and over the fowl of the air, and over every living thing that moveth upon the earth.
31 And God saw every thing that he had made, and, behold, it was very good. And the evening and the morning were the sixth day.

he was created, until iniquity was found in him." But his "heart was lifted up because of his beauty," and his wisdom was thus corrupted.

As no King of Tyrus answering this description has, as yet, existed, this passage is taken to be a prophetic portrait of the "Antichrist," and as Antichrist is to be an incarnation of Satan, it probably is a description of Satan before his fall. The intimation in this scripture then is, that Satan, with a host of angelic beings, was placed in charge of the original or primeval earth, and that he through pride (1 Tim. 3:6; Isa. 14:12-14) sought to be equal with God, and that to punish him the earth was thrown into a chaotic state, and Satan and his angels, amounting to a third of the angelic hosts (Rev. 12:4) were excluded from Heaven, and took up their abode in the heavenlies, the Second Heaven, located between the atmosphere of our earth and the Heaven where God dwells, and thus became the "Principalities and Powers," and "Rulers of the Darkness of this Age," and the "Spiritual Wickedness" in "High Places" (the Second Heaven), of whom we are warned in Eph. 6:12. This seems very plausible, for Satan is said to be the "Prince of the Powers of the Air" (Eph. 2:2), and the "God of this World" (Age), and it looks as if his plan for the Fall of man was a scheme to regain control of this earth.

If there were human beings on the Original or Pre-Adamite Earth, they were doubtless involved in Satan's fall and destroyed. In fact, the "demons" are believed by many to be the disembodied spirits of the inhabitants of the Pre-Adamite Earth, and their efforts to re-embody themselves in human beings, as in the days of Christ, is looked upon as evidence that they once possessed bodies similar to human bodies. Naturally the question arises, "if the inhabitants of the Pre-Adamite Earth were human beings like ourselves, and were destroyed when the Pre-Adamite Earth was thrown into a chaotic form, where are their fossil remains; why have we not discovered them in the soil or rocks of the earth?" The answer is, their "**bodies**" may have been consumed by fire, as will be the case with the rebellious hosts of Gog and Magog at the end of the Millennium (Rev. 20:7-9), and their escaping "**spirits**" became the demons referred to above. It is clear that the "demons" are not Satan's angels, for they are free, while the demons are confined in the Bottomless Pit and are only given liberty as it suits God's purpose. Rev. 9:1-21. Neither are they the "Fallen Angels" of 2 Pet. 2:4, and Jude 6-7, for they are reserved in chains under darkness against the Judgment of the Great Day. The "demons" then are in a class by themselves and for aught we know shall never be different. What we do know in reference to them is that the time is coming when they are to suffer "torment." Matt. 8:29.

If death reigned on the Pre-Adamite Earth, and the **bodies** of the Pre-Adamites were buried in the earth, they may still remain buried in that part of the earth which they occupied, which now may be the bed of the Atlantic or Pacific Ocean. If this be so, it helps to explain the Scripture passage which reads—"And the **SEA** gave up the dead which were in it; and '**Death**' and '**Hell**' (Hades) delivered up the dead which were in them; and they were judged every man according to his works." Rev. 20:13. Here we have the "**SEA**" differentiated from "**DEATH**," (the Grave), which swallows up the **body**, and "**HELL**" or "**HADES**," the abode of the **soul** between death and the resurrection, and this seems to imply that the "**DEAD OF THE SEA**" are a different class from mankind and may refer to the dead of the Pre-Adamite World as now resting at the bottom of the sea. As God's creatures are to be judged each in his own order, it would seem no more than right that the dead of the Pre-Adamite World should be judged before the wicked dead of this present world.

The manner in which the Pre-Adamite Earth was made "formless and void," and this refers only to the exterior surface, the habitableness of the earth, is clearly revealed by Peter, where he says—

"For this they willingly are ignorant of, that by the word of God the heavens were of old, and the earth standing out of the water and in the water; whereby **the world that then was, BEING OVERFLOWED WITH WATER, perished.**" 2 Pet. 3:5-6.

It is clear that Peter does not refer here to Noah's Flood, for the world of Noah's day did not perish, and Peter goes on to add that—

"The heavens and the earth which are now (that is, have been in existence since the restoration of the earth of Gen. 1:3-31), by the same word are kept in store, **reserved unto fire** against the day of judgment and perdition of ungodly men (Great White Throne Judgment)." Rev. 20:11-15.

The manner then in which the Pre-Adamite Earth was made "formless and void" was by **WATER**. The water which lies upon the surface of the earth is about 1/4950 part of the earth's mass. If the land surface was even the water would cover it to the depth of 11 miles. Violent convulsions must have wrecked the Pre-Adamite Earth and covered its surface with the waters of its oceans. Not a living creature remained alive upon it, and its atmosphere of murky darkness hid the light of the sun, moon and stars. To all intents and purposes it was a dead planet, though the seeds of its vegetable life remained entombed in its bosom ready to spring into resurrection life on the "Third Day." The absence of the warm rays of the sun caused the earth to pass through the "Winter" of its life, and the submerging waters were congealed into ice that preserved in "**COLD STORAGE**" the remains of immense quadrupeds and winged creatures, that we might know the kind of animal life that inhabited the Pre-Adamite Earth. This was probably the Glacial Period of Geologic Times. The Prophet Jeremiah records a vision of the time.

"I beheld the earth, and, lo, it was **WITHOUT FORM AND VOID**; and the heavens, and they had **NO LIGHT**. I beheld the mountains, and, lo, they **TREMBLED**, and all the hills **MOVED LIGHTLY**. I beheld, and, lo, there was **NO MAN**, and all the **BIRDS OF THE HEAVENS WERE FLED**. I beheld, and, lo, the **fruitful place was a WILDERNESS**, and all the **CITIES** thereof were **broken down** at the presence of the Lord, and by His fierce anger." Jer. 4:23-26.

If this was, as it appears, an account of the destruction of the Pre-Adamite Earth, then the Pre-Adamite Earth was inhabited, and its inhabitants dwelt in cities, and God's purpose in destroying the Pre-Adamite Earth was to efface all historic monuments and evidences of the sinfulness of its occupants.

How long a period elapsed between the creation of the earth and its becoming "formless and void" we do not know; neither do we know how long it continued in that condition, but when the time came in the purpose of God to restore the earth to its habitable state, and make it fit for the abode of man, He did it in six periods of longer or shorter duration. The Hebrew word translated "day" may mean either a day of 24 hours or a longer period of time. The probability is that the time was short.

3. THE PRESENT EARTH

The six days' work as described in Gen. 1:3-31 is not a description of how God made the Original earth, but how He restored it from its "formless and void" condition to its present state. If the Flood of Noah's day was only local and affected only that section of the world, then the geography of the restored earth was probably the same as that of the earth today.

THE SEVEN DAYS OF THE RESTORATION WEEK

Era of Matter
1. DAY—WORK, COSMIC LIGHT
2. DAY—WORK, READJUSTMENT OF THE ATMOSPHERE
3. DAY—
   1. WORK, DRY LAND REAPPEARS
   2. WORK, VEGETATION REAPPEARS

Era of Life
4. DAY—WORK, SOLAR LIGHT RESTORED
5. DAY—WORK, CREATION OF FISH AND FOWL
6. DAY—
   1. WORK, CREATION OF LAND ANIMALS
   2. WORK, CREATION OF MAN
7. DAY—NO WORK, THE SABBATH

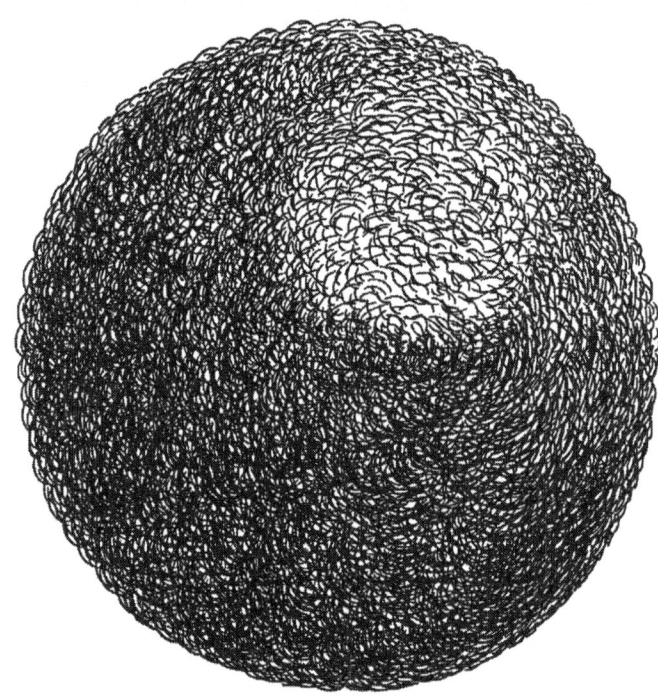

When the time came to restore the earth to a habitable condition, God began by reversing the process He took to make it uninhabitable. The Spirit of God "brooded" over the watery waste, and God said—

"LET THERE BE LIGHT."

God did not create the light, the word for create is not used. God simply said—"Let there be light," just as one might say—"Turn on the light." This light was not sunlight, for the clouds did not break away and permit the Sun to shine on the earth. That did not happen until the "Fourth Day." The light was doubtless "Electric Light," similar to the Aurora Borealis or North Lights, for we now know that Electricity is one of the primary forces and has always been in the atmosphere, although we have only in recent times learned how to harness it and compel it to light our cities. The incandescence of the atmosphere, and it doubtless was very strong and brilliant, generated a vast amount of heat that melted the icy covering of the earth and formed water, that, being evaporated, formed vaporous clouds that prepared the way for the work of the "Second Day." The change from "Darkness" to "Light" caused God to call the "Darkness" **NIGHT** and the "Light" **DAY**. Thus the earth passed out of the "Night" of its history into the brightness of its "Resurrection Day," and as each day's work was an advance on the previous day's work, each day begins with an evening and ends with a morning.

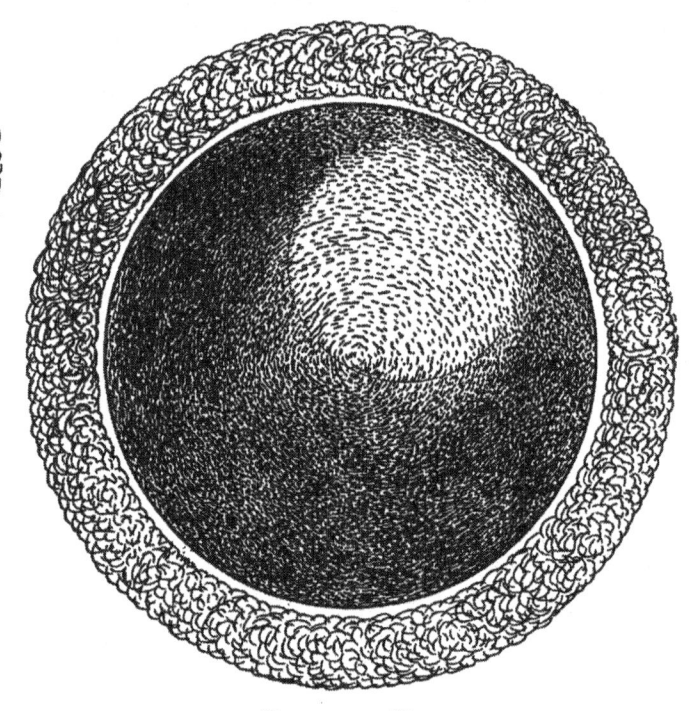

FIRST DAY
COSMIC LIGHT

THE FIRST DAY
Gen. 1:2-5

"And the Spirit of God moved (brooded) upon the face of the waters. And God said, **LET THERE BE LIGHT:** and there was light. And God saw the light, that it was good: and God divided the light from the darkness. And God called the light Day, and the darkness He called Night. And the evening and the morning were the 'First Day'."

SECOND DAY
FIRMAMENT FORMED

THE SECOND DAY
Gen. 1:6-8

"And God said, Let there be a **FIRMAMENT** in the midst of the waters, and let it divide the waters from the waters. And God made the **Firmament**, and divided the waters which were under the **Firmament** from the waters which were above the **Firmament**: and it was so. And God called the **Firmament HEAVEN**. And the evening and the morning were the 'Second Day'."

The fact that the "Firmament" is called "Heaven," and by the word Heaven we are to understand our Atmosphere, implies that the "Chaotic Earth" either had no atmosphere, or that it was not adapted to the formation of clouds, that in the form of vapor, would support water, and thus divide or separate the waters in the atmosphere from the waters on the earth. The Second Day's work then was the "Readjustment of the Atmosphere" to the needs of the present earth, and its evening and morning made up the "Second Day."

It is worthy of note that the words—"And God saw that it was **GOOD**," are not spoken of this Day's work, as it is spoken of the other days' work. This may not be without significance, for we read in Eph. 2:2 of the "Powers of the **AIR**," over whom Satan is the Prince, and it may have been that as soon as the atmosphere of the earth again became habitable that the "Powers of Evil," (Eph. 6:12), with Satan as their leader, swarmed into it, with the intention of making it their habitation, and so God could not say of the Firmament or Atmosphere that it was "**good**."

THE THIRD DAY

The work of the "Third Day" was twofold, the emergence of the land from the sea, and the reappearance of vegetable life.

FIRST WORK
Gen. 1:9-10

"And God said, Let the waters under the heaven be gathered together unto one place, and let the dry land appear: and it was so. And God called the dry land **EARTH**; and the gathering together of the waters called He **SEAS**: and God saw that it was good."

This is simply a reversal of the cataclysmic convulsions that submerged the Pre-Adamite Earth, and by upheaval caused the earth to emerge from its "Watery Grave."

SECOND WORK
Gen. 1:11-13

"And God said, Let the earth bring forth **grass**, the **herb yielding seed**, and the **fruit tree yielding fruit AFTER HIS KIND**, whose **seed is in itself UPON THE EARTH**: and it was so. And the earth brought forth grass and herb yielding seed **after his kind**, and the tree yielding fruit, whose seed was in itself, **after his kind**: and God saw that it was good. And the evening and the morning were the 'Third Day'."

This was not a new creation but a **RESURRECTION**. The earth rises up out of the "Waters of Death," and seeds, and the roots of plants and herbs and trees are called upon to germinate and sprout and grow as they did before the catastrophe that submerged the Pre-Adamite Earth. If that catastrophe was what we know as the "Glacial Period," the resurrection of plant life no more required a "creative act" than vegetation does in the spring of the year after the winter is over. That this was the case seems clear from the expression, "Whose seed is in itself, **UPON THE EARTH**." That is, the seed was already **in the earth**, having been buried by the waters that swept over the Pre-Adamite Earth, and, being indestructible, it only needed the proper conditions to spring up and cover the earth with verdure. This reveals the fact that the Pre-Adamite Earth was clothed with verdure, and covered with plants and trees like those of our present earth.

THE FOURTH DAY
Gen. 1:14-19

"And God said, Let there be '**LIGHTS**' in the Firmament of the heaven to divide the Day from the Night; and let them be for **signs**, and for **seasons**, and for **days**, and **years**; and let them be for **LIGHTS** in the Firmament of the heaven to give light upon the earth: and it was so. And God made **TWO GREAT LIGHTS**; the greater light to rule the day, and the lesser light to rule the night. He made the stars also. And God set them in the Firmament of the heaven to give light upon the earth, and to rule over the day and over the night, and to divide the light from the darkness: and God saw that it was good. And the evening and the morning were the 'Fourth Day'."

THIRD DAY
TWO WORKS
THE LAND REAPPEARS | VEGETATION REAPPEARS

The appearance of the sun and moon on the Fourth day was not a new creation. They had existed in connection with the Pre-Adamite Earth and had not been destroyed when it was made waste. The words translated "made" in the 16th verse is not the same word as is

FOURTH DAY
SOLAR LIGHT RESTORED

FIFTH DAY
CREATION OF FISH AND FOWL

THE FIFTH DAY
Gen. 1: 20-23

"And God said, Let the **WATERS BRING FORTH ABUNDANTLY THE MOVING CREATURE THAT HATH LIFE, AND FOWL THAT MAY FLY ABOVE THE EARTH IN THE OPEN FIRMAMENT OF HEAVEN.** And God **CREATED** (Bara) great whales, and every living creature that moveth, which the waters brought forth abundantly, **AFTER THEIR KIND**, and every winged fowl **AFTER HIS KIND**; and God saw that it was good. And God blessed them, saying, Be fruitful, and multiply, and fill the waters of the seas, and let fowl multiply in the earth. And the evening and the morning were the 'Fifth Day'."

The work of the "Fifth Day" was the **CREATION** of fish and fowl. Here is the first time we come across the word **"CREATE"** since we read of the original creation of the earth in verse one. This shows that all **animal life** was destroyed in the catastrophe that overtook the Pre-Adamite Earth. The fish and fowl that were created on the "Fifth Day" were the same that we have today. The fossil remains of huge marine animals and gigantic birds belong to the Pre-Adamite Earth.

translated "created" in verse one, and does not imply a "creative" act. What is meant is that the clouds broke away and permitted the sun and moon to be seen, and that from that time they were appointed to measure the days, and years, and seasons as we have them today. In other words, on the Fourth day "Time" in contrast with "Eternity" began.

SIXTH DAY
TWO WORKS
CREATION OF ANIMALS | CREATION OF MAN

THE SIXTH DAY

The creative work of the "Sixth Day" was twofold, that of land animals and of man.

FIRST WORK
Gen. 1:24-25

"And God said, Let the earth bring forth the **LIVING CREATURE AFTER HIS KIND, cattle, and creeping thing, and beast of the earth AFTER HIS KIND**; and it was so. And God made (created) the beast of the earth **AFTER HIS KIND**, and cattle **AFTER THEIR KIND**, and every thing that creepeth upon the earth **AFTER HIS KIND**; and God saw that it was good."

These land animals were doubtless the same kind as we have today. The fact that they were created,

"AFTER THEIR KIND,"

which is 5 times repeated, shows that they were not **"evolved"** from one common specie. That all the different species of animals were created **"separately"** is proven from the fact that when species are crossed their offspring are sterile. The crossing of the jackass and a mare is the mule, and a mule is a hybrid and is sterile. If the "Evolutionary Theory" of the development of animal and vegetable life was true, we should expect to find evidence to that effect in fossil remains of the intermediate links, and we should also see "evolutionary processes" at work now whereby higher orders of animal and plant life are coming into being. But we see nothing of the kind. Animal and plant life exists today in the same form that it has existed in the knowledge of man. The birds build their nests and raise their young as they always did. The beaver builds his dam, and the bee constructs his honeycomb as they have always done. Man alone has the faculty of improving his mode of construction. This is seen in the development of farming instruments from the crude plow and winnowing fan to the complex plow and cultivator, and the combined reaper, binder, and thresher. But here we can trace the various steps by the obsolete specimens of farming implements. This is not true in the animal and vegetable kingdoms, for there we find no intermediary links. If the Evolutionary Theory is correct, it should apply to man as well as animals, and we should see by the crossing of the best specimens of the human race the evolution of a **SUPERMAN**, but the history of the race disproves this.

SECOND WORK
Gen. 1:26-28

"And God said, Let **US** make man in **OUR IMAGE**, after **OUR LIKENESS**: and let them have dominion over the fish of the sea, and over the fowl of the air, and over the cattle, and over all the earth, and over every creeping thing that creepeth upon the earth. So God **CREATED** (Bara) man in His **OWN IMAGE**, in the **IMAGE OF GOD CREATED** (Bara) He him; male and female created He them. And God blessed them, and God said unto them, Be fruitful, and multiply, and **REPLENISH THE EARTH**, and subdue it; and have dominion over the fish of the sea, and over the fowl of the air, and over every living thing that moveth upon the earth."

That man also was **"CREATED"** (Bara) shows that he has not descended from an ape. Man was made in the **"IMAGE OF GOD,"** not in the image of an "Ape," and was not formed from a brute, but of the "Dust of the Earth." There is an **"Impassable Gulf"** between the lowest order of man and the highest type of beast that science has failed to bridge. The "Missing Link" has never been found. That the whole human race is of "One specie" and had a common origin (Acts 17:26) is clear from the fact that, when the different races of the earth's inhabitants marry, their offspring are not sterile but fertile. This nullifies the argument that the white and colored races are of different origin, and that the white race alone is the Adamic race.

There is no contradiction between the first and second chapters of Genesis as to the creation of man. The first chapter (Gen. 1:26-28) gives the **FACT** of his creation, the second, the **MANNER OF IT**. Gen. 2:7. One is supplementary to the other. In chapter one God is spoken of as **"ELOHIM,"** the Creator; in chapter two, He is called **"JEHOVAH"** (The Lord) because He there enters into covenant relations with man. At first the name **"Jehovah"** is joined with **"Elohim"** to remove all doubt as to the identity of the Being designated by the compound word. Now while **either** of these names would suit **some passages,** in others one would be more suitable than the other. This accounts for the discriminating use of these two names by the sacred writers, and is an answer to those critics who claim that the Scriptures are a clumsy compilation of incongruous and diverse documents which they call Elohistic and Jehovistic.

In Gen. 2:7 we are told that—"The **LORD God** formed (Yatsar, fashioned) man of the dust of the ground, and breathed into his nostrils the '**Breath of Life**;' and man became a living soul."

This may mean that the Lord God fashioned man out of the "dust of the ground" as a sculptor fashions the statue out of clay, and then breathed into the earthy form the "Breath of Life." However it was done we know the work was threefold:

1. The formation of the "**BODY**"—"And the Lord God **formed man of the dust of the ground.**"

2. The gift of the "**SPIRIT**"—"And breathed into his nostrils the '**Breath of Life**'." By this is not meant the "Holy Spirit," but the "Spirit" of the "natural man"—that part of man that must be indwelt by the Holy Spirit before he can be born again. It is the "God Conscious" nature of man.

3. The **SOULISH** part of man—"And man became a 'Living Soul'." This is the seat of the "Self-Conscious" nature, of memory, the affections, etc.

The two principal parts of man are the **BODY** and the **SPIRIT**, but as the functions of these are separate, one being physical and the other spiritual, a third part had to be supplied called the **SOUL**, intermediate between them, and through which they may communicate. Thus man became a "Threefold Being." I Thess. 5:23. Heb. 4:12. See the Chapter on "The Spirit World." Section, "The Threefold Nature of Man."

In Adam, as originally created, the Soul was such a perfect medium of communication between the Body and the Spirit that there was no conflict between them. The three blended together in one harmonious whole. When man fell the soul became the "battlefield" of the Body and the Spirit, and the conflict began that Paul so graphically describes in Rom. 7:7-24.

Eve was not fashioned in the same way as Adam. She was "made" sometime later. Adam had not found among all the creatures God had made a suitable companion, and God saw that it was not good for him to be alone, so He proceeded to make him an "helpmeet." To this end

"The Lord God caused a '**deep sleep**' to fall upon Adam and he slept; and He took one of his '**RIBS**,' and closed up the flesh instead thereof; and the '**RIB**,' which the Lord God had taken from man, made (builded) He a **WOMAN**, and brought her unto the man. And Adam said, This is now bone of my bones, and flesh of my flesh; she shall be called **WOMAN**, because she was taken **OUT OF MAN**." Gen. 2:21-23.

While Adam and Eve were not both fashioned in the same way, they were not evolved from some lower creature, but were direct creations of God, "**male and female created He them.**" Gen. 1:27. The reason why Eve was not fashioned separately from Adam, but was taken out of Adam's side, was to show that in their relation to each other as man and wife they were to be **ONE FLESH.** That is their interests and sympathies, etc., were to be one, and physically they were to be counterparts of each other. Adam and Eve in their physical relation to each other are a type of Christ and the Church. When Eve was presented to Adam he said—"This is now **bone of my bones, and flesh of my flesh;**" and the Apostle Paul in speaking of the Church says—"we are **members** of His **BODY**, and of His **FLESH**, and of His **BONES**. For this cause shall a man leave his father and mother, and shall be joined unto his wife, and they **two** shall be one flesh. This is a great '**mystery**;' but I speak concerning Christ and the Church." Eph. 5:30-32.

Adam was not created a baby or a primitive savage, but a full-grown man perfect in intellect and knowledge, else he could not have named the beasts of the field and the fowls of the air. And the fact that his descendants had such skill in the invention of musical instruments and mechanical devices and could build cities and towers and such a vessel as the Ark, proves that the men of Antediluvian times were men of gigantic intellect and attainments, and that instead of man having "evolved upward" he has "degenerated downward."

We see from Gen. 1:29-30, that animals and man were originally given only vegetable food, and that it was not until after the Fall that animals became carnivorous. And it was not until after the Flood that man was permitted to eat "**flesh**." "Every **moving thing that liveth** (animals) shall be meat for you; even as the green herb (which had been their food) have I given you **all things**. But '**flesh**' with the **life thereof**, which is the **BLOOD THEREOF**, shall ye not eat." Gen. 9:3-4.

That is, that in eating "flesh" they must first drain the "**blood**" from it, because the "**blood**" is the **LIFE** of the animal. It was not until after the Exodus, when the Law was given from Mt. Sinai, that God's chosen people the Jews were restricted as to the kind of creeping things, flying fowl, and beasts they should eat. Lev. 11:1-47.

Note that all that God created **was GOOD**. "And God saw everything that He had made, and, behold it was **VERY GOOD**. And the evening and the morning were the Sixth Day." Gen. 1:31. God is not the author of evil. Evil is the fruit of sin and disobedience. Thorns, thistles, poisonous vines, weeds, noxious beasts, as the serpent, are all the results of sin. Thus the heaven and the earth were restored and repopulated during the six days or periods of the "Restoration Week."

The Bible and Science are in exact accord as to the order of the 8 works of the Restoration Week. The following Diagram shows how these 8 works could be arranged in a different order 40,320 times ($1 \times 2 \times 3 \times 4 \times 5 \times 6 \times 7 \times 8 = 40,320$) without any two lines being alike. Surely Moses must have been inspired, for there was only **ONE** chance in **40,320**, that he would have recorded them in the order that science claims they occurred. This is one of the proofs of the Divine Inspiration of the Holy Scriptures.

SEVENTH DAY
Gen. 2:2-3.

"And on the 'Seventh Day' God ended His work which He had made; and He **RESTED** on the Seventh Day from all His work which He had made. And God blessed the 'Seventh Day,' and **SANCTIFIED IT**; because that in it He had **RESTED FROM ALL HIS WORK** which God created and made."

By God here is meant God in His Triune capacity, for, as has been well said, God the **FATHER created** the matter, God the **SON** took the matter and **made** the worlds and all that exists upon them, and then God the **HOLY SPIRIT** breathed the "Breath of Life" into the things that have life. John 1:1-3. Eph. 3:9. Col. 1:12-16. God rested because His work was **finished**. That is the only justifiable reason for resting. God rested because His work was not only **finished** but was **GOOD**. There could be no reflection upon it. But when God's perfect work was marred by sin, by the "Fall of Man," His "Sabbath Rest" was broken. As soon as man fell it was necessary for God to resume His work, this time not to continue the creation of material things, but for the purpose of the redemption of man that he might become a "**NEW CREATION**" in Christ Jesus. 2 Cor.

DIAGRAM OF THE EIGHT WORKS OF THE SIX DAYS

LIGHT	FIRMAMENT	LAND	VEGETATION	SUN	FISH	BEASTS	MAN
FIRMAMENT	LAND	VEGETATION	SUN	FISH	BEASTS	MAN	LIGHT
LAND	VEGETATION	SUN	FISH	BEASTS	MAN	LIGHT	FIRMAMENT
VEGETATION	SUN	FISH	BEASTS	MAN	LIGHT	FIRMAMENT	LAND
SUN	FISH	BEASTS	MAN	LIGHT	FIRMAMENT	LAND	VEGETATION
FISH	BEASTS	MAN	LIGHT	FIRMAMENT	LAND	VEGETATION	SUN
BEASTS	MAN	LIGHT	FIRMAMENT	LAND	VEGETATION	SUN	FISH
MAN	LIGHT	FIRMAMENT	LAND	VEGETATION	SUN	FISH	BEASTS

THE SEVEN COSMIC PHASES OF THE EARTH

ETERNITY — The Original Earth — "Without Form and Void" Gen. 1:2 — The Chaotic Earth — Six Days Of Restoration. Gen. 1:3-31 — The Edenic Earth — The Ground Cursed. Gen. 3:17-19 — The Antediluvian Earth — The Flood. Gen. 7:1-24 — The Present Earth — Physical Changes Zech. 14:4, Ezek. 47:1-12 — The Millennial Earth — Renovation Of The Earth By Fire. 2. Pet. 3:5-13 — The New Earth — ETERNITY

Designed and Drawn By Clarence Larkin, Fox Chase, Phil'a, PA.

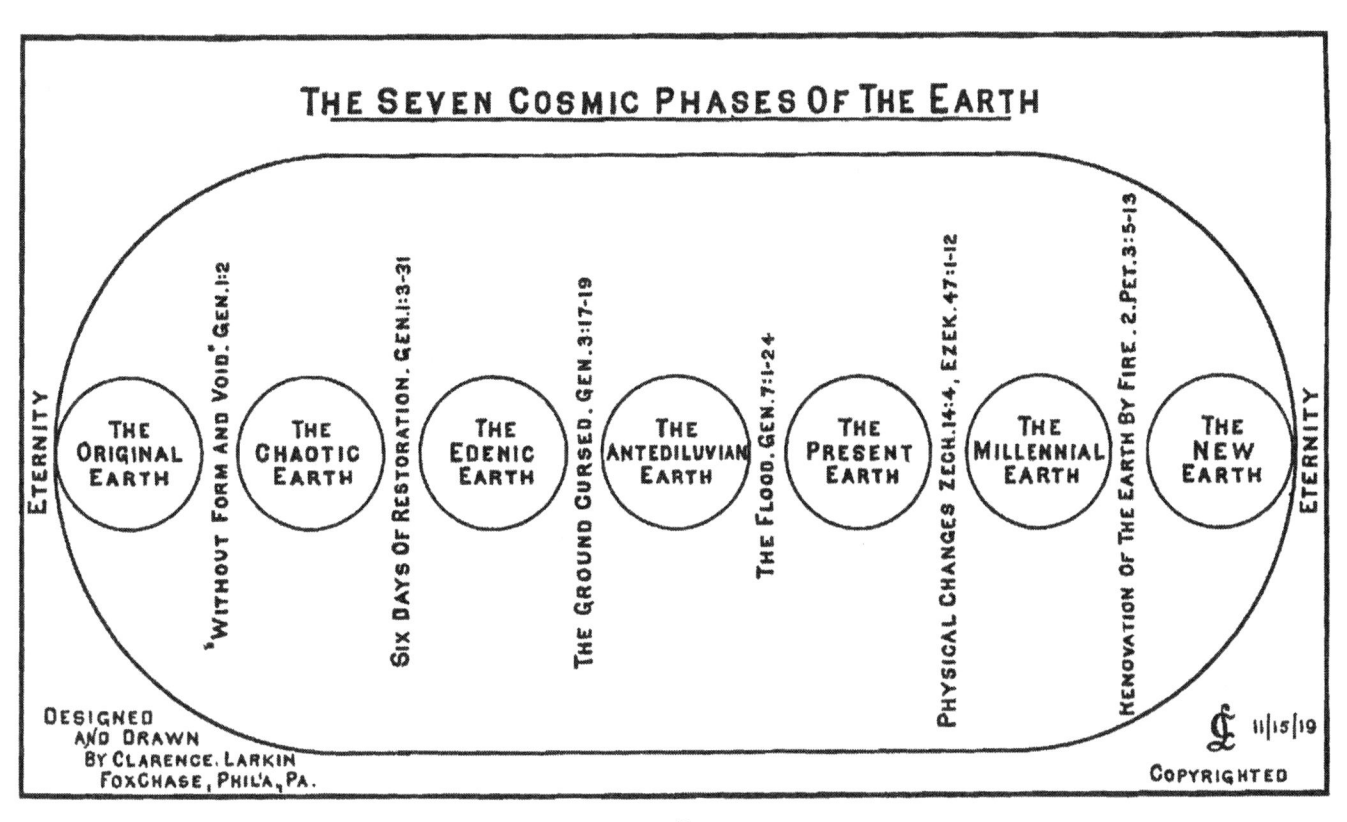

11/15/19 COPYRIGHTED

5:17. So Jesus in explaining His mission said—"My Father worketh hitherto (in creation), and I work (now in **REDEMPTION**)." John, 5:17.

In Gen. 2:1-3, we are simply told that God **rested** from His work of **creating on the "SEVENTH** Day." The Day is not called a **SABBATH** Day. We are told that God **BLESSED and SANCTIFIED** it. That is, set it apart as a **REST DAY**. We are not told the **length** of the **"SEVENTH** Day" of the Creative Week, but it should have corresponded with the length of the other days, if sin had not shortened it.

THE SABBATH

If God instituted the "Sabbath" before the "Fall of Man," it seems strange that the fact is not recorded in Genesis, and that Adam was not told to observe it. Nowhere in the Book of Genesis do we read of Adam, or any of his descendants, or Noah, or Abraham observing the Sabbath. The only hint we have of a "seven-fold" division of days is found in Gen. 7:4, 10, when **seven days of grace** were granted before the Flood came, and in Gen. 8:8-12, where a seven day period elapsed between the sending forth of the dove. The first place we read of the Sabbath is in Ex. 16:23-26, in connection with the gathering of the manna—"Six days ye shall gather it; but on the **SEVENTH** day, **WHICH IS THE SABBATH**, in it there shall be none." Here we have the **"SEVENTH"** day designated as **"THE SABBATH."** That the "Seventh Day" of the "Creative Week" was a **type** of the Sabbath is clear from Ex. 20:11—"For in six days the Lord made heaven and earth, the sea, and all that in them is, and rested the **SEVENTH** day; wherefore the Lord **blessed the SABBATH** day, and **hallowed** it." But we have no evidence that the Sabbath was commanded to be observed until after the Exodus, and the reason is clear. God's "Rest Day" was broken by the "Fall of Man," and there could be no "rest" until redemption was brought in, and this was **typically** brought in by the redemption of the Children of Israel from Egypt through the offering of the "Passover Lamb," a type of Christ. The purpose of their deliverance was that they might find **rest** in Canaan from the weary toil and slavery of Egypt. Deu. 5:15.

When a few weeks later the "Ten Commandments" were given on Mt. Sinai, the Lord said to Israel, **"REMEMBER** the Sabbath Day to keep it holy," (Ex. 20:8), the Sabbath Day they were to **remember** was not the "Seventh Day" on which God rested, but the "Day" that God had appointed as the Sabbath Day at the time of the giving of the manna.

The command to observe the Sabbath was given to Israel **EXCLUSIVELY**. It was not given to the Gentiles. It was given to Israel as the **"SIGN"** of the "Mosaic Covenant." "Verily my Sabbaths ye shall keep: for it is a **'SIGN'** between me and you **throughout your generations."** Ex. 31:13; Ezek. 20:12, 19-21. The Sabbath Day then belongs to the Jews alone and is not binding on the Gentiles (the world), or on the Church (Christians). Nowhere in the Bible do you find God finding fault with any nation or people, except the Jewish nation, for not observing the Sabbath. As a Jewish ordinance it has never been abrogated, changed, or transferred to any other day of the week, or to any other people. It is now in abeyance as foretold in Hosea 2:11 it would be. It is to be resumed when the Jews are nationally **restored** to their own land. Isa. 66:23. Ezek. 44:24; 46:1-3.

If this be true, then the "Sabbath" does not belong to the Church, and is not to be observed by Christians, for the "Sabbath Day" is a part of **"THE LAW,"** and Christians are not under **"LAW,"** but under **"GRACE."** Rom. 6:14. In his letter to the Galatian Christians Paul reproved them for going back to the "Law," and declared that those who did so were **"under the CURSE."** Gal. 3:10. "How turn ye again to the **'beggarly elements'** (religious ordinances) whereunto ye desire again to be **in bondage?** Ye observe **DAYS** (Sabbath and Feast Days), and months, and times, and years. I am **afraid of you,** lest I have bestowed upon you labor in vain." Gal. 4:9-11. "Let no man therefore judge you in **meats** or in **drink,** or in respect of a **holy day,** or of the **new moon,** or of the **SABBATH."** Col. 2:16. If Christians are under obligations to keep the "Jewish Sabbath," then they are under the Jewish "Ceremonial Law" and should observe all the ordinances and Feast Days of the Jewish Ritual.

As an institution of Judaism, the Sabbath, with all the "Feast Days" and other ritualistic ceremonies and offerings of Judaism, ceased to function with the close of the Jewish Dispensation. The **JEWISH** Sabbath was not changed to the **CHRISTIAN** Sabbath, any more than "Circumcision" was changed to "Baptism." There is no such thing as the **"CHRISTIAN** Sabbath." "Sabbath" has to do with **LAW,** and "Christian" with **GRACE,** and to join **"LAW"** and **"GRACE"** is to unite what God has forever separated.

After the Resurrection, Christ and His Disciples never met on the "Sabbath" but on the **"FIRST DAY** of the week." John 20:1, 19. Acts 20:7. 1. Cor. 16:2. It is true that they went into the Jewish Synagogues on the Sabbath, but not to worship, but that they might have opportunity to preach the Gospel. The "First Day of the Week" is the day to be observed for rest and worship by the Christian Church. It is prefigured in the Old Testament as the **"EIGHTH DAY,"** or the **"DAY AFTER THE SABBATH."** "Ye shall bring a sheaf of the **'FIRST-FRUITS'** of your harvest unto the priest, and he shall wave the sheaf before the Lord, to be accepted for you; on the **'MORROW AFTER THE SABBATH'** the priest shall wave it." Lev. 23:10-11. What did that **"First Fruits"** typify? Read 1. Cor. 15:20—"Now is Christ risen from the dead, and become the **'FIRST-FRUITS'** of them that slept." When did Christ rise from the dead and become the **"FIRST FRUITS?"** Not on the "Sabbath," for He lay dead in the tomb on that day, but on the **"FIRST DAY OF THE WEEK,"** on the **"MORROW AFTER THE SABBATH."**

The fact that the "Birthday" of the Church was at Pentecost, and that fell on the "First Day of the Week," is further proof that the Church should keep the "First Day of the Week" and not the "Seventh" day or **"SABBATH."**

The Jewish Sabbath links man with the "Old Dispensation," the "First Day of the Week" links man with the "New." It is claimed that the Roman Catholic Church changed the day of rest from the "Seventh Day" to the "First Day of the Week," but the claim is false, for the Papacy did not exist until a long time after the "First Day of the Week" had become a fixed day for Christian worship. It is a noteworthy fact that the whole of the "Ten Commandments" (Ex. 20:1-17) are reaffirmed in the New Testament, except the "Fourth Commandment" regarding the Sabbath. Rom. 13:8-10, Eph. 6:1-2, James 5:12, 1. John 5:21. Why this omission if the Law of the "Sabbath" is still in force? It is called the **"LORD'S DAY."** It belongs to Him. It is not called a "rest day" in the Bible. It is a day that should be filled with worship and service and holy activity. It is not a day to be spent in laziness or pleasure, or the giving of sacred concerts and the discussion of worldly betterment schemes, but a day for the teaching and preaching of the Word of God.

DEGENE

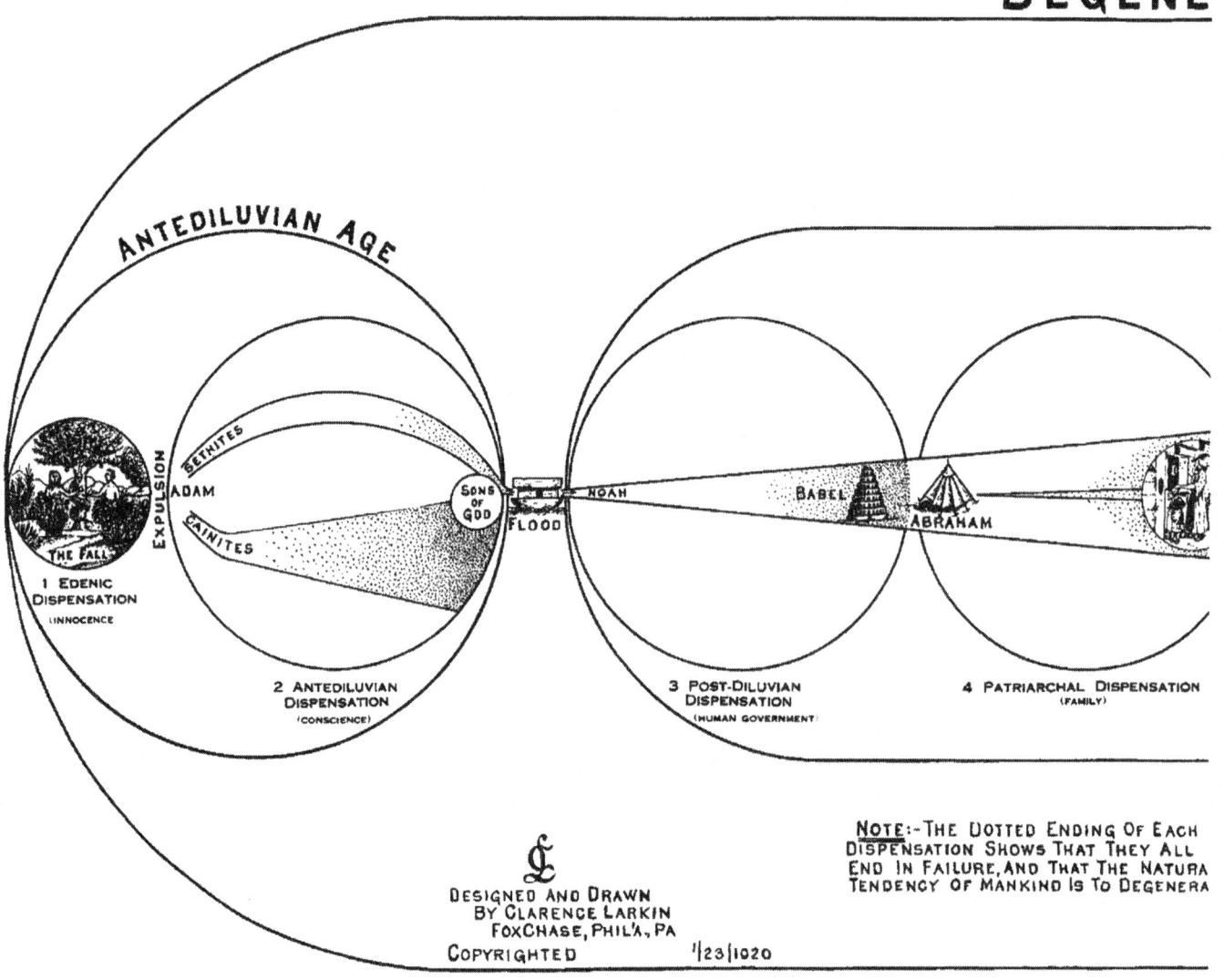

ANTEDILUVIAN AGE

1 EDENIC DISPENSATION
(INNOCENCE)

2 ANTEDILUVIAN DISPENSATION
(CONSCIENCE)

3 POST-DILUVIAN DISPENSATION
(HUMAN GOVERNMENT)

4 PATRIARCHAL DISPENSATION
(FAMILY)

THE FALL — EXPULSION — ADAM — SETHITES — CAINITES — SONS OF GOD — FLOOD — NOAH — BABEL — ABRAHAM

Designed and Drawn
By Clarence Larkin
FoxChase, Phil'a, PA
Copyrighted 1/23/1920

NOTE:— The Dotted Ending Of Each Dispensation Shows That They All End In Failure, And That The Natural Tendency Of Mankind Is To Degenera

RATION

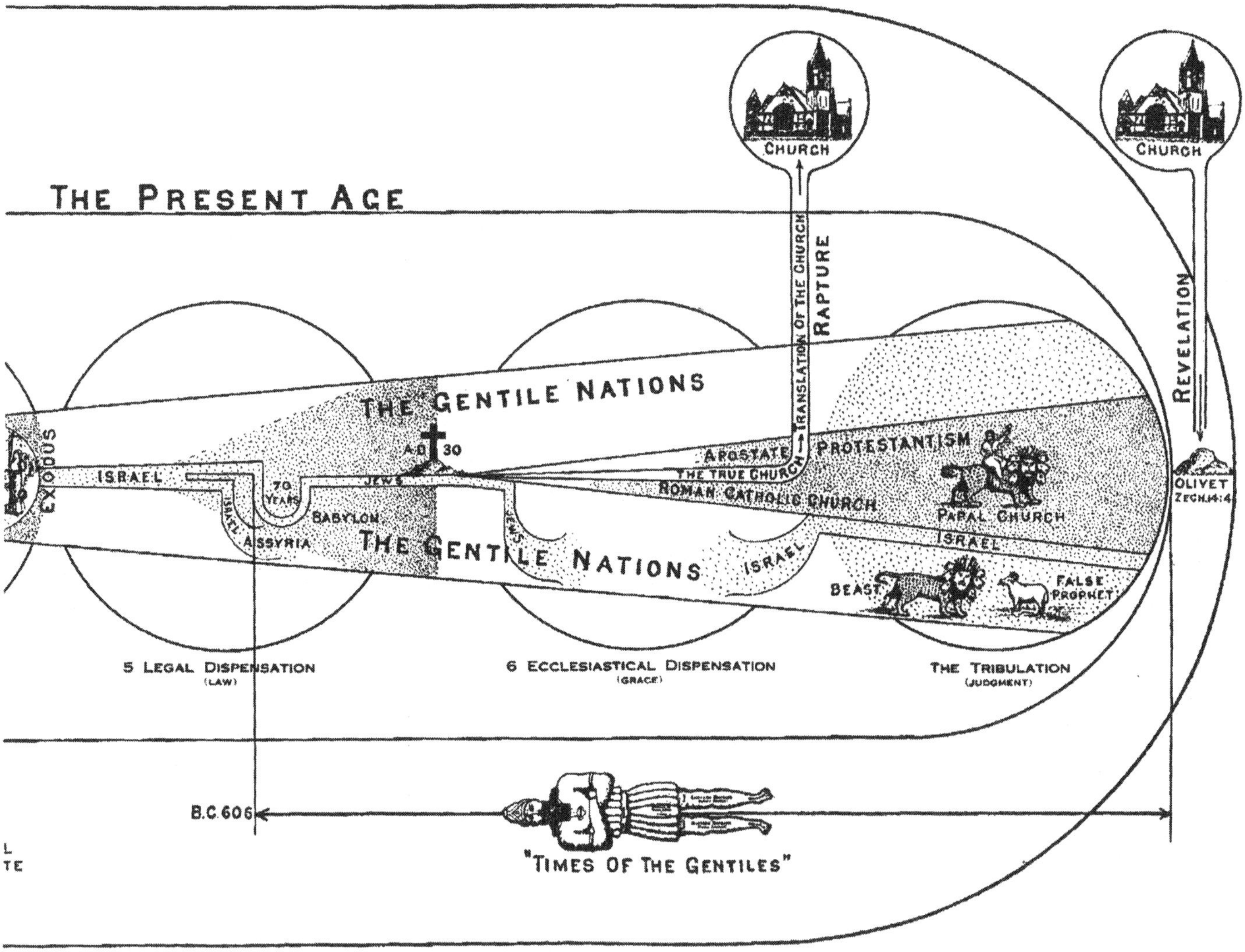
THE PRESENT AGE
CHURCH
CHURCH
TRANSLATION OF THE CHURCH
RAPTURE
REVELATION
THE GENTILE NATIONS
EXODUS
ISRAEL
A.D. 30
JEWS
70 YEARS
ISRAEL
ASSYRIA
BABYLON
APOSTATE PROTESTANTISM
THE TRUE CHURCH
ROMAN CATHOLIC CHURCH
PAPAL CHURCH
ISRAEL
OLIVET
ZECH.14:4
THE GENTILE NATIONS
JEWS
ISRAEL
BEAST
FALSE PROPHET
5 LEGAL DISPENSATION
(LAW)
6 ECCLESIASTICAL DISPENSATION
(GRACE)
THE TRIBULATION
(JUDGMENT)
B.C.606
"TIMES OF THE GENTILES"
L
TE

II. THE ANTEDILUVIAN AGE

This extends from the restoration of the earth from its chaotic condition to the Flood. It is divided into two Dispensations.

1. EDENIC DISPENSATION
(INNOCENCE)

1. The Edenic Dispensation.

This Dispensation extends from the creation of Adam to the Expulsion from the Garden. As to its duration we know nothing. It was probably very short, and was the "Dispensation of Innocence."

Man's existence on this planet began under the most favorable circumstances. The earth had been restored to its Primeval glory. The waters swarmed with fish and fowl. The land was one mass of luxuriant verdure, and hills and valleys and plains were covered with flocks and herds of sheep and cattle, and all kinds of beasts and animals. The air was alive with bird life, and filled with fragrance from fruits and flowers. There were no storms to terrify and destroy, for the earth was watered by a mist, and the beauty of the day and night must have been unspeakably grand. Everything must have been perfect of its kind, for we read that God saw everything He had made and behold, it was "very good."

But not good enough for man, for God took and planted a "Garden" eastward in Eden. A garden in which God caused to grow every tree that was pleasant to the sight and good for food, and in the midst of the garden He planted the "Tree of Life," and the tree of the "Knowledge of Good and Evil."

The garden was watered with a beautiful river, and when it was ready God placed Adam in it. In this garden of matchless delights, and amid scenes of indescribable loveliness, with God for his counselor, and angelic beings as visitors, with a sinless nature and environment most favorable to a pure and holy life, the progenitors of the human race were placed. The conditions were ideal.

But Adam had no companion like unto himself, and because it was not good for him to be alone, for he would be lonely even among such beautiful surroundings, God said, I will make a helpmeet for him, and so the Lord God caused a deep sleep to fall upon Adam, and while he slumbered, the Lord God took a rib from his side and from it made Eve. This is the first use of an anesthetic in the performance of a surgical operation of which we have any record. Whether Adam slept until his side was healed, or whether the Lord God healed it at once we are not told. What must have been his surprise, when he opened his eyes to see standing by him such a beautiful creature as Eve must have been. That Adam knew where she came from is clear from his statement—"This is now **bone of my bone**, and **flesh of my flesh**; she shall be called **WOMAN** (Isha) because she was taken **out of MAN** (Ish)." Gen. 2:23. It is clear that from the first Adam loved her, or he would not have risked death for her by eating of the forbidden fruit.

The first pair were happy in their sweet companionship, and doubtless believed that it would last forever. They knew nothing of the ruins of the Primeval Earth beneath their feet, now covered with the Edenic verdure of a renewed earth. Neither did they know that the heavens above them swarmed with fallen beings under the leadership of Satan, and that their happiness was to end in a "Fall" that would necessitate their expulsion from that "Garden of Delights," and that sooner or later they should taste of physical death.

If it be charged that God should have forewarned Adam of his danger of an attack by Satan, let it not be forgotten that the commandment not to eat of the "Tree of the Knowledge of Good and Evil" should have caused him to beware of any being who should tempt him to disobey the command of God and eat of it. To have plainly told him of the plan of Satan would have frustrated God's purpose in the testing of Adam. True obedience is to obey without knowing why.

The purpose God had in allowing Adam to be tempted and fall is revealed in the Gospel. If God had not permitted the human race to be tested and fall, the Universe would never have had the supreme spectacle of His forgiving love and redemptive grace as revealed on Calvary.

How long after Adam was created Eve was given to him we do not know. It must have been some time, for Adam required time to name all the living creatures that were brought to him, of cattle, of fowl, and of the beasts of the field. Neither are we told how long after Eve was given to Adam before the Temptation. It is hardly likely that it was immediately, for while they were mature physically they were but as children in experience, at least Eve was, and she was unfit to cope with the seductive wiles of the Serpent, the most powerful enemy of God and man.

Satan's purpose in the "Temptation" was to thwart God's purpose in the creation of man (the peopling of the earth with a holy race of beings), and to regain the earth, which he had lost by his rebellion. His hope was to excite God to destroy the first pair for their sin before they could populate the earth. He played his game with consummate skill. Fearing that if they were approached together they might withstand him, he awaited the time when Eve should be alone.

It is not improbable that Eve, curious to know the cause of the prohibition, had stolen away from Adam and gone off by herself to examine the Tree, and that Satan, discovering her there, was not slow to take advantage of his opportunity.

If Eve had avoided the vicinity of the Tree, she would not have been able to cast that look at it which made her desire to eat of its fruit. Satan saw that Eve was disgruntled about something. He wisely surmised that it was because God had forbidden Adam and Eve to eat of the Tree, so he approached her and spoke to her. The fact that Eve was not afraid to talk with the Serpent is an indication that it was not a loathsome creature, and that it was no stranger to her. She had seen it often, and probably talked with it before, for Satan does not make his supreme effort until he has first prepared the way. What the Serpent was like before it was cursed and caused to crawl instead of stand upright, we do not know, but it must have been a beautiful creature. Whether it had the power to talk, or simply became the mouthpiece of Satan we are not told. What we do know is that Satan incarnated himself in it.

Observing that Eve was casting longing glances at the "Fruit" of the Tree, the Serpent (Satan) opened the conversation by craftily asking—"Yea, hath God said, Ye shall not eat of every tree of the Garden?" The subtility of this question is seen in its insinuating suggestion that God did not love them, and was unfair and unkind to forbid them anything. In her answer Eve betrays her feeling toward God by adding to the prohibition, saying—"Neither shall ye TOUCH it," as if God was afraid to trust her. She also altered the penalty from—"thou shalt surely die," to "lest ye die," thus expressing doubt as to the certainty of death. It is a dangerous thing to add to or subtract from God's word. Rev. 22:18-19. The commencement of the Fall was the "deceitful handling" of the Word of God. 2 Cor. 4:2.

Satan was the first "Higher Critic." He was the creator of the "SEED OF DOUBT." It was deposited in the heart or mind of Eve by Satan's question—"Yea, hath GOD said?" This led Eve to question the love of God. This "MICROBE OF UNBELIEF" the human race has inherited from Eve. Men do not openly deny the goodness of God so much as they question the statements of the Word of God. They say—"Has God really said we must not do thus and so? Have we not misunderstood what He has said, or misinterpreted His meaning? Surely God is too loving and merciful to eternally punish the wicked."

Satan having sown the "Seed of Doubt" and perceiving that the poison was working, next declared that God was a liar by saying—"Ye shall not surely die." This is the "DEVIL'S LIE," and it has been incorporated into the religious systems of today that teach that man shall not be eternally punished. Satan then impugned God's motive by declaring that God did not want them to have a knowledge of "Good" and "Evil" lest they become "gods" like Himself. This appealed to Eve's curiosity and ambition, and stirred up a "torrent of desire" in her heart, and when she saw that the "Tree" was "good for food" (the Lust of the Flesh), and "pleasant to the eyes" (the Lust of the Eye), and "desirable to make one wise" (the Pride of Life), she did not wait to consult her husband, but put forth her hand and plucked and ate the fruit, and the days of her innocence were ended; and when Adam appeared, without contrition of heart, she in turn tempted him, and he not willing to be separated from her also ate, the result the ruin of the race. The Woman was deceived, but Adam was not deceived, nevertheless, the Apostle tells us, it was the "woman's" fault. 1 Tim. 2:13-14.

The inducement that Satan held out to Eve, that the acquisition of knowledge would put her and Adam on the same plane with God, and make them GOD-LIKE, is the same inducement that Satan offers to ambitious men today, and he is seeking through his dupes to build up a magnificent civilization on the discoveries and inventions of men, and exalt man without God, and his aim is the final

"DEIFICATION OF MAN,"

that will find its culmination in his

"SUPERMAN,"
"THE ANTICHRIST,"

who will sit in the Temple at Jerusalem and proclaim himself GOD. 2 Thess. 2:3-4. This accounts for all the "World Systems" of today for the social, religious, political and commercial betterment and advancement of the race.

Adam and Eve were created "INNOCENT." "Innocence" is not "RIGHTEOUSNESS." "Innocence" cannot become "Righteousness" until TESTED. If Adam and Eve had stood the "Test" they would have become "Righteous" or "Holy," they failed and became SINNERS. There is but one step from "Innocence" to "HOLINESS," or from "Innocence" to "SIN." Adam and Eve took the step from "Innocence" to SIN and became SINNERS. If they had taken the opposite step they would have become "Holy" and been beyond the possibility of "Sin." Now man cannot become "Holy" without the New Birth.

In the Fall of man the triumph of Satan was complete. The first effect of the disobedience of Adam and Eve was SELF-CONSCIOUSNESS. "They saw that they were NAKED." The result of this knowledge led them to invent clothing made of "FIG LEAVES." All living creatures are clothed by nature. Fish have scales, birds have feathers, beasts have hair, or fur, or wool; even serpents have a beautifully colored skin. Many are naked when ushered into existence, but it is not long until nature provides clothing. Man alone of all God's creatures is left without clothing, and is compelled to have recourse to artificial covering. Why is this? It is the result of SIN.

Adam and Eve at first wore no clothing, nor did they need to. Their state of innocence made them not ashamed. Some claim that their unfallen nature was clothed in a veil of radiant glory that hid their nakedness. This they lost in the Fall. At once, conscious of their shame, they resorted to artificial clothing. Clothes are the trappings of guilt. The style and character of clothing may change, but the guilt remains. Clothing may hide our shame from the eyes of man, but not from the eyes of God. A black heart may hide behind a white vest.

The sun set that day upon a scene that witnessed the downfall of the human race. It was a dark and fearful night. They both dreaded to meet God and so hid themselves in the forest when the Lord God came down to take His usual walk in the Garden in the cool of the day. Heretofore they had looked forward to the daily visit of the Lord God, but now they feared to face Him. Thus sin makes cowards of us all.

By questioning them the Lord God got them to sit in judgment on their own conduct. Adam blamed his fall on Eve, she blamed her fall on the Serpent. God patiently listened to them and gave them an opportunity to justify their conduct, then He passed judgment on them. But to the Serpent He gave no opportunity for justification, but said—

"Because thou hast done this, thou art cursed above all cattle, and above every beast of the field; upon thy belly shalt thou go, and dust thou shall eat all the days of thy life; and I will put enmity between thee and the woman, and between THY SEED and HER SEED, IT (her seed—CHRIST) shall bruise thy HEAD, and THOU shalt bruise His HEEL."

33

GEN
THE BOOK OF E
"SEED-BOOK"

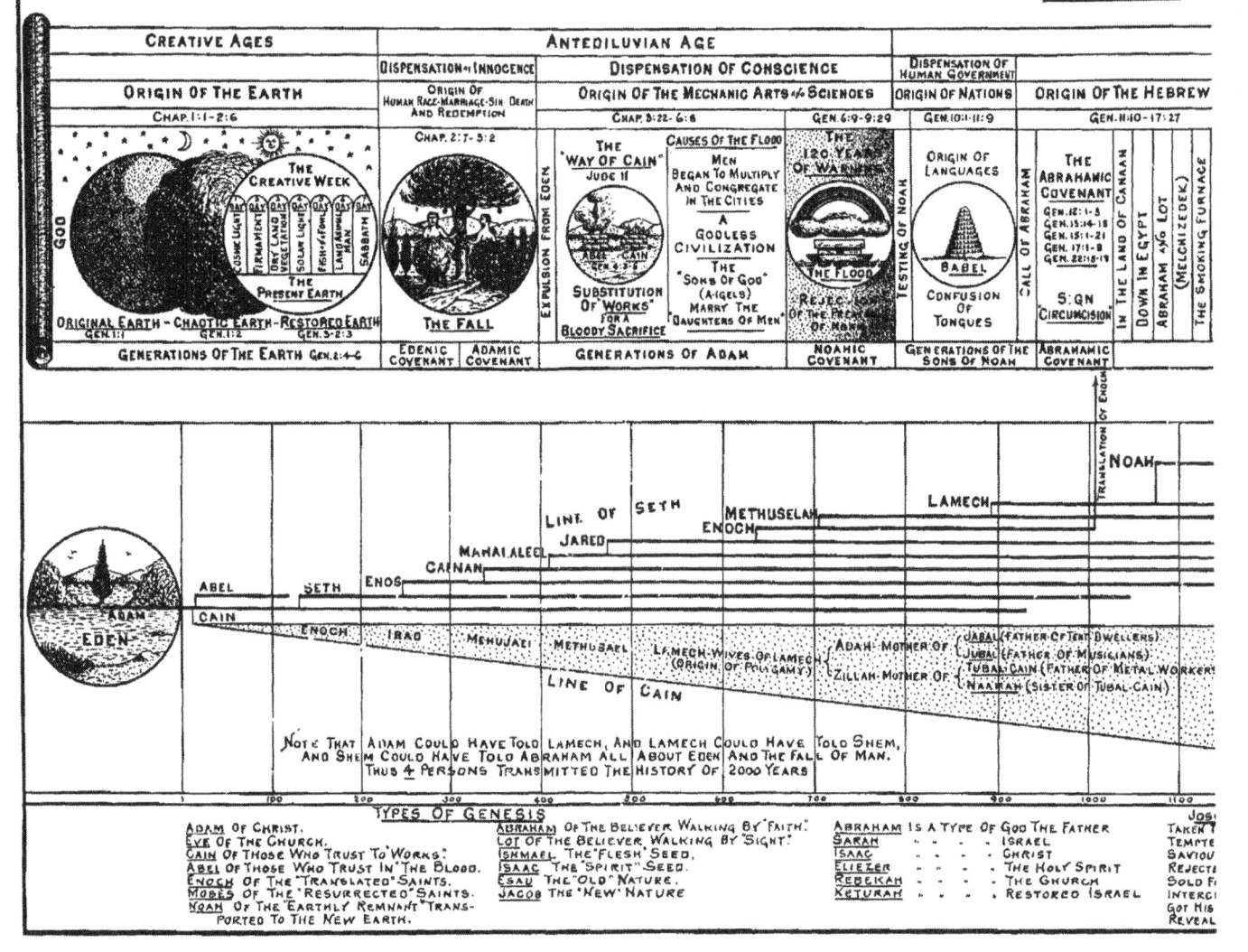

CREATIVE AGES	ANTEDILUVIAN AGE		DISPENSATION OF HUMAN GOVERNMENT	
	DISPENSATION OF INNOCENCE	DISPENSATION OF CONSCIENCE		
ORIGIN OF THE EARTH	ORIGIN OF HUMAN RACE-MARRIAGE-SIN-DEATH AND REDEMPTION	ORIGIN OF THE MECHANIC ARTS & SCIENCES	ORIGIN OF NATIONS	ORIGIN OF THE HEBREW
CHAP. 1:1-2:6	CHAP. 2:7-3:2	CHAP. 3:22-6:8	GEN. 6:9-9:29	GEN. 10:1-11:9	GEN. 11:10-17:27

Creative Week — Cosmic Light, Firmament, Dry Land & Vegetation, Solar Light, Fish & Fowl, Land Animals & Man, Sabbath — The Present Earth

ORIGINAL EARTH — CHAOTIC EARTH — RESTORED EARTH
GEN. 1:1 — GEN. 1:2 — GEN. 1:3-2:3

GENERATIONS OF THE EARTH GEN. 2:4-6

THE FALL
EDENIC COVENANT | ADAMIC COVENANT

EXPULSION FROM EDEN
"WAY OF CAIN" JUDE 11
SUBSTITUTION OF "WORKS" FOR A BLOODY SACRIFICE

CAUSES OF THE FLOOD
MEN BEGAN TO MULTIPLY AND CONGREGATE IN THE CITIES
A GODLESS CIVILIZATION
THE "SONS OF GOD" (ANGELS) MARRY THE "DAUGHTERS OF MEN"

THE 120 YEARS OF WARNING
THE FLOOD
REJECTION OF THE PREACHING OF NOAH

GENERATIONS OF ADAM
NOAHIC COVENANT

TESTING OF NOAH
ORIGIN OF LANGUAGES
BABEL
CONFUSION OF TONGUES

GENERATIONS OF THE SONS OF NOAH

CALL OF ABRAHAM
THE ABRAHAMIC COVENANT
GEN. 12:1-3
GEN. 13:14-18
GEN. 15:1-21
GEN. 17:1-8
GEN. 22:15-18
SIGN CIRCUMCISION

IN THE LAND OF CANAAN | DOWN IN EGYPT | ABRAHAM AND LOT (MELCHIZEDEK) | THE SMOKING FURNACE

ABRAHAMIC COVENANT

ADAM — EDEN

ABEL — SETH — ENOS — CAINAN — MAHALALEEL — JARED — ENOCH — METHUSELAH — LAMECH — NOAH
LINE OF SETH
TRANSLATION OF ENOCH

CAIN — ENOCH — IRAD — MEHUJAEL — METHUSAEL — LAMECH-WIVES OF LAMECH (ORIGIN OF POLYGAMY) — ADAH-MOTHER OF JABAL (FATHER OF TENT DWELLERS), JUBAL (FATHER OF MUSICIANS) — ZILLAH-MOTHER OF TUBAL CAIN (FATHER OF METAL WORKERS), NAAMAH (SISTER OF TUBAL-CAIN)
LINE OF CAIN

NOTE THAT ADAM COULD HAVE TOLD LAMECH, AND LAMECH COULD HAVE TOLD SHEM, AND SHEM COULD HAVE TOLD ABRAHAM ALL ABOUT EDEN AND THE FALL OF MAN. THUS **4** PERSONS TRANSMITTED THE HISTORY OF 2000 YEARS.

100 200 300 400 500 600 700 800 900 1000 1100

TYPES OF GENESIS

ADAM OF CHRIST.
EVE OF THE CHURCH.
CAIN OF THOSE WHO TRUST TO "WORKS."
ABEL OF THOSE WHO TRUST IN "THE BLOOD."
ENOCH OF THE "TRANSLATED" SAINTS.
MOSES OF THE "RESURRECTED" SAINTS.
NOAH OF THE "EARTHLY REMNANT" TRANSPORTED TO THE NEW EARTH.

ABRAHAM OF THE BELIEVER WALKING BY "FAITH."
LOT OF THE BELIEVER WALKING BY "SIGHT."
ISHMAEL THE "FLESH" SEED.
ISAAC THE "SPIRIT" SEED.
ESAU THE "OLD" NATURE.
JACOB THE "NEW" NATURE.

ABRAHAM IS A TYPE OF GOD THE FATHER
SARAH " " " " ISRAEL
ISAAC " " " " CHRIST
ELIEZER " " " " THE HOLY SPIRIT
REBEKAH " " " " THE CHURCH
KETURAH " " " " RESTORED ISRAEL

JOS
TAKEN
TEMPTE
SAVIOU
REJECTI
SOLD F
INTERCI
GOT HIS
REVEAL

ESIS.
BEGINNINGS, OR
OF THE BIBLE.

THE PRESENT AGE
DISPENSATION OF THE FAMILY

RACE

| GEN.18:1-19:38 | GEN.20:1-21:34 | GEN.22:1-24 | GEN.23:1-25:18 | GEN.25:19-28:22 | 29:1-31:55 | 32:1-32 | GEN.33:1-36:43 | CHAP.37:1-50:26 |

- BIRTH OF ISHMAEL
- SIGN OF CIRCUMCISION
- ISAAC PROMISED
- DESTRUCTION OF SODOM AND GOMORRAH
- ABRAHAM'S LAPSE AT GERAR
- BIRTH OF ISAAC
- (ISHMAEL CAST OUT)
- ABRAHAM AND ABIMELECH
- THE TEST OF ABRAHAM — MORIAH — OFFERING OF ISAAC
- DEATH OF SARAH
- ISAAC'S BRIDE-REBEKAH
- ABRAHAM MARRIES KETURAH
- DEATH OF ABRAHAM
- (GENERATIONS OF ISHMAEL)
- BIRTH OF ESAU AND JACOB
- THE BIRTHRIGHT SOLD
- COVENANT CONFIRMED TO ISAAC
- LAPSE OF ISAAC
- ISAAC THE "WELL DIGGER"
- THE STOLEN BLESSING
- BETHEL
- COVENANT CONFIRMED TO JACOB
- AT HARAN
- CALLED BACK TO BETHEL
- FLIGHT OF JACOB
- JABBOK THE NIGHT OF WRESTLING — FROM JACOB TO ISRAEL
- JACOB MEETS ESAU
- (DINAH'S SIN)
- BACK AT BETHEL
- DEATH OF RACHEL
- DEATH OF ISAAC
- (GENERATIONS OF ESAU)
- JOSEPH THE DREAMER
- JOSEPH CAST INTO THE PIT
- JOSEPH SOLD INTO SLAVERY
- (SHAME OF JUDAH)
- IN POTIPHAR'S HOUSE
- JOSEPH IN PRISON
- BUTLER AND BAKERS DREAMS
- PHAROAH'S DREAMS
- JOSEPH EXALTED
- JOSEPH'S BRETHEREN VISIT EGYPT
- JOSEPH REVEALS HIMSELF
- JACOB GOES DOWN TO EGYPT
- LAST DAYS OF JACOB
- DEATH OF JACOB
- BURIAL OF JACOB
- FEAR OF JOSEPH'S BRETHEREN
- DEATH OF JOSEPH

GENERATIONS OF ABRAHAM | GENERATIONS OF ISAAC | GENERATIONS OF JACOB

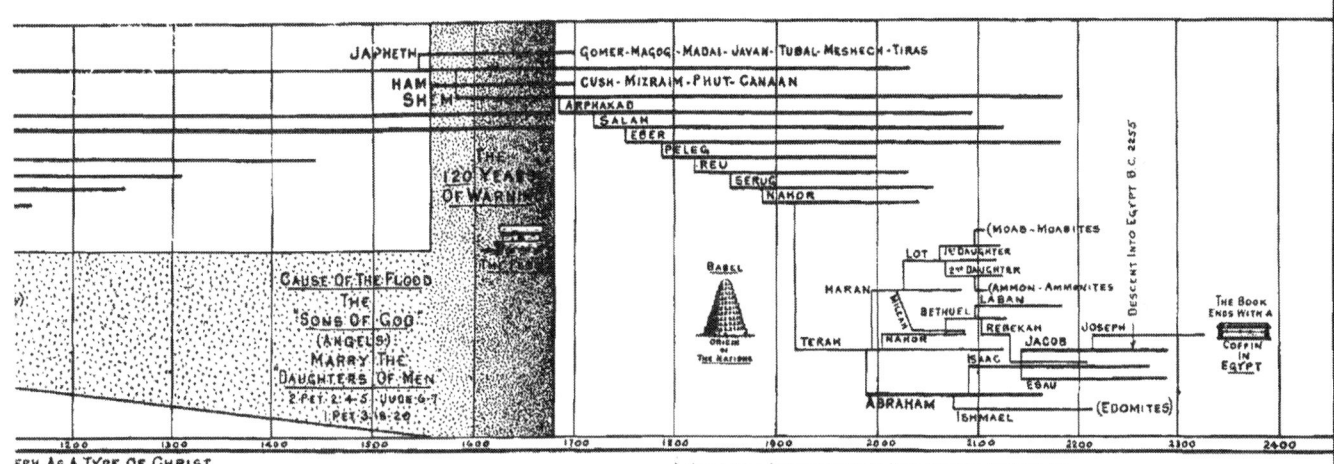

JAPHETH — GOMER - MAGOG - MADAI - JAVAN - TUBAL - MESHECH - TIRAS
HAM — CUSH - MIZRAIM - PHUT - CANAAN
SHEM — ARPHAXAD — SALAH — EBER — PELEG — REU — SERUG — NAHOR

120 YEARS OF WARNING

CAUSE OF THE FLOOD
THE SONS OF GOD (ANGELS) MARRY THE DAUGHTERS OF MEN
2 PET. 2:4-5. JUDE 6-7. 1 PET. 3:19-20

BABEL — ORIGIN OF THE NATIONS

(MOAB - MOABITES)
LOT — 1st DAUGHTER, 2nd DAUGHTER
(AMMON - AMMONITES)
HARAN — LABAN
BETHUEL — REBEKAH
TERAH — NAHOR — JACOB — JOSEPH
ABRAHAM — ISAAC — ESAU — (EDOMITES)
ISHMAEL

DESCENT INTO EGYPT B.C. 2255

THE BOOK ENDS WITH A COFFIN IN EGYPT

1200 1300 1400 1500 1600 1700 1800 1900 2000 2100 2200 2300 2400

EPH AS A TYPE OF CHRIST
O EGYPT.
O AND OVERCAME.
R OF THE WORLD.
D BY HIS BRETHREN.
R 20 PEICES OF SILVER.
DED FOR HIS BRETHREN.
BRIDE (GENTILE) BEFORE THE FAMINE (TRIBULATION).
S HIMSELF TO HIS BRETHREN AND IS ACCEPTED.

NOTE THE DIFFERENCE IN THE LENGTH OF LIFE OF THOSE BEFORE AND AFTER THE FLOOD, DUE PROBABLY TO CLIMATIC CHANGES AT THE TIME OF THE FLOOD. THESE CHANGES WILL BE REVERSED AT THE RETURN OF CHRIST TO OLIVET. (ZECH. 14:4. EZ. 47:6-12), AND HUMAN LIFE AGAIN EXTENDED. ISA. 65:20-22.

DESIGNED AND DRAWN BY
CLARENCE LARKIN
FOX CHASE PHILA., PA.

COPYRIGHTED.

In the expression **THY SEED** (Satan's seed) we have a prophetic reference to THE ANTICHRIST who as Satan's seed is called in 2 Thess. 2:3 the "**SON OF PERDITION.**"

These are the words of a Judge to a condemned criminal who is awaiting sentence, and is a confirmation of Satan's previous rebellion, who here hears his doom. At once the Serpent, the tool of Satan, is changed into a crawling, loathsome, venomous reptile. The Woman's sentence was that she should lose her position as man's equal and become subject to him, and that untold sorrow and misery in motherhood should be her lot. Unto Adam God said, "Cursed is the ground for thy sake, . . . thorns also and thistles shall it bring forth to thee, . . . in the sweat of thy face shalt thou eat bread, till thou return unto the ground." So what had been a pleasure to Adam, the care of the Garden, was henceforth to be a task, for driven out from the Garden he must make a living by tilling a soil that brought forth naturally nothing but thorns, thistles and weeds.

But Adam and Eve could not be expelled from the Garden without clothing. Their "Fig-leaf" raiment was not sufficient. It would not protect them from the **penalty of sin**, for it was man made, and man cannot be saved by his own works, so it was necessary for God to provide a suitable raiment, a raiment that would typify the putting away of sin. So we read "Unto Adam and his wife did the Lord God make '**COATS OF SKINS**,' and clothed him." Gen. 3:21.

Why did not the Lord God provide a more refined and beautiful dress? When Adam sinned did he become so "animalized" that skins were the only suitable dress for him to wear? No. The skins were typical. They could only be secured by the killing of some innocent animals, probably lambs, and were a type of the "**Lamb of God**," and proclaimed the great truth that sin can only be put away by the shedding of **BLOOD**. Heb. 9:22. They proclaim man's reclothing. They speak of the garments of glory of the resurrection body.

But the night of that awful day was not starless. One single "star of promise" lighted up the gloom. It was the promise that

"**The Seed of the Woman Should Bruise the Serpent's Head**,"

and eventually destroy the last trace of his slimy trail over the fields of this fair earth.

It is a significant fact that the giver of this "Promise" was Himself the promised

"**Seed of the Woman**";

and that He who clothed Adam and Eve in skins was the "**LORD GOD**," the second person of the Trinity, who was to become the

"**Lamb of God**,"

whose death on Calvary was foreshadowed by the slaying of the lambs whose skins were needed to cover the nakedness of Adam and Eve.

While the "World Systems" of this world are under the dominion of Satan, and God for some good reason permits them to be, He is not to be charged with inability to prevent Satan's work, or as being cruelly indifferent to man's lost condition, or blamed for not having stopped at once the reign of evil powers in the Universe, for immediately upon the "Fall of Man" God provided a redemptive remedy in the promise—"The 'Seed of the Woman' (Christ) should bruise the Serpent head," and men are lost, not because there is no way of escape from the toils of Satan, but because they will not accept God's way of escape through Christ.

The world would not be deluded by Satan's "**devices**" (2 Cor. 2:11) if it would give heed to the more "sure word of prophecy" (2 Pet. 1:19) which reveals his origin, purpose and doom. But the study of prophecy is not only neglected, but discouraged because of the way in which the scriptures are "**WRESTED**" (2 Pet. 3:16) by those who use prophecy to further their own doctrinal ends, so that many condemn the study of prophecy, and read the scriptures as if they said—"We have a very '**UNCERTAIN**' word of prophecy, to which you do well to pay no attention whatever."

The Edenic Dispensation was perfectly unique. It was characterized by the "**absence of sin**," and the "**presence of God**." There will be nothing like it again until "The Tabernacle of God is with men," and He will dwell with them on the New Earth. Rev. 21:3. In the Edenic Dispensation God dealt with Adam on the basis of "**INNOCENCE**," and He can never treat with man again on the same basis until the curse of sin shall be removed from the earth. Man is no longer under probation, but under condemnation. John 3:18. Ever since the Fall God has had to deal with man as a guilty, lost, helpless and ruined **sinner**. And not only a ruined **sinner**, a ruined **CREATURE**. There is no good thing in him, he is at "**enmity with God**," and is not "**subject to the law of God, neither indeed can be.**" Rom. 8:6-7. Man is a failure.

In mercy God drove the guilty, but forgiven pair, from the Garden lest they eat of the "Tree of Life" and be doomed to live "**forever**" in their sinful mortal bodies. Thus the First Dispensation ended in failure, the human race under condemnation, and the whole earth cursed. Men claim that innocence, and a perfect environment are safeguards against wrong-doing, but the catastrophe of Eden proves that this is not true.

2. The Antediluvian Dispensation.

This Dispensation extends from the "Fall" to the "Flood." It lasted for 1656 years, and was the Dispensation of "Conscience." It shows what man will do when guided only by his conscience. Adam and Eve had no conscience before the "Fall." Conscience is a knowledge of good and evil, and this Adam and Eve did not have until they ate of the fruit of the forbidden tree. Conscience may produce fear and remorse, but it will not keep men from doing wrong, for conscience imparts no "power."

It is probable that the Lord God explained to Adam and Eve the significance of a "Bloody Sacrifice" for sin, but it is a remarkable fact that Adam is not mentioned in the Scriptures as offering such a sacrifice, neither is he mentioned in the list of Old Testament worthies recorded in the eleventh chapter of Hebrews. The list begins with Abel, who is the first one mentioned as offering up a "bloody" sacrifice. Is this a silent hint that Adam and Eve were still unrepentant after their exclusion from the Garden?

Adam and Eve had no children before the "Fall." That they were created for that purpose is clear from the words God spoke to them after their creation, when He blessed them and said—

"Be fruitful and multiply and **replenish the earth.**" Gen. 1:28.

In the words "replenish the earth" we have unmistakable evidence that the earth had been peopled before it was thrown into a chaotic condition, and that its inhabitants in some way had been destroyed. It does not follow, however, that those inhabitants were human beings like ourselves. No human remains have been found antedating the creation of man.

How soon after the **expulsion** from the Garden the first child was born to Adam and Eve we are not told. Probably it was not very long. The first child was a son, Cain. The name means "gotten" or "acquired," and implies that Eve took him for the "Promised Seed." She seems to have been disappointed, and when Abel was born she called him "vapor." It does not follow that Abel was the second child. There may have been a number of children, both sons and daughters, born between Cain and Abel. Cain and Abel are "Repre-

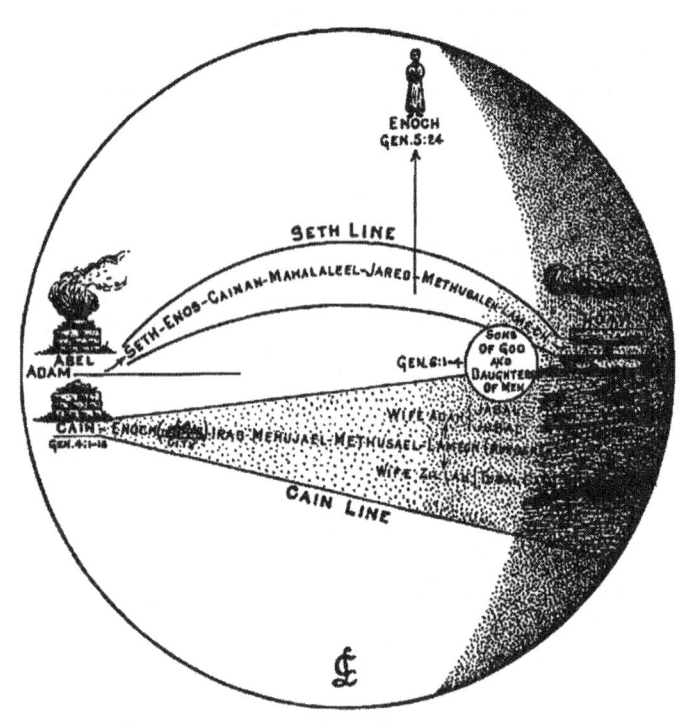

2. ANTEDILUVIAN DISPENSATION
(CONSCIENCE)

sentative" men—one of the wicked line, and the other of the righteous line from Adam.

There is an intimation in the curse imposed on Eve—"I will greatly **multiply thy conception,**" Gen. 3:16, that births were not only frequent, but that several children were born at a time. In no other way could the human race multiply as it did in those early days, and for some time after the Flood. Intermarriages among the children of the same family were not forbidden until after the Flood.

Cain and Abel were not children when Cain killed Abel. They were probably over 100 years of age. Abel was a "keeper of sheep," not his father's, but his own. He was a grown man and a cattle owner. Cain was an agriculturist and the possessor of large estates. We read that Adam was 130 years old when he begat Seth. Gen. 5:3. Seth was probably born soon after the death of Abel. Gen. 4:25. This would make Abel over 100 years of age at his death.

The death of Abel was probably due to a religious dispute between Cain and Abel on the merits of religious offerings. Abel claimed that a "Bloody Sacrifice" was necessary. Cain claimed that an offering of "works" taken from the soil which God had cursed was sufficient. They put the matter to a test. God accepted Abel's offering and rejected Cain's, probably answering as on Mt. Carmel by fire.

This angered Cain. He did not kill Abel that day. The Lord remonstrated with Cain and reminded him that there was still time to bring a "sin offering." The expression "sin lieth at the door" (Gen. 4:7), may be translated a "sin-offering lieth at the door." But Cain would not listen and nursed his anger, possibly for a long time. One day, while alone in the field, Cain brought the subject up again, for we read that Cain talked with Abel about the matter (Gen. 4:8), and Cain's anger became uncontrollable and he arose from the ground where they were sitting and killed his brother. The whole thing was a scheme of Satan's to destroy Abel, through whom the "Promised Seed" was to come. That Abel was childless, at least did not have a son to succeed him, is clear from the fact that Seth took his place.

Satan was not only the instigator of Abel's murder, he was the author of Cain's "Religion," spoken of by Jude as—

"The Way of Cain."

Here we see the origin of all human religions.

When Cain fled he took his wife with him. He did not get his wife in the land of Nod, he **"knew her"** there. That is, she there conceived and bore a son, Enoch. This was not the Enoch of the line of Seth who was translated.

After the birth of Enoch, Cain began to build a city. Here we have the beginning of the city with all its attendant evils. Among the descendants of Cain were Jubal, the inventor of musical instruments, and Tubal-Cain, an instructor of workers in brass and iron. Men in those days used their brains to improve and upbuild a "godless civilization," and when we recall that in that age men were not cut off at threescore and ten, but lived on for nearly **1000** years, their immense accumulation of knowledge, experience and skill must have advanced the arts and sciences and resulted in the invention and manufacture of all the appliances of a luxurious civilization, with a rapidity to us almost inconceivable. The building of such a ship as that constructed by Noah is an illustration. We have the echo of that skilled civilization in the construction, after the Flood, of the Tower of Babel, and later of the Great Pyramid, which involved in its construction such a knowledge of mathematics and astronomy as the world has never as yet surpassed.

The outcome of that brilliant but godless civilization was to promote the rapid increase of population. "Then men began to 'multiply' on the face of the earth." Gen. 6:1. As a result the godly descendants of Seth were, by intermarriage, swallowed up by the godless descendants of Cain, and as the sequel shows, only eight persons were fit to be saved from that foaming sea of sin in the Ark that Noah built.

In the midst of this godless civilization a startling event occurred.

"The '**Sons of God**' saw the '**Daughters of Men**' that they were fair; and they took them wives of all which they chose." Gen. 6:2.

This polygamous relation was not between the "Sons of Seth" and the "Daughters of Cain," an amalgamation of the godly and wicked people of that day, as some suppose, but it has a far deeper meaning. The expression "daughters of **MEN**" includes the daughters of Seth as well as the daughters of Cain, hence the expression "**Sons of God**" must mean beings **different from the human race.**

The title "**Sons of God**" has not the same meaning in the Old Testament that it has in the New. In the New Testament it applies to those who have become the "Sons of God" by the New Birth. John 1:12; Rom. 8:14-16; Gal. 4:6; 1 John 3:1-2. In the Old Testament it applies to the **angels,** and is so used five times. Twice in Genesis (Gen. 6:2-4) and three times in Job. Job 1:6, 2:1, 38:7. A "Son of God" denotes a being brought into existence by a **creative act** of God. Such were the angels, and such was Adam, and he is so called in Luke 3:38. But Adam's natural descendants are not the special creation of God. Adam was created in the **"likeness of God"** (Gen. 5:1), but his descendants were born in **his likeness**, for we read in Gen. 5:3, that Adam **"BEGAT** a son in **his own likeness, after his image."** Therefore all men born of Adam and his descendants by **natural generation** are the **"SONS OF MEN,"** and it is only by being **"BORN AGAIN"** (John 3:3-7), which is a **"NEW CREATION,"** that they can become the **"SONS OF GOD"** in the New Testament sense.

Now the "Sons of God" of Gen. 6:2, 4, could not be the "Sons of Seth," as some claim, because the "Sons of Seth" were only **MEN**, and could only be called **"Sons of MEN,"** not **"Sons of GOD."** This proves beyond question that the **"Sons of God"** of Gen. 6:2, 4, were **ANGELS**, and not godly descendants of Seth.

The objection is raised on the statement of Jesus that the righteous dead, when raised, "neither marry or are given in marriage. . . . for they are **equal to the angels."** (Luke 20:27-36), that the angels are "sexless" and therefore cannot cohabit either with themselves or human beings. While the passage implies that the angels "do not marry," it does not say that they are "sexless," for that would convey the idea that the righteous at the resurrection would also be sexless, a doctrine abhorrent to the belief that husbands and wives and brothers and sisters shall know each other "as such" in the other world.

What the passage does teach is that angels do not multiply by procreation. Angels were created as far as we know "en masse," and as they never die there is no necessity for marriage among them. Marriage is a human institution to prevent the extinction of the race by death. What Christ sought to teach the Sadducees was, that as the resurrection would make men and women immortal there would be no occasion for the marriage relation in heaven.

However much we may question the possibility of intercourse between angels and human beings, this account in Genesis seems to teach it. We have only to turn to the Epistles of Peter and Jude for confirmation.

"God spared not the 'angels' that sinned, but cast them down to hell (Tartarus), and delivered them into chains of darkness, to be reserved unto judgment." 2 Pet. 2:4-9.

"The 'angels' which kept not their first estate, but left their own habitation, he hath reserved in everlasting chains in darkness unto the judgment of the great day." Jude 6-7.

The angels here mentioned cannot be Satan's angels, for his angels are "free." They are not "reserved in everlasting chains in darkness," but are to be cast into the "Lake of Fire" (Gehenna), prepared for the Devil and his angels, when he is cast in. Matt. 25:41. These angels then must be a **special class of angels**, condemned for some particular sin, and when we read the context to these two passages the character of that sin is evident.

It was the sin of **"Fornication and Going After 'Strange Flesh.'"** Jude 7. The "time" of the sin is given as just **before the flood**. 2 Pet. 2:5. It is the same sin that caused the destruction of Sodom and Gomorrah, whose inhabitants demanded of Lot, the surrender of the two Angels that he had received into his home, that they might "know them," that is have carnal intercourse with them. 2 Pet. 2:6-8. Jude 7. Gen. 19:5.

The Scriptures clearly teach that **angels** can assume fleshly bodies and eat and drink with men. Gen. 18:1-8. So the difficulty vanishes when we see that the **"Sons of God"** assumed human bodies and **AS MEN** married the "Daughters of Men."

What the "First Estate" was that they lost we do not know. They may have been some of the angels who had already left their "first estate" of holiness and subjection to God to follow the lead of **Satan**. But we must not forget, that, as far as we know, the Garden of Eden was not destroyed until the Flood, and as the descendants of Adam doubtless lived in the vicinity, the "Heavenly Watchers," or keepers of the Garden, the "Sons of God" (Cherubim), Gen. 3:24, would, from time to time, see the "Daughters of Men," and that they left their own "Habitation" (the Garden) and mingled with the "Daughters of Men," thus going after

"STRANGE FLESH,"

and thus losing their "First Estate" as angelic beings and guardians of the Garden.

Another argument for the support of this view is the fact that the progeny of this union was a race of **GIANTS, "MIGHTY MEN," "MEN OF RENOWN."** Gen. 6:4. Now the "godly descendants" of men have married "ungodly women," but their offspring have never been such **"monstrosities"** as the offspring of the **"Sons of God"** and the **"Daughters of Men"** of Noah's day. The word translated "giant" means the "Fallen Ones," the "Nephilim." It is clear that those "Mighty Men" and "Men of Renown," were not the ordinary offspring of the daughters of men, else why did they not appear before? The "sons of Seth" and the "daughters of Cain" had doubtless often intermarried before this, but there were no such children born to them. In this irruption of angelic beings into the world of men we have the source or origin whence the classic writers of antiquity obtained their notions concerning the loves of the gods and demi-gods, and the legends of beings half human and half divine.

These angels who lost their "First Estate" are the "Spirits in Prison" of whom Peter speaks in 1 Pet. 3:18-20, and to whom Christ preached, not in person, but by the Holy Spirit, through Noah, in the days before the Flood.

The outcome of this invasion of the earth by the denizens of the air was the Flood, by which the contour and elevation of the Antediluvian Earth was changed, thus wiping out the Garden of Eden. This brought to an end the "Antediluvian Age."

In the Antediluvian Dispensation mankind was treated as a **whole.** There were no nations. That Dispensation is called in Acts 17:30, the **"TIMES OF IGNORANCE,"** and is contrasted with the "Times that are **NOW,"** and we are told that in that Dispensation God **"WINKED AT"** what He could not **"OVERLOOK"** in the Legal Dispensation. Conscience was then the standard of human conduct. It was the standard by which men **accused** or **excused** themselves. Rom. 2:15. The Sinaitic Law was not given until after the Exodus. Being without Law there was no legal standard for sin, for "by the Law is the **KNOWLEDGE OF SIN."** Rom. 3:20. But they were without **"excuse,"** for God was very near to mankind in those days, and His voice was heard in rebuke, as to Cain (Gen. 4:14), in communion with Enoch (Gen. 5:22-24), or in counsel as with Noah. Gen. 6:3. They were therefore not without a knowledge of God, but they glorified Him not, and God **"gave them over to VILE AFFECTIONS."** Their daughters to cohabit with "Fallen Angels." The character of that Dispensation is vividly disclosed in Rom. 1:20-32. In it man proved rather to be **"UNGODLY"** than **a sinner.**

The principles which governed God's administration of those **"TIMES OF IGNORANCE"** would not be appropriate then in the days of Moses, when God revealed His will in "The Law." We must then distinguish these two Dispensations as being one **"WITHOUT LAW,"** and the other **"UNDER LAW."** This therefore would affect the "Basis of Judgment" in these Dispensations. This distinction is brought out clearly in Rom. 2:12.

"For as many as have sinned 'WITHOUT LAW' shall also **PERISH WITHOUT LAW,** and as many as have sinned 'IN THE LAW' shall be **JUDGED BY THE LAW."**

This clearly shows us that "**ignorance of the Law**" is no excuse, and will not save us from punishment. This "Principle of Judgment" will prevail at the "Great White Throne Judgment," when the inhabitants of both the Antediluvian and Legal Dispensations will be judged, and doubtless will be the "Principle of Judgment" for those living in this present Gospel Dispensation, for there are two classes of persons on the earth today—(1) Those who sin without knowing of God through the Gospel, and (2) Those who know of the Gospel but who have not obeyed it. 2 Thess. 1:7-10.

While there was no "**WRITTEN LAW**" in the Dispensation before the Flood, there was an "**UNWRITTEN LAW**," and when the Gentiles who have not the Law, do "**BY NATURE**" the things contained in the Law, they show that they have the Law **WRITTEN IN THEIR HEART,** for not the hearers of the Law are just (justified) before God, but the "**DOERS**," or those who keep it. Rom. 2:11-16. This answers the question as to the salvation of the Heathen without the written or spoken Gospel. If they by nature seek after God, and show by their faith and conduct, according to their light, like Cornelius (Acts 10:1-6) that in their heart they have received Him, who dare say they will not be saved? But this does not excuse us from taking the Gospel to them.

The characteristics of the "Antediluvian Dispensation," as outlined by the late Dr. A. T. Pierson, were,

"First, an advance in fulness and clearness of revelation; then gradual spirit declension; then conformity to the world, ending with amalgamation with the world; then a gigantic civilization, brilliant but godless; then parallel development of evil and good; then an 'Apostasy,' and finally a **CATASTROPHE**."

This we shall find is the characteristic of every dispensation that follows, except the last.

III. THE PRESENT AGE

This "Age" extends from the Flood to the second stage of Christ's Second Coming, called the "Revelation." It covers four Dispensations.

1. The Post-Diluvian Dispensation.

This was the Dispensation of "Human Government."

If ever the human race had an opportunity to work out the theory of "Human Government" it was right after the Flood. Noah was an old man over 600 years of age, full of wisdom and experience, and his family, all of whom had reached manhood and womanhood, for the youngest, Shem, was 98 years old, were qualified for self-government. Behind them was the Flood with all its warnings, and in addition the accumulated knowledge from Adam down to their day. They had also the advantage of a New Covenant, called the "Noachic Covenant." Gen. 8:20-22. Noah also re-established the true mode of worship by erecting an altar and sacrificing thereon, but the Dispensation was a failure like its predecessors.

God commanded Noah and his sons to be fruitful and multiply and replenish the earth, but instead of scattering, their posterity kept together, and sought to build a capital city and "make themselves a name" by building a "Tower" to heaven. This was disobedience, and God came down and confused their speech, and scattered them abroad over the face of the earth. Gen. 11:1-9. Even the names of the builders, except Nimrod (Gen. 10:8-10) are unknown. Here we have the origin of the different languages of the earth. The miracle was reversed at Pentecost. Acts 2:4.

1. POST-DILUVIAN DISPENSATION
(HUMAN GOVERNMENT)

The Dispersion of the Babelites happened about 325 years after the Flood, for we read in Gen. 10:25 that in the days of Peleg, one of the descendants of Shem, that the "earth was divided," that is, apportioned among the nations, and Peleg did not die until 340 years after the Flood (Gen. 11:10-19). That Dispensation lasted 102 years longer, or 427 years in all, and ended in failure like those that preceded it.

THE SACRIFICIAL ALTAR

2. PATRIARCHAL DISPENSATION
(FAMILY)

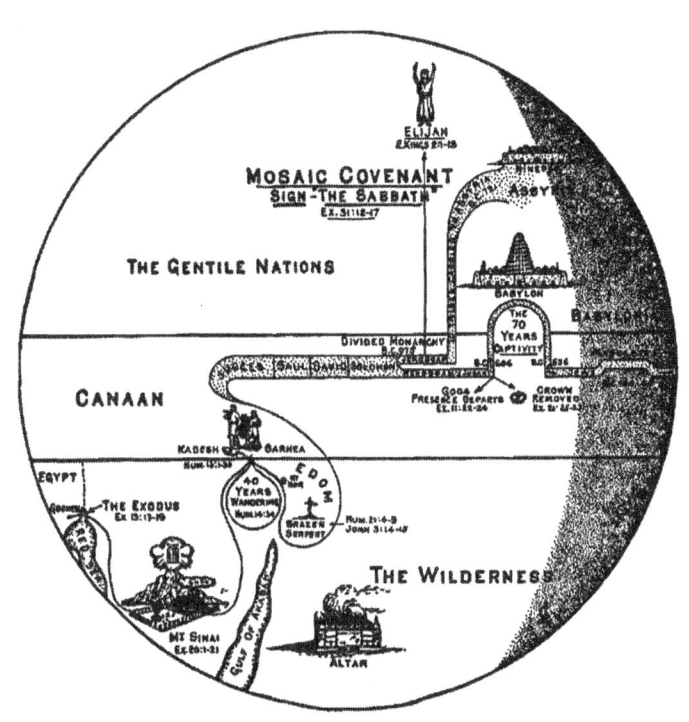

3. LEGAL DISPENSATION
(LAW)

2. The Patriarchal Dispensation.

This Dispensation extended from the "Call of Abraham" to the "Exodus," a period of 430 years, and is known as the Dispensation of "The Family."

After the Dispersion from Babel, the descendants of Noah and his sons became idolaters. No doubt God had His witnesses, but there is no record of any. Even Abraham's father was an idolater. So God decided to single out one family and start afresh. Abraham was chosen and he proved a mighty man of faith, but his righteousness waned in his descendants. Isaac was a good man, but not so good as his father, and Jacob, Isaac's son, who succeeded to the birthright, was still less so, and the twelve sons of Jacob, with the exception of Joseph, greatly degenerated from the parent stock, and that short Dispensation of only 430 years ended with all of Abraham's descendants working as abject slaves in the brickyards of Egypt.

The last words of the Book of Genesis, "a coffin in Egypt," are very suggestive. Was Egypt to be the "Graveyard" of all God's plan and purpose in the creation of the human race? Four times in the Book of Genesis God's plans for the human race were frustrated by Satan. First by the Fall in Eden, second by the Flood, third by the Dispersion at Babel, and fourth by the Captivity in Egypt. Is Satan mightier than God? Will he always prevail? We shall see.

3. The Legal Dispensation.

This Dispensation extended from the "Exodus" to the "Birth of Christ," a period of 1491 (?) years, and is known as the Dispensation of the "Law."

At the close of the preceding Dispensation the Children of Israel cried unto God in their bondage and He sent them a "Deliverer" in Moses. Heretofore God had allowed man to govern himself, now He purposed to organize a Commonwealth with laws and regulations and a "visible" system of worship with a local habitation or place of worship.

This government was to be "Theocratic." That is, it was God's intention to Himself rule on earth through a representative that He Himself would appoint. The person chosen was Moses. When Moses died he was succeeded by Joshua. After his death the Children of Israel had no ruler, except as by reason of bondage they cried unto the Lord, and He, as circumstances required, raised up "Judges" who governed them for about 450 years. Acts 13:20. Then they provoked God to give them a King, and Saul was selected, who reigned for 40 years. He was followed by David, who was succeeded by his son, Solomon, each of whom reigned 40 years.

At the death of Solomon, B. C. 975, the Kingdom was divided, Solomon's son Rehoboam getting two Tribes, spoken of as Judah, and Jeroboam, a usurper, ten Tribes, called Israel. Israel lasted for 254 years longer, and was carried captive to Assyria in B. C. 721, and 115 years later Judah went into exile to Babylon.

In B. C. 536, after 70 years' captivity, the Jews returned from Babylon, and from B. C. 166-40 strove under the Asmoneans to regain supremacy over Palestine, but in B. C. 40, Herod the Great, an Idumean, was made king by the Romans, and in A. D. 70 Jerusalem was sacked and burned by Titus, and the Jews driven out of Palestine.

In the "Legal Dispensation" God dealt with a chosen nation, Israel. His dealings with them was based on a **"WRITTEN LAW"** given at Mt. Sinai. This "Ceremonial Law" was given to Israel only, and not to any other nation. Israel then is to be judged according to their observance of it. The "Ceremonial Law," as far as its outward observance, ceased at the destruction of Jerusalem in A. D. 70.

The Law is based on the **JUSTICE** of God, and so knows no **MERCY**. It accounts for the destruction of the enemies of God, and of their cities and nations, and why God fought for His chosen people Israel. It also accounts for the "Imprecatory Psalms."

The Legal Dispensation was a wonderful period in that it was full of the "Miraculous Interposition" of God in behalf of His people. He delivered them from Egypt after visiting that land with plagues and destroying the first-born, and opening the Red Sea. He spoke to them in an awe-inspiring manner from Mt. Sinai. He took up His abode with them in the "Pillar of Cloud and of Fire." He fed them in the Wilderness in a miraculous manner for 40 years, and then walled back the waters of the Jordan and conducted them safely into the Promised Land, and helped them conquer it.

For centuries He watched over and protected them from their enemies, but when they forsook Him and became idolaters, His "Glory" left the Temple and He gave them over to their enemies, and when He sent the "Promised Seed" they were so filled with unbelief and hatred that they said this is the "Heir," let us kill Him, and they took and crucified the "Lord of Glory," and that Dispensation ended, as did all its predecessors, in the revelation that man is not only a failure, but blind and ungrateful.

4. The Ecclesiastical Dispensation.

This is the Dispensation of "Grace" and extends from the "Cross" to the "Crown" for Christ, and from the "Descent of the Holy Spirit" to the "Rapture of the Church" at the Second Coming of Christ for the Believer. This Dispensation is a

(PARENTHETICAL DISPENSATION)

thrown in between the "Dispersion" of Israel, and their "Restoration" to their own land. The purpose of this Dispensation is to gather out a "People for His Name," called

THE CHURCH,

composed of both Jew and Gentile.

This purpose of God was not revealed in the Old Testament Scriptures, and was unknown to the Patriarchs and Prophets. Christ was the first one to hint at it, when He said of Peter's confession,

"On this rock I will build **MY CHURCH.**" Matt. 16:18.

Paul calls it "The Mystery, which in other Ages (O. T. Ages), was not made known unto the sons of men" (Eph. 3:3-6), and adds that it was "hid in God" from the "beginning of the World." Eph. 3:9.

That the Gentiles were to be "saved" was no Mystery. Rom. 9:24-30. The "Mystery" was the fact of the purpose of God to "unite the Jew and the Gentile" in a wholly "new thing"—The Church,

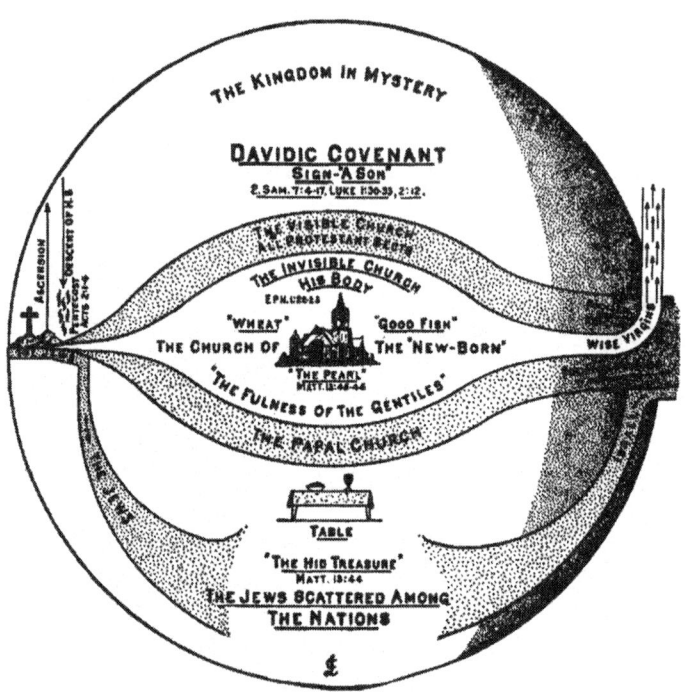

5. ECCLESIASTICAL DISPENSATION
(GRACE)

which is His (Christ's) **BODY.** 1 Cor. 12:12-13. This will be brought out fully in the chapter on "The Church."

In this Dispensation we are under the "Davidic Covenant," the sign of which is **"A SON"**—JESUS, and neither Jews nor Gentiles are dealt with as such. God is not dealing with the nations today but with **INDIVIDUALS.** The characteristic of this Dispensation is that— "Blindness **IN PART** is happened to **ISRAEL,** until the 'Fullness of the Gentiles' be come in." Rom. 11:25. God is calling out through the agency of the Holy Spirit individuals from both Jews and Gentiles to form a **NEW BODY,** the **CHURCH,** separate and distinct from both Jews and Gentiles. This "New Body" is not under **LAW** but **GRACE.** Rom. 6:14. The "Basis of Judgment" is our acceptance of the Lord Jesus Christ as our personal Saviour. When Christ took His seat upon the Father's Throne, He changed it from a "Throne of **JUSTICE**" to a "Throne of **GRACE,**" and God's attitude in this Dispensation is one of favor and longsuffering toward wicked men and nations. 2 Pet. 3:9.

So much for the "purpose" of this Dispensation. But how is it to end? We have seen that all the five preceding Dispensations have ended in failure—the Edenic in the "Fall," the Ante Diluvian in the "Flood," the Post Diluvian in the "Confusion of Tongues," the Patriarchal in "Egyptian Bondage," and the Legal in the "Crucifixion of Christ." Is this Dispensation to be an "exception" to all the preceding ones? What we know of the past Dispensations is History; how this Dispensation is to end is the subject of Prophecy.

The common view is that the World is to be converted by the preaching of the Gospel, which will usher in the Millennium, and that this Dispensation is to be a glorious success. But that is not the teaching of the Scriptures. The Scriptures teach that the "Wheat" and "Tares" are to continue growing side by side "until the Harvest," which is the end of this Dispensation; that the "Good" and "Bad Fish" are to be found in the "same Dragnet;" that the "Sheep" and "Goats" will continue to "browse together;" and that the "Wise and Foolish Virgins" shall keep on slumbering and sleeping "until the Bridegroom comes."

Christ Himself said that when He came back He would not find "Faith" (the Faith) on the earth. Luke 18:8.

And Paul warns us that in the last days of this Dispensation—"Perilous Times Shall Come." 2 Tim. 3:1-5.

Jesus told us that the closing days of this Dispensation would be like the days just before the flood.

"As the days of Noah were, **so shall also the coming of the Son of Man be.** For as in the days that were before the Flood they were eating and drinking, marrying and giving in marriage (this may refer to the marriage of the "Sons of God" and the "Daughters of Men"), until the day that Noah entered into the Ark, and knew not until the Flood came and took them all away; **so shall also the coming of the Son of Man be.**" Matt. 24:37-39.

Let us glance back for a moment at the characteristics of those "Noah Days" and we shall have an idea of the character of the closing days of this Dispensation. We mention but seven features.

1. **A Tendency to Worship God Simply as Creator, and Not as Jehovah Requiring Atonement for Sin.**

2. **There was a Rapid Advance in Civilization and in the Arts and Sciences.**

3. **There was a Union of the Holy Line of Seth and the Wicked Line of Cain.**

4. **A Vast Increase of Population and Congestion of Population in the Great Cities.**

5. **Undue Prominence of the Female Sex and Disregard of the Primal Law of Marriage.**

6. **Unlawful Intercourse of "Denizens of the Air" With the Daughters of Men.**

7. **The Rejection of the Preaching of Enoch and Noah.**

A careful observer of the "Signs of the Times" will note that all these features are characteristic of these days, and warn us that we are rapidly approaching the close of this Dispensation. We are living in the days of the revival of "Spiritism." The air is full of "Seducing Spirits," and there is a revival of the "Doctrine of Devils." 1 Tim. 4:1. It is no longer called Spiritualism but "Psychical Research" and now they have a new name—"Immortalism."

The preaching of today as to the "Coming of the Lord" is also largely rejected, thus fulfilling the words of Peter:

"Knowing this first, that there shall come in the last days **Scoffers,** walking after their own lusts and saying—**Where Is the Promise of His Coming?**" 2 Pet. 3:3-4.

Soon the Holy Spirit will no longer strive with men, as He ceased to do before the Flood, though God gave them 120 years' warning (Gen. 6:3), and will go back with the Church when it is called out of

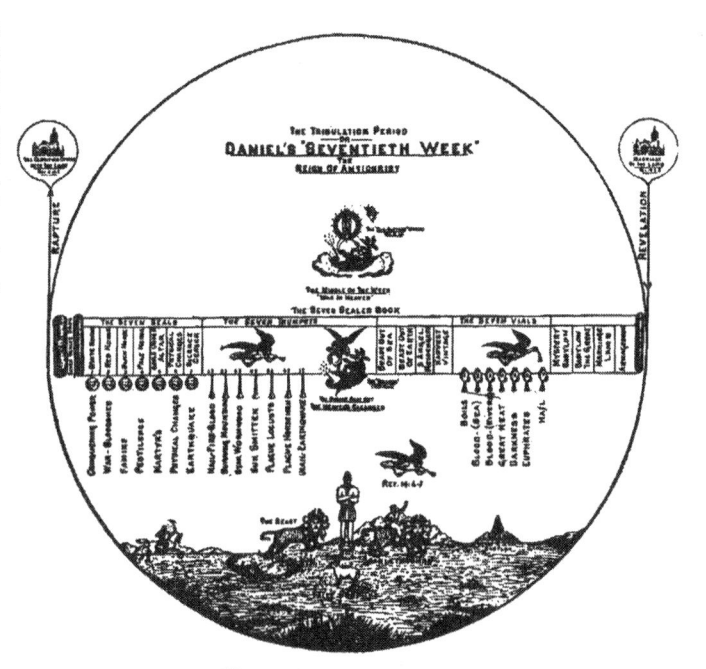

THE TRIBULATION
(JUDGMENT)

the world, and the world will be left for judgment. From this we see that this Dispensation, like all that have preceded it, will end in **Apostasy.**

DISPENSATION OF JUDGMENT

Between the "Ecclesiastical Dispensation" and the "Millennial Dispensation" there is another

PARENTHETICAL DISPENSATION,
the
DISPENSATION OF JUDGMENT,

during which the "Jews," the "Gentiles," and the "Church" are to be judged, not as individuals, but nationally or as bodies. The "Church" is to be caught out at the **beginning** of this Dispensation and judged at the "Judgment Seat of Christ." 2 Cor. 5:10. The Jews are to be judged **during** the Dispensation under Antichrist on the earth. Their Judgment is known as the "Time of Jacob's Trouble." Jer. 30:4-7. Dan. 12:1. The Gentiles (the Nations) are to be judged at the **close** of the Tribulation, when the Lord Jesus Christ shall descend from Heaven and sit on the "Throne of His Glory" at Jerusalem, and all nations shall be gathered in their representatives before Him, and the "Sheep Nations" shall be rewarded by entrance into the Millennial Kingdom, and the "Goat Nations," as **NATIONS,** shall be destroyed. Matt. 25:31-46.

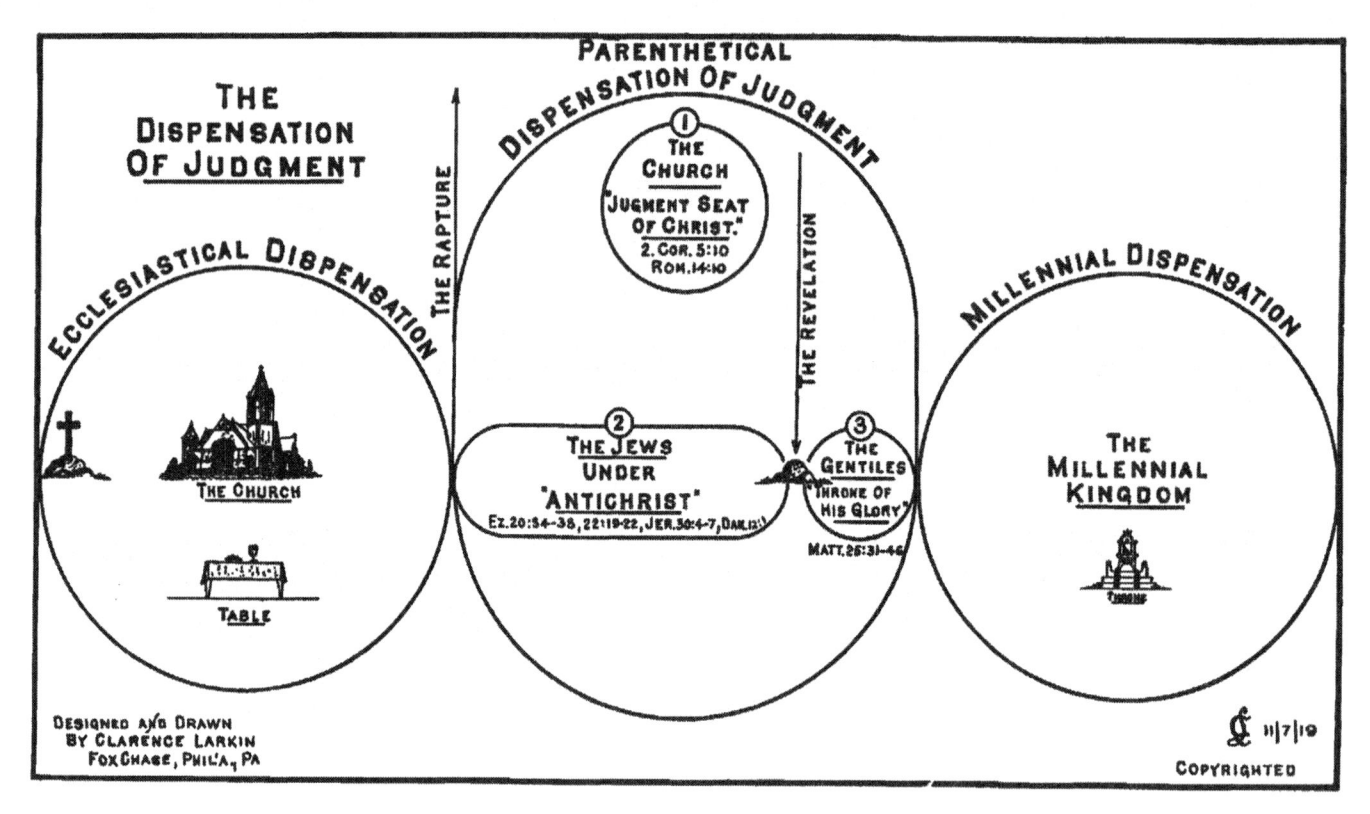

IV. THE AGE OF AGES

This is a "Dual Age" and includes the "Millennial Age" and the "Perfect Age," between which the earth is to be "Renovated by Fire." The Present Age is to end by the "Rapture" of the Church, followed by the "Great Tribulation," and the "Age of Ages" is to be ushered in by the "Revelation" of Christ, when He shall return to the earth, and after judging the "Nations," shall set up His Millennial Kingdom.

1. The Millennial Age.

Writers and poets have written and sung of a "Golden Age," an Age of universal righteousness and peace; and the Jews believe that the Seventh Thousand of years from the Creation is to be a "Sabbath of Rest," and that a description of that Age is given to us in the Old Testament Prophets. That there is to be a period of 1000 years during which Satan shall be bound and Christ shall reign on this earth is clearly revealed in the New Testament. This period is mentioned six times in the Book of Revelation. Rev. 20:1-7.

The Scriptures mention seven great "Dispensational Tests" of man from his creation until the New Heaven and the New Earth appear. He was tested in "Innocence" in the Garden of Eden; under "Conscience" before the Flood; under "Human Government" at Babel; under the "Headship of the Family" under the Patriarchs; under "Law" before Christ; he is now being tested under "Grace;" and he is to have one more test before God will give him up as hopelessly, incurably, incorrigibly God-hating and disobedient, and that test will be final and deprive him of his last shadow of excuse.

What is that excuse? Man charges his fall and his continuance in sin to Satan. "Take him away," he cries, "paralyze his power; cripple his malignant activity; bind him and deliver us from his dominating influence, and then you will see that man is radically good and virtuous, and is simply the victim of an unfavorable environment."

God answers it shall be done. Satan shall be bound so that he can no longer deceive men; and lest man shall say that sinful habits are too deeply rooted to be soon eradicated, the test shall last for a **thousand years**, and man shall have during that period of probation all the blessed influences of the Holy Spirit.

But we shall see as we study the outcome of the "Millennial Age" that when Satan is loosed, man will reveal the fact that he is still a rebellious creature, for that Dispensation, like all that preceded it, will end in **Apostasy.** Rev. 20:7-10.

In the Millennial Dispensation God will again deal with mankind as a **whole**, but as made up of nations. The Church will not be on the earth, only as it is represented by those who will assist Christ. **THE KING**, in His Administration of the Millennial Kingdom. The

41

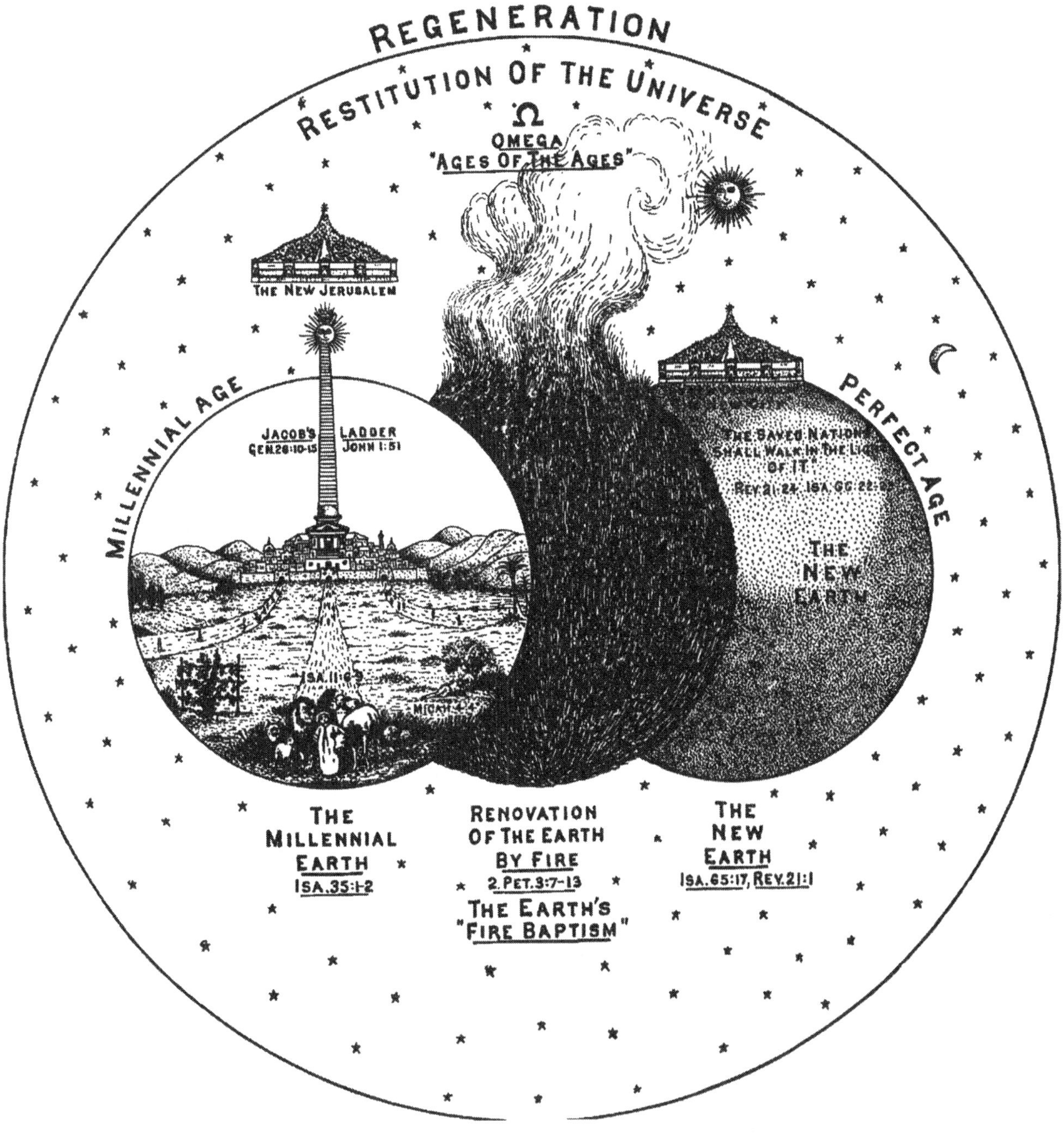
REGENERATION
RESTITUTION OF THE UNIVERSE
Ω
OMEGA
"AGES OF THE AGES"
THE NEW JERUSALEM
MILLENNIAL AGE
JACOB'S LADDER
GEN.28:10-15 JOHN 1:51
ISA.11:6-9
PERFECT AGE
THE SAVED NATION
SHALL WALK IN THE
OF IT
REV 21:24
THE NEW EARTH
THE MILLENNIAL EARTH
ISA.35:1-2
RENOVATION OF THE EARTH BY FIRE
2.PET.3:7-13
THE EARTH'S "FIRE BAPTISM"
THE NEW EARTH
ISA.65:17, REV.21:1

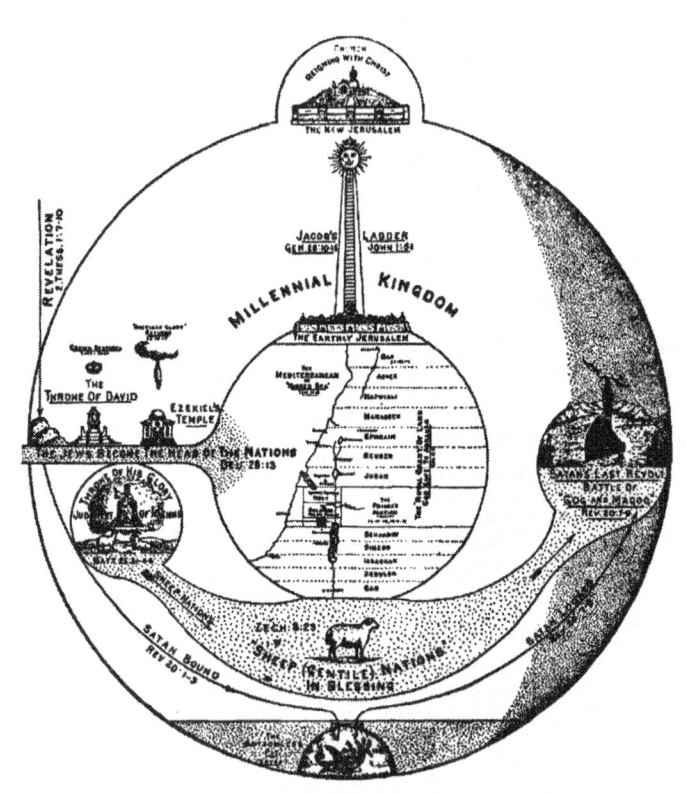

MESSIANIC DISPENSATION
(RIGHTEOUSNESS)

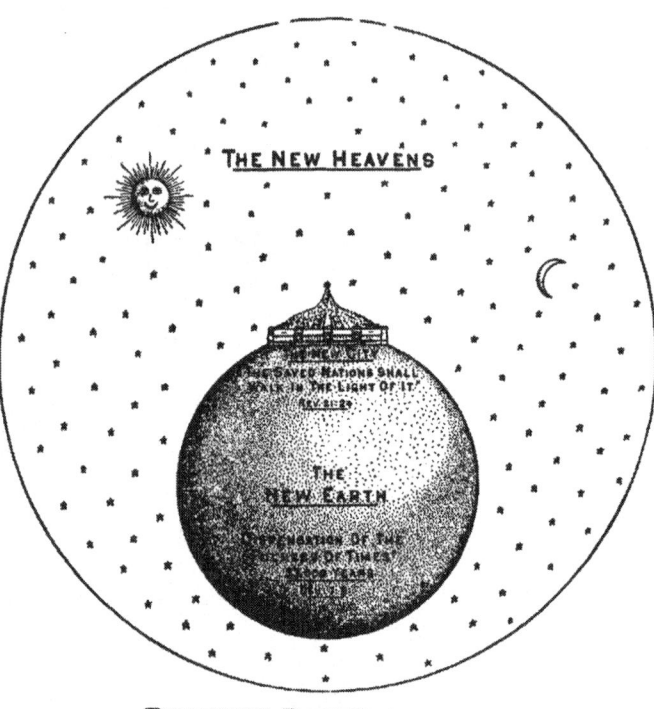

Jews, as a nation, will then be the **HEAD OF THE NATIONS.** Deu. 28:13. While they will in part observe the "Ceremonial Law," they will be under a **"NEW COVENANT."** Jer. 31:31-37. Heb. 8:7-13. The principle under which God will deal with men in those days will not be Law, Grace or Judgment, but **RIGHTEOUSNESS.** The Government will be based on "Righteousness." It will be an "Autocratic Government," for Christ will rule with a **"ROD OF IRON"** (Isa. 11:1, 4; Rev. 2:27, 19:15; Psa. 2:9), but that rule will be based on **LOVE.** As Satan will be bound at that time, the character of the Millennial Dispensation will be entirely different from all preceding Dispensations, and cannot be classed with them.

2. The Perfect Age.

At the close of the "Millennial Age," the present earth is to be "Renovated by Fire," the outcome of which will be a "New Heaven" and a "New Earth" **Wherein Dwelleth Righteousness.** 2 Pet. 3:13.

It is this "Perfect Kingdom that Christ surrenders to the Father," (1 Cor. 15:28), for the "Millennial Kingdom" is not perfect, there is sin in it, and it ends in "Apostasy." This "Perfect Kingdom" is also a Dispensation, the "Dispensation of the Fulness of Times." Eph. 1:10. The "Millennial Kingdom" and the "Perfect Kingdom" make up the **"Kingdom of the SON OF MAN."**

V. THE AGES OF THE AGES

As the "Creative Ages" were the "Alpha" Ages, these will be the "Omega" Ages. With the surrender of the "Perfect Kingdom" to the Father, what we speak of as "Time" ceases, and the "Eternal Ages," called the "Ages of the Ages," begin. They correspond to what the Apostle Paul in his Letter to the Ephesians calls the "Ages to Come." Eph. 2:7. And John in the Book of Revelation says that the "Devil" and the "Beast" and the "False Prophet" shall be tormented day and night **forever and ever,** or for the **"Aions"** of the **"Aions,"** the **"Ages of the Ages,"** (Rev. 20:10), and that the "Servants of God" shall reign for the same period. Rev. 22:5.

What those "Ages of Ages" shall reveal of the Plan and Purpose of God we do not know, but if we are His we shall live to **know,** and possibly take part in their development. What we do know **is** that we are but in the **beginning of things,** and as concerning **the "Ages,"** Eternity is still **young.**

43

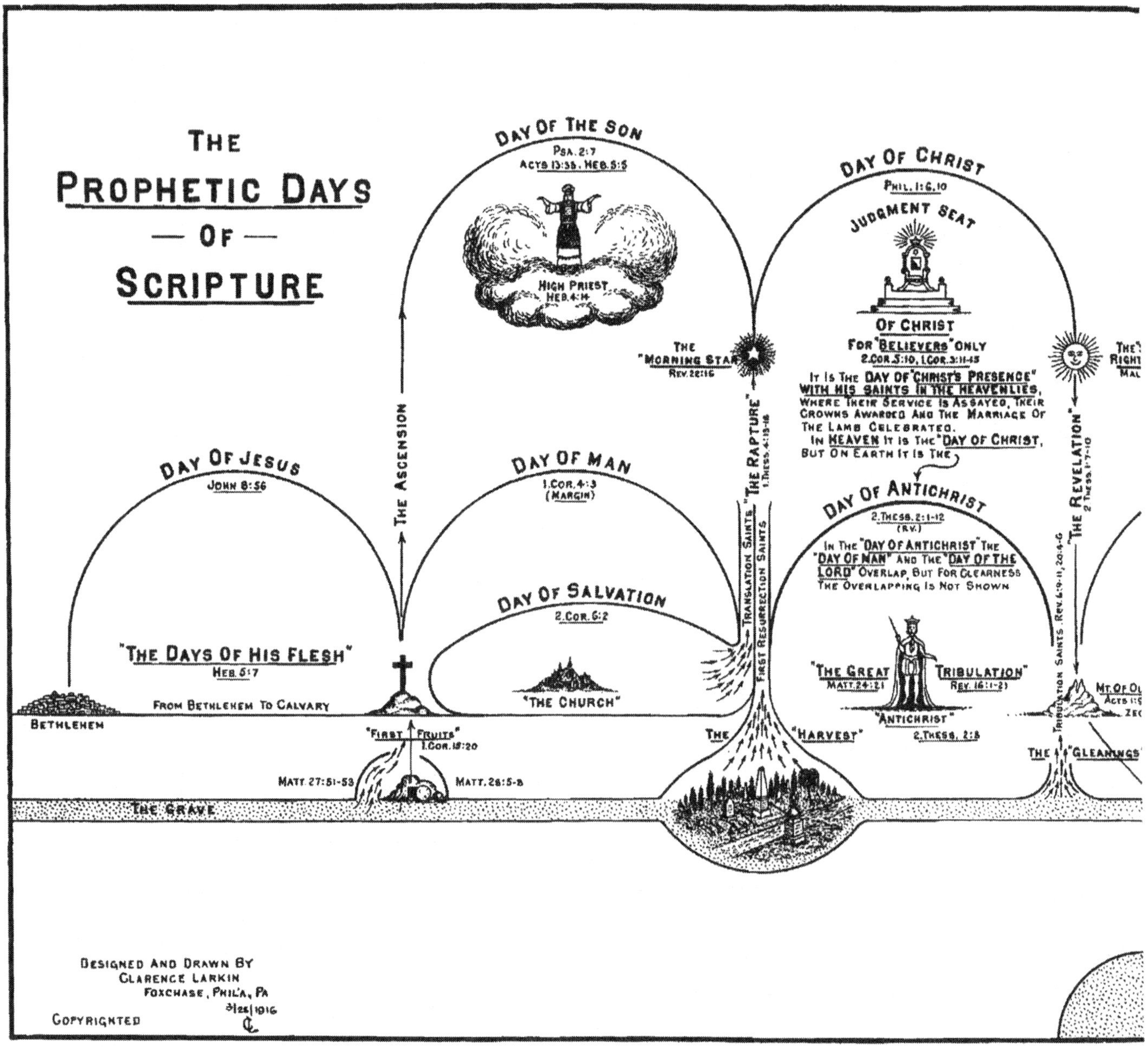
THE
PROPHETIC DAYS
— OF —
SCRIPTURE
DAY OF THE SON
PSA. 2:7
ACTS 13:33. HEB. 5:5
HIGH PRIEST
HEB. 4:14
DAY OF CHRIST
PHIL. 1:6, 10
JUDGMENT SEAT
OF CHRIST
FOR "BELIEVERS" ONLY
2. COR. 5:10, 1. COR. 3:11-15
IT IS THE DAY OF "CHRIST'S PRESENCE" WITH HIS SAINTS IN THE HEAVENLIES, WHERE THEIR SERVICE IS ASSAYED, THEIR CROWNS AWARDED AND THE MARRIAGE OF THE LAMB CELEBRATED.
IN HEAVEN IT IS THE "DAY OF CHRIST, BUT ON EARTH IT IS THE
THE "MORNING STAR"
REV. 22:16
THE ASCENSION
"THE RAPTURE"
1. THESS. 4:13-18
TRANSLATION SAINTS
FIRST RESURRECTION SAINTS
"THE REVELATION"
2 THESS. 1:7-10
TRIBULATION SAINTS. REV. 6:9-11, 20:4-6
DAY OF JESUS
JOHN 8:56
DAY OF MAN
1. COR. 4:3
(MARGIN)
DAY OF ANTICHRIST
2. THESS. 2:1-12
(R.V.)
IN THE "DAY OF ANTICHRIST" THE "DAY OF MAN" AND THE "DAY OF THE LORD" OVERLAP, BUT FOR CLEARNESS THE OVERLAPPING IS NOT SHOWN
DAY OF SALVATION
2. COR. 6:2
"THE DAYS OF HIS FLESH"
HEB. 5:7
FROM BETHLEHEM TO CALVARY
BETHLEHEM
"THE CHURCH"
"THE GREAT TRIBULATION"
MATT. 24:21
REV. 16:1-21
"ANTICHRIST"
2. THESS. 2:8
"FIRST FRUITS"
1. COR. 15:20
MATT. 27:51-53
MATT. 28:5-8
THE "HARVEST"
THE "GLEANINGS"
THE GRAVE
DESIGNED AND DRAWN BY
CLARENCE LARKIN
FOXCHASE, PHIL'A, PA
3/25/1916
COPYRIGHTED

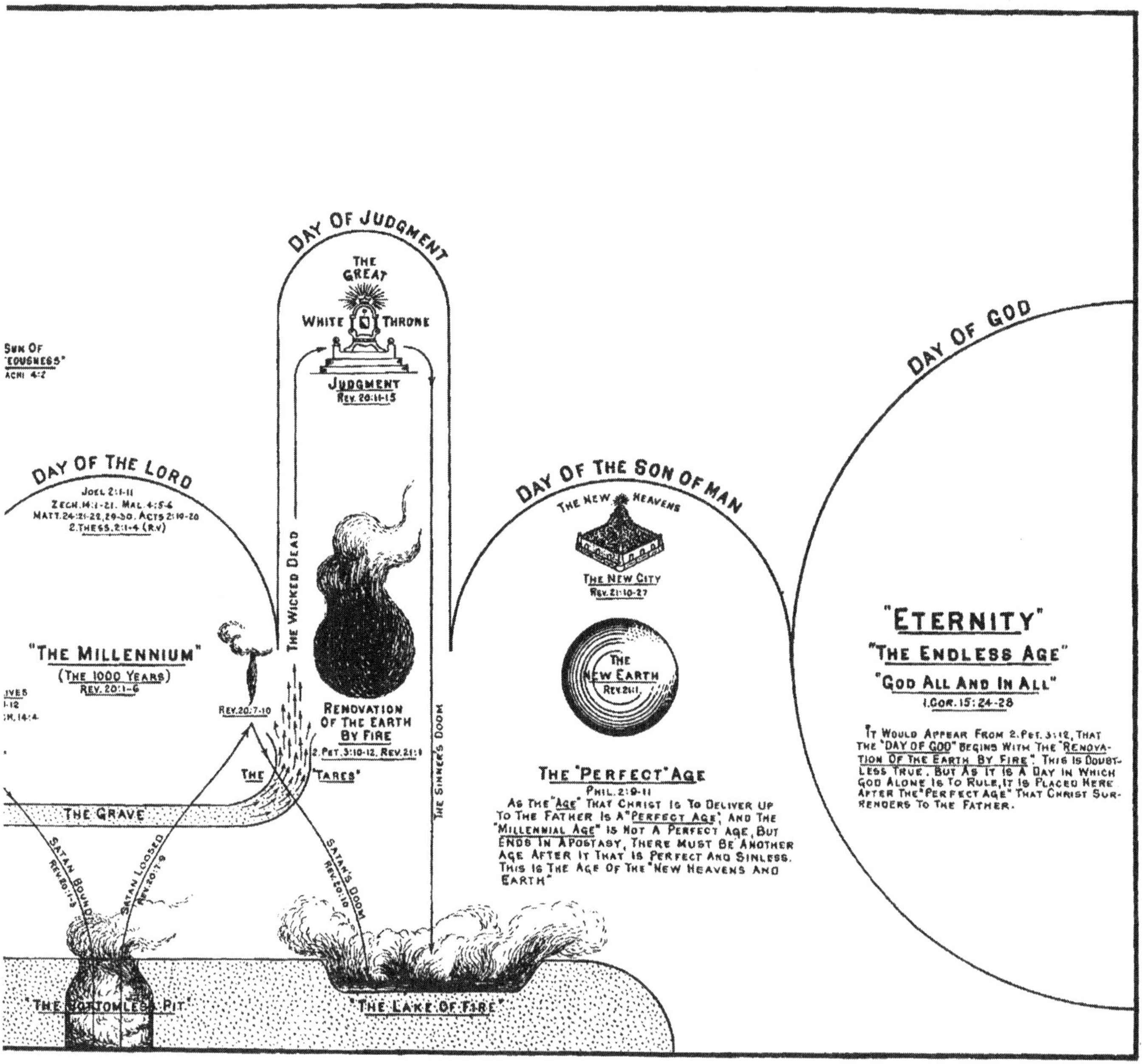
DAY OF JUDGMENT
THE GREAT WHITE THRONE
JUDGMENT
REV. 20:11-15
DAY OF GOD
DAY OF THE LORD
JOEL 2:1-11
ZECH. 14:1-21. MAL. 4:5-6
MATT. 24:21-22, 29-30. ACTS 2:19-20
2. THESS. 2:1-4 (R.V)
"THE MILLENNIUM"
(THE 1000 YEARS)
REV. 20:1-6
REV. 20:7-10
THE WICKED DEAD
RENOVATION OF THE EARTH BY FIRE
2. PET. 3:10-12. REV. 21:1
THE SINNER'S DOOM
THE "TARES"
THE GRAVE
SATAN BOUND
SATAN LOOSED
REV. 20:7-9
SATAN'S DOOM
REV. 20:10
"THE BOTTOMLESS PIT"
"THE LAKE OF FIRE"
DAY OF THE SON OF MAN
THE NEW HEAVENS
THE NEW CITY
REV. 21:10-27
THE NEW EARTH
REV. 21:1
THE "PERFECT" AGE
PHIL. 2:9-11
AS THE "AGE" THAT CHRIST IS TO DELIVER UP TO THE FATHER IS A "PERFECT AGE", AND THE "MILLENNIAL AGE" IS NOT A PERFECT AGE, BUT ENDS IN APOSTASY, THERE MUST BE ANOTHER AGE AFTER IT THAT IS PERFECT AND SINLESS. THIS IS THE AGE OF THE "NEW HEAVENS AND EARTH"
"ETERNITY"
"THE ENDLESS AGE"
"GOD ALL AND IN ALL"
1. COR. 15:24-28
IT WOULD APPEAR FROM 2. PET. 3:12, THAT THE "DAY OF GOD" BEGINS WITH THE "RENOVATION OF THE EARTH BY FIRE". THIS IS DOUBTLESS TRUE. BUT AS IT IS A DAY IN WHICH GOD ALONE IS TO RULE, IT IS PLACED HERE AFTER THE "PERFECT AGE" THAT CHRIST SURRENDERS TO THE FATHER.

VI

THE PRESENT EVIL WORLD

While this is the "Dispensation of Grace," and God's purpose during it is to gather out a "People for His Name"—the CHURCH, the world out of which the Church is being gathered is called—

"THE PRESENT EVIL AGE."
Gal. 1:4. (R. V.).

That this "Age" is EVIL is seen in the character of its civilization. After nearly 1900 years of Gospel preaching the world is in a worse state, in proportion to its light, than it was in the days of Christ, and seems headed toward some great crisis. The spirit of lawlessness is in the air, and despite all efforts to quench it, it is strangely becoming unmanageable and perverse and determined to break away from all authority and law.

How are we to account for this? Has God lost His control over the world, or is He permitting some other agency to have its way?

The answer is that there are

"TWO OPPOSING SPIRITS"

at work in the world in this Dispensation. The "HOLY SPIRIT" who is engaged in gathering out the elect body of the Church, and the "SPIRIT OF EVIL." These are called in 1 Cor. 2:12. the "SPIRIT WHICH IS OF GOD," and the "SPIRIT OF THE WORLD," and in 1 John 4:5-6, the "SPIRIT OF TRUTH" and the "SPIRIT OF ERROR." The Spirit of Error is the source of all the "STRONG DELUSIONS" (2 Thess. 2:11) that are in the world today, and as the "End of the Age" draws near they are being rapidly multiplied, and it requires the utmost vigilance not to be caught in their net. Just as the Church is indwelt and guided by the "HOLY SPIRIT," so the World outside the Church is indwelt and guided by the "SPIRIT OF THE WORLD" (1 Cor. 2:12), or "UNHOLY SPIRIT." And as the "HOLY SPIRIT" is a PERSON, so the "SPIRIT OF THE WORLD" is a PERSON.

"And you hath He quickened, (by His Holy Spirit), who were dead in trespasses and sins; wherein in time past ye walked according to the 'COURSE (AGE) OF THIS WORLD,' according to the Prince of the 'Power of the Air,' (Satan) the 'SPIRIT' (Evil Spirit) that now worketh (energizes) in the—

'CHILDREN OF DISOBEDIENCE.'"
Eph. 2:1-2.

From this we see that the "SPIRIT OF THE WORLD" is SATAN.

The world refused to accept the rule of God when it crucified His Son, and chose Barabbas instead of Christ, thus exalting Satan to the position of the "GOD OF THIS AGE," for Satan is not spoken of as the God of any other Age than this. It was Satan's ambition to be like God that caused his fall (Isa. 14:13-14), and he has not as yet given up that ambition, and it is his purpose and plan to exalt himself in the person of Antichrist, whom he will indwell, and sit in the "Temple of God," (the rebuilt Jewish Temple in Jerusalem), AS GOD, and have the people worship him as such. 2 Thess. 2:3-4. Rev. 13:4, 11-12.

MAN'S DAY.

This Dispensation is spoken of in the Scriptures as "MAN'S DAY." Writing to the Corinthians Paul says, "But with me it is a very small thing that I should be judged of you, or of 'man's judgment.'" The margin reads of—"MAN'S DAY." 1 Cor. 4:3. This then is the day of the GLORIFICATION OF MAN. The day in which the works of man are exalted and praised. We cannot explain the great advance in knowledge and the mechanic arts of the past one hundred years, apart from God, only on the supposition that there is some superhuman being who imparts this knowledge and who controls the affairs of the mechanical and commercial world. And it is worthy of note that it was not the descendants of Seth, the godly people of the Antediluvian Dispensation, but the descendants of Cain, the ungodly people of that period, who invented metal working, devised musical instruments (doubtless for pleasure), and built great cities for commercial and other purposes. Now we know that Satan's gospel is the—

"GOSPEL OF PROGRESS."

He preached it in the Garden of Eden when he promised Eve that if she would eat of the fruit of the Tree of the "Knowledge of Good and Evil," her eyes would be opened, and she and Adam be as "Gods," knowing good and evil. Gen. 3:5.

It was the promise of KNOWLEDGE that caused the downfall of the human race, and when Adam and Eve followed Satan's advice they committed the race to the acceptance of his LEADERSHIP AND PROGRAM.

It is not likely that the Holy God imparted to the ungodly race of Cain the knowledge to invent things that would lead to the downfall of the race and help to bring on the Flood. Neither is it to be supposed that a God of Love would impart to men the knowledge that would enable them to invent such hellish instruments of warfare as were used in the great European War. It is clear then that there is some "SUPERNATURAL BEING" who is at the head of the "WORLD SYSTEM," and that that "Being" is—"SATAN." His Program is to build up a magnificent Civilization without God. The phrase "Christian Civilization" is an invention of the "God of this Age." There can be no such thing, for Christianity and Civilization have nothing in common. There can be no Christian civilization without Christ, and when He comes back He will bring to an end the boasted civilization of this Age, and set up a NEW CIVILIZATION over which Satan shall have no control, for he will then be a prisoner in the Pit. It is clear that if this world could be made a fit place for men to live in without God, it could not have had a more masterly leader than Satan, and that if he has failed it is not his fault, but is due to the wilfulness of man.

There are but two classes of people spoken of in the New Testament. The "CHILDREN OF GOD," and the "CHILDREN OF THE DEVIL." "In this the 'CHILDREN OF GOD' are manifest, and the 'CHILDREN OF THE DEVIL:' whosoever doeth not righteousness is not of God." 1 John 3:10. Here all who "doeth not righteousness" are classed as "CHILDREN OF THE DEVIL," and in Eph. 2:2 are called the "CHILDREN OF DISOBEDIENCE." There is no possibility of union between them, therefore there cannot be any such thing as the "BROTHERHOOD OF MAN," which popularly understood is the union of all religious bodies and sects, such as Christians, Jews, Atheists, Unitarians, Mohammedans, Buddhists, Confucianists, etc., in a Federation of Religions.

The word "disobedience" means obstinate rebellion. How futile then is the effort of the "Children of Disobedience" to make the earth a more comfortable habitation for man, and bring in a Millennium by a Federation of all Religious Bodies, when the bulk of mankind is in **OBSTINATE REBELLION** against God, and will not have His Son to reign over them, but are spending every energy to produce a **"Godless Civilization"** and make way for Satan's **"MASTERPIECE,"** the **"MAN OF SIN."**

Satan is the **"DECEIVER OF THE WORLD."** Rev. 12:9. He raises "false hopes," and deludes by the—**"DECEITFULNESS OF RICHES"** (Matt. 13:22), the **"DECEITFULNESS OF SIN"** (Heb. 3.13), and the **"DECEITFULNESS OF UNRIGHTEOUSNESS."** 2 Thess. 2:9-11. He causes the **"exercise of the imagination,"** and by **"strong delusions,"** and **"seducing spirits,"** he tries to make men believe that his plans for the world's betterment are right. His advocates point to the great increase in scientific knowledge and invention, the great advance in methods of world-wide communication by land, sea, and air, and the various inventions that lighten labor and add to domestic comfort, and claim that the world is growing better, not only because of these, but because of the great philanthropies of men that have founded colleges, libraries, hospitals and great charitable institutions, forgetting that these things only tend to the physical helpfulness of man and have little to do with his moral character, and overlooking the fact that, in spite of all this advancement of civilization, the world today sits on the mouth of a volcano, whose interior is a "foaming cauldron" of social unrest and commercial rottenness.

When the "God of this Age" discovered that he could not stamp out the Church by **PERSECUTION**, he changed his tactics and now seeks to neutralize her efforts by **SEDUCTION**. His method is to divert her efforts for the evangelization of the world, to methods of "Social Betterment," and thus make the world a better place to live in, forgetting that, as the natural man cannot be spiritually saved by **CULTURE**, neither can the world, therefore all efforts to save the world by "Social Betterment" are futile. And when the Church lends her aid to such methods she confesses that Christ's method of saving the world **IS INSUFFICIENT**, and thus discounts the power of the Gospel. Christian men give vast sums of money for the "Social, Intellectual, and Physical Betterment of the world," rather than for the evangelization of the world. They even go farther and form societies for the investigation of "adverse social conditions," such as poverty, vice, ignorance, etc., and appoint specialists at high salaries to investigate and see if they can discover the cause of all the sin, misery and wretchedness there is in the world, forgetting that in so doing they are wasting their money, for the Bible told us centuries ago that the **cause was SIN**. If the proper thing to do is to remedy a thing at its source, let the Church apply the remedy of the Gospel and save the individual, and by thus doing save society.

The common opinion is, that all the "ills of society" are in men's surroundings, or environment, whereas they are in **MAN HIMSELF**. Hence all human schemes for the "Betterment of Society" must begin in the man himself. That is, man must first be **REGENERATED** by the Holy Spirit. All the schemes of men to make this world a better place to "live in," seem to be to make the world a better place to **"SIN IN,"** because they increase the facilities for sin.

The "God of this Age" knows that if the Church was to give herself exclusively to the work of "World Evangelization" he would lose her service in building his great "Civilization Structure," so he is just as anxious to keep her in his power, and postpone the time of her "Exodus," (1 Thess. 4:15-18), as Pharaoh was to keep Israel in Egypt at work on his stone cities Rameses and Pithom. To this end he keeps her busy "making bricks without straw," and thus blinds her eyes to the light of the "Glorious Gospel of Christ," (the doctrine of the Pre-Millennial Coming of the Lord), knowing that once she gets a vision of that she will refuse to any longer work for his "World Betterment" schemes.

The unification of the nations of the earth is a scheme to reverse the judgment of God on Babel, and resume the building of **"THE TOWER"** that is to exalt the name of man. Gen. 11:1-9.

There are two "Distinct Bodies" in this "Present Evil Age" in the process of formation.

1. The **"BODY OF CHRIST"—THE CHURCH.**
2. The **"BODY OF ANTICHRIST."**

The first is being gathered by the **"SPIRIT OF GOD"** (Holy Spirit,) 1 Cor. 12:3, 13, and the second by the **"SPIRIT OF EVIL,"** that now worketh (energizes) in the **"Children of Disobedience."** Eph. 2:1-2. The difference between the "Body" the Holy Spirit is forming, and the "Body" the "Spirit of Evil" is forming, is, that the former is united to a **"LIVING HEAD,"** (Christ—Eph. 1:20-23), while the latter has no living head, for it is simply an **"Organization,"** while the "Body of Christ" is an **"ORGANISM."** Since the "Fall" and death of Adam the human race has been **headless**, but when the "Body," or "Organization," that the "Spirit of Evil" (Satan) is forming is complete, he (Satan) will produce its **"HEAD,"** who will be the **ANTICHRIST**, thus reversing the Divine order of first the **"HEAD"** (Christ) and then the **"BODY"**—the Church.

We are told that the Lord at His "Second Coming" will depose and punish two distinct governing bodies. Isa. 24:21.

1. "The 'HIGH ONES' that are on high."

That is Satan and the "Evil Powers of the Air." Eph. 6:12.

2. "The 'KINGS OF THE EARTH' upon the earth."

That is the Anti-Christian World Powers represented by the "Ten Federated Kings" under the control of Antichrist. Rev. 19:17-21.

The heavens will then be cleansed of all the "Powers of Evil," and their place will be taken and occupied by Christ and the Saints who constitute the Church, and they will reign during the Millennium from the heavens over the earth, as Satan and his hosts do now. Rev. 20:4.

VII

THE DISPENSATIONAL WORK OF THE LORD JESUS CHRIST

The study of the "Life and Work of Christ" is confined by most students to His "Earthly Life," that is to the **"DAYS OF HIS FLESH."** But we must not forget that Jesus was—

"THE ETERNAL CHRIST."

The reason therefore why so many have a defective view of Christ's "Life and Work" is because they have but a **partial** view of Him. His work of Atonement on the Cross was but one phase of His work, which began in the Creation of the Universe, and will continue as long as God exists. The "Greater Life and Work of Christ" is a circle of which the circumference is "Eternity," and the centre is **CALVARY.**

In tracing the lineage of Jesus Matthew traces Him back to Abraham, (Matt. 1:1-17), Luke to Adam, (Luke 3:23-38), and John to God. (John 1:1-2.) Jesus said of Himself "I am **'Alpha'** and **'Omega,'** the **'BEGINNING'** and the **'ENDING,'** the **'FIRST'** and the **'LAST,'** which IS, and which WAS, and which is TO COME, the ALMIGHTY." Rev. 1:8, 11. Jesus thus identifies Himself with God, and confirms His earthly statement—"I and my Father are ONE." John 10:30. John tells us (John 1:14) that—**"THE WORD was made flesh,** and dwelt among us, and we beheld His **GLORY** (on the Mount of Transfiguration), the **GLORY** as of the **ONLY BEGOTTEN OF THE FATHER."** And in His prayer in the "upper room" before going out to Gethsemane Jesus prayed, "And now, O Father, glorify thou me with **Thine own self** with the **GLORY** which I had with **Thee BEFORE THE WORLD WAS."** John 17:5. Thus we see that Jesus existed **before the World was** and is the **ETERNAL CHRIST.**

In studying the Dispensational or Greater Life and Work of the Lord Jesus Christ we shall for simplicity divide it into three parts, His Past, Present and Future Life and Work. See my Chart on "The Greater Life and Work of Christ."

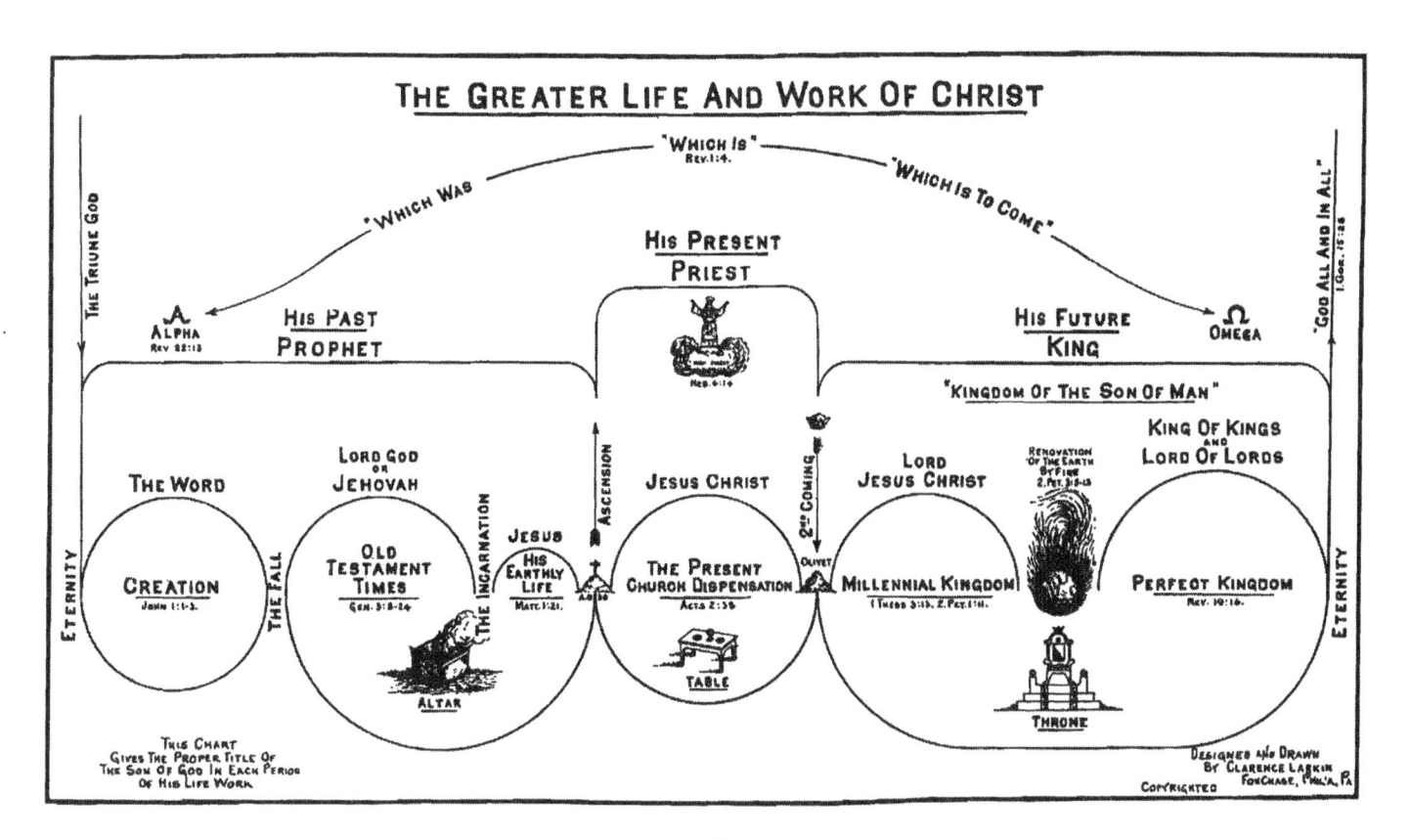

I. CHRIST'S PAST LIFE AND WORK.

The "Office Work" of Christ is "**Threefold**," that of **"PROPHET," "PRIEST"** and **"KING."** But He does not hold these offices conjointly but successively. His "Prophetic Work" extended from Creation to His Ascension; His "Priestly Work" extends from His Ascension to the Rapture of the Church; and His "Kingly Work" from His Revelation at the close of the Tribulation Period, until He surrenders the Kingdom to the Father, that "God may be All in All." 1 Cor. 15:28. His Past Life and Work we may divide into Three Periods.

1. CHRIST'S WORK IN CREATION.

The Scriptures begin with the sublime statement, "**In the beginning GOD.**" Gen. 1:1. The finite mind cannot grasp the thought that there was a time when there was absolutely nothing but God. Whether the Father existed at first alone, and the Son, and the Holy Spirit proceeded from Him, thus making the Divine Three, is not clear. If the expression—"The Only Begotten of the Father" (John 1:14) as applied to Jesus, refers to His **Eternal** origin, then He was not co-existent with the Father, if it refers to His **Earthly** origin, to His birth of the Virgin Mary, then He was the "Only Begotten of the Father" in the sense of being begotten by the Father through the agency of the Holy Spirit. Luke 1:30-35. But there is another passage that is confusing. In writing to the Colossians in regard to Christ Paul says—

"In whom we have redemption through His blood, even the forgiveness of sins; who is the '**Image of the Invisible God,**' the **FIRSTBORN OF EVERY CREATURE.**" Col. 1:14-15.

What are we to understand by this? Is Jesus only a "**Creature**" and therefore not a part of God from the beginning? It can hardly mean that, for in the next verse He is described as the Creator of all things. The probable explanation is that as Jesus became by His human birth—"**God manifest in the FLESH,**" (1 Tim. 3:16), thus becoming to men the "**IMAGE of the Invisible God,**" that He thus became the "**Firstborn**" of the "**NEW CREATION**" of God, of which race the "Second" or "Last Adam" (Christ) is the **HEAD**. 1 Cor. 15:45, 2 Cor. 5:17. However this may be it is the clear teaching of Scripture that the "Divine Three" existed in a co-ordinate relation to each other before anything else existed.

In His "Creative Work" Jesus is spoken of in the Scripture as

"THE WORD."

"In the Beginning was the '**WORD**' and the '**WORD**' was with God, and the '**WORD**' **WAS GOD**. The same was in the Beginning with God. **ALL THINGS WERE MADE BY HIM**; and without **Him was not anything made that was made.**" John 1:1-3. This is corroborated by Paul in Col. 1:16-17:

"For **BY HIM** were **all things created**, that are in **Heaven**, and that are in **earth**, visible and invisible, whether they be **thrones**, or **dominions**, or **principalities**, or **powers**; **ALL THINGS** were created **BY HIM**, and **FOR HIM**; and He is **BEFORE ALL THINGS**, and **BY HIM** all things **consist.**"

While all things were made by Christ, He was aided by the Father and the Holy Spirit. This is clearly revealed in Gen. 1:26, where it says—"And God (the Divine Three) said, Let **US** make man in **OUR IMAGE**, after **OUR likeness.**" The work of the Father was the creation of matter, that of the Son, the formation of matter into all its various forms, and that of the Holy Spirit to give **LIFE** to such forms as have life. Christ's work in Creation is beautifully described in Isa. 40:12:

"Who hath **measured the waters in the hollow of His hand**, and **meted out heaven with the span**, and **comprehended the dust of the earth in a measure**, and **weighed the mountains in scales**, and **the hills in a balance.**"

Job, the oldest book in the Bible, is particularly rich in its account of the Creative Work of Christ. See the 38th and 39th chapters of Job. We have a beautiful illustration of Christ's Creative Power in the miracle of making wine out of water. John 2:1-11. In that miracle He produced from **water** without the natural process of the vine, **WINE**, and thus manifested His Creative Glory.

2. CHRIST'S WORK FROM CREATION TO HIS INCARNATION.

With the Creation of Man the "Creative Work" of Christ ceased, for we read in Gen. 2:2, that—"On the Seventh Day God ended His Work which He had made; and He rested on the Seventh Day." From that time His work has been that of "Supervision" and "Redemption." In Gen. 2:4 we find the word God changed to "**LORD** God." Why is this? The Hebrew name for God as "**Creator**" is ELOHIM, as "**Revealer**" it is JEHOVAH, translated "**LORD**." The name "God" is used over 6000 times in the Old Testament, and when in the Authorized Version we find the word "God" or "Lord" printed in small capitals, the original is JEHOVAH.

In the first part of the Book of Genesis four names are given, each of which reveals some distinct attribute of God. They are God (Elohim), **LORD** (Jehovah), God Almighty (El Shaddai), and Most High (El Elyon). They are all used in Psa. 91:1-2. "He that dwelleth in the secret place of the Most High shall abide under the shadow of the **Almighty**. I will say of **Jehovah**, He is my refuge and my fortress; my **God** in whom I trust." JEHOVAH has seven compound names that reveal Him as meeting every need of man.

1. JEHOVAH-JIREH—"The Lord will provide." Gen. **22:** 13-14. That is, provide a sacrifice.

2. JEHOVAH-RAPHA—"The Lord that healeth." Ex. 15:26.

3. JEHOVAH-NISSI—"The Lord our Banner." Ex. 17:8-15.

4. JEHOVAH-SHALOM—"The Lord our peace." Judges 6:23-24.

5. JEHOVAH-RĀ-AH—"The Lord my Shepherd." Psa. 23.

6. JEHOVAH-TSIDKENU—"The Lord our righteousness." Jer. 23:6.

7. JEHOVAH-SHAMMAH—"The Lord is present." Ez. 48:35.

It is therefore only as we know the meaning of the different titles of God that we can understand their significance. The word for Christ as "Creator" is "**ELOHIM**," for Christ as "Revealer and Redeemer" is **Jehovah** (translated **LORD**). As "Creator" (Elohim) Christ is revealed in His Covenant Relationship to man, as "Revealer and Redeemer" (Jehovah). He is revealed not only as a God of Love, but righteous and just, and who will punish evil. The use of the words separately or together will reveal their significance. In the Old Testament Dispensations Christ is called either "Elohim," or "Jehovah," or "Jehovah-Elohim" (**LORD** God), according to whether He is referred to as "Creator" or "Preserver," that is Revealer or Redeemer. With this in mind let us now trace Christ's work from Creation to

His Incarnation. It was the "LORD God" or Christ that planted the Garden eastward in Eden, and placed Adam and Eve in it, and instructed them what, and what not, to do. It was Christ who came to them in the cool of the evening charging them with disobedience, and gave them the promise that the Seed of the Woman should bruise the Serpent's head, and it was Christ who drove them from the Garden. Gen. 3:8-23. It was Christ who charged Cain with killing his brother Abel. Gen. 4:9. It was Christ who warned Noah of the Flood, and told him to build the Ark. Gen. 6:1-22. It was Christ who called Abraham from Ur of the Chaldees and directed him to Canaan. Gen. 12:1-3. It was Christ who appeared with two angels at Abraham's tent door and foretold the birth of Isaac, and the destruction of the Cities of the Plain, Sodom and Gomorrah. Gen. 18:1-22. It was Christ who wrestled with Jacob at the ford Jabbok. Gen. 32:24-30. It was Christ who appeared to Moses at the Burning Bush in the Wilderness. When Moses asked the "Angel of the LORD" His name, He replied—"I AM THAT I AM," and added—"Say unto the Children of Israel 'I AM' hath sent me to you." Ex. 3:13-14. The "I AM" of the Burning Bush is the "I AM" of the New Testament, who said—"I am the Way, and the Truth, and the Life." It was Christ who sent the Plagues on the Egyptians, who commanded the slaying of the Passover Lamb, a type of Himself, Ex. 12:1-30, and who opened the Red Sea for the Children of Israel to cross over. It was Christ who fed Israel in the Wilderness with manna and quails. Ex. 16:1-15. It was Christ who gave the "Ten Commandments" from Mt. Sinai, (Ex. 20:1-26), and who appeared in the Shekinah glory of the Tabernacle and Temple of Solomon, and who in the "Pillar of Cloud and Fire," led the Children of Israel throughout their Wilderness Wandering. Ex. 13:21-22.

It was Christ, who as "Captain of the Lord's Host" (Joshua 5:13-15), opened the River Jordan that Israel might cross over, and helped them in the siege of Jericho and the conquest of the land. It was Christ who called for the Judges in the Days following Joshua, and commissioned them to fight for Israel. He was with Gideon, Samson and Samuel. It was Christ who chose Saul the first king of Israel, (1 Sam. 9:15-17), and blessed him until his disobedience compelled Christ to choose David in his place. 1 Sam. 16:1-13. It was Christ who called the prophets and fitted them for their work. It was a vision of Christ that Isaiah saw in the Temple in the year that King Uzziah died, and before whose glory Isaiah saw himself to be a man of unclean lips. Isa. 6:1-8. It was Christ who, in answer to Daniel's prayer as to the expiration of the "Seventy Years of Captivity," sent the Angel Gabriel, and revealed to Daniel the exact date of His (Christ's) death on the Cross, in the Vision of the "SEVENTY WEEKS," Dan. 9:1-27. From all these references we see how active Christ was from Creation until His Incarnation in supervising the affairs of men, particularly those of His own chosen people Israel.

While Moses asked the LORD to show him "HIS GLORY," and the LORD said—"Thou canst not see my face, for there shall no man see ME, and LIVE, (Ex. 33:17-23), we are told in Verse 11, "And the LORD spake unto Moses face to face, as a man speaketh unto his friend." The only way we can reconcile these two statements is on the supposition that the "LORD God" when He personally appeared to men, as to Abraham at his tent door, did so in disguise, or, as some have supposed, in a "form" that He provided Himself with before the Creation of man, in anticipation of the need of personally appearing to men, and that "form" was the form of a man, for we know that in the creation of man, God said—"Let US make man IN OUR IMAGE, after OUR likeness." But that "Image" does not necessarily imply "flesh and blood." As these appearances were but occasional, and comparatively few, there was no need for Christ to incarnate Himself in the Flesh in Old Testament times, but when that became necessary for the purpose of Redemption, then He "took upon Him the form of a servant, and was made in the LIKENESS OF MEN." Phil. 2:5-8. This was a physical likeness that required a human bodily form of flesh.

3. CHRIST'S WORK FROM HIS INCARNATION TO HIS ASCENSION.

While Christ as a Prophet foretold many things before His Incarnation, it was not until after His Incarnation that He entered fully on His Prophetic Office. He was the Prophet foretold by Moses. "The LORD thy God will raise up unto thee a Prophet from the midst of thee, of thy brethren, like unto me; unto Him ye shall hearken." Deu. 18:15. And Peter in his sermon in the Temple declared that Christ was that Prophet. Acts 3:19-26. As a Prophet Christ foretold His Death and Resurrection. His Parabolic Teaching was full of prophetic statements, and in His "Olivet Discourse" (Matt. 24:1, 25:46) He outlined events that should come to pass from the time of His Ascension until His Return. But the main purpose of His Incarnation was to make an Atonement for the sin of the human race. This He only could do by becoming a MAN. For only as the "SINLESS MAN" could He atone for the sin of sinful men. This He did by His death on the Cross. To understand the need of the Atonement we must understand what sin is. Sin is

"THE WORLD'S BLOOD POISON."

It takes no Bible, or standard of morals, to make a man realize that when he would do good, evil is present with him. And we all recognize that there is a conflict between our conscience and our conduct, between our better judgment and our carnal appetites. Men may call this "Moral Inharmony" or what they will, the Bible calls it SIN. And the sins we commit only reveal the "PRINCIPLE OF SIN" that is within us, as the boils, carbuncles, etc., reveal the bad state of the blood in a human body. This "Principle of Sin" we inherit. King David said—"Behold, I was shapen in iniquity and in sin did my mother conceive me." Psa. 51:5. He did not mean by that, that he was born out of wedlock, or was the son of an adultress, he meant that he was born with a sinful nature. By "Original Sin" or "Natural Depravity" is not meant that there is nothing good in man, but that the natural tendency of the human heart is toward evil. Sin is not the result of environment or temptation, but is the outcome of a SINFUL INCLINATION. James 1:13-14. Christ pictures the human heart as the source of all kinds of specific sins. Mark 7:20-23. We must distinguish between "SIN" and "SINS." "SIN" is the natural disposition that we inherit from Adam, "SINS" are the specific acts of sin that we commit because of the disposition to sin in us. Sin is to the natural man what the tendency to rot is to the apple. Adam was born innocent, there was but a step between his innocence and righteousness, and but a step between his innocence and sin. He chose to take the latter step and became a sinner. If he had taken the former step he would have become righteous and would have been permitted to eat of the "Tree of Life" and live forever in a state of holiness. Adam and Eve had no children before the Fall. If they had had they would have been born innocent. The children Adam begat after the Fall were born sinners, so the human race became sinners by inheritance. "Wherefore, as by one man (ADAM) sin entered into the world, and death by sin; and so death passed upon all men, for that all have sinned." Rom. 5:12. The fact that all men die is therefore proof that all men are sinners. Now the penalty of Adam's sin was both spiritual and physical death, and the only way the human race can be saved from spiritual and physical death is by some one paying that penalty for them. This Christ came into the world to do. To this end it was necessary that He should become a **MAN**. This required that he should be born of a **woman**. But He must be **a SINLESS MAN**, that is He must have no inherited taint of **SIN** in His nature, therefore He could not have a **human** father. Wherefore the **"HOLY THING"** that was born of Mary (Luke 1:35) was generated in her womb by the Holy Ghost, and was sinless because Mary only imparted to it its physical body. Being sinless Jesus was qualified to make an atonement for sin.

Now it is a "Principle of Law" **THAT THE PENALTY OF A BROKEN LAW MUST FALL ON THE BREAKER OF THE LAW, OR ON A SUBSTITUTE, OTHERWISE THE LAW IS OF NO EFFECT.**

An **"ATONEMENT"** then is any "Provision" that may be introduced into the Administration of a Government, whereby that Government may on **JUST, SAFE,** and **HONORABLE GROUNDS** grant a **PARDON** to the Offender.

Now Adam broke the Law, the penalty for breaking the Law was **DEATH**. Spiritual and physical death. God could have set aside the Law, but that would have defrauded the Law of its rights, and been unjust, more, it would have been an impeachment of the integrity of God's word. The Penalty therefore must be paid by Adam or by a substitute. But as Adam was unable to provide a substitute, God, in his love and justice, at once took steps to provide one, and at once notified Adam and Eve to that effect. The substitute was to be Himself in the person of His Son Jesus. Gen. 3:15. This substitute however was not provided at once. It was not until 4000 years later that Jesus bore the penalty of Adam's sin, and the sin of the race, on the Cross. But during those 4000 years, by the shedding of the blood of bullocks, goats, and innocent lambs, whose bodies were laid smoking and quivering on Hebrew altars, God, in one great "Object Lesson," kept before the people the fact that without the **SHEDDING OF BLOOD** there could be no remission for sin. The sprinkling of the blood of every Passover Lamb was a reminder of Him who was to be the "Lamb of God" who should take away the sin of the world. John 1:29. And when the hour had come for the offering up of **THE SACRIFICE**, we see Justice and Mercy standing on the Hill Calvary, and hear Justice say to Mercy—"Where is He who, over 4000 years ago, in the Garden of Eden, offered Himself a **SUBSTITUTE** for the sin of the world?" "Behold Him," said Mercy, "coming up the Hill bearing His Cross." When He reached the top of the Hill Justice presented the "Bond," executed centuries before, and demanded its payment. The Son of God replied—"I will this day cancel it." Soon all the preparations for the sacrifice were complete, and the "Lamb of God" was laid on the **ALTAR OF THE CROSS**. As Jesus laid His hand upon the crossbar of the Cross, He held in it, invisible to human eyes, the "Bond" to be cancelled, and when the Roman soldier drove the nail through that hand, there was fulfilled the words of the Apostle—

"And you, being dead in your sins and the uncircumcision of your flesh, hath He quickened together with Him, having forgiven you all trespasses; **BLOTTING OUT THE HANDWRITING OF ORDINANCES that was against us,** which was contrary to us, and took IT out of the way, NAILING IT TO HIS CROSS." Col. 2:13-14.

By the cancellation of the "Bond" the Law and Justice of God were satisfied, and it was possible for God to—"Be **JUST** and the **JUSTIFIER** of them who **BELIEVE IN JESUS**." Rom. 3:26. The penalty of **"Spiritual Death"** was paid when Jesus cried—"My God, My God, why hast Thou forsaken Me?" and the penalty of **"Physical Death"** when He cried "It is Finished," and yielded up the Ghost.

The efficacy and "Substitutionary" character of the Atonement of Christ on the Cross is beautifully illustrated in the story of Barabbas. Barabbas was a robber, who had been arrested, tried, found guilty of insurrection and murder, and had been condemned to die. John 18:39-40. Matt. 27:15-26. Mark 15:6-15. It was the "Feast of Passover," at which time it was customary to liberate some notable criminal, and when the multitude demanded the death of Jesus, Pilate gave them the choice between Jesus or Barabbas. They chose Barabbas, and Jesus was turned over to the Officers of the Law for death by crucifixion; and by His death, as a **SUBSTITUTE** for Barabbas, Jesus, who was innocent, satisfied the "Law" and Barabbas was freed. The "Barabbas" or "Substitutionary View" of the Atonement is the Scriptural view of the Atonement. If Barabbas, after his liberation, had gone out to Calvary to witness the Crucifixion, and had informed himself as to who it was that had taken his place on the central cross, he would have known five things.

1. That he was a **JUSTLY CONDEMNED SINNER**.

2. That Jesus was an **INNOCENT SUFFERER**.

3. That that "Innocent Sufferer" had taken **HIS PLACE**.

4. That he **HAD DONE NOTHING TO MERIT THAT SUBSTITUTION**.

5. That Christ's substitution in his place **SATISFIED THE LAW**.

If Barabbas had thus gone out to Calvary to witness the Crucifixion and had been recognized and some one had threatened to point him out to the Centurion as an escaped convict, Barabbas could have said—"Oh, the Centurion cannot arrest me. It was he who set me free this morning and told me that Jesus of Nazareth was to take **MY** place on the Cross, and his death **SATISFIES THE LAW FOR ME**, and I am free." Barabbas was the first man to have a practical experience of the Atonement. If Jesus had not hung on that central cross Barabbas would have had to. There was at least one man in Jerusalem that day who understood the meaning of Jesus' death, and experienced its saving power, and that man was Barabbas. As believers our position is that of Barabbas, free from the Law.

As sinners we were under the "Curse of the Law," but as believers "Christ hath redeemed us from the **CURSE OF THE LAW**, being **MADE A CURSE FOR US**; for it is written **CURSED IS EVERY ONE THAT HANGETH ON A TREE**." Gal. 3:13. The "Tree" that Christ hung on was the "**CROSS.**" As we inherited our sinful state from Adam, we now by faith in Christ, the second Adam, inherit all that He did for us on the Cross, and our position now is that of having been crucified, dead, buried, risen and ascended with Christ, so we can say with the Apostle Paul—

"I am crucified with Christ; nevertheless I live; yet not I, but **CHRIST LIVETH IN ME**; and the Life which I now live in the flesh I live by the **faith of the Son of God**, who loved me, and gave Himself for me." Gal. 2:20.

In the preceding verse (Gal. 2:19) Paul says—"For I through the Law am **DEAD TO THE LAW**, that I might live unto God." Now Paul does not mean that he was **physically** dead, but that he was **JUDICIALLY** dead. That is, that the penalty of the Law, which was death, was paid for us by Christ when He died on the Cross, and cannot be required of us, for "He was wounded for **OUR** transgressions. He was bruised for **OUR** iniquities; the chastisement of **OUR** peace was **UPON HIM**; and with **HIS STRIPES WE ARE HEALED."** Isa. 53:5. It follows therefore that if our iniquities are **UPON HIM**, they are **not UPON US**.

But some one may say, how could an innocent person assume the guilt of another? This can only be done by the innocent person entering into **"Corporate Oneness"** with the guilty person, and thus becoming **IDENTIFIED WITH HIM**. For illustration the debts of a poor widow could not be justly charged up to a millionaire neighbor, but if he entered into "Corporate Oneness" with her by marrying her, and thus assuming all her obligations, then he could justly and legally be held responsible for her debts. Now this is just what the Apostle says—

"Wherefore, my brethren, ye also are become **DEAD TO THE LAW** (our first husband) by the body of Christ (that is by Christ's death); that ye should be **MARRIED TO ANOTHER**, even to Him (Christ) who is **RAISED FROM THE DEAD."** Rom. 7:4.

This union with Christ results in a **"LEGAL ANSWERABLENESS"** by Him for all our debts to the Law, and Jesus recognized the justice of all His sufferings on the Cross, when He said to the two disciples on the Road to Emmaus—"O fools, and slow of heart to believe all that the prophets have spoken: **OUGHT NOT CHRIST TO HAVE SUFFERED THESE THINGS**, and to enter into His Glory?" Luke 24:25-26. We see then that the Atonement of Christ means more than mere **Substitution**," it means a **"CORPORATE ONENESS,"** a union in which it was perfectly just for God to exact from His Son the penalty of "Spiritual" and "Physical" death in satisfaction of the broken Law. We are therefore as believers to **"RECKON OURSELVES DEAD TO THE LAW."** Rom. 6:11. That is, we are to believe and act as those who have been freed from the Law, for "there is therefore now **NO CONDEMNATION** to them who are in Christ Jesus," (Rom. 8:1), for we were judged for sin in Christ on the Cross, and our Judgment for **"Sin" IS PAST**.

We see then that Christ's work from the Incarnation to His Ascension was to make an Atonement for Sin.

II. CHRIST'S PRESENT LIFE AND WORK

Christ's present work is that of a High Priest. He is now **"TARRYING WITHIN THE VAIL."** As the High Priest entered through the "veil" into the "Most Holy Place" once a year, on the "Day of Atonement," to present the blood of the sacrifice and make intercession for the **SINS** of the people, so Jesus entered into the "Holy of Holies" of the Heavenly Tabernacle when He ascended and passed through the "Veil of the Cloud" and disappeared from earthly view. Acts 1:9. Heb. 4:14. "For Christ is not entered into the Holy Places made with hands (such as the Tabernacle or Temple), which are the figures of the true; but **INTO HEAVEN ITSELF, now to appear in the presence of God for us."** Heb. 9:24. Heaven, not earth, is the sphere of Christ's **PRIESTLY** Ministry. He never appeared as a Priest in the Temple at Jerusalem. He went there to teach, but never to offer sacrifices or burn incense.

The sacrifices and ceremonies of the Tabernacle and Temple services did not make the offerers perfect, or they would not have ceased to be offered. They were but **SHADOWS** or Types of things to come. Heb. 10:1-3. Among them was the "Day of Atonement." On that day the High Priest entered alone into the Holy Place, and having divested himself of his garments of "Glory and Beauty," he washed himself, and arrayed himself in linen clothes with a linen Mitre upon his head. He then filled a Censer with burning coals from off the Incense Altar and entered through the "Veil" into the "Most Holy Place," and putting incense upon the coals of the Censer, so that the smoke would cover the "Mercy Seat" on the "Ark of the Covenant" and hide it from view lest he die, he withdrew from the "Most Holy Place" and passed out into the Court of the Tabernacle, where he slew a bullock for a "Sin Offering" for himself and his house, and taking of its blood he re-entered the Tabernacle and passing through the "Veil" he sprinkled with his finger of the blood seven times eastward before the "Mercy Seat," thus making Atonement for himself and his household. He then returned to the Court of the Tabernacle and slew the goat that had been selected by lot for the "Sin Offering," and took of its blood and re-entered for the third time the "Most Holy Place," and did with its blood as he had done with the blood of his bullock, thus making Atonement for the sins of the Congregation. He then returned to the Court, and going to the "Brazen Altar" he made Atonement for it by sprinkling of the mixed blood of the bullock and goat upon it with his finger seven times, after he had first anointed the Horns of the Altar with the blood.

He then took the live goat, called the "Scapegoat," and laying both of his hands upon its head, he confessed the sins of the Children of Israel, thus placing them upon the head of the "Scapegoat," and then he sent it by a "fit man" into the wilderness, into a land uninhabited, where it was left, thus carrying away the iniquities of the people.

Aaron then returned to the Holy Place of the Tabernacle and took off his linen garments, washed himself, and robed himself again in his garments of "Glory and Beauty," and then returned to the Court of the Tabernacle. Until he thus appeared the people were in doubt as to whether God had accepted the "Sin Offering" or not. If his stay was unduly prolonged they would fear that the offering had been rejected and the High Priest smitten with death. They listened then for the tinkling of the bells upon the bottom of the High Priest's robe, and when they heard them they were assured that the sacrifice had been accepted.

When the High Priest came out in his garments of "Glory and Beauty" he went to the "Brazen Altar" and offered a "Burnt Offering" for himself, and one for the people, as a token of their revived consecration to God.

Let us take the work of the High Priest on the "Day of Atonement" and apply it to our High Priest, Jesus Christ. When Jesus "emptied Himself" of His Heavenly Glory (Phil. 2:5-8), He laid aside His garments of "Glory and Beauty," and put on the "Linen Garment" of humanity in which to minister. He had no occasion to offer incense in the "Most Holy Place," or to offer a bullock as a "Sin Offering" for Himself, for He was sinless, but He had to offer a Sin Offering for the world. It is here that we see that no single offering could typify the work of Christ, for Christ's work is twofold. First He died as a "Sin Offering" for **SIN**, and then rose from the dead and ascended through the "Veil of the Cloud" into the "Holy of Holies" of the "Heavenly Tabernacle" and offered **HIS OWN BLOOD** as an Atonement for the sin of the world. This could only be foreshadowed by the use of two goats. The first was made a "Sin Offering" and as such had to die, the second was called the "Scapegoat" and bore away the sins of the people into the wilderness. Lev. 16:8-10, 20-22. So in connection with the cleansing of the leper, two birds were necessary. One was killed in an earthen vessel over running water, and the living bird was to be dipped in the blood of the slain bird, and let fly in the open field, after the blood of the slain bird had been sprinkled seven times upon him who was to be cleansed of his leprosy. Lev. 14:1-7.

THE HEAVENLY TABERNACLE

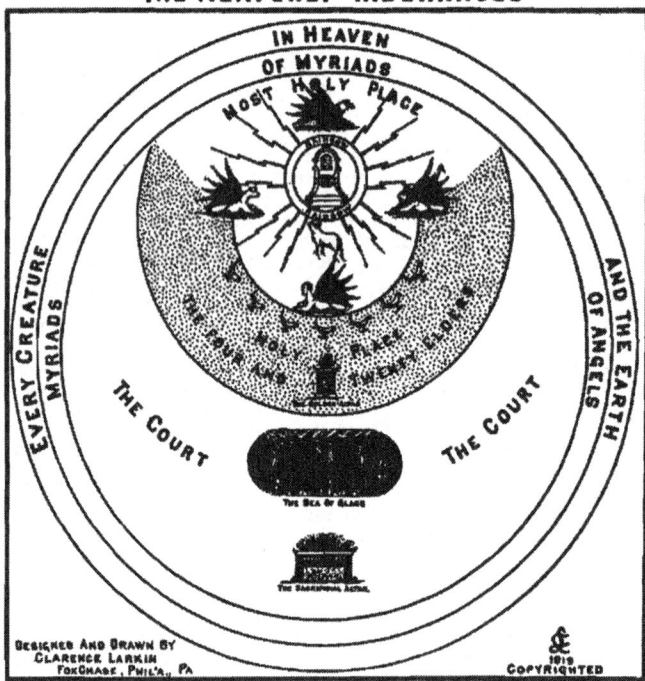

Designed and drawn by Clarence Larkin, Fox Chase, Phil'a, PA. 1919 Copyrighted.

The High Priest entered into the "Most Holy Place" once a year with the blood of others, but Jesus Christ our High Priest entered **once for all** with His **OWN BLOOD** into the "Holy of Holies" of the "Heavenly Tabernacle," otherwise He must have suffered yearly since the foundation of the world (Ages), "but now once in the **END OF THE AGE** (the Old Testament Age) hath He appeared to put away sin by the sacrifice of Himself." Heb. 9:24-26.

Having, as our High Priest, taken His own blood within the "Veil," Jesus still tarries engaged in His High Priestly work, and will continue to tarry throughout this

"GREAT DAY OF ATONEMENT,"

and at its close he will lay aside His High Priestly robes and come forth in His Kingly dress of "Glory and Beauty" to rule and reign in Kingly splendor.

There was no provision made for sitting down in the Tabernacle or Temple, for there was no time for sitting down, as sacrifices were continuously being offered; but Jesus our High Priest offered the sacrifice of Himself **"ONCE FOR ALL,"** and then **"SAT DOWN"** at the right hand of God, on God's Throne (Heb. 12:2), which is in this Dispensation the "Throne of Grace." Heb. 4:16. In Acts 7:55-56, we read that Stephen saw Jesus **STANDING** at the right hand of God. This may mean either of two things. Either Jesus rose to receive Stephen or that He had not yet sat down, for we must not forget that Jesus really did not begin His High Priestly work until after His final rejection by the Jews, that culminated in the stoning of Stephen, who charged them with being "stiffnecked" and resisting the Holy Ghost. Acts 7:51.

It is worthy of note that the "Divine Three" were rejected in succession by the Jewish nation. They rejected "God the Father" in the days of Samuel (1 Sam. 8:6-7); "God the Son" in the "Days of His Flesh," saying—"We will not have this man to rule over us" (Matt. 21:37-39); and God the Holy Ghost when they resisted the Holy Ghost who spoke through Stephen. Acts 7:51.

1. MEDIATOR.

Paul writing to Timothy said that the will of God was that all men might be saved, and that he had appointed to that end a "**MEDIATOR**" between God and man, the **MAN CHRIST JESUS**. 1 Tim. 2:3-6. He is a "Mediator" for both believers and unbelievers, but He had to become a MAN to "Mediate" between God and man. A man can mediate between two men, but he cannot mediate between a man and a horse, because he has not the nature of both a man and a horse. So the Son of God could not mediate between God and man until He became the "Divine **MAN**," that is, had the nature of both God and man. It was necessary then for the Son of God to become a **MAN** that He might mediate between God and man, and when He ascended He took up His **MANHOOD** with Him, and He is now in Heaven the **MAN CHRIST JESUS**. 1 Tim. 2:5.

2. ADVOCATE.

In 1 John 2:1 we read—"My little children, these things write I unto you, that ye sin not. And if any man sin, we have an **ADVOCATE** with the Father, Jesus Christ the righteous." From this we see that Jesus is the Advocate of the righteous only, for the Epistle is addressed to "My Little Children," and to those who were entitled to call God **FATHER**. The sinner does not need an Advocate; he needs a **SAVIOUR**. What is the use of an Advocate when the trial is over, the jury has rendered its decision, the Judge pronounced sentence and the day of execution set? What a condemned man needs then is not an Advocate, but a **PARDON**. The Bible distinctly states that, "he that believeth not **IS CONDEMNED ALREADY**," and, "that the **WRATH OF GOD ABIDETH ON HIM**." John 3:18, 36. What the sinner needs to do is not to ask Jesus to intercede for him, but to **accept the FINISHED WORK** of Christ on the Cross in his behalf.

There are some who claim that Jesus is the Advocate for everyone, because the next verse says—"And He is the 'Propitiation' for our sins: and not for our's **only**, but also for the sins of the **WHOLE WORLD**." The word "Propitiation" does not mean that the Atonement of Christ **saves the whole world**, but that it makes **possible** the salvation of the whole world. There are three views of the Atonement.

1. Some hold that the Atonement was in the nature of a **COMMERCIAL TRANSACTION**. In a commercial transaction there must be a "buyer" and a "seller," a "thing to be sold," and a "price to be paid," and if the thing sold was 100 horses, the "buyer" would want to be sure that he not only got the right number, but the right **ONES**. On this view of the Atonement Jesus paid with His blood only for a certain number, and they the ones He had chosen,

the ELECT. The advocates of this view hold to the theory of a LIMITED ATONEMENT.

2. Others claim that as the Bible represents the Atonement as made for ALL men, therefore all men will be saved. These persons are consistently UNIVERSALISTS.

3. The third class holds the view that the nature of Christ's Atonement was not the mere payment of the debt of a few, the elect; neither does it save all men, but it was such an assumption of the penalty of the Law, that God can now honorably and justly forgive any man his sin who repents and accepts Christ as his Saviour. This latter view must be the correct view, for it is the only view that corresponds with the facts. For the Scriptures distinctly teach in such passages as—"WHOSOEVER cometh unto Me I will in no wise cast out" (John 6:37), that salvation is not limited to any special class; and the demand for repentance and faith shows that if men are to be saved, they are to be saved on **certain conditions**, and not merely because Jesus died on the Cross. Jesus then is the "**Advocate**" of only those who are saved.

If Jesus is our Advocate then, what is He our Advocate for? Not for SIN, for that was Atoned for on the Cross. He is our Advocate for the "**sins**" we commit since we became a Christian. "My Little Children, these things write I unto you, that ye SIN NOT. And if any man SIN, we have an Advocate." 1 John 2:1. Our Advocate then is to intercede for us because we SIN, that is His business, that is why He remains constantly beside the Father. If a man break the law, or is accused of breaking it, the first thing he needs is a lawyer, or advocate, one who will plead his cause and see that he gets justice. So the believer when he sins needs an Advocate.

Many Christians are disheartened and discouraged because they sin and feel that it is a sign that they were never converted. But the Scriptures teach that they will sin. The Apostle says—"If we say that we have NO SIN, we deceive ourselves, and the truth is not in us." 1 John 1:8. We must learn to distinguish between our

STANDING AND STATE.

Our "Standing" is that of a SON. John 1:12-13. 1 John 3:1-2. And we are a "Son" NOW. 1 John 3:2. And this "Sonship" makes us "HEIRS." Rom. 8:17. And this "Heirship" guarantees our PRESERVATION. 1 Pet. 1:4-5. John 3:16. John 6:39. And no man shall be able to pluck us out of our Father's hand (John 10:27-29), for we are "Sealed" unto the Day of Redemption. Eph. 4:30, and our "life" is HID WITH CHRIST IN GOD. Col. 3:3.

But while our "Standing" is SETTLED and SURE, our "State" is VARIABLE. This is owing to the fact that after our "New Birth" we have "TWO NATURES," where before we had but one. We do not lose the "Old Adam," or "Flesh Nature," when we receive the "New Adam" or "Spiritual Nature." For that which was born of the "Flesh" is STILL FLESH, and only that which is born of the "Holy Spirit" is SPIRIT. John 3:6. This explains the "SPIRITUAL WARFARE" so vividly portrayed by the Apostle Paul in Rom. 7:14-25. This was the Apostle's own experience after his conversion, and reveals the fact that the believer has a DUAL NATURE, and he is sinful or sinless according to which nature is uppermost, for that which is "born of God" in him, his "Spiritual Nature," cannot sin. 1 John 3:9. As to "Experience," the believer may be in any one of three places. (1) He may be in EGYPT, the "Type of the World." The Children of Israel were SAFE in Egypt the moment they sprinkled the "Blood" of the "Passover Lamb" on their doorposts. So the believer is SAFE, or SAVED, the moment he applies the Blood of Christ by faith to his soul, though he may in experience be still living in Egypt a type of the world. (2) He may be in the WILDERNESS, the "Type of the Flesh." But as to experience living on the Egyptian side of the Wilderness, longing for the leeks, onions and garlic of his old Egyptian life, and murmuring, restless and unfruitful, fearing to return to Egypt, and yet not happy in his Christian life. (3) He may be in CANAAN, a "Type of the Rest of Faith," but fighting for the possession of the land against the Canaanites, Hittites, Hivites, Perizzites, Girgashites, Amorites, and Jebusites of his soul. Joshua 3:10.

The Scriptures mention three ways in which the believer may overcome the Flesh. (1) By AMPUTATION. Matt. 18:8-9. (2) By MORTIFICATION. Rom. 8:13. Col. 3:5-10. (3) by LIMITATION. Heb. 12:1. From what has been said we see that our "Fellowship" with the Father may be broken, but our RELATIONSHIP never. 1 John 1:3, 7.

There is a vast difference between a "SINNER'S SINS" and a "BELIEVER'S SINS." Not that God does not hate both alike, the Believers it may be the most because he sins with greater light, but the difference is not in the sin, but in the WAY GOD TREATS IT. Here is a father who sends his son and his hired servant to do a piece of work. They are lazy and inefficient, and do not do the work. He bears with them, and tries them again, but it is no use. His son and his servant are good for nothing, and his son perhaps the worse of the two. Now what does he do? He discharges the servant. He puts him out of the house. He will have nothing more to do with him. But does he discharge his son? Does he send him away from the house? Does he disinherit him? Nothing of the kind. He may rebuke him, cut off his allowance, punish him worse than he punished the servant, but he will not send him away because he is his son. We see then that "Sonship" is a REAL THING. Is "Sonship" then a shield from the punishment of sin? Does my "Sonship" make it safer for me to sin? Oh, no! It simply gives me the blessed privilege of having an Advocate, and since it is inevitable that I will sin, it is better to sin as a SON than as an unbeliever.

III. CHRIST'S FUTURE LIFE AND WORK

Christ's future work is that of KING. When Christ has finished His High Priestly work He will leave His Father's Throne and descend into the atmosphere of this earth to meet His espoused Bride—THE CHURCH. 1 Thess. 4:15-18. He will then accompany His Bride back to Heaven, and taking His place upon the "Judgment Seat of Christ" (Rom. 14:10) will judge the saints and reward them according to their works, after which He will present the Church to Himself, "a glorious Church, not having spot, or wrinkle, or any such thing." Eph. 5:27. Then follows the Marriage of the Lamb. Rev. 19:6-9. Then, having received the Kingdom from the Father, Christ, accompanied by the armies of Heaven, will descend to the earth, and the Battle of Armageddon will be fought (Rev. 19:11-21), following which He will sit upon the "Throne of His Glory" and judge the nations (Matt. 25:31-46), after which the Millennial Kingdom will be set up. At its close Satan will be loosed from the Bottomless Pit, there will be a great Apostasy, and fire will descend from heaven and destroy the wicked. The heaven and the earth will then be renovated by Fire, and the New Heaven and Earth will appear, upon which shall be placed righteous nations taken from the old earth, over which Christ shall reign as King of Kings and Lord of Lords, until such a time as He shall see fit to surrender the Kingdom to the Father, that GOD MAY BE ALL IN ALL. 1 Cor. 15:28.

VIII

THE DISPENSATIONAL WORK OF THE HOLY SPIRIT

As the Holy Spirit, the **THIRD PERSON** in the Godhead, has existed from all eternity (Heb. 9:14), it stands to reason that if we would pursue the same course of speaking and writing about Him, as we do about the person and work of Christ, much of the mystery and misunderstanding as to His person and work would disappear. Let us therefore take up His work in each Dispensation.

1. THE WORK OF THE HOLY SPIRIT IN CREATION

We read in Job 26:13, "By His **SPIRIT** He hath garnished the heavens." That is, made them beautiful with stars and suns. The work of the Trinity in Creation has been described thus: God the **FATHER created the matter,** God the **SON** moulded it into shape, as seen in the heavens, and earth, and every visible object, and God the **HOLY SPIRIT** breathed into all animate creation life. This seems confirmed by the account of the creation of man in Gen. 2:7, "And the **LORD GOD** (the Triune God) formed man of the **dust of the ground,** and **breathed into his nostrils the BREATH OF LIFE: and** man became a **LIVING SOUL."** Here we see the threefold work of God. The Father made the "dust of the ground," the Son, like a sculptor molds the clay into a statue, formed the dust into the shape of a man, and the Holy Spirit breathed into its nostrils the **"BREATH OF LIFE."**

In Gen. 1:2, we read that—"The Earth was without form, and void; and darkness was upon the face of the deep. And the **SPIRIT OF GOD** (Holy Spirit) **moved upon the face of the waters."** Here we have the work of the **HOLY SPIRIT** in the restoration of the Earth to its Primeval State. This reveals to us that the work of the Holy Spirit in Creation was to impart and restore life.

2. THE WORK OF THE HOLY SPIRIT IN THE DISPENSATION FROM THE FALL TO THE FLOOD.

This was the "Dispensation of **CONSCIENCE,"** and the work of the Holy Spirit during that Dispensation seems to have been to **"strive"** with men through their conscience to live better lives, for we read in Gen. 6:3, "And the Lord said, My Spirit shall not always **STRIVE** with man, for that he also is flesh: yet his days shall be a hundred and twenty years." That is He would bear with them for 120 years longer, and if they did not repent and turn to Him, He would send the Flood.

3. THE WORK OF THE HOLY SPIRIT IN THE DISPENSATION FROM THE FLOOD TO THE BIRTH OF JESUS.

This Period included Three Dispensations, the "Post-Diluvian," the "Patriarchal" and the "Legal." The work of the Holy Spirit in these Dispensations seems to have been about the same, and was neither constant nor specific. He came upon individual men and women and filled them for some special service or specific work without reference to their character, such as Balaam (Num. 24:2-9), Samson (Judges 13:24-25), and King Saul. 1 Sam. 10:6-13. The Holy Spirit came upon these men not because they were good men, but on account of their official position, and was given for a special service. With few exceptions, such as Joseph (Gen. 41:38-39), Joshua (Num. 27:18), and Daniel (Dan. 4:8, 9, 18; 5:11-14), the Holy Spirit did not abide on men for any length of time during this Dispensation, but came and went, as, in the case of Samson, His presence was necessary.

When the time came to construct the Tabernacle and its furnishings, God specially endowed Bezaleel for the work by filling him with the Holy Spirit. Ex. 31:1-5. Thus the whole of the work of the Tabernacle in its exquisite perfection and glorious beauty, was the work of the **HOLY SPIRIT** through Bezaleel. So the people could not praise Bezaleel, and say—"Bezaleel, what a wonderful and skilful workman you are", but were compelled to say—"See how wondrously the **SPIRIT OF GOD** has wrought through Bezaleel." So it was with the Old Testament prophets—"the prophecy came not in old time by the **will of man:** but holy men of God spake as they were moved by the **HOLY GHOST."** 2 Pet. 1:21. The work of the Holy Spirit in this Dispensation was mainly to fit men for some special work.

4. THE WORK OF THE HOLY SPIRIT IN THE "PARENTHETICAL DISPENSATION" BETWEEN THE OLD AND NEW TESTAMENT DISPENSATIONS.

The work of the Holy Spirit during this "Parenthetical Dispensation" has to do mainly with the earthly life of Jesus, and throws additional light on the relation of the three persons of the Godhead to each other, and shows that even God the **SON,** could not take on our human nature and do the work He did for the redemption of the race without the aid and co-operation of the **"HOLY SPIRIT."** The work of the Holy Spirit in Jesus is very clearly outlined in the New Testament.

1. He was **CONCEIVED** by the Holy Spirit. Luke 1:30-31, 34-35. Matt. 1:18-20.

2. He was **BAPTIZED** by the Holy Spirit. Matt. 3:16. Luke 4:1.

3. He was led by the Holy Spirit into the Wilderness to be **TEMPTED** (Tested). Matt. 4:1. Luke 4:1-2.

4. He performed all His **MIGHTY WORKS** by the power of the Holy Spirit. Acts 10:38.

5. He was **ANOINTED TO PREACH** by the Holy Spirit. Luke 4:18.

6. He **DIED ON THE CROSS** through the Holy Spirit. Heb. 9:14.

7. He was **RAISED FROM THE DEAD** by the Holy Spirit. 1 Pet. 3:18.

8. He gave His **POST RESURRECTION DIRECTIONS** to the Apostles through the Holy Spirit. Acts 1:1-2.

5. THE WORK OF THE HOLY SPIRIT IN THE DISPENSATION FROM PENTECOST TO THE SECOND COMING OF CHRIST.

This is preeminently the **"DISPENSATION OF THE HOLY SPIRIT."** The Old Testament Dispensation was that of the **FATHER**, the Millennial Dispensation will be that of the **SON**, and this is that of the **HOLY SPIRIT.** Jesus said to His Disciples—"It is **expedient** for you that I go away: for if I go not away the **COMFORTER** (Holy Spirit) **WILL NOT COME UNTO YOU**; but if I depart, I will send him unto you." John 16:7. This clearly teaches that the Holy Spirit is a **PERSON**, and that He and Jesus cannot both reside at the same time on the earth. The Holy Spirit has a specific work in this Dispensation. It is the formation of the **"BODY OF CHRIST"—THE CHURCH,** into which we are baptized by the Holy Spirit. 1 Cor. 12:13, 27. The Holy Spirit took up His residence on the earth at Pentecost (Acts 2:1-4), and will remain on the earth until the Church is complete and then He will escort it to meet the Lord in the air at the Rapture.

But you ask—"If the Holy Spirit is now residing on the earth, where may He be seen? Is He in the Holy Land or in some other part of the world?" The Holy Spirit at Pentecost did not assume a bodily form, but took up His residence in the Church. The Apostle Paul, writing to the saints at Corinth, said—"What! Know ye not that your **BODY** is the **TEMPLE OF THE HOLY GHOST?"** 1 Cor. 6:19. And in 1 Cor. 3:16, he speaks of them as being collectively the **"TEMPLE OF GOD,"** and that the **"SPIRIT OF GOD"** (Holy Spirit) **dwelt in them,** that is, had his residence among them. And in Eph. 2:21-22 he speaks of the Church as a **Building,** "fitly framed together" for a **"HOLY TEMPLE,"** into which the saints are being built, as building stone is built into a building, and that the purpose of the building was to make a **"HABITATION FOR GOD"** in which He could dwell on the earth in the Person of the Holy Spirit. In John 14:22-23, in anticipation of His going away, and in answer to Judas Iscariot's question as to how He would manifest Himself to His disciples after His departure, and not to the world, Jesus said—"If a man love me he will keep my words: and my Father will love him and **WE** (the Triune God) will come unto him, and make our **ABODE** with him." And in the "appendix" to the "Great Commission" (Matt. 28:20) Jesus said—"Lo, **I AM WITH YOU ALWAYS, EVEN UNTO THE END OF THE AGE,"** that is, the end of this Church Dispensation. Now the idea is, not that Jesus Himself **IN PERSON** will be with us in this Dispensation, for He cannot leave His High Priestly duties at the Right Hand of God, but that He will be with us in the Person of the Holy Spirit, for the Holy Spirit is now the **REPRESENTATIVE** of the Godhead on the earth, for when Jesus said "I will be with you," He meant by **"I"** the Godhead, and the Godhead is represented on the earth whenever one of its members is resident on the earth, as it was represented in Jesus when He was on the earth (John 1:14. 1 Tim. 3:16), and is now represented by the Holy Spirit.

It follows therefore, as every true believer is a "Temple of the Holy Spirit," if we would see the Holy Spirit during His residence on the earth we must see Him in the glowing face and Christlike behavior of the sanctified child of God.

THE WORK OF THE HOLY SPIRIT IN THE CHURCH

The Holy Spirit, by virtue of His residence in the Church, is the

PRESIDING OFFICER OF THE CHURCH.

Says Dr. A. J. Gordon, in his work on the "Ministry of the Spirit"—"The Holy Spirit has rightly been called the **'VICAR OF JESUS CHRIST.'** To him has been committed the administration of the affairs of the Church. There is but one 'Holy See' upon earth, and that is the **'Seat' of the Holy Spirit** in the Church. There is but one **'Infallible POPE,'** and He is the Holy Spirit. He alone can speak 'Ex Cathedra'.

This is clearly brought out in Acts 15:13-29 in the account of the First Church Council, where the record states (Vs. 28), "For it seemed good to the **HOLY GHOST** and to us," implying that the Holy Ghost was present in the Council, and acted in an official capacity.

When Ananias and Sapphira were arraigned for conspiracy and falsehood in the sale of a certain piece of property, Peter said to Ananias—"Why hath Satan filled thine heart to lie to the **HOLY GHOST?"** (Acts 5:3), thus implying that the invisible presiding officer at that trial was the Holy Spirit Himself.

As Jesus chose and sent forth His Apostles, so the Holy Spirit chooses and sends forth His Apostles; for we read in Acts 13:2-4—

"As they ministered to the Lord, and fasted, the Holy Ghost said, (He must have been personally present)—'Separate me Barnabas and Saul for the work whereunto I have called them. And when they had fasted and prayed, and laid their hands on them, they sent them away. So they, **BEING SENT FORTH BY THE HOLY GHOST,** departed to Seleucia; and from thence they sailed to Cyprus."

Paul's last words to the Ephesian Elders were—"Take heed therefore unto yourselves, and to all the flock over which the **HOLY GHOST HATH MADE YOU OVERSEERS,** to feed the 'Church of God,' which He hath purchased with His own blood." Acts 20:28. Clearly the pastors or bishops of the Apostolic Church were chosen by the Holy Spirit, and not by the suffrage of the people.

As an illustration of the mistake that may be made in filling an official position in the Church without consulting the Holy Spirit, we have the case of Matthias. A vacancy had occurred in the "Apostolate" by the suicide of Judas. Standing in the upper-room, surrounded by the 120, Peter boldly affirmed that the vacancy must be filled, and of the men who had companied with them during the Lord's earthly ministry—"One must be ordained to be a **witness with us** of **HIS RESURRECTION."** Acts 1:22. But the Apostles had hitherto had no voice in choosing Apostles. The Lord had done this of His own sovereign will—"Have I not chosen you twelve." John 6:70, 13:18. Now the Lord had gone back to heaven having commanded His disciples to do **NOTHING** until His "Vicar" the "Holy Spirit" should come (Luke 24:49), and as he had not yet arrived no business that they might transact would be **LEGAL.** But in spite of the Lord's command a nomination was made, and an election held but there is no indication that their choice was ratified by the Holy Spirit when He came. On the contrary, Matthias, who was chosen from that time, passed into obscurity, and his name is never again mentioned. A few years later, on the road to Damascus, the Lord Himself chose Saul of Tarsus to be an Apostle in Judas' place, certifying to the choice by filling him with the Holy Spirit (Acts 9:15-17), so that the Apostle could say of himself—"Paul, an **APOSTLE, NOT OF MEN, NEITHER BY MAN, BUT BY JESUS CHRIST, AND GOD THE FATHER."** Gal. 1:1.

While the Apostolic Office ceased with the death of the Apostle John, for its qualification was that the holder should be a witness of the Lord's resurrection, and Paul was a witness of that (1 Cor. 15:3-8), it is still the Divine plan that the office of the successors of the Apostles, the pastors, elders, bishops, and teachers of the flock should be filled by Holy Spirit chosen men. Acts 20:28. There is no certainty when an Archbishop, or Bishop, or some other church

Functionary, appoints a pastor over a flock, whether the appointment is of the Holy Spirit or not. We see therefore that while it is easier to get—"**the sense of the meeting by a show of hands**" in the choice of a pastor, that it is not the Apostolic way, and accounts for the mistakes and misfits that occur in filling the pastoral office. It also accounts for the decline and death of many church organizations. It is far better by prayer and fasting to wait upon God until the "**MIND OF THE SPIRIT**" is made manifest, and the right man sent.

And not only should a church consult the Holy Spirit in the choice of a pastor, but the pastor should consult the Holy Ghost as to a field of service. Of Paul and Timotheus we read—"Now when they had gone throughout Phrygia, and the region of Galatia, and were **FORBIDDEN OF THE HOLY GHOST** to preach the word in Asia, after they were come to Mysia, they assayed (attempted) to go unto Bithynia; '**BUT THE SPIRIT SUFFERED THEM NOT**.'" Acts 16:6-7. We naturally ask—"Why not?" And we do not have far to go for an answer, for in the next three verses we read—"And they passing by Mysia came down to Troas, and a vision appeared to Paul in the night: there stood a man of Macedonia, and prayed him, saying, **COME OVER INTO MACEDONIA AND HELP US**. And after he had seen the vision, **IMMEDIATELY WE ENDEAVORED TO GO INTO MACEDONIA, ASSUREDLY GATHERING THAT THE LORD HAD CALLED US FOR TO PREACH THE GOSPEL UNTO THEM**." Acts 16:8-10. And into Macedonia they went and were blessed in their work. We see then that the pastor, and missionary, and every Christian worker, should follow the Holy Spirit's guidance in the choice of a sphere of work. The Holy Spirit makes no "**Misfits**." This is beautifully illustrated in the experiences of Adoniram Judson, William Carey, and David Livingstone. Judson purposed going to India, the Holy Spirit sent him to Burmah. Carey purposed going to Tahiti, the Holy Spirit landed him in India. Livingstone purposed going to China, but the Holy Spirit led him to Africa.

When Jesus was on the earth the Father spoke and said—"This is my beloved Son **HEAR YE HIM**." The night before His Crucifixion Jesus said to His Disciples—"I have yet many things to say unto you, but ye cannot bear them now. Howbeit when He, the 'Spirit of Truth' (H. S.), is come, He will guide you into **ALL TRUTH**: He will show you things **TO COME**." John 16:12-13. The reason was that the teachings of Jesus required to be illumined by the light of the Cross and of the Resurrection, and the further light that He would be able to furnish after His Ascension. There were certain limitations to Christ's knowledge while on the earth. When asked as to the time of His Second Advent, He replied—"Of that day and that hour knoweth no man, no, not the angels which are in Heaven, neither (not yet) the Son, but the Father." Mark 13:32. But as soon as Jesus was "Glorified" He knew all about it, and 66 years after His Ascension He revealed it to the Apostle John on the Isle of Patmos. The Book of Revelation is the Revelation of Jesus Christ, which **GOD GAVE UNTO HIM**, to show unto His servants **THINGS WHICH MUST SHORTLY COME TO PASS**" (Rev. 1:1), and in the Messages to the Seven Churches of Asia, which are typical churches (Rev. 2:1, 3:22), we find, **SEVEN TIMES REPEATED**, the command—"He that hath an ear, let him **HEAR** what '**THE SPIRIT**' **SAITH UNTO THE CHURCHES**."

The Holy Spirit's Teachings and communications are not His own, but **CHRIST'S**. "Howbeit when He, the 'Spirit of Truth,' is come, He will guide you into all truth: for **He shall not speak of Himself**; but **WHATSOEVER HE SHALL HEAR**, that shall He speak; and He will show you things to come. He shall **GLORIFY ME**: for He shall **RECEIVE OF MINE, AND SHALL SHOW IT UNTO YOU**." John 16:13-14. The office-work then of the Holy Spirit in this Dispensation is to reveal the things of the Glorified Christ to the Church.

To this end the preacher and teacher of the "Word" should be a Holy Spirit filled person. Peter said—"We have preached the Gospel unto you **WITH THE HOLY GHOST SENT DOWN FROM HEAVEN**." 1 Pet. 1:12. And Paul said—"And my speech and my preaching was not with enticing words of man's wisdom, but in **DEMONSTRATION OF THE SPIRIT AND OF POWER**." 1 Cor. 2:4. Education is not enough. The Disciples were in training with Jesus for three years, but He forbade them to preach until they were **ENDUED WITH POWER FROM ON HIGH**. Luke 24:49. Acts 1:8, 2:1-4. Peter, the fisherman, could never have preached the sermon he did on the Day of Pentecost without the help of the Holy Spirit. The preacher is to "Rightly Divide the Word" (2 Tim. 2:15), and Peter could not have done so in his apt quotations from the Scriptures if the Holy Spirit had not aided him. The "Instrument" that the Holy Spirit uses to convict and convert men is the "**WORD OF GOD**." "The 'Seed' is the WORD OF GOD." Luke 8:11. But as in the Natural World the seed must be alive to germinate, and there can be no life without—"**PRE-EXISTING LIFE**," for there is no such thing as "**SPONTANEOUS GENERATION OF LIFE**," so in the Spiritual World the "Seed" (the Word of God) must be vitalized by the Holy Spirit, otherwise it is **BARREN**. This explains why sceptics and scientists and philosophers and others may know the Scriptures and be able to quote them glibly and yet not be converted by them. To use another figure the Scriptures are "Burglar Proof" to those who have not the "**Spiritual Combination**," for "the **NATURAL** man receiveth not (cannot understand) the things of the 'Spirit of God': for they are foolishness unto him; neither can he **know them**, because they are **SPIRITUALLY DISCERNED**." 1 Cor. 2:14. A spiritual revelation cannot be comprehended by the natural understanding. Says Dr. R. A. Torrey, "I would as soon think of setting a man to teach art merely because he understood paints, as to set him to teach the Bible merely because he understood Greek or Hebrew."

In the Natural World there can be no offspring without the union of the two sexes. There must be a father and a mother. How was the "Son of God" born? The Holy Spirit was his Father, and the Virgin Mary his mother. Luke 1:30-33. As the womb of the Virgin was the place of conception of the Son of God, so the **HUMAN HEART** is the place of conception of the "Children of God." Similarly "**Sin**" is generated in the human heart by Satan the "Father of Lies." Peter said—"Ananias, why hath Satan **filled thine heart** to lie to the Holy Ghost, and to keep back part of the price of the land? While it remained, was it not thine own? and after it was sold, was it not in thine own power? Why hast thou **CONCEIVED** this thing in thine heart? Thou hast not lied unto men, but unto God." Acts 5:3-4.

The "New Birth" then is the **COMMUNICATION** of a "**New Life**", the **IMPLANTATION** of a "**New Nature**" by the **SPIRIT OF GOD**. When as he sat under a Numidian Fig-Tree there fell into the heart of Augustine, who was living a profligate life, the "Seed" of Rom. 13:13-14, "Let us walk honestly, as in the day; not in rioting and drunkenness, not in chambering and wantonness, not in strife and envying, but **PUT YE ON THE LORD JESUS CHRIST, AND MAKE NOT PROVISION FOR THE FLESH, TO FULFIL THE LUSTS THEREOF**," and Augustine's heart received the words by **faith**, they being vitalized by the Holy Spirit, caused Augustine to become a "**NEW CREATURE**," and he arose to his feet no longer a child of the Devil, but a **SON OF GOD**.

What every minister of the Gospel and Bible Teacher should do, is to so familiarize himself with the Scriptures, and saturate his mind with them, that he shall be able skilfully to use the instrument that the Holy Spirit has provided, for the "Sword of the Spirit" is the "**WORD OF GOD.**" And it is only by the proper use of it that men are convicted of sin and regenerated.

But it is just as important that we have the Holy Spirit's help in our **PRAYING** as in our preaching. Ought we to prepare and write out our prayers and memorize them, or read them from a book? For an answer we turn to the Scriptures. In Eph. 6:18, we read, "Praying always with all prayer and supplication **IN THE SPIRIT.**" Paul says—"Likewise '**THE SPIRIT**' (H. S.) also helpeth our infirmities: for we know not what we should pray for as we ought: but 'THE SPIRIT' HIMSELF (R. V.) **MAKETH INTERCESSION FOR US** with groanings which cannot be uttered. And He that searcheth the hearts knoweth what is the '**MIND OF THE SPIRIT**,' because He maketh intercession for the saints **ACCORDING TO THE WILL OF GOD.**" Rom. 8:26-27. There is a promise which Christians love to quote—"If two of you shall **AGREE ON EARTH** as touching anything that they shall ask, **it shall be done for them** of my Father **which is in Heaven.**" Matt. 18:19. This is generally taken to mean that if two persons mutually agree to pray for a certain thing they have God's promise that they shall have it.

The word here translated "**AGREE**" is the Greek word from which our word "**SYMPHONY**" comes. In tuning an organ all the notes must be keyed to the standard pitch or harmony is impossible. So in prayer the suppliants must not only agree, they must **SYMPHONIZE**, and this must be done by the "**DIVINE TUNER,**" the **HOLY SPIRIT**, else they will not be in agreement with the "**MIND OF THE SPIRIT,**" and cannot ask according to the "**WILL OF GOD.**" If two persons find themselves, without previous arrangement, praying for the same individual, they have doubtless been prompted so to do by the Holy Spirit, and their prayer will be answered.

There may be an agreement which is **SINFUL**. "How is it that ye have **AGREED TOGETHER** to tempt the 'Spirit of the Lord' (H. S.)?" (Acts 5:9), asked Peter of Sapphira. Here there was "**mutual accord,**" but guilty "**discord**" with the Holy Spirit. It is not enough that two persons **agree with each other**; they must be in accord with a "**THIRD**"—the **HOLY SPIRIT.**

Having thus dwelt at length on the Holy Spirit's work in this Dispensation in the Church, let us now briefly note

HIS WORK IN THE WORLD

His work in the world is outlined in John 16:8-11. "And He, when He is come, will **CONVICT THE WORLD IN RESPECT OF SIN, and OF RIGHTEOUSNESS, and OF JUDGMENT**: of Sin, because they **BELIEVE NOT ON ME**; of Righteousness, because I **GO TO THE FATHER**, and ye behold Me no more; of Judgment, because the 'Prince of this World' **HATH BEEN JUDGED.**" (R. V.)

The Holy Spirit's work then as to the World is threefold—

1. TO CONVICT THE WORLD OF "SIN."

Some hold that "Conscience" is all-sufficient to convict men of sin, and they quote Rom. 2:15, where, speaking of the Gentiles, Paul says—"Which show the work of the Law written in their hearts, their **conscience also bearing witness**, and their **thoughts** the meanwhile **ACCUSING** or else **EXCUSING**, one another." But there is a vast difference between "**LEGAL**" conviction, and "**SPIRITUAL**" conviction. Conscience only begets "Legal" conviction, while the Holy Spirit begets **SPIRITUAL** conviction. Conscience may produce fear and remorse, but it will not keep men from doing wrong, for Conscience imparts no "power," but the Holy Spirit imparts "power" and begets **HOPE**. Conscience only "**Accuses**" or "**Excuses**," while the Holy Spirit **CONDEMNS**. Conscience convicts men of sin against the "Law," for the "Law" says—Thou shalt not **steal**, or **covet**, or **commit adultery**, or kill, and so when men steal, or covet, or commit adultery, or kill, conscience convicts them of those sins. But the "**SIN**" that the Holy Spirit convicts the world of is none of these, but of the special sin of **UNBELIEF**. "He will convince the World of sin, because they **BELIEVE NOT ON ME.**" The entrance of Jesus into the world rendered possible a sin hitherto unknown, the sin of **REJECTING HIM AS THE WORLD'S SAVIOUR**. What was the sin that Peter charged his audience with on the Day of Pentecost? Listen! "Ye men of Israel, hear these words: Jesus of Nazareth, a man approved of God among you by miracles and wonders and signs, which God did by Him, in the midst of you, as ye yourselves also know: Him, being delivered by the determinate counsel and foreknowledge of God, **YE HAVE TAKEN AND BY WICKED HANDS HAVE CRUCIFIED AND SLAIN.**" Acts 2:22-23. Their sin then was the **REJECTION AND CRUCIFIXION OF JESUS BECAUSE OF UNBELIEF**. And we read (Acts 2:37) that they were **PRICKED** (Convicted) **IN THEIR HEART**, and cried out—"Men and brethren, what shall we do?" Now what produced that conviction for sin? The presence of the Holy Spirit, who, using Peter as a mouthpiece, charged His hearers of the awful sin of "**UNBELIEF**" in rejecting the claims of Jesus.

The sin then that it is the work of the Holy Spirit to convict men of in this Dispensation is the sin of **REJECTING JESUS**. Conscience may convict men of "legal sins," such as murder, theft, covetousness, adultery, etc., but only the Holy Spirit can convict of the **SIN OF UNBELIEF**, the most awful and damning sin of the World today. So it is no longer the "**SINS QUESTION,**" but the "**SON QUESTION**"—"What shall we do with **JESUS?**"

It is only then as we present and press home the "Sin of UNBELIEF IN JESUS," that we may expect the co-operation of the Holy Spirit, and the conviction of sin in the unbeliever.

2. TO CONVICT THE WORLD OF "RIGHTEOUSNESS."

What is "Righteousness?" It is to be conformed to the Divine standard of right and justice, to be upright and blameless. But it is not the "World's Righteousness" that is here meant, for it has none, it is the "**Righteousness**" of Jesus. When Jesus was on the earth He claimed to be the "Son of God." He claimed to forgive sins, and to be Himself holy and sinless, and that whosoever believed on Him should have "Eternal Life." But He died an ignominious death. He went to the Cross under charges of sedition and blasphemy, even amid His dying agonies the challenge was hurled at Him—"If Thou **BE THE SON OF GOD**, come down from the Cross." Matt. 27:40-42. He failed to justify His claim by coming down from the Cross. He died as an ordinary mortal dies. The shades of night found Him locked in the Tomb of Joseph of Arimathaea, and a Roman guard keeping watch. Where now are all His claims to Deity? Was that to be the end of all His pretensions? Suppose He had remained in the Tomb and had not risen, what evidence would we have had that He was not an imposter, a false Messiah, like many before Him? None. "If Christ **BE NOT RISEN**, then is our preaching vain, and your faith is also vain." 1 Cor. 15:14.

If Jesus had not risen from the grave that would have been the end of His Righteousness, for three times He had declared that he would, and it was for fear that He would that a guard was placed at the Tomb. Matt. 27:63-64. The fact then that Jesus rose from the dead is proof that His claims were true, and thus His **RIGHTEOUSNESS** was established, and He was "**DECLARED TO BE THE SON OF GOD** with power, according to the Spirit of Holiness, (Holy Spirit), by the **RESURRECTION FROM THE DEAD**." Rom. 1:4.

The standard miracle of the Old Testament is the opening of the Red Sea, and the standard miracle of the New Testament is the Resurrection and Exaltation of Jesus to the Right Hand of God. Eph. 1:19-20. We read in Phil. 2:8-11, that, because He was "**obedient unto death, even the death of the cross**," that God hath **HIGHLY EXALTED HIM**.

The "Resurrection" and "Exaltation" of Jesus then is indisputable proof of His **RIGHTEOUSNESS**. But how is the world to know and be convinced of this? That is the work of the Holy Spirit. That is what He is to convince the world of in this Dispensation. How is He to do it? How did He do it at Pentecost? In John 14:16, Jesus said—"I will pray the Father, and He shall give you another Comforter." That the Father had acceded to Jesus' request is clear from Luke 24:49, where, after His Resurrection and just previous to His Ascension, He said to His Disciples—"Behold, I send the '**PROMISE OF MY FATHER**' upon you: but tarry ye in the city of Jerusalem, until ye be **endued with power FROM ON HIGH**." "And when the Day of Pentecost was fully come, they were with one accord in one place. And suddenly there came a **sound from heaven as of a rushing mighty wind, and it FILLED ALL THE HOUSE WHERE THEY WERE SITTING**. (That is, the sound filled the house). And there appeared unto them '**CLOVEN TONGUES**' **like as of fire**, and it (a cloven tongue) sat upon each of them. And they were all **FILLED WITH THE HOLY GHOST**, (that is, the Holy Ghost took up His residence in them, and they became 'Temples of the Holy Ghost'—1 Cor. 6:19), and began to speak with other tongues, as the **SPIRIT** (H. S.) **gave them utterance**." When this was "voiced abroad" a crowd collected and wanted to know the meaning of the strange proceeding, and Peter stood up, and having charged them with having crucified Jesus, he declared that God had raised Him from the dead, and exalted Him, thus justifying His claims, and—"Therefore, being by the Right Hand of God **EXALTED**, and **having received of the Father THE PROMISE OF THE HOLY GHOST**, He (Jesus) hath shed forth **this** which ye **NOW SEE and HEAR**." Acts 2:33.

While the disciples of Jesus knew that He had been raised from the dead, they did not know whether He had been "Exalted," and could not unless a "**WITNESS**" was sent from Heaven, and the "**Witness**" sent was the "Holy Ghost." If a friend should tell you that He was going to take a trip to the Holy Land, and that when he reached there he would send you a "box of figs," though you did not hear from him by cable or letter, the receipt of the "box of figs" would be evidence sufficient that he had reached his destination. So the receipt of the "**promised gift**" of the Holy Spirit on the Day of Pentecost was visible and sufficient evidence to the Disciples that Jesus had reached Heaven, that the Father had approved of His work on earth, and accepted the sacrifice of the Cross, and as an acknowledgment of His **RIGHTEOUSNESS** had **EXALTED** Him to a seat beside Himself on His Throne.

In Peter's defense before the Council he said—

"The God of our fathers **raised up Jesus**, whom ye slew and hanged on a tree. Him hath God **EXALTED** with His Right Hand (that is, drew Him up with His right hand, to a seat at His right hand on His Throne) to be a '**PRINCE**' (He is not yet a King) and a **SAVIOUR**, for to give repentance to Israel and forgiveness of sins. And we (the Disciples) are His **WITNESSES** of these things; and so is also the **HOLY GHOST**." Acts 5:30-32.

The Law required two witnesses. Deu. 17:6. While the Disciples could bear witness to the Crucifixion, Resurrection, and Ascension of Jesus, they could not testify to His "**EXALTATION**" as that was beyond their human vision, but the Holy Ghost could, for He had witnessed in the presence of Angels, Archangels, and all the Principalities of Heaven the **EXALTATION OF JESUS**, and had been sent to the earth to bear witness to the fact.

If Jesus had not been what He claimed to be, the Father would never have received Him back and "Exalted" Him, and the Holy Spirit would never have been sent to testify to His **EXALTATION**. The Holy Spirit then is the only one who can convince the world of Jesus' **RIGHTEOUSNESS**.

3. TO CONVICT THE WORLD OF "JUDGMENT."

Many in quoting this passage say—"Of a Judgment to come." But the words, "to come," are not there. It was Paul before Felix who "reasoned of Righteousness, Temperance, and Judgment to come," and the result was that Felix trembled. But it was only the conviction of conscience, not Holy Spirit conviction, for though Felix trembled he did not change his course of life, but dismissed Paul with the words—"Go thy way for this time; when I have a convenient season, I will call for thee." Acts 24:25.

The Judgment that the Holy Spirit is to convict the world of in this Dispensation is not a future Judgment, but a Judgment that is **PAST**. Neither is it a Judgment of the Righteous or the Wicked; it is a Judgment of **SATAN**, the "Prince of this World." John 16:11. And it does not refer to a future judgment of him, but declares—"**IS JUDGED**." When was Satan Judged? In the first place he was Judged in the Garden when God passed the sentence on him—"I will put enmity between thee and the woman, and between thy seed and her seed (Christ); it (He) shall bruise thy head and thou shall bruise His heel." Gen. 3:15. In the second place Satan was judged on the Cross. Satan is the author of "**Death**." To overcome the work of Satan it was necessary for Jesus to die on the Cross, and by rising from the dead to "**ABOLISH DEATH**." 2 Tim. 1:10. The purpose of Christ's death then was—"That **THROUGH DEATH** He might **DESTROY HIM THAT HATH THE 'POWER OF DEATH**.' That is, **THE DEVIL**; and **DELIVER THEM** who through 'fear of Death' were all their lifetime subject to bondage." Heb. 2:14-15.

While the "Prince of this World" (Satan) has been Judged, and condemned to the Bottomless Pit for a **thousand years**, (Rev. 20:1-3), and finally is to be cast forever into the "Lake of Fire," (Rev. 20:10), his sentence has not yet gone into effect. But he does not want the world to know this lest he lose his influence, and it is the work of the Holy Spirit in this Dispensation to convince the world that Satan has been Judged and that his power is on the wane, and that "Death" will soon be swallowed up in the victory that the Resurrection shall have over the grave. For if the "Tomb" could not hold Jesus, neither shall the "Grave" hold us.

But there is one more work the Holy Spirit is engaged in in this Dispensation, and that is to hinder Satan in his efforts to produce His Masterpiece, the "**MAN OF SIN**." Writing to the Thessalonians Paul said—

"And now ye know what **WITHHOLDETH** that he (the "Man of Sin"—**THE ANTICHRIST**, 2 Thess. 2:3-4) might be revealed in his time. For the 'Mystery of Iniquity' doth already work; only he who now letteth (restraineth, R. V.) will let, until he be taken out of the way. And then shall that **WICKED** Antichrist be revealed, whom the Lord shall consume with the 'Spirit of His Mouth,' and shall destroy with the Brightness of His Coming: even him, whose coming is after the workings of Satan with all power and signs and lying wonders." 2 Thess. 2:6-9.

There has been a great deal of controversy about who or what is meant by the "Restrainer" or "Withholder" in this passage, but the Apostle John clears it up —

"Hereby know ye the '**SPIRIT OF GOD**': every spirit that **confesseth that Jesus Christ is come in the flesh is OF GOD**: and every spirit that **confesseth not that Jesus Christ is come in the flesh is NOT OF GOD**: and this is that '**SPIRIT OF ANTICHRIST**,' whereof ye have heard that it should come: and even now already is it in the World." 1 John 4:2-3.

Here we have two **opposing** Spirits, one the "**SPIRIT OF GOD**" and the other the "**SPIRIT OF ANTICHRIST**." The "**SPIRIT OF GOD**," or the "**HOLY SPIRIT**," must therefore be the "**RESTRAINER**" who keeps Satan from producing his "Man of Sin," the Antichrist.

A part of the Holy Spirit's work in this Dispensation then is to hold in check the full development of evil until the Church is complete. Then He will be "**Taken away**" and there will be nothing to prevent the manifestation of the "Mystery of Iniquity."

6. THE WORK OF THE HOLY SPIRIT IN THE PARENTHETICAL DISPENSATION BETWEEN THE RAPTURE AND REVELATION.

As we have seen, the Holy Spirit who came at Pentecost to form the "Body of Christ," the Church, will, when the Church is complete and caught out, return with the Church to Heaven. This will leave the world without the presence of the Holy Spirit, and as no man can be "Born again" (John 3:3, 5-7), or call Jesus **LORD** but by the Holy Ghost (1 Cor. 12:3), the world will be in a bad plight. And as the "**SALT**" of "Pure Christianity" will have been removed from the earth, the earth's "Moral Rottenness" will rapidly develop into such a state of "Putrefaction" that only the return of the Lord can stop. But we read that during this period between the "Rapture" and the "Revelation" a "great multitude" shall be saved, out of all nations, and kindreds, and people, and tongues. Rev. 7:9-17. Now how is this "great multitude" to be saved if the Holy Spirit is no longer resident on the earth? They will be saved as the Old Testament Saints were saved, by the Holy Spirit coming to individuals and regenerating them. The work of the Holy Spirit then in the "Parenthetical Dispensation" between the "Rapture" and the "Revelation" will be individualistic only.

7. THE WORK OF THE HOLY SPIRIT IN THE DISPENSATION FROM THE REVELATION OF CHRIST TO THE RENOVATION OF THE EARTH BY FIRE.

This is the Dispensation commonly spoken of as "The Millennium." The work of the Holy Spirit in this Dispensation is foretold in Joel 2:28-32.

"And it shall come to pass **afterward** (after Israel shall have returned to their own land, which will be before the Millennium, Joel 2:21-27), that I will pour out **MY SPIRIT** (H. S.) upon **ALL FLESH**; and your (Israel's) **sons and your daughters shall PROPHESY, your old men shall DREAM DREAMS, your young men shall see VISIONS**: and also upon your **servants** and upon the **handmaids** in those days will I pour out **MY SPIRIT**. And I will show **wonders in the heavens and in the earth, BLOOD** and **FIRE**, and **PILLARS OF SMOKE**. The sun **shall be turned into darkness**, and the **moon into blood**, before the great and the terrible 'Day of the Lord' come. And it shall come to pass, that whosoever shall call on the name of the Lord shall be delivered; for in Mount Zion and in Jerusalem shall be deliverance, as the Lord hath said, and in the remnant whom the Lord shall call."

But you say this was fulfilled at Pentecost. Yes, in part only. That was the "First Fruits" of a future and greater outpouring of the Holy Spirit, for while Peter quoted all but the last few lines of Joel's prophecy, the physical phenomenon that is to attend this outpouring of the Holy Spirit did not take place at Pentecost. There were no **wonders in the heavens and in the earth**, such as **blood and fire, and pillars of smoke**. The sun was not **darkened**, nor the moon turned into **blood**, and as these things are to occur during the Tribulation Period and just previous to the Millennium, it is clear that the prophecy has reference to the Millennial Dispensation.

Whether this "Baptism of the Holy Spirit" shall be on the Jews only is not clear, but it will overflow on the Gentiles, for in those days a King (the Lord Jesus Christ) shall reign in **righteousness** (Isa. 32:1), and the work of righteousness shall be **peace** (Isa. 32:17-18) and upon the bells of the horses shall be inscribed "**HOLINESS TO THE LORD**." Zech. 14:20-21. All this will be largely possible because Satan will be bound, but the Holy Spirit will doubtless have much to do with the righteousness of those days.

THE PASSOVER

IX
THE JEWS

For upwards of 4000 years, amid all civilizations and countries, and under all conditions of government, there has existed a distinct people, with laws, habits and customs distinctively their own. The history of the Jewish race reads like a story from the Arabian Nights, and is without a parallel in human history. Though oppressed, downtrodden, carried captive to other lands, scattered among the nations, like the fabled Phoenix they have risen from the ashes of their dispersions, and appear now and again upon the page of history.

They are remarkable in the first place for their "Antiquity." No nation can trace back its lineage by the clear light of reliable history so far as they. In comparison with the Jews the nations which are making the history of the world today are young.

The "Golden Age" of Israel's glory was long before the palmy days of Greece and Rome. Long before Socrates and Plato taught philosophy, or Herodotus wrote history; in the dim ages of which Homer's Iliad preserves traditions and memorials; before all other authentic and circumstantial records, the nation of Israel was an organized, civilized, and well-established people.

They had a literature before most nations had letters, a literature that today, in the Scriptures, is more widely diffused than the literature of any other people.

Assyria has perished, Babylon is in heaps, Rome has tottered and fallen, Egypt has become a "base" kingdom, but the Jew has outlived all his conquerors and walks unscathed amid the general wreck. Dispersed for centuries among all nations, without a national centre, capital, government, flag, or rallying point, secular or religious, he has never been absorbed by the nations, nor lost his identity or national peculiarities and characteristics, and we have the unique spectacle of a nation without a king, government, or land, retaining its national existence, and a land that seems to be under a curse, awaiting the return of its legal owners.

No nation has ever had such manifest and visible tokens of the "Divine Presence." For them the Red Sea was driven back and the Jordan parted. They were miraculously fed in the Wilderness, and divinely sheltered and guided by the Pillar of Cloud and Fire. At the blowing of rams' horns the walls of a besieged city fell, and the Sun and Moon stayed in their courses that they might have time to slay their enemies. The Angel of the Lord encamped about them, and one angel slew 185,000 of the army of Assyria for their deliverance.

No nation has given to the world such a number of great men. Such a man of faith as Abraham; such a great leader and lawgiver as Moses; such statesmen as Joseph in Egypt and Daniel in Babylon; such a king as David, and wise man as Solomon.

No nation has produced such seers as the Hebrew prophets, Isaiah, Jeremiah, Ezekiel and Daniel and no such man as that man above all men, the

"MAN OF GALILEE."

In the first century there is no name that shines more resplendent than that of the Apostle Paul. And in modern days the men who have been and are making history are Jews.

The preservation of the Jewish people is the

"MIRACLE OF HISTORY."

When Frederick the Great asked the court preacher for an unanswerable proof, in one word, of the inspiration of the Bible, he replied —"The Jew, your Majesty." The emblem of the Jewish Race is a

Bush Burning and Unconsumed.

How are we to account for the wonderful preservation of the Jewish Race? We can only account for it on the supposition that God had, and still has, some great work for them to do. We believe that God raises up individuals for special ministries. Why not a nation?

In the first place the Jewish Race was raised up to reaffirm and teach that there is but one God. In the days of Abraham the nations of the earth were given over to universal idolatry, pantheism and polytheism. For 2000 years (B. C. 1921 to A. D. 30) no other people but the Jews believed the "Unity" of God, or taught it. The Jews have been the teachers of "Monotheism" to the nations. No Gentile nation, untouched by Jewish influence, ever became Monotheistic.

In the second place the Jewish Race was raised up to be the **Writers, Preservers,** and **Transmitters of the Holy Scriptures.** To them were committed the **"Oracles of God."** Rom. 3:1, 2.

Every page and book in the Bible were written by Jews. The Jews took especial care to preserve the Scriptures and keep them from being tampered with, and if it had not been for them they would have been lost long ago.

In the third place the Jewish Race was raised up that God through them might give the world a—Saviour. Who was Jesus? A Jew. How carefully His genealogy has been preserved in the Scriptures from Adam to His Birth at Bethlehem.

In the fourth place the Jewish Race was raised up that they might **save the world from moral putrefaction.**

When Jesus said—

"Salvation Is of the Jews,"

John 4:22, did He simply mean that from them should come the Saviour of the world—**Jesus?** Or did He mean when He said

"YE Are the Salt of the Earth,"

that the Jewish Race were to be the means of preventing the

Moral Putrefaction

of the world, and that if they **became extinct as a nation,** that God would destroy all mankind from off the earth, as He destroyed the Antediluvians when Noah and his family were safely shut in the Ark, or as He destroyed the "Cities of the Plain," Sodom and Gomorrah, when Lot had escaped from them?

A careful study of Peter's speech, as quoted by James, at the First Church Council (Acts 15:13-18), and the words of Paul in his letter to the Romans (Rom. 11:1-5, 11, 12, 15, 17, 23-27) clearly show that Christ meant the latter.

That is, the Salvation of the Nations, morally and physically, and the preservation of the human race on the earth depends on the

Preservation and Continuance of the Jews as a
RACE.

The present degenerate condition of the world is owing to the fact that the Jews have lost their savor, as the salt its saltness, and until the Jews recover their savor degeneration will continue to develop until the time comes that the smell of decomposition of the decaying nationalities of the earth shall call for Divine interposition and the salt be resavored by the conversion of the Jews, and the Jewish nation again take its place among the nations of the earth.

Let us as briefly as possible trace the history of this people.

I. THEIR PAST

In the morning time of history, in B. C. 1936, 412 years after the Flood, God called Abraham, a Shemite, from Ur of the Caldees, to be the father of a new nation.

"Now the Lord had said unto Abraham, Get thee out of thy country, and from thy kindred, and from thy father's

THE JEWS

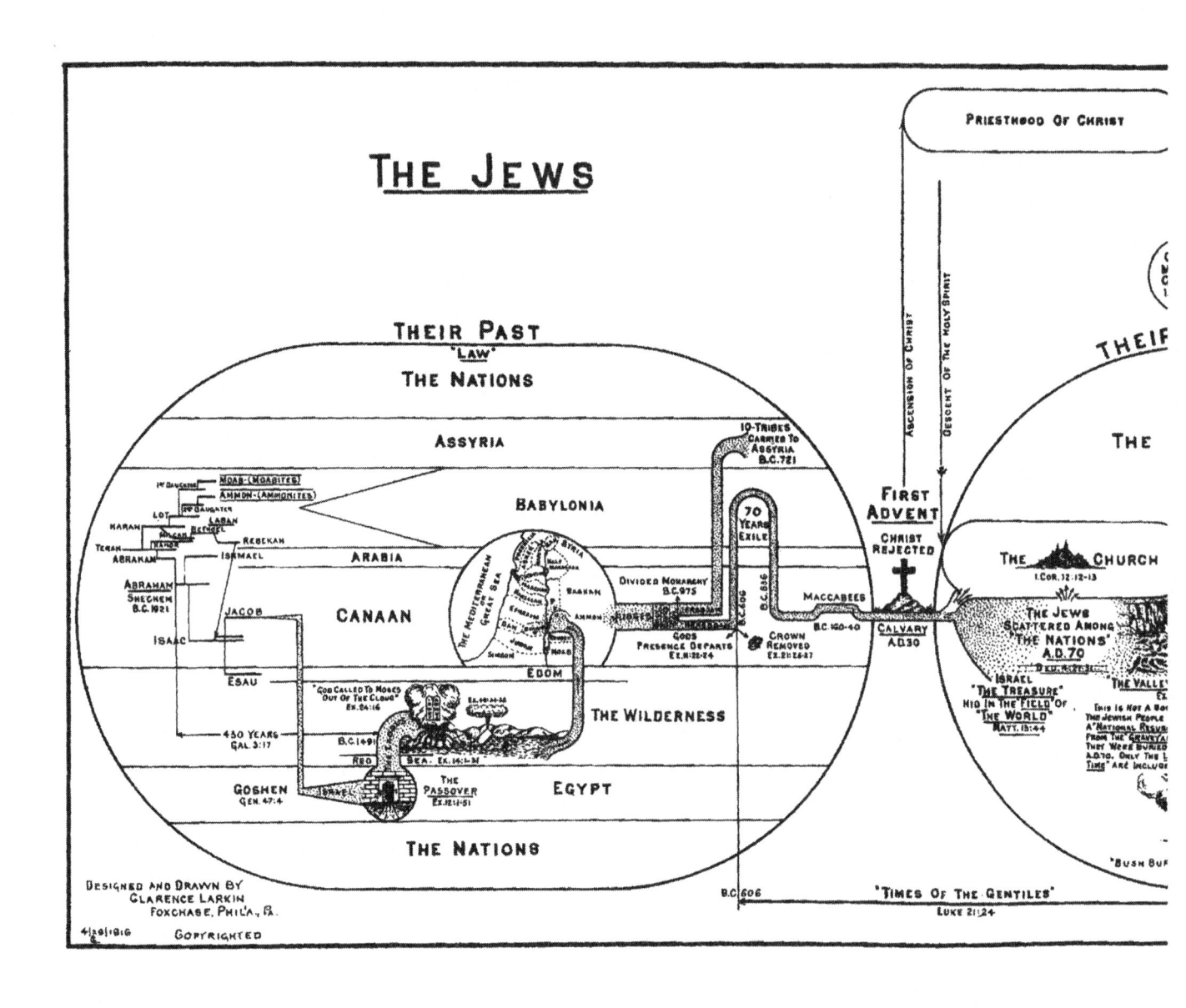

Their Past
"Law"
The Nations

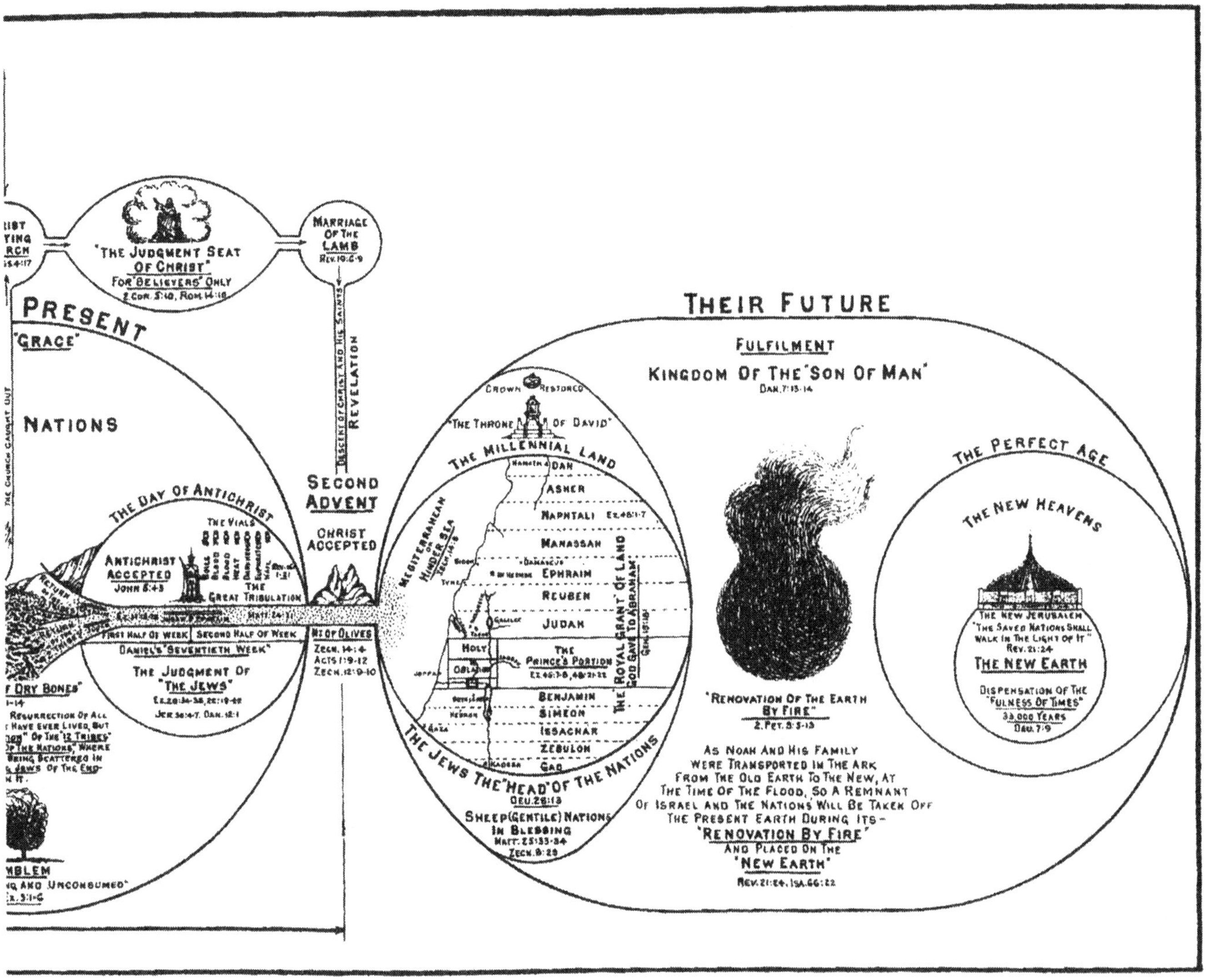

"The Judgment Seat Of Christ"
For "Believers" Only
2 Cor. 5:10, Rom. 14:10
Marriage Of The Lamb
Rev. 19:6-9
Present
"Grace"
Nations
Descent Of Christ And His Saints
Revelation
Second Advent
Christ Accepted
The Day Of Antichrist
The Vials
Antichrist Accepted
John 5:43
The Great Tribulation
First Half Of Week
Second Half Of Week
Daniel's "Seventieth Week"
The Judgment Of "The Jews"
Mt. Of Olives
Zech. 14:4
Acts 1:9-12
Zech. 12:9-10
Their Future
Fulfilment
Kingdom Of The "Son Of Man"
Dan. 7:13-14
Crown Restored
"The Throne Of David"
The Millennial Land
Dan
Asher
Naphtali
Ez. 48:1-7
Manasseh
Ephraim
Reuben
Judah
Holy
Oblation
The Prince's Portion
Benjamin
Simeon
Issachar
Zebulon
Gad
Mediterranean Sea
The "Royal Grant" Of Land
God Gave To Abraham
The Jews The "Head" Of The Nations
Deu. 28:13
Sheep (Gentile) Nations In Blessing
Matt. 25:33-34
Zech. 8:23
"Renovation Of The Earth By Fire"
2 Pet. 3:5-13
As Noah And His Family Were Transported In The Ark From The Old Earth To The New, At The Time Of The Flood, So A Remnant Of Israel And The Nations Will Be Taken Off The Present Earth During Its "Renovation By Fire" And Placed On The "New Earth"
Rev. 21:24, Isa. 66:22
The Perfect Age
The New Heavens
The New Jerusalem
"The Saved Nations Shall Walk In The Light Of It"
Rev. 21:24
The New Earth
Dispensation Of The "Fulness Of Times"
Dry Bones"
Emblem
Unconsumed"

EX
THE BOOK

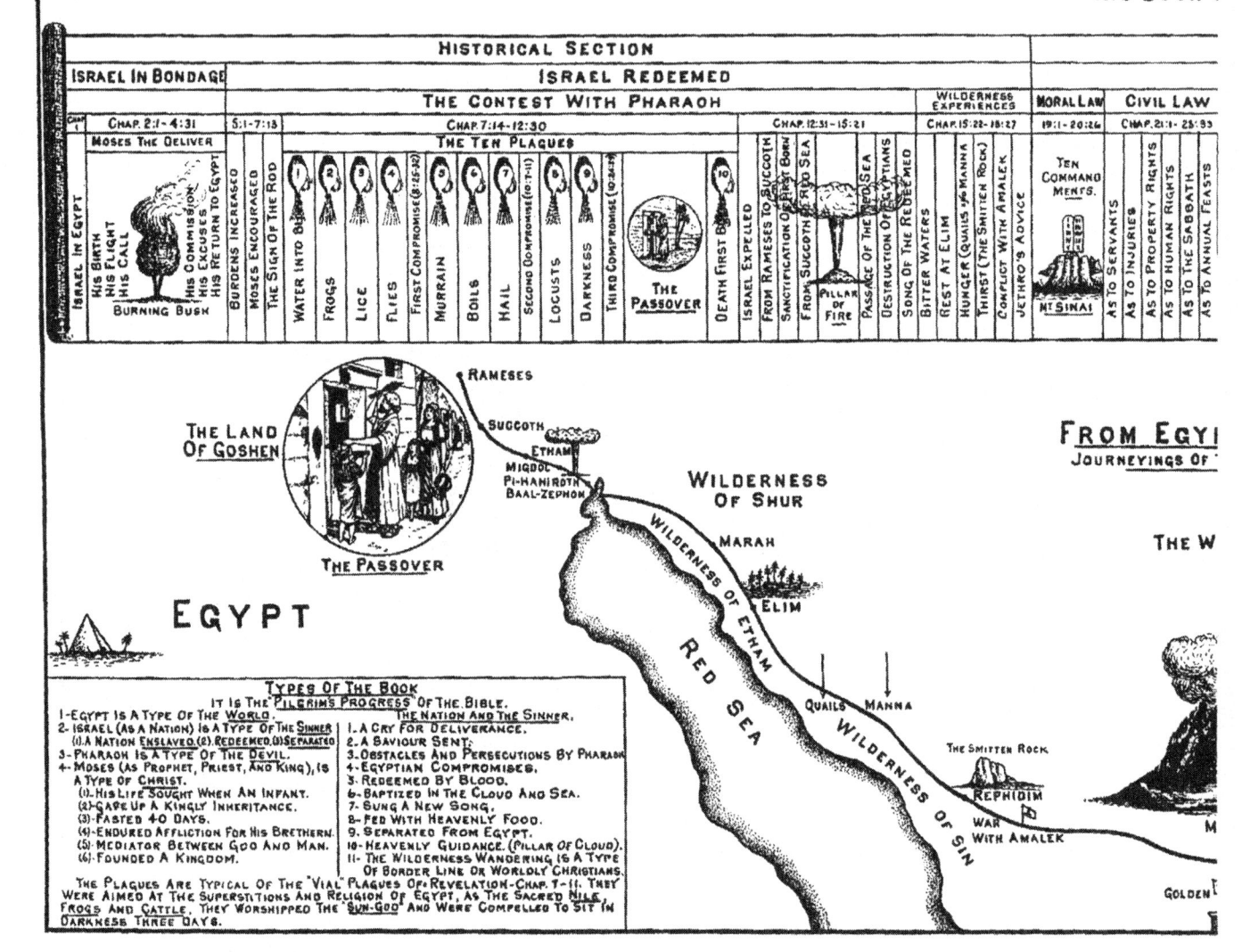

HISTORICAL SECTION

ISRAEL IN BONDAGE	ISRAEL REDEEMED						
	THE CONTEST WITH PHARAOH			WILDERNESS EXPERIENCES	MORAL LAW	CIVIL LAW
CHAP. 2:1-4:31	5:1-7:13	CHAP. 7:14-12:30		CHAP. 12:31-15:21	CHAP. 15:22-18:27	19:1-20:26	CHAP. 21:1-23:33
MOSES THE DELIVER		THE TEN PLAGUES					

Israel In Egypt | His Birth, His Flight, His Call, His Commission, His Excuses, His Return To Egypt | BURNING BUSH | Burdens Increased | Moses Encouraged | The Sign Of The Rod | 1. Water Into Blood | 2. Frogs | 3. Lice | 4. Flies | 5. First Compromise (8:25-32) Murrain | 6. Boils | 7. Hail | 8. Second Compromise (10:7-11) Locusts | 9. Darkness | 10. Third Compromise (10:24) The Passover | Death First Born | Israel Expelled | From Rameses To Succoth | Sanctification Of First Born | From Succoth To Red Sea | Pillar Of Fire | Passage Of The Red Sea | Destruction Of Egyptians | Song Of The Redeemed | Bitter Waters | Rest At Elim | Hunger (Quails & Manna) | Thirst (The Smitten Rock) | Conflict With Amalek | Jethro's Advice | Ten Commandments (Mt Sinai) | As To Servants | As To Injuries | As To Property Rights | As To Human Rights | As To The Sabbath | As To Annual Feasts

---

THE LAND OF GOSHEN

THE PASSOVER

RAMESES — SUCCOTH — ETHAM — MIGDOL — PI-HAHIROTH — BAAL-ZEPHON

WILDERNESS OF SHUR — MARAH — ELIM

WILDERNESS OF ETHAM

RED SEA

WILDERNESS OF SIN

QUAILS — MANNA

THE SMITTEN ROCK — REPHIDIM — WAR WITH AMALEK

GOLDEN

EGYPT

FROM EGY
JOURNEYINGS OF

THE W

TYPES OF THE BOOK
IT IS THE PILGRIM'S PROGRESS OF THE BIBLE.

1. EGYPT IS A TYPE OF THE WORLD.
2. ISRAEL (AS A NATION) IS A TYPE OF THE SINNER.
   (1) A NATION ENSLAVED. (2) REDEEMED. (3) SEPARATED.
3. PHARAOH IS A TYPE OF THE DEVIL.
4. MOSES (AS PROPHET, PRIEST, AND KING), IS A TYPE OF CHRIST.
   (1) HIS LIFE SOUGHT WHEN AN INFANT.
   (2) GAVE UP A KINGLY INHERITANCE.
   (3) FASTED 40 DAYS.
   (4) ENDURED AFFLICTION FOR HIS BRETHREN.
   (5) MEDIATOR BETWEEN GOD AND MAN.
   (6) FOUNDED A KINGDOM.

THE NATION AND THE SINNER.
1. A CRY FOR DELIVERANCE.
2. A SAVIOUR SENT.
3. OBSTACLES AND PERSECUTIONS BY PHARAOH.
4. EGYPTIAN COMPROMISES.
5. REDEEMED BY BLOOD.
6. BAPTIZED IN THE CLOUD AND SEA.
7. SUNG A NEW SONG.
8. FED WITH HEAVENLY FOOD.
9. SEPARATED FROM EGYPT.
10. HEAVENLY GUIDANCE. (PILLAR OF CLOUD).
11. THE WILDERNESS WANDERING IS A TYPE OF BORDER LINE OR WORLDLY CHRISTIANS.

THE PLAGUES ARE TYPICAL OF THE "VIAL" PLAGUES OF REVELATION CHAP. 7-11. THEY WERE AIMED AT THE SUPERSTITIONS AND RELIGION OF EGYPT, AS THE SACRED NILE, FROGS AND CATTLE. THEY WORSHIPPED THE SUN-GOD AND WERE COMPELLED TO SIT IN DARKNESS THREE DAYS.

ODUS
OF "REDEMPTION"

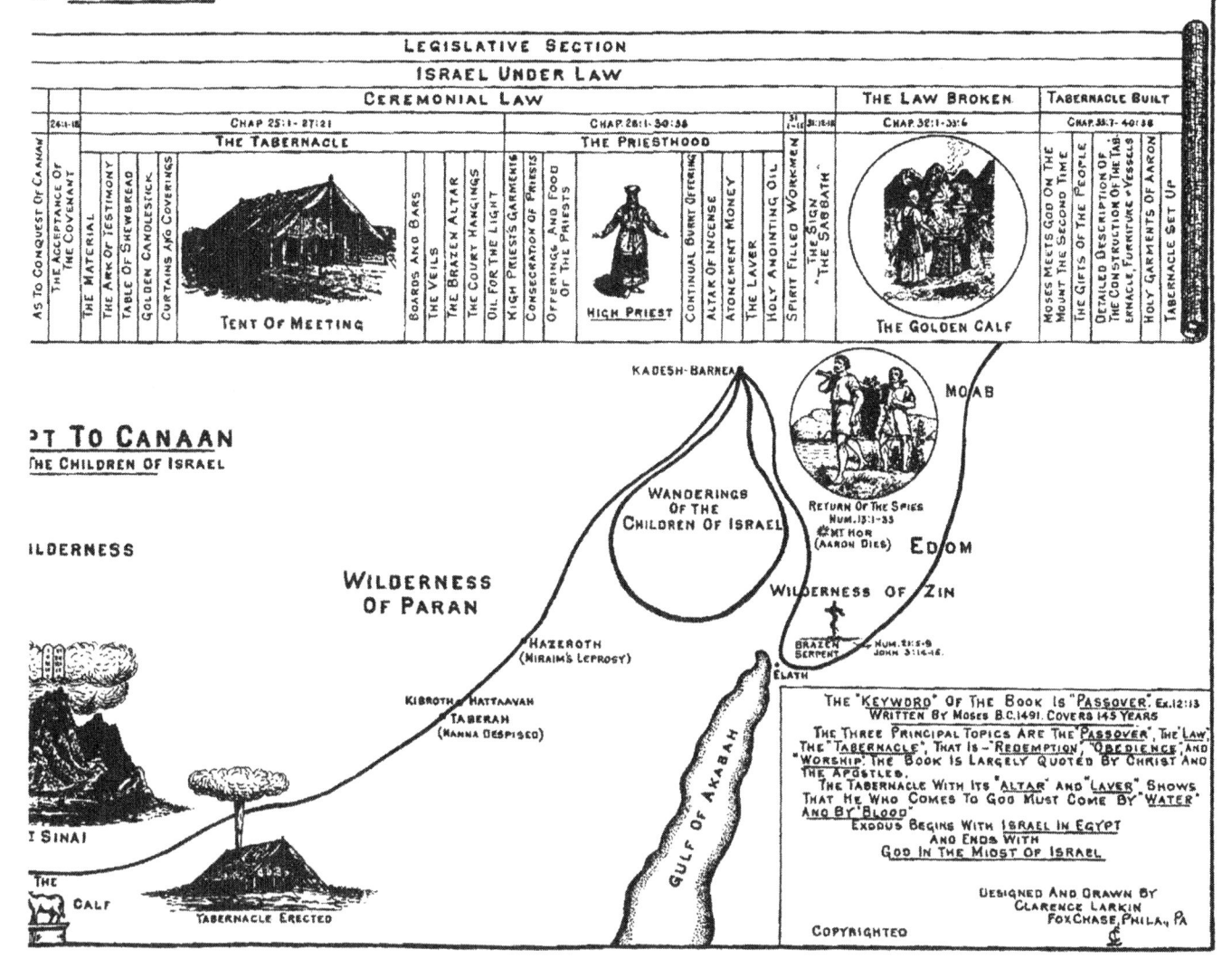

LEGISLATIVE SECTION
ISRAEL UNDER LAW

CEREMONIAL LAW		THE LAW BROKEN	TABERNACLE BUILT
CHAP. 25:1-27:21 — THE TABERNACLE	CHAP. 28:1-30:38 — THE PRIESTHOOD	CHAP. 32:1-33:6	CHAP. 33:7-40:38

Columns (left to right):
- As To Conquest Of Canaan
- The Acceptance Of The Covenant
- The Material
- The Ark Of Testimony
- Table Of Shewbread
- Golden Candlestick
- Curtains And Coverings
- **Tent Of Meeting**
- Boards And Bars
- The Veils
- The Brazen Altar
- The Court Hangings
- Oil For The Light
- High Priest's Garments
- Consecration Of Priests
- Offerings And Food Of The Priests
- **High Priest**
- Continual Burnt Offering
- Altar Of Incense
- Atonement Money
- The Laver
- Holy Anointing Oil
- Spirit Filled Workmen
- "The Sign" The Sabbath
- **The Golden Calf**
- Moses Meets God On The Mount The Second Time
- The Gifts Of The People
- Detailed Description Of The Construction Of The Tabernacle, Furniture & Vessels
- Holy Garments Of Aaron
- Tabernacle Set Up

PT TO CANAAN
THE CHILDREN OF ISRAEL

KADESH-BARNEA
MOAB
WANDERINGS OF THE CHILDREN OF ISRAEL
RETURN OF THE SPIES
NUM. 13:1-33
MT. HOR (AARON DIES)
EDOM
WILDERNESS OF ZIN
WILDERNESS OF PARAN
HAZEROTH (Miriam's Leprosy)
KIBROTH-HATTAAVAH
TABERAH (Manna Despised)
BRAZEN SERPENT — NUM. 21:5-9, JOHN 3:14-16
ELATH
GULF OF AKABAH
ILDERNESS
SINAI
THE CALF
TABERNACLE ERECTED

THE "KEYWORD" OF THE BOOK IS "PASSOVER". Ex.12:13
WRITTEN BY MOSES B.C.1491. COVERS 145 YEARS
THE THREE PRINCIPAL TOPICS ARE THE "PASSOVER", THE "LAW",
THE "TABERNACLE", THAT IS — <u>REDEMPTION</u>, <u>OBEDIENCE</u> AND
<u>WORSHIP</u>. THE BOOK IS LARGELY QUOTED BY CHRIST AND
THE APOSTLES.
THE TABERNACLE WITH ITS "ALTAR" AND "LAVER" SHOWS
THAT HE WHO COMES TO GOD MUST COME BY "WATER"
AND BY "BLOOD"
EXODUS BEGINS WITH <u>ISRAEL IN EGYPT</u>
AND ENDS WITH
<u>GOD IN THE MIDST OF ISRAEL</u>

DESIGNED AND DRAWN BY
CLARENCE LARKIN
FOX CHASE, PHILA., PA

COPYRIGHTED

house, unto a land that I will show thee; and I will make of thee a great nation, and I will bless thee, and make thy name great, and thou shalt be a blessing; and I will bless them that bless thee, and curse him that curseth thee, and in thee shall all families of the earth be blessed." Gen. 12: 1-3.

Notice that this is not a conditional promise, and there is not a passage in the Bible anywhere that revokes it.

Abraham was 60 years old when he was called, but tarried at Haran for 15 years until his father, who was an idolater, died, when he started for the "Land of Promise." God appeared to him 10 times. These appearances were called "Theophanies."

God's promises to Abraham were progressive. At Ur the promises were the "Land," and that his seed should "become a great nation." Gen. 12:1, 2. At Shechem the promise of the "ownership of the land to his descendants." Gen. 12:7. At Bethel, all the land "thou seest," and that his seed should be as the "dust of the Earth for number." Gen. 13:15, 16. At Mamre, that his seed should be for numbers as the "stars of the heavens," and that the "Land" should extend from the "River of Egypt" to the "River Euphrates." Gen. 15:5, 18. And at Moriah the promise as to the number of his seed was repeated. Gen. 22:16, 17.

These promises were unconditionally confirmed to his son, Isaac (Gen. 26:1-4), and to his grandson, Jacob. Gen. 28:10-15.

When the descendants of Abraham had increased to about 70, in fulfillment of a prophecy made by God to Abraham that his seed should be as strangers in another land, where they would be afflicted for 400 years (Gen. 15:13, 14); and to prevent contamination by intermarriages, and to give them time to grow into a nation, God paved the way for their leaving Canaan, by sending Joseph down into Egypt to make provision for them when the famine He was going to send would fall on the land. There they were segregated in the land of Goshen.

The next great event in their history was the Exodus. When the time for their deliverance from Egypt came, God weaned them by increasing the hardness of their lot, and when they cried to God He sent Moses to deliver them. Within a year after their escape from Egypt the Law was given, the Tabernacle built, a sacrificial system of worship inaugurated and the "Jewish Commonwealth" set up. But when at the end of the year they reached Kadesh Barnea and refused to go up and take possession of the Land, God punished them by compelling them to wander for 40 years in the Wilderness, where they were miraculously clothed and fed, and were divinely guided by the "Pillar of Cloud and Fire."

At the end of the 40 years, under the leadership of Joshua, they crossed the Jordan and entered the Promised Land and took possession of it.

Then began the third period of their history, the "Times of the Judges," which lasted about 450 years. The government was a Theocracy, administered at first through elders, and then by Judges. The people, however, were not satisfied with being ruled by an invisible King, they wanted a king like the other nations around them had, so they went to Samuel the Prophet and asked him for a king. Samuel was displeased and felt it was aimed at his administration, but when he took the matter to God, God said—

"Hearken unto the voice of the people . . . for they have not rejected thee, but they have rejected ME." 1 Sam. 8:7.

Samuel then warned the people of what the king they would chose would do to them, but the warning did not avail and Saul was chosen. This was the beginning of the fourth period of their history.

Saul reigned for 40 years and was succeeded by David, a man of God's choice, who also reigned 40 years, and was succeeded by his son Solomon, who in turn reigned 40 years. During the reign of Solomon the First Temple was built. His reign was most glorious, but its weak feature was that he married so many heathen wives, and permitted them to introduce at Jerusalem idolatrous worship. This was the beginning of the downfall of the Jewish nation.

After the death of Solomon, B. C. 975, the Kingdom was divided, his son Rehoboam retaining possession of two Tribes, Judah and Benjamin, and with them Jerusalem and the Temple; and Jeroboam, a usurper, as ruler over the remaining ten Tribes, set up his capital at Samaria. This division of the Kingdom, known as "Israel," rapidly declined, and in B. C. 721 the Ten Tribes were carried captive to Assyria. The Two Tribes, known as "Judah," survived over 100 years longer, but in B. C. 606 they were carried in Captivity to Babylon, and Jerusalem was destroyed by Nebuchadnezzar in B. C. 587. Thus ended a period of deadly tribal wars which was made illustrious by the ministry of a noble succession of great prophets.

With the Captivity of Judah and the destruction of Jerusalem, began that long period which still continues, known in the Scriptures as

"The Times of the Gentiles,"

and which is so fully outlined and described in the Book of Daniel.

The fifth period of Jewish History began in B. C. 536, when the 70 years of the Captivity ended, as prophesied (Jer. 25:11); and some 40,000 of those of the Captivity returned to Jerusalem to rebuild the City and the Temple. The Temple was not finished and dedicated until 20 years later, and the walls of the city were not rebuilt until 70 more years had passed by, B. C. 445.

But while the Jews were permitted to return to their own land, they never again secured supremacy. They remained subject to the different conquerors of their land, though for the most part governed by rulers of their own race, in fulfillment of the prophecy that the Sceptre should not depart from Judah until Shiloh came.

In B. C. 168 Antiochus Epiphanes, King of Syria, wrested Palestine from Egypt, twice took and sacked Jerusalem, desecrated and closed the Temple, and cruelly persecuted the Jews, until they became so incensed as to rise in rebellion under the leadership of the "Maccabees." This rebellion lasted from B. C. 166 to B. C. 40.

In B. C. 63 Judea became subject to Rome, and during the next 60 years the Roman Empire tightened its grip on the Holy Land. About this time, B. C. 5, many of the students of prophecy, knowing that the time set for the coming of "Messiah the Prince" by Daniel the Prophet (Dan. 9:25) was not far distant, frequented the Temple waiting for the "Consolation of Israel." Luke 2:25, 26.

In December of that year Jesus was born at Bethlehem, was visited by the Shepherds, acknowledged a few weeks later in the Temple by Simeon and Anna, the Wise men from the East did Him homage, He was taken to Egypt, and returned to Nazareth where He spent His youth and young manhood, and at 30 years of age appeared at the Jordan, was baptized of John and entered upon His public ministry.

But His claim of being the Messiah was rejected by His own people. They joined hands with the Gentiles in crucifying the "Lord of Glory," and in A. D. 70 the Roman armies came, Jerusalem and the Temple were destroyed by Titus and the Jews were scattered among the nations of the earth.

II. THEIR PRESENT.

With the Crucifixion of Christ the sorrows of the Jewish race began. Their cry—**His Blood Be on Us and on Our Children** (Matt. 27:25) has been literally fulfilled.

In A. D. 50, 30,000 were killed in Jerusalem in a tumult with the Romans, but their worst sufferings commenced in A. D. 66 under Gessius Florus, the Roman Governor of Judea. His oppressions led to a widespread revolt. Nero sent Vespasian, accompanied by his son Titus, with an army of 60,000. He was met in upper Galilee by Josephus, a famous general of the Asmonean race, and a noted historian, who entrenched himself at Jotapata, but was finally overpowered, after a siege of 47 days, with a loss of over 40,000 men. The subjugation of Galilee followed. Thousands perished in the war. Judea and Jerusalem were spared because Vespasian was called back to Rome by the death of Nero. When Vespasian was made King he sent his son Titus to complete the subjugation of the Holy Land and capture Jerusalem.

It was in April, A. D. 70, that the Roman army, numbering 100,000 men, marched against Jerusalem. The city was poorly prepared to stand a siege. Rival factions disputed among themselves for control. The city was surrounded by a triple wall, defended by 90 towers. The siege lasted 4 months. Great engines of elastic timbers, aided by the twisting of great cables, hurled huge stones against the massive walls. Within the city famine reigned, wives snatched food from their husbands, children from their parents, mothers from their babes, and some mothers, lost to all sense of motherhood, killed, cooked and ate their own children. Many fled from the city to meet a worse fate, for being captured by Titus, they were crucified as a warning outside the city walls. So horrible became the condition of the besieged that Titus called God to witness that he was not responsible.

At last, on August 5, A. D. 70, the Tower Antonia was taken, the Romans swarmed into the Temple enclosure, and though Titus had commanded his soldiers to spare the beautiful Temple building, for it was looked upon, even by Rome, as one of the wonders of the world, yet a soldier threw a blazing torch through a doorway and in the conflagration that followed the Temple of Herod was destroyed, leaving nothing but the rock upon which it stood.

Josephus says that over 1,000,000 perished in the siege, while 97,000 survived as captives, of whom the handsomest young men were taken to Rome to grace the triumph of the Conqueror, and thus was fulfilled the prophecy of Daniel, that "the 'People' of the Prince that shall come (Antichrist) shall destroy the City and the Sanctuary." Dan. 9:26.

While the destruction of Jerusalem by Titus scattered the Jews far and wide, the end was not yet. Sixty-five years later, A. D. 135, the Jews had sufficiently recovered from that crushing blow to rise afresh in revolt against the Roman power. Hadrian then completed the work of Dispersion. In a war lasting three and a half years he devastated Palestine, destroyed 580,000 persons, ran a ploughshare over Zion, thus fulfilling the prophecy of Mich 3:12, uttered 885 years before, and forbade the Jews, on pain of death, even to approach Aelia Capitolina, the new Roman city which he erected on the site of Jerusalem. The Jews since that time have been few in Palestine.

In A. D. 362 the Emperor Julian the Apostate made an attempt to rebuild the walls of Jerusalem, thus to falsify the prediction of the Lord, but his workmen were driven off by fire that burst from the ruins.

The interval from Hadrian, A. D. 140, to Constantine saw the Jewish people in a measure prosperous and flourishing in the lands of their exile throughout the Roman World. They even took part in pagan persecutions of the early Church. But the conversion of Constantine to Christianity in A. D. 312, changed all this. The Jews then became a condemned and persecuted sect. They lost the imperial favor and privileges they had enjoyed, and were excluded from one sphere after another, though they were still free to observe their own religion and retained their rights as citizens.

The gloom deepened until A. D. 1096, the time of the First Crusade, known in history as the "Holy War;" when the pall of midnight blackness fell upon them, and did not lift until long after the Reformation.

The Frown of England.

In A. D. 1020 Canute banished all Jews from England. In A. D. 1068 the only burial place in all England allowed the Jews was Cripplegate, London. In A. D. 1096 the "Holy War" began by attempting to murder all the Jews in Europe who would not submit to baptism. Henry II ordered the Jews to pay £60,000 toward defraying his expenses during one of the Crusades. At the accession of Richard I (Coeur de Leon), A. D. 1189, murderous riots were instigated against the Jews and not a Jewish household in London escaped robbery and murder.

The following year occurred the "Tragedy of York Castle," in which the chief Rabbi of York, with 500 followers were besieged in York Castle, and when escape became hopeless they slew one another and the chief Rabbi, the last to die, started a conflagration, then took his own life, and when the besiegers broke in they found the besieged in one great pile like the sacrifice upon the altar.

Up to the time of Edward I, A. D. 1272, the Crown claimed to own the Jew and all he possessed, and from time to time would allow him to gather riches that he might squeeze them from him, like water from a sponge. Edward I drove all the Jews, 16,500 in number, from England, and for nearly four centuries there is no evidence that British soil was pressed by a Jewish foot.

The Curse of France.

In A. D. 1306, on the morning of the fast commemorating the Destruction of Jerusalem all the Jews of France, men, women and children to the number of 100,000, were stripped of their possessions for the benefit of the royal treasury, and cast out of the land. In 10 years they were allowed to return, but soon the "Pastoureaux," bands of fanatical shepherds and malefactors, swept them away by thousands. In A. D. 1683 the Jews were ordered to quit all the French Colonies, and it was not until A. D. 1723, when Louis XV gave the Jews permission to hold real estate in France, that the tide began to turn.

The Bloody Hand of Germany.

The Plague of the "Black Death," which swept over Europe in A. D. 1348-1350, and which carried off one-fourth of the population, afflicted the Jews but lightly, owing to their simple life and observance of the hygienic requirements of the Levitical Law. Their comparative exemption caused them to be suspected as the source of the Plague, and they were charged with poisoning the wells and springs. In Germany the composition of the poison, the color of the packages in which it was transported, and the persons who conveyed them, were all declared to be known. The result was that they suffered the torture, the caldron and the devouring flame at the hands of the "Flagellants," an order of fanatics who swarmed through Germany preaching extermination to all unbelievers. The entire community at Strasburg, 2000 souls, was dragged upon an immense scaffold, and it set on fire. They were also charged with stealing the children of Christians and crucifying them for Passover Lambs, and also with stealing the consecrated "Host" and piercing it with knives. In A. D. 1560 they were banished from Prague and later in Constantinople 3000 houses in the Jews' quarters were burned and property to the value of 50,000,000 crowns confiscated.

THE HOLOCAUSTS OF SPAIN

In Spain the machinery of

"The Inquisition"

held full sway. It was established to terrify into faithfulness apostate Jews. Men and women disappeared by hundreds, as if the ground had opened and swallowed them up. Some never returned, others reappeared in after years human wrecks, pale and emaciated and semi-insane through long incarceration in dark and chilly subterranean dungeons. Now and then processions wound through the streets to the place of burning, the victims being tortured with the hope that they would recant before being thrown into the flames.

Many found themselves led from the Hall of Judgment along subterraneous passage ways to the chamber of the

"Iron Maiden,"

the rude hollow figure of a woman, made of iron, which at the touch of a spring flew open and disclosed its inner surface studded with iron nails rusted by the blood of its numerous victims. No sooner did the condemned step inside than the figure began to close, hugging in its iron grasp the victim, until the nails, entering the body amid the shrieks of the victim, pierced some vital part, and when all was over the "Iron Figure" again opened and allowed the body to fall into the yawning pit below.

But this was not all. Ferdinand and Isabella in A. D. 1492 issued an edict of banishment against all the Jews in Spain. A Jew offered 600,000 crowns for a revocation of the edict. The King and Queen hesitated and were inclined to accept when the Spanish Inquisitor, Torquemada, stalked into the presence of the abashed rulers and holding up a "Crucifix" before them cried—

"Behold Him Whom Judas Iscariot Sold for 30 Pieces of Silver. Sell Ye Him Now for a Higher Price and Render an Account of Your Bargain Before God."

The sovereigns trembled before the stern Dominican and the Jews had to go. They were given four months in which to prepare. Whither to go they knew not, for there was no hospitable shore to which to fly. Some embarked for Africa and were sold into slavery. A number reached Italy. Their sufferings were indescribable. Two hundred years later, A. D. 1680, the spirit of Spain toward the Jews was unchanged.

And so, like a horrible nightmare, for centuries history records the terrible punishments and persecutions that befell the seed of Abraham.

But the long night of persecution came to a close. The tide began to turn when England passed the

"Naturalization Bill" in A. D. 1753,

and received its greatest impulse when our own

"Declaration of Independence" Was Signed in A. D. 1776,

and, with the exception of Russia the Jews today, in all lands enjoy comparative freedom.

The miracle of the preservation of the Jews during the long night of their persecutions cannot be accounted for, only on the supposition that they have been preserved for a purpose.

The secret of their endurance is twofold.

1. **Their National Law.**

It preserved them from disease, controlled and regulated their passions, checked the baser impulses of their nature, and secured the vigor of their offspring.

2. **Their National Hope.**

Amid all the vicissitudes of their history the Jewish people have been upheld by their "National Hope." A "Hope" so radiant, and a "Faith" so beautiful, that the world has never seen its like. The "Hope of a

Coming Messiah.

The "Hope" of the coming of this "Messiah" has flamed like a "Morning Star" through the darkness of Israel's long night, and has turned their thoughts toward the dawning of that day when the

"Sun of Righteousness"

shall arise and dispel the gloom and usher in that bright "Millennial Day" when Righteousness and Peace shall cover the earth as the waters cover the deep.

For the Jews today there is no "Pillar of Cloud" by day, nor "Shechinah Flame" by night. They have no altars, no sacrifices, no priesthood as in former days. They observe the "Passover," but no paschal lamb is slain. They keep the "Great Day of Atonement," but no blood is shed to make reconciliation for sin. All sacrifices and oblations have ceased. They have no King, no Judges, no Prophets, no inspired writers. The "Urim" and "Thummin" give no Divine token. The word of God is precious, but there is no "open vision." Their last Great Prophet was the "Man of Galilee," but Him they rejected. Like their forefathers, who took Joseph, after they had rejected him, and sold him for 20 pieces of silver, and he was hidden from their view in Egypt on the Throne of Pharaoh, so the Jews took Jesus, their Joseph, and having rejected Him, sold Him for 30 pieces of silver, and He is now hidden from them on His Father's Throne.

Why Is This? Have they been supplanted as a "Nation" by the Gentiles, and as "God's People" by the Church? Are they never again to have a land of their own, and a King, and a Capital City, and a National Existence?

Is not their condition today the fulfillment of the prophecy of Hosea 3:4.

"The Children of Israel shall abide MANY DAYS without a King, and without a Prince, and without a Sacrifice, and without an Image, and without an Ephod, and without Teraphim?"

Is it not that Jerusalem must be—

"Trodden down of the Gentiles until the 'Times of the Gentiles' be fulfilled?" Luke 21:24.

What does Paul say—

"Blindness in part is happened to Israel until the 'Fulness of the Gentiles' be come in. And so All Israel Shall Be Saved." Rom. 11:25, 26.

We see then that the Jews (Israel) have not been supplanted by the Church, or by the Gentile nations. They are again to take the lead among the nations of the earth. For this they have been preserved.

The eleventh chapter of Romans begins with the question—

"Hath God Cast Away His People?"

Paul answers his own question by replying "God Hath Not Cast Away His People Which He Foreknew." Vs. 2.

In the eleventh verse Paul asks a second question. "Have they stumbled That They Should Fall?" That is, have they fallen down so that they shall Never Rise Again? He replies,

"God forbid; but rather through their fall salvation is come unto the Gentiles for to provoke them to jealousy."

Now two things are revealed here, first, the Jews have fallen that the Gentiles may have a chance to be saved, and second, that the sight of seeing the Gentiles saved may make the Jews "jealous." Why should God want to provoke the Jews to jealousy if He has cast them off?

The Apostle then adds—

"If the **Fall** of them be the **riches of the world** and the **Diminishing** of them the **riches of the Gentiles** (that is, if the giving of the Gospel to the Gentiles is such a blessing to them), how much more will be their **Fulness?**" Vs. 12.

That is, how much greater blessing there will be for **the world** when the Jews rise up again and take their place among the nations. For Paul goes on to say—

"If the **casting away** of them be the **reconciling of the world**, what shall the **receiving** of them be, but

LIFE FROM THE DEAD?"

That is, when the Jews come back to God it will be like **a resurrection**, not of individuals, but a

"National Resurrection."

Then the Apostle changes the figure and speaks of

Two Olive Trees.

One he calls the "Good" Olive Tree, the other a "Wild" Olive Tree. Of the "Good" Olive Tree he speaks of "Some" (not all) of the branches being broken off, for there is a "Remnant of Grace," vs. 5, as there were 7000 men in Elijah's day who had not bowed the knee to Baal. And we must not forget that the "**Root**" and "**Trunk**" of the Tree were **still alive**, and where some of the "Good" branches were broken off, the "Wild" Olive branches were grafted in "among" them, not "instead of," and thus became "partaker" of the "**Root**" and "**Fatness**" of the "Good Olive Tree."

We see from this that the "Good Olive Tree" is not **rooted up and destroyed** and a "Wild Olive Tree" **planted in its place**, but it still remains **alive** and gives life to both the "**Good**" and "**Wild**" olive branches.

The Apostle then goes on to reprove the Gentile members of the Church at Rome, who were boasting of their independence of the Jews, and that Christianity had supplanted Judaism, just as so many in the Church today claim that the Church has supplanted Judaism and fallen heir to all its promises. saying to them—

"Boast not against the branches . . . for Thou bearest not the root, but the "**Root**" thee.

And he reminded them that the branches were broken off, not that they might be grafted in, but because of "Unbelief," and thus the "unbelief" of the Jews redounded to their benefit, and he goes on to tell them that if the "Good" Olive branches that had been cut off should repent, they would be **grafted back again**, for **GOD is able to graft them in again.** Rom. 11:17-26.

Here we see that if the Jews repent and turn from their unbelief, God will restore them to their old time place among the nations.

III. THEIR FUTURE.

If it were suggested that we discuss the future of any other nation than the Jewish nation, I, for one, would not attempt it, for the task would be simply a speculative one, based on probabilities that would be likely to be upset by unforeseen circumstances. But the Jewish nation has the unique distinction of having for its historian the "Holy Spirit," who has not simply recorded the past history of that nation, but has outlined its future.

We indulge then in no idle and profitless speculations when we attempt to forecast the future of the Jewish People. All we have to do is to gather together and place in their logical order what the Holy Spirit through the Prophets, has foretold of their future. The method is as simple as the result is sure.

THE RESTORATION OF THE JEWS.

1. **As to the Fact.**

"Therefore fear not, O my servant Jacob, saith the Lord; neither be dismayed, O Israel; . . . . . For I am with thee, saith the Lord, to save thee; though I make a full end of all nations whither I have scattered thee, yet will **I not make a full end of thee.**" Jer. 30:10, 11.

"And I will bring again the captivity of my people 'Israel' and they shall build the waste cities, and inhabit them; and they shall plant vineyards and drink the wine thereof; they shall also make gardens, and eat the fruit of them. And I will plant them upon their land, and they shall **no more be pulled up out of their land.**" Amos 9:14, 15.

But you say this prophecy was fulfilled in the restoration from the "Babylonian Captivity." Not so, for they were driven out of the land after that, and this promise is, that they shall **no more be pulled up out of their land**, and must refer to some **future** restoration. The return from the "Babylonian Captivity" was the **First** restoration, and the Scriptures speak of a **Second**.

"And it shall come to pass in '**That Day**' (Millennial Day) that the Lord shall set his hand again the '**Second Time**' to recover the remnant of His People, which shall be left, from Assyria, and from Egypt, and from Pathros, and from Cush, and from Elam, and from Shinar, and from Hamath, and from the islands of the Sea." Isa. 11:11.

The Jews have never been **restored** but **ONCE,** and that was from Babylon. The march from Egypt to Canaan was not a restoration. You cannot have anything restored to you unless it **has been in your possession before**, and Palestine was never in possession of the Children of Israel until **after** its conquest by Joshua.

Again the Jews are to come this time, not from the "**East,**" as when they returned from the "Babylonish Captivity," but from the "**North,**" and from "**All Countries.**"

"Therefore, behold, the days come, saith the Lord, that it shall no more be said, The Lord liveth, that brought up the Children of Israel out of the Land of Egypt; but the Lord liveth that brought up the Children of Israel **from the land of the** NORTH **and from ALL THE LANDS** whither He had **driven them**; and I will bring them again into their land that I gave unto their fathers." Jer. 16:14, 15. Also Isa. 43:5-7. And they shall never again be dispersed.

"For I will set mine eyes upon them for good, and I will bring them again to this land: and I will build them, and **not pull them down**; and I will plant them, and **not pluck them up.**" Jer. 24:6.

The certainty of it is seen in Jer. 31:35, 36.

"Thus saith the Lord, which giveth the sun for a light by day and the ordinances of the moon and of the stars for a light by night, which divideth the sea when the waves thereof roar: the Lord of Hosts is His name: if those ordinances depart from me, said the Lord, **then the seed of Israel also shall cease from being a nation before Me forever.**"

When the Children of Israel shall be restored to their own land the whole "Twelve Tribes" will return. In Rom. 11:26, Paul says—"ALL Israel shall be saved," and Ezekiel in his vision of the

"Valley of Dry Bones"

was told that the bones represented the "**Whole House of Israel.**" Ez. 37:11.

There are some who teach that what is here meant is, that, previous to the Millennium God will resurrect all the descendants of Israel and put them back in the Land of Palestine, and they base it on the statement in Ez. 37:12—

"Behold, O my people, I will open your **graves**, and cause you to **come up out of your graves**, and **bring you into the Land of Israel**."

Now such an interpretation cannot be true for several reasons. First, the Land of Palestine is not large enough to hold and sustain such a great multitude, and secondly this is not a description of a **physical resurrection of dead bodies**, but of a "**National Resurrection**" of a people. The cry of the "bones" in verse 11, where they say—

"Our bones are dried, and our hope is lost: we are cut off for our parts,"

is not the cry of **individual dead Israelites**, but the cry of a **dead nation** that has been "cut off" from its own land. It is the cry of a Spiritually and **nationally** dead people.

By the word "graves" we are not to understand "literal graves," for the bones were **not in graves** but **scattered** over the valley. What the passage means is, that God is going to bring back His People Israel, who are buried in captivity in the "**Graveyard of the Nations**," and place them again in their own land. This is clear from what follows—

"I will open your **graves**, (among the nations), and cause you to come up out of your graves (that is back from among the nations), and bring you **into the Land of Israel**."

Notice that nothing is said here of the opening of any **graves in the Land of Israel**. This therefore could not be a **general resurrection of the Dead of Israel**, but only of Israelites who lived in other countries.

But **the** next two verses settle the question, for the Lord says—

"**When I have opened your graves, O my people, and brought you up out of your graves**" (that is, back into their own land), and **THERE shall put my spirit** (Holy Spirit) **in you, and ye shall live** (nationally) and I shall **place you in your own land:** (according to your Tribes, as described in Ez. 48:1-29), **then shall ye know that I the Lord have spoken it, and performed it, said the Lord**." Ez. 37:13, 14.

This is in exact accord with other scriptures that teach that Israel is to be gathered back to their own land, where they are to be first judged, (Ez. 20:34-38; 22:19-22), and **then converted**. Ez. 36:24-27.

If we are to take the resurrection spoken of by Daniel (Dan. 12:2), as referring to his "People" only, then we are still more certain that there is not to be a "General Physical Resurrection" of Daniel's "People," the Jews, before the Millennium, for he distinctly says that only **some shall** rise at that time.

That what is meant is a

National Restoration

of the **Whole Twelve Tribes**, is clear from what follows the Vision of the "Valley of Dry Bones." Ez. 37:15-28.

The Prophet is told to take a stick and write on it,

"**For Judah and for the Children of Israel** his companions,"

which means the Two Tribes, Judah and Benjamin, known as "**Judah.**"
Then he was told to take another stick, and write on it,

"**For Joseph**, the stick of Ephraim,"

the son of Joseph who represented him among the Twelve Tribes, and by whose name (Ephraim) the Ten Tribes, after Jeroboam's insurrection were sometimes called. Isa. 7:17.

When Ezekiel had done so, he was told to join the two sticks together, **end to end**, so as to make **one stick**, which when he had done, the Lord said—

"When the children of thy people shall speak unto thee saying, Wilt thou not shew us what thou meanest by these? Thou shalt say, Behold, I will take the Children of Israel from among the heathen, whither they be gone, and will gather them on every side, and bring them into their own land: and I will make them **ONE NATION** in the land upon the mountains of Israel, and one king shall be king to them all; and **they shall be no more two nations, neither shall they be divided into two kingdoms any more at all**." Ez. 37:18-22.

From this we see that the

"WHOLE HOUSE OF ISRAEL,"

that is, the **Whole Twelve Tribes**, are to be gathered back to their own land, and redistributed upon it according to the manner described in Ez. 48.

"In those days the 'House of Judah' shall walk with the 'House of Israel,' and they shall come together out of the land of the North to the land that I have given for an inheritance unto your fathers." Jer. 3:18.

The Lost Ten Tribes.

If the whole Twelve Tribes are to be restored to the Holy Land, naturally the question arises, "**Where Are They Now?**" The Jews are the descendants of the Tribes of Judah and Benjamin, but where are the remaining "**Ten Tribes?**" How are they to be identified?

Much has been written to try to prove that the "**Anglo Saxons,**" the English speaking race, are the descendants of the lost Ten Tribes. But they cannot be, for it is said of Israel, that "they shall **dwell alone, and not be reckoned among the nations**" (Num. 23:9), but the "Anglo-Saxons **are numbered among the nations**. Israel is to remain many days **without a King, a Prince or a Temple** (Hosea 3:4), but the "Anglo-Saxons" have **kings, presidents and princes**, and centres of religious worship. Again, Israel, out of the Holy Land, were to be few in number, and under national curse, (Deu. 4:26, 27; 28:62-68), but neither of these are true of the "Anglo-Saxons." Once more, the penalty of "**Uncircumcision**" is "**Excision**," (Gen. 17:10-14), the "Anglo-Saxons" are "**Uncircumcised**" and therefore not entitled to Jewish privileges.

The Jews Today Are Representative of the Whole Twelve Tribes.

1. A portion of Israel, **out of all the tribes**, fell away to Judah at the time of the division of Solomon's Kingdom, B. C. 975. 2 Chron. 11:5, 13-17.

2. A number **deserted from Israel** to Judah in the days of Asa, grandson of Rehoboam. 2 Chron. 15:8, 9.

3. Ninety-six years **after the Ten Tribes were carried captive**, in B. C. 625, Josiah, great grandson of Hezekiah, observed the

"Passover" at Jerusalem, and many were present of the "Remnant of Israel." 2 Chron. 35:17, 18.

4. In B. C. 605-587, Judah was carried captive to Babylon, and many Israelites were carried away with them.

5. In B. C. 536, when the Jews returned from the Babylonian Captivity, Babylon and Assyria had become identical, and Israel was as free to return as Judah. Ezra tells us that he took up some Israelites (Ezra 7:28), and when the Temple was dedicated they offered sacrifices for the **Whole Twelve Tribes**. Ezra 6:16, 17.

The conclusion therefore is, that those who returned from the Captivity were fairly representative of the whole Twelve Tribes. Now as the descendants of those who returned from Babylon were scattered in A. D. 70 and A. D. 135, we may well ask, "the 'Ten Tribes' **Where Are They Not?**"

But the above explanation will not completely satisfy the careful Bible student, for Ezek. 37:15-25 clearly teaches that the "Ten Tribes," as **tribes** are to be gathered back in the future. They must therefore be **somewhere**.

Says Sir John Wilkinson in his book "Israel My Glory," **search for a thing where it was lost.**" When God called Abraham from Ur of the Chaldeans it was from an idolatrous country, and he was called a Hebrew, (one who has crossed over), and when Israel relapsed into idolatry God sent them back to the other side of the Euphrates. History says the Ten Tribes were taken to Assyria, and prophecy says they are to be **brought out of Assyria** (Isa. 11:11, 16), the plain inference is **they are still there**.

Josephus says they were there in A. D. 70; so does Jerome in his notes on Hosea, written in the Fifth Century. We have never heard of their leaving, and so they have been identified with certain peoples living in the fastnesses of the mountains of Kurdistan, by Lake Oroomiah, in Persia. These people have many modified observances of the Mosaic Ritual, as Peace Offerings, Vows, First-Fruits, Tithes, etc. (Wilkinson.)

2. As To The TIME.

a. When the "TIMES OF THE GENTILES" Have Been Fulfilled.

"And they shall fall by the edge of the sword, and shall be led away captive into all nations; and Jerusalem shall be trodden down of the Gentiles, until the **"Times of the Gentiles" be fulfilled.**" Luke 21:24.

b. When Christ Returns.

"For I say unto you, Ye shall not see me henceforth, till ye shall say blessed **is He that cometh in the Name of the Lord.**" Matt. 23:39.

3. As To The Manner.

a. Gathered Back UNCONVERTED.

"I will take you from among the heathen, and gather you out of all countries, and will bring you into your own land. **THEN will I sprinkle clean water upon you,** and ye shall be clean: from all your filthiness, and from all your idols will I cleanse you. A **New Heart** also will I give you, and a **New Spirit** will I put within you: and I will give you an **Heart of Flesh.** And I will put **My Spirit within you,** and cause you to walk in my statutes; and ye shall keep my judgments, and do them." Ezek. 36:24-27.

b. Before Conversion They Are To Be JUDGED.

"I will bring you out from the people, and will gather you out of the countries wherein ye are scattered, with a mighty hand, and with a stretched out arm, and with fury poured out. And I will bring you into the wilderness of the people, and there will I plead with you face to face. . . . And I will cause you to

'**Pass Under The Rod,**'

and I will bring you into the bond of the Covenant; and I will **purge out from among you the rebels,** and them that **transgress against Me:** I will bring them forth out of the country where they sojourn, and they shall not enter into the Land of Israel." Ezek. 20:34-38.

Then God will cast them into His

"Melting Pot."

"Therefore thus saith the Lord God; Because ye are all become **dross,** behold, therefore I will gather you into the **midst of Jerusalem.** As they gather silver, and brass, and iron, and lead, and tin, into the midst of the furnace, to blow the fire upon it, to melt it; **so will I gather you in mine anger and in My fury and I will leave you there, and MELT YOU.** Yea I will gather you, and blow upon you in the fire of my wrath, and ye shall be **melted in the midst thereof.** As silver is melted in the midst of the furnace, **so shall ye be melted in the midst thereof;** and ye shall know that I the Lord have poured out my fury upon you." Ezek. 22:19-22.

"Behold, I will send my messenger (Elijah—Malachi 4:5, 6), and he shall prepare the way before me, and the Lord, whom ye seek, shall **suddenly come to His Temple,** even the Messenger of the Covenant, whom ye delight in: behold, He shall come, saith the Lord of hosts. But who may abide the day of His coming? and who shall stand when He appeareth? for He is like a **Refiner's Fire,** and like Fuller's Soap: and He shall sit as a **Refiner and Purifier of Silver:** and He shall **Purify the Sons of Levi,** and purge them as gold and silver, that they may offer unto the Lord an offering in righteousness." Malachi 3:1-3.

"And I will bring the **third part through the fire, and will refine them as silver is refined,** and will try them as **gold is tried:** they shall call on my name and I will hear them: I will say, it is my people; and they shall say, the Lord is my God." Zech. 13:9.

The Jews have never as yet had such an experience as this. It is spoken of in Jer. 30:4-7, and Dan. 12:1, as the

"**Time Of 'Jacob's Trouble,'**"

and Christ called it

"**THE GREAT TRIBULATION,**"

and He and Zechariah the Prophet associate it with the **Return of the Lord.** Matt. 24:21-31. Zech. 14:1-11.

The result of these terrible judgments will be that the Jews will call in their misery upon the Lord.

"And I will pour upon the 'House of David,' and upon the inhabitants of Jerusalem **The Spirit of Grace and of Supplications.**" Zech. 12:10.

Then Christ will come back to Jerusalem—

"And His feet shall stand in that day upon the **Mount of Olives which is before Jerusalem on the east.**" Zech. 14:4.

"And they shall look upon ME Whom They Have Pierced." Zech. 12:10.

And a nation, the Jewish Nation, shall be born (converted) IN A DAY.

"Who hath heard such a thing? who hath seen such things? Shall the earth be made to bring forth in one day? or shall a Nation Be Born At Once? for as soon as Zion Travailed, She Brought Forth Her Children." Isa. 66:8.

Speaking of the appearance of Christ after His Resurrection, Paul says,

"And last of all He was seen of me also, as of one born out of due time." 1 Cor. 15:8.

What Paul means is, that he was born before the time, that his was a premature birth, and that his "New Birth" is a type of the Birth of the Jewish Nation when the Lord returns, and not of the "New Birth" of a Christian. As Paul saw the glory of the Lord, and heard his voice, so shall it be with the Jewish Nation assembled at Jerusalem when Christ shall reveal Himself on the Mount of Olives at His return.

As to the Children of Israel, when they came out of Egypt they took with them of the "Riches of the Egyptians," Ex. 12:35, 36, so when they return to their own land they will take with them the "Riches of the Gentiles." Isa. 60:9; 61:6.

When the Children of Israel return to their own land it will be to possess and occupy all that was promised to Abraham.

"The Royal Grant"

given by the Almighty to Abraham, extended from the "River of Egypt" unto the "Great River," the River Euphrates (Gen. 15:18); and according to Ezekiel (Ezek. 48:1-29), from Hamath, north-east of Damascus, to Kadesh on the south. The Temple will be rebuilt. The Glory of the Lord will return. Sacrifices will again be offered. The Government shall be reestablished, and the nations of the earth will be blessed through Israel. Zech. 8:20-23.

For a continued account of the future of the Jews, see the chapters on "The Great Tribulation," and "The Kingdom." Also carefully study the chart on "The Jews," and "The Millennial Land."

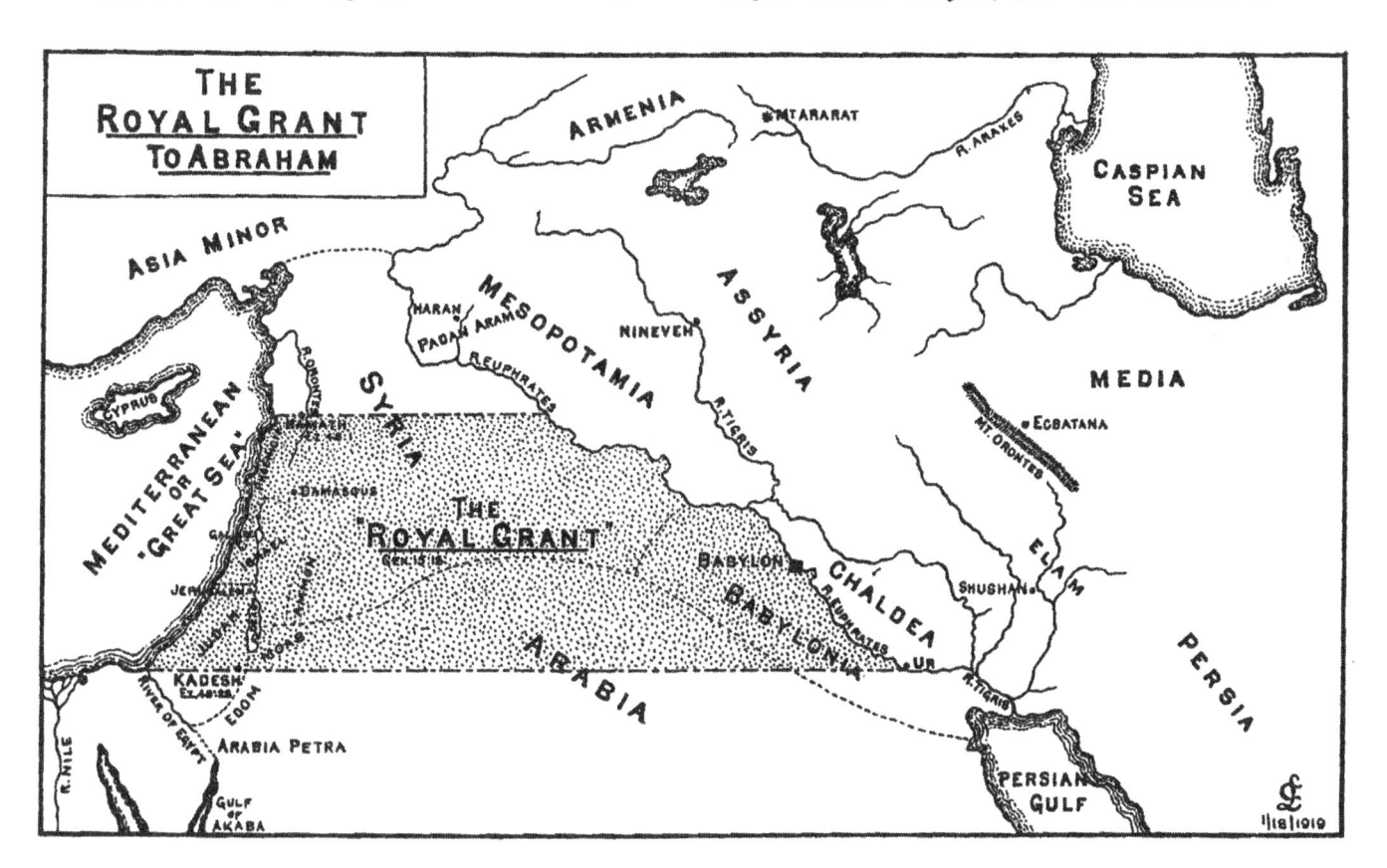

X

THE GENTILES

The Scriptures speak of three classes of people on the earth, the Jews, the Gentile, and the Church. The Church is made up of both Jew and Gentile. Outside of the Church all who are not Jews are Gentiles. Up to the call of Abraham all the people of the earth were Gentiles. Abraham was the first Hebrew. His grandson Jacob, whose name was changed to Israel (Gen. 32:24-28), had twelve sons. They became the heads of twelve tribes, known as the "Twelve Tribes of Israel." After the death of King Solomon these "Tribes" were divided. Ten of them became known as Israel, and two (Judah and Benjamin) as Judah. In B. C. 721 Israel was carried captive to Assyria, and in B. C. 606 Judah was carried captive to Babylon. When Judah, after seventy years, returned from captivity, a fair representation of the whole Twelve Tribes returned with them. From that time they have been known as the Jews.

The Jews were God's chosen people, but when they fell into idolatry and were carried into captivity, they were supplanted by the Gentiles. The nations of Egypt, Assyria, and Babylon were anxious to conquer and supplant Israel (The Jews), but God held them in an unseen leash until the iniquity of Israel was full, and then He permitted the world power to pass into the hands of Nebuchadnezzar, King of Babylon. Jer. 27:5-7. This happened in B. C. 606 and marked the beginning of the

"Times Of The Gentiles,"

spoken of by Christ in Luke 21:24, and which is a period that in the mind of God has certain chronological limits. It is not to be confounded with the "Fulness of the Gentiles" spoken of by Paul in Rom. 11:25. The "Fulness of the Gentiles" refers to the Gentiles that are "gathered out" to make up the Church, and "blindness in part" will continue among the Jews until the "Fulness" (the whole number of the elect) of the Gentiles be come in, then the Church is "caught out," and the Jews restored to their own land. The "Fulness of the Gentiles" began at Pentecost, and ends at least seven years before the "Times of the Gentiles" end.

The "Times of the Gentiles" are fully outlined in the Book of Daniel.

The Book of Daniel (see chart) contains one "Dream" by Nebuchadnezzar, and four "Visions" by Daniel all relating to the "Times of the Gentiles."

1. Nebuchadnezzar's Dream.

In the second year of Nebuchadnezzar's reign he had a dream, but when he awoke it had gone from him. He demanded of his magicians and astrologers that they should not only reproduce the dream, but that they should interpret it. This they were unable to do and their destruction was ordered, but was stayed by Daniel's petition for a little time. Then Daniel and his companions betook themselves to prayer, and in a night vision the "Dream" and its meaning was made known to Daniel. The interpretation is certainly one that human ingenuity could not have hit upon. The wise men and flatterers of the Chaldean court would never have dared to announce the **End of Gentile Supremacy.**

The "Colossus" (Image) symbolized the **"World Kingdoms"** in their **Unity** and **Historical Succession.** Gentile dominion is represented by a huge **"Metallic" Man.** The degeneration of the "World Kingdoms" is seen in the diminishing **value** of the metals used. Silver is worth less than gold, brass than silver, iron than brass, and clay than iron. The **weight** of the image also declines, the specific gravity of gold is 19.5, of silver 10.47, of brass 8, of cast-iron 5, and of clay 1.93. The "Colossus" is **Top-Heavy.**

The four metals of which the "Colossus" was composed represent

Four Worldwide Empires.

which were to arise in succession. Dan. 2:37-40. Four great Empires, and only four, are to succeed each other in the government of the world, from Nebuchadnezzar to the "Second Coming" of Christ—the Babylonian, Medo-Persian, Grecian, and Roman. These Kingdoms are not only made known as to **number,** but their **names,** in the **order of their succession,** are given. The First Kingdom—"Babylon" is indicated by Daniel while interpreting the vision to Nebuchadnezzar. "**THOU** art this **Head of Gold.**" Dan. 2:38. The Second—the "Medo-Persian," he points out in his account of Belshazzar's Feast, by the emphatic words—"In that night was Belshazzar the king of the Chaldeans slain, and Darius the **Median** took the Kingdom." Dan. 5:30, 31. The Third—the "Grecian," is mentioned in Dan. 8:20-21, "the ram which thou sawest having two horns are **The** kings of Media and Persia. And the rough goat is the **King of Grecia.**" The Fourth—the "Roman" is referred to in Dan. 9:26, as—"the **People** of the Prince that should destroy the city (Jerusalem) and the Sanctuary"; and we know that it was the **Romans** under Titus, that destroyed Jerusalem in A. D. 70.

We have seen that the deterioration of the "Colossus" is shown in the character of the metals composing it. This was prophetic of the character of the governments as they were to succeed one another. The power of Nebuchadnezzar was **Absolute,** of him Daniel said—

"All people, nations, and languages, trembled and feared him; **whom he would he slew; and whom he would he kept alive; and whom he would he set up; and whom he would he put down.**" Dan. 5:19.

The second Kingdom was inferior to the first. It was a Monarchy dependent upon the support of an **Hereditary Aristocracy.** The king could by no means do as he willed. This is seen in the case of Darius, who desired to save Daniel from the "Lions' Den," and could not, Dan. 6:12-16; and in the case of Ahasuerus who could only save the Jews from slaughter by a counter-decree. Esther 8:3-12. The metal of the third Kingdom was **brass,** and the government of Alexander the Great was a Monarchy supported by a **Military Aristocracy,** that was as weak as the ambitions of its leaders.

The iron power of the fourth Kingdom shows a still further depreciation. The Caesars were nominally elected by the people; they were merely called First Magistrates of the State or Generals; and for a long time they wore no diadem, but only the laurel crown of a successful commander. They had also a Senate which was supposed to counsel and control them. The people were neither allowed to legislate for them, nor to interfere with them, and if a Senator became too independent he was banished. Thus the Empire remained metallic and coherent. Iron is more perishable, more easily corroded or rusted than brass, or silver, or gold; but in the form of **STEEL** it is harder than any of them, and cuts through every other metal. Such has been Rome with her **iron** rule.

But the "Colossus" grows weaker and weaker until the feet and toes become a **mixture of Iron and Clay.** In other words the government degenerates from an **Absolute Monarchy** to an

Autocratic Democracy,

a form of government in which the people largely have the say.

Book Of Daniel

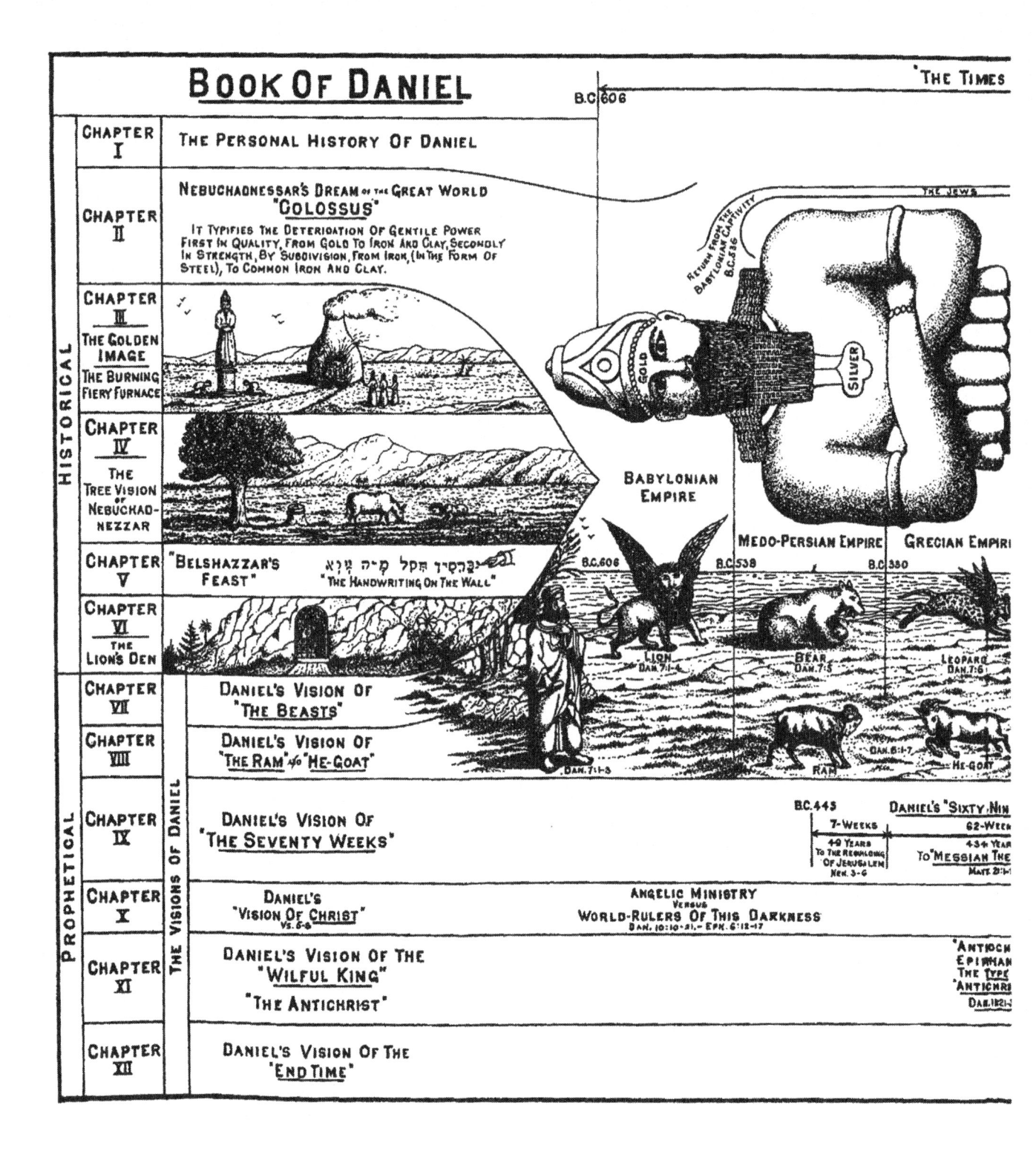

HISTORICAL	Chapter I	The Personal History Of Daniel
	Chapter II	Nebuchadnezzar's Dream of the Great World "Colossus" — It Typifies The Deterioration Of Gentile Power First In Quality, From Gold To Iron And Clay, Secondly In Strength, By Subdivision, From Iron, (In The Form Of Steel), To Common Iron And Clay.
	Chapter III	The Golden Image — The Burning Fiery Furnace
	Chapter IV	The Tree Vision of Nebuchadnezzar
	Chapter V	"Belshazzar's Feast" — "The Handwriting On The Wall"
	Chapter VI	The Lion's Den
PROPHETICAL	Chapter VII	Daniel's Vision Of "The Beasts"
	Chapter VIII	Daniel's Vision Of "The Ram" and "He-Goat"
	Chapter IX	Daniel's Vision Of "The Seventy Weeks"
	Chapter X	Daniel's "Vision Of Christ" vs. 5-8
	Chapter XI	Daniel's Vision Of The "Wilful King" — "The Antichrist"
	Chapter XII	Daniel's Vision Of The "End Time"

"The Times"

B.C. 606

Return From The Babylonian Captivity B.C. 536 — The Jews

Gold — **Silver**

Babylonian Empire — Medo-Persian Empire — Grecian Empire
B.C. 606 — B.C. 538 — B.C. 330

Lion Dan. 7:1-4 — Bear Dan. 7:5 — Leopard Dan. 7:6

Ram — He-Goat Dan. 8:1-7

B.C. 445
7-Weeks — 62-Weeks
49 Years To The Rebuilding Of Jerusalem Neh. 3-6 — 434 Years To "Messiah The Prince" Matt. 21:1-11

Daniel's "Sixty Nine Weeks"

Angelic Ministry versus World-Rulers Of This Darkness
Dan. 10:10-21 — Eph. 6:12-17

Antiochus Epiphanes The Type of Antichrist Dan. 18:21

The Visions Of Daniel

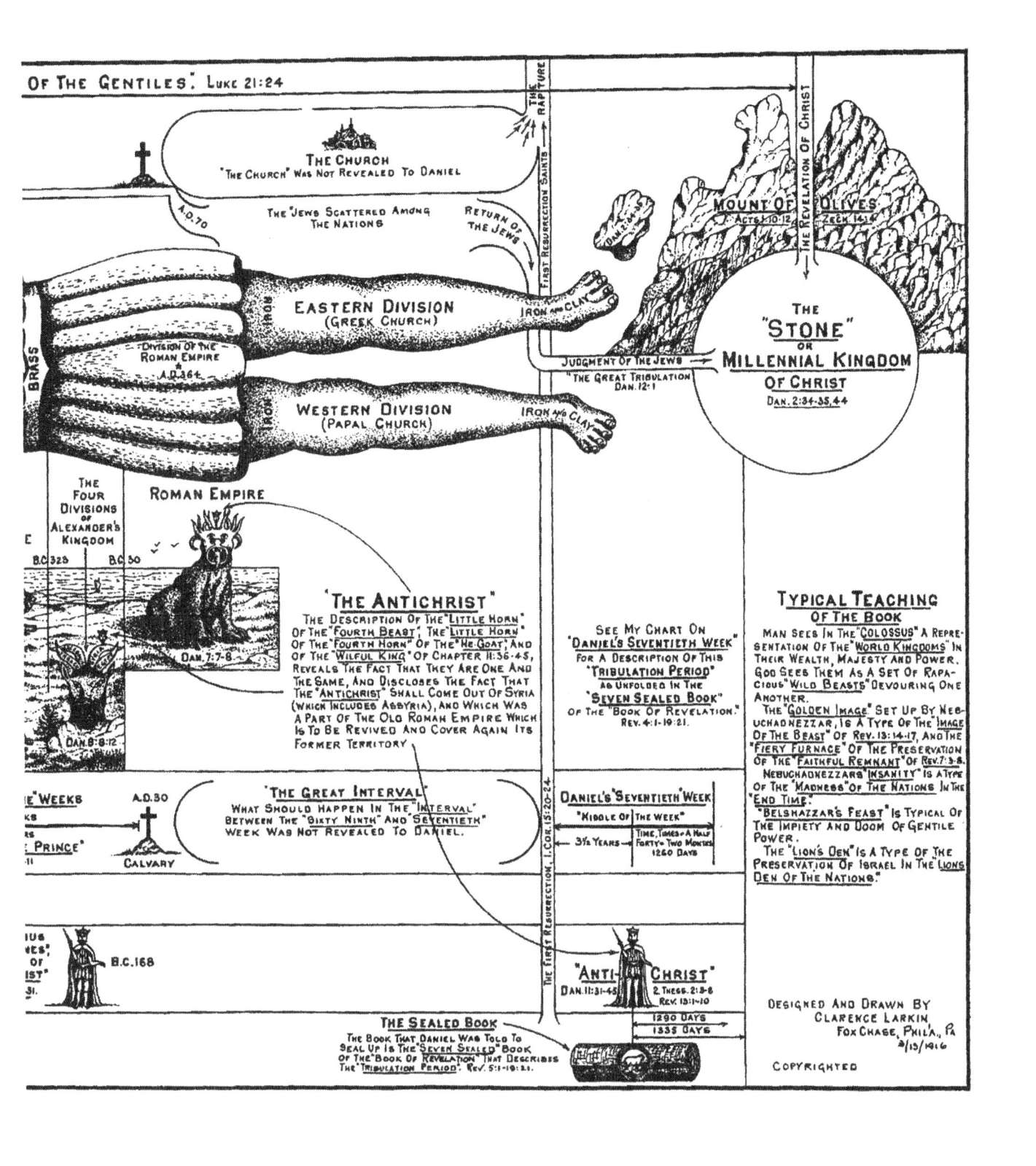

"OF THE GENTILES." Luke 21:24

THE CHURCH
"The Church" Was Not Revealed To Daniel

The Jews Scattered Among The Nations

Return Of The Jews

MOUNT OF OLIVES Acts 1:10-12 — The Revelation Of Christ — Zech 14:4

A.D. 70

EASTERN DIVISION (Greek Church) — IRON — IRON AND CLAY

BRASS — Division Of The Roman Empire A.D. 364

WESTERN DIVISION (Papal Church) — IRON — IRON AND CLAY

Judgment Of The Jews — "The Great Tribulation" Dan. 12:1

The **"STONE"** OR **MILLENNIAL KINGDOM** OF CHRIST
Dan. 2:34-35, 44

The Four Divisions Of Alexander's Kingdom
B.C. 323 — B.C. 30

ROMAN EMPIRE
Dan. 7:7-8

Dan. 8:8-12

"THE ANTICHRIST"
The Description Of The "Little Horn" Of The "Fourth Beast", The "Little Horn" Of The "Fourth Horn" Of The "He Goat", And Of The "Wilful King" Of Chapter 11:36-45, Reveals The Fact That They Are One And The Same, And Discloses The Fact That The "Antichrist" Shall Come Out Of Syria (Which Includes Assyria), And Which Was A Part Of The Old Roman Empire Which Is To Be Revived And Cover Again Its Former Territory

See My Chart On **"DANIEL'S SEVENTIETH WEEK"** For A Description Of This "Tribulation Period" As Unfolded In The **"SEVEN SEALED BOOK"** Of The "Book Of Revelation." Rev. 4:1-19:21.

TYPICAL TEACHING OF THE BOOK

Man Sees In The "Colossus" A Representation Of The "World Kingdoms" In Their Wealth, Majesty And Power. God Sees Them As A Set Of Rapacious "Wild Beasts" Devouring One Another.

The "Golden Image" Set Up By Nebuchadnezzar, Is A Type Of The "Image Of The Beast" Of Rev. 13:14-17, And The "Fiery Furnace" Of The Preservation Of The "Faithful Remnant" Of Rev. 7:3-8. Nebuchadnezzar's Insanity Is A Type Of The Madness Of The Nations In The "End Time".

"Belshazzar's Feast" Is Typical Of The Impiety And Doom Of Gentile Power.

The "Lion's Den" Is A Type Of The Preservation Of Israel In The "Lion's Den Of The Nations."

"THE GREAT INTERVAL"
What Should Happen In The "Interval" Between The "Sixty Ninth" And "Seventieth" Week Was Not Revealed To Daniel.

WEEKS — A.D. 30 — CALVARY — "PRINCE"

DANIEL'S SEVENTIETH WEEK
Middle Of The Week
3½ Years | Time, Times & A Half — Forty-Two Months — 1260 Days

B.C. 168

"ANTI-CHRIST"
Dan. 11:31-45
2. Thess. 2:3-8
Rev. 13:1-10
1290 Days
1335 Days

THE SEALED BOOK
The Book That Daniel Was Told To Seal Up Is The "Seven Sealed" Book Of The "Book Of Revelation" That Describes The "Tribulation Period". Rev. 5:1-19:21.

Designed And Drawn By
CLARENCE LARKIN
Fox Chase, Phila., Pa
2/15/1916

COPYRIGHTED

In short the "Colossus" shows that Gentile dominion passes gradually from the **Head**, the organ which ought to direct the members, to the **Feet**, which are only made to carry the body whither the head directs. We see then that the first of these Kingdoms was a **Unit**, the second **Dual**, the third became **Quadruple** (Dan. 7:6, 8:8), and the fourth, in its final form, becomes **Ten-Toed**.

The "Colossus" comes to an end by being smitten on the **Feet** by a "**Stone Cut Out of a Mountain.**" The "**Stone**" does not fill the earth **by degrees**, and thus crowd the "Colossus" out, it at **One Blow DEMOLISHES IT.** The action of the "**Stone**" is **JUDGMENT**, not grace. It therefore cannot mean Christianity, for it is a "process" whereas the action of the "**Stone**" is **SUDDEN** and **CALAMITOUS**.

Again the Time of the destruction is not until **after the formation of the toes**, and we know that the "**Two Limbs**" of the "Colossus" did not appear until A. D. 364, and the "**Ten Toes**" have not yet developed. The Time when the "Stone" falls on the "Colossus" is distinctly stated in the interpretation as "**in the days of those kings,**" that is, in the days of the kings represented by the "**Ten Toes.**"

The "**Stone**" which smites the "Colossus" must be interpreted **as Christ** who is called a "**Stone**" in Scripture. "Whosoever shall fall on this stone (Christ) shall be broken (softened by repentance), but on whomsoever it shall fall, **it will grind him to powder.**" Matt. 21:44. This is exactly what the prophet foretells of the smiting of the "Colossus."

> "Then was the iron, the clay, the brass, the silver, and the gold, broken to pieces together, and became like **the chaff of the summer threshing floors; and the wind carried them away, that no place was found for them;** and the Stone that smote the image **became a great mountain, and filled the whole earth.**" Dan. 2:35.

As the four Kingdoms typified by the "Colossus" are literal Kingdoms, it follows that the "**Stone Kingdom**" must be a literal Kingdom, for it takes the place of the Kingdoms that are destroyed, and **conquers the whole earth.** The "**Stone Kingdom**" then is the "**Millennial Kingdom of Christ**" and the "Colossus," or the

"Times of the Gentiles"

typified by it, cannot come to an end until the "**revelation of Christ**" at His Second Coming.

2. The Vision of the "FOUR BEASTS."

This was a vision of Daniel's 48 years after Nebuchadnezzar had his dream, and occurred in the first year of Belshazzar, B. C. 555. In vision Daniel stood on the shore of the "Great Sea" (the Mediterranean), from which region the four Kingdoms arose. Out of the sea four "Great Beasts" came up in succession. We have no difficulty in identifying these "Four Beasts" with the "Four Kingdoms" represented by the "Colossus." "The first was like a **Lion** and had **Eagle's Wings,**" and as the Prophet watched it, he saw it "lifted up from the earth, and made stand upon its feet as a Man, and a **Man's Heart** was given to it. Dan. 7:4. We have only to visit the British Museum, London, and examine the colossal stone lions with the "wings of an eagle" and the "head of a man," disinterred from the ruins of Babylon and Assyria by Sir Henry Layard between the years 1840 and 1850 A. D., to see that the "First Beast" of Daniel's vision represented the First World Kingdom—Babylon, and its King Nebuchadnezzar.

The peculiarity of the "First Beast" was that it had "**Eagle's Wings.**" This combination of the **lion**, the "King of Beasts," and the **eagle**, the "King of Birds," corresponded to the Royalty of the "Head of Gold" of the Colossus, and typified the "Eagle-like" swiftness of the armies of Nebuchadnezzar. The "Plucking of the Wings" doubtless referred to the "Beastly Insanity" of Nebuchadnezzar (Dan. 4:20-27), and the "lifting up," and causing to stand upon its feet "as a man" to his restoration to sanity.

The Second Beast was "like to a **Bear,** and it raised up itself on one side, and it had **Three Ribs** in the mouth of it, between the teeth of it; and they said thus unto it, **Arise, Devour Much Flesh.**" Dan. 7:5. The bear is the strongest beast after the lion and is distinguished for its voracity, but it has none of the agility and majesty of the lion, is awkward in its movements, and effects its purpose with comparative slowness, and by brute force and sheer strength. These were the characteristics of the Medo-Persian Empire. It was ponderous in its movements. It did not gain its victories by bravery or skill, but overwhelmed its enemies by hurling vast masses of troops upon them. Xerxes' expedition against Greece was undertaken with 2,500,000 fighting men, who with the camp followers made up an army of 5,000,000. Other Persian generals had armies running up into the 100,000's of men. It is easy to be seen that the movements of such enormous bodies of men would "devour much flesh," not only in the destruction of their enemies, but thousands would die of disease and exposure and the countries through which they passed would become famine-stricken by the loss of food seized to feed such armies. The side of the Bear which raised up to attack typified Persia, in which lay the greatest military strength, and corresponded to the right shoulder and arm of the "Colossus." The "Three Ribs" stood for the three Kingdoms of Lydia, Babylon and Egypt, which formed a "Triple Alliance" to check the Medo-Persian power, but were all destroyed by it.

The Third Beast was "like a **Leopard,** which had upon the back of it **four wings of a fowl**; the Beast had also **four heads**; and dominion was given to it." Dan. 7:6. The leopard is the most agile and graceful of creatures; but its speed is here still further assisted by "wings." Slight in its frame, but strong, swift and fierce, its characteristics render it a fitting symbol of the rapid conquests of the Greeks under Alexander the Great, who, followed by small but well-equipped and splendidly brave armies, moved with great celerity and in about 10 years overthrew the unwieldy forces of Persia, and subdued the whole civilized world. The "four wings of a Fowl" indicate, that, as a "fowl" does not fly high, the armies of Alexander were fitted mainly for lowland fighting. There is an incongruity between the number of "wings" and the number of "heads" of the Leopard. "Four heads" call for "four pair of wings." Why only "four" wings we do not know, unless they denote the four quarters of the earth into which Alexander sought to extend his Kingdom.

The "Four Heads" of the Leopard represent the "Four Kingdoms" into which the Empire of Alexander was divided by his generals, namely Egypt, Syria, Thrace and Macedonia. From B. C. 323 to B. C. 30 there was no world-wide Kingdom, there being this break or parenthesis between the Medo-Persian and Roman Empires, showing that while there was to be "four" and "only four" world-wide Empires it did not necessarily follow that there should be no break between them. The Third Beast, the Leopard, corresponds to the abdomen and hips of the Colossus.

The Fourth Beast was unlike any beast that Daniel had ever seen or heard about, it was "**dreadful and terrible, and strong exceedingly,** and it had great **IRON TEETH.** It devoured and brake in pieces, and stamped the residue (the other Beasts) with the feet of it; and it was diverse from all the Beasts that were before it and it had "**Ten Horns.**"

The fact that the Fourth Beast had "**Iron Teeth,**" and that there were "**Ten Horns**" on its head, the "iron" corresponding to the "**Iron Limbs**" and the "ten horns" to the "**Ten Toes**" of the Colossus, would cause Daniel to see that the Fourth Beast represented the Fourth World Kingdom.

But as Daniel "considered" the "Ten Horns," he was amazed to see another Horn, a "LITTLE" one, come up among them, and before whom there were "three" of the "First Horns" plucked up by the roots, that is destroyed; and as he examined the "Little Horn" more closely he noticed that it had Eyes like the eyes of a Man, and the Mouth of a Man speaking great things. Dan. 7:7, 8. This mystified and troubled Daniel. He had seen nothing corresponding to it on the "Ten Toes" of the Colossus. It must mean some new and additional revelation that God did not see fit to impart to the Gentile King Nebuchadnezzar, and that was reserved for Daniel and his people (the Jews), for we must not forget that Daniel's own visions, in the last six chapters of the Book, have to do with God's dealings with the Jewish People in the "Latter Days." Dan. 10:14.

Before Daniel could ask for an explanation of the meaning of the "Little Horn," he had another vision, a vision of a Judgment. Dan. 7:9-14. Daniel's vision of the destruction of the Beast (vs. 11) locates this Judgment as just before the Millennium. Daniel at the same time saw the "Son of Man" (Christ) receive His Kingdom (the Stone Kingdom). Vs. 13, 14. These visions added to Daniel's perplexity, and he was "grieved in his spirit," and the visions of his head "troubled him" (vs. 15), so he approached one of the "Heavenly Messengers" that stood by and asked him the meaning. He was told that the "Four Beasts" stood for Four Kings, or Kingdoms (vs. 23), that should arise out of the earth. Then Daniel wanted to know the "truth" about the "Fourth Beast," which was so diverse from the other three. The "Little Horn" of the Fourth Beast was what troubled him the most because it was to make war against the

"Saints of the Most High,"

and they were Daniel's own people, the God-fearing Jews of the "End Time," who were to pass through the "Great Tribulation" and to be prevailed against, until the time came that the people (the Jews) of the "Saints of the Most High" should possess the Kingdom.

In explanation Daniel was told that the "Ten Horns" on the Fourth Beast represented "Ten Kings" that shall arise, and that the "Little Horn" was a king that should rise among them and subdue three of them, and that he would be a "person" of remarkable intelligence and great oratorical powers, having a mouth speaking great things (vs. 8, 20). That he would be audacious, arrogant, imperious and persecuting and change "times and laws," and that the "Saints of the Most High" would be given into his hands for a "Time, and Times, and the Dividing of Time," or 3½ years. For a further description of the "Little Horn" see the Chapter on "The Antichrist."

In this vision of the Four Beasts we see "Degeneration" just as we saw it in the metals of the Colossus. The descent is from the Lion, the "King of Beasts," to a nondescript monster that defies description. The reason why these Four Kingdoms are represented first as a "Golden Headed Metallic Image," and then as a succession of "Wild Beasts," is to show the difference between man's view and God's view of the World Kingdoms. Man sees in them the concentration of wealth, majesty and power; God sees them as a succession of rapacious wild beasts devouring one another.

3. The Vision of the "RAM" and the "HE-GOAT."

The explanation as to the meaning of the "Little Horn" perplexed Daniel, and he voiced it by saying, "My 'cogitations' much troubled me, and my countenance changed in me; but I kept the matter in 'my heart.'" Dan. 7:28. To comfort His servant, God, two years later, transported Daniel in vision to Shushan, the capital of Persia, and as he stood on the bank of the river Ulai, he saw a Ram which had "Two Horns," one higher than the other, and the higher came up last. He saw the Ram push "Westward" and "Northward" and "Southward" and nothing could stand before it, and it did according to its will. Dan. 8:4. While Daniel was "considering" what the vision of the Ram meant, he saw a He-Goat come from the West unmolested, and he noticed it had a "Notable Horn" between its eyes, and when it reached the Ram it was moved with "choler" or anger against it, and smote it with "fury," and broke its "Two Horns," and knocked it down and stamped upon it.

Then the He-Goat waxed great, but when it became strong its "Great Horn" was broken off, and "Four Notable Horns" came up in its place, and out of one of them sprang a "Little Horn" which waxed exceeding great toward the "South" and toward the "East," and toward the "Pleasant Land" (Palestine). Dan. 8:5-9.

When Daniel sought for the meaning of the vision he heard a voice say—"Gabriel, make this man to understand the vision." Then Gabriel said to Daniel: The vision belongs to the 'Time of the End,' and is to make thee know what shall come to pass in the "Last End of the Indignation." Dan. 8:15-19. Gabriel then informed Daniel that the "Ram" stood for the Medo-Persian Kingdom, with its two Kings, Darius and his nephew Cyrus; that the He-Goat stood for the Grecian Kingdom, the "Great Horn" between its eyes for its first King (Alexander the Great), and that the "Four Horns" that took the place of the "Great Horn" stood for Four Kingdoms into which the Grecian Kingdom should be divided.

This explanation cleared up things considerably for Daniel. It revealed to him that the "Two Horns" of the Ram, one higher than the other, and the "Two Shoulders" of the Bear, one higher than the other, of his vision of the "Four Wild Beasts;" and the "Two Arms" of the Colossus of Nebuchadnezzar's dream, must stand for the same thing, and that the double Kingdom of Medo-Persia. He also saw that the "Four Horns" that came up in the place of the "Great Horn" corresponded to the "Four Heads" of the Third Wild Beast (the Leopard) and that therefore the He-Goat and the Third Wild Beast and the "Abdomen and Hips" of the Colossus stood for the Grecian Kingdom, and its fourfold division among the generals of Alexander the Great.

We have already anticipated this in our explanation of the "Colossus" and of the "Four Wild Beasts," but we must not forget that Daniel's information was progressive, and that each new vision threw light on his previous visions. For instance the Ram's pushing "Westward" and "Northward" and "Southward," identifies it with the Bear crunching "Three Ribs" in its mouth which we saw was prophetic of the subjugation of Lydia to the "West," Babylon to the "North," and Egypt to the "South."

If the He-Goat had not been pointed out as the "King of Grecia" it would not be difficult for us to identify him, for the "Goat" was the national emblem of Macedonia, and is found on the coins of that country, the ancient capital of which was called "Aegae" or the "Goat City."

The same may be said as to the identification of the Ram with the Medo-Persian Kingdom.

Persian coins have been found which display a "Ram's Head" on one side, and a "Ram" incumbent on the other. We also read of a Persian king riding in front of his army wearing a golden figure of a "Ram's Head" set with gems, instead of a diadem. In the Zendavesta, Ized Behram, the guardian spirit of Persia, appears as a "Ram," with clean feet and sharp-pointed horns.

The fury and violence of the He-Goat well depicts the vigor of Alexander the Great's attacks which carried everything before them. Rushing from the West, Alexander, in three great battles, made himself master of the world. But the "Great Horn" was suddenly broken off, for Alexander, with plans inconceivably vast, succumbed to marsh fever and intemperance at Babylon, in the thirty-third year of his life, and, in fulfillment of the prophecy "Four Horns" sprang up in the place of the "Great Horn."

These "Four Horns" stood for the four Generals of Alexander's army who divided his Kingdom among themselves. Cassander took possession of Macedonia. Lysimachus seized upon Thrace, Western Bithynia, Lower Phrygia, Mysia and Lydia. Seleucus took the remainder of Asia Minor and the East, including Syria and Assyria. Ptolemy took possession of Egypt. These Four Kingdoms were in time all absorbed into the Fourth World Kingdom, the Roman Empire. The last to lose its identity being Egypt, which succumbed in B. C. 30.

Soon after the appearance of these "Four Horns" on the head of the He-Goat Daniel saw a "Little Horn" come up on one of them. Gabriel explained the significance of this "Little Horn" to Daniel.

He told him that it stood for a King of "Fierce Countenance" who should stand up in the "Latter Time" of the Kingdom, and who should stand up against the "Prince of Princes" (Christ). Dan. 8: 23-25. The description of this "Little Horn" so clearly corresponds with the description of the "Little Horn" that rose among the "Ten Horns" on the head of the Fourth Wild Beast that it was not difficult for Daniel to see that they described and stood for the same Person—THE ANTICHRIST. The revelation so overcame Daniel that he "fainted" and was sick certain days. Dan. 8: 27.

4. The Vision of the "KINGS OF THE NORTH AND SOUTH."

While Daniel foresaw that the Kingdom of Alexander the Great would be divided into Four Kingdoms and that out of one of them would come the "Antichrist," he was not told at that time which one it would be, but 20 years later, in B. C. 533, he had another vision in which he saw two kings warring against each other. One was called the "King of the North," the other the "King of the South." This chapter (Dan. 11: 1-45) is one of the most wonderfully minute as to prophetic details of any chapter in the Bible. It corresponds exactly with the profane history of the kings of Egypt and Syria for over 350 years. From verse 5 to verse 31 we have an account of what is called the "wars" of the "Kings of the North" (Syria) and of the "Kings of the South" (Egypt). These end with the close of the reign of Antiochus Epiphanes, B. C. 164. Verses 32-35 cover the whole period from B. C. 164 down to the "Time of the End." At verse 36 "The Wilful King" (Antichrist) appears, and from that verse down to the end of the Book, we have an account of what is to befall Daniel's People in the "Latter Days." This vision of the "King of the North" (Syria), and of the "King of the South" (Egypt), in which the "King of the North" prevailed, revealed to Daniel that Antichrist would arise in the "Syrian" division of Alexander's Kingdom, for the description of the "King of the North" corresponded with the description of the "Little Horn" that came up on one of the "Four Horns" of the He-Goat, and also with the "Little Horn" that came up among the "Ten Horns" on the head of the Fourth Beast.

Thus to Daniel was revealed the whole course of the "Times of the Gentiles."

5. The Vision of the "SEVENTY WEEKS."

In chapter nine Daniel had a Vision of "Seventy Weeks" that were determined on his "People" (the Jews) and the Holy City (Jerusalem) to finish "their transgressions," and make an "end of their sins," and bring in "everlasting righteousness." Dan. 9: 24. This Vision of the

"Seventy Weeks"

is the most important revelation in many respects made in the Scriptures. It set the date of the First Coming of Christ, and gives the length of the reign of Antichrist.

The date of the "Vision" is important. The first verse of the chapter locates it in the "First Year" of Darius the Median, or the same year as the "Fall of Babylon," B. C. 538. Daniel had been studying the Prophecy of Jeremiah, and learned from it that the 70 years of "Captivity" of his people were drawing to a close, for the "Captivity" began in B. C. 606, and 68 years had elapsed since then. Jer. 25: 11. This discovery thrilled Daniel and he set his face toward God and poured out his soul in one of the most wonderful prayers recorded in the Scriptures. Verses 3-19. It is a model of confession, supplication and intercession. His prayer was interrupted by the appearance of the angel Gabriel, who had been sent at its commencement to give him "understanding in the matter." Vs. 20-23. Daniel was concerned about the end of the "seventy years" of the "Captivity," and doubtless Gabriel relieved his mind as to that, but Gabriel had something more important to reveal to Daniel and that was the period of "Seventy Weeks."

The purpose of Gabriel's visit was to show Daniel that while his people would be restored to their own land at the end of the "Seventy Years," that did not mean the restoration of their National Life, but was only the commencement of a longer period, which the angel called the "Seventy Weeks," that must elapse before they should again be in control of their own land. This period was "determined" upon Daniel's people, and upon the Holy City. This is very important. It discloses the fact that the "Seventy Weeks" have nothing to do with the Gentiles or the Church. It also discloses another fact that the "Seventy Weeks," or 490 years, only cover the period when the Jews are, by God's permission, dwelling as a people in their own land. It does not cover the present period of their Dispersion.

THE SEVENTY WEEKS

The expression "Seventy Weeks" should read "Seventy Sevens." Whether those "sevens" are days, weeks or years is to be determined by the context. The "Period" of the "Seventy Weeks" is divided into three periods of "Seven Weeks," "Threescore and Two Weeks" and "One Week," and it was to be 7+62=69 weeks from the going forth of the "commandment" to Restore and Build Jerusalem Unto

"MESSIAH THE PRINCE."

The date of the "commandment" is given in Nehemiah 2: 1 as the month "Nisan" in the twentieth year of Artaxerxes the king, which was the 14th day of March, B. C. 445. The day when Jesus rode in Trumphal Entry into Jerusalem as "Messiah the Prince," was Palm Sunday, April 2, A. D. 30. Luke 19: 37-40. But the time between March 14, B. C. 445, and April 2, A. D. 30, is more than 69 literal "weeks." It is 445+30=475 years. What explanation can we give for this? It is clear to every careful student of the Word of God that there is a "Time Element" in the Scriptures. We come across such divisions of time as "hours;" "days;" "weeks;" "months;" "years;" "times;" "time and the dividing of time." To be intelligible and avoid confusion they must all be interpreted on the same scale. What is that scale? It is given in Num. 14: 34. "After the number of the days in which ye searched the land, even forty days—Each Day FOR A YEAR, shall ye bear your iniquities, even forty years." See also Ezek. 4: 6

The "Lord's Scale" then is—

"A Day Stands for a Year."

Let us apply this scale to the "Seventy Weeks." We found that the time between the "commandment" to restore and build Jerusalem, and "Messiah the Prince," was to be 69 weeks, or 69×7=483 days, or if a "day" stands for a year, 483 years. But we found that from B. C. 445 to A. D. 30 was 475 years, a difference of 8 years. How can we account for the difference?

We must not forget that there are years of different lengths. The Lunar year has 354 days. The Calendar year has 360 days. The Solar year has 365 days. The Julian, or Astronomical year, has 365¼ days, and it is necessary to add one day every 4 years to the calendar.

Now which of these years shall we use in our calculation? We find the "Key" in the Word of God. In Gen. 7:11-24; 8:3, 4, in the account of the Flood, we find that the 5 months from the 17th day of the 2d month, until the 17th day of the 7th month, are reckoned as 150 days, or 30 days to a month, or 360 days to a year. So we see that we are to use in "Prophetical Chronology" a "Calendar" year of 360 days.

According to ordinary chronology, the 475 years from B. C. 445 to A. D. 30 are "Solar" years of 365 days each. Now counting the years from B. C. 445 to A. D. 30, inclusively, we have 476 solar years. Multiplying these 476 years by 365 (the number of days in a Solar year), we have 173,740 days, to which add 119 days for leap years, and we have 173,859 days. Add to these 20 days inclusive from March 14 to April 2, and we have 173,879 days. Divide 173,879 by 360 (the number of days in a "Prophetical Year"), and we have 483 years all to one day, the exact number of days (483) in 69 weeks, each day standing for a year. Could there be anything more conclusive to prove that Daniel's 69 weeks ran out on April 2, A. D. 30, the day that Jesus rode in triumph into the City of Jerusalem.

We must carefully notice that nothing is mentioned as occurring between the "Seven Weeks" and the "Threescore and Two Weeks," and that Daniel was to understand that the latter followed the former without a break. The words that follow, "the street shall be built, and the wall, even in troublous times," doubtless refers to the "first period" or 49 years, occupied by Ezra and Nehemiah in the work of restoring and rebuilding the City of Jerusalem.

We see from this that if the "Students of Prophecy" of Christ's day had been on the alert, and had understood Daniel's prophecy of the "Seventy Weeks," they would have been looking for Him, and would have known to a certainty whether He was the Messiah or not.

While there was no break between the "Seven Weeks" and the "Threescore and Two Weeks," there is a break between the "Sixty-ninth" and "Seventieth Week," in which several things were to happen.

First we read that **"Messiah Was to Be Cut Off, But Not for Himself."** This refers to Christ's rejection and crucifixion. He died for others. Then we read that the people of the **"Prince That Shall Come"** shall destroy the City and the Sanctuary. Note that it does not say that the **"Prince"** will destroy the City and Sanctuary, but the People of the Prince. The people who destroyed the City of Jerusalem and the Temple in A. D. 70 were the Romans, therefore the "Prince (Antichrist) must be a Roman Citizen. This does not mean that he cannot be a Syrian Jew, for Syria will then be a part of the revived Roman Empire, and Saul of Tarsus was a Roman citizen as well as a Jew.

We are then told that the desolation of the land of Palestine shall continue until the "End of the War" (probably Armageddon). As this "desolation" still continues we see that the "GAP" between the "Sixty-ninth" and "Seventieth Week" takes in the whole of this PRESENT DISPENSATION.

The next verse (vs. 27) introduces the "Seventieth Week."

"And He (the "Prince"—Antichrist) shall confirm the Covenant with many for ONE WEEK (the Seventieth Week); and in the MIDST (middle) of the Week He (the Antichrist), shall cause the sacrifice and oblation to cease," etc.

For a description of the "Seventieth Week" see the chapter on "The Tribulation."

THE TIMES OF THE GENTILES

In Luke 21:24 Jesus says that Jerusalem shall be trodden down of the Gentiles until the "Times of the Gentiles" be fulfilled.

We have seen that the "Times of the Gentiles" began in B. C. 606; is there any way of telling when they will end?

There are those who claim that Jesus meant by the word "Times," "Prophetical Times," and that a Prophetical "Time" is a year of 360 days, each day standing for a year, thus making a "Time" equal to 360 years. They also claim that Moses in the Book of Leviticus (Lev. 26:18-21, 24-28), foretold, and four times repeated it, that if the Children of Israel disobeyed God, He would punish them "Seven Times" for their sins and that Jesus referred to these "Seven Times" when He spoke of the "TIMES" of the Gentiles. Therefore if a "Time" is 360 years, "Seven Times" would be 7×360=2520 years; and as the "Times of the Gentiles" began in B. C. 606, they should end in A. D. 1914.

Can this claim be substantiated? In the Book of Revelation the last "half" of the "Seventieth Week" of Daniel is described by three statements of time. First by 42 months (Rev. 11:2; 13:5); second by 1260 days (Rev. 11:3; 12:6); third by "Time, and Times, and Half a time" (Rev. 12:14); this last corresponding with Daniel's "Time and times and the dividing of time." Dan 7:25; 12:7. Now as all these statements of time apply to the same period it is clear that the things that are equal to the same thing are equal to each other; and as a "thousand, two hundred and threescore days" equal 1260 days, and 1260 days equal 42 months of 30 days each, and 42 months equal 3½ years, then "Time, Times and Half a Time" (or the dividing of time), must equal 3½ years. That is, a "Time" must equal one year; and "Times," two years; and a "Half a Time," half a year. So we see that in "Prophetical Chronology" a "Time" is equal to a year of 360 days, and not a year of 360 years. There is therefore no scriptural authority for calling a "Time" 360 ordinary years.

If a "Time" was 360 ordinary years, then the "times, and times, and half a time" of Rev. 12:14 would be equal to 360+720+180 or 1260 years, making the "Last Week" of Daniel's "Seventy Weeks" 2520 years long; the absurdity of which is seen when we remember that the last week of the "Seventy Weeks" must be on the same scale as the "Weeks" of the 69 Week Period, which we proved from history were only 7 years long.

If the claim that the "Times of the Gentiles" is 2520 years long is correct, then we must not forget that those years are years of 360 days each. Now 2520 years of 360 days each, make 907,200 days. But exactly 2523 Julian or "Astronomical Years" of 365¼ days each, or 921,516 days, have elapsed since B. C. 606 up to the present time (A. D. 1917), a difference of 14,316 days. If we reduce these 2523 years of 365¼ days to years of 360 days, then we must divide 921,516 by 360, which gives us 2559¾ years, which is 39¾ years more than 2520 years, so that the 2520 years of the "Times of the Gentiles" ran out 39¾ years ago, or in A. D. 1877.

As further proof that the "Seven Times" of Leviticus are not Prophetic "Times," we have the fact (shown on the chart on "Prophetical Chronology"), that the Children of Israel have been punished, or given over to "Servitude" and "Captivity" exactly SEVEN times. Their present "Dispersion" is neither a "Servitude" or "Captivity," and does not count.

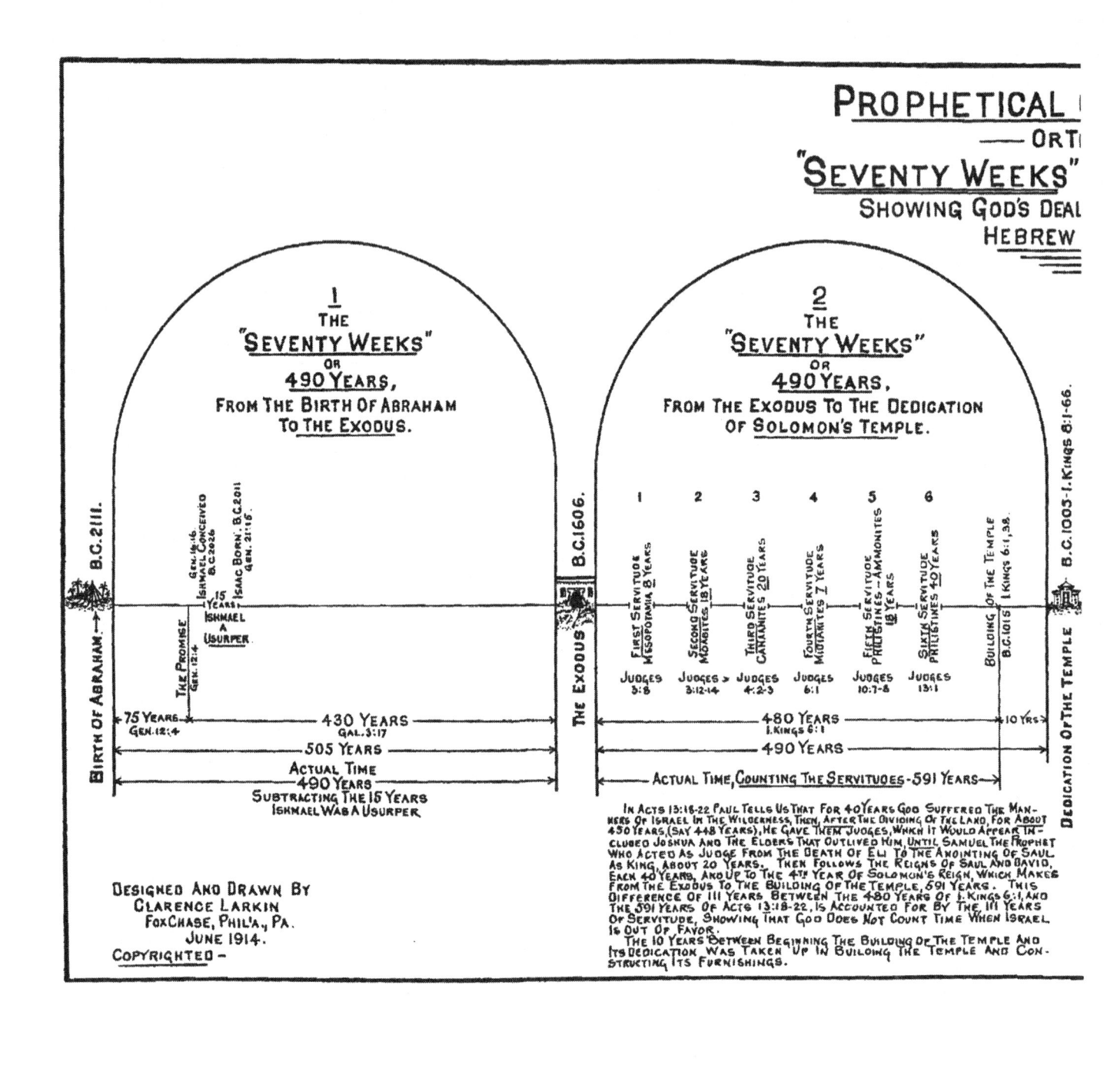

PROPHETICAL
—— OR T...
"SEVENTY WEEKS"
SHOWING GOD'S DEAL...
HEBREW...

1. THE "SEVENTY WEEKS" OR 490 YEARS, FROM THE BIRTH OF ABRAHAM TO THE EXODUS.

- B.C. 2111 — Birth of Abraham
- 75 Years — Gen. 12:4
- The Promise — Gen. 12:4
- Gen. 16 — Ishmael Conceived B.C. 2026
- Isaac Born B.C. 2011 — Gen. 21:1-6
- 15 Years — Ishmael a Usurper
- 430 Years — Gal. 3:17
- 505 Years Actual Time
- 490 Years Subtracting the 15 Years Ishmael Was a Usurper

Designed and Drawn By
Clarence Larkin
FoxChase, Phil'a., Pa.
June 1914.
Copyrighted —

2. THE "SEVENTY WEEKS" OR 490 YEARS, FROM THE EXODUS TO THE DEDICATION OF SOLOMON'S TEMPLE.

- The Exodus — B.C. 1606
- 1. First Servitude Mesopotamia 8 Years — Judges 3:8
- 2. Second Servitude Moabites 18 Years — Judges 3:12-14
- 3. Third Servitude Canaanites 20 Years — Judges 4:2-3
- 4. Fourth Servitude Midianites 7 Years — Judges 6:1
- 5. Fifth Servitude Philistines – Ammonites 18 Years — Judges 10:7-8
- 6. Sixth Servitude Philistines 40 Years — Judges 13:1
- Building of the Temple — B.C. 1015 — I. Kings 6:1, 38
- Dedication of the Temple — B.C. 1005 — I. Kings 8:1-66
- 480 Years — I. Kings 6:1
- 10 Yrs
- 490 Years
- Actual Time, Counting the Servitudes — 591 Years

In Acts 13:18-22 Paul tells us that for 40 years God suffered the manners of Israel in the Wilderness, then, after the dividing of the land, for about 450 years, (say 448 years), He gave them Judges, which it would appear included Joshua and the Elders that outlived him, until Samuel the Prophet who acted as Judge from the death of Eli to the anointing of Saul as King, about 20 years. Then follows the reigns of Saul and David, each 40 years, and up to the 4th year of Solomon's reign, which makes from the Exodus to the building of the Temple, 591 years. This difference of 111 years between the 480 years of I. Kings 6:1, and the 591 years of Acts 13:18-22, is accounted for by the 111 years of Servitude, showing that God does not count time when Israel is out of favor.

The 10 years between beginning the building of the Temple and its Dedication was taken up in building the Temple and constructing its furnishings.

CHRONOLOGY
HE ——
OF SCRIPTURE
..INGS WITH THE
RACE

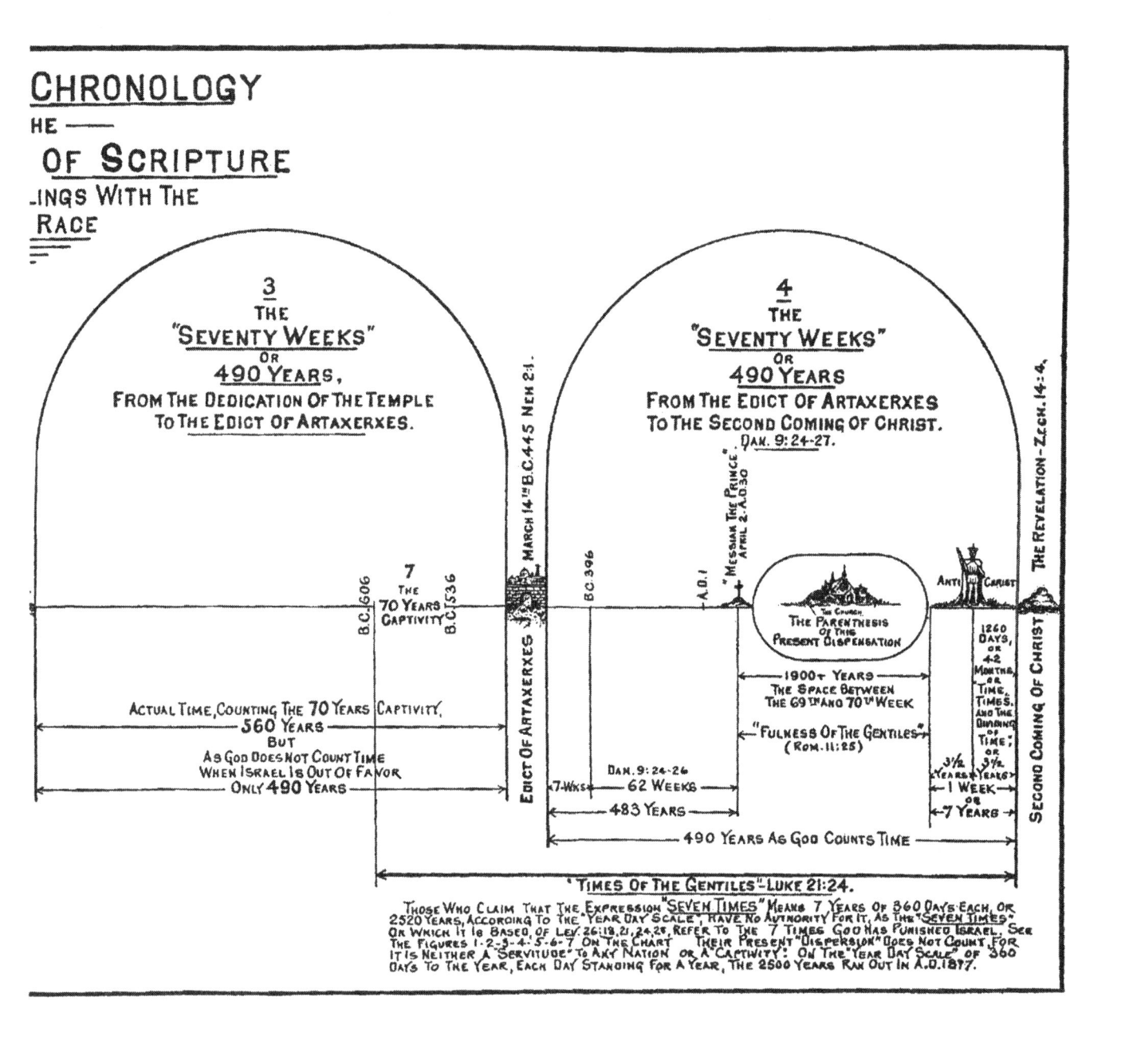

3
THE
"SEVENTY WEEKS"
OR
490 YEARS,
FROM THE DEDICATION OF THE TEMPLE TO THE EDICT OF ARTAXERXES.

B.C. 606 — 7 THE 70 YEARS CAPTIVITY — B.C. 536

ACTUAL TIME, COUNTING THE 70 YEARS CAPTIVITY, 560 YEARS
BUT AS GOD DOES NOT COUNT TIME WHEN ISRAEL IS OUT OF FAVOR ONLY 490 YEARS

EDICT OF ARTAXERXES — MARCH 14TH B.C. 445 NEH 2:1.

4
THE
"SEVENTY WEEKS"
OR
490 YEARS
FROM THE EDICT OF ARTAXERXES TO THE SECOND COMING OF CHRIST.
DAN. 9:24-27.

B.C. 396   A.D. 1   "MESSIAH THE PRINCE" APRIL 2, A.D. 30

THE CHURCH
THE PARENTHESIS OF THE PRESENT DISPENSATION

1900+ YEARS THE SPACE BETWEEN THE 69TH AND 70TH WEEK
"FULNESS OF THE GENTILES" (ROM. 11:25)

ANTICHRIST

1260 DAYS, OR 42 MONTHS, OR TIME, TIMES, AND THE DIVIDING OF TIME; OR 3½ YEARS & 3½ YEARS

THE REVELATION – ZECH. 14:4.

SECOND COMING OF CHRIST

7 WKS — DAN. 9:24-26 — 62 WEEKS
483 YEARS
1 WEEK OR 7 YEARS
490 YEARS AS GOD COUNTS TIME

"TIMES OF THE GENTILES" – LUKE 21:24.

THOSE WHO CLAIM THAT THE EXPRESSION "SEVEN TIMES" MEANS 7 YEARS OF 360 DAYS EACH, OR 2520 YEARS, ACCORDING TO THE "YEAR DAY SCALE," HAVE NO AUTHORITY FOR IT, AS THE "SEVEN TIMES," OR WHICH IT IS BASED, OF LEV. 26:18,21,24,28, REFER TO THE 7 TIMES GOD HAS PUNISHED ISRAEL, SEE THE FIGURES 1-2-3-4-5-6-7 ON THE CHART. THEIR PRESENT "DISPERSION" DOES NOT COUNT, FOR IT IS NEITHER A "SERVITUDE" TO ANY NATION OR A "CAPTIVITY": ON THE "YEAR DAY SCALE" OF 360 DAYS TO THE YEAR, EACH DAY STANDING FOR A YEAR, THE 2520 YEARS RAN OUT IN A.D. 1877.

If the "Seven Times" of Leviticus are Prophetic "Times" and a "Time" is **one year**, then **"Seven Times"** would be **seven years**, the length of the "Last Week" of Daniel's "Seventy Weeks," and would make the statement of Leviticus a **Prophetic reference** to the length of the "**Tribulation Period**" through which the Jews must go as a punishment for their sins.

The 1000 years of Rev. 20: 2-7 are ordinary years, just as the 70 years of the Babylonian Captivity were. The context will show whether ordinary or prophetical years are meant. It is this confusion in interpreting "Prophetical Chronology" that has led to the "time setting" that has brought discredit upon the whole system of Premillennial Truth.

The "Times of the Gentiles" will end with the end of Daniel's "Seventieth Week." When that will begin and end **no one knows**, for the Scriptures teach that it is not for us to know the

"Times and Seasons."

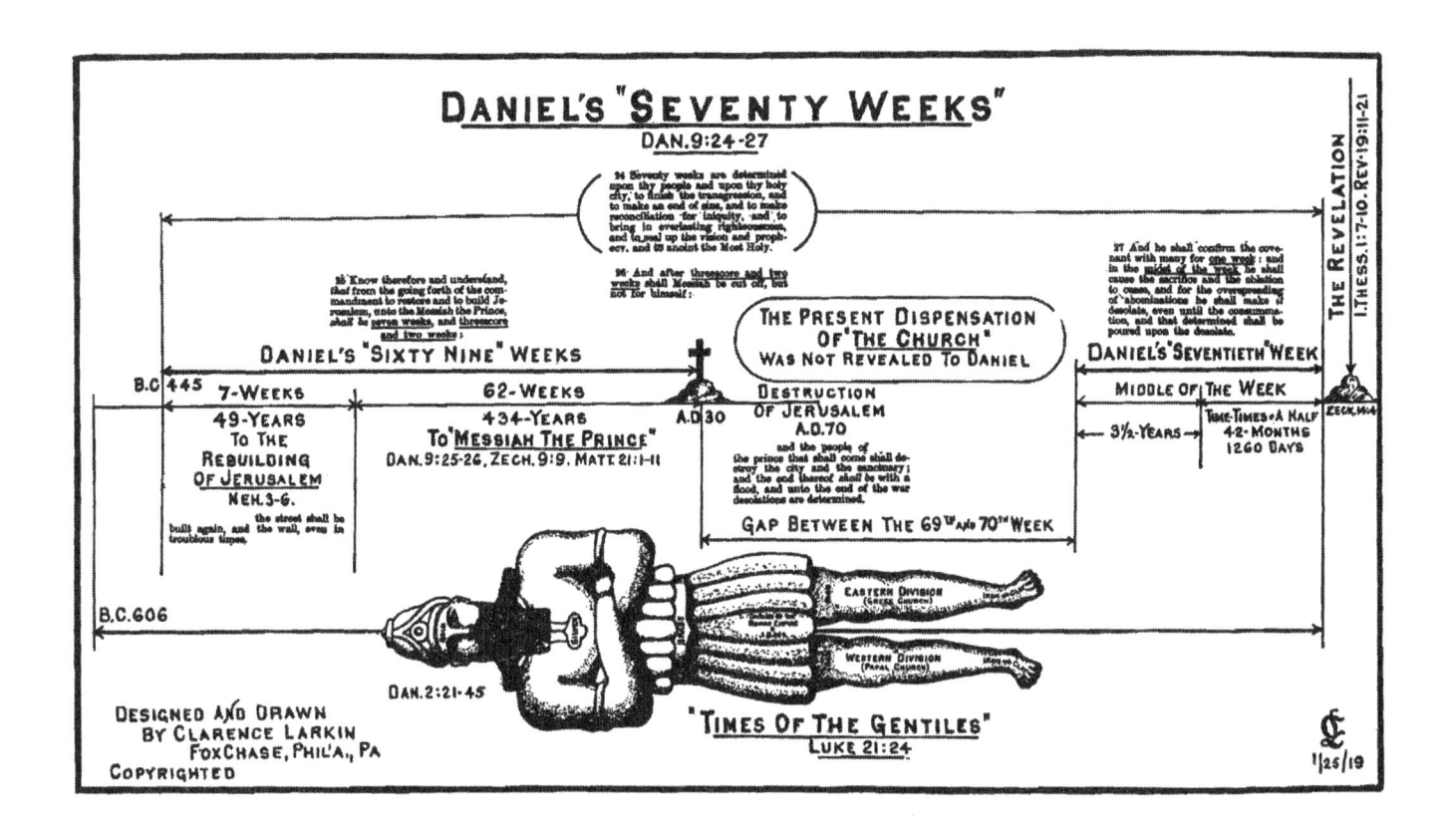

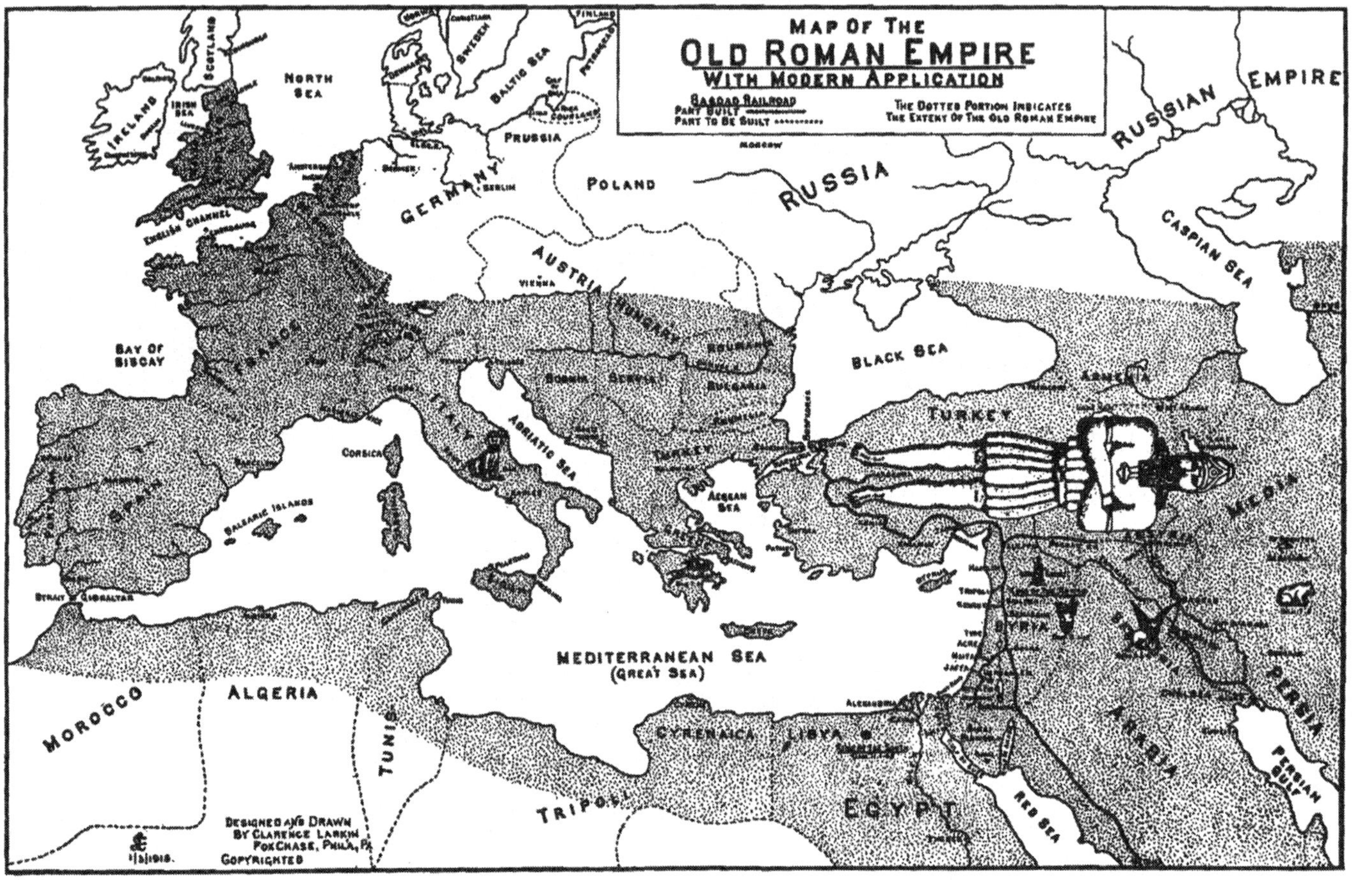
MAP OF THE
OLD ROMAN EMPIRE
WITH MODERN APPLICATION
BAGDAD RAILROAD
PART BUILT
PART TO BE BUILT
THE DOTTED PORTION INDICATES
THE EXTENT OF THE OLD ROMAN EMPIRE
NORTH SEA
SCOTLAND
IRELAND
IRISH SEA
ENGLISH CHANNEL
PRUSSIA
GERMANY
BERLIN
POLAND
RUSSIA
RUSSIAN EMPIRE
CASPIAN SEA
AUSTRIA HUNGARY
VIENNA
BAY OF BISCAY
FRANCE
SPAIN
ITALY
CORSICA
BALEARIC ISLANDS
ADRIATIC SEA
BOSNIA
SERVIA
ROUMANIA
BULGARIA
BLACK SEA
TURKEY
AEGEAN SEA
ARMENIA
MEDIA
SYRIA
ARABIA
PERSIA
PERSIAN GULF
RED SEA
MEDITERRANEAN SEA
(GREAT SEA)
STRAIT GIBRALTAR
MOROCCO
ALGERIA
TUNIS
TRIPOLI
CYRENAICA
LIBYA
EGYPT
DESIGNED AND DRAWN
BY CLARENCE LARKIN
FOX CHASE, PHILA, PA.
COPYRIGHTED
1/5/1918.

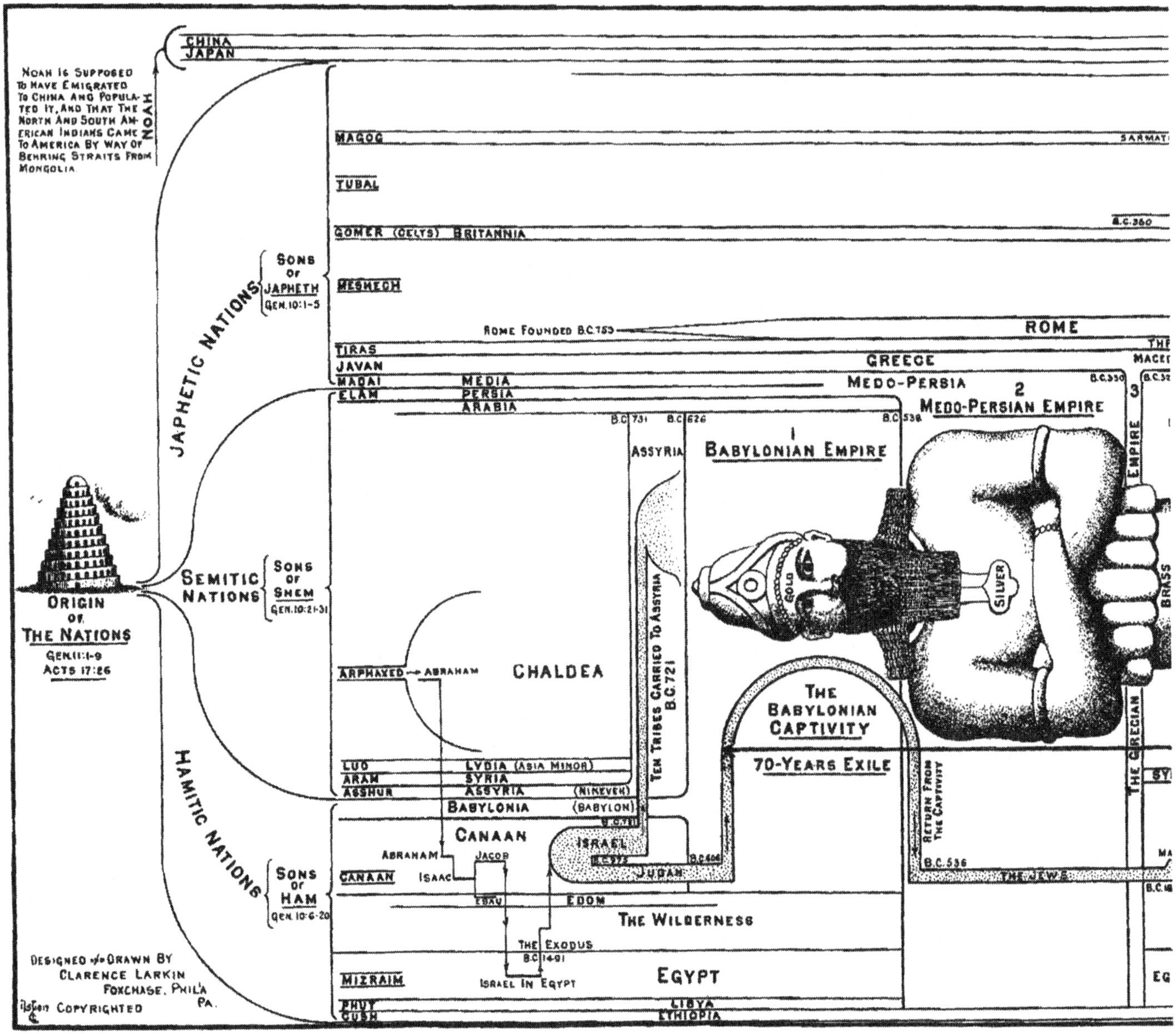

CHINA
JAPAN
NOAH IS SUPPOSED TO HAVE EMIGRATED TO CHINA AND POPULATED IT, AND THAT THE NORTH AND SOUTH AMERICAN INDIANS CAME TO AMERICA BY WAY OF BEHRING STRAITS FROM MONGOLIA.
NOAH
MAGOG
SARMATI
TUBAL
GOMER (CELTS) BRITANNIA
B.C. 360
SONS OF JAPHETH GEN. 10:1-5
MESHECH
JAPHETIC NATIONS
ROME FOUNDED B.C. 753
ROME
TIRAS
JAVAN
GREECE
MADAI
MEDIA
MEDO-PERSIA
ELAM
PERSIA
ARABIA
2
MEDO-PERSIAN EMPIRE
3
B.C. 731
B.C. 626
B.C. 538
ASSYRIA
1
BABYLONIAN EMPIRE
GOLD
SILVER
BRASS
EMPIRE
THE GRECIAN
SEMITIC NATIONS
SONS OF SHEM GEN. 10:21-31
ORIGIN OF THE NATIONS
GEN. 11:1-9
ACTS 17:26
ARPHAXED → ABRAHAM
CHALDEA
TEN TRIBES CARRIED TO ASSYRIA B.C. 721
THE BABYLONIAN CAPTIVITY
70-YEARS EXILE
RETURN FROM THE CAPTIVITY
LUD
LYDIA (ASIA MINOR)
ARAM
SYRIA
ASSHUR
ASSYRIA
(NINEVEH)
BABYLONIA
(BABYLON)
HAMITIC NATIONS
CANAAN
ISRAEL
ABRAHAM
JACOB
ISAAC
B.C. 606
B.C. 536
SONS OF HAM GEN. 10:6-20
CANAAN
ESAU
EDOM
JUDAH
THE JEWS
THE WILDERNESS
THE EXODUS
B.C. 1491
DESIGNED AND DRAWN BY CLARENCE LARKIN FOXCHASE, PHIL'A PA.
COPYRIGHTED
MIZRAIM
ISRAEL IN EGYPT
EGYPT
PHUT
LIBYA
CUSH
ETHIOPIA

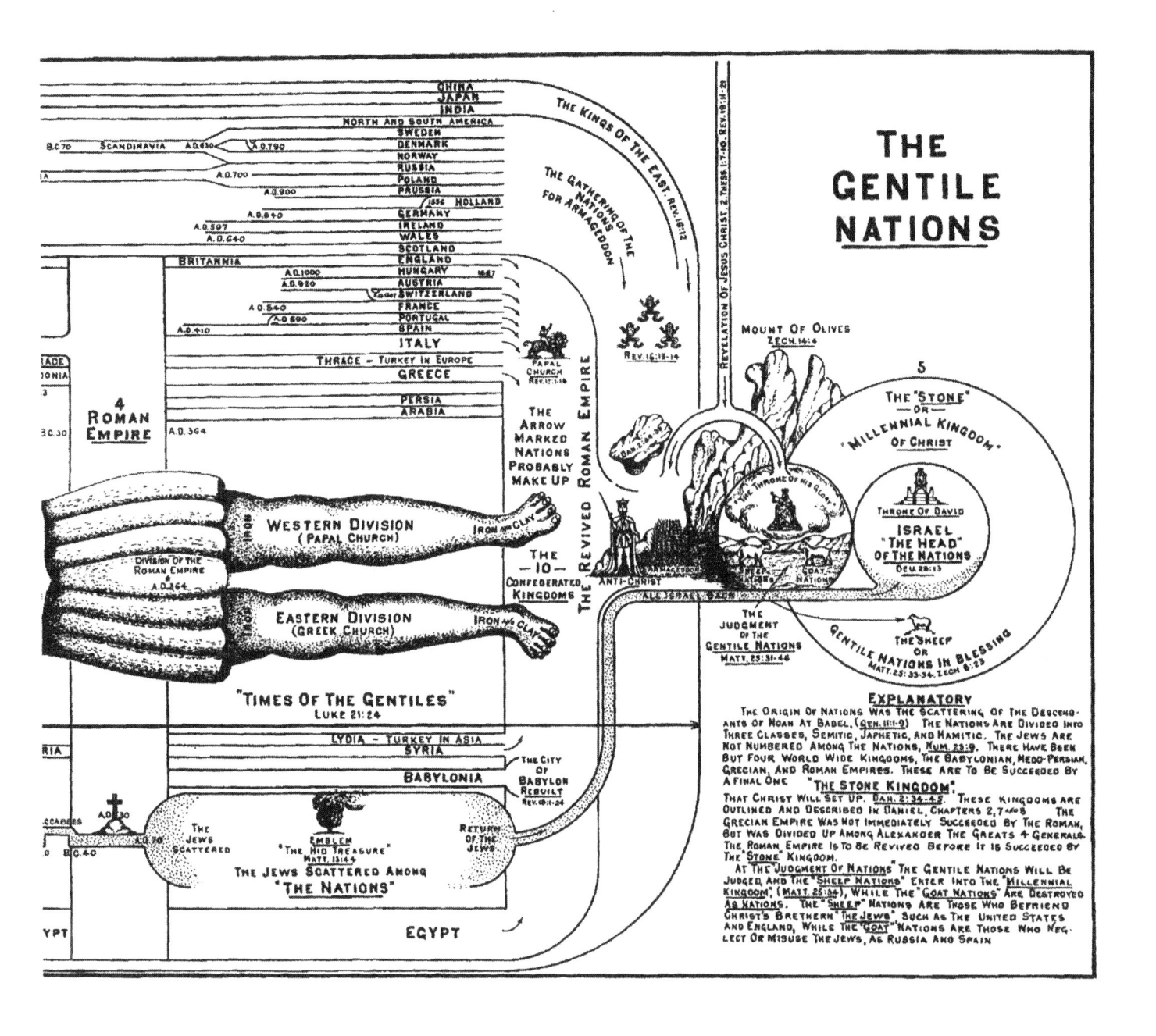

THE GENTILE NATIONS

EXPLANATORY

The origin of nations was the scattering of the descendants of Noah at Babel. (Gen. 11:1-9.) The nations are divided into three classes, Semitic, Japhetic, and Hamitic. The Jews are not numbered among the nations, Num. 23:9. There have been but four world wide kingdoms, the Babylonian, Medo-Persian, Grecian, and Roman Empires. These are to be succeeded by a final one "THE STONE KINGDOM" that Christ will set up. Dan. 2:34-45. These kingdoms are outlined and described in Daniel, Chapters 2, 7 and 8. The Grecian Empire was not immediately succeeded by the Roman, but was divided up among Alexander the Great's 4 generals. The Roman Empire is to be revived before it is succeeded by the STONE Kingdom.

At the "JUDGMENT OF NATIONS" the Gentile nations will be judged, and the "SHEEP NATIONS" enter into the MILLENNIAL KINGDOM, (Matt. 25:34), while the "GOAT NATIONS" are destroyed as nations. The "SHEEP" Nations are those who befriend Christ's brethren "THE JEWS" such as the United States and England, while the "GOAT" Nations are those who neglect or misuse the Jews, as Russia and Spain.

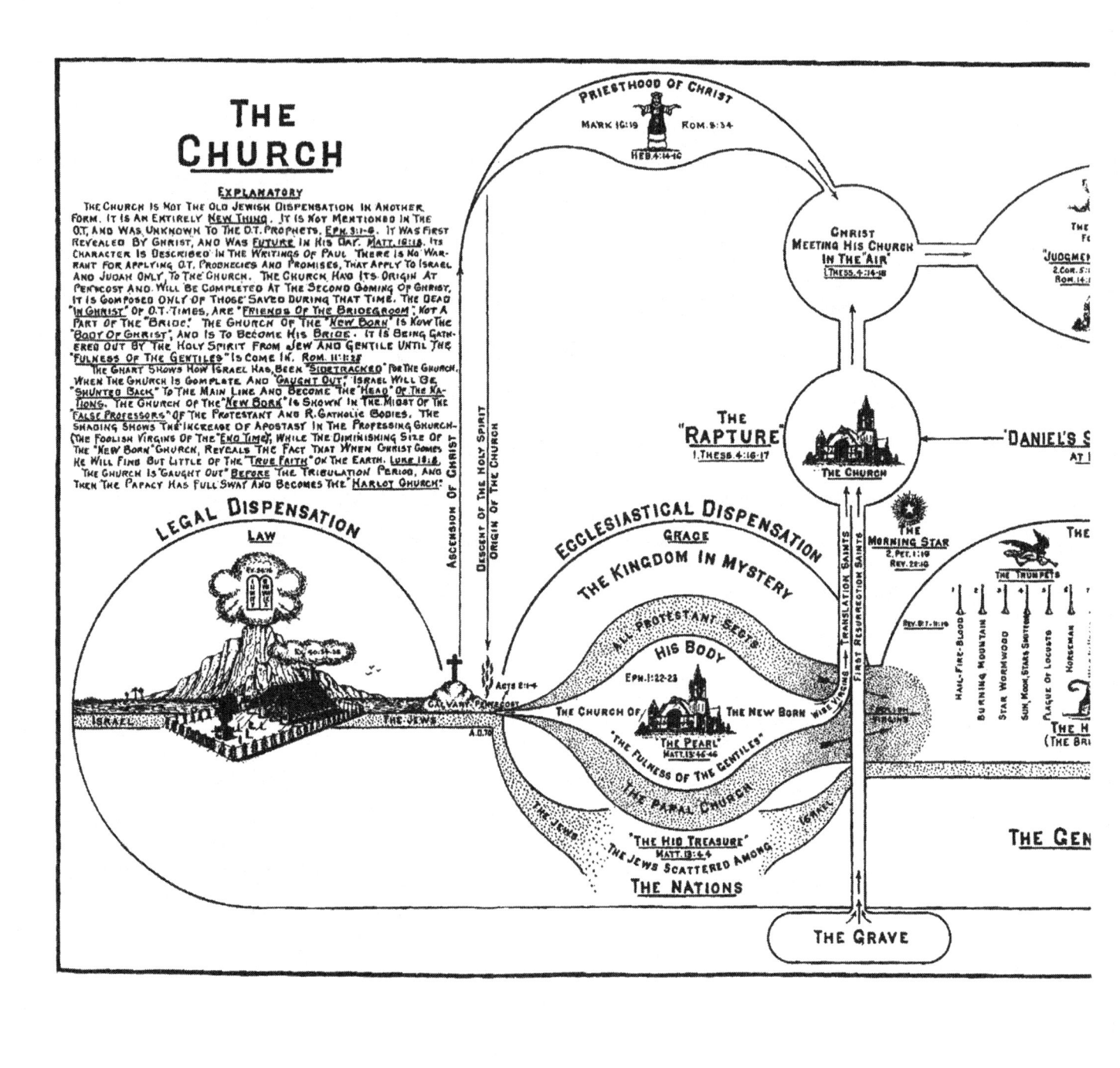

THE CHURCH

EXPLANATORY

The Church is not the Old Jewish Dispensation in another form. It is an entirely NEW THING. It is not mentioned in the O.T., and was unknown to the O.T. prophets. EPH. 3:1-6. It was first revealed by Christ, and was FUTURE in His day. MATT. 16:18. Its character is described in the writings of Paul. There is no warrant for applying O.T. prophecies and promises, that apply to Israel and Judah only, to the Church. The Church had its origin at Pentecost and will be completed at the Second Coming of Christ. It is composed only of those saved during that time. The dead "IN CHRIST" of O.T. times, are "FRIENDS OF THE BRIDEGROOM", not a part of the "BRIDE". The Church of the "NEW BORN" is now the "BODY OF CHRIST", and is to become His BRIDE. It is being gathered out by the Holy Spirit from Jew and Gentile until the "FULNESS OF THE GENTILES" is come in. ROM. 11:25.

The Chart shows how Israel has been "SIDETRACKED" for the Church. When the Church is complete and "CAUGHT OUT", Israel will be "SHUNTED BACK" to the main line and become the "HEAD" of the NATIONS. The Church of the "NEW BORN" is shown in the midst of the "FALSE PROFESSORS" of the Protestant and R. Catholic bodies. The shading shows the increase of apostasy in the professing Church. (The Foolish Virgins of the "END TIMES", while the diminishing size of the "NEW BORN" Church, reveals the fact that when Christ comes He will find but little of the "TRUE FAITH" on the earth. LUKE 18:8. The Church is "CAUGHT OUT" BEFORE the Tribulation Period, and then the Papacy has full sway and becomes the "HARLOT CHURCH".

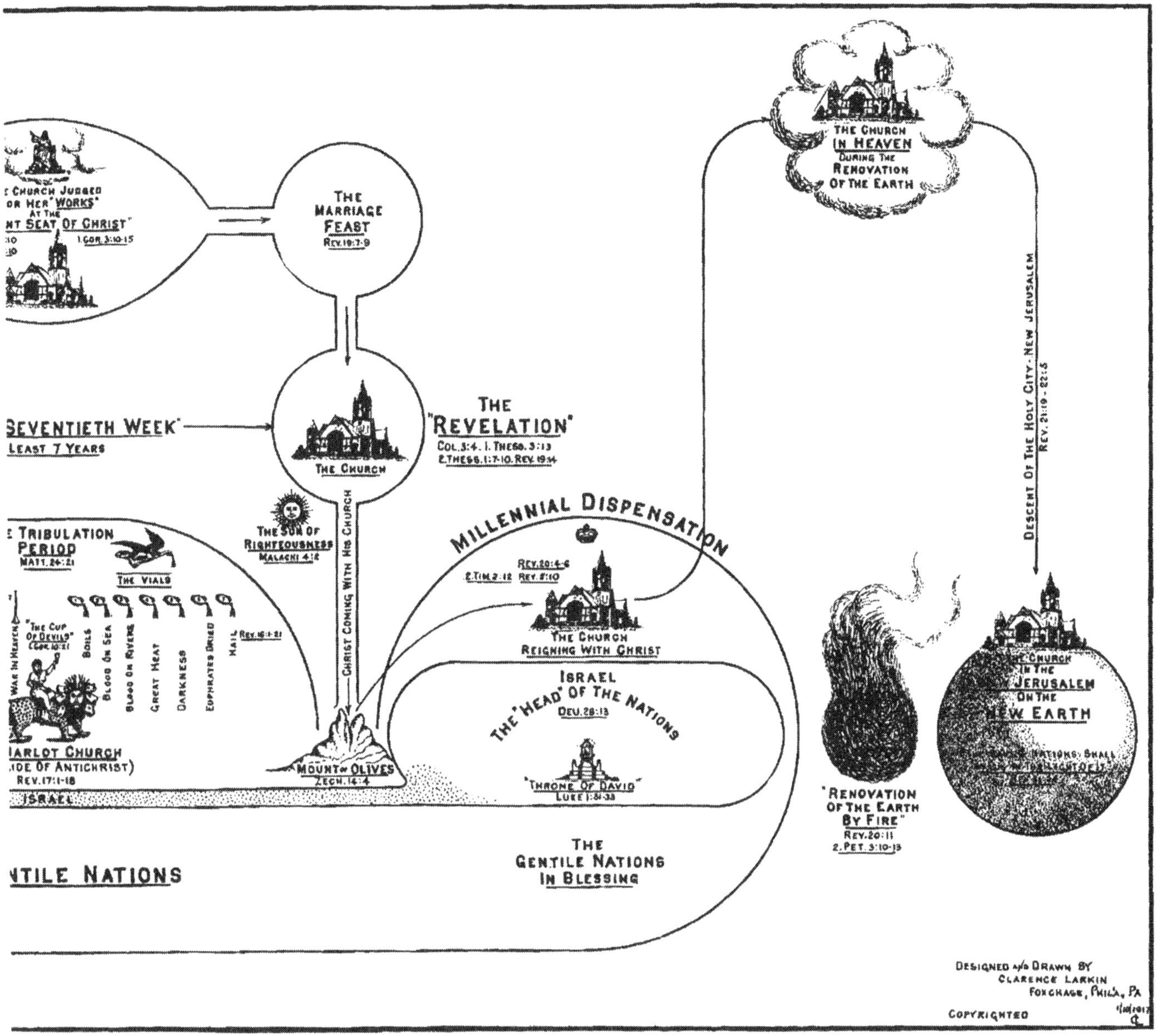

THE MARRIAGE FEAST
REV. 19:7-9
SEAT OF CHRIST"
1 COR. 3:10-15
SEVENTIETH WEEK"
LEAST 7 YEARS
THE CHURCH
THE "REVELATION"
COL. 3:4. 1. THESS. 3:13
2. THESS. 1:7-10. REV. 19:14
THE SUN OF RIGHTEOUSNESS
MALACHI 4:2
CHRIST COMING WITH HIS CHURCH
TRIBULATION PERIOD
MATT. 24:21
THE VIALS
BOILS
BLOOD ON SEA
BLOOD ON RIVERS
GREAT HEAT
DARKNESS
EUPHRATES DRIED
HAIL
REV. 16:1-21
"THE CUP OF DEVILS"
1 COR. 10:21
REV. 17:1-18
MOUNT OF OLIVES
ZECH. 14:4
ISRAEL
MILLENNIAL DISPENSATION
REV. 20:4-6
2. TIM. 2:12 REV. 5:10
THE CHURCH REIGNING WITH CHRIST
ISRAEL
THE "HEAD" OF THE NATIONS
DEU. 28:13
"THRONE OF DAVID"
LUKE 1:31-33
THE GENTILE NATIONS IN BLESSING
NTILE NATIONS
THE CHURCH IN HEAVEN DURING THE RENOVATION OF THE EARTH
DESCENT OF THE HOLY CITY - NEW JERUSALEM
REV. 21:19 - 22:5
"RENOVATION OF THE EARTH BY FIRE"
REV. 20:11
2. PET. 3:10-13
JERUSALEM
ON THE
NEW EARTH
DESIGNED AND DRAWN BY
CLARENCE LARKIN
FOXCHASE, PHILA, PA
COPYRIGHTED

XI
THE CHURCH

For the sake of clearness we will consider the Church under seven heads.

I. What the Church Is NOT.

1. It is not a continuation of the "Jewish Dispensation" under another name.

As we have seen in the chapter on the Jews, the Jews have been **shunted to a sidetrack** that the "Main Line" may be clear for the passage of the Church. Jesus said—"The Law and the Prophets are until John." If the Scriptures put **Moses** and **Law** in one Dispensation and **Christ** and **Grace** in another let us respect the Divine order and not join together what God has put asunder.

It is because some religious bodies believe that the Christian Church is but another phase of what they call the "Jewish Church," that they insist on a "ceremonial ritual" and retain the Priesthood with its altar, vestments, etc., and Temple-like buildings; and call the ordinances of the Christian Church "Sacrifices" and "Sacraments." They also go further and advocate a "State Church," with the Church as the head, and claim that all the Old Testament promises of riches and glory have been transferred from the Jew to the Church. This we shall see is unscriptural.

2. It is not "The Kingdom."

John the Baptist came preaching that the "Kingdom of Heaven" was "at hand" and Jesus sent out the Twelve and the Seventy to do the same, but the Jewish people rejected their King, and the setting up of the Kingdom was postponed. There cannot be any Kingdom until the "Nobleman Farmer" who has gone into a "far country" to receive the Kingdom returns. Luke 19:11-27.

The Church is never confounded with the Kingdom in the Scriptures. The Church is compared to a **"House"** (I Tim. 3:15), to a **"Temple"** (I Cor. 3:16, 17), to a **"Body"** (I Cor. 12:27-31), but never to a **Kingdom**. Christ is the **"HEAD"** of His Church (Eph. 1:22; 4:15; Col. 1:18), but He is never spoken of as its **King**. The Church's relation to **Christ is** to be that of a **"Bride."** Eph. 5:23-32; Rev. 21:2, 9, 10.

II. What the Church IS.

1. It is a "Mystery."

The Kingdom was no **mystery**. The Old Testament prophets describe it in glowing terms. But there was something that was a "Mystery" to them, and that was what was to come in between the **"Sufferings and Glory"** of Christ. 1 Pet. 1:9-12.

That is, between the **Cross** and the **Crown**. Jesus intimated that there was to be something that He called the "Church," but He did not say when it should appear, or what it would be like. Matt. 16:13-20.

The "Mystery of the Church" was first revealed to Paul.

"For this cause I, Paul, the prisoner of Jesus Christ for you Gentiles, if ye have heard of '**The Dispensation of the Grace of God**' which is given me to you-ward; how that by **revelation** He made known unto me

'THE MYSTERY'

which in **other ages** was not made known unto the sons of men, as it is **now revealed unto His holy apostles and prophets by the Spirit**; that

THE GENTILES

should be fellow heirs and of

THE SAME BODY,

and partakers of His promise in Christ by the **Gospel** . . . according to the

'Eternal Purpose'

which He purposes in Christ Jesus our Lord." Eph. 3:1-11.

(See the Chart on "God's Eternal Purpose as to the Earth.")

From this we see that the Church was **unknown** to the Old Testament patriarchs and prophets.

That the Gentiles were to be **saved** was no mystery. Rom. 9:24-30. The "Mystery" was, that God was going to form an entirely **"NEW THING,"** composed of **Both Jew and Gentile,** to be called— **"THE CHURCH."**

2. It is a "Called Out" Body.

The word Church comes from the Greek word "ecclesia" which means "Assembly" or a congregation of "called out ones."

But the word is not used exclusively as to the Church. Israel was an "ecclesia" or an Assembly of people "called out" from other peoples and nations, and is called in Acts 7:38, "The Church in the Wilderness."

Any Assembly of worshippers banded together as a church or congregation is an "ecclesia." Matt. 18:17; I Cor. 14:19, 35.

The Guild of Ephesian Craftsmen and a Town Meeting is an "ecclesia," because distinct or called out from the body of citizens Acts 19:32, 39. The context will show what is meant.

The purpose of this Dispensation is seen in the "Divine Program," outlined by the Apostle James in his address to the First Church

Council (Acts 15:13-18), where he declares that God has visited the Gentiles to

"Take Out of Them
A 'PEOPLE' for His Name."

The purpose of this Dispensation then is not the **Conversion of the World**, but the **"Gathering Out" of the Church**.

While Israel is a "called out body" it is a "National Body," composed exclusively of the descendants of Abraham, but the Church is not a "National Body" for it is not composed of the people of any one nation, but of individuals from **every kindred, people, tribe and nation**.

That Israel and the Church are distinct and **separate** and cannot be blended, is clear from the fact that their "election" was made at different dates, and that the "election" of the Church **antedates** the "election" of Israel, for Israel was chosen in Abraham from the **foundation of the world** (Matt. 25:34), while the Church was chosen in **HIM** (Jesus) **BEFORE the Foundation of the World**. Eph. 1:4-6.

3. **It is the "Body of Christ."**

In Eph. 1:22, 23 we read—

"And hath put all things under His feet, and gave HIM (Jesus), to be the **HEAD** over all things to the Church which is His **BODY**."

The context shows (vs. 20), that this "Headship" was not possible until Jesus had been **raised from the dead, and seated at the right hand of the Father**. The Church, therefore, could not have been in existence before there was a **Head**, for God does not make **headless things**. The Church then is the **Body** of which Christ is the Head.

In I Cor. 12:12, 13 we are told how this "Body" is formed.

"For as the body is one, and hath many members; and all the members of that one body, being many, are one body; **so also is Christ**. For by one Spirit are we all **baptized into One Body**, whether we be Jew or Gentile, whether we be bond or free; and have been all made to drink into **ONE SPIRIT**."

From this we see that it is the

"Baptism of the Spirit"

that incorporates us into the

"BODY OF CHRIST."

Therefore there could be no Church until the "Day of Pentecost." Acts 1:4, 5; 2:1-4.

Paul in his Letter to the Ephesians, that deals mainly with the Church, emphasizes this **baptism**.

"There is **One Body** (the Church) and **One Spirit** (the Holy Spirit), even as ye are called in one hope of your calling; **One Lord** (Jesus), **One Faith, ONE BAPTISM** (of the Holy Spirit), **One God and Father** of all, who is above all, and through all, and in you all." Eph. 4:4-6.

That there should be no mistake as to what Paul meant by the "one body" of 1 Cor. 12:13 he says, verse 27, "Now ye are the **Body of Christ**." And in Rom. 12:5 he reaffirms it—

"So we, being many, are 'One Body in Christ,' and every one members one of another."

The fact that the Church is a "Body" made up of "living members" shows that it is not an "Organization," but an **"ORGANISM."** An "Organization" is made up of distinct units like the doors, windows, roof, floors, etc., of a building, that may be removed and replaced by new parts without destroying the integrity of the building; but a human body is an **organism**. You cannot remove an eye, or ear, or arm, or foot, or even a finger nail or tooth, without destroying the integrity of the body and causing a mutilation. So we see from this for Christ to lose **One Member of His Body** (the Church) is to **MUTILATE** it.

Neither can the Church, as the "Body of Christ" die, for who ever saw a **dead** body attached to a **living** head. Christ the Head is **ALIVE** and can **NEVER DIE AGAIN**, for He tells us in Rev. 1:18, "I am He that **liveth** and was dead (on the Cross), and behold, I am **ALIVE FOR EVERMORE**." It follows therefore that "when Christ, who is our **LIFE**, shall appear, then **Shall We Also Appear With Him in Glory**." Col. 3:4. Jesus Christ not only gave His life for the Church, but **to** the Church.

But why call the Church the "Body of Christ?" What is a body for? It is for the

Manifestation of a Personality.

A person can exist without a physical body, as the Soul exists without a physical body between death and the resurrection of the body, but that existence cannot be made manifest. So the only way Christ, who is now in glory, can manifest Himself to the world is through **His Body—THE CHURCH**.

The only way the world can see Christ today is in Christian believers. This is probably what Paul meant when he wrote to the Philippians,

"For to me to live Is Christ."

(Phil. 1:21). That is, for **Christ** to live again in Paul, so that the world might see Christ **manifested in Paul**.

The Perfect Man.

If Christ is the Head, and the Church is the Body, then the two should make a **Perfect Man**, for we cannot conceive of a perfect Head like Christ, joined to an imperfect body. This is just what Paul tells us should be.

"And He gave some, Apostles; and some, Prophets; and some, Evangelists; and some, Pastors and Teachers; **for the**

Perfecting of the Saints,

for the work of the ministry, for the edifying of the

'Body of Christ;'

till we all come in the unity of the faith, and of **the knowledge of the Son of God, unto a**

PERFECT MAN,

unto the measure of the stature of the fulness of Christ. Eph. 4:11-13.

In 1 Cor. 3:9-17, Paul speaks of the Church, under the figure of a **Building** or **Temple**, of which Christ is the **Chief Corner Stone**, "in whom all the building fitly framed together groweth unto an Holy Temple in the Lord; in whom ye also are builded together for an **HABITATION OF GOD** through the Spirit." Eph. 2:19-22.

Here we see that as God's presence was manifested in the Tabernacle in the "Shekinah Glory," so now in this Dispensation, when Israel, nationally, is out of fellowship with God, and there is no Temple at Jerusalem, the Church, since Pentecost is the visible "**Habitation of God**" on earth, where He manifests Himself through the Holy Spirit.

John tells us (John 1:14), that the "WORD" (Jesus) Tabernacled among us, and spoke of His Body as a Temple, John 2:19-21, so between God's manifesting Himself in the "Shekinah Glory" of the Temple, and now through His Spirit in the Church, He manifested Himself in the "person" of Jesus, and John tells us that he and Peter and James saw the "Glory of God" in the person of Jesus on the Mt. of Transfiguration. John 1:14.

4. It is to be the "Bride of Christ."

At present the Church is a virgin espoused.

Paul said to the Church at Corinth,

"I am jealous over you with godly jealousy; for I have espoused you to one husband, that I may present you as a chaste VIRGIN to Christ." 2 Cor. 11:2.

In Christ's day an espousal was as sacred as a marriage.

The First Adam had his Bride, and the Second or Last Adam must have His Bride. In Gen. 2:18, 21-24, we are told how the First Adam got his Bride.

"The Lord God caused a deep sleep to fall upon Adam and he slept; and He took one of his ribs, and closed up the flesh instead thereof; and with the rib, which the Lord God had taken from man, made (builded) He a woman, and brought her unto the man. And Adam said, This is now bone of my bones and flesh of my flesh; she shall be called woman because she was taken out of man."

Now Jesus during His life on the earth as a man, abode alone, but a deep sleep—the sleep of death—fell on Him, and out of His wounded side, as the result of the Atonement He made on the Cross, there came that from which the Church was formed, and to which the Holy Spirit gave life on the Day of Pentecost; so that, as Adam said of Eve—"This is now bone of my bones, and flesh of my flesh," so we can say of the Church—"We are members of His Body, of his Flesh, and of his Bones." Eph. 5:29-33.

The Woman was brought to Adam and presented to him, but Christ will present the Church to Himself, Eph. 5:27. That Eve was married to Adam is indicated in Gen. 2:24 and referred to in Matt. 19:4, 5, and Eph. 5:31.

We have a beautiful illustration of how Christ is gathering out His Bride, the Church, in the story of how Isaac got his bride.

In the Scriptures—

>   Abraham is a type of God.
>   Sarah is a type of Israel.
>   Isaac is a type of Jesus.
>   Eliezer is a type of the Holy Spirit.
>   Rebekah is a type of the Church.
>   Keturah a type of Israel Restored.

When the time came for Isaac to have a wife his father Abraham did not want him to marry a Canaanitish woman, and so he sent his servant Eliezer over to Padan Aram to get one for him from among Abraham's kindred. When Eliezer reached Padan Aram he was divinely directed to the home of Laban, a grandnephew of Abraham, whose sister Rebekah God had chosen to be the wife of Isaac. Gen. 24:12-14. Rebekah consented to become the wife of a man she had never seen solely on the representations of Eliezer, and she departed with him, leaving her kinsfolk behind. As the caravan neared the home of Abraham we read that "Isaac went out to meditate in the field at the Eventide" and saw the camels of his father returning, and Rebekah alighted from off her camel and was introduced by Eliezer to Isaac and she became his wife.

So God has sent the Holy Spirit into this world in this Dispensation to get a wife for His Son Jesus, and when the full number of the Church is complete, the Holy Spirit will take her back with him to the Father's home, and Jesus, whose Bride she is to be, will come out into the midair at the "Eventide" of this Dispensation to meet her. 1 Thess. 4:15-17.

Some hold that because Isaac's bride was taken from his own kin, that, therefore, to complete the type, Jesus' Bride must be Israel, His own kin, and not the Church composed mainly of Gentiles. But we must not forget that while Abraham was the first Hebrew his kin were Gentiles. Abraham was not, strictly speaking, a Jew, for the Jews are the descendants of Judah, the fourth son of Jacob or Israel. So we see that Rebekah was not an Israelite, but a Gentile, so the type holds good.

We must not forget that there are "Two Brides" mentioned in the Scriptures. One in the Old Testament, and the other in the New Testament. The one in the Old Testament is Israel, the Bride of Jehovah; the one in the New Testament is the Church, the Bride of Christ. Of Israel it is said—"Thy Maker is thine husband." Isa. 54:5-8. Because of her Whoredoms, Israel is a cast off wife, but God, her husband, promises to take her back when she ceases from her adulteries. Jer. 3:1-18; Ez. 16:1-63; Hosea 2:1-23, 3:1-5. Sarah is a type of Israel before her fall, and Keturah of Israel when God shall take her back again. She will not be taken back as a Virgin, but as a Wife. But it is a VIRGIN that the Lamb (Christ) is to marry. So the Wife (Israel) of the Old Testament cannot be the Bride (Virgin) of the New Testament.

Again the "Wife" (Israel) is to reside in the earthly Jerusalem during the Millennium, while the "Bride" (the Church) will reside in the New Jerusalem. These distinctions make it clear that Israel cannot be the "Bride" of Christ.

As to the Church being both the "Body" and "Bride" of Christ, we have the type of Eve who was of the "body" of Adam before she was his "bride."

III. The ORIGIN of the Church.

While, as we have seen, the Church had its origin in the mind of God

"Before the Foundation of the World,"

yet it did not exist until after Christ's Ascension.

In the summer of the third year of Christ's ministry, when Israel had practically rejected Him and He was entering the "Shadow of the Cross," knowing that the offer of the Kingdom would soon be withdrawn, and the Church be set up, and wishing to prepare His Disciples for what was coming, He took them over into Cesarea Philippi, and there asked the question—"Whom do men say that I, the Son of Man, am?" Matt. 16:13-20. After they had told Him what others said of Him, He said to them—"But whom say Ye that I am?" And Simon Peter answered and said—"Thou Art the Christ, the Son of the Living God." And Jesus answered and said unto Peter—"Thou art Peter, and upon this Rock I will build my Church; and the 'Gates of Hell' (Hades) shall not prevail against it." Notice that there is here a little play upon words. It is from the Greek word "petros" that the word Peter is taken. "Petros" in the Greek means a stone, the small fragment of a rock, while the Greek word "Petra" means a rock, or large mass of stone. It is significant that in the Greek the word "Petros" is masculine, while the word "Petra" is feminine. The change of gender then is not without significance, as if it would distinguish Peter the man, from his confession that

"Christ Was the Son of God,"

and that upon that confession, or upon Christ—THE ROCK, Christ would build His Church. That the "**Rock**" means Christ Himself is in harmony with other scriptures that speak of Him as a "Rock." That Peter understood that Christ meant that He Himself was the "Rock" is evident from Peter's address in Acts 4: 5-12, where he says of Christ

"This Is the STONE

which was set at nought of you builders, which is become the **head of the corner**"—that is the **Corner Stone of the Building**.

Peter reaffirms this in his First Epistle (1 Pet. 2: 3-8), and thus disclaims that he was the "rock" Christ meant.

The Apostle Paul also declares that by the "Rock" Christ is meant. Writing to the Corinthians he says—

"Other **foundation** can no man lay than that which is laid which is—**Jesus Christ**." 1 Cor. 3: 11.

In Eph. 2: 20-22, Paul declares of the Church that it is being built upon the foundation of the Apostles and Prophets, **Jesus Christ Himself Being the CHIEF Corner Stone**,"

in whom all the building fitly framed together groweth into a

HOLY TEMPLE

in the Lord; in whom we also are builded together for an

Habitation of God

through the Spirit.

There could be no foundation for the Church until Christ's death, resurrection and ascension. Then Christ became the **Rock** and upon Him the **Foundation of the Apostles and Prophets** (New Testament Prophets) was laid, and the first layer of the superstructure of 3000 "**Living Stones**" was laid on the Day of Pentecost (Acts 2: 41), and a few days later the second layer of 5000 was added (Acts 4: 4), and so on, down the centuries, the Church has been growing as a "Holy Temple" for the "Habitation of God," through the Spirit. The Church then had its origin at Pentecost. If Peter was the "rock" upon which the Church was to be built, it seems reasonable that the "Mystery of the Church" should have been revealed to him instead of to Paul.

By the "Gates of Hell" is meant the "Gates of Hades" or the "Underworld." The "Underworld" is composed of two sections with an "Impassible Gulf" between. See the chapter and chart on the "Spirit World." One of the sections was called "Paradise," the other "Hell." Luke 16: 19-31. To the "Paradise" section Jesus went to meet the penitent thief after His death on the Cross, and when He came back from Paradise He took all the "captives" that Death had locked up there, with Him, and locked up that compartment of the Underworld, and HE now has the **Keys** of "**Death and Hades**," and so the "Gates of Hell" shall not prevail against the Church. The Roman Catholic Church claims that Peter was the "Rock" on which the Church was to be built, and as Christ promised to Peter the "Keys of the Kingdom of Heaven" that therefore the Pope and his successors can unlock the "Gates of Purgatory." But Peter never did have, and never will have the "Keys of **Hades**," for the Keys of the "Kingdom of Heaven" are not the "Keys of **Hades**." The "Keys of **Hades**" are in the hand of Peter's **MASTER**, who said to the beloved John on the Isle of Patmos—

"Fear not; I am the First and the Last; I am He that **liveth** and was **dead**; and, behold, I am **alive forever more**, Amen, and have the '**Keys**' of HELL (Hades), and of **DEATH**." Rev. 1: 17, 18.

This at one stroke destroys the claim of Rome.

As we have seen that the Church is not the Kingdom, the Keys of the "Kingdom of Heaven" therefore cannot be the Keys of the Church. The "Kingdom of Heaven" is the "Mystery Form" of the Kingdom during the absence of the King, and is broader than the Church, and takes in the World, particularly that part known as Christendom. This is seen in the "Kingdom of Heaven Parables" of Matt. 13. The Keys of the "Kingdom of Heaven" that were given to Peter were the "Keys" by which he opened the way into the "Kingdom of Heaven" to the Jews at Pentecost, Acts 2: 14-40, and later to the Gentiles in the house of Cornelius at Caesarea. Acts 10: 34-48.

Who Belong to the Church?

If the Church had its origin at Pentecost, and ends at the Second Coming of Christ for His saints at the "Rapture," who belong to the Church, and therefore constitute the "Bride?" Necessarily only those who are saved between those two events. The Old Testament saints could not belong to the Church for it did not then exist. At every wedding that is a public function there are others present beside the Bridegroom and the Bride. There is the groomsman, the bridesmaids, the ushers, flower girls, relatives and invited guests.

In Rev. 19: 9 we read—

"Blessed are they which are **called** unto the "Marriage Supper' of the Lamb."

Now the "Bride" would not be "called" (invited), she has a place there of her own right. The "called" are the "Guests." And in the Parable of the "Marriage of the King's Son" (Matt. 22: 1-14), those who were "bidden to the Wedding" were "Guests" not the Bride. John the Baptist, who stands for the Old Jewish Dispensation, claimed to be only the "Friend of the Bridegroom." John 3: 29.

At the Rapture all the "Dead in Christ" will rise, and that includes all the Old Testament Saints, and there will be present at the

Marriage of the Lamb

the "Blood Washed Multitude" that come out of the "Tribulation," after the Church is caught out. These will all be "Blessed" but they will not be a part of the Bride. Angels will be spectators of the scene, but they cannot be "Guests," that honor is reserved for those who have been redeemed by the Blood of the Lamb.

IV. The "MISSION" Of The Church.

As we have seen the Church is not an "Organization" but an "**Organism**." Therefore it is not a "Social Club," organized and supported solely for the benefit of its members. It is not a "Place of Amusement" to pander to the carnal nature of man. It is not a "House of Merchandise" for the sale of "Indulgences," or other commodities, whereby the money of the ungodly can be secured to save the penurious church member a little self sacrifice. Neither is it a "Reform Bureau" to save the "bodies" of men. The reformation of men is very commendable, as are all forms of "Social Service," but that is not the work or mission of the Church. The world was just as full, if not fuller, of the evils that afflict society today, in the days of Christ, but He never, nor did the Apostles, organize any reform agencies. He knew that the source of all the evils in the world is SIN, and the only way to eradicate sin is to **Regenerate the Human Heart**, and so He gave to the world **The Gospel**, and the **Mission of the**

The Failure of Christianity

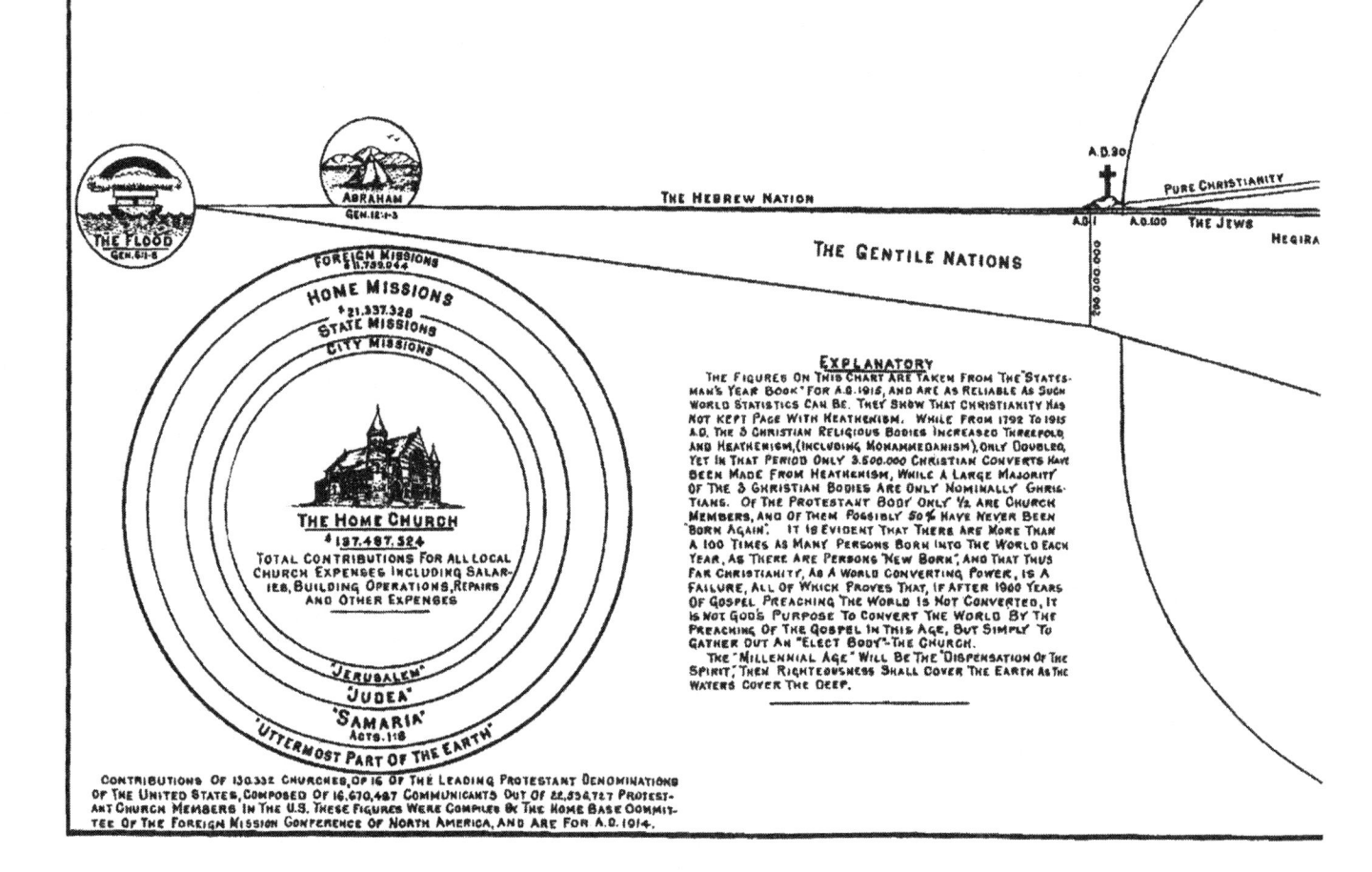

THE FLOOD GEN. 6:1-5

ABRAHAM GEN. 12:1-3

THE HEBREW NATION

A.D. 30 — PURE CHRISTIANITY

A.D. 1 — A.D. 100 — THE JEWS — HEGIRA

THE GENTILE NATIONS

FOREIGN MISSIONS $1,733,044
HOME MISSIONS $21,337,328
STATE MISSIONS
CITY MISSIONS

THE HOME CHURCH $137,487,524
Total Contributions For All Local Church Expenses Including Salaries, Building Operations, Repairs And Other Expenses

"JERUSALEM"
"JUDEA"
"SAMARIA"
"UTTERMOST PART OF THE EARTH"
ACTS 1:8

Contributions Of 130,332 Churches, Of 16 Of The Leading Protestant Denominations Of The United States, Composed Of 16,670,487 Communicants Out Of 22,334,727 Protestant Church Members In The U.S. These Figures Were Compiled By The Home Base Committee Of The Foreign Mission Conference Of North America, And Are For A.D. 1914.

Explanatory

The figures on this chart are taken from the "Statesman's Year Book" for A.D. 1915, and are as reliable as such world statistics can be. They show that Christianity has not kept pace with heathenism. While from 1792 to 1915 A.D. the 3 Christian religious bodies increased threefold and heathenism, (including Mohammedanism), only doubled, yet in that period only 3,500,000 Christian converts have been made from heathenism, while a large majority of the 3 Christian bodies are only nominally Christians. Of the Protestant body only ½ are church members, and of them possibly 50% have never been "born again". It is evident that there are more than a 100 times as many persons born into the world each year, as there are persons "new born", and that thus far Christianity, as a world converting power, is a failure, all of which proves that, if after 1900 years of Gospel preaching the world is not converted, it is not God's purpose to convert the world by the preaching of the Gospel in this age, but simply to gather out an "Elect Body"—the Church.

The "Millennial Age" will be the "Dispensation of the Spirit", then righteousness shall cover the earth as the waters cover the deep.

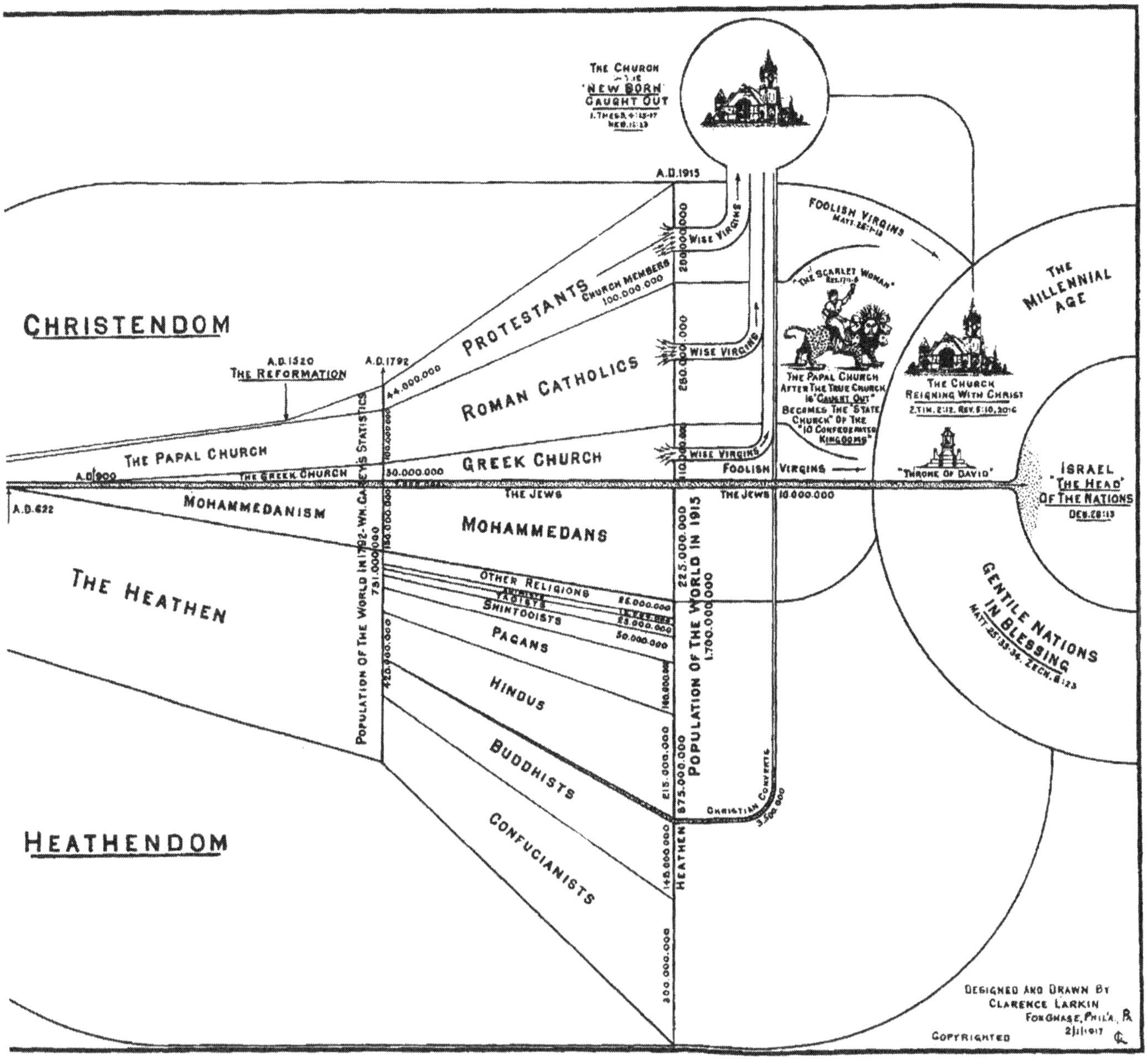

Church is to carry that **Gospel** to the **Whole World**. Mark 16:15. The Gospel is not a system of "Ethics," or a "Code of Morals," it is a

Proclamation of Salvation.

"I am not ashamed of the **Gospel of Christ**
For It Is
THE POWER OF GOD UNTO SALVATION
To Every One That Believeth
To The Jew FIRST
And Also To The Greek (Gentile)."
Rom. 1:16.

The purpose of the Gospel in this Dispensation is not to **Save Society**, but to save the **Individual Members** that are to compose the "**Body of Christ**"—THE CHURCH.

The great mistake the Church has made is in appropriating to herself, in this Dispensation, the promises of earthly conquest and glory which belong exclusively to Israel in the Millennial, or "Kingdom Age." As soon as the Church enters into an "Alliance With the World," and seeks the help of Parliaments, Congresses, Legislatures, Federations and Reform Societies, largely made up of ungodly men and women, she loses her spiritual power and becomes helpless as a redeeming force.

V. The "DESTINY" Of The Church.

The Church is to be "caught out." The "event" will be twofold.

1. Of the Dead in Christ.
2. Of the Living Saints.

They are to be caught up simultaneously to meet the Lord in the air.

"For the Lord Himself shall descend from heaven with a shout, with the voice of the Archangel (Michael), and with the Trump of God: and the

'Dead In Christ'

shall rise first: then we which

'Are Alive And Remain'

shall be caught up together with them in the clouds, **To Meet the Lord IN THE AIR**: and so shall we ever be with the Lord." 1 Thess. 4:16,17.

The "taking up" of Enoch in the days before the Flood (Gen. 5:24), and of Elijah in the days of the kings of Israel (2 Kings 2:11), are types of the "Translation" of the Saints.

The appearance of Moses and Elijah on the Mt. of Transfiguration with Christ (Luke 9:28-31), is a type of the

"Rapture of the Church."

It pictures the meeting of Christ and the Church in the air. Moses is a type of the "Resurrected Saints," and Elijah of the "Translated Saints."

Jesus revealed to Martha, before He raised Lazarus, what should happen at the First Resurrection. He said to her—

"I am the '**Resurrection and Life**,' he that believeth in Me, though he were dead yet shall he **live**: (First Resurrection Saints); and whosoever LIVETH, (is alive when I come back) and believeth in Me shall **NEVER DIE**." John 11:25, 26.

Note how exactly this harmonizes with Paul's statement in 1 Thess. 4:16, 17. When Jesus comes back He will be the "**Resurrection**" to the "**Dead in Christ**," and the "**Life**" to those who are "**Living**" and **Believe In Him**.

In his immortal chapter on the Resurrection, 1 Cor. 15:1-58, after describing the "order" of the Resurrection (verses 22-24), Paul proceeds to describe what shall happen to the "living saints."

"Behold, I show you a **Mystery**, we shall not all **Sleep**, but we shall **All Be Changed** in a moment, in the twinkling of an eye, at the last trump: for the trumpet shall sound, and the **dead** shall be **raised**, and **we** shall be **changed**. For this **Corruptible** (the dead in Christ) must put on **incorruption**, and this **mortal** (the living saints) must put on **immortality**. So when this **corruptible** shall have put on **incorruption**, and this **mortal** shall have put on **immortality**, **then** shall be brought to pass the saying that is written, DEATH IS SWALLOWED UP IN VICTORY.

O DEATH, WHERE IS THY STING?
O GRAVE, WHERE IS THY VICTORY?"
1 Cor. 15:51-57.

The last two lines refer only to those who are "changed without dying," for it is only those who will not die who can shout—

"O Death, Where Is Thy Sting?
"O Grave, Where Is Thy Victory?"

This passage also corresponds with 1 Thess. 4:16, 17, and declares that the "Resurrection" and "Translation" of the Saints shall be at the **same time**, and in a **moment**, in the **twinkling of an eye**, and agrees with Christ's statement as to its "suddenness." "For as the lightning cometh out of the east, and shineth even unto the west; so shall also the **coming of the Son of Man Be**." Matt. 24:27.

In 2 Cor. 5:1-4, Paul expresses his longing, and the longing of the Saints, to be among those who should not be "unclothed" by Death, but who should be "clothed upon" by Immortality "without dying."

"For we know that if our earthly house of this tabernacle, (the body), were dissolved, (that is die), we have a building of God, an house not made with hands eternal in the heavens. For in this (body) we groan, earnestly desiring to be 'clothed upon' with our house which is from heaven: if so be that being 'clothed' we shall not be found naked. For we that are in this tabernacle (the body) do groan, being burdened; not for that we would be 'unclothed' (by death), but 'clothed upon' (by immortality), that 'mortality' might be "swallowed up of life."

In his letter to the Philippians, while Paul hopes that—

"If by any means he may attain unto **The** (out from among the dead) **Resurrection**, yet he pressed toward the mark for the '**prize**' of the **High** (out and up) **Calling** of God in Christ Jesus." Phil. 3:11-14.

That is, while Paul would esteem it a great thing to "rise from the dead" at the First Resurrection, and be "caught up" with those who should be "changed," yet he would esteem it a "prize" if he could be caught up "without dying," that is, live until Jesus came back.

The Time of Rapture.

Some claim that "all" the Church are to pass through the Tribulation; others that "all" the Church are to be caught out before the Tribulation, while some claim that only the "Waiting" and "Watching" Saints shall be caught out before the Tribulation, and that the rest must pass through it. The latter base their claim on Heb. 9:28, where it says—"Unto them that look for Him shall He appear the second time without sin unto salvation." While this might apply to the living when He appears, it certainly cannot apply to the dead. There are tens and hundreds of thousands who "fell asleep in Jesus" who never heard of the Premillennial Coming of the Lord, or at least never grasped its meaning, and who therefore never "watched" and "waited" and "looked" for His Appearing. They surely are "In Christ"; and the "Dead in Christ" are to rise at the Rapture. Paul does not say in 1 Thess. 4:16, 17, that it will be the "dead" who "watched" and "waited" and "looked," and those who are "alive" and "watch" and "wait" and "look" for His Appearing that shall be "caught out," but the dead "In Christ," and we who **Are Alive And Remain."**

The order of the Resurrections is—"Christ the 'First Fruits,' afterward they that 'are Christ's at His Coming." Paul says—"Behold, I show you a Mystery: we shall not all 'sleep,' but we shall **ALL Be Changed."** 1 Cor. 15:51.

Then there is another fact that we must not forget, and that is, the Unity of the Church.

"For as the **Body Is One,** and hath many members, and **ALL the Members Of That One Body, Being Many ARE ONE BODY**; so also is Christ. For by One Spirit are we **ALL Baptized Into One Body."** 1 Cor. 12:12, 13.

All then who have been "born again" (John 3:3-7) are part of Christ's "Body," and we cannot conceive of Christ's "Body" being divided; part of it remaining "asleep" in the grave, and part of it "raised in glory"; part of it left to pass through the Tribulation, and part of it "changed" and caught up to meet Him in the air.

If "all" the Church are to pass through the Tribulation, then instead of waiting and watching "for the Lord," we should be waiting and watching "for the Tribulation," which is contrary to the teaching of Christ Himself. Matt. 24:42-44.

The Tribulation is not for the perfecting "of the Saints." It has nothing to do with the Church. It is the time of "Jacob's Trouble" (Jer. 30:7), and is the "Judgment of Israel," and it is God's purpose to keep the Church Out Of It. Rev. 2:10. The Book of Revelation is written in chronological order. After the fourth chapter the Church is seen no more upon the earth until she appears in the nineteenth chapter coming with the Bridegroom "from" Heaven. The entire time between these two chapters is filled with appalling judgments that fall upon those that "dwell on the earth," and as the Church is not of the earth, but is supposed to "sit together in "Heavenly Places" in Christ Jesus," (Eph. 2:6), she will not be among those who "dwell on the earth" in those days.

Rapture And Revelation.

The confusion is largely due to the fact that students of Prophetic Truth do not distinguish between Christ's coming "for" His Saints, and "with" His Saints. The former is called the "Rapture" the latter the "Revelation." Between the two there is an interval of at least seven years, during which the Church is "judged," and the "Marriage of the Lamb" takes place in the heavenlies, and on the earth Antichrist manifests himself and the Tribulation runs its course.

Numerous passages in scripture speak of Christ coming "with" His Saints (Zech. 14:5, Col. 3:4, 1 Thess. 3:13, 1 Thess. 4:14, Jude 14), but it is evident that they cannot come "with" Him, if they had not been previously caught out "to" Him. All such passages refer therefore to the "Revelation" and not the "Rapture."

The typical teaching of the Scriptures demand that the Church be caught out "before" the Tribulation. Joseph was a type of Christ and he was espoused to, and married Asenath, a Gentile bride, during the time of his "rejection by his brethren," and "before the famine," which typified the Tribulation, because it was the time of "Judgment of his Brethren." This is the time of Christ's rejection by "His Brethren"—the Jews, and to complete the type He must get His Bride—the church, "before" the Tribulation.

Moses, who is also a type of Christ, got his bride, and she a Gentile, "after" his rejection by his brethren, and "before" they passed through the Tribulation under Pharoah. Ex. 2:23-25.

Enoch, a type of the "Translation Saints," was caught out "before" the Flood, and the Flood is a type of the Tribulation, and Noah and his family of the "Jewish Remnant" or 144,000 sealed ones of Rev. 7:1-8, who will be preserved through the Tribulation.

The Rapture.

The "Rapture" will be the most startling "event" of this Age and Dispensation. As it is to occur in the **"twinkling of an eye"** and **all over the earth at the same time**, that part of the world that is not asleep will witness the event. As to the "Shout of the Lord," the "Voice of the Archangel," and the "Trump of God" we do not know whether their sound will be heard and distinguished by others than the "dead in Christ" and the "living saints." We know that one day the Father spoke to Christ in a voice that He understood, but the people who stood by mistook it for "thunder." John 12:28, 29. When the Lord appeared to Saul of Tarsus on the road to Damascus and spoke to him, the men that journeyed with him stood speechless, "hearing a voice," but seeing no man, and not understanding what was said. Acts 9:3-7. We know, however, that the "dead in Christ" will hear the sound, for it will be "intensely penetrating." There will be no graves so deep, no catacombs so rock covered, no pyramids or mausoleums so thick, but what the sound shall reach their depths and the "dead in Christ" shall hear the cry—**"awake ye sleeping saints and arise from the dead, it is MORNING, the morning of the FIRST RESURRECTION."**

The Voice Of The Archangel.

The statement in Dan. 12:1, 2 that Michael (the Great Prince) will be busy helping Daniel's People (the Jews), at the time of the Second Coming of Christ, and that there will be an "out from among the dead resurrection" at that time; and the fact that Michael the Archangel contended with the Devil about the dead body of Moses when it was raised from the dead, as we are told in Jude 9, makes it clear that Michael the Archangel will have a part to play in the resurrection of the dead at the Rapture. The "voice" of the Archangel then will be the "voice" of Michael, for he is the only Archangel mentioned in the Scriptures.

As Satan tried to prevent the resurrection of the body of Moses, and as he will not be cast out of the Heavenlies until "after" the First Resurrection, the inference is that he will try to prevent the resurrection of the "dead in Christ," and that he will be opposed by Michael at the head of "Armies of Heaven," and that the "voice of the Archangel" refers to his commands to the Heavenly Army.

The Trump Of God.

What is meant by the "Trump of God" is not so clear. That there is a Trumpet to sound at the "first" Resurrection is certain, for Paul mentions it in his discourse on the Resurrection in 1 Cor. 15:52, and calls it the "Last Trump." Some hold that Paul refers to the last of the "Seven Trumpets" mentioned in the Book of Revelation (Rev. 8:1, 2, 6; 10:7), and as that does not sound until the "Middle of the Week," that therefore the Church is not caught out until the "Middle of the Week."

But as the Church is to be caught out at the "beginning" of the Week. this cannot be true. What then is meant by the "Last Trump?"

The Trumpet is a military instrument. It was used in the Camp of Israel to call the Assembly together. The First Trumpet called them to arise and be ready to depart, the Second (last) Trumpet was the signal to march. When God descended upon Mt. Sinai the people were assembled at the sound of the "Trumpet of God." Ex. 19: 9-11, 16-20. And when God was ready to speak to the people it sounded the second time (verse 19). It has been suggested that the descent of God to Mt. Sinai is a type of the "Descent of the Lord" into the Air to meet His Church, and that at the sounding of the First Trumpet, the "dead in Christ" will be raised, and at the sounding of the Second (last) Trumpet, the "living Saints" will be changed and together with the risen dead ascend to meet the Lord. The probability of this is seen in the fact that the "Last Trump" is connected with the "changing" of the living Saints, rather than with the resurrection of the dead. 1 Cor. 15: 51, 52.

We know that the "Elect of Israel" are to be gathered back to their own land with a "great sound of a trumpet." Matt. 24: 30, 31. This will occur at the

"Feast of Trumpets"

(the Jewish New Year) at the close of the Tribulation Period. The "Feast of Trumpets" was associated with the "Feast of Tabernacles" and occurred in the fall of the year, and as Jesus was crucified at the time of the "Passover Feast," and the Holy Spirit was given at the time of the "Feast of Pentecost," it has been suggested, that as Jesus will reveal Himself to His brethren, the Jews, at the "Feast of Tabernacles," a type of Israel's rest in the Millennial Land, that He will call out His Church with the "sound of a Trumpet" at the "Feast of Trumpets" **seven years before** the "Elect of Israel" are called out. This however is mere speculation.

If the sainted dead shall slip out of their sepulchres without disturbing them, as Christ arose and left the tomb without breaking the seal, the angel rolling away the stone simply to show that the tomb was empty, the First Resurrection will be secret and probably unknown to the world, but it will not be so with the "Living Saints" who are translated.

If it is night on our side of the earth when the Rapture occurs, the community will wake up in the morning to find all the real Christians gone, disappeared in the night. The world will awake to the fact that the Bible is true, and the much despised doctrine of the Premillennial Coming of the Lord to gather out His Saints is no fanciful interpretation of Scripture.

"I tell you, in **that night** there shall be two men (omit men) in one bed: the one shall be **taken**, and the other shall be **left**. Two women (omit women) shall be grinding together; the one shall be **taken** and the other left. Two men (omit men) shall be in the field; the one shall be **taken**, and the other left." Luke 17: 34-36.

Here we have the "rotundity" of the Earth taught by Christ before it was demonstrated by Columbus. Two in one bed, that means night; two grinding grain for the morning or evening meal, that means sunrise or sunset; two in the field, that means midday, and this is another proof that when the Rapture occurs it will be instantaneous, in the "twinkling of an eye," and shall girdle the earth like **lightning**.

If it be day with us when the Rapture occurs the event will be "startling." As it was in the days of Noah (Matt. 24: 36-39), the people will be eating and drinking, marrying and giving in marriage, buying and selling, planting and building. If it be at a pleasant time of the year, the boats, and cars, and parks, will be filled with pleasure seekers. If it be in the midst of the week and during the business hours of the day, the shops and stores and mills will be filled with toilers and shoppers, and the streets of the cities lined with men and women and children on pleasure and business bent. Suddenly a noise from heaven will be heard. To the vast majority it will be but a startling "sound," but to many it will be the

"Voice Of The Lord."

When the people shall recover from their affrighted condition they will discover that a great many people are missing, and that the missing ones were the best people in the community.

Confusion for a time will reign. The working force in the stores, banking institutions, manufacturing plants, and other places of business will find their force depleted by the loss of faithful employes. Street car lines and other means of transportation will be blocked owing to a shortage of men. At first, the whole thing will be a **Mystery**, until some one who has heard of the Doctrine of the "Rapture" explains the situation. The surprise will be that so many professing Christians are left behind, among them many ministers of the Gospel, while many who were not known to be Christian will be missing.

For a few days the excitement will be intense. Then the people will settle down to the inevitable. With the exception of a few who will repent and turn to God, the mass of the people will become more hardened and wicked. As the Holy Spirit will have gone back with the "Raptured Ones," and the Saints, the "salt" of the earth, been taken out, there will be nothing to prevent the rapid degeneration and "Moral Putrefaction" of those who are "left," and sin and iniquity and all manner of crime and worldliness will increase and pave the way for the manifestation of Antichrist, under whose administration the world will rapidly ripen for judgment.

VI. The "Judgment" of the Church.

After the Church has been taken out of the World it is to be "judged." Not for sin, but for works, at the "Judgment Seat of Christ." See Judgment No. 2, in the Chapter on "The Judgments," and on the Chart of "The Resurrections and Judgments."

VII. The "MARRIAGE" Of The Church.

The "Marriage" of the Church is prophetically referred to by Jesus in the Parable of the "Marriage of the King's Son" (Matt. 22: 1-14), and is consummated in Rev. 19: 7-9.

"Let us be glad and rejoice and give honor to Him; for the

'Marriage of the Lamb'

is come, and His wife hath made herself ready. And to her was granted that she should be arrayed in fine linen, clean and white; for the fine linen is the righteousness of Saints. And he saith unto me, write, **Blessed are they which are called unto the MARRIAGE SUPPER OF THE LAMB."**

Notice that it does not say the "Marriage of the Bride," but the "Marriage of the **LAMB**." That grand event will be not so much the consummation of the hopes of the Bride, as it will be the consummation of the **plan of God for His Son**, arranged for **before the foundation of the World**. Eph. 1: 4. The "Marriage of the Lamb" is the consummation of the joy of Christ as a **MAN**. It would not have been possible if Christ had not been born in **the flesh**. Otherwise it would have been the union of "dissimilar natures" for the "Bride" is of "human origin." This is why Jesus took His "human nature" back with Him to Heaven, and today we have in Heaven the **MAN** Christ Jesus. 1 Tim. 2:5.

While the "Bride" was chosen for Christ "before the foundation of the world," the "espousal" could not take place until Christ assumed humanity and ascended to Heaven as the **Man** Christ Jesus. There have been many long betrothals but Christ's has been the longest on record. He has been waiting for His Bride nearly 1900 years, but He will not have to wait much longer. Soon Heaven shall resound with **the cry—**

"Let us be glad and rejoice, and give honor to Him, for the **Marriage of the Lamb is Come.**" Rev. 19:7.

There have been many royal weddings of international interest, where the invited guests and spectators witnessed a spectacle magnificent in its appointments, and rejoiced in a union that bound together different nations. But the wedding of the Lamb and His Bride the Church will surpass them all, for it shall unite Heaven and Earth in a bond that shall never be broken, for what God (the Father) shall join together, no man shall ever put asunder, and that union no divorce shall ever break.

The Bride shall be "arrayed in fine linen, clean and white; for the fine linen is the righteousness of Saints." Rev. 19:7, 8. The word "righteousness" is plural, and should read "righteousnesses." Not the imputed righteousness of Christ, but the "righteous acts and works" of the saints themselves, that shall remain after they have passed through the "fiery test" of the "Judgment for Works" at the "Judgment Seat of Christ." 1 Cor. 3:11-15. What a contrast there will be between the purple and scarlet colored dress, and jewel bedecked person, of the "Harlot Wife" of Antichrist (Rev. 17:3, 4), and **the spotless white robe of fine linen of the Bride of the Lamb.**

After the Marriage, the Heavenly Bridegroom, having received His Kingdom, will return to this earth where He bled and died, and from whence He got His Bride, and the Lord God will give unto Him the "Throne of David," and He shall reign on the earth for **a Thousand Years."** What a sweet and delightful **"Honey-Moon"** that will be. But it will end, not for the Bridegroom and the Bride, but for the earth, by their return to the Father's House. Then after the earth has had its "Baptism of Fire," they will return with the descent of the "Holy City" to abide on the New Earth forever. See the **chart on "The Church."**

HE IS COMING

He is coming, coming for us;
   Soon we'll see His light afar,
On the dark horizon rising,
   As the Bright and Morning Star,
Cheering many a waking watcher,
   As the star whose kindly ray
Heralds the approaching morning
   Just before the break of day.
     Oh! what joy, as night hangs round us,
      'Tis to think of morning's ray;
     Sweet to know He's coming for us,
      Just before the break of day.

He is coming, coming for us;
   Soon we'll hear His voice on high;
Dead and living, rising, changing,
   In the twinkling of an eye
Shall be caught up altogether,
   For the meeting in the air;
With a shout the Lord, descending,
   Shall Himself await us there.
     Oh! what joy that great foregathering,
      Trysted meeting in the air;
     Sweet to know He's coming for us,
      Calling us to join Him there.

He is coming as the Bridegroom,
   Coming to unfold at last
The great secret of His purpose,
   Mystery of ages past.
And the Bride, to her is granted
   In His beauty now to shine,
As in rapture she exclaimeth,
   "I am His and He is mine."
     Oh! what joy that marriage union,
      Mystery of love divine;
     Sweet to sing in all its fulness,
      "I am His and He is mine."

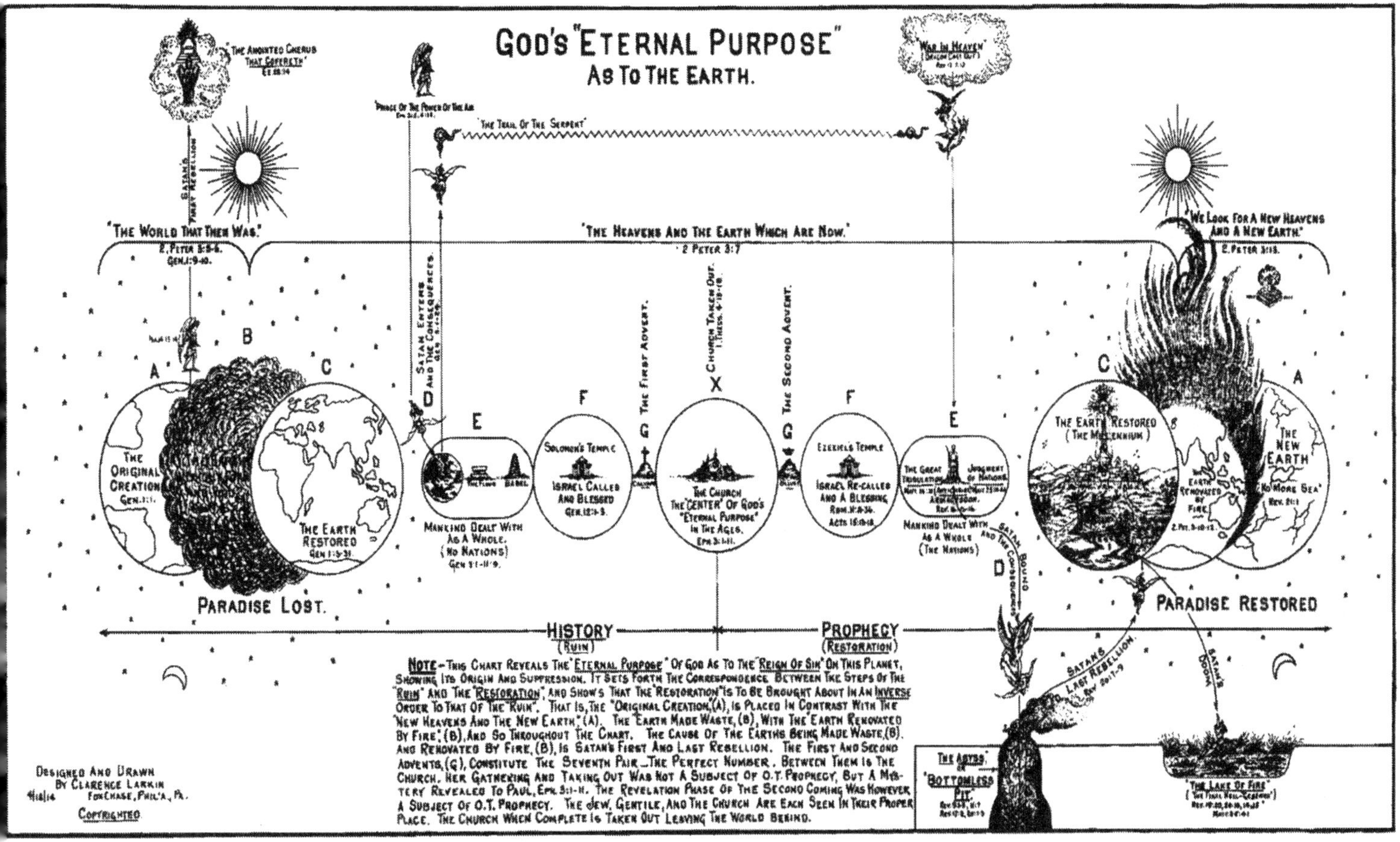

GOD'S "ETERNAL PURPOSE"
AS TO THE EARTH.
"The Anointed Cherub That Covereth"
"War In Heaven"
"The Trail Of The Serpent"
Satan's First Rebellion
"The World That Then Was."
2. Peter 3:5-6.
Gen. 1:9-10.
"The Heavens And The Earth Which Are Now."
2 Peter 3:7
"We Look For A New Heavens And A New Earth."
2. Peter 3:13.
Satan Enters And The Consequences.
The First Advent.
Church Taken Out.
1. Thess. 4:15-18.
The Second Advent.
A
B
C
D
E
F
G
X
The Original Creation Gen. 1:1.
The Earth Restored Gen 1:3-31.
Babel
Mankind Dealt With As A Whole. (No Nations)
Solomon's Temple
Israel Called And Blessed
Gen. 12:1-3.
The Church The "Center" Of God's "Eternal Purpose" In The Ages.
Eph. 3:1-11.
Ezekiel's Temple
Israel Re-called And A Blessing
Acts 15:13-18.
The Great Tribulation
Judgment Of Nations
Armageddon.
Mankind Dealt With As A Whole (The Nations)
Satan Bound And The Consequences
The Earth Restored (The Millennium)
Earth Renovated By Fire.
The New Earth "No More Sea" Rev. 21:1
Paradise Lost.
Paradise Restored
HISTORY (Ruin)
PROPHECY (Restoration)
Satan's Last Rebellion.
Satan's Doom
The Abyss, or "Bottomless Pit"
"The Lake Of Fire"
Note—This Chart Reveals The "Eternal Purpose" Of God As To The "Reign Of Sin" On This Planet, Showing Its Origin And Suppression. It Sets Forth The Correspondence Between The Steps Of The "Ruin" And The "Restoration", And Shows That The "Restoration" Is To Be Brought About In An Inverse Order To That Of The "Ruin". That Is, The "Original Creation," (A), Is Placed In Contrast With The "New Heavens And The New Earth," (A). The "Earth Made Waste, (B), With The "Earth Renovated By Fire," (B), And So Throughout The Chart. The Cause Of The Earths Being Made Waste, (B), And Renovated By Fire, (B), Is Satan's First And Last Rebellion. The First And Second Advents, (G), Constitute The Seventh Pair—The Perfect Number. Between Them Is The Church. Her Gathering And Taking Out Was Not A Subject Of O.T. Prophecy, But A Mystery Revealed To Paul, Eph. 3:1-11. The Revelation Phase Of The Second Coming Was However A Subject Of O.T. Prophecy. The Jew, Gentile, And The Church Are Each Seen In Their Proper Place. The Church When Complete Is Taken Out Leaving The World Behind.
Designed And Drawn By Clarence Larkin Fox Chase, Phil'a, Pa.
Copyrighted.

THE KING

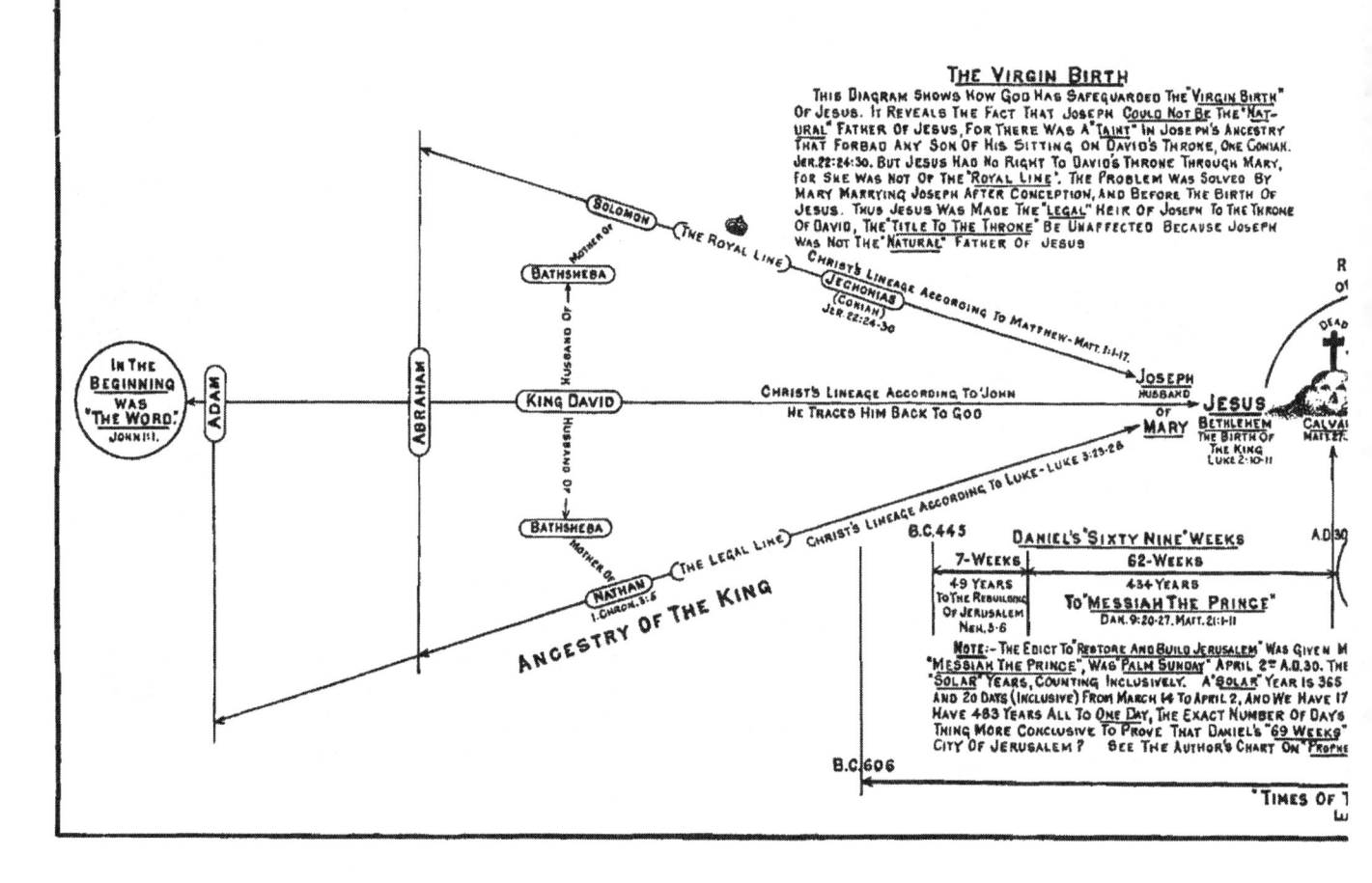

THE VIRGIN BIRTH
This diagram shows how God has safeguarded the "Virgin Birth" of Jesus. It reveals the fact that Joseph could not be the "Natural" Father of Jesus, for there was a "Taint" in Joseph's ancestry that forbad any son of his sitting on David's Throne, one Coniah. Jer. 22:24-30. But Jesus had no right to David's Throne through Mary, for she was not of the "Royal Line". The problem was solved by Mary marrying Joseph after conception, and before the birth of Jesus. Thus Jesus was made the "Legal" heir of Joseph to the Throne of David, the "Title to the Throne" be unaffected because Joseph was not the "Natural" Father of Jesus.

The Royal Line — Solomon — Bathsheba (Mother of) — Jechonias (Coniah) Jer. 22:24-30

Christ's Lineage According to Matthew — Matt. 1:1-17

"In the Beginning was The Word." John 1:1

Adam — Abraham — King David (Husband of Bathsheba) — Joseph (Husband of Mary) — Jesus, Bethlehem, The Birth of the King, Luke 2:10-11

Christ's Lineage According to John — He Traces Him Back to God

Bathsheba (Mother of) — Nathan 1 Chron. 3:5 — **The Legal Line**

Christ's Lineage According to Luke — Luke 3:23-28

ANCESTRY OF THE KING

Daniel's "Sixty Nine" Weeks

7-Weeks	62-Weeks
49 Years to the Rebuilding of Jerusalem Neh. 3-6	434 Years to "Messiah the Prince" Dan. 9:20-27, Matt. 21:1-11

B.C. 445

Note: — The Edict to "Restore and Build Jerusalem" was given... "Messiah the Prince", was "Palm Sunday" April 2nd A.D. 30. The "Solar" Years, counting inclusively. A "Solar" year is 365... and 20 days (inclusive) from March 14 to April 2, and we have 17... have 483 years all to one day, the exact number of days... thing more conclusive to prove that Daniel's "69 Weeks"... City of Jerusalem? See the Author's Chart on "Prophe...

B.C. 606

Calvary Matt. 27

A.D. 30

"Times of T...

The Kingdom

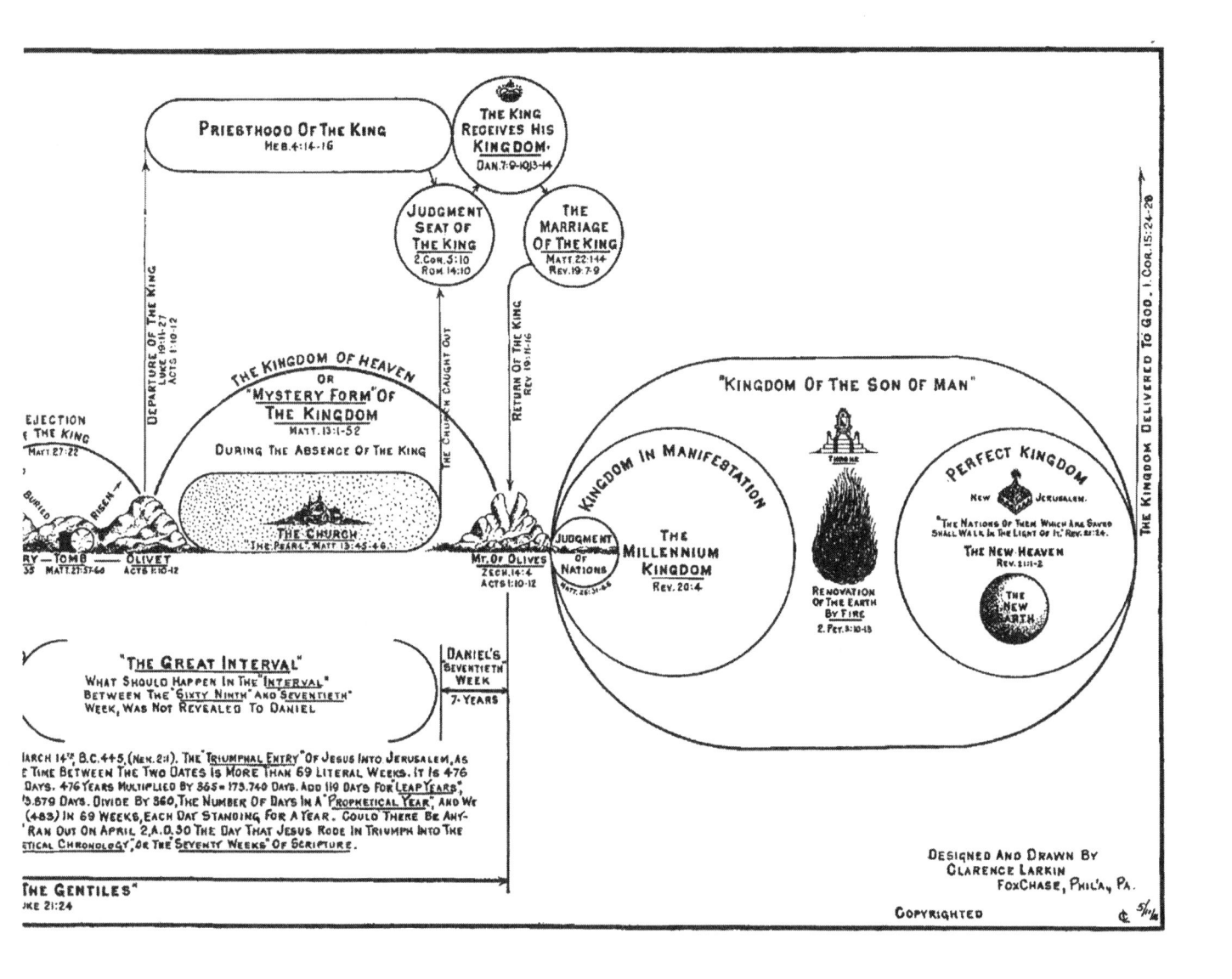

- **Priesthood Of The King** — Heb. 4:14-16
- **The King Receives His Kingdom** — Dan. 7:9-10, 13-14
- **Judgment Seat Of The King** — 2. Cor. 5:10; Rom. 14:10
- **The Marriage Of The King** — Matt. 22:1-14; Rev. 19:7-9
- **Departure Of The King** — Luke 19:11-27; Acts 1:10-12
- **Return Of The King** — Rev. 19:11-16
- **The Kingdom Of Heaven** or **"Mystery Form" Of The Kingdom** — Matt. 13:1-52. During The Absence Of The King
- **The Church Caught Out**
- **Rejection Of The King** — Matt. 27:22
- Buried — Risen — Tomb — Olivet — Matt. 27:57-60; Acts 1:10-12
- **The Church** — The Pearl, Matt. 13:45-46
- **Mt. Of Olives** — Zech. 14:4; Acts 1:10-12
- **Judgment Of Nations** — Matt. 25:31-46
- **"Kingdom Of The Son Of Man"**
- **Kingdom In Manifestation** — **The Millennium Kingdom** — Rev. 20:4
- **Renovation Of The Earth By Fire** — 2. Pet. 3:10-13
- **Perfect Kingdom** — New Jerusalem. "The Nations Of Them Which Are Saved Shall Walk In The Light Of It." Rev. 21:24. **The New Heaven** — Rev. 21:1-2. **The New Earth**
- **The Kingdom Delivered To God** — 1. Cor. 15:24-28

"The Great Interval" — What Should Happen In The "Interval" Between The "Sixty Ninth" And "Seventieth" Week, Was Not Revealed To Daniel.

Daniel's Seventieth Week — 7 Years

March 14th, B.C. 445 (Neh. 2:1). The "Triumphal Entry" Of Jesus Into Jerusalem. As The Time Between The Two Dates Is More Than 69 Literal Weeks. It Is 476 Days. 476 Years Multiplied By 365 = 173,740 Days. Add 119 Days For Leap Years. 173,879 Days. Divide By 360, The Number Of Days In A "Prophetical Year", And We (483) In 69 Weeks, Each Day Standing For A Year. Could There Be Any— Ran Out On April 2, A.D. 30 The Day That Jesus Rode In Triumph Into The ...etical Chronology, Or The "Seventy Weeks" Of Scripture.

"The Gentiles" — Luke 21:24

Designed And Drawn By
Clarence Larkin
FoxChase, Phil'a, Pa.

Copyrighted

XII
THE KING

If it is the purpose of God to set up a Kingdom on this earth, the question naturally arises who is to be the King. Is there any intimation in the Scriptures as to who he shall be? In the Old Testament we have a "Prophetic Portrait" of the King, and in the New Testament the "Historic Portrait." These correspond as the die to the matrix. As the cartoonist first outlines his picture and then fills in the details, so it is the Divine method of revelation to begin with an outline, and then gradually fill in its details until we have the complete picture.

The first outline of the "Prophetic Portrait" of the King we find in the book of Genesis. The Lord God said unto the Serpent—

"I will put enmity between **thee** and the **woman**, and between **thy seed** and **her seed**; it shall bruise thy **head**, and thou shalt bruise his **heel**." Gen. 3:15.

Here we have a reference to some future "descendant" of the woman who should be victorious over the Serpent. How luminous this becomes in the light of the New Testament's statements as to Christ's final victory over Satan.

We have to wait for 1700 years, until after the Flood, for our second outline of the "Prophetic Portrait," when God tells us in Gen. 9:26, 27, that the promised seed of the woman shall come through the line of Shem.

The third outline is given 400 years later, when God singles out Abraham to be the father of the race from whom the King shall come. Gen. 12:1-3. At that time Abraham had no heir, and humanly speaking there was no likelihood of his having one, so Abraham besought the Lord that his steward Eliezer, who had been born in his house, should be his heir, but God said "he shall not be thine heir, but he that shall come forth out of 'thine own bowels' shall be thine heir." Gen. 15, 1-4. Now Sarah, Abraham's wife was "past age," and the only solution of the problem to her was that Abraham should take her handmaid, Hagar, an Egyptian, as his wife, to which Abraham consented, and in due time Ishmael was born to Abraham of Hagar. Gen. 16:1-16. This pleased Abraham and he said unto God: "O that Ishmael might live before Thee!" And God said—

"**Sarah, thy wife, shall bear thee a son indeed**, and thou shalt call his name **Isaac**; and I will establish my covenant with him for an everlasting covenant, and with his seed after him. And as for **Ishmael**, I have heard thee. Behold I have blessed him and will make him fruitful, and will multiply him exceedingly; twelve princes shall he beget, and I will make him a great nation. But my **Covenant** will I establish with **Isaac**, which Sarah shall bear unto thee at this set time in the next year." Gen. 17:18-21.

Here again we see the principle of selection, or limitation. If in the days of Christ an Ishmaelite had claimed to be the Messiah because he was a "lineal descendant of Abraham," his claim would have been rejected because the Messiah was to come from Abraham through **Isaac**.

In course of time Isaac was married and unto him and Rebekah twin sons were born, Esau and Jacob. Then another choice had to be made, and at Bethel God revealed to Jacob that he was the one chosen. Gen. 28:10-15. Here we see that the Abrahamic Covenant passes over Esau, the "first-born," and falls on **Jacob**. No descendant of Esau therefore may claim the Messianic title.

To Jacob twelve sons were born, to which one shall the promise descend? To Reuben, the first-born, or to Joseph, the favorite? To our surprise God chooses neither, but selects Judah, the fourth son of Leah.

"**Judah**, thou art he whom thy brethren shall praise; thy hand shall be in the neck of thine enemies; **thy father's children shall bow down before thee**. . . . The **sceptre** shall not depart from **Judah**, nor a lawgiver from between his feet

UNTIL SHILOH COME;

and unto **Him** shall the gathering of the people be." Gen. 49:8-10.

Here the promise gains in definiteness. The Messiah must come through **Judah**, not through Levi, the progenitor of the Priestly order. The word "sceptre" indicates Kingly power, and the word "Shiloh" is a name for the Messiah.

The promise now skips 475 years to the time of David, who was of the tribe of Judah. God said to David, through Nathan the prophet—

"Thine **House** and thy **Kingdom** shall be established **forever** before thee; thy **throne** shall be established **forever**." 2 Sam. 7:-16.

This promise God afterward confirmed with an oath, saying—

"I have made a Covenant with my chosen, I have **sworn** unto David my servant, thy **seed** will I establish **forever**, and build up thy **throne to all generations**. . . . Once have I **sworn** by **My Holiness** that I will not lie unto David. His **seed** shall endure **forever**, and his **throne as the sun before ME**. It shall be established **forever as the moon**, and as a **faithful witness in heaven**." Psa. 89:3, 4, 35-37.

This Covenant was unconditional and was reaffirmed to Israel through Jeremiah the prophet, many years after David's death when Israel had lapsed into idolatry (Jer. 33:17-26), in which God promised that David should never want a **man** (son) to sit upon **his throne forever**.

That these promises did not mean, as we now see, that there should be an "unbroken" line of successors on David's throne, is clear from the fact that, after Solomon, the kingdom was divided, and in B. C. 587 the last king of Judah was carried captive to Babylon. Jeremiah refers to a "future" king that God would raise up to sit on the "Throne of David."

"Behold, the days come, saith the Lord, that I will raise unto David a righteous **Branch**, and a **King** shall reign and prosper, and shall execute judgment and justice in the earth. **In His days** Judah shall be saved, and Israel shall dwell safely, and this is his name whereby he shall be called—**THE LORD OUR RIGHTEOUSNESS**." Jer. 23:5, 6.

When we compare this prophecy with Isa. 11:1, 2—

"There shall come forth a rod out of the stem of Jesse, and a **Branch** shall grow out of his **roots**; and the **Spirit of the Lord** shall rest upon Him, the spirit of wisdom and understanding, the spirit of counsel and might, the spirit of knowledge and of the fear of the Lord,"

and note the word "**Branch**" that is common to both, and then note the last words of Isaiah's prophecy—"The **Spirit of the Lord** shall rest upon him, etc.," and recall Luke's description of the Child Jesus—"And the Child grew, and waxed strong in Spirit, filled with wisdom;

and the Grace of God was upon Him"—Luke 2:40, we have no difficulty in identifying who the Prophet meant.

But the Messiah was not only to come from the line so clearly marked out in the Old Testament Scriptures. He was also to be of

Divine Parentage.

How this could be was a riddle until the Prophet Isaiah solved it by saying—

"Behold a **virgin** shall conceive and bear a son, and shall call his name **Immanuel**." Isa. 7:14.

An obscure passage in Jer. 31:22 may refer to the same event—"A woman shall 'encompass a man.'" That is, a woman shall enclose in her womb a "man-child" without human parentage.

Later Isaiah says—

"For unto us a **Child is born**, unto us a **Son is given**; and the government shall be upon his shoulder; and his name shall be called **Wonderful, Counsellor, the Mighty God, the Everlasting Father, the Prince of Peace**. Of the increase of his government and peace there shall be no end, upon the

Throne of David,

and upon his **Kingdom**, to order it, and to establish it with judgment and with justice from henceforth, even **forever**." Isa. 9:6, 7.

Where is the key that will unlock this passage? Listen.

"In the sixth month the angel Gabriel was sent from God unto a city of Galilee, named Nazareth, to a **virgin espoused to a man whose name was Joseph**, of the

House of David;

and the virgin's name was Mary. . . . And the angel said unto her—Fear not, Mary; for thou hast found favor with God. And, behold, thou shalt conceive in thy womb, and bring forth a **son**, and shalt call His name **Jesus**. He shall be great and shall be called the **Son of the Highest** and the Lord God shall give unto Him

The Throne of His Father David;

and He shall **reign** over the **House of Jacob** (Israel) **FOREVER**; and of His Kingdom **There Shall Be NO END**." Luke 1:26-33.

That this was not to be a natural birth after marriage with Joseph, is clear from the fact that when Joseph learned of Mary's condition he was minded to put her away privately, but was told not to do so by the angel Gabriel, for that which was conceived in her was of the Holy Ghost. Matt. 1:18-20. This is confirmed by the words of Gabriel to Mary herself.

"The **Holy Ghost** shall come upon thee, and the power of **THE HIGHEST** shall overshadow thee; therefore also that **Holy Thing** which shall be born of thee shall be called the **SON OF GOD**." Luke 1:35.

Some have maintained that the Prophet Isaiah in his prophecy. "Behold a 'virgin' shall conceive and bear a son and shall call his name Immanuel;" referred to some maiden of his own time, but this is refuted by Matthew, who says—"Now all this was done that it might be fulfilled which was spoken of the Lord by the prophet, saying—

"Behold, a **virgin** shall be with child and shall bring forth a **son**, and they shall call his name **Emmanuel**, which being interpreted is **God With Us**." Matt. 1:23.

The "Virgin Birth" of Jesus is still further confirmed by the statement of Matthew that Joseph "knew her not" until she had brought forth her firstborn son. Matt. 1:24, 25.

The promise in Gen. 3:15 was to be fulfilled through the "**seed of the woman**." The word "seed" is always in the Scriptures, with this exception, applied to the "male" of man and beast, and the promise could only be fulfilled, as Luke tells us it was fulfilled, by Mary being with child by the **Holy Ghost**.

That we may have no difficulty in tracing the ancestry of Jesus, two genealogical tables are given us. The first, in Matthew, is of Joseph, and traces Jesus' ancestry back to Abraham. The second, in Luke, is of Mary, and traces Jesus' ancestry back to Adam. See the Chart on "The King." A careful examination of these genealogies shows what a safeguard God threw about the birth of Jesus and how careful He was to see that the Scriptures were literally fulfilled in Him. Matthew traces the genealogy of Jesus back to David, through Solomon; Luke traces it back to David through Nathan. That there are similar names in the two tables presents no difficulty as such a thing is common in tracing any long line of descent. Again the statement in Matthew that "Jacob begat Joseph, the husband of Mary," and the statement in Luke that Joseph was (as supposed) the son of Heli is easily reconciled, for Joseph could not be the son of both **Jacob and Heli**. The fact that the translators of the King James version use the word "supposed" and that the word "son" is in italics (which indicates that it is not in the original but is placed there to make sense), shows that some other word could be inserted that would make sense, and that word is "son-in-law," and so it should read, "Joseph which was the 'son-in-law' of Heli." This makes the genealogy of Luke that of Mary, for two genealogies so clearly unalike could not both be the genealogy of Joseph.

But why two lines of descent, one through Nathan and the other through Solomon? Why was not Mary's genealogy sufficient? During King David's residence at Hebron, while he was as yet only the king of Judah, six sons were born to him. Of these, three appear to have died in infancy. Of the other three, Amnon was murdered, Absalom perished while in rebellion against his father, and Adonijah, having attempted to usurp the throne, was subsequently put to death by Solomon. The right of succession to the crown was thus secured to the sons of David born "after" he was enthroned king over all Israel.

The children that were born to David after he was crowned king over all Israel are also enumerated. I Chron. 3:1-9. Of these two only need be mentioned, Nathan and Solomon. Solomon, as we know, succeeded his father as king, but Nathan was older than Solomon, and on that ground might have contested Solomon's right of succession, though we are not told that he did. Nevertheless Solomon's title had the shadow of Nathan's claim upon it, and that there should be no cloud upon Jesus' title to the "Throne of David," God ordained that Mary, the mother of Jesus, should be a direct descendant of David through Nathan, the "legal heir" to the throne. But Jesus had no right to David's **Throne** through Mary, for she was not in the "Kingly Line" of descent through Solomon. How then was Jesus' right to David's Throne to be brought about? Only by **marriage**.

Here we see the wonderful way in which God safeguarded the "**Virgin Birth**" of Jesus. He saw to it that Mary married (after conception) a man who could not be the **natural** father of Jesus, because of a **taint** or defect in his ancestry.

Joseph was a lineal descendant of David through the "Kingly Line" of Solomon, but in that line there was one Jechonias (Matt. 1:11, 12), called in Jer. 22:24-30, Coniah, of whom God had said,

"No man of his seed **shall prosper**, sitting upon the 'Throne of David' and ruling any more in Judah."

MATT
BOOK OF

I. THE KING	II. THE KINGDOM — SERMON ON THE MOUNT	III. KING'S GALILEAN MINISTRY	IV. THE "MYSTERIES" OF THE KINGDOM

I. THE KING
- His Pedigree. 1:1-17
- His Birth. 1:18-25
- His Infancy. 2:1-23
- His Baptism. 3:1-17
- His Testing. 4:1-11
- Begins His Public Ministry

II. THE KINGDOM — Sermon on the Mount

Its Citizens
- Their Character. 5:1-12
- Their Influence. 5:13-16
- Relation of the King to the Law

Its Laws — Man's Relation to Man
- As to Murder. 5:21-26
- As to Adultery. 5:27-30
- As to Divorce. 5:31-32
- As to Perjury. 5:33-37
- As to Retaliation. 5:38-42
- As to Enemies. 5:43-48

Man's Relation to God — Spiritual
- As to Almsgiving. 6:1-4
- As to Prayer. 6:5-15
- As to Fasting. 6:16-18

Temporal
- As to Money. 6:19-24
- As to Food–Raiment 6:25-34
- As to Judgment. 7:1-6
- The Conditions of Entrance 7:7-29

III. KING'S GALILEAN MINISTRY — Reveals His Deity
- By His Power Over Disease. 8:1-22
- By His Power Over Nature. 8:23-27
- By His Power Over Demons. 8:28-34
- By His Power to Forgive Sin. 9:1-8
- By His Power Over Death. 9:18-26
- By His Power Over Bodily Affliction
- Calls and Commissions Disciples. 10:1-42
- Testimony to John the Baptist. 11:1-19
- Upbraids Cities. 11:20-30
- Relation to the Sabbath Day. 12:1-13
- Pharisees Conspire Against Him
- The Sign of Jonah. 12:14-50

IV. THE "MYSTERIES" OF THE KINGDOM

1 Mystery	2 Mystery	3 Mystery	4 Mystery	5 Mystery	6 Mystery	7 Mystery
"The Sower" 13:1-23	"The Wheat and Tares" 13:24-30 13:36-43	"The Mustard Tree" 13:31-32	"The Leaven" 13:33	"The Hid Treasure" 13:44	"The Pearl" 13:45,46	"The Drag-Net" 13:47-58

EXPLANATORY NOTE

The Scroll gives the events in Christ's life in chronological order according to Matthew's Gospel.

The Geography of His Life is shown in the seven horizontal bands on the lower part of the chart that correspond to the divisions of Palestine in Christ's Day. Dotted horizontal lines mark the cities and towns He visited and by following the heavy black line that traces the course of His life from country to country and city to city, it is easy to locate the place and country in which the principal events of His life occurred, as also the year and month.

The Passovers are indicated by dotted vertical columns. The events of the last week of His life are shown by days and hours, and His Post-Resurrection Appearances are outlined. It is to be noted that John is the only one of the Gospel writers who mentions and outlines Christ's JUDEAN MINISTRY.

Designed and Drawn By—
CLARENCE LARKIN
Fox Chase, Phil'a, Pa
Copyrighted

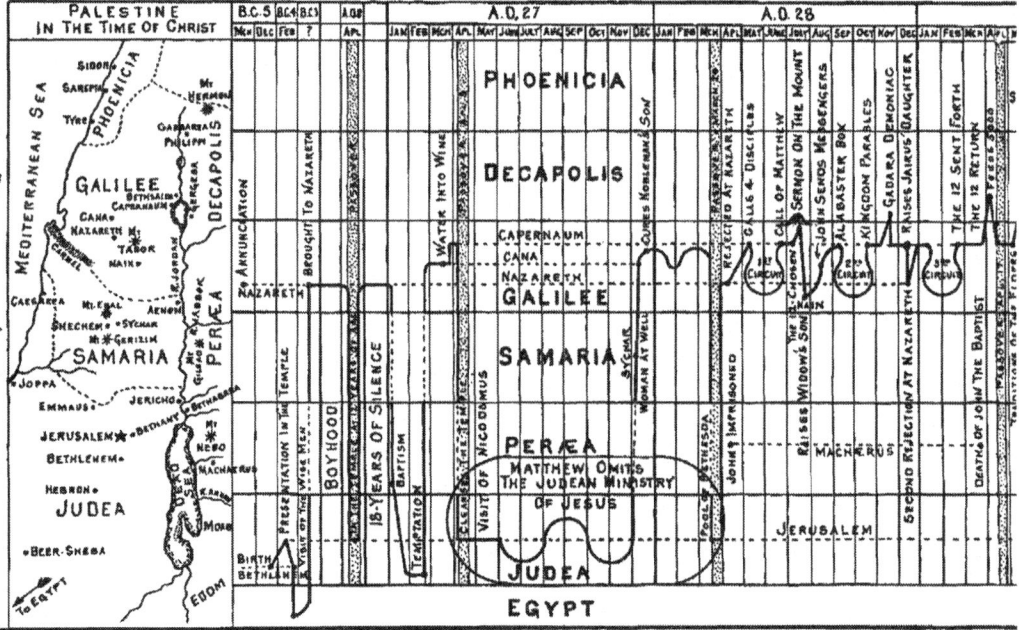

'HEW
"THE KING"

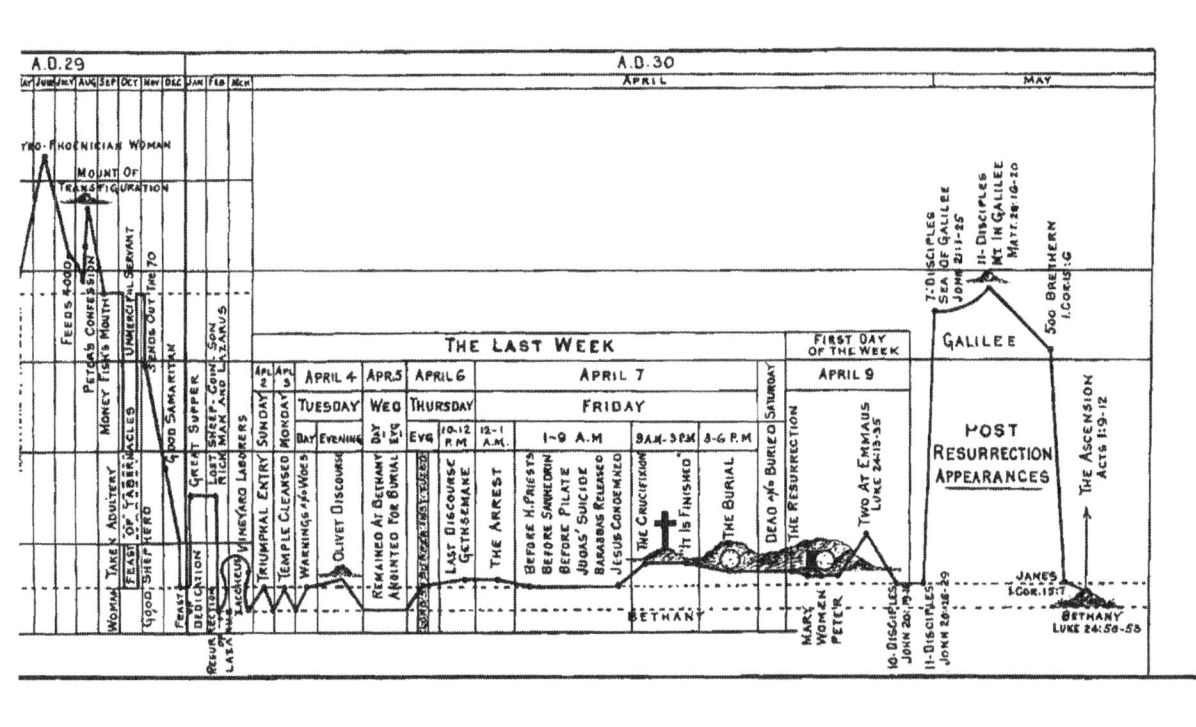

V. The King's Galilean and Decapolis Ministry	VI. Perean Ministry	VII. The King's Last Week											
		Sunday	Monday	Tuesday Day	Tuesday Evening (Olivet Discourse)	Wednesday Evg	Thursday P.M 10-11	Friday A.M 4-6	Friday A.M 7-9	Friday A.M 9-3	Friday P.M 3-6	Sunday (Dawn)

Death of John the Baptist 14:1-13 | Feeds the 5000 14:14-21 | Walks on the Sea 14:22-36 | Rebukes Scribes & Pharisees 15:1-20 | The Syro-Phoenician Woman 15:21-28 | Feeds the 4000 15:29-39 | Pharisees and Sadducees 16:1-12 | "The Church" — Peter's Confession 16:13-18 | "Mt of Transfiguration" — "The Transfiguration" 17:1-27 | "The Unmerciful Servant" 18:15-35 — True Greatness 18:1-14 | The King's Teaching — As to Marriage-Divorce 19:1-12 | As to Children 19:13-15 | As to Riches 19:16-26 | "The Vineyard Laborers" 19:27-20:28 — As to the Hireling Spirit | Journeys to Jerusalem 20:29-34 | The King Enters His Capital 21:1-11 | The King in His Own House 21:12-17 | The King and His Enemies 21:18-23:35 | "The Marriage Feast" 22:1-14 | The King Bids His Capital Farewell 23:34 — The King as a Prophet 24:1-51 | "The Virgins" | "The Talents" | "Judgment of Nations" — The King as a Judge 25:1-46 | The King Anointed for Burial 26:1-13 | The King Eats the Passover 26:17-35 | The King in Gethsemane 26:36-46 | The King's Betrayal-Arrest 26:47-56 | The King's Trial 26:57-27:14 | The King Condemned 27:15-26 | The King Crucified 27:27-56 | The King Buried 27:57-66 | The King Risen 28:1-15 | The Great Commission Matt. 28:16-20

A.D. 29										A.D. 30			
May	June	July	Aug	Sept	Oct	Nov	Dec	Jan	Feb	Mch	April		May

Two Phoenician Woman | Mount of Transfiguration | Feeds 4000 | Peter's Confession | Money Fish's Mouth | Unmerciful Servant | Sends Out the 70 | Woman Taken Adultery | Feast of Tabernacles | Good Shepherd | Feast of Dedication | Resur. Reciter Lazarus | Great Supper | Lost Sheep, Coin, Prod, Son, Mark and Lazarus | Vineyard Laborers | Zacchaeus

The Last Week — Apl 2, Apl 3 | April 4 Sunday Triumphal Entry | April 5 Monday Temple Cleansed Day / Evening | April 6 Tuesday Olivet Discourse Day / Warnings & Woes Evg | Apr 5 Wednesday Remained at Bethany Anointed for Burial | April 7 Thursday Last Discourse Gethsemane Evg / The Arrest 10-12 P.M. / Before H. Priests Before Sanhedrin 12-1 A.M. | April 7 Friday 1-9 A.M. Before Pilate Judas' Suicide Barabbas Released Jesus Condemned | 9 A.M.-3 P.M. The Crucifixion "It Is Finished" | 3-6 P.M. The Burial | Dead & Buried Saturday The Resurrection — BETHANY

First Day of the Week April 9 — Mary, Women, Peter | 10 Disciples John 20:19-23 | Two at Emmaus Luke 24:13-35 | 11 Disciples John 20:26-29

GALILEE — 7 Disciples Sea of Galilee John 21:1-25 | 11 Disciples Mt In Galilee Matt. 28:16-20 | 500 Brethren I Cor 15:6

POST RESURRECTION APPEARANCES — James I Cor 15:7 | The Ascension Acts 1:9-12 | BETHANY Luke 24:50-53

So we see that Joseph could not be the "natural" father of Jesus, for no descendant of his could sit on the Throne of David and "prosper." This forever sets at rest the claim that Joseph was the "natural" father of Jesus, and establishes the fact of His **"Virgin Birth."**

The marriage of Joseph and Mary made Jesus the adopted son and "legal heir" of Joseph. The title, unaffected by the curse pronounced upon Coniah, was thus conveyed to Jesus, in whom there centres, through both Nathan and Solomon, exclusive right to the "Throne of David."

That there might be no question as to Joseph's and Mary's ancestors, God, when the time came for Jesus to be born, put it into the heart of the Roman Emperor, Caesar Augustus, to call for an enrollment, and this required that every Jewish citizen should be enrolled in the city where his family had lived, and as Joseph was of the "House and Lineage of David" (Luke 2: 1-5), this required him to go to Bethlehem to be enrolled. And as Mary was of the same family, Joseph took her with him. They could not have been enrolled unless their names were **on the Register**, and that they were enrolled proves that they could **at that time** trace their ancestry back to King David. It was doubtless from this register that Matthew and Luke got their genealogy.

If the claim of Jesus to the "Throne of David" had not been known in Jerusalem to be absolutely without a flaw, the Jews would have denounced Him as an imposter and pretender on the day He entered Jerusalem and was received with royal acclamation as the Son of David. Matt. 21: 9-11. Up to the time of Jesus' rejection as King, all genealogical records were preserved in the Temple, and easily accessible to all the people, but when Titus in A. D. 70 destroyed the city and the Temple those records were all destroyed, and since that day the genealogical tables of Matthew and Luke alone remain to give us the lineal descent of Jesus from King David.

Therefore the **only living man** who today can establish an **unbroken genealogy** directly and incontrovertibly from King David, is the **MAN** Christ Jesus, (I Tim. 2: 5), born "**King of the Jews**," (Matt. 2: 2), crucified "**King of the Jews**," (John 19:19), and to come again "**King of the Jews.**"

It has been said that Jesus never claimed to be the "Messiah," but this is not true. He made the claim to the "Woman at the Well" (John 4: 26), and to Pilate (John 18: 33-37).

But the Old Testament Scriptures not only give the Messiah's ancestry, but the **time and place** of His birth. If we can locate the "time" of His birth, we shall have strong evidence of His identification. If, according to the Scriptures, He was to appear at the time Jesus "did appear," and Jesus fulfilled the other scriptures relating to Him, then our identification of Jesus as the Messiah is beyond question.

In Dan. 9: 24, 25, we read that it was to be 69 Weeks from the going forth of the commandment to restore and to build Jerusalem unto the "**Messiah the Prince.**" Now here is a definite period of time mentioned—"**69 Weeks**," and these weeks were to date from a certain edict—"The commandment to **Restore and Rebuild Jerusalem.**" The date of this "commandment" is given in Neh. 2: 1, as the month Nisan, in the twentieth year of Artaxerxes the king, which was the 14th day of March, B. C. 445. Now we found in the Chapter on "The Gentiles," under the head of "Prophetical Chronology," using the "Year Day Scale," that those "69 Weeks" expired within **one day** of April 2nd, A. D. 30, the day on which Jesus rode in triumph into Jerusalem as "Messiah the Prince."

If the students of prophecy of Jesus' day had been on the watch they would have known for a certainty whether Jesus was the Messiah or not; for in all probability they had among their archives a copy of the famous edict of Artaxerxes Longimanus, dated March 14, B. C. 445, and they could have computed from the prophecy of Daniel the year, if not the day, when "Messiah the Prince" would come. What a rebuke is this to the teachers and preachers of today who make light of the prophetical statements of God's word. The Second Coming of Jesus will find them just as much unprepared to receive Him, as the Jews were to receive Him at His First Coming.

But not only was the time of the Messiah's appearing given, but the place of His birth.

"But thou, **Bethlehem Ephratah**, though thou be little among the thousands of Judah, yet out of thee shall he come forth unto me that is to be 'Ruler in Israel' whose goings forth have been from of old, from everlasting." Micah 5: 2.

This prophecy we know was literally fulfilled. There are four prophecies in reference to the origin of the Messiah that seemed irreconcilable previous to their fulfilment. They were, that he was to be born at Bethlehem, born of a Virgin, was to come out of Egypt, and that he should be called a Nazarene, and yet, as we know, every one of them was literally fulfilled in Jesus.

But the very passage from Daniel which gives us the "time" of the coming of "Messiah the Prince," also tells us that almost immediately "**He Shall Be Cut Off But Not for Himself.**" Dan. 9: 26. How then could be fulfilled the prophecy that declared that He was to be given the "Throne of David," and that He should reign over the "House of Jacob forever, and of His Kingdom there shall be **NO END**? There is but one answer. His coming was to be in **Two Stages.** He was to come first as a "Suffering Saviour," and then as a "King." Here is where the Jews of Jesus' day misread the Scriptures. They did not distinguish between the **Sufferings of the Messiah** and **His Glory.** 1 Peter 1: 11. They could not understand how the Messiah was to be a mighty King and also be "cut off" for the sins and iniquities of His people. There was but one possible answer and that was by **Resurrection.** They accepted Psa. 16, as Messianic, and yet did not see that it prophesied the "**Resurrection of Jesus**" in the words—

"Thou wilt not leave my soul in hell (Hades); neither wilt thou suffer thine 'Holy One' to see corruption." Psa. 16: 10.

This passage Peter in his sermon on the Day of Pentecost, quoted saying that David, being a prophet, here speaks of the Resurrection of Christ," and added—"This JESUS hath God raised up, whereof we all are witnesses." Acts 2: 25-32

There can be no question but what "Jesus of Nazareth" was the promised "Son of David," who is to reign upon the "Throne of David." But being rejected and crucified, and risen from the dead, He now sits on His Father's Throne until the time comes for Him to take the Kingdom.

The "Throne of David" was on the earth, and can never be anywhere else. To say that Christ now reigns on the "Throne of David," and that His Kingdom is "spiritual," is to subvert the meaning of the Old Testament prophecies. The "Throne of David" is now vacant, and has been for 2500 years, but when the "Times of the Gentiles" have run their course, and the time has come to set up again the "Tabernacle (House) of David" which has fallen down (Acts 15: 13-18), the "**Throne of David**" will be re-established and given to Christ.

XIII
THE KINGDOM

It is clear from the Scriptures that God has been trying to set up a "visible" Kingdom on this earth ever since the creation of man, to whom He gave dominion. Gen. 1:26-28. But that dominion was lost by the "Fall," and Satan set himself up as the "Prince of this world." Matt. 4:8-10. John 14:30.

In the "Call" of Abraham God took the first step toward the setting up of a "visible" Kingdom on this earth, which assumed an outward form in the "Jewish Commonwealth," under Moses, and during the administration of Moses, Joshua, the Elders that outlived Joshua, the Judges, David, Solomon, the kings of Israel and Judah down to the Babylonish Captivity, God reigned through these men under the form of a "Theocracy."

Under the Judgeship of Samuel there was a revolt against the "Theocracy," and Saul was chosen by the people as King. 1 Sam. 8:6, 7. This was followed by God's selection of David. But the misrule of his successors, and the idolatry of the people, caused the cessation of the Theocratic reign in B. C. 606, and the "Times of the Gentiles" began.

I. The Kingdom at Hand.

But when 600 years of the "Times of the Gentiles" had run their course, God again made the attempt to set up His Kingdom on the earth, and the angel Gabriel announced to Mary the birth of the King. Luke 1:26-33.

Thirty years later the King's forerunner, John the Baptist, announced that the Kingdom was "at hand," (Matt. 3:1, 2); and when the King manifested Himself to Israel He Himself made the same announcement, (Matt. 4:17-23), and later He sent out the "Twelve," (Matt. 10:7), and the "Seventy" to proclaim the same thing. Luke 10:1-9.

But the King was rejected and crucified, and the setting up of the Kingdom postponed, and the Kingdom took on its "Mystery Form" under the name of the "Kingdom of Heaven."

Here we must distinguish between the "Kingdom of God" and the "Kingdom of Heaven." The "Kingdom of God" is the "Reign of God" in the Universe over all His created creatures, and includes time and eternity, heaven and earth. It is spiritual and "cometh not with observation." Luke 17:20, 21. It is entered by the "New Birth," (John 3:5); and is not "meat" and "drink," but "Righteousness and Peace, and Joy in the Holy Ghost." Rom. 14:17.

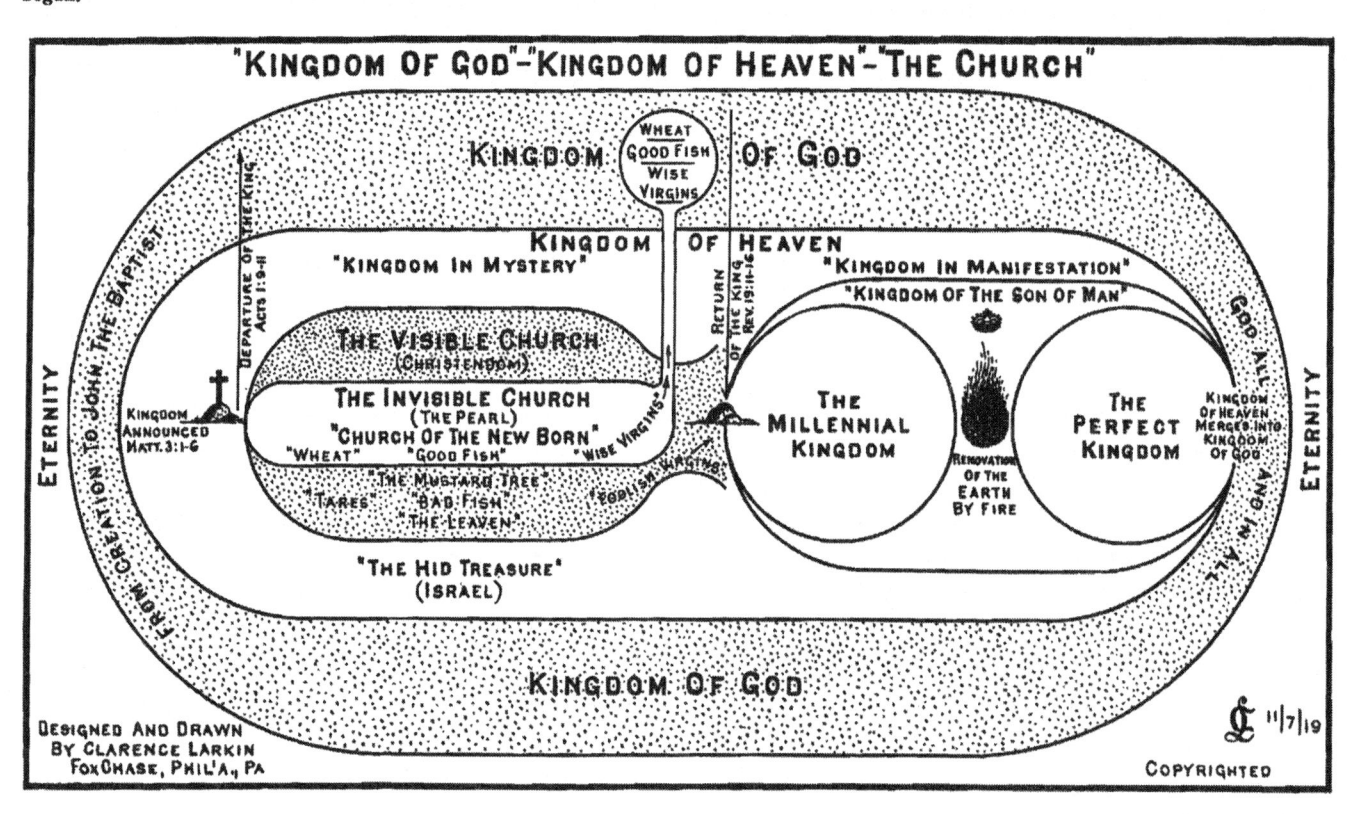

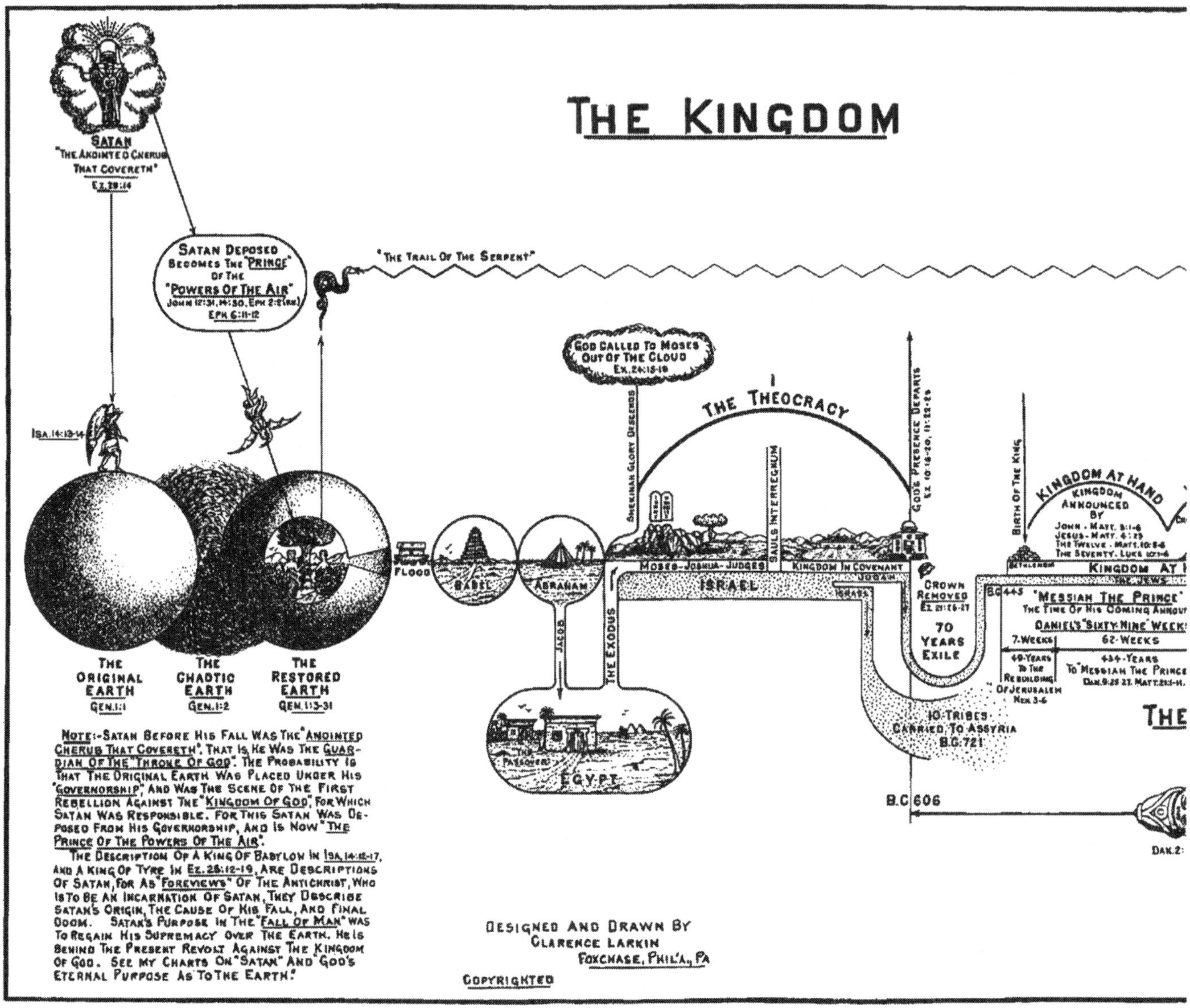
THE KINGDOM
SATAN
"THE ANOINTED CHERUB THAT COVERETH"
EZ.28:14
SATAN DEPOSED BECOMES THE "PRINCE" OF THE "POWERS OF THE AIR"
JOHN 12:31, 14:30, EPH 2:2(RV.)
EPH 6:11-12
"THE TRAIL OF THE SERPENT"
ISA.14:13-14
THE ORIGINAL EARTH
GEN.1:1
THE CHAOTIC EARTH
GEN.1:2
THE RESTORED EARTH
GEN.1:3-31
FLOOD
BABEL
ABRAHAM
JACOB
EGYPT
PASSOVER
THE EXODUS
GOD CALLED TO MOSES OUT OF THE CLOUD
EX.24:15-18
SHEKINAH GLORY DESCENDS
THE THEOCRACY
MOSES-JOSHUA-JUDGES
SAULS INTERREGNUM
KINGDOM IN COVENANT
ISRAEL
JUDAH
GODS PRESENCE DEPARTS
EZ.10:18-20, 11:22-23
CROWN REMOVED
EZ.21:25-27
70 YEARS EXILE
10 TRIBES CARRIED TO ASSYRIA B.C.721
B.C 606
BIRTH OF THE KING
BETHLEHEM
KINGDOM AT HAND
KINGDOM ANNOUNCED BY
JOHN - MATT. 3:1-6
JESUS - MATT. 4:17
THE TWELVE - MATT.10:5-6
THE SEVENTY - LUKE 10:1-6
KINGDOM AT
B.C 445
"MESSIAH THE PRINCE"
THE TIME OF HIS COMING ANNOU
DANIEL'S "SIXTY-NINE" WEEKS
7-WEEKS
62-WEEKS
49-YEARS TO THE REBUILDING OF JERUSALEM
NEH 3-6
434-YEARS TO "MESSIAH THE PRINCE"
DAN.9:25-27. MATT.21:1-11.
THE
DAN.2:
NOTE:- SATAN BEFORE HIS FALL WAS THE "ANOINTED CHERUB THAT COVERETH". THAT IS HE WAS THE GUARDIAN OF THE "THRONE OF GOD". THE PROBABILITY IS THAT THE ORIGINAL EARTH WAS PLACED UNDER HIS "GOVERNORSHIP", AND WAS THE SCENE OF THE FIRST REBELLION AGAINST THE "KINGDOM OF GOD", FOR WHICH SATAN WAS RESPONSIBLE. FOR THIS SATAN WAS DEPOSED FROM HIS GOVERNORSHIP, AND IS NOW "THE PRINCE OF THE POWERS OF THE AIR".
THE DESCRIPTION OF A KING OF BABYLON IN ISA.14:12-17, AND A KING OF TYRE IN EZ.28:12-19, ARE DESCRIPTIONS OF SATAN, FOR AS "FOREVIEWS" OF THE ANTICHRIST, WHO IS TO BE AN INCARNATION OF SATAN, THEY DESCRIBE SATAN'S ORIGIN, THE CAUSE OF HIS FALL, AND FINAL DOOM. SATAN'S PURPOSE IN THE "FALL OF MAN" WAS TO REGAIN HIS SUPREMACY OVER THE EARTH. HE IS BEHIND THE PRESENT REVOLT AGAINST THE KINGDOM OF GOD. SEE MY CHARTS ON "SATAN" AND "GOD'S ETERNAL PURPOSE AS TO THE EARTH."
DESIGNED AND DRAWN BY
CLARENCE LARKIN
FOXCHASE, PHIL'A, PA
COPYRIGHTED

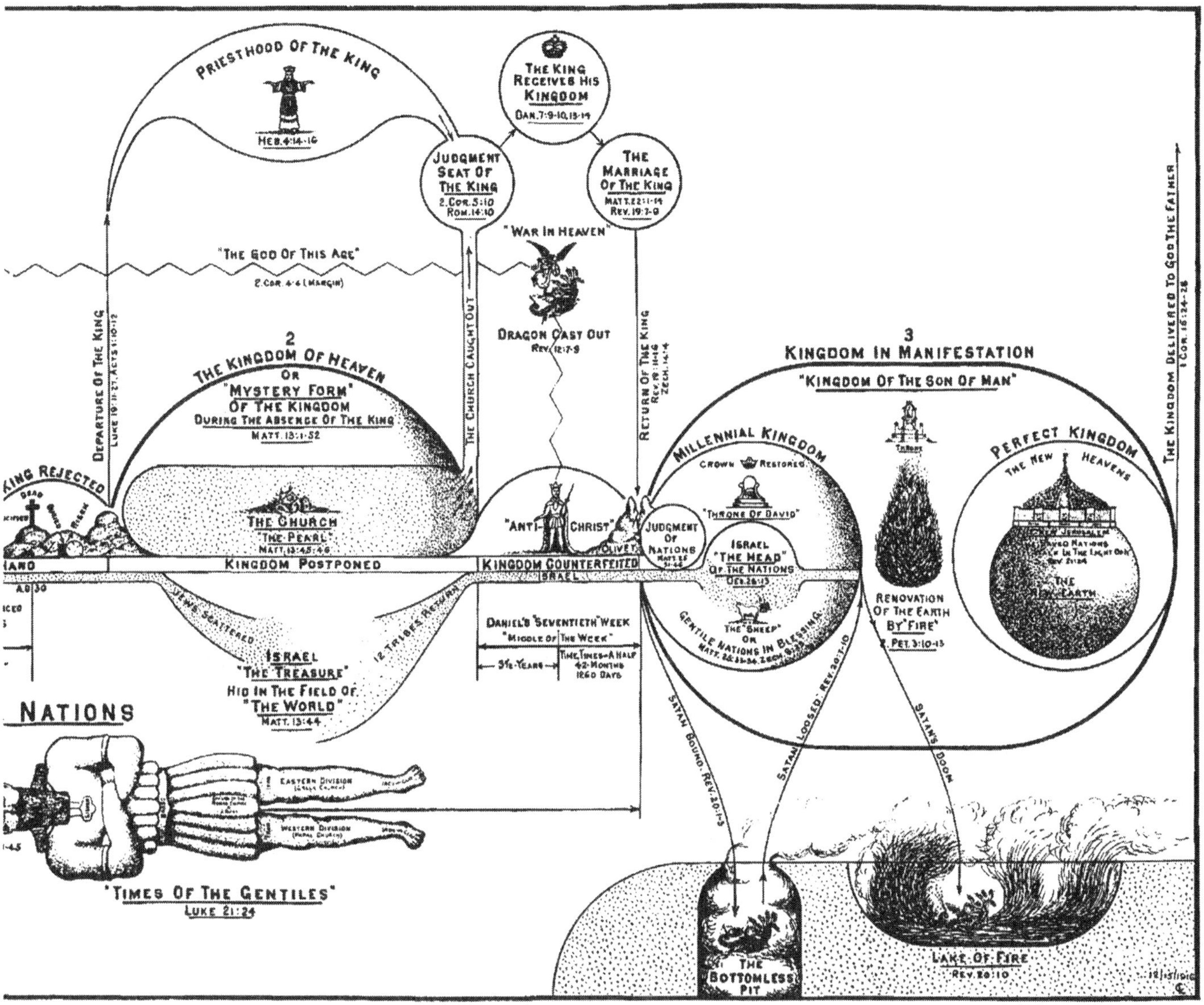

Priesthood Of The King
Heb. 4:14-16
The King Receives His Kingdom
Dan. 7:9-10, 13-14
Judgment Seat Of The King
2 Cor. 5:10
Rom. 14:10
The Marriage Of The King
Matt. 22:1-14
Rev. 19:7-9
"War In Heaven"
"The God Of This Age"
2 Cor. 4:4 (Margin)
Departure Of The King
Luke 19:11-27, Acts 1:10-12
The Church Caught Out
Dragon Cast Out
Rev. 12:7-9
Return Of The King
Rev. 19:11-16
Zech. 14:4
2
The Kingdom Of Heaven
Or
"Mystery Form" Of The Kingdom
During The Absence Of The King
Matt. 13:1-52
3
Kingdom In Manifestation
"Kingdom Of The Son Of Man"
King Rejected
The Church
"The Pearl"
Matt. 13:45-46
"Anti-Christ"
Olivet
Judgment Of Nations
Millennial Kingdom
Crown Restored
"Throne Of David"
Israel
"The Head"
Of The Nations
Perfect Kingdom
The New Heavens
The New Earth
Kingdom Postponed
Kingdom Counterfeited
A.D. 30
Jews Scattered
12 Tribes Return
Israel
"The Treasure"
Hid In The Field Of "The World"
Matt. 13:44
Daniel's "Seventieth" Week
"Middle Of The Week"
3½ Years
Time, Times & A Half
42 Months
1260 Days
The "Sheep"
Or
Gentile Nations In Blessing
Renovation Of The Earth By "Fire"
2 Pet. 3:10-13
The Kingdom Delivered To God The Father
1 Cor. 15:24-28
Nations
Eastern Division
Western Division
Satan Bound. Rev. 20:1-3
Satan Loosed. Rev. 20:7-10
Satan's Doom
"Times Of The Gentiles"
Luke 21:24
The Bottomless Pit
Lake Of Fire
Rev. 20:10

The Church versus The Kingdom

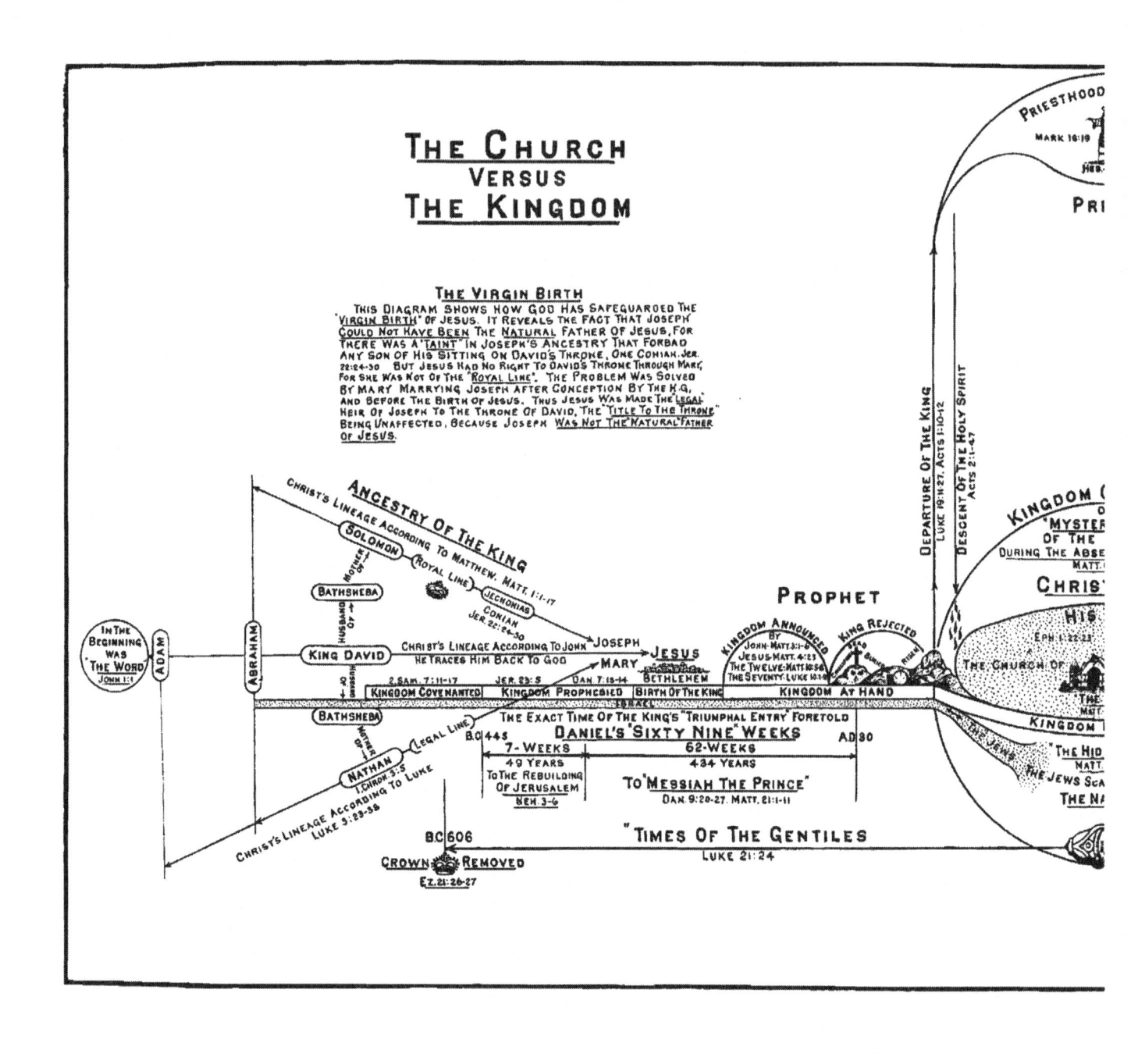

The Virgin Birth

This diagram shows how God has safeguarded the "Virgin Birth" of Jesus. It reveals the fact that Joseph could not have been the natural father of Jesus, for there was a "taint" in Joseph's ancestry that forbad any son of his sitting on David's throne, one Coniah. Jer. 22:24-30. But Jesus had no right to David's throne through Mary, for she was not of the "Royal Line". The problem was solved by Mary marrying Joseph after conception by the H.G. and before the birth of Jesus. Thus Jesus was made the legal heir of Joseph to the throne of David, the "Title to the Throne" being unaffected, because Joseph was not the natural father of Jesus.

Ancestry of the King

- Christ's Lineage According to Matthew. Matt. 1:1-17
- Solomon — Royal Line — Jechonias / Coniah (Jer. 22:24-30)
- Bathsheba (Mother of) — King David (Husband of) — Joseph → Jesus (Bethlehem) ← Mary
- Christ's Lineage According to John. He traces Him back to God
- "In the Beginning was the Word" John 1:1 — Adam — Abraham
- Bathsheba (Mother of) — Nathan (Legal Line)
- Christ's Lineage According to Luke. Luke 3:23-38

2 Sam. 7:11-17 — Jer. 23:5 — Dan. 7:13-14
ISRAEL: Kingdom Covenanted | Kingdom Prophesied | Birth of the King | Kingdom at Hand

Kingdom Announced by John - Matt. 3:1-6; Jesus - Matt. 4:23; The Twelve - Matt. 10:5-6; The Seventy - Luke 10:1-9
King Rejected

The Exact Time of the King's "Triumphal Entry" Foretold

Daniel's "Sixty Nine" Weeks

BC 445 — 7-Weeks (49 Years To the Rebuilding of Jerusalem, Neh. 3-6) — 62-Weeks (434 Years) — AD 30

To "Messiah the Prince" Dan. 9:20-27, Matt. 21:1-11

"Times of the Gentiles" Luke 21:24

BC 606 — Crown Removed — Ez. 21:26-27

Prophet

Priesthood — Mark 16:19

Departure of the King — Luke 24:44-27, Acts 1:10-12
Descent of the Holy Spirit — Acts 2:1-47

Kingdom... "Mystery" of the... During the Absence... Matt....

Christ... His...

The Church of... Eph 1:22-23

The Hid... Matt...
The Jews Sca...
The Na...

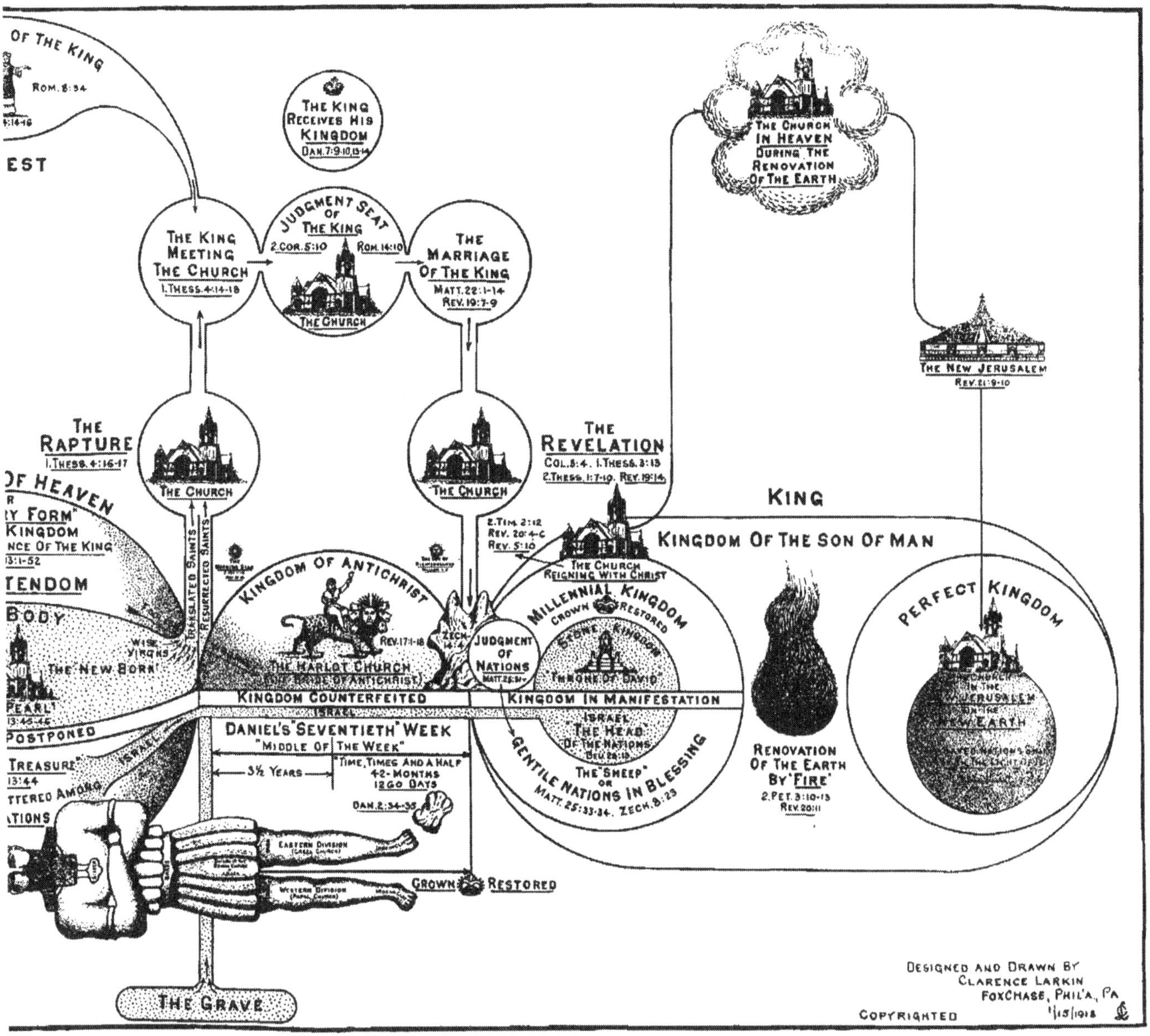

Of The King
Rom. 8:34
EST
The King Receives His Kingdom
Dan. 7:9-10, 13-14
The King Meeting The Church
1. Thess. 4:14-18
Judgment Seat Of The King
2. Cor. 5:10
Rom. 14:10
The Church
The Marriage Of The King
Matt. 22:1-14
Rev. 19:7-9
The Church In Heaven During The Renovation Of The Earth
The New Jerusalem
Rev. 21:9-10
The Rapture
1. Thess. 4:16-17
The Church
The Church
The Revelation
Col. 3:4. 1. Thess. 3:13
2. Thess. 1:7-10. Rev. 19:14
King
Kingdom Of The Son Of Man
2. Tim. 2:12
Rev. 20:4-6
Rev. 5:10
The Church Reigning With Christ
Of Heaven
Kingdom
Tendom
Body
Translated Saints
Resurrected Saints
Kingdom Of Antichrist
Rev. 17:1-18
The Harlot Church
Zech. 14:4
Judgment Of Nations
Millennial Kingdom
Crown Restored
Stone Kingdom
"Throne Of David"
Perfect Kingdom
Wise Virgins
The New Born
Pearl
13:45-46
Kingdom Counterfeited
Israel
Kingdom In Manifestation
Postponed
Daniel's "Seventieth" Week
"Middle Of The Week"
3½ Years
"Time, Times And A Half
42 Months
1260 Days
Israel "The Head" Of The Nations
The "Sheep" Or
Gentile Nations In Blessing
Matt. 25:33-34. Zech. 8:23
Renovation Of The Earth By "Fire"
2. Pet. 3:10-13
Rev. 20:11
The New Earth
Treasure
13:44
Israel
Attered Among
Ations
Dan. 2:34-35
Eastern Division
Western Division
Crown Restored
The Grave
Designed And Drawn By
Clarence Larkin
Foxchase, Phil'a, Pa
Copyrighted
1/15/1918

The "Kingdom of Heaven" is a New Testament term, and is found in Matthew's Gospel only, where it is mentioned 32 times. Its character is described in the 12 "Kingdom of Heaven Parables" given in **Matt. 13: 1-50; 18: 23-25; 20: 1-16; 22: 1-14; 25: 1-30.** From these Parables we see that the "Kingdom of Heaven" is limited as to its Time and its Sphere. Its Time is from the First to the Second Coming of Christ, and its Sphere is over that part of the world that we call Christendom. In the "Kingdom of Heaven" there is a mixture of good and evil, of "Wheat" and "Tares," of "Good Fish" and "Bad Fish," of "Wise Virgins" and "Foolish Virgins."

THE POSTPONEMENT THEORY

There are some who object to what they call the "Postponement Theory," and claim that the Kingdom which was **"At Hand"** was not an outward visible Kingdom, but a **spiritual** Kingdom, and that it was not withdrawn but is seen today in "New Born" believers. They base their claim on the fact that the earthly visible Kingdom of Christ could not be set up until after He had suffered and died on the Cross as the Saviour of men, and had risen from the dead, and ascended to the Father and received the Kingdom, and that therefore the offer of an **outward visible and earthly** Kingdom at that time was not a "bona fide" offer, and that John the Baptist and Jesus must have meant by the "Kingdom of Heaven" something else than an outward visible and earthly Kingdom. What are the facts? First that the Old Testament scriptures teach that there is to be an earthly and visible Kingdom over which the Son of Man is to rule (Dan. 7: 13-14, 2: 34-35, 44-45; Jer. 23: 5; Zech. 14: 9), and we know that at the time of Jesus' birth there was a widespread expectation of the coming of the Messiah, and that Simeon and Anna waited in the Temple for the "Consolation of Israel." Luke 2: 25-38. We are also told that "Wise Men" came from the East to Jerusalem inquiring "Where is He that is born **KING OF THE JEWS?**" and when they had found Jesus they worshipped Him as **KING.** Matt. 2: 1-11. There can be no question but what Jesus was born to be a **KING.** It was not until Jesus was 30 years old that John the Baptist appeared at the Jordan preaching—"Repent ye: for the Kingdom of Heaven is **AT HAND."** Matt. 3: 2. And we are told that his mission was to **"Prepare the Way of the Lord."** Matt. 3: 3. Isa. 40: 3. Prepare the way of the Lord for what? Not for the "Cross" but the "Kingdom." John's message had no meaning to those who heard him and were looking for the setting up of the "Messianic Kingdom," if he did not mean by the "Kingdom of Heaven" an outward and visible earthly Kingdom. That John himself so believed is evident from the question he sent his disciples while in prison to ask Jesus—"Art Thou He that should come or do we look for another?" Matt. 11: 3. The fact that Jesus answered John's question by a number of miracles of healing, which are the "signs" of the Messianic Kingdom (Isa. 35: 1-10), and were proofs of Christ's Messiahship, and told John's disciples to so report, is proof that both John and Jesus had in mind the earthly Messianic Kingdom when they proclaimed that the "Kingdom of Heaven was **AT HAND."** It was the "Kingdom of Heaven," not because it was a Heavenly or Spiritual Kingdom, but because it was not received from men, but was given from Heaven by God the Father.

While it is true that John the Baptist pointed out to two of his own disciples Jesus as the "Lamb of God" (John 1: 29), this was after Jesus' return from the "Wilderness Temptation," and had been revealed to John at the Baptism of Jesus, and does not nullify or alter the character of his previous proclamation that the Kingdom of Heaven was at hand. We must not forget that as soon as Jesus was baptised He was **"immediately"** driven into the Wilderness to be tempted of the Devil (Matt. 4: 1-11, Mark 1: 11-13), and it was not until 40 days after His Baptism that John pointed out to his disciples Jesus as "the Lamb of God, which taketh away the sin of the world." The words "next day" (John 1: 29) refer not to the day after Jesus' Baptism, but the next day after the Priests and Levites had inquired of John whether he was the Christ or Elias. John 1: 19-28. In John 1: 32-34, John the Baptist testifies that he knew not Jesus as the "Lamb of God" until His Baptism. Then he knew by the descent of the Holy Spirit in the form of a dove upon Christ that He was the **"SON OF GOD."** Therefore John the Baptist knew nothing about Christ's sacrificial work at the beginning of his ministry, and his proclamation that the Kingdom of Heaven was at hand could have had no reference to a Spiritual Kingdom.

When Nathanael exclaimed—"Rabbi, Thou art the Son of God; Thou art the **KING OF ISRAEL"** (John 1: 49), Jesus did not disclaim the title. When Jesus entered on His own ministry His message was the same as John the Baptist's—"Repent, for the Kingdom of Heaven is **AT HAND."** Matt. 4: 17. The repentance called for was a **"NATIONAL REPENTANCE."** The Old Testament scriptures clearly teach that the Messianic Kingdom cannot be set up until Israel as **a nation** REPENTS. In Matt. 4: 23 we read—"And Jesus went about all Galilee, teaching in their synagogues and preaching the **'Gospel of The Kingdom'."** While this was attended with "signs of **bodily healing"** we are nowhere told that the "Gospel of the Kingdom" had anything to do with the salvation of the soul, and as it is to be preached again after the Rapture of the Church, for a "witness" unto all nations, that the time has come for the setting up of the Kingdom (Matt. 24: 14), the inference is that the "Gospel of the Kingdom" has nothing to do with "salvation," but is simply an announcement that the "Messianic Kingdom" is AT HAND.

When Jesus sent forth the Twelve Disciples He commanded them, saying, "Go not into the way of the Gentiles, and into any city of the Samaritans enter ye not; but go rather to the 'lost sheep' of the **HOUSE OF ISRAEL,** and as ye go, preach, saying—'The **Kingdom of Heaven is AT HAND.'** Heal the sick, cleanse the lepers, raise the dead, cast out devils (demons)." Matt. 10: 5-8. Note again that the works they were to perform were "Kingdom SIGNS," and had no reference to the salvation of the soul. They did not preach the "Gospel of Salvation," but the "Gospel of the Kingdom." And further the "Gospel of Salvation" is for the whole world, but the Disciples were forbidden to go to any but the **"House of Israel,"** thus showing that what they preached was exclusively for Israel. That the Disciples were expecting the setting up of a visible earthly Kingdom is evidenced by the request of James and John that they might sit, one on the right hand, and the other on the left hand of Jesus in His Kingdom. Mark 10: 35-41. If there was to be no earthly Kingdom Jesus would have disabused their minds of that idea, but He confirmed it by saying that the place of honor was not for Him to give, but would be bestowed by His Father. Matt. 20: 23.

The fact that after the miracle of the "Loaves and Fishes" the multitude was desirous to take Jesus by force and make Him a **KING** (John 6: 15), reveals what they understood by the preaching of the Kingdom of Heaven being **AT HAND.** That Jesus prevented their doing so by escaping to a mountain is no evidence that He repudiated the idea of Kingship over a visible earthly Kingdom, but that to have received the Kingdom from them would have been wrong, for He is to receive the Kingdom from the **FATHER,** and not from men. Dan. 7: 13-14. That Jesus did not deny His Kingship of an outward and visible earthly Kingdom is clear from the fact that He accepted the

"Hosannahs" of the multitude when He rode into Jerusalem on **Palm Sunday** in fulfilment of the Messianic prophecy of Zech. 9:9. John 12:12-15. And it was as **"KING OF THE JEWS"** He was crucified. Matt. 27:37. When Pilate asked Jesus—"Art Thou the King of the **JEWS?"** He evaded the question, but admitted that He was a **KING**, and to that end had been born, but that His Kingdom was **"not of this world,"** that is, it would be given to Him by God the Father, and therefore would be from Heaven. John 18:33-37.

But some one may ask, "What would have happened if the Jews, as a nation, had **repented**, and accepted Jesus as King, would the earthly Messianic Kingdom have been set up?" Certainly, but not necessarily immediately, for certain Old Testament prophecies as to Jesus' death and resurrection had to be fulfilled, for He had to die for the redemption of the race, before He could assume His office as King. But this could and would have been fulfilled by the Roman Government seizing Jesus and crucifying Him as a usurper, and with Jesus' Resurrection and Ascension, Daniel's 69th week would have terminated, and the 70th week begun without a break, and at its close Jesus would have descended and set up His earthly Kingdom.

But you ask, "What about the Church? If it was God's Eternal Purpose to form the Church (Eph. 1:4), how could it have been formed if there was no break or gap between Daniel's 69th and 70th week, and how therefore could there have been a 'bona fide' offer of an earthly Kingdom to Israel?" The question is hypothetical and based on the supposition that something might have happened that God foresaw would not happen. God's foreknowledge that the Jewish nation would not at that time heed the announcement that the Kingdom of Heaven was **at hand** and repent, does not militate against the sincerity of the announcement any more than the offer of spiritual salvation by a preacher of the Gospel to an audience of sinners who he has every reason to believe will refuse his offer, is not a sincere and "bona fide" offer.

God's Plan and Purpose in the Ages is based upon His **FOREKNOWLEDGE**. If God had not foreseen that the Jews would reject the King and therefore the Kingdom. He would have planned for the formation of the Church at some other time than this present Dispensation. As the Church was to be purchased by the precious blood of Christ (Acts 20:28, 1 Pet. 1:18-21), it was necessary that Jesus should be rejected and crucified, and that by His own nation, for the Prophet Zechariah (Zech. 12:10) foretold that the Jews should look upon Him whom they had **PIERCED**. But God's foreknowledge did not require or compel the Jewish nation to reject Jesus, any more than Jesus' foreknowledge that Judas would betray Him compelled Judas to so do. The possibility of the Church being crowded out by the repentance of the Jewish nation did not enter into the "Plan of God," who foresaw the refusal of Israel to accept Jesus as King, and that Israel would not nationally repent until after the Church had been formed and taken out of the world.

In expounding the Scriptures we are not to take something that belongs to a **"PAST"** and a **"FUTURE"** Dispensation and put it in the **"PRESENT"** Dispensation. For instance, **"THE KINGDOM."** The **"PAST"** and **"COMING"** Dispensations have to do with **"THE KINGDOM,"** but the "Present" has to do with the **CHURCH**. The "Kingdom" is an outward, visible and earthly **"POLITICAL ORGANIZATION,"** and is to be **"set up"** on the earth (Dan. 2:44); while the "Church" is an invisible and heavenly **"SPIRITUAL ORGANISM"** that is to be **"caught out."** 1 Thess. 4:16-17. The "Kingdom" was prepared **FROM** the "Foundation of the World." Matt. 25:34. The "Church" was chosen in Him **"BEFORE** the Foundation of the World." Eph. 1:4. The "Church" then is not the "Kingdom."

THE SERMON ON THE MOUNT

A good illustration of the confusion that results when we take things that belong to a **FUTURE** Dispensation and put them in this **PRESENT** Dispensation is seen in the "Sermon on the Mount." It is found in Matthew 5:1-7:29. Matthew's Gospel is Jewish and must so be **interpreted**, though there are teachings in it that have eternal application and may be applied to any Dispensation, as "Till heaven and earth pass, one jot or one tittle shall in no wise pass from the Law, till all be fulfilled (Matt. 5:18); or "Where your treasure is, there will your heart be also." Matt. 6:21. But the instructions as to "fasting" (6:16-18); the "danger of the Council" (5:22); the "Judge," the "Officer," and the "Altar" (5:24-25), and the profession "I never knew you," and such like, have no application to the Christian, but only to those who are under the Law, and therefore must apply to another Dispensation than this.

The absurdity of the application is seen when we note that many professing Christians instead of "loving their enemies," do not even "love their brethren." Instead of agreeing with their "adversary quickly," they are unwilling to agree with their "brethren slowly." Instead of not judging others it is the one thing to which they are most addicted. If any sue them and would take away their coat, instead of letting them have their cloak also, they let them have the law. Take the command "Give to him that asketh of thee, and from him that would borrow of thee turn not thou away." Try that upon the average church member and see what you would get. How many if they were smitten on one cheek would turn the other?

Take the "Lord's Prayer," (Matt. 6:9-13), which is a part of the "Sermon on the Mount." It asks that—**"The Kingdom"** may come, not that the "Church" may increase and prosper. There is no petition for "Salvation from sin" in it. It asks that "God's will may be done in earth, as it is done in heaven." It is a prayer for those who shall be living in the "Tribulation Period" who in their persecutions will long for the return of the King, that the Kingdom may be set up, and God's will be done, as it will be done then, on earth as it is done in Heaven. At that time the "Beast" (Antichrist) will be in power and no one shall be able to "buy" or "sell" except he that hath the "Mark of the Beast," and this explains the petition—"Give us this day our **DAILY BREAD,"** for unless food is supplied **miraculously** they will perish. And it will be a time when they shall particularly need to be delivered, not from evil, but the **EVIL ONE**—Satan, who will tempt them to recant and worship the Beast.

The "Sermon on the Mount" was spoken by Christ before His rejection, and was the Constitution of the then offered Kingdom; now that the Kingdom has been withdrawn it is not in force, but will be in the Millennial Kingdom. So we see that we must discriminate between the Dispensations and not dislocate scripture.

THE DISCIPLES, QUESTION

After the Resurrection of Jesus the hope of a visible Kingdom was revived, and just before His Ascension the Disciples asked Him—

"Lord wilt Thou **at this time** restore the Kingdom of Israel?" His reply was— "It is not for you to know 'The Times' or 'The Seasons' which the Father hath put in His own power." **Acts 1:6, 7.**

THE "KINGDOM OF

THE MESSAGES TO TH

I. THE EPHESUS PERIOD (AD 70 – AD 170)
Rev. 2:1-7

"A Backslidden Church" Who Had Lost Its "First Love," But It Hated The "Nicolaitanes," A Sect That Wanted To Introduce "Holy Orders."

II. THE SMYRNA PERIOD (AD 170 – AD 312)
Rev. 2:8-11

"A Persecuted Church" They Were Persecuted By The Jews And The Teachers Who Wanted To Return To The "Works Of The Law."

III. THE PERGAMOS PERIOD (AD 312 – AD 606)
Rev. 2:12-17

"A Licentious Church" The Licentious Character Of This Period Is Seen In The Union Of Church And State Under Constantine, Called The "Doctrine Of Balaamism."

IV. THE THYATIR...
Rev. 2:...

"A La Ch...

This Church Is Charged With Permitting A "Prophetess" Called "Jezebel" To Teach That The Papal Church Introduced Its Many "Heathen" Practices, Enumerated Be... "Baptismal Regeneration," Justification By Works, "Image Worship," Celibacy, A.D. 300...

"The Sower" — Matt. 13:1-23

This Parable Reveals The Fact That This Dispensation Is An "Agricultural" One For The Purpose Of Getting The "Wheat Of The Church."

"The Wheat And Tares" — Matt. 13:24-30, 36-43

There Is No Fault In The Soil. It Is Equally Good All Over The Field. The Trouble Is Lack Of Cultivation. The "Wayside," "Stony Ground" And "Thorny Ground" Hearers Reveal The Causes That Prevent The Entrance And Growth Of...

"The Mustard Seed" — Matt. 13:31-32

This Parable Reveals That "The Field" Is Not Left To The Wheat. The Devil Sows Tares. Notice That The Devil Cannot Change The Wheat, But He Can Sow Tares In Such Quantities As To Completely Change The Aspect Of The Field. The Servants...

The Seed, And The "Good Ground" Hearers Are Not Equally Fruitful. Why? Because They Have Lost Their "First Love" And Are In A "Backslidden State." This Parable Corresponds With The Ephesus Church Period. As The Proportionate Reception And Fruitfulness Of The Soil Remains Same, The Conversion Of The World In This Dispensation Is Not Taught In...

IV. "The Leaven" — Matt. 13:33

Are Forbidden To At Present Gather Out The Tares. They Are To Let Them Grow Teaches That There Is To Be A "Twofold Development Of 'Good' And 'Evil.' Christ Will Come Back When The Wheat Of The Church Is Ripe, And That Will Ready For Burning. This Is Being Done Now In The Bundles Of Christian Science Wheat Will Be Taken Into The "Heavenly Garner" Before The Ta...

As This Is A "Kingdom Of Heaven" Parable It Must Be Interpreted Like The Two Mustard Tree "Represents The "Visible Church, And Represents Its External G Here It Is A Large Overgrown Tree, In Which The "Birds Of The Air Lodge (The E Of The Sower) And Therefore Agents Of The Devil, And As They Continue To Lo Represent Converted People, But Are The "Arabians." Simon Magus, Hymeneus...

ISRAEL

Ascension Of Jesus / Descent Of The Holy Spirit / Destruction Of Jerusalem, A.D. 70

A.D. 30 — CALVARY — ISRAEL

The Field Here, As In The Other Parables, Is The World. The Sinner Is Not To Purchase Is Not For Sale, Neither Can Salvation Be Bought. It Is A Free Gift. Rom. 6:23 Field. The Devil Claims He Owns The Field. The Treasure Is "Israel," Hidden By Only Way Christ Could Get The Treasure Was To Purchase The Field, Having Demption Of The Purchased Possession. Eph. 1:14. God Calls "Israel" His P...

THE CHURCH

The "Merchant-Man" In This Parable Is Not The Sinner, Nor The "Pearl" Christ Or Salvation. For As We Have Seen In The Preceding Parable They Cannot Be Bought. The "Merchant-Man" Is Christ. The Pearl Is "The Church." Acts 20:28. The Pearl Is A Beautiful Symbol Of The Church. It Is Grown By Accretion. It Is Found In The Pearl Oyster. In This Dispensation Christ Is After The Pearl Only. No Conversion Of The World Here.

THE CHURCH OF TH...
Heb. 12:...

"THE FIELD IS...

VIII. "The Unmerciful Servant" — Matt. 18:23-35

IX. "The Vineyard Laborers" — Matt. 20:1-16

This Parable Has To Do With The Conduct Of The Members Of The Kingdom Of Heaven Towards Each Other During This Dispensation. It Was Given Because Of A Dispute Between The Disciples And Teaches That The Offended Should Seek Reconciliation. (Matt. 18:15-17), And That Forgiveness Should Be Without Limit. Matt. 18:21-22. The "Certain King" Is God. The Servant Who Owed 10,000 Talents Is The Sinner. A Forgiven Man Should Forgive As Freely As He Has Been Forgiven. If He Will Not, Then There Is A Question As To Whether He Is A Forgiven Man.

THIRD HOUR — **SIXTH HOUR**

The Dispensation Of The King... And Unforgiv... The End Of Th...

The "Penny" That The Laborers Received For Their Labor Does Not Represent "Salvation," For Salvation Is A Gift, Not Wages. Neither Do The Hours When The Laborers Were Employed Represent The Different Ages At Which Sinners May Come To Christ. The Laborers Stood In The Market Place Not Because They Were Unwilling To Work, But Because No Man Had Hired Them. The Content (Matt. 19:16-30) Shows That The Parable Was Spoken In Answer To The Question Of Peter: "What Shall We Have Therefore?" And Was Spoken To Show The "Hireling Spirit" Of Peter. There Is Nothing Unusual In The Parable But The "Settling Time." Men Who Unbusiness Like Way Of Paying Off First Those Who...

THIS PARABLE GOES BACK TO MOSES AND THE PROPHETS

This Parable Is Not To Be Confounded With The Parable Of The Great Supper Recorded In Luke 14:16-24, That Refer To The Gospel Feast. This Goes Back To The Days Of Moses And Reaches To The Judgment Of Reward. The "Certain King" Is God. The "Son" Is Christ. Those Bidden Were The Jewish Nation. Moses And The Prophets Announced The Feast. John The Baptist, The Twelve, And The Seventy Notified The Jewish Nation That It Was About Ready. When Jesus, "The Lamb," Was Offered On Calvary, The Feast Was Ready, And Peter, John, & Others Were The Other Servants Sent Forth. This Was The "Second Call." Acts 3:19-21. But The Nation Made Light Of It. Then The Remnant Took Stephen And...

Had Been Hired Had Been Hired Spirit" Is A Ch... Coming In The...

James, And Others His Armies And B Destruction Of J And Others Were In Those Who We...

X. "The Marriage Feast" — Matt. 22:1-14

NOTE: Jesus Spoke 12 "Kingdom Of Heaven Parables." Matthew Alone Records Them. They Reveal The Character Of This Dispensation Up To The Return Of The Lord. The 7 Given In Matt. 13 Correspond With The 7 Church Periods Of Rev. 2 And 3, And Are So Shown Above. The Chart Shows The Character Of This Dispensation, And What Becomes Of The Righteous And The Wicked At Its Close, And Discloses The Fact That The "Kingdom Of Heaven" Is Of A Twofold Character, And That There Is To Be No Conversion Of The World In This Dispensation.

Designed And Drawn By
Clarence Larkin
Foxchase, Phila., PA
Copyrighted

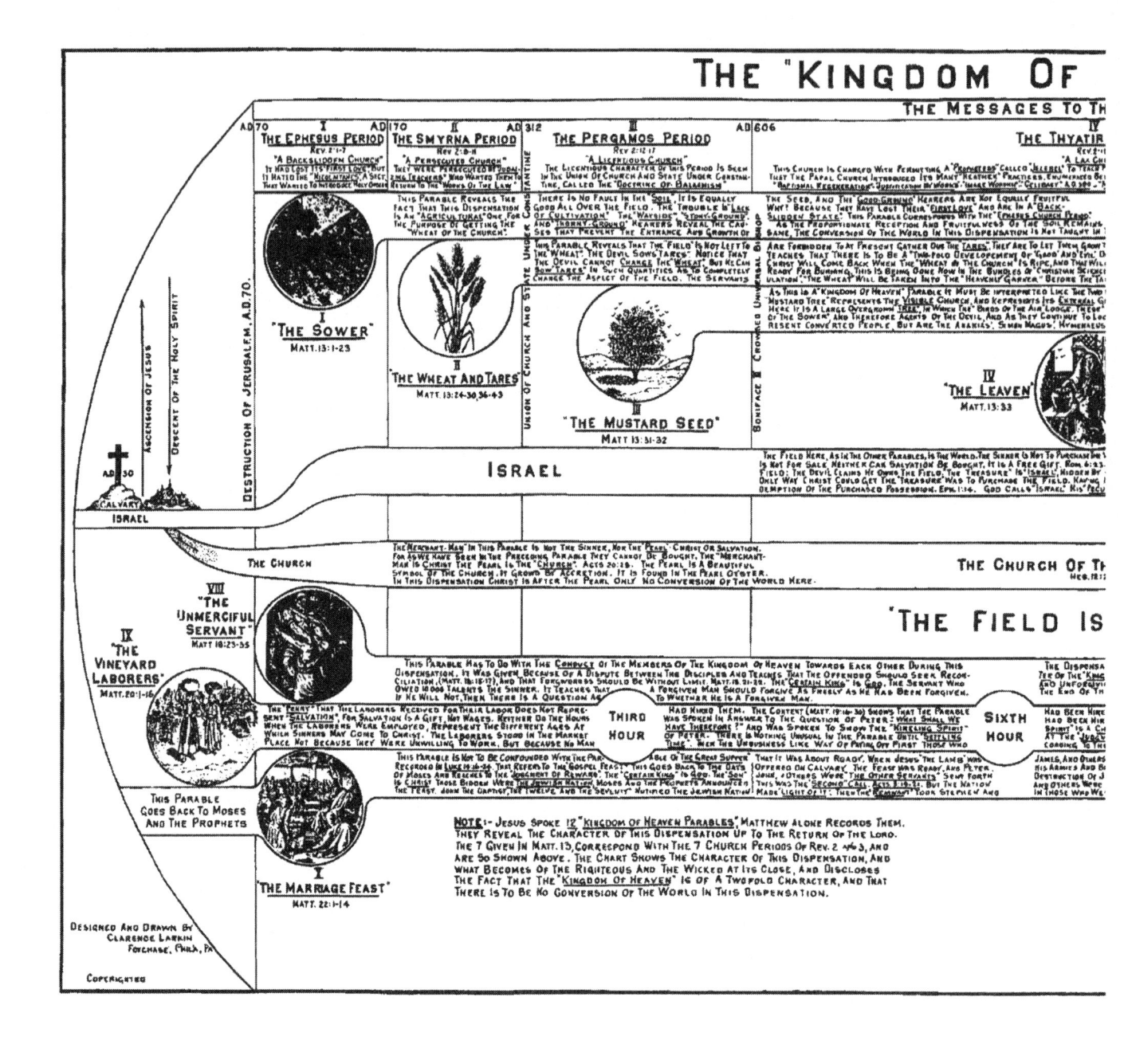

"HEAVEN" PARABLES.

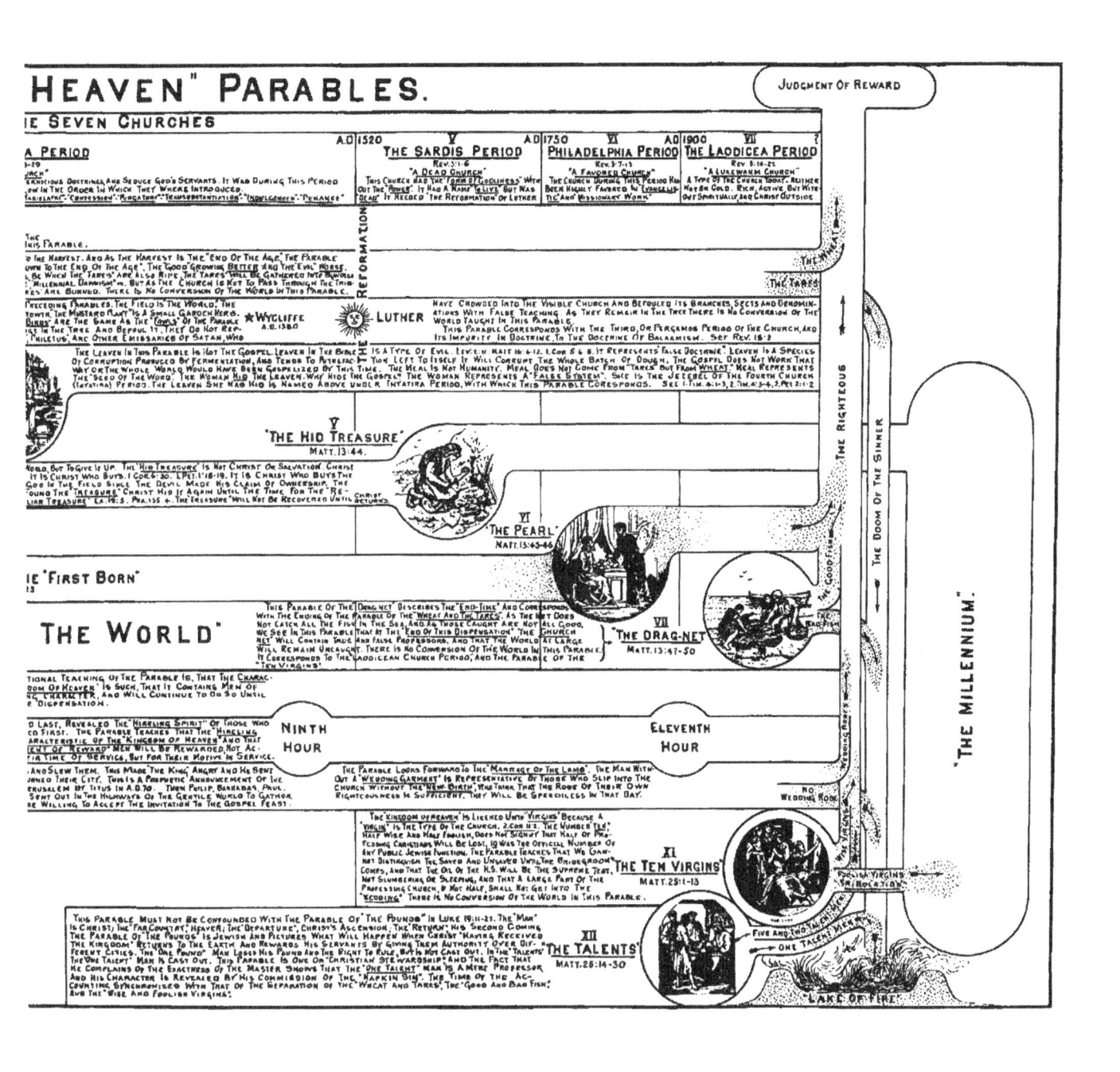

It is clear from this that the Disciples were looking for an **Earthly and Visible** Kingdom, and not a spiritual one. If Jesus came simply to set up a "**Spiritual Kingdom**" in this Dispensation, as many claim, then common honesty demanded that He at that solemn moment when He was about to leave His Disciples and go back to the Father, should have disabused His Disciples' minds of their false hope, and told them plainly that the Kingdom he came to set up was "**spiritual**" and not earthly. But He did no such thing. He confirmed their hope and told them that there was to be an "**Earthly Kingdom**," but the time and season for setting it up had not yet come.

In Luke 19:11, 12, we read—

"Because He was nigh to Jerusalem, and because they thought that the **Kingdom of God Should 'IMMEDIATELY' Appear**; He spake this parable. A certain nobleman went into a far country to receive for himself a Kingdom, and to return."

From this we see that Jesus is the "Certain Nobleman" who has gone into a "Far Country" (Heaven), to receive the Kingdom and that, when He has received it, He will return.

There is nothing in the Scriptures to prove that Jesus is a King now. David was anointed King over Israel long before King Saul died in anticipation of that event, but he did not become King, and take the throne, until **after Saul's death**. So while Jesus was born "King of the Jews," He does not become King until He actually takes the Throne. At present He is engaged in His High Priestly functions, and is seated on His Father's Throne and not on His own Throne.

II. The Kingdom in Mystery.

The King having been rejected it was impossible then to set up the Kingdom, so the Kingdom took on another aspect known as

The Kingdom in Mystery.

This "Mystery Form" of the Kingdom is described in the "Kingdom of Heaven Parables" found in Matthew's Gospel alone. If we want to know the character of this Period, which covers the time between the Ascension of Christ, and the Rapture of the Church, we must study these Parables. They are 12 in number.

After Jesus had spoken the Parable of "The Sower," the Disciples came to Him and said, "Why speakest Thou unto them in **Parables?**" He answered—"Because it is given unto you to know

THE MYSTERIES
Of the Kingdom of Heaven."

In verse 35 He gives as His reason for speaking to them in Parables, that it might be fulfilled as spoken by the prophet—

"I will open my mouth in **Parables**; I will utter things which have been kept **SECRET** from the foundation of the world."

The "Kingdom of Heaven Parables" therefore cannot describe the "Messianic" or "Millennial Kingdom," for it was no "secret" to the old Testament Prophets. Neither do they describe a "Spiritual Kingdom," for the figures they use are all of an "earthly" nature. They must then describe the character of the Present Dispensation, in its **earthly aspect**, during the **absence of The King**.

Our Lord's Parables are not "Allegories." A vein of falsehood characterizes all allegories. Things are represented "fictitiously." The Parables of our Lord present things truthfully. He used Parables so that those who were not disposed to believe might not understand, and that the word of God might be fulfilled as spoken by the Prophet Isaiah. **Isa. 6:9-11. Matt. 13:13-17.** Also because "blindness in part" had fallen upon Israel, (Rom. 11:25), and a clear revelation would only discourage them or drive them further into unbelief.

Seven of the "Kingdom of Heaven" Parables are found in Matthew 13. All of the twelve, except the Parable of "The Sower," begin with "The Kingdom of Heaven is like unto."

1. The Sower.

The purpose of the "Parable of the Sower" seems to be, not so much to show the "character" of the "Kingdom of Heaven," that is, the "proportion" of those who hear the Gospel and fail to profit by it, though that is clearly revealed, as it is to show the **causes that hinder the growth of the Seed**. The Parable mentions four classes of "Hearers."

(1) The "Wayside" Hearer.

Here the seed does not have a chance to "take root." The "Devil's Birds," (vs. 19), "Criticism," "Doubt," "Unbelief," "Prejudice," "Preoccupation," etc., snatch up the seed before it can be worked into the soil.

(2) The "Stony Ground" Hearer.

Here the seed takes "root" but dies before it can grow up because of the "shallowness" of the soil. Emotional souls caught by some sudden fear of hell, or moved by some strong appeal, profess conversion, but not counting the cost they soon fall away. Jesus mentioned "two stones" that underlie the soil of the heart of the "Stony-Ground Hearer," "Tribulation" and "Persecution."

(3) The "Thorny-Ground" Hearer.

Here the seed takes "root," "grows up," but does not bear fruit. The soil of the heart of the "Thorny-Ground Hearer" contains the seeds or roots of "thorns" and these spring up, and outgrow, and overshadow the wheat, and absorb from the soil the nutriment needed by it. Matthew mentions two of these "thorns," the "Cares of the World" and the "Deceitfulness of riches." Mark (4:19) mentions another, the "Lust of other things," and Luke (8:14) a fourth, the "Pleasures of this life."

(4) The "Good-Ground" Hearer.

Here the seed takes "root," "grows up," "bears fruit," but the amount varies. Some brings forth a 100 fold, some 60, some only 30. Why is this? It was not the fault of the soil. That was equally good all over the field, even on the "Wayside," and in the "Stony" and "Thorny" parts. Why then? It was the lack of cultivation. If the soil had been properly cleared, tilled, and cultivated, and the proper atmospheric conditions prevailed, it would have brought forth a uniform crop of 100 fold.

This Parable teaches us that Christianity is a **New Thing**, that it is not like weeds that grow up spontaneously of themselves, but it must be sown and cultivated like wheat. The figure is a lowly agricultural one, that of a farmer sowing seed, and not of a King **Setting Up a Kingdom**. In other words this Dispensation is an "**Agricultural One**" for the purpose of getting the "**WHEAT OF THE CHURCH**."

The apparent fruitlessness of the soil, only one-quarter bringing forth any fruit, and that in unequal proportions, seems to indicate the comparative failure of the Gospel in this Dispensation. Surely this Parable does not teach that the World is to be **converted in this Dispensation by the preaching of the Gospel**.

2. The Wheat and Tares.

The Parable of the "Wheat and Tares" (Matt. 13:24-30), Christ Himself interprets (vs. 37-43), and this forbids any fanciful or unscriptural interpretation. He tells us that the "Man" who sowed the good seed is the "Son of Man" (vs. 37), that He sowed it in His "own field" (vs. 24), and that the "Field" is not the Church, but the "world." This at one stroke demolishes the argument of those who claim that the "Field" is the Church, and that the "Wheat" and the "Tares" represent "true" and "false" professors.

The Son of Man, the "Sower," in the first Parable sowed the seed of "The Word." In this Parable He sows "Men" (the Children of the Kingdom). This is beautifully illustrated in the persecution that followed the martyrdom of Stephen. Acts 8: 1-4. It was the Son of Man Himself, through the agency of Saul of Tarsus, and not Satan, who scattered the Church broadcast throughout Judea and Samaria. This is where the Parable begins. This scattering has been going on down the centuries.

But the "Field" was not left to the "Wheat." The Devil came and sowed Tares." The "Tares," or "Darnel," so closely resembles Wheat that its true nature cannot be seen until it has matured. This sowing of the "Tares" was done, not while the Sower slept, for He never slumbers or sleeps, but while the "men" He left to look after the Field slept. Vs. 25. This sowing is still going on.

The "Tares" are called the "Children of the Wicked One." They are men of the character of those Jews to whom Jesus said—"Ye are of your father the Devil." John 8: 44.

It is important to note that the Devil cannot "change" the "Wheat;" he can only sow "Tares;" but he can sow in such large quantities as to completely change the "aspect" of the whole field. When the servants saw what was done they said—"Wilt thou then that we go and gather them up?" The master said—"Nay; lest while ye gather up the tares ye root up also the wheat with them." This is no argument for "laxness" in Church Discipline. This Parable has no reference to the Church, as a church. Men and women in these days are trying to root out all manner of obnoxious evils, it is an idle dream. It does more harm than good. There is to be a **Twofold Development of "Good" and "Evil" DOWN TO THE END OF THE AGE**, the "Good" growing better and the "Evil" worse. The Parable teaches that as the time for the "Harvest" approaches the difference between the "Wheat" and the "Tares" will become more strikingly and clearly manifest.

How long is this conflict between "Good" and "Evil" to last? "**Until the Harvest.**" Vs. 30. When is the Harvest. At the "**End of This Age**," and the "reapers" are the **Angels** (vs. 39). As soon as the "**Wheat of the Church Is Ripe**" Jesus will come back.

Some are perplexed by the words

"Gather ye together first the 'Tares,' and bind them in bundles to burn them; but gather the 'Wheat' into my barn" (vs. 30),

and claim that the Church is to remain on the earth until the "Tares" are burned, and that this necessitates the Church's going through the Tribulation.

The fact is that the "Tares" are gathered together in "bundles," not to burn them "before" the "Wheat" is harvested, but to have them "separated" and in readiness to burn "after" the "Wheat" has been garnered in the "Heavenly Barn." This gathering together of the "Tares" into bundles is going on now in the formation of false religious systems such as "Christian Science," "New Thought," "Millennial Dawnism," "Spiritualism," "Mormonism," "Theosophy," etc. This Parable teaches that the "Wheat" and the "Tares" **are inseparable until the End of This Dispensation**, and therefore there can be no Millennium until Christ returns.

3. The Mustard Tree.

The Parable of the "Mustard Tree," and the one that follows it, the "Leaven," both begin with the phrase "The Kingdom of Heaven is like unto," and therefore their teaching should not contradict the teaching of the Parable of the "Wheat and Tares." The same is true of all the "Kingdom of Heaven" parables. Yet these two parables have both been used to teach the "expansion of the Church" until it shall be universal in its supremacy. We repeat again that the "Kingdom of Heaven" is not the Church, but Christendom. Yet for clearness sake we will let the "Mustard Tree" represent the "visible" Church, composed of all churches called Christian. Of these two Parables the "Mustard Tree" represents the "external" growth and condition of the visible Church and the "Leaven" the "internal" development.

The "Mustard Plant" is a "garden herb," and is cultivated for its seed, used as a condiment. It grows wild, often to the height of seven or eight feet. To obtain the best results it should be cultivated in a garden. In the Parable we find the seed sown in a "Field," (the World), not in a garden, and it grows "wild" until it is no longer called an "herb" but a "tree." The seed does not produce, after its kind," an humble "herb," but becomes a vain-glorious **Tree**, a "**Monstrosity**," in which the "**Birds of the Air**" **Lodge**. Who are these "birds?" They are the "fowls" of the Parable of the Sower, for the same word is used, and are therefore the agents of the "Wicked One," the Devil. Matt. 13: 4, 19. It is clear then that the "birds" in this parable do not represent persons converted by the preaching of the Gospel, but the emissaries of Satan, and they do not lodge in the branches of the "Tree" so much for shelter as for worldly advantage, and they "befoul" it by their presence.

The "Mustard Tree" began with the 120 believers who received the Baptism of the Holy Spirit on the Day of Pentecost and continued to enlarge until its branches spread all over the Roman world. But the "Birds of the Air," the Ananias and Sapphiras, the Simon Maguses, the Hymenaeus and Philetus and other emissaries of Satan, began to lodge in its branches and "befoul" its purity, and when in A. D. 324 the Emperor Constantine united Church and State, thousands, and tens of thousands, crowded into the Church as a matter of policy, interest and fashion, and crouched beneath its shadow, lodged in its branches, fattened on its fruit, and have continued to do so until this day.

According to this Parable the "Kingdom of Heaven" is a

Vast Worldly System,

rooted in the earth, bearing the name of Christ, possessed of wealth, standing, and power, but **sheltering the agents of the "Ruler of the Darkness of This Age."** Such we know is the condition of the visible Church today. Where is the picture of "pure" Christianity spreading through the world until the knowledge of the Lord shall cover the earth as the waters cover the deep, thus ushering in a Millennium, in this Parable? In fact, it teaches the contrary and is proof of Jesus' own declaration that when He shall come back He shall **Not Find 'THE FAITH' on the Earth**. Luke 18: 8.

4. The Leaven.

The common interpretation of the Parable of the "Leaven" (Matt. 13: 33), is, that the "Woman" represents the Church, the "Leaven," the Gospel, and the "Three Measures of Meal," Humanity; and that the "Leaven of the Gospel" is to be so introduced by the Church into the "Meal of Humanity" that the whole world will be converted to Christ. But the "Leaven" cannot mean the "Gospel," Leaven in the Scriptures is the

Symbol of Evil.

It is a species of corruption produced by fermentation, and tends to putrefaction, and will "corrupt" everything with which it comes in contact. The Children of Israel were commanded to put it out of their houses at the time of the "Passover" on penalty of "excommunication." Ex. 12:15. It must not come in contact with any sacrifice. Ex. 34:25; Lev. 2:11; 10:12. Three times Christ uses the word "Leaven" beside here in this Parable. He speaks of the "Leaven of the Pharisees," the "Leaven of the Sadducees" and the "Leaven of Herod." Matt. 16:6-12; Mark 8:15. He calls the "Leaven" of the Pharisees and Sadducees "false doctrine." The "False Doctrine" of the Pharisees was "Legalism," the "form of godliness without the power." The "False Doctrine" of the Sadducees was "Scepticism," the denial of the resurrection of the body, saying there was neither angel or spirit. The "False Doctrine" of Herod was "Materialism," a mixture of religion and worldliness.

Christ never used the word "Leaven" except in an "evil" sense. It is used in the same way by the Apostle Paul. Writing to the Corinthians he said—"Purge out therefore the 'old leaven' that ye may be a 'new lump.'" 1 Cor. 5:6-8. In the same passage he calls Leaven "malice and wickedness," as contrasted with "sincerity and truth." Writing to the Corinthians and Galatians about "evil practices," he warns them that "a little leaven leaveneth the whole lump." 1 Cor. 5:6; Gal. 5:9.

There are but two exceptions to this universal rule. In Lev. 23:6-14 we read that the "Wave Sheaf" of "First Fruits" was to contain no Leaven because it represented Christ, the "First Fruits" of the Resurrection, who was "without sin." But the new "Meat Offering," of "two wave loaves," offered 50 days later, at the Feast of Pentecost (Lev. 23:15-17), was to contain Leaven, because the Feast of Pentecost was typical of the bestowal of the Holy Spirit on the Disciples on the Day of Pentecost (Acts 2:1-4), and those who received it were not free from sin.

The other exception is in Amos 4:4, 5, where the Lord is "rebuking transgression," and "sarcastically" refers to the use of Leaven as a "multiplying of transgression." We see then that even where the use of Leaven is commanded, or permitted, it is a symbol of evil. It is clear then that what is meant by "Leaven" in this Parable is false or corrupting doctrine.

If by "Leaven" is meant the Gospel we have a queer contradiction, for the Gospel does not work like leaven. Leaven when put in meal works by "itself," and if left "alone" will leaven the whole batch of dough. But this is not the way the Gospel works; if it were, every village, town, city and country where the Gospel has once been implanted, should by this time be so thoroughly "Leavened" as to be now completely Christian, but this we know is not true. The Gospel as far as converting the world is concerned is a failure.

We are not left in the dark as to the "character" of the Leaven. Paul writing to Timothy said—

> "The time will come when they will not **endure sound doctrine**; but after their **own lusts** shall they heap to themselves teachers having **'itching ears;'** and they shall turn away their ears from the truth, and shall be turned unto fables." 2 Tim. 4:3, 4.

The Apostle Peter also sounds a warning.

> "But there were false prophets also among the people, even as there shall be **false teachers** among you, who **privily** (like hiding the Leaven in the meal) shall bring in **damnable heresies**, denying the Lord **that bought them,** and bring upon themselves swift destruction. And **many shall follow their 'Pernicious Ways,'** by reason of whom the **'Way of Truth' SHALL BE EVIL SPOKEN OF."** 2 Pet. 2:1, 2.

So much for the "Leaven." Now what is meant by the "three measures of meal?" Where do we get meal? Not from Tares. They would not yield fine wholesome flour. Meal comes from corn. Hence the "Meal" cannot represent the "unregenerate mass of humanity," but the pure seed of the Word of God. It is a striking coincidence that the professing Church is divided today into three great parts, the Roman Catholic, the Greek, and the Protestant churches, which may represent the "three measures" into the "Meal" of which has been placed the false and corrupting doctrines of "Baptismal Regeneration," "Prayers for the Dead," "Image Worship," the "Sacrifice of the Mass" and other false doctrines.

The "Woman" who hides the "Leaven" corresponds to the woman Jezebel of the Church of Thyatira (Rev. 2:20), and foreshadows the "System" (Papal) referred to in Rev. 17:5, as the **Mother of Harlots and Abominations of the Earth."** As further proof that the "Leaven" is "bad" and "corrupting" is the fact that the Woman "hides" it in the "Meal." If the Leaven is the Gospel there was no reason why she should hide it.

The purpose of these four Parables is to warn us of what to expect as the result of the preaching of the Gospel in this Age, so that we shall not be discouraged and disheartened by what we see to be the apparent failure of the Gospel. They teach that at no time during Christ's absence will there be a universal reception of the Gospel; that it will be opposed by the World, the Flesh and the Devil until the End of the Age, that the Church will grow unwatchful and fall asleep, that the Devil will take advantage of such unwatchfulness to put his own children into the professing Church to introduce corrupting doctrine, and that all this shall continue in an increasing measure until the Lord shall come with "fiery" judgments, for fire alone can arrest the work of leaven. This then is to be the outcome of all the "religionism" of the Age. Where is there a place in these Parables for a Millennium before Christ comes back?

5. The Hid Treasure.

The Parables of the "Hid Treasure," and the "Pearl" have been interpreted to mean that Christ is the "Hid Treasure" and also the "Pearl," and that we are to sell all, that is, give up everything for Him. But such an interpretation is contrary to the Gospel plan of salvation and breaks down in every particular.

The "Field" in this Parable is the "World," the same as in the Parable of the "Wheat and Tares," and the sinner is not to "purchase" the "World" but to "give it up." Furthermore, the sinner has "nothing to sell," nor is Christ "for sale," nor is He "hidden in a field," nor having found Christ does the sinner "hide him again." Salvation is not something that can be "bought." It is a "free gift." Rom. 6:23. The sinner does not buy Christ, Christ buys him. 1 Cor. 6:20. Salvation is "free," and is something to be "received" (John 1:12), and that "without money" and "without price." Isa. 55:1.

As in the preceding Parables the "Field" is the World, and the "Man" is the Son of Man, or Christ. Christ is the "purchaser" of the "Field." But why should He purchase the "Field?" Does not the World belong to His Father? And if He found the "Treasure" in the "Field" why should He "hide" it until He was able to purchase the "Field?" Would it be considered honest to discover that, under the surface of a man's farm there were hidden treasures of coal, iron, oil or copper, and, without letting him know, try to secure the farm at a small cost, thus deceiving him until the property was secured? The answer is that a "usurper," the Devil, had taken possession of the

"Field." The Hid Treasure was not in the field when he took possession. It was placed their afterward. It did not belong to the Devil, it belonged to God who had hid in it the "Field" from the Devil. Christ found it, and as the only way to get the "Treasure" was to buy the "Field," Christ hid it again, and then purchased the "Field." The price He paid was all He possessed. 2 Cor. 8:9.

The Hid Treasure is Israel. God said to Israel at Sinai—

"Ye shall be a **Peculiar Treasure** unto me above all people; for all the earth (world) is mine." Ex. 19:5.

"For the Lord hath chosen Jacob for Himself and **Israel for His Peculiar Treasure.**" Psa. 135:4.

The "Treasure" still remains "hid" in the "Field." Christ purchased the "Field" on the Cross, but He has not taken possession as yet, and will not until the time comes for the "**Redemption of the PURCHASED POSSESSION.**" Eph. 1:14.

Until that time Israel must remain hid among the Nations. This is one of the "Mysteries" of the "Kingdom of Heaven."

"For I would not, brethren, that ye should be ignorant of this **'Mystery,'** lest ye should be wise in your own conceits, that **blindness in part is happened to Israel, until the Fulness of the Gentiles Be Come in.**" Rom. 11:25.

Israel must remain hid in the "Field" until the "Fulness of the Gentiles" be come in. Then Christ will come back and claim His "Hid Treasure," and Israel will be resurrected from the "Graveyard of the Nations" where she is buried and restored to her own land.

6. The Pearl.

In the Parable of the "Pearl" the "Merchant Man" is Christ. The "Pearl" is the Church. In the Parable of the "Hid Treasure," the Treasure was not purchased but the Field. In this Parable it is the "Pearl" that is purchased. Once Christ comes into full possession of the "Pearl" it will never be on the market again. It will be His forever. We see from this Parable that the purpose of this Dispensation is not the conversion of the World, but the securing (formation) of the Church.

7. The Drag Net.

The Parable of the "Drag Net," like all the preceeding, covers the present Dispensation. The "net" here mentioned is the "Gospel Net." The Parable is descriptive of the work the Disciples were to do when Jesus said unto them—"I will make you 'Fishers of Men.'" While men in this "Gospel Age" are mostly caught one by one, yet in times of revival they are caught as in a net in large quantities. The Parable is descriptive of the method used in this Gospel Dispensation of gathering people into our churches by the "Drag-net of Solicitation."

The result is that there are "Good" and "Bad" fish in the net. But while fishermen can separate the "bad" fish from the "good," that is the eatable and marketable from those that are not, the officers of a church are not always omniscient enough to do this. The ending of this Parable corresponds with the ending of the Parable of the "Wheat and Tares." As there the separation does not come until the "Harvest," and the "Harvest" is the "End of the Age," and the separation will be made by the "Angel Reapers," so in this Parable the separation between the "Good" and "Bad" fish will not be until the "end of this Age," and angels will do the separating.

We should notice also that as the "Tares" were gathered together "first," but not burned until the "Wheat" had been garnered in the "Heavenly Barn," so here, the "Good" fish are separated from the "Bad" and the "Good" gathered into "vessels" (Heaven), before the "Bad" are cast away.

When a net is cast into the sea, even though the net is filled to the point of breaking, the great bulk of the fish in the sea remain uncaught, and where there is a separation of those caught, as in the Parable, comparatively few are saved. If this is true of this Gospel Dispensation, as the Parable seems to teach, then the world is not to be converted before the "Angel Fishermen" separate the "Righteous" and the "Wicked" at the coming of the Lord.

Of the five remaining "Kingdom of Heaven" Parables we have only space to speak briefly. The Parable of the "Unmerciful Servant" (Matt. 18:23-35), has to do with the "conduct" of the members of the "Kingdom of Heaven" towards each other during this Dispensation.

The Parable of the "Vineyard Laborers" (Matt. 20:1-16) does not teach that the "penny" that the laborers received for their labor represents "Salvation," for "Salvation" is a Gift, and cannot be "earned" as wages, or "merited" as a reward. Neither does the Parable teach, as some claim, that those who were hired early in the morning, and at the third, sixth, ninth and eleventh hours, represent the different ages at which sinners may come to Christ. Neither does the Parable teach that because each one received a "penny" that men shall be "equally" rewarded in the next world. What then does the Parable teach? The context shows (Matt. 19:27-30), that the Parable was spoken to rebuke the "hireling spirit" of Peter, and is to teach that men will be judged for the "motive" of their service, and not for the "amount." The Parable teaches that the "Hireling Spirit" will be a characteristic of the "Kingdom of Heaven," and therefore of this Dispensation, and that it will be revealed at the "Judgment of Reward" by the consumption of the "wood," "hay" and "stubble" works of all "Hireling Laborers." 1 Cor. 3:9-15.

The Parable of the "Marriage Feast" (Matt. 22:1-14) must not be confounded with the Parable of the "Great Supper" recorded in Luke 14:16-24. That Parable was spoken in the house of a chief Pharisee in Perea, three months before Christ's death, and refers to the "Gospel Feast." This Parable was spoken in the Temple at Jerusalem on the morning of the Tuesday preceding His Crucifixion, and was spoken to the multitude. In the scope of its teaching and outlook this Parable of the "Marriage Feast" is the broadest of all the parables of Jesus. In its perspective it extends from the giving of the "Mosaic Law" to the "Marriage of the Lamb." The "certain king" is God, the "son" is Christ. Those first bidden were the Jewish Nation. Moses and the Prophets announced the "Feast." John the Baptist, the Twelve, and the Seventy, notified the Jewish Nation that it was about ready. When Jesus the "Lamb" was offered on Calvary the Feast was ready, and Peter, John and others were the "other servants" sent forth. This was the "second" call. Acts 3:19-21. But the Jewish Nation made "light of it." Then the "remnant" took Stephen, James and others, and "entreated them spitefully" and "slew them." This made the King angry and He sent His armies and "burned their city." This is a prophetic announcement of the destruction of Jerusalem by Titus in A. D. 70. Then Philip, Barnabas, Paul and others, were sent out into the Highways of the "Gentile World" to gather in those who were willing to accept the invitation to the "Marriage Feast." This is still going on. The Parable looks forward to the "Marriage of the Lamb," and reveals that there is to be a "separation" among the guests, and that all those who have not on a "Wedding Garment" will be excluded from the "Feast." The ending of the Parable synchronizes with the separation of the "Wise" and "Foolish" Virgins, and reveals the fact that many professing Christians will be found without a "Wedding Garment," and "speechless," when they are called upon to face God.

The Parable of the "Ten Virgins" (Matt. 25:1-13), is a picture of what will happen to the professing Church when Christ comes to gather out His Saints. It teaches that we cannot distinguish the

"True" from the "False" professors in the Church until the time for separation comes, and that the possession of the Holy Spirit (represented by the "oil" in the Parable) will be the supreme test. If possibly half the "Professing Church" is shut out from the "Wedding," and all of the great multitude outside the Church, who show by their lives that they are unsaved, where is the Conversion of the World in this Dispensation to be seen in this Parable?

The Parable of the "Talents" (Matt. 25:14-30) must not be confounded with the Parable of the "Pounds" in Luke 19:11-27. The "Man" is Christ. The "far country," Heaven. The "departure," Christ's Ascension. The "return," His Second Coming.

The Parable of the "Pounds" is Jewish and pictures what will happen when Christ, "having received the Kingdom," returns to the earth and rewards His Servants (the Jews), by giving them authority over different cities. The "One Pound" man loses his Pound and the right to rule, but is not "cast out." In this Parable of the "Talents" the "One Talent" man is "cast out." The theme of the Parable is "Christian Stewardship" and the fact that the "One Talent" man complains of the strict accountability required of him shows that the "One Talent" man is a mere professor, and his character is revealed by his commission of the "Napkin Sin." The time of the accounting synchronizes with that of the separation of the "Wheat" and "Tares," the "Good" and "Bad" Fish, and the "Wise" and "Foolish" Virgins, and reveals the fact that unfaithfulness in "Christian Stewardship" will be punished.

See the Chart on the "Kingdom of Heaven" Parables.

III. The Kingdom in Manifestation.

That there is to be a period of a 1000 years during which Satan shall be bound and Christ shall reign on this earth, is plainly stated in the New Testament. This period is mentioned 6 times in Rev. 20:1-7, and is generally called

"The Millennium,"

from the Latin words "Mille" (1000) and "Annum" (year). It is to be regretted, however, that the word "Millennium" ever supplanted the Biblical word "Kingdom," for it is this period that Christ taught His Disciples to pray for in the petition—"Thy Kingdom Come."

Let us drop then for the present the word "Millennium" and look at the word "Kingdom." In the chapter on "The Gentiles" we saw that there were to be "Four World-wide Kingdoms" that were to succeed each other on the earth and that they were to be destroyed in turn by a Kingdom called the

"Stone Kingdom."

As those "Four Kingdoms" were "literal" Kingdoms it follows that the "Stone Kingdom" must be a "literal" Kingdom, for it takes the place of those Kingdoms and "fills the whole earth." This "Stone Kingdom" is the "Millennial Kingdom of Christ."

The time when this "Stone Kingdom" shall be set up is at the "Revelation of Christ," when He shall come with the "armies of Heaven" and destroy Antichrist (Rev. 19:11-21) and judge the Nations.

"When the Son of Man shall come **in His glory**, and all the holy angels with Him, then shall He sit upon the

'Throne of His Glory;'

and before Him shall be gathered **all nations**; and He shall separate them one from another as a shepherd divideth his sheep from the goats, and He shall set the **Sheep** (Sheep Nations) on His **right** hand, but the **Goats** (Goat Nations) on the left. Then shall the King say unto them on His **right hand,** Come, ye blessed of my Father, inherit the **Kingdom Prepared for You From the Foundation of the World.**" Matt. 25:31-34.

This Kingdom is an earthly, visible Kingdom, and is the "Millennial Kingdom" of the Lord Jesus Christ.

1. The Form of Government.

It will be a "Theocracy." God will rule in the person of the Lord Jesus Christ.

"And the angel said unto Mary, thou shalt bring forth a son and shalt call His name Jesus. He shall be great and shall be called the 'Son of the Highest,' and the Lord God shall give unto Him the **Throne of His Father David**; and He shall **reign over the House of Jacob FOREVER,** and of **His Kingdom There Shall Be NO END.**" Luke 1:30-33.

There are 7 of God's "**shalls**" in this passage. Four of them have been fulfilled, for Mary did bring forth a "son," He was called "Jesus," He was "great," and was called the "Son of the Highest;" the other three must and will be fulfilled.

Daniel the Prophet describes the event.

"I saw in the night visions, and, behold, one like the 'Son of Man' came with the clouds of heaven, and came to the 'Ancient of Days' (God), and they brought Him near before Him. And there was given Him **Dominion**, and **Glory** and a **KINGDOM** that all people, nations, and languages, should serve Him; His **Dominion** is an **Everlasting Dominion, Which Shall Not Pass Away**, and His **KINGDOM** that which **Shall Not Be Destroyed.**" Dan. 7:13, 14.

Whether Christ shall sit in person on the Throne at Jerusalem, or whether He shall rule through another is not so clear. There are several passages of Scripture that seem to teach that King David will be raised and placed on the throne again, and that the Children of Israel will seek him, or it may mean that the new King shall be named David.

"Afterward shall the Children of Israel return, and seek the Lord their God, and **David Their King**; and shall fear the Lord and His goodness in the **Latter Days.**" Hosea 3:5.

"They shall serve the Lord their God, and **David Their King**, whom I will **Raise Up Unto Them.**" Jer. 30:9.

"And **David**, my servant, shall be **King Over Them.**" Ezek. 37:24.

"I Jehovah will be their God, and my servant **David a Prince in Their Midst.**" Ezek. 34:24.

"My servant **David** shall be their **Prince Forever.**" Ezek. 37:25.

As the "Lord of Hosts" shall reign in Mt. Zion, and in Jerusalem, and before His ancients "gloriously" (Isa. 24:23), the inference is that King David will reign simply as "Regent," and will be called "King" or "Prince" as circumstances may require. It is very clear from Ezekiel that the "Prince," whoever he may be, is not perfect, and has to offer sacrifices for himself. Ezek. 45:22.

We have a hint of the manner of government in the Parable of the Pounds. That Parable was spoken to show what Jesus will do to His servants (the Jews) when He shall have "received the Kingdom and returned." The man whose Pound shall have gained "Ten Pounds" will be rewarded by being placed in authority over "ten cities." The man whose Pound shall have gained "Five Pounds" will have authority over "five cities." The man who failed to use his Pound is simply deprived of it and loses all opportunity of authority. Luke 19:11-26.

The promise that Jesus made to His Disciples that

"In the Regeneration when the Son of Man shall sit on the Throne of His Glory, ye also shall sit upon Twelve Thrones, Judging the Twelve Tribes of Israel." Matt. 19:28,

in all probability does not refer to the "Millennial Age," but to the "Perfect Age," the "Age" that is to follow the renovation of the Earth by fire. The use of the word "regeneration" suggests this, as it refers to the time when the present earth is to be "re-created" and made "new." It has occurred to the writer that we have not as yet the proper perspective as to all the Old Testament prophecies, and that we are putting in the "Millennial Age" some things that belong to the "Perfect Age." The one just mentioned, for example.

Some object to the "visible reign" of King David, or the Disciples on the earth during the Millennium because it involves the anomaly of intercourse between men in the flesh and those who are clad in resurrected and glorified bodies. But why should this be an objection? Did not Jesus appear "eleven" times "after His resurrection," during a period of "forty days," to His disciples? Did He not "eat" and "drink" with them during that period? Did they not "walk" with Him to the Mount of Olives and see Him go up in that Same Resurrection Body? Did not angels appear in human form and "eat" and "drink" with men in Old Testament times? Gen. 18:1-8.

We must not forget that they who shall be accounted worthy to obtain "That Age," and the "Resurrection From Among the Dead," shall be "Angel Like" (Luke 20:35, 36), and like the angels can mingle with earth's inhabitants, having visible bodily forms, can eat and drink, and there is probably more truth than poetry in the Prophet's utterance that in those days,

"They that wait upon the Lord (as messengers) shall renew their strength; they shall mount up with wings as eagles (Angels); they shall run and not be weary; and they shall walk and not faint." Isa. 40:31.

This can be said of only those who have been "Raised in Power." 1 Cor. 15:42, 43.

2. **The Seat of Government.**

The Seat of Government will be at Jerusalem. Jerusalem is to be trodden down of the Gentiles, until the "Times of the Gentiles be fulfilled." Luke 21:24. Then it will be rebuilt. The Prophet Ezekiel gives us a detailed description of the restored Land and City in Ezek. 48:1-35. See Chart of the Millennial Land.

The "Royal Grant" of land that God gave to Abraham and his descendants extended from the "River of Egypt" unto the "Great River," the river Euphrates. Gen. 15:18. Ezekiel fixes the Northern boundary at Hamath, about 100 miles north of Damascus (Ezek. 48:1), and the Southern boundary at Kadesh, about 100 miles south of Jerusalem. Ezek. 48:28. This "Royal Grant" was not conditional and was never revoked. It is 8 times as large as that formerly occupied by the Twelve Tribes.

This "Royal Grant" is to be divided among the restored Twelve Tribes in parallel horizontal sections, beginning at Hamath on the North with a section for Dan, next comes Asher, then Naphtali, Manassah, Ephraim, Reuben, Judah. Then comes the

"Holy Oblation,"

a square tract on the west of Jordan, 25,000 reeds, or 50 miles on a side. A "Reed," according to Ezek. 40:5, is 6 cubits long, the cubit being an ordinary cubit 18 inches long plus a hand-breadth, 3 inches, making the "reed cubit" 21 inches. Six of such cubits make the "reed" 10½ feet long. South of the "Holy Oblation" will be the Tribes of Benjamin, Simeon, Issachar, Zebulon and Gad.

The "Holy Oblation" is divided into three horizontal sections. The Northern section is 25,000 reeds long, from East to West, and 10,000 reeds wide. It is called the "Levites' Portion." South of it is the "Priests' Portion" of equal size. South of the "Priests' Portion" is the section for the "City" with its suburbs and farming sections. This section is 25,000 reeds long, from East to West, and 5000 reeds wide. Ezek. 48:15-19.

In the centre of this section the City (Jerusalem) is located. This helps us to map out the whole of the "Holy Oblation," as the "New City" is to be located on the site of the Old. The "New City," however, is to be much larger than the Old. It is to be 9 miles square, and with its suburbs, ½ a mile on a side, 10 miles square. It will have a wall around it with 3 gates on each side like the New Jerusalem (Ezek. 48:15-18, 30-35), these gates being named after the 12 sons of Jacob.

The "Temple," or "Sanctuary," will not be rebuilt in the "New City," but in the "midst" or middle of the "Holy Oblation." Ezek. 48:10, 20, 21. This will locate it at or near Shiloh, where the Tabernacle rested after the Children of Israel conquered the Land, and where it remained until the Temple of Solomon was finished. A "Highway" shall lead from the "Sanctuary" to the "New City." Isa. 35:8. It will be a magnificent boulevard, 12 miles long, lined with beautiful shade trees.

The "New Temple" or "Sanctuary" will occupy a space of 500 reeds on a side, or nearly a mile square. Ezek. 42:15-20. The old Temple was not a mile in circuit.

The Prophet Zechariah tells us (Zech. 14:8), that in **"That Day"** (the Millennial Day)—

"**Living Waters Shall Go Out From Jerusalem,**" half of them toward the Former Sea (Red Sea) and half of them toward the Hinder Sea (Mediterranean); in summer and in winter shall it be."

But those "Living Waters" will not have their "source" in Jerusalem. The life-giving spring from which they flow will be located under the "Sanctuary." Ezekiel tells us how he saw in vision the "New Temple" or "Sanctuary" and how the Lord took him to the eastern door of the "House" or Sanctuary," where he saw the waters come forth from under the Threshold of the door, and flow past the "Altar of Burnt Offering" on the south side eastward until the stream was deep enough to swim in.

"Then said he unto me, These waters . . . go down into the desert (by way of Jerusalem) and go into the sea (Dead Sea), which being brought forth into the sea, the waters (of the Dead Sea) shall be healed (lose their saltness). . . . And everything shall live whither the river cometh. And it shall come to pass that the fishers shall stand upon it (Dead Sea), from Engedi (on the west shore) even unto Eneglaim (on the east shore); they shall be a place to spread forth nets; their fish shall be according to their kinds, as the fish of the Great Sea (Mediterranean) exceeding many. . . . And by the River upon the banks thereof, on this side and on that side, shall grow all trees for meat, whose leaf shall not fade, neither shall the fruit thereof be consumed; it shall bring forth new fruit according to its months, because the waters they issued out of the "Sanctuary;" and the "Fruit" thereof shall be for meat and the "Leaf" thereof for medicine." Ezek. 47:8-12. Compare Rev. 22:1, 2.

The size of the "New City," the location of the "New Sanctuary" and the elevation of the Dead Sea, which is now 1200 feet below the

THE MILLENNIAL LAND

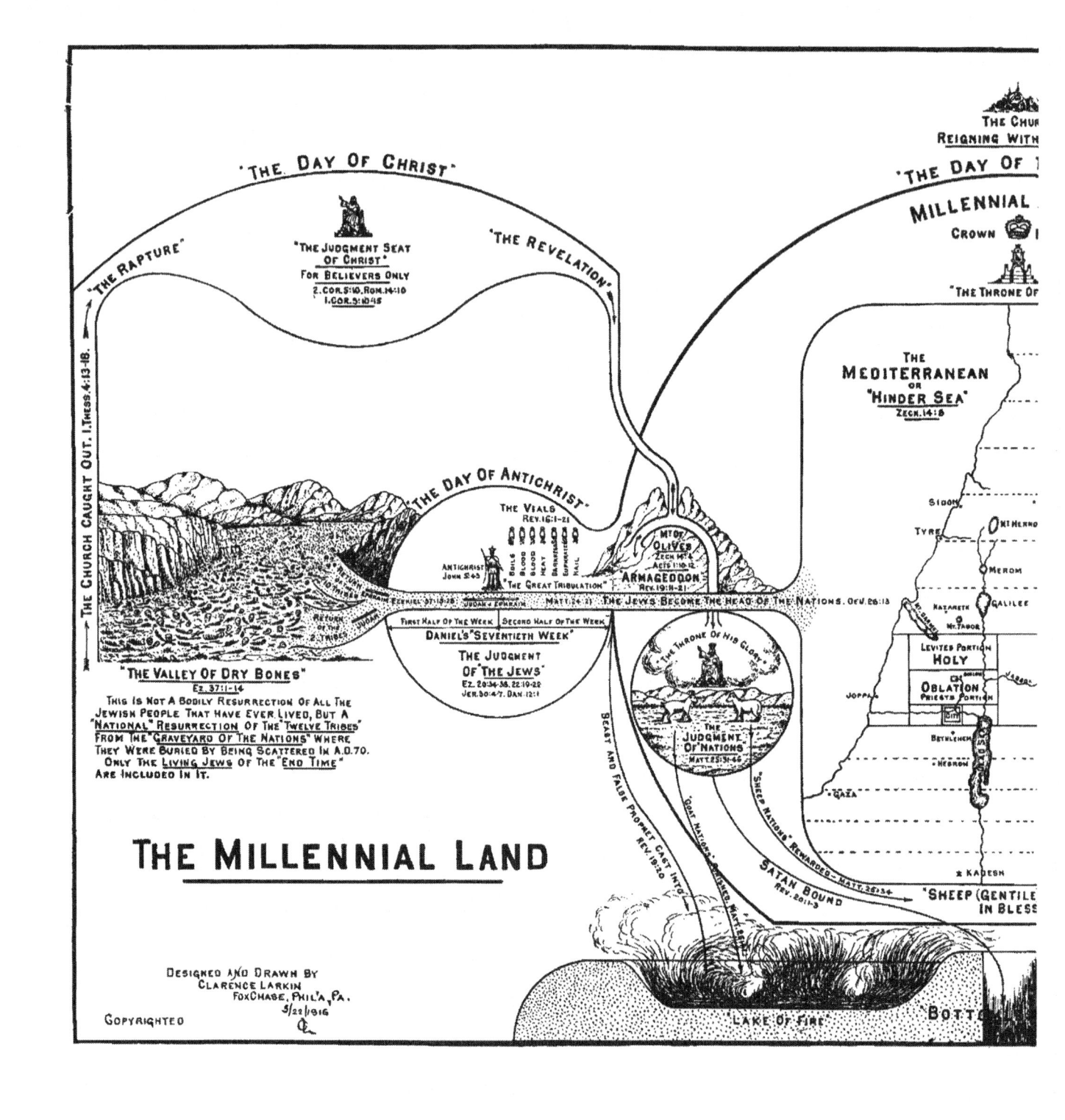

Designed and Drawn By
Clarence Larkin
Fox Chase, Phil'a, Pa.
5/22/1916
Copyrighted

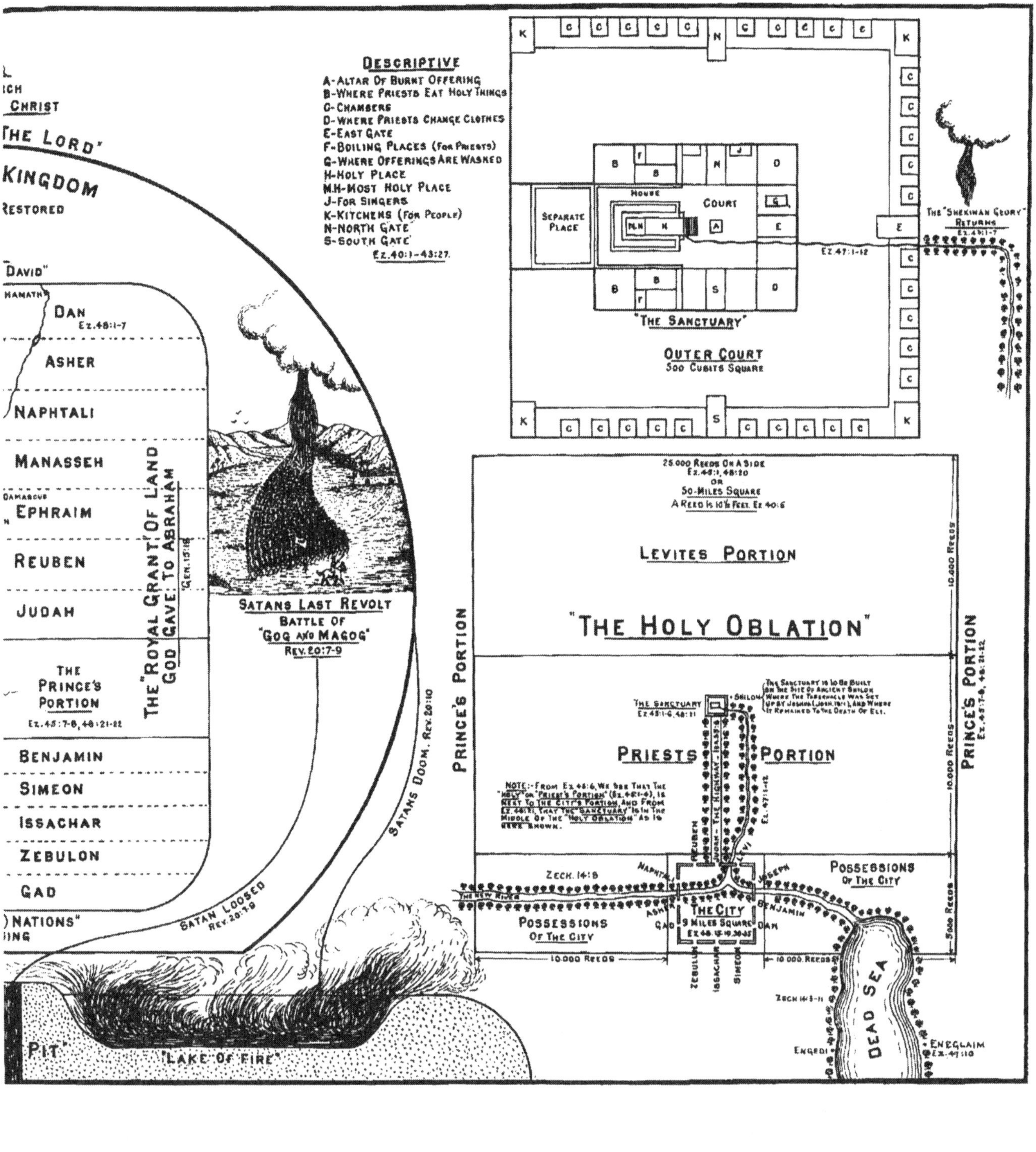
CHRIST
"THE LORD"
KINGDOM
RESTORED
"DAVID"
HAMATH
DAN
Ez. 48:1-7
ASHER
NAPHTALI
MANASSEH
DAMASCUS
EPHRAIM
REUBEN
JUDAH
THE PRINCE'S PORTION
Ez. 45:7-8, 48:21-22
BENJAMIN
SIMEON
ISSACHAR
ZEBULON
GAD
NATIONS"
THE "ROYAL GRANT" OF LAND GOD GAVE TO ABRAHAM
GEN. 13:15
SATANS LAST REVOLT
BATTLE OF
"GOG AND MAGOG"
REV. 20:7-9
SATANS DOOM. REV. 20:10
SATAN LOOSED
REV. 20:7-9
"PIT"
"LAKE OF FIRE"
DESCRIPTIVE
A-ALTAR OF BURNT OFFERING
B-WHERE PRIESTS EAT HOLY THINGS
C-CHAMBERS
D-WHERE PRIESTS CHANGE CLOTHES
E-EAST GATE
F-BOILING PLACES (FOR PRIESTS)
G-WHERE OFFERINGS ARE WASHED
H-HOLY PLACE
M.H-MOST HOLY PLACE
J-FOR SINGERS
K-KITCHENS (FOR PEOPLE)
N-NORTH GATE
S-SOUTH GATE
EZ. 40:1-43:27.
SEPARATE PLACE
HOUSE
COURT
EZ. 47:1-12
"THE SANCTUARY"
OUTER COURT
500 CUBITS SQUARE
THE "SHEKINAH GLORY" RETURNS
EZ. 43:1-7
25,000 REEDS ON A SIDE
EZ. 45:1, 48:20
OR
50-MILES SQUARE
A REED IS 10½ FEET. EZ. 40:5
LEVITES PORTION
10,000 REEDS
"THE HOLY OBLATION"
PRINCE'S PORTION
PRINCE'S PORTION
EZ. 45:7-8, 48:21-22
THE SANCTUARY
EZ. 45:1-6, 48:21
SHILOH
THE SANCTUARY IS TO BE BUILT ON THE SITE OF ANCIENT SHILOH WHERE THE TABERNACLE WAS SET UP BY JOSHUA (JOSH. 18:1), AND WHERE IT REMAINED TO THE DEATH OF ELI.
PRIESTS PORTION
JUDAH - THE HIGHWAY - ISA. 35:8
EZ. 47:1-12
NOTE:- FROM EZ. 48:6, WE SEE THAT THE "HOLY" OR "PRIEST'S PORTION" (EZ. 48:1-4), IS NEXT TO THE CITY'S PORTION, AND FROM EZ. 48:21, THAT THE "SANCTUARY" IS IN THE MIDDLE OF THE "HOLY OBLATION" AS IS HERE SHOWN.
REUBEN
LEVI
NAPHTALI
JOSEPH
ZECH. 14:8
THE NEW RIVER
POSSESSIONS OF THE CITY
ASHER
GAD
THE CITY
9 MILES SQUARE
EZ. 48:15-19, 30-35
BENJAMIN
DAN
POSSESSIONS OF THE CITY
ZEBULUN
ISSACHAR
SIMEON
10,000 REEDS
10,000 REEDS
5000 REEDS
ZECH. 14:8-11
DEAD SEA
ENGEDI
ENEGLAIM
EZ. 47:10

level of the Mediterranean Sea, call for great physical changes in the land surface of Palestine. How are these changes to come about?

When Christ comes back it will be to the Mount of Olives from whence He went up. Acts 1:9-12. The Prophet Zechariah describes what will then happen.

"His (Christ's) feet shall stand in **That Day** (the day of His return) upon the **Mount of Olives**, which is before Jerusalem on the east and the **Mount of Olives shall Cleave in the midst Thereof Toward the East and Toward the West, and There Shall Be a Very Great Valley; and Half of the Mountain Shall Remove Toward the North and Half of It Toward the South**. . . .

"**All the Land Shall Be Turned as a Plain From Geba to Rimmon South of Jerusalem; and it shall be LIFTED UP AND INHABITED.**" Zech. 14:4, 10, 11.

These great changes will probably be brought about by earthquakes or volcanic action.

"Behold, the Lord cometh forth out of His place, and will come down, and tread upon the high places of the earth. And the **mountains** shall be **Molten Under Him**, and the **valleys** shall be **Cleft as Wax Before the Fire, and as the Waters That Are Poured Down a Steep Place.**" Micah 1:3, 4.

These great physical changes will level the land surface of Palestine, and make room for the "New City," and raise the Dead Sea, so its waters can flow into both the Red and Mediterranean Seas. Ezekiel tells us that the name of Jerusalem in that day shall be "**Jehovah-Shammah,**" the **Lord Is There**. Ezek. 48:35. See the Chart of "The Millennial Land."

3. The Temple and Its Worship.

As we have seen the Temple or Sanctuary will be located in the centre of the "Holy Oblation." A full description of the Temple and its courts is given in Ezek. 40:1-44:31. No such building as Ezekiel so minutely describes has ever yet been built, and so the prophecy cannot refer to either Zerubbabel's or Herod's Temple, and as there is to be no Temple in the New Jerusalem, it must be a description of the Temple that is to be on the earth during the Millennium. That it does not belong to the New Earth is also clear, for the land in which it is located is bounded by the Sea, and the waters that flow from it, flow "into the Sea," but in the New Earth there is "no more sea." Rev. 21:1. This is still further confirmed by the Prophet's mention of the "desert," the "River Jordan," the "Mediterranean Sea," and other localities that will not be found on the New Earth after its renovation by fire.

The "Aaronic Priesthood" will be re-established, and the sons of Zadok shall officiate and offer sacrifices. Ezek. 44:15-31. The New Temple, however, will lack many things that were the features of the old Temple. There will be no "Ark of the Covenant," no "Pot of Manna," no "Aaron's Rod" to bud, no "Tables of the Law," no "Cherubim," no "Mercy Seat," no "Golden Candlestick," no "Shew Bread," no "Altar of Incense," no "Veil," no unapproachable "Holy of Holies" where the High Priest alone might enter, nor is there any "High Priest" to offer atonement for sin, or to make intercession for the people, unless a rather obscure passage in Zech. 6:12, 13 means that Christ (The Branch, Jer. 23:5, 6) shall be a "King-Priest," and perform the duties of High Priest conjointly with His Kingly office.

While the Levites as a class shall perform Temple service they shall be barred from Priestly duties for their past sins. Ezek. 44:10-14. There shall be a daily "morning" sacrifice, but no evening sacrifice. Ezek. 46:13-15. The offerings will be the "Burnt," the "Meal," the "Drink," the "Sin," the "Peace" (Ezek. 45:17), and the "Trespass" offering. Ezek. 42:13. Two Feasts are to be observed, "The Passover," but no Passover Lamb will be offered as Jesus fulfilled that Type (Ezek. 45:21-24), and the "Feast of Tabernacles," Zech. 14:16-19. This Feast is to be observed by all the nations under penalty of "Drought" or "Plague."

The "Feast of Pentecost" will be done away with on account of its fulfillment. The "Day of Pentecost," recorded in Acts 2:1-4, was only a partial fulfillment of the prophecy of Joel 2:28-32. No such wonders in the heavens and the earth as "blood," and "fire" and "pillars of smoke" the "Sun turned to darkness," and the "Moon into blood," occurred at Pentecost. But all those things will happen before "The Great and Terrible Day of the Lord."

The conversion of the Jewish Nation will be sealed with a great outpouring of the Holy Spirit. Whether this shall be universal, or only upon Israel is not clear. The original prophecy in Joel was given to Israel, and its partial fulfillment at Pentecost seems to have been limited to them. The knowledge of the Lord, however, will be world-wide, and "it shall come to pass that ten men of all languages and nations shall take hold of the skirt of him that is a Jew, saying, **We will go with you; for we have heard that God is with you.**" Zech. 8:22, 23. There will be one "universal religion" in that day. Malachi 1:11. The "Shekinah Glory" that departed from the Temple at the time of the Babylonian Captivity (Ezek. 10:18-20; 11:22, 23), will again take up its residence in the "New Temple." Ezek. 43:1-5.

4. The Character of the Millennium.

(1.) **Satan Bound.** Rev. 20:1-3.

That man may be "without excuse" God is going to subject him to a final test under the most favorable circumstances. Man has charged his fall and continuance in sin to Satan. "Take him away," he cries, "paralyze his power; cripple his malignant activity; bind and imprison him and deliver us from his dominating influence, and then you will see that man is radically good and virtuous and is simply the victim of an unfavorable environment."

God answers it shall be done. Satan shall be bound and imprisoned so that he can no longer deceive men, and lest man shall say that sinful habits are too deeply rooted to be soon eradicated the test shall last for a **Thousand Years,** and man shall have during that period of probation all the blessed influences of the Holy Spirit and the presence of **Christ Himself.**

Man has never known and therefore cannot conceive what this world would be like free from Satanic influence. It would certainly be a marvelously different world. There would be no one to stir up hate and passion, and engender strife and turmoil. True, man would still have an evil heart of unbelief to contend against, but it would be like a magazine of gunpowder without a spark to ignite it. That the evil heart of man has not been eradicated will be evident when at the close of the Millennium Satan is loosed and finds no difficulty in deceiving the nations. Rev. 20:8.

During the Millennium the "Prince of the Powers of the Air" will be "dethroned" and the "Prince of Peace" "enthroned." When the "Great Red Dragon" (Satan) is cast out of the Heavenlies there will be cast out with him all the "Principalities and Powers" and "Age Rulers of Darkness" (Eph. 6:12), and the Heavens which now are "not clean" in His sight (Job 15:15), will be "cleansed" of all Evil Powers.

There will be no universal peace until the Lord comes back. Then the nations will beat their swords into "plow-shares" and their spears into "pruning-hooks" (Mich. 4:3, 4), and shall be no longer impoverished by the enormous tax on their revenues for the support of armies and navies and the building of "Dreadnoughts." Then ships of war and armorclad vessels will rust and rot in the navy yards and guns and cannon will be recast into implements of agriculture. The great armies of earth will be disbanded, and in the pursuits of peace and the tilling of the soil, the depleted treasuries of the world will be replenished. There will be little if any political graft. Corporations and combines will not be run in restraint of trade, and there will be no entailed estates if the law of the "Year of Jubilee" is re-established. Lev. 25: 8-17. Num. 36: 4.

(2) **The Revival of the Land of Palestine.**

The Land of Palestine when it was first occupied by the Children of Israel under Joshua, was a land of "milk" and "honey" and of "all manner of fruits," and its soil brought forth "abundantly," and this continued as long as the Children of Israel kept its Sabbaths. But God had warned them that if they did not obey Him and turned aside to worship other Gods He would shut up the heavens and the harvests would fail. Deut. 11: 13-17. Palestine today has the same fertile soil it had in Joshua's time, but it lacks rain and irrigation. God has withheld the "early" and "latter" rain, but they are now becoming more frequent and copious. The "early" rain falls in October and November, and prepares the land for ploughing and sowing; the "latter" rain falls in April and May and insures a good crop.

In the Millennium the Land of Palestine will be restored to its former fertility. This will be aided not only by the rains, but by numerous rivers and streams that shall flow from the "New River" that shall have its source in the Sanctuary.

> "It shall come to pass in **That Day** (Millennium) that the **mountains shall drop new wine**, and the **hills shall flow with milk**, and all the **Rivers of Judah** (where the New River will be) shall **flow with waters**, and a **fountain shall come forth of the House of the Lord**, and shall water the **Valley of Shittim**," the country about the Dead Sea. Joel 3: 18.

The "mountains dropping new wine," and the "hills flowing with milk," are figures of speech declaring that the mountain sides will be covered with vineyards from which an abundance of wine shall be obtained, and that the pasture lands will be so productive that they will sustain vast herds of milk cattle.

The harvests will be so great and abundant that the ploughman will "overtake the reaper," and the treader of grapes him that "soweth seed." Amos 9: 13.

> "The wilderness and the solitary place shall be glad for them; and the desert shall rejoice, and blossom as the rose." Isa. 35: 1.

> "Instead of the thorn shall come up the fir-tree, and instead of the briar shall come up the myrtle tree; and it shall be to the Lord for a name, for an everlasting sign that shall not be cut off." Isa. 55: 13.

> "Then shall the earth yield her increase." Psa. 67: 6.

> "And the floors shall be **full of wheat**, and the vats shall **overflow with wine and oil**. And I will **restore to you the years** that the locust hath eaten, the **cankerworm** and the **caterpillar**, and the **palmerworm**, my great army which I sent among you. And ye shall **eat in plenty** and be **satisfied**, and praise the name of the Lord your God that hath dealt wondrously with you; and **My People** (the Jews) shall never be ashamed." Joel 2: 24-26.

(3) **There Will Be Changes in the Animal Kingdom.**

> "The wolf also shall dwell with the lamb, and the leopard shall lie down with the kid; and the calf and the young lion and the fatling together; and a little child shall lead them. And the cow and the bear shall feed; their young ones shall lie down together, and the lion shall eat straw like the ox. And the sucking child shall play on the hole of the asp and the weaned child shall put his hand on the cockatrice's den. They shall not hurt nor destroy in all my holy mountain (Jerusalem), for the earth shall be full of the knowledge of the Lord, as the waters cover the sea." Isa. 11: 6-9.

We cannot spiritualize these words. This was the character of these animals in Eden before the Fall, and in the Ark. The ferocity of the brute creation is the outcome of the "Fall of Man." While the context seems to imply that this change in the brute creation has reference to the "Millennial Earth," where it may be partially true, yet the fact that the Edenic condition of the earth is not to be restored until the appearance of the New Earth may postpone the fulfillment of this prophecy until then.

The Apostle Paul says—

> "We know that the **Whole Creation** groaneth and travaileth in pain together until now. . . . Waiting for the adoption, to wit, the **Redemption of Our Body**." Rom. 8: 23.

That is, until the human race is redeemed from the results of the "Fall, and fitted to occupy the New Earth, Creation must wait for its restoration to "Edenic conditions."

(4.) **Human Life Will Be Prolonged.**

> "There shall be no more thence an **infant of days**, . . . for the **child shall die a hundred years old**." Isa. 65: 20.

That is, a person dying 100 years old shall be considered only a child. Therefore a man, to be called a man, must live for several hundred years.

> "For as the days of a **Tree** (oak tree) are the days of my people." Isa. 65: 22.

> "Thus saith the Lord of **Hosts**: There shall yet **Old Men** and **Old Women** dwell in the streets of Jerusalem, and every man with his staff in his hand **For Very Age**." Zech. 8: 4.

Patriarchal Years will be restored, and men shall live as long as they did before the Flood. This may be due to some climatic or atmospheric change, or to the healing or life-giving qualities of the water of the "New River" that shall flow from the "Sanctuary," and the leaves of the trees that line the banks of the River, which shall be for "Medicine." Ezek. 47:12.

(5) **There Will Be a Sevenfold Increase of Light.**

> "Moreover the light of the moon shall be as the light of **the sun**, and the light of the sun shall be **SEVENFOLD** as the light of **seven days**, in the day that the Lord bindeth up the breach of His people, and healeth the stroke of their wound." Isa. 30:26.

The "atmosphere" of the Millennial Earth will be of such a character as to make **moonlight nights as bright as day**, and the days **seven times as bright.**

> "The sun shall be no more thy light by day: neither for brightness shall the moon give light unto thee; but the Lord **Shall Be Unto Thee An Everlasting Light, and Thy God Thy Glory**." Isa. 60: 19-20.

EZEKIEL

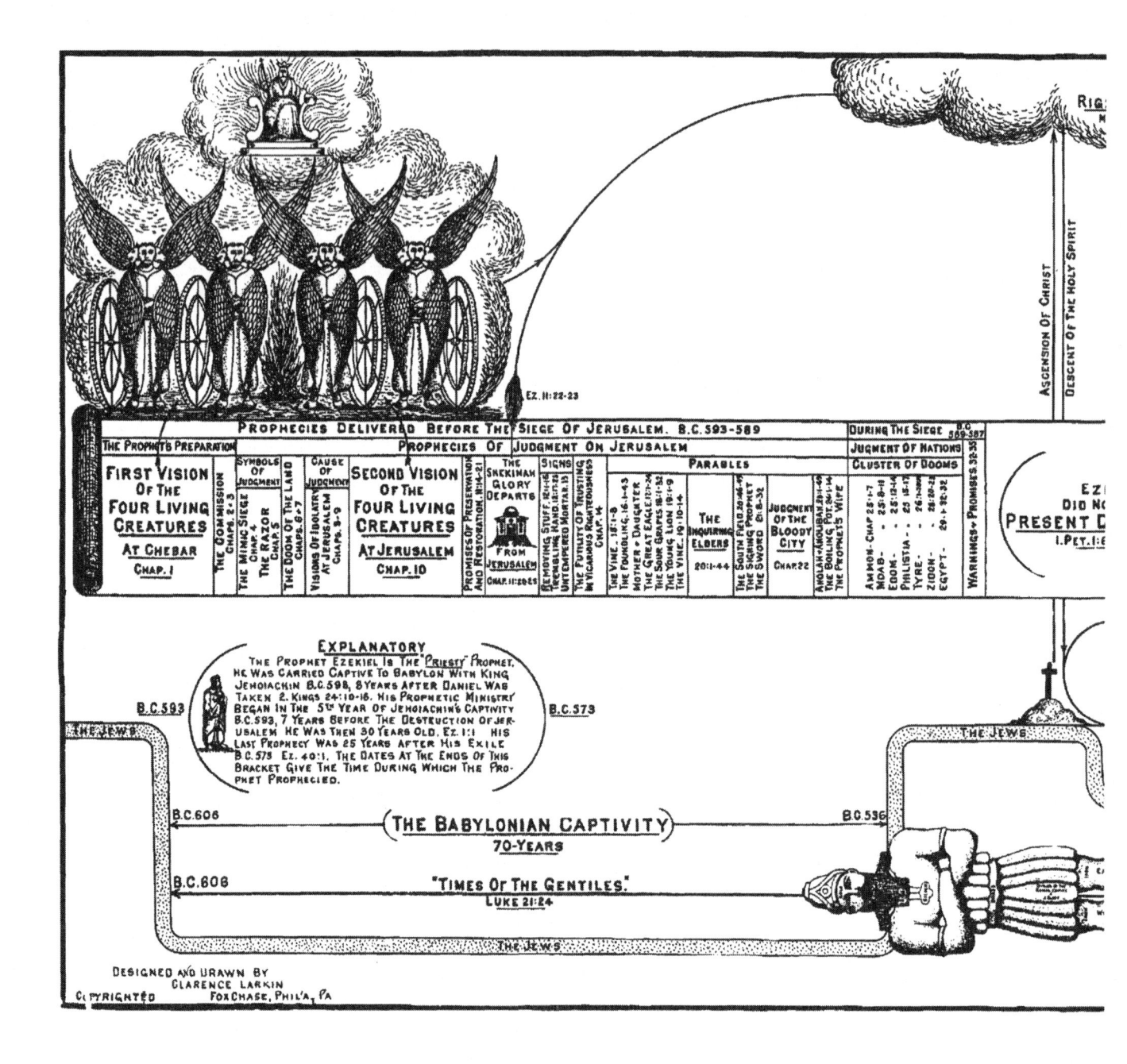

THE PROPHET'S PREPARATION	PROPHECIES DELIVERED BEFORE THE SIEGE OF JERUSALEM. B.C. 593-589	DURING THE SIEGE B.C. 589-587
	PROPHECIES OF JUDGMENT ON JERUSALEM	JUDGMENT OF NATIONS

FIRST VISION OF THE FOUR LIVING CREATURES AT CHEBAR CHAP. 1	SYMBOLS OF JUDGMENT	CAUSE OF JUDGMENT	SECOND VISION OF THE FOUR LIVING CREATURES AT JERUSALEM CHAP. 10	THE SHEKINAH GLORY DEPARTS	SIGNS	PARABLES	CLUSTER OF DOOMS	
	THE COMMISSION CHAPS. 2-3 — THE MIMIC SIEGE CHAP. 4 — THE RAZOR CHAP. 5	THE DOOM OF THE LAND CHAPS. 6-7 — VISIONS OF IDOLATRY AT JERUSALEM CHAPS. 8-9		PROMISES OF PRESERVATION AND RESTORATION. 11:14-21 — FROM JERUSALEM CHAP. 11:20-25	REMOVING STUFF 12:1-16 — TREMBLING MAN 12:17-28 — UNTEMPERED MORTAR 13 — THE FUTILITY OF TRUSTING IN VICARIOUS RIGHTEOUSNESS CHAP. 14	THE VINE. 15:1-8 — THE FOUNDLING. 16:1-43 — MOTHER + DAUGHTER — THE GREAT EAGLE 17:1-24 — THE SOUR GRAPES 18:1-32 — THE YOUNG LION 19:1-9 — THE VINE. 19:10-14	THE INQUIRING ELDERS 20:1-44	THE SOUTH FIELD 20:45-49 — THE SIGHING PROPHET — THE SWORD 21:1-32 — JUDGMENT OF THE BLOODY CITY CHAP. 22	AMMON — CHAP 25:1-7 — MOAB — 25:8-11 — EDOM — 25:12-14 — PHILISTIA — 25:15-17 — TYRE — 26:1—28:19 — ZIDON — 28:20-24 — EGYPT — 29:1—32:32	WARNINGS + PROMISES 33:1-33

EXPLANATORY

The Prophet Ezekiel is the "Priest" Prophet. He was carried captive to Babylon with King Jehoiachin B.C. 598, 8 Years after Daniel was taken. 2 Kings 24:10-16. His Prophetic Ministry began in the 5th Year of Jehoiachin's Captivity B.C. 593, 7 Years Before the Destruction of Jerusalem. He was then 30 Years Old. Ez. 1:1. His Last Prophecy was 25 Years after his Exile B.C. 575. Ez. 40:1. The Dates at the Ends of this Bracket Give the Time During Which the Prophet Prophesied.

B.C. 593 — B.C. 573

THE JEWS

B.C. 606 — (THE BABYLONIAN CAPTIVITY) — B.C. 536
70 YEARS

B.C. 606 — "TIMES OF THE GENTILES." — LUKE 21:24

THE JEWS

DESIGNED AND DRAWN BY
CLARENCE LARKIN
COPYRIGHTED   FOX CHASE, PHIL'A, PA

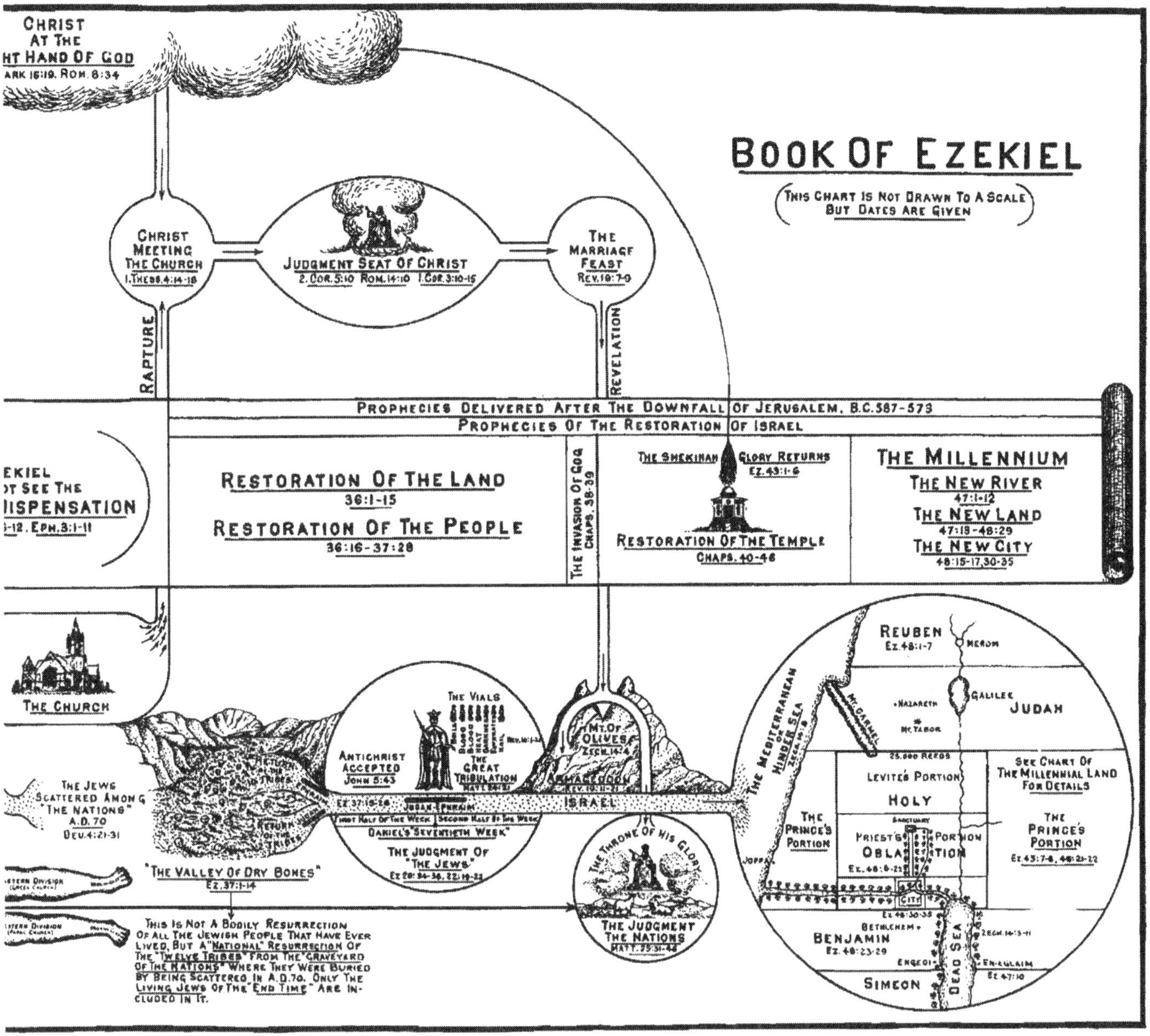

Book Of Ezekiel
(This Chart Is Not Drawn To A Scale But Dates Are Given)
Christ At The ...ht Hand Of God
...ark 16:19. Rom. 8:34
Christ Meeting The Church
1. Thess. 4:14-18
Judgment Seat Of Christ
2. Cor. 5:10 Rom. 14:10 1. Cor. 3:10-15
The Marriage Feast
Rev. 19:7-9
Rapture
Revelation
Prophecies Delivered After The Downfall Of Jerusalem, B.C. 587-573
Prophecies Of The Restoration Of Israel
...ekiel ...ot See The ...ispensation
...-12. Eph. 3:1-11
Restoration Of The Land
36:1-15
Restoration Of The People
36:16-37:28
The Invasion Of Gog
Chaps. 38-39
The Shekinah Glory Returns
Ez. 43:1-6
Restoration Of The Temple
Chaps. 40-46
The Millennium
The New River
47:1-12
The New Land
47:13-48:29
The New City
48:15-17,30-35
The Church
The Jews Scattered Among "The Nations" A.D. 70
Deu. 4:21-31
"The Valley Of Dry Bones"
Ez. 37:1-14
This Is Not A Bodily Resurrection Of All The Jewish People That Have Ever Lived, But A "National" Resurrection Of The "Twelve Tribes" From The "Graveyard Of The Nations" Where They Were Buried By Being Scattered In A.D. 70. Only The Living Jews Of The "End Time" Are Included In It.
Return Of The Tribes
The Vials
Antichrist Accepted
John 5:43
The Great Tribulation
Ez. 37:15-28
Judah-Ephraim
First Half Of The Week
Second Half Of The Week
Daniel's "Seventieth Week"
The Judgment Of "The Jews"
Mt. Of Olives
Zech. 14:4
Armageddon
Rev. 19:11-21
Israel
The Throne Of His Glory
The Judgment The Nations
Matt. 25:31-46
The Mediterranean Or Hinder Sea
Reuben
Ez. 48:1-7
Merom
Galilee
Judah
Nazareth
Mt. Tabor
Mt. Carmel
25,000 Reeds
Levite's Portion
Holy
Sanctuary
Priest's Portion
Oblation
Ex. 48:8-22
The Prince's Portion
See Chart Of The Millennial Land For Details
The Prince's Portion
Ez. 45:7-8, 48:21-22
Joppa
City
Ez. 48:30-35
Bethlehem
Benjamin
Ez. 48:23-29
Engedi
Dead Sea
En-eglaim
Ez. 47:10
Simeon

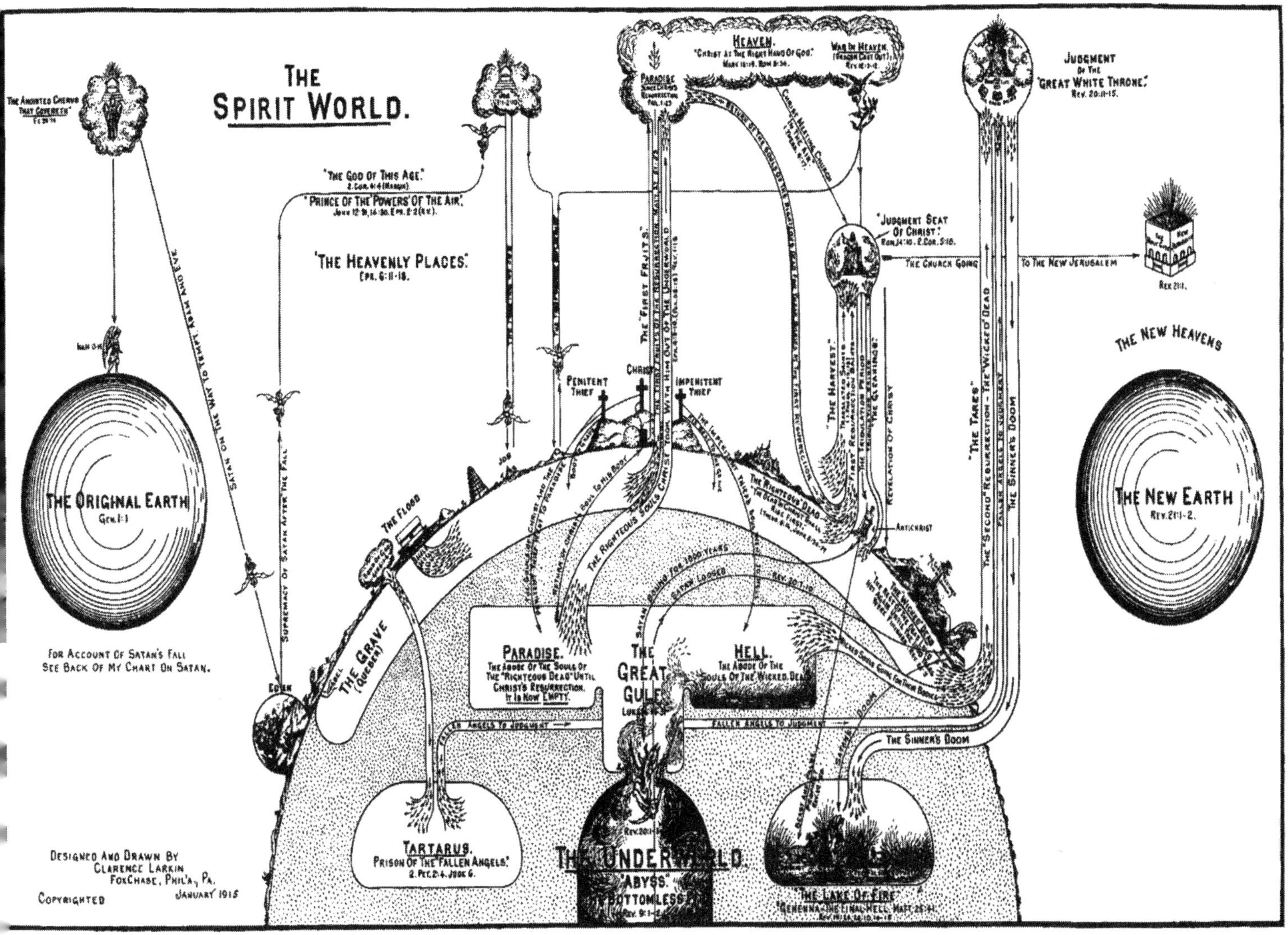
THE SPIRIT WORLD.
"The Heavenly Places." Eph. 6:11-18.
"The God Of This Age." 2 Cor. 4:4 (Margin).
"Prince Of The Powers Of The Air." John 12:31, 14:30. Eph. 2:2 (R.V.).
Heaven. "Christ At The Right Hand Of God." Mark 16:19. Rom. 8:34.
War In Heaven.
Judgment Of The "Great White Throne." Rev. 20:11-15.
"Judgment Seat Of Christ." Rom. 14:10. 2 Cor. 5:10.
The Church Going
To The New Jerusalem
Rev. 21:1.
The New Heavens
The Original Earth Gen. 1:1
The New Earth Rev. 21:1-2.
For Account Of Satan's Fall See Back Of My Chart On Satan.
Satan On The Way To Tempt Adam And Eve.
Supremacy Of Satan After The Fall
Penitent Thief
Christ
Impenitent Thief
The "First Fruits."
"The Harvest."
"The Tares."
The "Second" Resurrection - The "Wicked" Dead
Fallen Angels To Judgment
The Sinner's Doom
Revelation Of Christ
Antichrist
The Flood
Eden
The Grave ("Queber")
Paradise. The Abode Of The Souls Of The "Righteous Dead" Until Christ's Resurrection. It Is Now Empty.
The Great Gulf. Luke 16:26.
Hell. The Abode Of The Souls Of The Wicked Dead.
Satan Bound For 1000 Years
Satan Loosed
Tartarus. Prison Of The Fallen Angels. 2 Pet. 2:4. Jude 6.
The Underworld.
"Abyss." "Bottomless Pit." Rev. 9:1-2.
The Lake Of Fire. "Gehenna" - The Final Hell. Matt. 25:41.
Designed And Drawn By Clarence Larkin Fox Chase, Phil'a, Pa. January 1915
Copyrighted

This may refer to that part of the Holy Land that shall be illuminated by the "Shekinah Glory," where it will make no difference whether the sun shines or not. It will have its complete fulfillment when the nations of the New Earth shall walk in the Light of the New Jerusalem. Rev. 21:23-24.

Israel's Mission during the "Millennial Age" will be that of "blessing" to the Gentile nations. Of the nation of Israel, that has never as yet been a leading nation, God says—

"I will make thee the Head, and not the Tail." Deu. 28:13.

The nations today are a "Headless" body. There is no "Chief Nation" today. In that day Israel shall be the "Chief Nation," and the nation that will not serve her shall perish. Isa. 60:12.

But those nations will only be kept in subjection by the "Iron Rule" of Christ. This is brought out in the "Messianic Psalm," Psa. 2:6-9. It is very clear that during the "Millennial Age" the "will of God" will not be done on earth as it is done in heaven. The peace among the nations will be more superficial than real. It will only be signed obedience, more the result of fear than of love. As the "afternoon" of that long "Millennial Day" draws to a close the shadows deepen. As soon as Satan is loosed from his prison in the "Bottomless Pit," he will find a vast multitude ready to believe his lie, and to serve and obey him. He will gather them from the "Four Quarters of the Earth" to battle. They will be in number as the "sand of the sea." Rev. 20:8-9. The revolt will be Worldwide, and will mean the Mobilizing of Vast Armies. Satan will conduct them across the "Breadth of the Earth" until they compass the "Camp of the Saints" (the Holy Land), and lay siege once more to the "Beloved City." This time the armies of heaven are not sent to destroy the rebels, but "Fire from Heaven" devours the rebellious host, and Satan, who deceives them, is cast into the "Lake of Fire" to be tormented day and night for the "Ages of Ages."

From this we see that the "Millennial Dispensation," like all the six Dispensations before it, will end in failure. God will have tested man in "Innocence," under "Conscience," under "Self-Government," under the "Headship of the Family," under "Law," under "Grace," and finally under the influence of the "Holy Spirit," free from Satanic influences, and under them all he will prove himself to be hopelessly, incurably and incorrigibly bad.

If after a 1000 years of the Presence of the King, and of universal peace and blessing, man still persists in rebelling against his Maker, what will there be left for God to do? Humanly speaking, there will seem to be nothing for God to do but destroy the human race. To send another Flood and wipe out mankind. But this He cannot do, for He promised Noah that He would never again destroy the earth with a flood of waters. Gen. 9:11. But do something He must, so He is going to purge the earth with Fire. 2 Pet. 3:7.

XIV
THE SPIRIT WORLD

The Scriptures are full of the "Supernatural." The only cure for the "Materialism" of the present day is to discover what the Scriptures reveal as to the "Spirit World." There is but a step from the "Natural" World to the "Spirit" World. The dividing veil is our "fleshy" bodies. The "Heavenlies" are peopled with Spirit Beings. They are of two classes, good and evil. They are classified as "Seraphim," "Cherubim," "Angels" (Good and Bad), "Principalities," "Powers," "Age Rulers of Darkness," "Wicked Spirits," (Eph. 6:12), "Thrones," "Dominions," (Col. 1:16), "Fallen Angels," (2 Pet. 2:4), "Spirits in Prison," (1 Peter 3:18-20), "Demons," "Seducing Spirits," 1 Tim. 4:1.

The "Seraphim" have three pair of wings. They are the attendants of the "Lord of Hosts" and call attention to His holiness. Isa. 6:1-8.

The "Cherubim" or "Living Creatures," as described in Ezek. 1:4-25; 10:1-22, have only two pair of wings, but they have "four faces" on their head, the front face that of a "Man," the right side that of a "Lion," the left side that of an "Ox" (calf), and the back that of an "Eagle." They also have the "hand of a man" under their wings on each of their four sides. They are the Guardians of the Throne of God.

The "Four Beasts" or "Living Creatures" of Rev. 4:6-8, differ from the "Living Creatures" of Ezekiel, in that each Beast instead of having four faces has but one. The first Beast having the face of a lion, the second that of a calf, the third that of a man, and the fourth that of a flying eagle, and each "Beast" has "six wings" and "eyes before and behind." The mention of a "Rainbow" by both Ezekiel and John (Ez. 1:28, Rev. 4:3) identifies the two visions as relating to the Throne of God.

The "Seraphim," "Cherubim," "Angels," and all other "Heavenly Beings" are created beings. They did not exist from all eternity. (Col. 1:16.)

The Angels are "innumerable in number." Heb. 12:22. They are "mighty in power" but not almighty. 2 Thess. 1:7. They excel in strength. One angel destroyed 185,000 of the Assyrian army in a night. An angel rolled away the stone from the Tomb of Christ, and one angel shall bind Satan and cast him into the "Bottomless Pit." They are "Glorious" beings (Luke 9:26), and have "great knowledge, but are not Omniscient. They neither marry nor are given in marriage. Matt. 22:30. That does not mean that they are "sexless" and have not the power of procreation. All the angels in the Scriptures are spoken of as men, and were so created in great numbers, and as they do not die (Luke 20:36), there is no need for "procreation," but that they have such power seems indisputable from Gen. 6:1-4, where we are told that the "Sons of God" (angels), had intercourse with the "daughters of men," and the result was a race of "Mighty Men." See Chapter two on the cause of the Flood. From this we see that the angels can sin.

The Angels are "Ministering Spirits" to them who are "heirs of salvation," (Heb. 1:13, 14), and "Executioners of God's Wrath" on the "wicked." 2 Thess. 1:7-8. They will gather the "elect of Israel" from the four corners of the earth, (Matt. 24:31), and are commissioned to supply the physical needs of God's people. Matt. 4:11; 1 Kings 19:4-8.

The Demons are not to be classed as angels. They appear to be "disembodied spirits," some think of the Pre-Adamite Earth, the

96

inhabitants being disembodied because of the sin that caused the Pre Adamite Earth to become chaotic. This is plausible, because they seek to re-embody themselves in human beings. They are **wicked, unclean, vicious,** and have power to derange both mind and body. Matt. 12:22; 15:22; Luke 4:35; 8:26-36; 9:42. They are the "Familiar Spirits" of the Old Testament, and the "Seducing Spirits" of which Paul warned Timothy. 1 Tim. 4:1.

There are three prominent Personages spoken of in the Scriptures outside of the Triune God.

1. Michael.

He is mentioned three times in Daniel (Dan. 10:13, 21; 12:1), where he is called a "Prince" who stands for Daniel's People—the Jews. He is called in Jude 9 the Archangel. In Rev. 12:7 he is seen in command of the Angelic "Army of Heaven." His work seems to be to deliver God's people, particularly the Jews, from the power of Satan, and finally to oust him and his angels from the Heavenlies, and cast them down on to the earth. Rev. 12:7-9. He also has something to do with the resurrection of the dead, for he is associated with the "Resurrection mentioned in Dan. 12:1, 2, and he contested with the Devil the resurrection of Moses, (Jude 9) and the "voice" of the Archangel that will be heard when the "Dead in Christ" shall rise, (1 Thess. 4: 16), will be the "voice" of Michael, for he is the only Archangel mentioned in the Scriptures.

2. Gabriel.

He is mentioned by name four times. In Daniel twice and in Luke twice. He seems to be associated with the redemptive work of God. He appeared to Daniel (Dan. 8:16; 9:21-27), to inform him as to the "time" of Christ's "First Coming," and when the "time had come" he announced to Zacharias the birth of Christ's "Forerunner" —John the Baptist, and later to Mary the birth of Jesus. Luke 1:19, 26, 27. His position in heaven is lofty, for he said of himself to Zacharias—"I am Gabriel that **Stand in the Presence of God.**"

3. Satan.

We speak of Satan last not because he is the least of the three, for in many ways he is the greatest, but because of his evil character. He is the source of all the anarchy and rebellion in the Universe. See the Chart and Chapter on "Satan" for his history.

Let us now consider man's relation to the Spirit World. Man in his physical and spirit makeup, was made for two worlds, the Physical and the Spirit world. Writing to the Thessalonians Paul says—

"I pray God your whole 'Spirit' and 'Soul' and 'Body' be preserved blameless unto the coming of our Lord Jesus Christ." 1 Thess. 5:23. Writing to the Hebrews he says—

"The Word of God is quick (alive), and powerful, and sharper than any two edged sword, piercing even to the **dividing asunder** of 'Soul' and 'Spirit,' and of the 'Joints and Marrow' (body), and is a discerner of the thoughts and intents of the heart." Heb. 4:12.

From these references we see that man is a **Trinity,** and is composed of a "**Body,**" "**Soul,**" and "**Spirit.**" Man was made in the "**Image of God**" and God is a **Trinity.** The difference between plant and animal life is, that the plant has not "conscious" life, while the animal has a "living (conscious) soul." The difference between animal life and human life is, that while animals have a "living soul" man has more, he has a "spirit."

While man differs from a beast in having a "spirit," yet he is as to his "body" only an animal. That is, his body, as to its functions, is like the body of an animal in its vital processes of respiration, digestion, assimilation and general makeup; so when the Apostle speaks of the "Natural" body he refers to the "animal" body of man. And when he speaks of man's "Spiritual" body, he means a "body" not some "ethereal substance," but a body with form and shape, but controlled and regulated by spiritual rather than natural laws. In other words both our "Natural" and "Spirit bodies" are composed of "matter," the only difference being that the matter of our "Natural" bodies is adapted to this "Physical" world, while the matter of our "Spirit" bodies is adapted to the "Spirit" world. It makes the subject clearer to speak of a "Spirit" body, rather than a "Spiritual" body, for the word "Spiritual" refers more to the "religious" attribute of a body, than to the material.

The "Threefold Nature of Man" may be illustrated by the Tabernacle. The Tabernacle was a tent surrounded by a court, which court was enclosed by a curtain fence. (See diagram of the Tabernacle.) The tent was divided into two parts, one twice the length of the other, by a "veil" or curtain. The larger part was entered from without by a curtained doorway, and contained the "Table of Shewbread," the "Altar of Incense," and the "Seven Branched Candlestick." This part was called the "Holy Place." The smaller part was entered from the "Holy Place" through the "veil" or dividing curtain, and contained the "Ark of the Covenant," on the lid of which, between the "Cherubims," God took up His residence in the "Shekinah Glory." This part was called the "Most Holy Place." There were no windows in the Tabernacle, and the only entrance was through the curtained doorway into the "Holy Place."

The Tabernacle and its Courtyard is a type of the "Threefold Nature of Man." The "Courtyard" represents his Body, the "Holy Place" his Soul, and the "Most Holy Place" his Spirit, and as there could be no communication between the "Courtyard" and the "Most Holy Place," only through the "Holy Place," so there can be no communication between a man's Body and Spirit only through his Soul.

After the completion of the Tabernacle it remained empty of the "Presence of God" until the "Spirit of God" descended and took up His abode in the "Most Holy Place." So a man may be complete as to body, soul and spirit, but his spiritual nature will remain unregenerate until the Holy Spirit enters and takes possession of the "spirit" compartment of his nature. This happens when the "New Birth" takes place.

When a man dies his soul and spirit separate from the body, and the body is laid in the grave, but the "spirit" is not "bodiless," it has what Paul calls its "Psychical" or "Soulish" body. This may be illustrated by a peach. A peach is a trinity. It is composed of the "flesh of the peach," the "stone," and the "kernel." Let the "flesh" correspond to the "body" of man, the "stone" to the "soul," and the "kernel" to the "spirit." Remove the "flesh" of the peach from the stone, and the "kernel" still has a "body," the "stone." So when a man's "body" is separated from his "soul" and "spirit" at death, the "spirit" is not "bodiless," it still has its "Soulish body." As this "Soulish body" can hear, and speak, and think, and feel, it must have some "tangible" form. It is not a "ghostlike" structure. There are doubtless limitations in its use, or there would be no need for it to recover its physical body at the Resurrection.

That there is such a thing as the "Soulish Body" is brought out in the story of the "Rich Man and Lazarus." Luke 16: 19-31.

The story is not a Parable, but a description by Christ of something that really happened in the other world to his own personal knowledge. It declares that both Lazarus and the "Rich Man" **died** and were **buried.** That is, their **bodies** were left on the earth. What happened to them in the "Underworld" then, is descriptive of what happened to them in their "**disembodied state.**" In that state they were **conscious** and the Rich Man **recognized** Lazarus, which he could not have done if Lazarus had not a **body**, not his "physical" body, he left that on the earth, but his "Soulish" body. This is proof that the "Soulish" body is not simply a body, but that in its outward form and appearance it **conforms** to the **earthly** body of the owner, otherwise he would not be recognizable in the other world.

Again the "Rich Man" could **see**, and **feel**, and **thirst**, and **talk**, and **remember**, proving that he possessed his senses and had not lost his personality. This proves that there is no break, as "Soul Sleep," in the **Continuity of Existence**, or **Consciousness**, in passing from the "**Earth-Life**" to the "**Spirit-Life**." The one life merges into the other, just as the "infant-life" merges into the "boy-life," and at the Resurrection the "**Spirit-Life**" will merge into the "**Resurrection-Life**," just as the "boy-life" merges into the "man-life." I am just as much myself when I am stripped of my clothing, as when I had it on. So death, though it strips me of my "material" body, only changes my environment but does not destroy my **Personality** or **BODILY FORM**.

Sleep in the Scriptures always refers to the "body," not to the soul, and the expression, "Asleep in Jesus" refers to the Believer only.

The "Threefold Nature of Man" is clearly brought out in the Diagram.

"The Threefold Nature of Man."

The outer circle stands for the "body" of man, the middle for the "soul," and the inner for the spirit, or what Paul calls the "Carnal" (1 Cor. 3:1-3); the "Natural" (1 Cor. 2:14); and the "Spiritual" (1 Cor. 3:1); parts of man.

In the outer circle the "body" is shown as touching the Material world through the five senses of "sight," "smell," "hearing," "taste" and "touch." The soul uses the "Five Senses" of the body as its agents in the exploration of the phenomena of matter and historical research, and for its self expression and communion with the outside world. The "Gates" to the soul are "imagination," "conscience," "memory," "reason" and the "affections." The "Gate of Imagination" of the soul **corresponds** to the "Gate of Sight" of the body, being the "eye" by which the soul sees. The "Gate of Conscience" corresponds to the "Gate of Smell," by which the soul detects the **presence of good** and evil.

The "Gate of Memory" corresponds to the "Gate of Hearing," by which the soul recalls what it heard. The "Gate of Reason" corresponds to the "Gate of Taste," permitting the soul to compare facts as the taste compares foods. The "Gate of the Affections" corresponds to the "Gate of Touch," being the hand by which the soul feels the person of the one it loves.

The Spirit receives impressions of outward and material things through the soul and body. The "Sense Faculties" of the spirit are the "Spiritual faculties" of "Faith," "Hope," "Reverence," "Prayer," and "Worship." In his unfallen state the "spirit" of man was illuminated from Heaven, but when the human race fell in Adam, sin closed the window of the spirit, and pulled down the curtain, and the "chamber of the spirit" became a **Death Chamber**, and remains so in every unregenerate heart, until the "Life" and "Light" giving power of the Holy Spirit floods that chamber with the "**Life**" and "**Light**" giving power of the **NEW LIFE IN CHRIST JESUS**. We see then why the "natural" man cannot understand spiritual things. He cannot understand them until his spiritual nature has been renewed.

But the spirit of the Natural man is not only darkened, his "Will" stands as a "guard" at the door, and prevents the entrance of the Holy Spirit, and it is not until the "Will" surrenders through the power of the "Sword of the Spirit," the "'Word of God," that the Holy Spirit can enter and take up his abode in the "spirit" of man.

The battlefield of "Good" and "Evil" is in the "soul" of man. It is not enough that the Holy Spirit should take up His residence in the "spirit" of a man, He must have access to the "soul" and "body," as shown on the Diagram. Not until then can a man become "Sanctified"; for "Holiness" is conditioned on a "Spirit Filled" spirit, soul and body. A healthy soul and spirit need a healthy body, and if the body is given over to carnality and the lusts of the flesh, even to fasting that weakens it, the soul and spirit suffer, and the whole man becomes spiritually sick.

Let us now trace the life of the soul and spirit after they have left the body. In the story of the "Rich Man and Lazarus," we have a description of the "Underworld." We find that it is made up of two compartments, "Paradise" and "Hell," with an "Impassable Gulf" between. At the bottom of the Gulf is the "Bottomless Pit" or "Abyss." This is a place of temporary confinement for "Evil Spirits" (Demons). It has a King—"Apollyon," but is kept locked by God, who commissions an angel to open it when He so desires. Rev. 9:1-11; 17:8; 20:1-3. Study in this connection the charts on "The Spirit World" and "The Resurrections and the Judgments."

Before the resurrection of Christ the soul and spirit of the righteous dead went to the "Paradise" compartment of the Underworld. There Christ met the "Penitent Thief" after His death on the Cross. On the day of His Resurrection Christ's soul and spirit returned from the Underworld, but He did not return alone, He brought back with Him all the occupants of the Paradise section and locked it up, and He now has the "Keys of Death and Hades." Rev. 1:18 R. V. Here "Death" stands for the "grave" and "Hades" for the Underworld. Some of those who came back from the Underworld with Christ got their "bodies," and rose and ascended with Him as the "First-Fruits" of the resurrection "from among the dead." Matt. 27:52, 53. The rest were taken up to the "Third Heaven," where Paul was caught up, 2 Cor. 12:1-4. Paul called it Paradise. There all the Righteous dead that have died since Christ's resurrection go, that they may be "**With the LORD.**" Phil. 1:23. 2 Cor. 5:8.

There the souls of the Righteous dead shall remain until the time comes for the resurrection of their bodies, then when Christ comes back to meet His Church in the Air, He will bring back the souls of the Righteous dead from the Paradise of the "Third Heaven," for we are told that He will bring them who "**Sleep in Jesus**" WITH Him (1 Thess. 4:14), and they shall continue on to the earth and get their "bodies" from the grave, and then ascend again with the "Translated Saints" to meet Christ **IN THE AIR**.

So far as we know the souls of the "Wicked Dead" are still in the "Hell Compartment" of the Underworld, and will remain there until the Second Resurrection, when they will return to the earth and get their bodies, and then go to the "Great White Throne" Judgment. After judgment they will be sentenced to the "Second Death," which means that they shall die again, in the sense of losing their bodies again, and as "disembodied spirits" be cast into the "Lake of Fire," (Gehenna, the "Final Hell"), to suffer in flames forever. As soul and spirit are impervious to flames, this explains how the wicked, after being disembodied again by the "Second Death," can exist forever in literal fire.

When the earth is "Renovated by Fire," Satan and all the "Evil Powers" of the Heavenlies will be imprisoned, and the heavens will be "cleansed" of all evil and rebellious spirits. In the New Heavens and Earth man will be restored to the condition Adam was in before the Fall, and the "veil" between the Natural and Spirit Worlds will be removed.

The Threefold Nature of Man

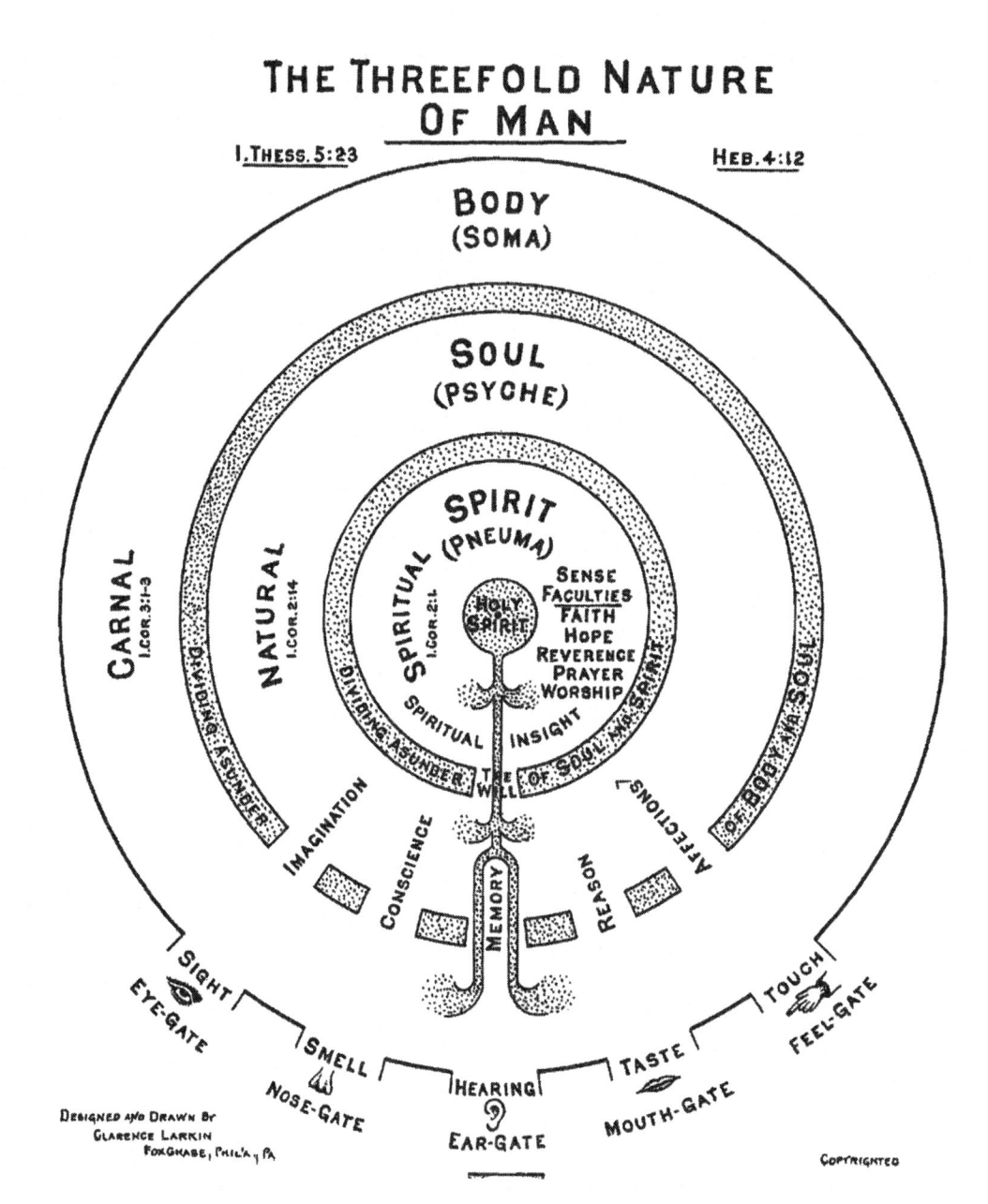

I. Thess. 5:23   Heb. 4:12

- **Body (Soma)**
- **Soul (Psyche)**
- **Spirit (Pneuma)**

Carnal — I. Cor. 3:1-3
Natural — I. Cor. 2:14
Spiritual — I. Cor. 2:1

Holy Spirit

Sense Faculties, Faith, Hope, Reverence, Prayer, Worship

Spiritual Insight

Dividing Asunder of Soul and Spirit
Dividing Asunder of Body and Soul

The Well

Imagination, Conscience, Memory, Reason, Affections

- Sight — Eye-Gate
- Smell — Nose-Gate
- Hearing — Ear-Gate
- Taste — Mouth-Gate
- Touch — Feel-Gate

Designed and Drawn by Clarence Larkin, Fox Chase, Phil'a, PA

Copyrighted

THE THREE TABERNACLES

THE HEAVENLY TABERNACLE
THE EARTHLY TABERNACLE
THE TABERNACLE OF MAN

Designed And Drawn By Clarence Larkin, Fox Chase, Phil'a, PA. 1919 Copyrighted.

XV

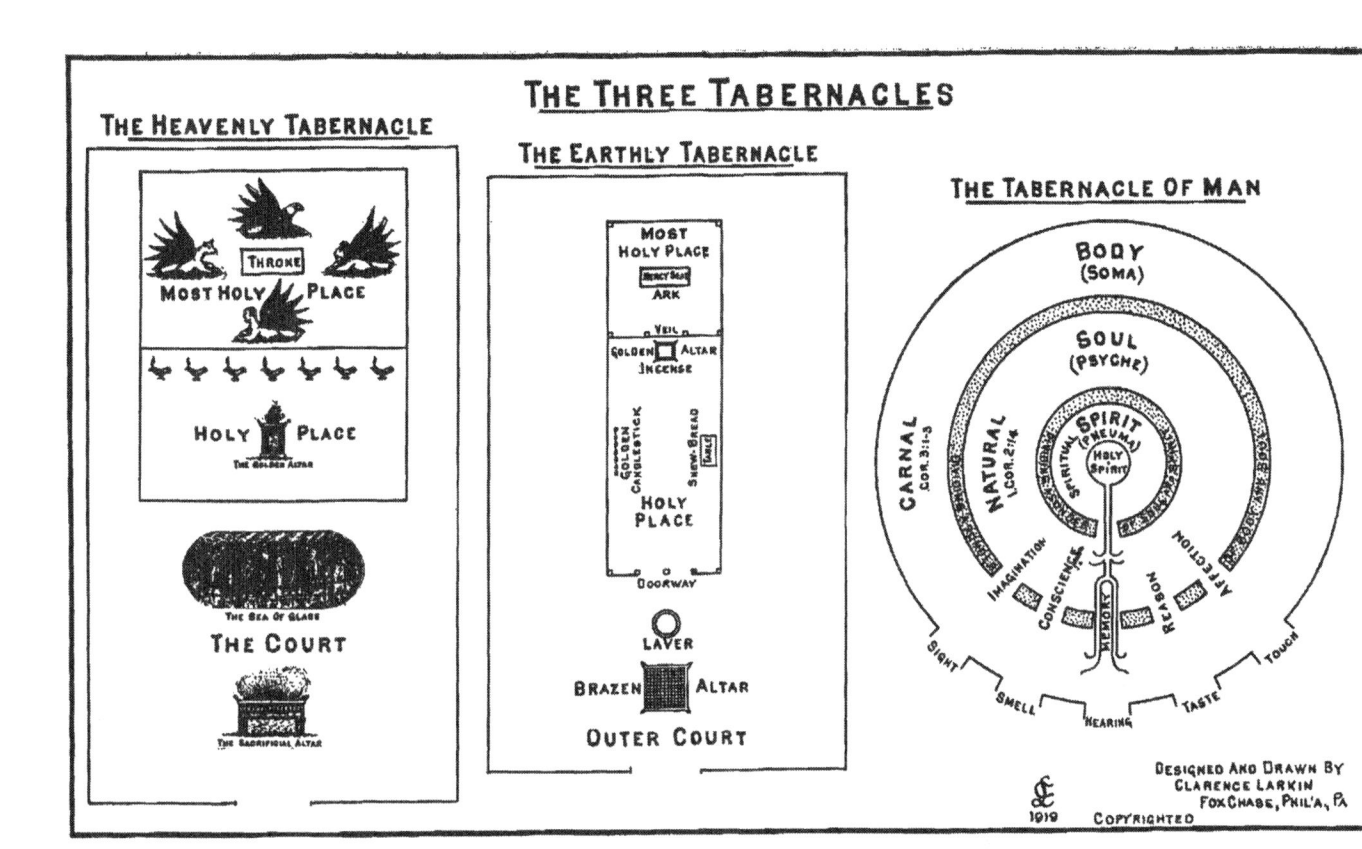

SPIRITISM

Spiritualism, or "**SPIRITISM**" as it should more properly be called, is an attempt to hold communication with the "spirits" of the departed dead. It has another name, "**IMMORTALISM**," and its investigations are carried on in these days under the title of "**PSYCHICAL RESEARCH**." The Biblical name for it is "**DEMONISM**."

It is forbidden in the Scriptures.

"The soul that turneth after such as have '**FAMILIAR SPIRITS**,' and after '**Wizards**,' to go a whoring after them, I will even set my face against that soul, and will **CUT HIM OFF FROM AMONG HIS PEOPLE**." Lev. 20:6.

"A man or woman that hath a '**FAMILIAR SPIRIT**,' or that is a 'Wizard,' shall surely be put to death; they shall **STONE THEM WITH STONES**." Lev. 20:27.

"There shall not be found among you any one * * * that useth 'Divination,' * * * or a 'Witch,' * * * or a consulter with 'Familiar Spirits,' or a 'Wizard.'" Deu. 18:10-11.

"When they shall say unto you, Seek unto them that have '**FAMILIAR SPIRITS**' and unto the 'Wizards,' that chirp and that mutter; should not a people seek unto their God on behalf of the living, should they seek unto the dead?" Isa. 8:19 R. V.

The "Familiar Spirits" of the Old Testament are the same as the "Demons" and "Seducing Spirits" of the New Testament.

Of the revival of "Spiritism" in these days we have been fully warned in the New Testament. The Apostle Paul, writing to Timothy, says—

"Now the Spirit (Holy Spirit) speaketh expressly, that in the '**LATTER TIMES**' (the last days of this Dispensation) some shall depart from the Faith (that is, give up the Christian Faith) giving heed to '**SEDUCING SPIRITS**,' and '**DOCTRINES OF DEVILS**' (Demons), * * * forbidding to marry, and commanding to abstain from meats." 1 Tim. 4:1-3.

The phrase **"forbidding to marry"** does not refer to **"celibacy,"** but to the **abrogation of the marriage relation,** the practice of **"FREE LOVE"** and the doctrine of **"AFFINITIES,"** which Spiritism leads to. The phrase **"Abstain From Meats"** is not a reference to fasting, but the requirement of a **"vegetable diet."** It is a well known fact that a "vegetable diet" renders the body more susceptible to spiritual forces than a meat diet.

The close connection of this warning of the Apostle with the words—"Refuse profane and **'OLD WIVES' FABLES,'** in verse seven, is doubtless a reference to some of the **"ISMS"** of these last days. For "Christian Science" is but an **"OLD WIFE'S"** Fable, for Mrs. Eddy was an "Old Wife" in the sense that she had been many times married.

It is an indisputable fact that most of the "Witches" and "Mediums" of Scripture, and these "Latter Days," were and are women. It was through Eve and not Adam that Satan sought to destroy the race. The reason may be that the nervous and impressionable character of women is better adapted to demon influence.

We are also told in Rev. 9:1-12, of an invasion of "Infernal Cherubim" or "Locusts" from the "Bottomless Pit" in the "Last Days." And we are told that "Three Unclean Spirits," or "Spirits of Demons" are to gather the Kings of the Earth for the great Battle of Armageddon. Rev. 16:13-16. And we read in Rev. 18:2, that the restored and rebuilt City of Babylon, shall, before its destruction, "become the **HABITATION OF DEVILS,** and the **HOLD OF EVERY FOUL SPIRIT,** and a cage of every **UNCLEAN AND HATEFUL BIRD."**

The revival of "Spiritism" then is one of the "Signs of the Times," and should be a warning to every true child of God of the approaching end of the Age. But alas! because of the absence of warning from the pulpit, thousands of God's Children are entering these "Perilous Times" unprepared to meet the subtle attack of "Spiritism" because they have not been taught the doctrine of

DEMONOLOGY.

The authorized English version of the New Testament is less clear in its presentation of "Demonology" than is the original Greek, because it translates **"diabolus," "daimonion,"** and **"daimon,"** by the same word—**"Devil."** The word **"diabolus"** (Devil), meaning **"slanderer"** or **"false accuser,"** is only used in the New Testament in the singular, and appears 35 times. The words **"daimonion"** and **"daimon"** are used in the New Testament both in the singular and plural, but never interchangeably with **"diabolus,"** and should be translated **"demon,"** or **"evil"** or **"unclean spirit."** The word "daimonion" occurs 56 times, and "daimon" 5 times.

There is but **one** Devil (Satan), but multitudes of **"demons,"** and Beelzebub (Satan) is the "Prince of the Demons." Matt. 12:24-30. Satan has not the power of omnipresence, and so many things attributed to him should be attributed to demons. On important occasions, as the Temptation of Jesus in the Wilderness, Satan himself is the agent. The "Demons" belong to the "Powers of Darkness." They are not few in number, but are a great "Martialed Host," veterans in the service of Satan. Their central camp or abode, is the "Bottomless Pit" from which they "sally forth" at the command of their leader. Rev. 9:1-11. They are not angels. Angels have bodies. But the fact that demons can enter in, and take possession of, and control human beings and animals (swine), is proof that they are **"Disembodied Spirits."** They are supposed by many to be the "spirits" of the inhabitants of the "Pre-Adamite Earth," whose sin caused its wreck, and whose bodies were destroyed in the catastrophe that overwhelmed it, and their desire and purpose in entering human bodies is to re-embody themselves again on the earth where they once lived. That the "Demons" have a **personality** is clear from the fact that Jesus conversed with them, asked them questions, and received answers. Luke 8:26-33. They are possessed of more than ordinary intelligence. They know that Jesus is the **"Son of God,"** and that they are finally to be confined in a place of **"Torment."** Matt. 8:29.

THE POWER OF DEMONS OVER THE HUMAN BODY

They can cause **DUMBNESS** (Matt. 9:32-33), and **BLINDNESS** (Matt. 12:22), and **INSANITY** (Luke 8:26-35), and the **SUICIDAL MANIA** (Mark 9:22), and **PERSONAL INJURIES** (Mark 9:18), and impart **SUPERNATURAL STRENGTH** (Luke 8:29), and inflict **PHYSICAL DEFECTS AND DEFORMITIES.** Luke 13:11-17. Once they have got control over a human body they can come and go at will. Luke 11:24-26.

The Devilish character of "Demons" is seen in the use they make of their victims. They use them as **"instruments of unrighteousness,"** (Rom. 6:13), for the proclamation of the **"DOCTRINES OF DEVILS,"** (1 Tim. 4:1), and the teaching of **"DAMNABLE HERESIES."** 2 Pet. 2:1. The effect of such use of the victim is not only **unmoral,** it is **IMMORAL.** It leads to vicious and inhuman conduct. The conduct of **"demonized"** men and women seems to indicate that the "Demon" takes possession of them for the purpose of **physical sensual gratification,** thus letting us into the secret of the cause of the wreck of the Pre-Adamite Earth, the **SIN OF SENSUALITY.** This accounts for the desire of the victim to live in a state of nudity; to have lustful and licentious thoughts. In these days of increasing tendency to yield to **"Seducing Spirits"** it may account for the immodesty of fashionable attire, and the craze of dancing. The purpose of the "Demon" is often to alienate husband and wife, and break up homes by preaching the doctrine of **"FREE LOVE."** In short, the "Demon," for personal gratification, has the power, once he is in control of his victim, to derange both mind and body, and wreck the victim's health, and if deliverance is not obtained by turning to Christ, who alone has power to cast out the Demon, the victim will be lost soul and body.

Demon-possession must not be confounded with diseases, such as "Epilepsy," which causes the victim to fall in convulsions, foam at the mouth and gnash the teeth, for the Scriptures make a clear distinction between them.

"And His fame went throughout all Syria; and they brought unto Him all sick people that were taken with **divers diseases** and **torments,** and those which were **POSSESSED WITH DEVILS** (Demons—"daimonizomai," demonized or demon possessed), and those which were **lunatic,** and those that had the **palsy;** and He healed them." Matt. 4:24.

In 1 Cor. 10:20-21 we read—

"But I say, that the things which the Gentiles sacrifice, they **SACRIFICE TO DEVILS** (Demons), and not to God; and I would not that ye should have **FELLOWSHIP WITH DEVILS** (Demons). Ye cannot drink the **'Cup of the Lord'** (Communion Cup), and the **'Cup OF DEVILS';** ye cannot be partakers of the **'Lord's Table,'** and of the **TABLE OF DEVILS** (Demons)"

This passage proves that behind all heathen worship there is the "Spirit of Demonism," or "**DEVIL WORSHIP**," and accounts for the "wild orgies" and voluptuous and licentious mode of worship of the heathen.

That the "Demons" have the power of "**DIVINATION**" is clearly revealed in the New Testament.

"And it came to pass, as we went to prayer, a certain damsel **POSSESSED WITH A SPIRIT OF DIVINATION** met us, which brought her masters much gain by **SOOTH-SAYING**. The same followed Paul and us, and cried, saying, These men are the servants of the 'Most High God,' which shew unto us the Way of Salvation. And this did she many days. But Paul, being grieved, turned and said to the '**SPIRIT**' (the Evil Spirit, or Demon), I command thee in the **name of JESUS CHRIST** to come out of her. And he came out the same hour." Acts 16:16-18.

It is clear from the context that this young woman was a **MEDIUM**, and that she performed her work through the instrumentality of an "Evil Spirit" or "Demon." This reveals the source of information of modern "Mediums." The information they furnish is given, not by the person they profess to call up, but by an "Evil Spirit" or "Demon," who, for the purpose impersonates the person called for.

If there ever was an exception to this method of communication between this and the world of departed spirits, it was the case of Samuel, recorded in 1 Sam. 28:6-25. There is a diversity of opinion as to whether Samuel really appeared, or was impersonated by an "Evil Spirit." But the account is so circumstantial, and the evident and undisguised surprise of the Witch of Endor at the appearance of Samuel, whom she doubtless had known, and the conversation between Saul and Samuel without the aid of the Witch as a **MEDIUM**, seems conclusive evidence that Samuel did really appear. But the Witch did not bring him up. God sent him as a rebuke to Saul. Thus the exception proves the rule.

Some claim that because Samuel said—"To-morrow shalt thou and thy sons be with me," that it was not Samuel that appeared, but an "Evil Spirit," for Saul and his sons would not go to the same place in the other world as Samuel. But we must not forget from our study of the chapter on the "Spirit World," that "Paradise" and "Hell" were at that time both in the heart of the earth, from which Samuel came up, but were separated by a "Great Gulf." So the words "Tomorrow shalt thou and thy sons be with me," meant that they should be with Samuel in the "Underworld," but in separate compartments, separated by a "Great Gulf." And the fact that we are told that Saul's death was partly caused by his asking counsel of a "Familiar Spirit" (1 Chron. 10:13), reveals God's displeasure with those who resort to Spiritism.

The account of the Transfiguration, in which Moses and Elijah appeared on the Mount with Jesus, and in the presence of Peter, James and John (Matt. 17:1-8), is used by Spiritualists to prove that our departed ones can come back again to the earth. But we must not forget that Moses and Elijah were not in the state of the dead. Moses had been resurrected, and Elijah had never died, and the Transfiguration scene is a foreview of the condition of the dead after the **FIRST RESURRECTION**, when those who are with Christ shall return to the region of the air to reign with Christ over the earth. In that day the saints will have communication with the earth, but not in this Dispensation.

The story of the rich man and Lazarus (Luke 16:19-31) reveals the fact that communication with the spirits of our departed dead, is not only unnecessary, but is not permitted. It is not necessary, for we have Moses and the Prophets, that is, the Holy Scriptures, to give us all we need to know of the state of the dead. And it is not permitted, or Lazarus, or the rich man himself, would have been allowed to return to the earth and warn his brethren. The inevitable conclusion to be drawn from this story is, that the spirit of a good man **MAY** not, and the spirit of a bad man **CANNOT** return to this earth. If this be true then Spiritism is a fraud, and is one of the devices of Satan in these latter days to lead astray the unwary. Those who dabble in Spiritism are in great danger of having their "**understanding darkened**" (Eph. 4:17-19) and come under the power and control of Demons.

The Apostle John says—"Believe not every spirit, but **TRY THE SPIRITS** whether they are of God, because many false prophets are gone out into the world." 1 John 4:1. The test is—"Every spirit that confesseth not that Jesus Christ **IS COME IN THE FLESH** is not of God." 1 John 4:3. Ask the "**spirit**" that comes to you personally seeking entrance, or speaks to you through a "Medium," if Jesus Christ **IS COME IN THE FLESH**, that is, was born of the Virgin, and is the "**SON OF GOD**," and if it says—**YES!** that is the Holy Spirit, for no man can say that Jesus is the **LORD**, but by the Holy Spirit. 1 Cor. 12:3. But if the "Spirit" gets angry, and denies the Deity of the Lord Jesus, and the authority of the Word of God, then it is clear that the "spirit" is an "Evil Spirit" or "Demon." The Holy Spirit will not teach anything contrary to the Scriptures, so a person to be able to "**TEST THE SPIRITS**" must be thoroughly conversant with the Word of God.

Another of the "Signs of the Times" is the revival of what is called the

"GIFT OF TONGUES,"

in which the recipient claims that he is taken possession of by the "Spirit of God" and empowered to speak in an "unknown" or "foreign tongue." But the conduct of those thus possessed, in which they fall to the ground and writhe in contortions, causing disarrangement of the clothing and disgraceful scenes, is more a characteristic of "demon possession," than a work of the Holy Spirit, for the Holy Spirit does not lend Himself to such vile impersonations.

From what has been said we see that we are living in "Perilous Times," and that all about us are "Seducing Spirits," and that they will become more active as the Dispensation draws to its close, and that we must exert the greatest care lest we be led astray by them.

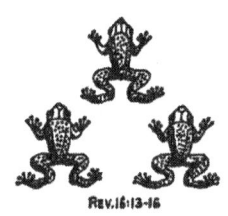

REV. 16:13-16

XVI
THE RESURRECTION

The Scriptures speak of three kinds of resurrection.

I. National.

This refers to Israel. In Hosea 6:1, 2 we read—

"Come and let us return unto the Lord for He hath torn, and He will heal us; He hath smitten, and He will bind us up.

After Two Days

will He revive us; in the third day He will raise us up, and we shall live in His sight."

There are several things in this passage worth noting. First we see from the context that the words of the prophet are addressed exclusively to the Jewish people and to the whole "Twelve Tribes" represented by Ephraim and Judah. Hosea 6:4. And it is the "Whole House of Israel" that says—"Come, and let us return unto the Lord." It is the cry of repentance of a "nation" that has been torn and smitten by the Lord, and not the cry of persons "dead in their graves." The "healing" does not refer to a resurrection from "the dead," and the "binding" means that the whole Twelve Tribes, now scattered, will be "rebound into one nation" again in their own land.

The expression "Will 'revive' us," does not mean a resurrection from physical death, for the word "revive" simply means what we mean when we speak of a "Revival of Religion," which is a "spiritual" and not a physical resurrection.

The remarkable statement in the passage is the "time" of the Revival. It says—"after TWO Days." It is clear that those "two days" are not literal days of 24 hours, for more than 2 such days have gone by and Israel has not yet been revived. They were spoken by the prophet about B. C. 780, or 2700 years ago, and therefore must be interpreted on the scale that **one day** is with the Lord as a **Thousand Years.** 2 Pet. 3:8.

Israel is now well along in the third Thousand Years of her rejection; and it is to be some time in this third Thousand Years, corresponding to the "Third Day" of Hosea, that Israel is to be revived and restored to her own land. For a full account of this "National Resurrection of Israel" see the Chapter on "The Jews."

II. Spiritual.

Writing to the Ephesians, Paul said—"And you hath he quickened, who **were dead in trespasses and sins**. . . . . and hath **raised us** up together, and made us sit together in heavenly places in Christ Jesus." Eph. 2:1-6.

"Awake thou that sleepest, and **arise from the dead**, and Christ shall give thee light." Eph. 5:14.

Writing to the Romans Paul says—"Reckon ye also yourselves to be **dead indeed unto sin**, but **alive unto God** through Jesus Christ our Lord." Rom. 6:11.

The Resurrection referred to in these passages is "Spiritual" and is a "present" Resurrection, and is going on continually. Every time a soul is "born again" there is a passing from "death" unto "life," a "Spiritual resurrection." John 5:24.

III. Material.

This is of the dead body. The spirit of man does not die, it goes back to God who gave it. See the Chapter on "The Spirit World." All that goes into the grave is the body, and all that can come out of the grave is the body.

Jesus clearly and distinctly taught a resurrection "from the grave."

"Marvel not at this; for the hour is coming in the which all that are **in the graves** shall hear His voice, and shall **come forth**; they that have done good unto the '**Resurrection of LIFE**,' and they that have done evil unto the '**Resurrection of DAMNATION**.'" John 5:28, 29.

Here Jesus teaches the resurrection of both the "Righteous" and the "Wicked." The Apostle Paul taught the same thing.

"And have hope toward God, which they themselves also allow, that there shall be a **resurrection of the Dead**, both of the **Just** (justified), and of the **Unjust** (unjustified)." Acts 24:15.

"For as in Adam **all die** (physically), even so in Christ shall **all be made alive** (physically)." 1 Cor. 15:22.

That the Apostle means "physical" death, and "physical" resurrection here, is clear, for it is the body, and not the spirit that he is discoursing about, and so the Universalist has no "proof text" here for the doctrine of "Universal Salvation."

These passages clearly teach that there is to be a resurrection of "all the dead," and if we did not look any further, we would be led to believe that the Righteous and the Wicked are not only to rise, but that they are to rise at the "same time." But when we turn to the Book of Revelation we find that the Righteous are to rise "before" the Wicked, and not simply precede them, but that there is a space of a 1000 years between the two Resurrections. Rev. 20:4, 5.

"And I saw thrones, and they sat upon them, and judgment was given unto them."

This refers to the saints of the First Resurrection, who, represented by the "Four and Twenty Elders" of Rev. 4:4, are seen seated on thrones surrounding the Throne of God.

"And I saw the **souls of them that were beheaded for the witness of Jesus, and for the Word of God, and which had not worshipped The Beast, neither His Image, neither had received His Mark upon their foreheads, or in their hands; and they LIVED and Reigned With Christ a THOUSAND YEARS.**"

These are the "Tribulation Saints." John first saw them in their "martyred" condition (as souls), then he saw them **rise from the dead (they lived again)**, and they, with the First Resurrection Saints, **reigned with Christ a Thousand Years.**

"But the **rest of the dead** (the wicked), lived not again until the 'Thousand Years' were finished."

The rest of the verse—"This is the 'First Resurrection,'" refers not to the "rest of the dead," but to those in verse 4, who lived and reigned with Christ for a 1000 years, for

"Blessed and holy is he that hath part in the **First Resurrection**, on such the **Second Death** (the doom of the Wicked, Rev. 20:14, 15), hath no power, but they shall be **Priests of God and of Christ**, and shall **Reign With Him a THOUSAND YEARS.**" Rev. 20:6.

That the Dead are to rise in different bands or cohorts, with an "interval of time" between, is beautifully brought out in 1 Cor. 15:22-24.

"For as in Adam all die (physically), even so in Christ shall all be made alive (physically). But every man in his **own order.**"

The word translated "order" is a military expression, and means a band, cohort, brigade or division of an army. Paul then gives the order

1. "Christ the **First Fruits.**"
2. "Afterward they that **Are Christ's At His Coming.**"
3. "Then cometh **The End.**"

Now we know that between "Christ the First Fruits," and they that "are Christ's at His Coming," there has already been nearly 1900 years, and as we have seen there will be 1000 years between the resurrection of those that **"are Christ's at His Coming"** and the "Wicked dead," we see that there is not to be a **simultaneous resurrection** of the Righteous and the Wicked.

See the small square diagram on The Resurrections.

But some one may say what authority have we for thus dividing up Scripture and locating "intervals of time?" We have the authority of Christ Himself. In Luke 4:16-20 we read that He went into the Synagogue on the Sabbath Day, and they handed Him the Book of Isaiah from which to read, and that He turned to Isa. 61:1, 2, and read—

"The Spirit of the Lord is upon me, because He hath anointed me to preach the gospel to the poor; He hath sent me to heal the broken hearted, to preach deliverance to the captives, and recovering of sight to the blind, to set at liberty them that are bruised, to preach the acceptable year of the Lord,"

and there He stopped at a "comma," as we see by referring to Isa. 61:2, and left unsaid the words, "and the 'Day of Vengeance' of our God."

Why did Christ stop at that comma? Because the time had not come to declare the "Day of Vengeance." That "comma" has been nearly 19 centuries long and will continue until the "Lord Jesus shall be revealed from Heaven with His mighty angels, in flaming fire taking 'vengeance' on them that know not God, and that obey not the Gospel of our Lord Jesus Christ." 2 Thess. 1:7, 8.

But it has been objected that the passage in Rev. 20:4, 5, is the "only" place in the Bible where a "length of time" is given between the resurrection of the Righteous and the Wicked, and that it is not fair to base such an important fact upon a single statement found in such a symbolic Book. While the Book of Revelation contains many symbols they are explained in the Book, and we must not forget that it is not a mysterious book, for it is the **Revelation of Jesus Christ**, and is the only book in the Bible that promises a blessing to the reader. Rev. 1:1-3. The Book is to be taken literally.

Suppose that Rev. 20:4-6 is the "only" place in the Bible where a "length of time" is given between the resurrection of the Righteous and the Wicked, that is no reason for questioning its truthfulness. The most marvelous fact in the life of our Lord —"The Virgin Birth," until it was fulfilled at His birth, rested for centuries on a "single" prophecy in the Old Testament. "Behold a 'virgin' shall conceive and bear a son." Isa. 7:14.

But we do not have to depend on Rev. 20:4-6 to prove that there is to be an "out" Resurrection "from among the dead." There are a number of passages referring to the resurrection of the dead that are unexplainable only on the supposition that there is a "time space" between the resurrection of the Righteous and the Wicked.

In the reply that Jesus made to the Sadducees, in answer to their question as to whose wife the woman would be in the next world, who had had seven husbands in this, He said—

"They which shall be accounted worthy to obtain that world (Age), and the resurrection from the **dead**, neither **marry**, nor are given in marriage; neither can they **die any more** (Second Death); for they are equal unto the angels; and are the 'Children of God' being the children of **THE** (out) **Resurrection.**" Luke 20:35, 36.

This is a very important statement. The use of the Greek word "Aion," translated "world," but which means "Age," shows that Jesus is speaking of a "class of dead" who are to be raised "before" the next or "Millennial Age," and that those thus raised can "die no more," there is no "**Second Death**" for them. Why? Because they are "**equal unto the angels**" and are the "**Children of God,**" having been "**born again,**" and are the "**Children of THE Resurrection,** the "**Out FROM AMONG The Dead** or **FIRST RESURRECTION,**" for only the "Children" of the "First Resurrection" shall live again "before" the Millennium."

In Luke 14:14 Jesus speaks of a "special" resurrection, that He calls the **Resurrection of the "JUST."** This is an "Out Resurrection" from "among the dead," and is only for the "Justified," and must refer to the "First" Resurrection.

The writer to the Hebrews (Heb. 11:35) speaks of a "better" Resurrection, and it is a significant fact that the Apostles preached through Jesus the Resurrection "from the dead." Not the Resurrection "of" the dead, that they always believed, but the Resurrection "from among" the dead, that was a "New Doctrine."

There is no question but what Paul believed in the resurrection "of" the dead, and that he expected to rise "some time," but in his letter to the Philippians (3:11) he expresses the hope that he might "attain unto 'the' resurrection of the dead." Paul must therefore have had in mind some "special" Resurrection. What Paul meant is clear when we turn to 1 Thess. 4:15-17, where he speaks of the resurrection of the "dead in Christ" and "translation of the living saints," at the Second Coming of the Lord, and as Christ is to come back to usher in the Millennium, then that event must "precede" the Millennium, and be an "Out Resurrection from among the dead," for the "rest of the dead" live not again until the 1000 years "are finished."

But the resurrection of the Righteous and Wicked is not only to be different as to "time" but as to "character." They that have done "good" (the Righteous) shall rise unto the "resurrection of Life," while they that have done "evil" (the Wicked) shall rise unto the "resurrection of Damnation." John 5:28, 29. And we read in Rev. 20:12-15, that those who are raised at the Second Resurrection or the "Resurrection of Damnation" must appear at the Judgment of the "Great White Throne," and that their names shall "not" be found written in the "Book of Life," and they shall be cast into the "Lake of Fire" which is the "Second Death."

The "Manner" of the Resurrection.

Some claim that the departure of the soul and spirit from the body is what is meant by the resurrection. But that cannot be so, for as we have seen, the dead are to arise from their "graves," and only that can come out of the grave that went into it, and that is the "body."

Then there is the "Germ Theory," that in every human body there is a "living germ" that is "indestructible," and though the body turn to dust that "living germ" will exist in the grave until at the Resurrection a new body shall spring from it. This theory explains how the body may be eaten by animals, destroyed by quick lime, blown to

THE RESURRECTIONS
As Outlined In - I. Cor. 15:22-25, Rev. 20:4-6

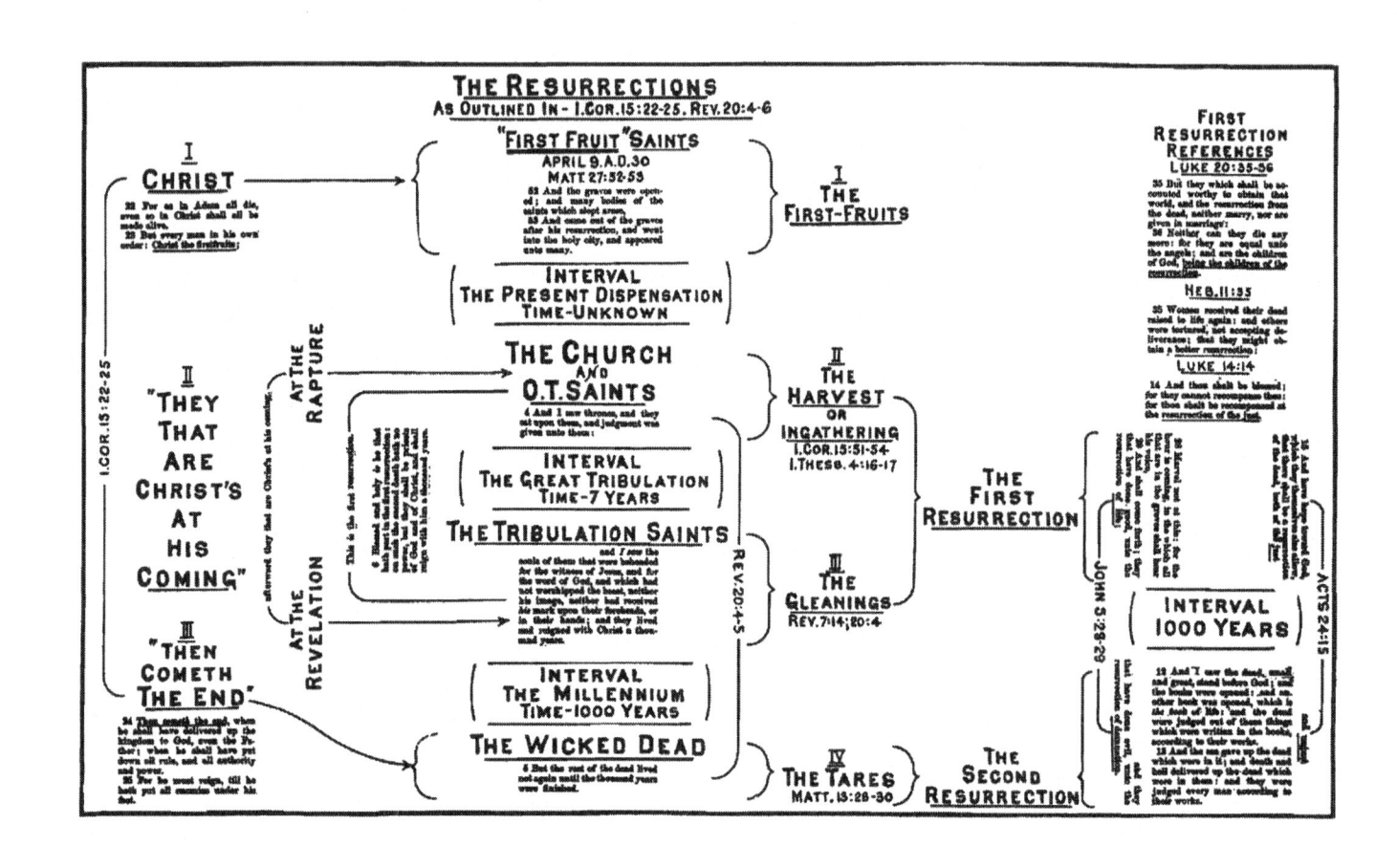

I. CHRIST
22 For as in Adam all die, even so in Christ shall all be made alive.
23 But every man in his own order: Christ the firstfruits;

→ **"FIRST FRUIT" SAINTS**
APRIL 9, A.D. 30
MATT 27:52-53
52 And the graves were opened; and many bodies of the saints which slept arose,
53 And came out of the graves after his resurrection, and went into the holy city, and appeared unto many.

I. THE FIRST-FRUITS

INTERVAL — THE PRESENT DISPENSATION — TIME-UNKNOWN

II. "THEY THAT ARE CHRIST'S AT HIS COMING"

At the Rapture →

THE CHURCH AND O.T. SAINTS
4 And I saw thrones, and they sat upon them, and judgment was given unto them:

II. THE HARVEST OR INGATHERING
I. Cor. 15:51-54
I. Thess. 4:16-17

INTERVAL — THE GREAT TRIBULATION — TIME-7 YEARS

At the Revelation →

THE TRIBULATION SAINTS
and I saw the souls of them that were beheaded for the witness of Jesus, and for the word of God, and which had not worshipped the beast, neither his image, neither had received his mark upon their foreheads, or in their hands; and they lived and reigned with Christ a thousand years.

III. THE GLEANINGS
Rev. 7:14; 20:4

THE FIRST RESURRECTION

INTERVAL — THE MILLENNIUM — TIME-1000 YEARS

III. "THEN COMETH THE END"
24 Then cometh the end, when he shall have delivered up the kingdom to God, even the Father; when he shall have put down all rule, and all authority and power.
25 For he must reign, till he hath put all enemies under his feet.

→ **THE WICKED DEAD**
5 But the rest of the dead lived not again until the thousand years were finished.

IV. THE TARES
Matt. 13:25-30

THE SECOND RESURRECTION

FIRST RESURRECTION REFERENCES

LUKE 20:35-36
35 But they which shall be accounted worthy to obtain that world, and the resurrection from the dead, neither marry, nor are given in marriage:
36 Neither can they die any more: for they are equal unto the angels; and are the children of God, being the children of the resurrection.

HEB. 11:35
35 Women received their dead raised to life again: and others were tortured, not accepting deliverance; that they might obtain a better resurrection:

LUKE 14:14
14 And thou shalt be blessed; for they cannot recompense thee: for thou shalt be recompensed at the resurrection of the just.

JOHN 5:28-29

INTERVAL 1000 YEARS

ACTS 24:15

12 And I saw the dead, small and great, stand before God; and the books were opened: and another book was opened, which is the book of life: and the dead were judged out of those things which were written in the books, according to their works.
13 And the sea gave up the dead which were in it; and death and hell delivered up the dead which were in them: and they were judged every man according to their works.

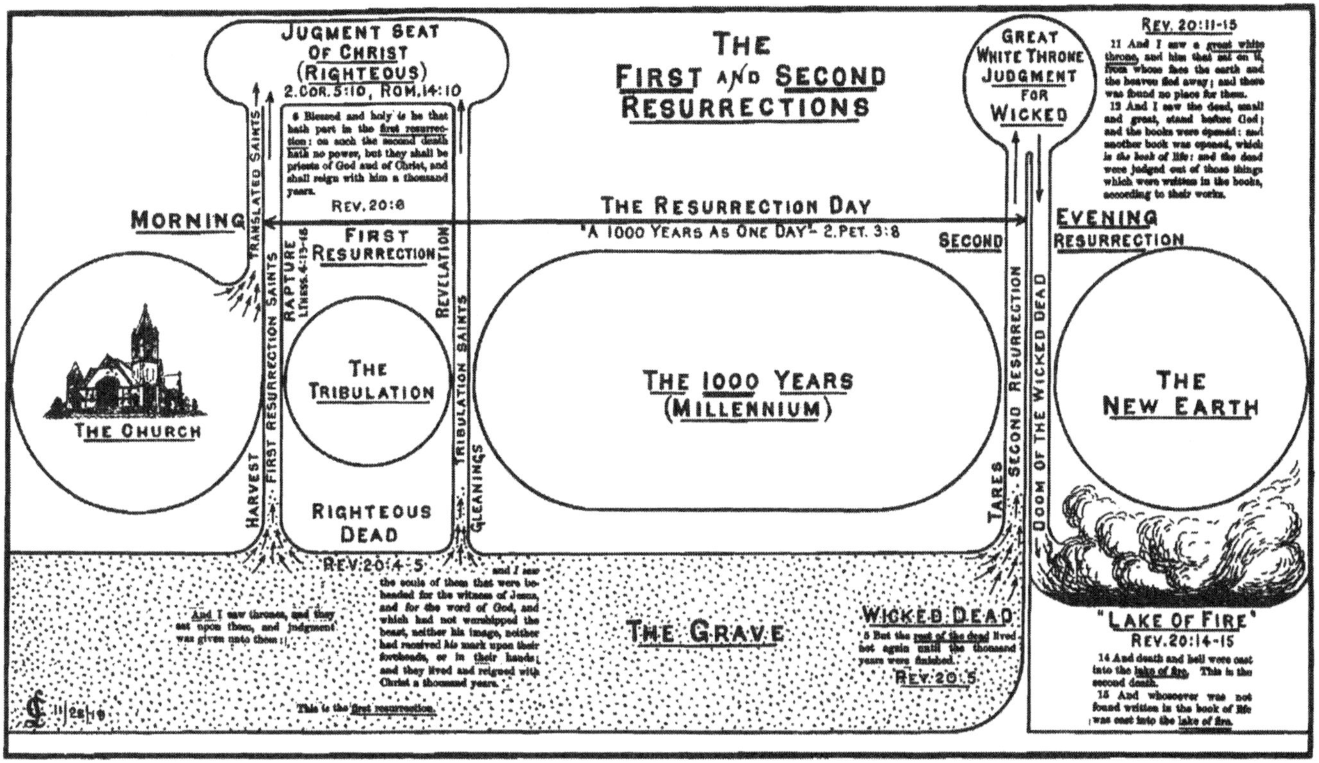
THE FIRST AND SECOND RESURRECTIONS
JUGMENT SEAT OF CHRIST (RIGHTEOUS)
2.COR.5:10, ROM.14:10
6 Blessed and holy is he that hath part in the first resurrection: on such the second death hath no power, but they shall be priests of God and of Christ, and shall reign with him a thousand years.
REV. 20:6
MORNING
TRANSLATED SAINTS
FIRST RESURRECTION SAINTS
HARVEST
RAPTURE
1.THESS.4:13-18
FIRST RESURRECTION
REVELATION
TRIBULATION SAINTS
GLEANINGS
THE RESURRECTION DAY
"A 1000 YEARS AS ONE DAY" - 2.PET. 3:8
THE CHURCH
THE TRIBULATION
THE 1000 YEARS (MILLENNIUM)
RIGHTEOUS DEAD
REV.20:4-5
And I saw thrones, and they sat upon them, and judgment was given unto them:
and I saw the souls of them that were beheaded for the witness of Jesus, and for the word of God, and which had not worshipped the beast, neither his image, neither had received his mark upon their foreheads, or in their hands; and they lived and reigned with Christ a thousand years.
This is the first resurrection.
THE GRAVE
WICKED DEAD
5 But the rest of the dead lived not again until the thousand years were finished.
REV.20:5
GREAT WHITE THRONE JUDGMENT FOR WICKED
REV. 20:11-15
11 And I saw a great white throne, and him that sat on it, from whose face the earth and the heaven fled away; and there was found no place for them.
12 And I saw the dead, small and great, stand before God; and the books were opened: and another book was opened, which is the book of life: and the dead were judged out of those things which were written in the books, according to their works.
SECOND
TARES
SECOND RESURRECTION
DOOM OF THE WICKED DEAD
EVENING RESURRECTION
THE NEW EARTH
"LAKE OF FIRE"
REV.20:14-15
14 And death and hell were cast into the lake of fire. This is the second death.
15 And whosoever was not found written in the book of life was cast into the lake of fire.
11/28/18

atoms, or mutilated by the loss of limbs, etc., and still the "life germ" exist from which shall come the resurrection body.

The advocates of this theory claim that Paul teaches it in 1 Cor. 15: 35-38, where he compares the resurrection of the body with the plant that comes up from the seed. We know that the seed is different from the plant that bore it, just as the acorn is different from the oak tree, but the plant that springs from the seed will be like the plant that bore it, so the body that comes from the indestructible "life germ" should be alike in kind to the body that produced the "germ."

But while the resurrection body shall be alike in kind, it will be different in character and possess different qualities. This Paul declares when he says that "All 'flesh' is not the same flesh; but there is one kind of flesh of 'men,' another flesh of 'beast,'' another of 'fishes,' and another of 'birds.' That is, the flesh of God's creatures is adapted to their "environment." "Fish flesh" cannot fly in the air, nor "Bird flesh" swim in the sea. So there are bodies "terrestial" and bodies "celestial." The human body as it is now constituted could not exist in Heaven. There must be a change, and this change is brought about by the resurrection. This change Paul portrays. He says—

"So also is the **Resurrection of the Dead.** It is sown in **corruption**; it is raised in **incorruption**; it is sown in **dishonor**, it is raised in **Glory**; **it is sown in weakness**; it is raised in **Power**; it is sown a **Natural body**; it is raised a **Spiritual body**."

This does not mean that it will have no "substance." We cannot conceive of a "body" that is to have the faculties of the "Spirit Body" not having "form" and "substance."

Christ's resurrection body is a "sample" of what ours is to be. While it is true that His body did not see "corruption" and He rose in the "same body" that was laid in the grave; while it was the same in "identity," it was different in "character."

While the "nail prints" and "spear wound" were visible it could pass through closed doors, and appear and disappear at will. It had "flesh" and "bones." (Luke 24: 39-43), but not "**blood**," for "flesh and blood" cannot enter the Kingdom of God, (1 Cor. 15: 50), for "**blood**" is that which causes "corruption." To preserve a body it must be drained of blood, or the blood chemically preserved by an embalming fluid. As the sacrifice was to be bled, so Jesus left His blood on the earth.

As our resurrection bodies will have visible "form" and "shape" it stands to reason that they will have a framework of "flesh" and "bones," but it will be "flesh" and "bones" adapted to its new environment. We must not forget that Enoch and Elijah went up in their "bodies." Presumably their bodies were "glorified" in the transit, but they were not "disembodied," and if they have use for a "body" in Heaven, why not we? Is it reasonable to suppose that only those two saints shall be in Heaven in their bodies? Why did Michael the Archangel contend with the Devil over the "body" of Moses, if Moses had no further need of it? Did not he and Elijah have use for their bodies when they appeared on the Mt. of Transfiguration with Jesus? And if they were "the" two men that stood by in "white apparel" when Jesus ascended (Acts 1: 9-11), and are to be the "Two Witnesses" of Rev. 11: 3-6, we see, that as they are the "type" of the Resurrected and Translated Saints, that the Saints at the Rapture will have "bodies" like Moses and Elijah now have.

XVII
THE JUDGMENTS

The common opinion that the Millennium is to be ushered in by the preaching of the Gospel, and that after the Millennium there is to be a "General Resurrection" followed by a "General Judgment," and then the earth is to be destroyed by fire is not scriptural.

There can be no "General" Judgment because the Scriptures speak of one Judgment as being in the "Air" (1 Thess. 4: 16, 17; 2 Cor. 5: 6-10); another on the "Earth" (Matt. 25: 31-46); and a third in "Heaven," the earth and its atmosphere having fled away. Rev. 20: 11-15. And to make sure that these three separate Judgments should not be combined into one General Judgment scene, three different Thrones are mentioned.

1. **The "Judgment Seat of Christ."** 2 Cor. 5: 10.
   "In the Air." For "Believers" only.
2. **The "Throne of Glory."** Matt. 25: 31, 32.
   "On the Earth." For "The Nations."
3. **The "Great White Throne."** Rev. 20: 11, 12.
   "In Heaven." For the "Wicked Dead."

The Scriptures speak of

Five Separate Judgments.

They differ in five general aspects. As to "Subjects," "Time," "Place," "Basis of Judgment" and "Result."

Judgment No. 1.

1. Subjects—Believers as to "SIN."
2. Time—A. D. 30.
3. Place—Calvary.
4. Basis of Judgment. Christ's "FINISHED WORK."
5. Result—
   1. Death as to Christ.
   2. Justification as to the Believer.

This Judgment is **PAST.** The Bible proofs of the results of this Judgment are Rom. 10: 4.

"For Christ is the **END OF THE LAW** for righteousness to every one that Believeth."

"Christ Hath Redeemed us from the **CURSE OF THE LAW**, being made a curse for us; for it is written, Cursed is every one that hangeth on a tree." Gal. 3: 13.

"Who His own self bare our sins in His own body on the tree, that we, **BEING DEAD TO SINS**, should live unto righteousness." 1 Pet. 2: 24.

"There is therefore NOW no condemnation (Judgment) to them which are IN CHRIST JESUS, who walk not after the flesh, but after the Spirit. For the **Law of the 'SPIRIT OF LIFE'** in Christ Jesus hath made me FREE From the Law of 'Sin and Death.'" Rom. 8: 1, 2.

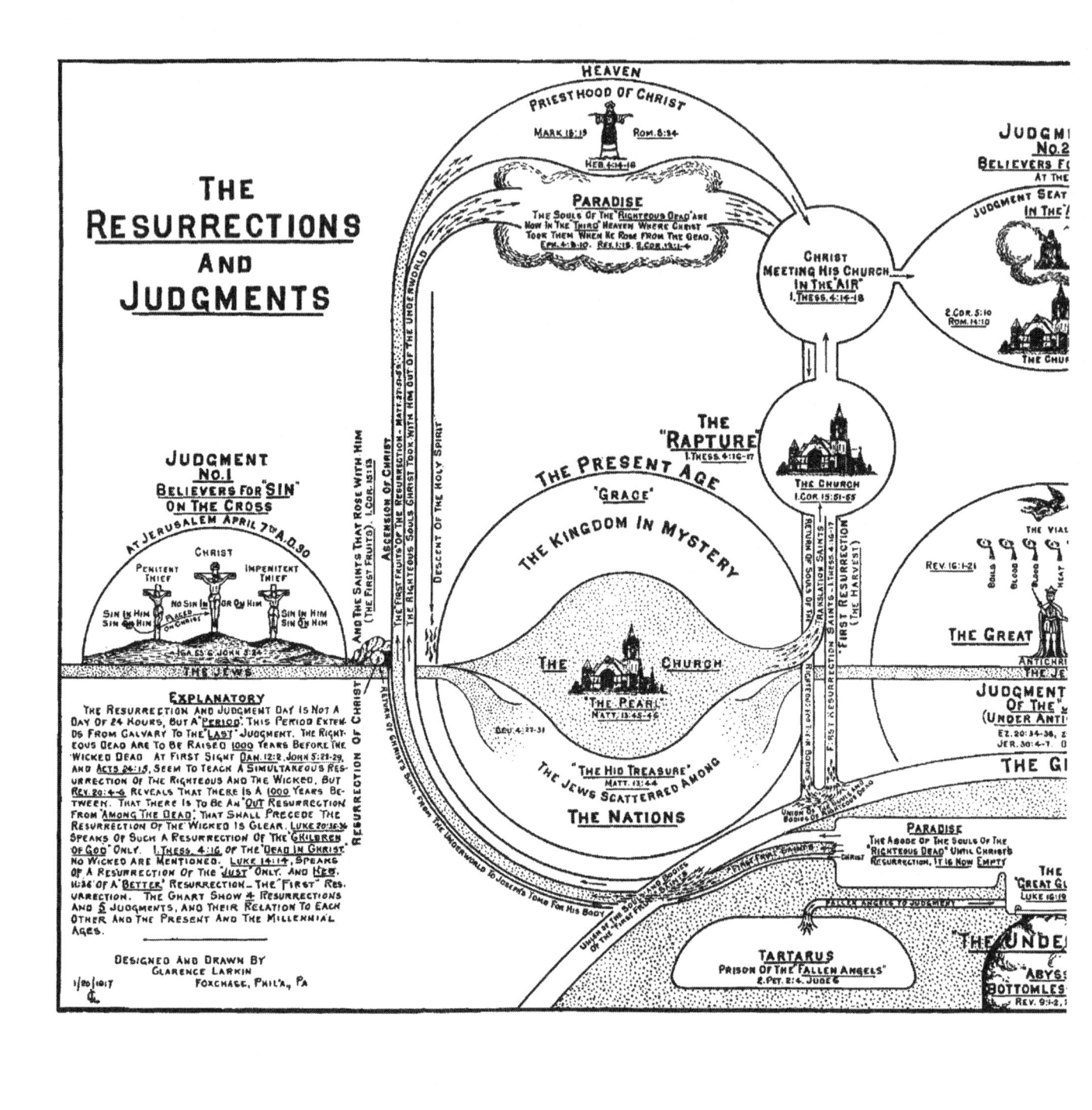

The Resurrections and Judgments

Heaven
Priesthood of Christ
Mark 16:19 Rom. 8:34
Heb. 4:14-16

Paradise
The Souls Of The "Righteous Dead" Are Now In The "Third" Heaven Where Christ Took Them When He Rose From The Dead.
Eph. 4:8-10, Rev. 1:18, 2. Cor. 12:1-4

Christ Meeting His Church In The "Air"
I. Thess. 4:16-18

Judgment No. 2
Believers For
At The
Judgment Seat
In The
2 Cor. 5:10
Rom. 14:10
The Church

Judgment No. 1
Believers For "Sin" On The Cross
At Jerusalem April 7th A.D. 30

Penitent Thief | Christ | Impenitent Thief
Sin In Him / Sin Off Him | No Sin In Nor On Him / Placed On Christ | Sin In Him / Sin On Him
Isa. 53:6, John 3:34
THE JEWS

The "Rapture"
I. Thess. 4:16-17
The Church
I. Cor. 15:51-55

The Present Age
"Grace"
The Kingdom In Mystery

The Church
"The Pearl"
Matt. 13:45-46
Rev. 4:27-31

"The Hid Treasure"
Matt. 13:44

The Jews Scattered Among The Nations

(vertical labels: Resurrection Of Christ — And The Saints That Rose With Him (The First Fruits) I. Cor. 15:20 — Ascension Of Christ — The First Fruits Of The Resurrection — Matt. 27:52-53 — The Righteous Souls Christ Took With Him Out Of The Underworld — Descent Of The Holy Spirit — Change Of Living Saints To Spiritual Bodies — Christ Brings Soul From The Underworld To Joseph's Tomb For His Body — Righteous Dead Raised In Spiritual Bodies — Translation Saints I. Thess. 4:16-17 — First Resurrection (The Harvest))

Explanatory
The Resurrection And Judgment Day Is Not A Day Of 24 Hours, But A "Period". This Period Extends From Calvary To The "Last" Judgment. The Righteous Dead Are To Be Raised 1000 Years Before The Wicked Dead. At First Sight Dan. 12:2, John 5:28-29, And Acts 24:15, Seem To Teach A Simultaneous Resurrection Of The Righteous And The Wicked, But Rev. 20:4-6 Reveals That There Is A 1000 Years Between. That There Is To Be An "Out" Resurrection From "Among The Dead", That Shall Precede The Resurrection Of The Wicked Is Clear. Luke 20:35-36, Speaks Of Such A Resurrection Of The "Children Of God" Only. I. Thess. 4:16, Of The "Dead In Christ". No Wicked Are Mentioned. Luke 14:14, Speaks Of A Resurrection Of The "Just" Only. And Heb. 11:35 Of A "Better" Resurrection - The "First" Resurrection. The Chart Show 4 Resurrections And 5 Judgments, And Their Relation To Each Other And The Present And The Millennial Ages.

Designed And Drawn By
Clarence Larkin
Foxchase, Phil'a, Pa
1/20/1917

The Great
Antichrist
The J
Rev. 16:1-21
Bowls, Boils, Blood, Heat, The Vials

Judgment Of The
(Under Antichrist)
Ez. 20:34-38,
Jer. 30:4-7

THE G

Paradise
"The Abode Of The Souls Of The "Righteous Dead" Until Christ's Resurrection. It Is Now Empty"

The
"Great Gu
Luke 16:19

Union Of The Souls And Bodies Of The Righteous Dead
First Resu
Christ

Fallen Angels To Judgment

Tartarus
"Prison Of The Fallen Angels"
2. Pet. 2:4, Jude 6

"The Unde
Abyss
Bottomles
Rev. 9:1-2,

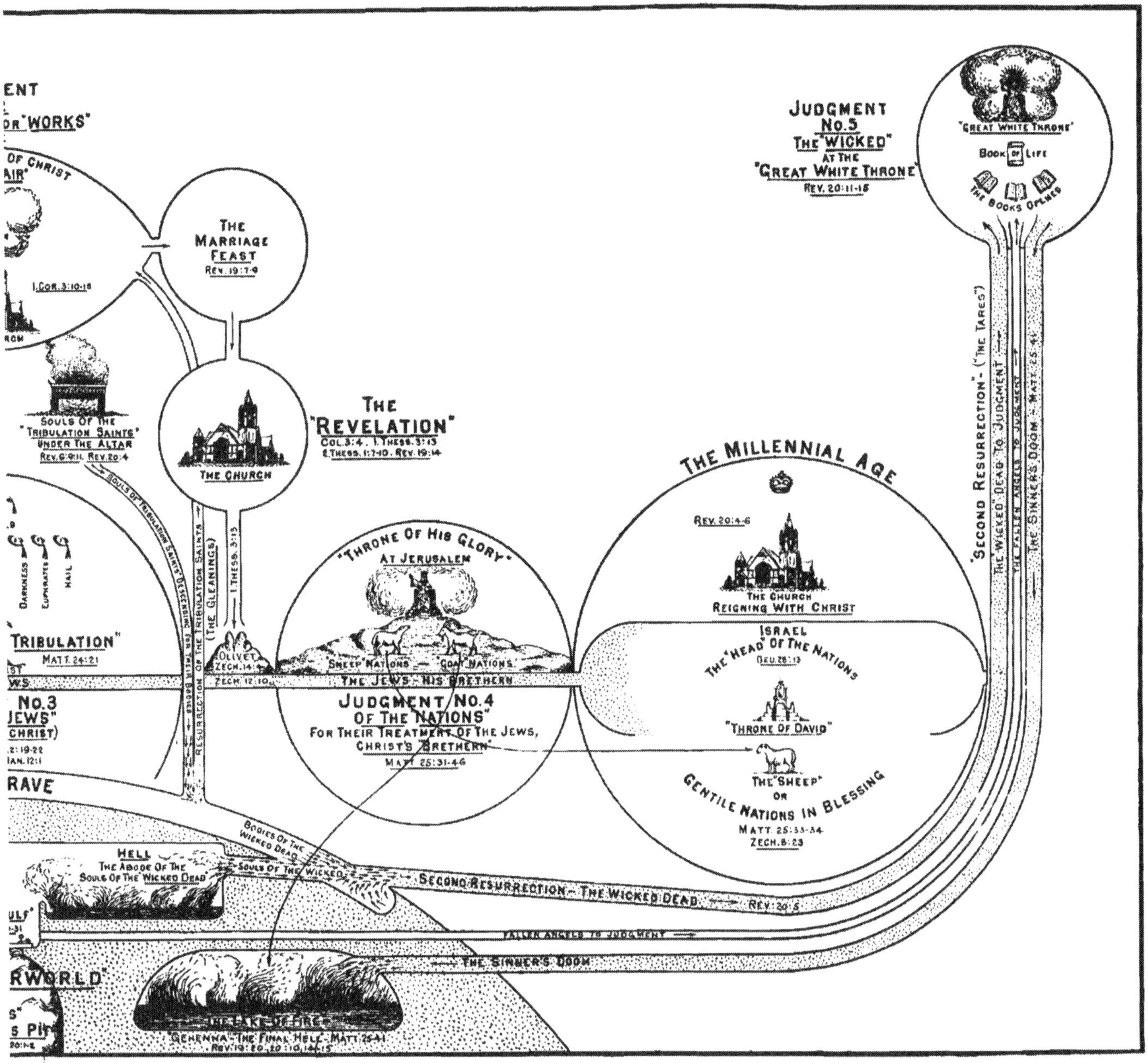

JUDGMENT
No.5
THE "WICKED"
AT THE
"GREAT WHITE THRONE"
REV. 20:11-15
"GREAT WHITE THRONE"
BOOK OF LIFE
THE BOOKS OPENED
THE MARRIAGE FEAST
REV. 19:7-9
1 COR. 3:10-15
SOULS OF THE "TRIBULATION SAINTS" UNDER THE ALTAR
REV. 6:9-11. REV. 20:4
THE CHURCH
THE "REVELATION"
COL. 3:4. 1 THESS. 3:13
2 THESS. 1:7-10. REV. 19:14
THE MILLENNIAL AGE
REV. 20:4-6
THE CHURCH
REIGNING WITH CHRIST
ISRAEL
THE "HEAD" OF THE NATIONS
DEU. 28:13
"THRONE OF DAVID"
THE "SHEEP" OR
GENTILE NATIONS IN BLESSING
MATT. 25:33-34
ZECH. 8:23
"THRONE OF HIS GLORY"
AT JERUSALEM
"SHEEP" NATIONS — "GOAT" NATIONS
OLIVET
ZECH. 14:4
ZECH. 12:10
THE JEWS - HIS BRETHERN
JUDGMENT No.4
OF THE "NATIONS"
FOR THEIR TREATMENT OF THE JEWS, CHRIST'S "BRETHERN"
MATT. 25:31-46
1 THESS. 3:13
(THE GLEANINGS)
RESURRECTION OF THE TRIBULATION SAINTS
"TRIBULATION"
MATT. 24:21
DARKNESS
EUPHRATES
HAIL
RAVE
HELL
THE ABODE OF THE SOULS OF THE WICKED DEAD
BODIES OF THE WICKED DEAD
SOULS OF THE WICKED
SECOND RESURRECTION — THE WICKED DEAD
REV. 20:5
FALLEN ANGELS TO JUDGMENT
THE SINNER'S DOOM
THE LAKE OF FIRE
GEHENNA - THE FINAL HELL - MATT. 25:41
REV. 19:20. 20:10, 14-15
"SECOND RESURRECTION" - ("THE TARES")
THE "WICKED" DEAD TO JUDGMENT
THE FALLEN ANGELS TO JUDGMENT
THE SINNERS DOOM - MATT. 25:41

"Verily, verily, I say unto you, He that heareth my word, and believeth on Him that sent me,

HATH EVERLASTING LIFE

and shall not come into condemnation (Judgment) but

IS PASSED

From Death Unto Life."

John 5:24.

The "Believer's" Judgment for Sin then is **PAST**, and was settled at the Cross.

But we must not forget that the Judgment of the Believer is threefold.

1. As a "Sinner."
2. As a "Son."
3. As a "Servant."

As we have already seen his Judgment as a "Sinner" is **Past**. Let us look at his judgment

2. As a "Son."

As soon as the sinner accepts Christ as his personal Saviour that settles the "Sin" question for him. For if our iniquities are laid on Him (Jesus), then they are not on Us. Isa. 53:5, 6. But the "Sin" question, and the "Sins" question are two different things. Christ died on the Cross to atone for "sin," to pay the penalty of Adam's disobedience in the Garden of Eden. "Sin" is that tendency in mankind to do wrong which we call "Natural Depravity." We do not get rid of this "tendency" by the "New Birth," but we get a "counteracting force" called the "New Nature." We become a "dual personality," composed of the "Old" and "New Natures," and which shall predominate depends on which we feed and which we starve. This explains the "warfare" that Paul describes as his experience, after his conversion, in Rom. 7:1-25. This warfare will continue until the "Old" nature is eradicated at death.

"Sins" are the outward acts of wrong-doing that we commit as the result of our tendency to sin. These sins must be put away daily by "confession."

"My little children, these things write I unto you, that ye sin not. And if any man sin, we have an 'Advocate' with the Father, Jesus Christ the righteous." 1 John 2:1.

"If we confess our sins, He is faithful and just to forgive us our sins, and to cleanse us from all unrighteousness." 1 John 1:9.

Our Judgment as "Sons" is for "unconfessed sins." The punishment is chastisement. This explains much of the chastisement of Christians, and should show them that they are "Sons" and not "Bastards." Heb. 12:5-11. Paul says—

"If we would 'judge ourselves' we should not be judged. But when we are chastened of the Lord, that we should not be condemned (Judged) with the world." 1 Cor. 11:31, 32.

Our duty then as "Sons" is to "self-judge" ourselves daily, "confess our sins," and so avert the chastisement of our Heavenly Father.

3. As a Servant.

This leads us to—

Judgment No. 2.

1. Subjects—Believers as to "WORKS."
2. Time—After The Church is caught out.
3. Place—"Judgment Seat of Christ" (in the Air).
4. Basis of Judgment—Their "WORKS."
5. Result—Reward or Loss.

This Judgment is **FUTURE**.

"We must all appear before the 'Judgment Seat of Christ,' that every one may receive the things 'done in the body' according to that he hath done, whether it be 'good' or 'bad' (worthless)." 2 Cor. 5:10.

The pronoun "We" occurs 26 times in the chapter, and in every instance it means the Believer, and the Epistle is addressed to the "Church" and "Saints" at Corinth, so the Judgment here spoken of is for Believers "only." The "Time" of this Judgment is when the Lord comes (1 Cor. 4:5), and the "Place" is "in the air" (1 Thess. 4:17) and before the Judgment Seat of Christ.

It will not be a Judgment in the sense of a "trial" to see whether the judged are innocent (saved) or guilty (lost), for it is a Judgment of the "saved only." It will be like the Judges' stand at a Fair, or Race Track, where rewards are distributed to the successful contestants. Paul describes such a scene in 1 Cor. 9:24-27.

It is not a Judgment for sin, but for "works." This Judgment is described in 1 Cor. 3:11-15.

"Other foundation can no man lay than that is laid, which is Jesus Christ. Now if any man build upon this foundation **gold, silver, precious stones** (valuable building stones, as marble, etc.), **wood, hay, stubble**; every man's 'Work' shall be made manifest; for the 'Day' (Judgment Day) shall declare it, because it shall be revealed by 'fire,' and the fire shall try every man's 'work' of what sort it is. If any man's work 'abide' which he hath built there upon he shall receive a 'reward.' If any man's work shall be 'burned' he shall suffer 'loss;' but 'he himself shall be saved;' yet so as by fire."

The result of this Judgment is "reward" or "loss." All our "bad" and "dead works," represented by the wood, hay and stubble, will be consumed, and only our "good works" shall remain. There is much which passes for Christian service which is merely human and secular, and does not count in our eternal reward. For those who deserve a "reward" it will be

The Crowning Day.

After the Grecian games were all over the runners, wrestlers, and successful contestants assembled before the "Bema," or Judges' stand, which was an elevated seat on which the Umpire sat, and the winners received a "corruptible crown" of "laurel leaves." Some had no reward, they had lost the "Victor's Crown." But while there was no reward there was no punishment, they were not cast out.

The New Testament speaks of Five Crowns.

1. The Crown of "LIFE."

This is the "Martyr's" crown, and is mentioned twice.

"Blessed is the man that endureth temptation (testing), for when he is 'tried' (at the Judgment Seat of Christ), he shall receive the 'Crown of Life' which the Lord hath promised to them that love Him." James 1:12.

"Fear none of those things which thou shalt suffer; behold, the Devil shall cast some of you into prison, that ye may be tried (tested) and ye shall have tribulation ten days; be thou faithful 'unto death,' and I will give thee a 'Crown of Life.'" Rev. 2:10

Notice it does not say "until" death, but "unto" death. They were not to recant but to remain faithful unto a martyr's death. To recant was to lose the crown. This refers to the martyrs of the Tribulation Period.

2. The Crown of "GLORY."

This is the "Elder's" or "Pastor's" crown, given by the Chief Shepherd when He shall appear. But it is not for those who serve for "filthy lucre" or "lord it over God's heritage." I Pet. 5:2-4.

3. The Crown of "REJOICING."

This is the "Soul Winner's" crown. Those brought to Jesus by us will be our "crown of rejoicing" at His Coming. 1 Thess. 2:19, 20. Phil. 4:1.

4. The Crown of "RIGHTEOUSNESS"

This is the crown of those who "love His appearing" and will be given in "that day"—the Day of His Appearing. 2 Tim. 4:8.

5. The Crown "INCORRUPTIBLE."

This is the "Victor's" crown, and is for those who "keep under their body." 1 Cor. 9:25-27. Who do not yield to their fleshly lusts. Who do not permit themselves to be diverted from the Master's work by worldly amusements and pleasure, nor saturate their body with drugs.

If we do not want to be "ashamed at His Coming," 1 John 2:28, let us see to it that we keep our body "under" and so live that we shall secure a crown.

Judgment No. 3.

1. **Subjects**—The JEWS.
2. **Time**—"The Great Tribulation."
3. **Place**—Jerusalem and Vicinity.
4. **Basis of Judgment**—Rejection of the Godhead.
5. **Result**—Their Conversion and Reception of Christ as Their Messiah.

This Judgment is **FUTURE**.

While the Church is being judged at the Judgment Seat of Christ in the air, the Jews will be judged under Antichrist on the earth. The Jews are an "earthly" people; and as all the promises to them are "earthly," it follows that their Judgment must be of an "earthly" character. The basis of their Judgment is their "rejection of the Godhead." In the days of Samuel they rejected God the Father. 1 Sam. 8:7. In the days of Christ they rejected God the Son. Luke 23:18. In the days of Stephen they rejected God the Holy Spirit. Acts 7:51, 54-60. For their sin they have been scattered among the nations until the Times of the Gentiles are fulfilled. When the Times of the Gentiles are about to end the Jews will be gathered back to the Holy Land "unconverted," and caused to "pass under the rod." Ez. 20:34-38. They will be cast into God's **"Melting Pot"** (Ez. 22:19-22), and pass through an experience spoken of by Jeremiah and Daniel as the **"TIME OF JACOB'S TROUBLE."** Jer. 30:4-7. Dan. 12:1.

Christ calls it "The Great Tribulation," and He and Zechariah the Prophet associate it with the "Return of the Lord." Matt. 24:21-31. Zech. 14:1-11.

The human agent the Lord will use will be Antichrist, the awfulness of whose rule will be supplemented by the pouring out of the "Vials of God's wrath" upon the earth. Rev. 15:1, 5-8; 16:21. See the chapter on "The Tribulation."

The result of these terrible Judgments will be that the Jews will call in their misery upon the Lord. Zech. 12:10. Then Christ will come back to the Mt. of Olives (Zech. 14:3) and the Jews will look upon Him whom they "pierced" (Zech. 12:10), and a nation, the Jewish Nation, shall be "born (converted) in a day." Isa. 66:8. This will complete the Judgment of the Jews. See the chapter on the Jews.

Judgment No. 4.

1. **Subjects**—The Nations (Gentiles).
2. **Time**—The "Revelation of Christ."
3. **Place**—The "Throne of His Glory." On the Earth—"Valley of Jehoshaphat."
4. **Basis of Judgment**—Their Treatment of Christ's Brethren—The Jews.
5. **Result**—Some Nations "SAVED," Others "DESTROYED."

This Judgment is **FUTURE**.

The account of this Judgment is given in Matt. 25:31-46. The description of this Judgment, and of the one given in Rev. 20:11-15 are combined by many, and taken to teach the doctrine of a general Judgment. But when we compare them, they differ so widely, that it is evident that they do not describe the same event. What God has put asunder let no man join together. The following comparison will show the difference in the two accounts:

Matt. 25:31-46.	Rev. 20:11-15.
1. No Resurrection.	1. A Resurrection.
2. Living Nations Judged.	2. Dead Judged.
3. On the Earth. Joel 3:2.	3. Heaven and Earth Gone.
4. No Books Mentioned.	4. Books Opened.
5. Three Classes Named. "Sheep," "Goats," "Brethren."	5. One Class Named. "The Dead."
6. Time—Before the Millennium.	6. Time—After the Millennium.

This comparison reveals the fact that one of these Judgments is "on the earth," the other in the "heavens," and that they are separated by 1000 years.

The Greek word "ethnos" here translated "Nations," occurs 158 times in the New Testament. It is translated "Gentiles" 92 times, "Nation" or "Nations" 61 times, and "The Heathen" 5 times, but it is never in any instance (unless it be this) applied either to the "dead" or the "resurrected."

As this is a Judgment of nations only, the Jews cannot be in it, for they are not reckoned among the nations. Num. 23:9. And as the Church will be associated with Christ in this Judgment, for the "Saints" (the Church) shall judge the "World" (the Nations), (1 Cor. 6:2), the Church cannot be in this Judgment either. As we have seen the Church and the Jews have been already judged, so the "Judgment of the Nations" cannot be a general Judgment. Who then, is asked, are meant by the Sheep? Do they not represent the Righteous, and all the Righteous from the beginning of the world to the end of Time? And do not the Goats in like manner represent all the Wicked?

If the Sheep are the Righteous, and the Goats the Wicked, then who are the Brethren? If they are the "followers of Christ," as some claim, they should be classed with the Sheep. The Scriptures teach that the Righteous are saved by "faith," and the Wicked are lost because they "reject Christ," but in this Judgment scene the Sheep inherit a "Kingdom" and the Goats are commanded to "depart," because of their **treatment of the Brethren.**

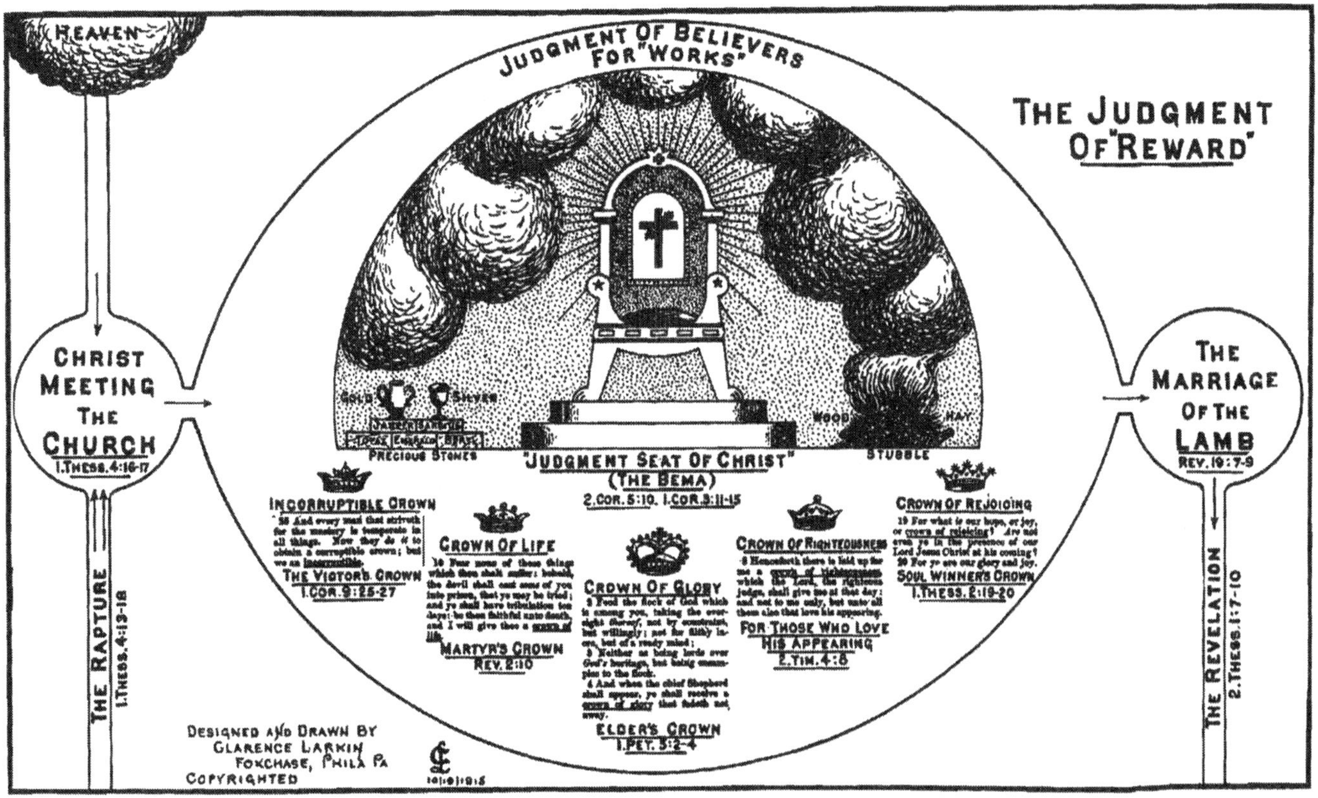
HEAVEN
JUDGMENT OF BELIEVERS FOR "WORKS"
THE JUDGMENT OF "REWARD"
CHRIST MEETING THE CHURCH
1.THESS.4:16-17
THE RAPTURE
1.THESS.4:13-18
GOLD
SILVER
PRECIOUS STONES
WOOD
HAY
STUBBLE
"JUDGMENT SEAT OF CHRIST"
(THE BEMA)
2.COR.5:10. 1.COR.3:11-15
THE MARRIAGE OF THE LAMB
REV.19:7-9
THE REVELATION
2.THESS.1:7-10
INCORRUPTIBLE CROWN
THE VICTOR'S CROWN
1.COR.9:25-27
CROWN OF LIFE
MARTYR'S CROWN
REV.2:10
CROWN OF GLORY
ELDER'S CROWN
1.PET.5:2-4
CROWN OF RIGHTEOUSNESS
FOR THOSE WHO LOVE HIS APPEARING
2.TIM.4:8
CROWN OF REJOICING
SOUL WINNER'S CROWN
1.THESS.2:19-20
DESIGNED AND DRAWN BY
CLARENCE LARKIN
FOXCHASE, PHILA PA
COPYRIGHTED
CL
1918

All the confusion is caused by trying to make a Judgment of "nations" mean a Judgment of "individuals." The Sheep represent one class of Nations, and the Goats another class, while the Brethren represent the Jews (Christ's brethren).

We must bear in mind the **time** and **place** of this Judgment. The **time** is at the "Revelation of Christ," when He comes to set up His "Millennial Kingdom" on the earth. The **place** is the "Valley of Jehoshaphat" in the vicinity of Jerusalem.

"For, behold, in **those days**, and in **that time, when I shall bring again the captivity** of Judah and Jerusalem, I will also gather **ALL NATIONS**, and will bring them down into the '**Valley of Jehoshaphat,**' and will plead with them there for **MY PEOPLE** and for my heritage **ISRAEL**, whom they have scattered among the Nations, and parted my land." Joel 3:1, 2.

This prophecy clearly states that there is to be a "Judgment of Nations" on the earth in the "Valley of Jehoshaphat" at the time of the restoration of the Jews to their own land, and that the basis of Judgment is the treatment by the nations of Christ's brethren—**The Jews.**

During the "Tribulation Period" the Nations that treat the Jewish People kindly, feeding and clothing them, and visiting them in prison, will be the "Sheep Nations," while those who neglect to do so will be the "Goat Nations."

At the "Judgment of Nations" the King (Christ) will say to the "Sheep Nations," inasmuch as ye have been kind to My brethren (the Jews), "Come, ye blessed of my Father, inherit the Kingdom prepared for you from the foundation of the world." This Kingdom is the "Millennial Kingdom" that the "Sheep Nations" **as Nations** will "inherit" and possess during the Millennium. And as they are to be among the "saved nations" of the New Earth (Rev. 21:24) it can be said of them that they, or at least the righteous individuals of them, shall enter into life eternal. Matt. 25:46.

Christ's sentence upon the "Goat Nations" will be—"Depart from Me, ye cursed, into **everlasting fire**, prepared for the Devil and his angels," and "these shall go away into **everlasting punishment**." The "Goat Nations" will at once be destroyed **as Nations**, not one of them shall get into the Millennium, and the wicked individuals that compose them will perish and be eternally lost.

Judgment No. 5.

1. Subjects—The Wicked Dead.
2. Time—During the Renovation of the Earth by Fire.
3. Place—Before "The Great White Throne."
4. Basis of Judgment—Their "Works."
5. Result—Cast Into the "Lake of Fire."

This Judgment is **FUTURE.**

The account of it is given in Rev. 20:11-15. It will take place at the close of the Millennium a 1000 years after the Judgment of the Nations, and before the "Great White Throne."

The "Great White Throne" will not be on the earth, for the "Great White Throne Judgment" will take place during the renovation of the earth by fire, for the "renovation" of this Earth is reserved or kept until the time of that Judgment, which Peter calls "The **Day of Judgment and Perdition of Ungodly Men**" (2 Pet. 3:7), because the Judgment of the "Great White Throne" is the Judgment of the **wicked dead.**

All the Righteous dead will arise at the First Resurrection. If any Righteous die between the First Resurrection and the Resurrection of the "wicked" or Second Resurrection, they will rise with the wicked dead at that Resurrection. The words—"Whosoever was not found written in the Book of Life (vs. 15), implies that there will be "some," probably very few, Righteous at the Second Resurrection.

At the close of the Millennium and just before the renovation of the earth by fire, the living Righteous will probably be translated, and the living Wicked or Ungodly will be destroyed in the flames that will consume the earth's atmosphere and exterior surface.

The Wicked or Ungodly will not be judged to see whether they are entitled to Eternal Life, but to ascertain the "degree" of their punishment. The sad feature of this Judgment will be that there will be many kind and lovable people there who were not saved, and who will be classed among the "ungodly" because they rejected Christ as a Saviour. The "Books" will be opened in which the "Recording Angel" has kept a record of every person's life, and they will be judged every man according to his "works." Some will be sentenced to a more severe punishment than others, but none will escape. The worst of all is, that those who were not so bad must spend eternity with the ungodly, and that in the "Lake of Fire." Their punishment includes the **second death,** which means that they shall lose their resurrection bodies, in which they were judged, and become "disembodied spirits" again, and so exist in the "Lake of Fire" **FOREVER.**

The "Fallen Angels" (not the Devil's angels), who are "reserved in everlasting chains under darkness" will be judged at this time, which Jude calls the Judgment of the "Great Day." Jude 6. When this Judgment is over the Devil and his angels, and all the ungodly, will have been consigned to the "Lake of Fire," and the Universe purged of all evil, and righteousness shall reign supreme on the New Earth.

XVIII

SATAN

There are many who deny the existence of Satan. They claim that what we call Satan is only a "principle of evil." That this "evil" is a sort of "malaria," an intangible thing like disease germs that floats about in the atmosphere and attacks people's hearts under certain conditions. The existence of Satan cannot be determined by the opinions of men. The only source of information is the Bible. That is the reason why Satan tries to discredit the Word of God. He is not a "principle of evil" he is a—Person.

"Be sober, be vigilant; because your adversary the Devil, as a 'roaring lion,' walketh about, seeking whom he may devour." 1 Pet. 5:8.

He "walketh," he "roareth," he is to be "chained." Rev. 20:1-3. These could not be said of a "principle of evil." He has many names or aliases—"Satan," "Devil," "Beelzebub," "Belial," "Adversary," "Dragon," "Serpent." He is mentioned by one or the other of these names 174 times in the Bible.

He is a great "Celestial Potentate." He is

"**The Prince of the Powers of the Air.**"
Eph. 2:2.

"**The God of this World**" (Age.)
2 Cor. 4:4.

SATAN
"The God of this World"

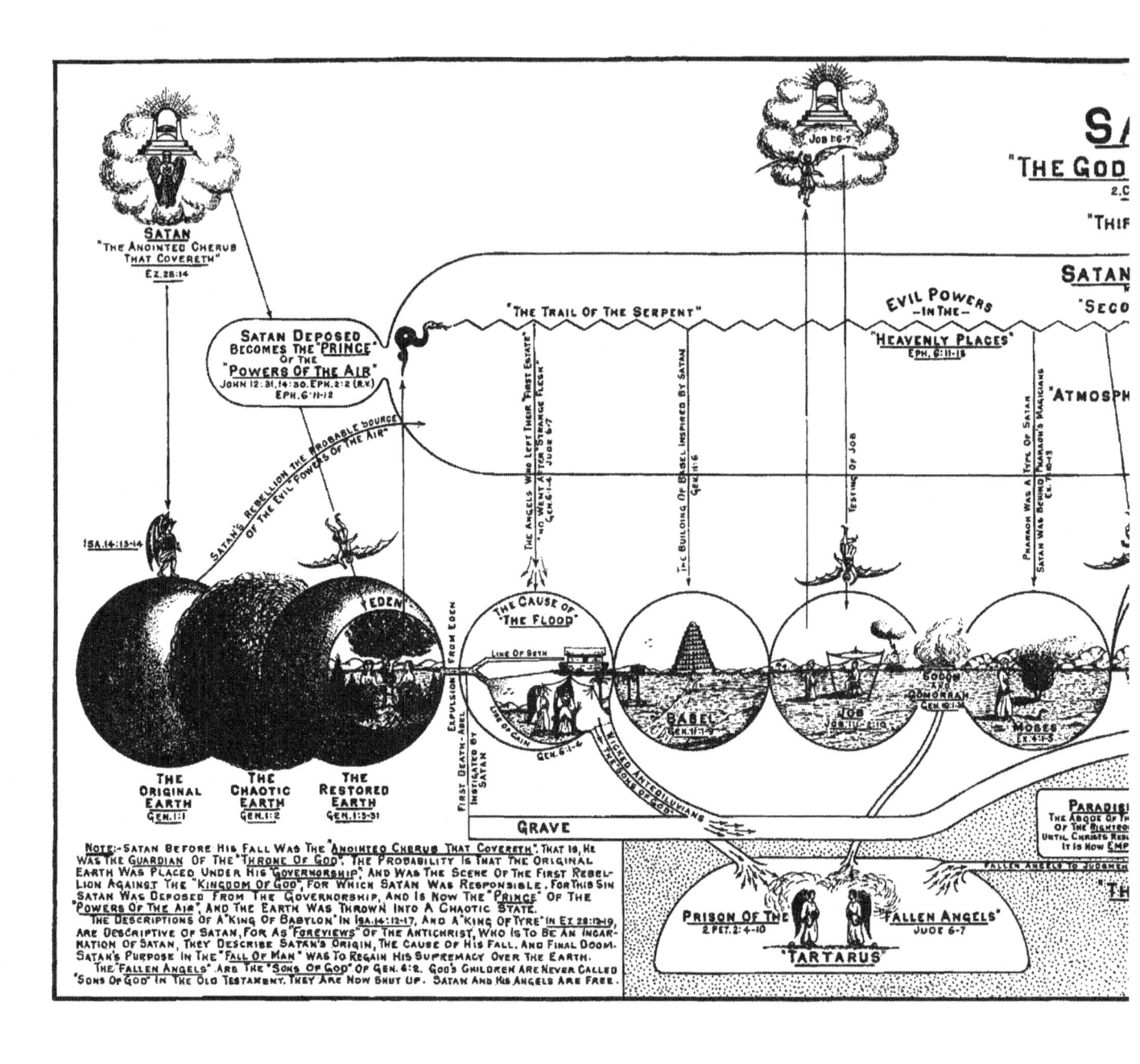

SATAN — "The Anointed Cherub That Covereth" Ez. 28:14

Satan Deposed Becomes the "Prince" of the "Powers of the Air" John 12:31, 14:30, Eph. 2:2 (R.V.) Eph. 6:11-12

"The Trail of the Serpent"

Evil Powers — in the — "Heavenly Places" Eph. 6:11-18

Satan's Rebellion the Probable Source of the Evil Powers of the Air

The Angels Who Left Their First Estate Who Went After Strange Flesh Jude 6-7

The Building of Babel Inspired by Satan Gen. 11:6

Testing of Job

Pharaoh was a Type of Satan — Satan was Behind Pharaoh's Magicians Ex. 7:10-13

Isa. 14:13-14

First Death — Abel Instigated by Satan

Expulsion from Eden

The Cause of The Flood

Line of Seth — Line of Cain Gen. 6:1-4

The Original Earth Gen. 1:1

The Chaotic Earth Gen. 1:2

The Restored Earth Gen. 1:3-31

EDEN

BABEL Gen. 11:7

JOB Gen. 1:1-10

SODOM and GOMORRAH Gen. 19:1

MOSES Ex. 14:15

Wicked Antediluvians — Sons of God

GRAVE

Prison of the 2 Pet. 2:4-10 — "Fallen Angels" Jude 6-7
"TARTARUS"

PARADISE — The Abode of the ... of the Righteous Until Christ's Res... It is Now Empty

Fallen Angels to Judgment

NOTE: — Satan Before His Fall was the "Anointed Cherub That Covereth". That is, He was the Guardian of the "Throne of God". The Probability is that the Original Earth was Placed Under His Governorship, and was the Scene of the First Rebellion Against the "Kingdom of God", For Which Satan was Responsible. For This Sin Satan was Deposed From the Governorship, and is Now the "Prince" of the "Powers of the Air", and the Earth was Thrown Into a Chaotic State.

The Descriptions of a "King of Babylon" in Isa. 14:12-17, and a "King of Tyre" in Ez. 28:12-19, are Descriptive of Satan, For as "Foreviews" of the Antichrist, Who is to Be an Incarnation of Satan, They Describe Satan's Origin, The Cause of His Fall, and Final Doom. Satan's Purpose in the "Fall of Man" was to Regain His Supremacy Over the Earth.

The "Fallen Angels" Are the "Sons of God" of Gen. 6:2. God's Children Are Never Called "Sons of God" in the Old Testament. They Are Now Shut Up. Satan and His Angels Are Free.

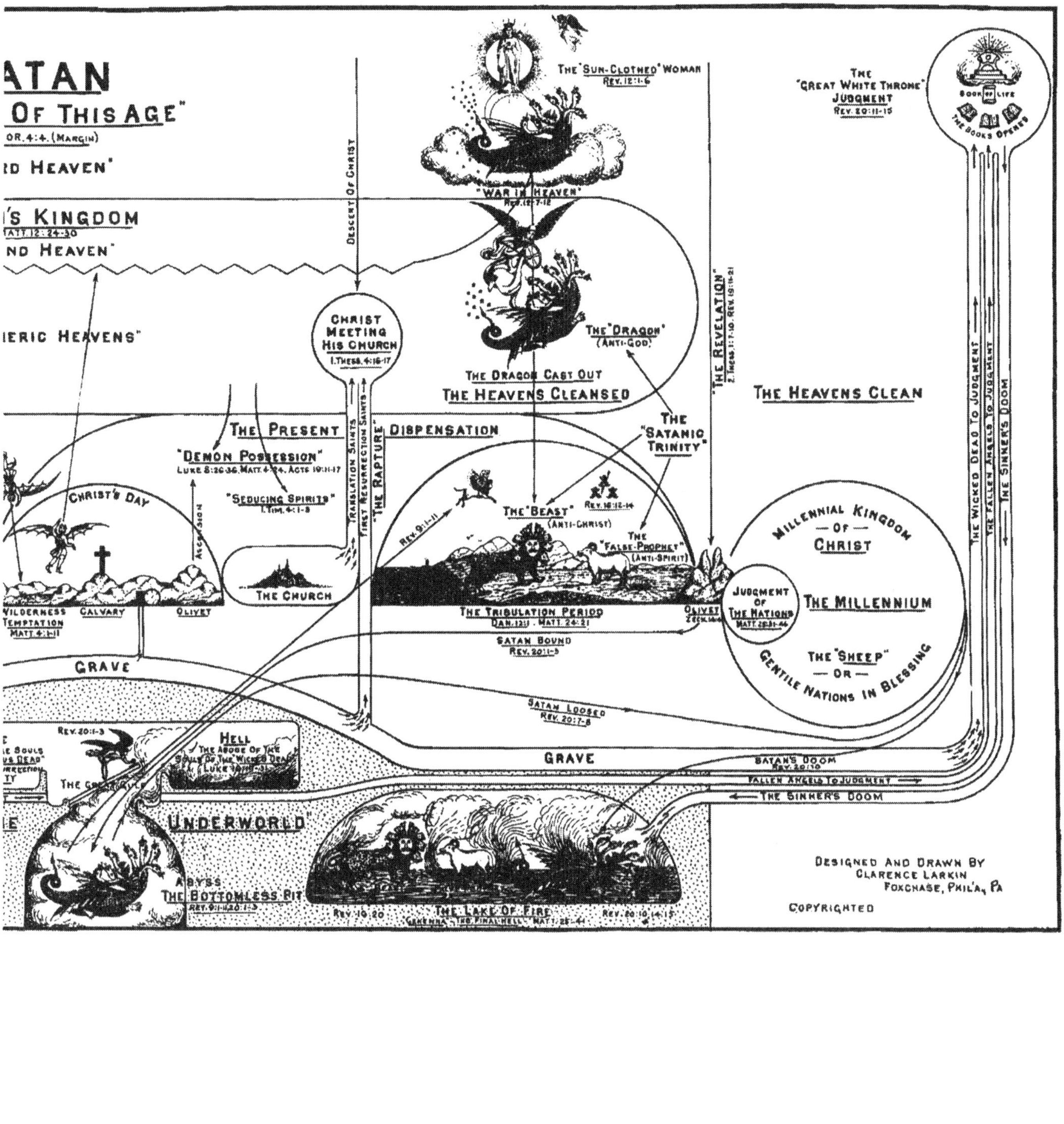

ATAN
OF THIS AGE"
OR. 4:4. (MARGIN)
RD HEAVEN"
'S KINGDOM
MATT. 12: 24-30
ND HEAVEN"
IERIC HEAVENS"
THE "SUN-CLOTHED" WOMAN
REV. 12:1-6
"WAR IN HEAVEN"
REV. 12:7-12
DESCENT OF CHRIST
CHRIST MEETING HIS CHURCH
I. THESS. 4:16-17
THE "DRAGON"
(ANTI-GOD)
THE DRAGON CAST OUT
THE HEAVENS CLEANSED
"THE REVELATION"
II. THESS. 1:7-10. REV. 19:11-21
THE "GREAT WHITE THRONE" JUDGMENT
REV. 20:11-15
BOOK OF LIFE
THE BOOKS OPENED
THE HEAVENS CLEAN
THE PRESENT DISPENSATION
"DEMON POSSESSION"
LUKE 8:26-36. MATT. 4:24. ACTS 19:11-17
"SEDUCING SPIRITS"
I. TIM. 4:1-3
CHRIST'S DAY
ASCENSION
TRANSLATION SAINTS
FIRST RESURRECTION SAINTS
"THE RAPTURE"
THE "SATANIC TRINITY"
THE "BEAST"
(ANTI-CHRIST)
REV. 16:13-14
REV. 9:1-11
THE "FALSE-PROPHET"
(ANTI-SPIRIT)
MILLENNIAL KINGDOM — OF — CHRIST
JUDGMENT OF THE NATIONS
MATT. 25:31-46
THE MILLENNIUM
THE "SHEEP" — OR — GENTILE NATIONS IN BLESSING
WILDERNESS TEMPTATION
MATT. 4:1-11
CALVARY
OLIVET
THE CHURCH
THE TRIBULATION PERIOD
DAN. 12:1. MATT. 24:21
OLIVET
ZECH. 14:4
SATAN BOUND
REV. 20:1-3
GRAVE
SATAN LOOSED
REV. 20:7-8
GRAVE
SATAN'S DOOM
REV. 20:10
FALLEN ANGELS TO JUDGMENT
THE SINNER'S DOOM
THE WICKED DEAD TO JUDGMENT
THE FALLEN ANGELS TO JUDGMENT
THE SINNER'S DOOM
REV. 20:1-3
HELL
THE ABODE OF THE SOULS OF THE WICKED DEAD
LUKE 16:19-31
UNDERWORLD"
ABYSS
THE BOTTOMLESS PIT
REV. 9:1-11. 20:1-3
THE LAKE OF FIRE
GEHENNA — THE FINAL HELL — MATT. 25:41
REV. 19:20
REV. 20:10. 14:15
DESIGNED AND DRAWN BY
CLARENCE LARKIN
FOXCHASE, PHIL'A, PA
COPYRIGHTED

He is the "God" not of the earth, for that belongs to its Maker—God. "The earth is the Lord's and the fulness thereof." Satan is the God of the "World Systems" of the habitable earth. These "World Systems" embrace business, society, politics, and religion. Satan is the Ruler of the "Powers of Darkness" of the "Spirit World," (Eph. 6:11, 12), and his position is so exalted that even Michael the Archangel dare not insult him. Jude 9. So mighty is he that man cannot successfully resist him without Divine help.

I. His Origin.

This is more or less shrouded in mystery. One thing is certain, he is a "created being," and that of the most exalted type. He was before his fall

"The Anointed Cherub That Covereth."

That is, he was the guardian or protector of the "Throne of God." He was perfect in all his ways from the day that he was created, until iniquity was found in him. In him was the "fulness of wisdom," and the "perfection of beauty," but it was his "beauty" that caused the pride that was his downfall. He was clothed in a garment that was covered with the most rare and precious gems, the sardius, topaz, diamond, beryl, onyx, jasper, sapphire, emerald, carbuncle, all woven in with gold. He dwelt in Eden, the "Garden of God."

This probably refers not to the earthly Eden, but to the "Paradise of God" on high, for Satan dwelt on the "Holy Mount of God." All this we learn from Ezek. 28:11-19, where the Prophet has a "foreview" of the Antichrist under the title of the "King of Tyrus," and as Antichrist is to be an incarnation of Satan, the Prophet here describes Satan's original glory from which he fell. There never has been as yet such a King of Tyrus as is here described.

The cause of Satan's fall is given in Isa. 14:12-20. He is there called—

Lucifer, Son of the Morning.

This was his glorious title when he was created, and this world of ours was made, at which time—

"The 'Morning Stars,' (probably other glorious created ruling beings like himself), sang together, and all the 'Sons of God,' (angels), shouted for joy." Job 38:7.

It is well to note that the one here called "Lucifer, Son of the Morning," is in verse four, (Isa. 14:4), also called the "King of Babylon." As there never has been a King of Babylon like the one here described, the description must be that of a "future" King of Babylon. And as Antichrist is to have for his Capital City Babylon rebuilt," this is probably a "foreview" by the Prophet of Antichrist, as indwelt by "Lucifer," or "Satan," in that day when he shall be "King of Babylon."

Some think that when this world was created and fit for habitation, Satan was placed in charge of it, and it was then, as Isaiah declares, that Satan said in his heart—

"I will ascend into heaven, I will exalt my throne above the 'Stars of God' (other ruling powers); I will sit also upon the Mount of the Congregation, in the sides of the North. I will ascend above the heights of the clouds; I will be like

The MOST HIGH:"

and that it was for this presumptuous act that the "Pre-Adamite World" became a chaos, and "without form and void," as described in Gen. 1:2.

This would justify the claim of Satan that this world belongs to him, and that he had the right and power to transfer the "kingdoms of this world" to Christ, if He would only acknowledge Satan's supremacy. (Matt. 4:8, 9.) And it accounts for the persistent war Satan is waging against the Almighty to retain his possession of the earth.

II. His Present Location.

The common notion is that Satan and his angels are imprisoned in Hell. This is not true. The angels described in 2 Pet. 2:4, and Jude 6, as having left their "first estate," and being "reserved in everlasting chains under darkness," are not Satan's angels. They are a special class of angels whose sin caused the Flood. They are the "Spirits in Prison" of whom Peter speaks in I Pet. 3:18-20. See the chapter on "Rightly Dividing the Word," under the cause of the Flood. Satan and his angels are at liberty. We read in the first and second chapters of Job that it was the custom in Job's day for the "Sons of God" (angels), to appear at stated times in the presence of God to give an account of their stewardship, and that Satan always appeared with them.

When the Lord said to Satan—"Whence comest thou?" he replied, "From going to and fro in the earth and from walking up and down in it." Job 1:7; 2:2. Satan then was at liberty "on the earth," and had "access to God," and was "not cast out of Heaven" in Job's day, B. C. 2000. Milton in his book "Paradise Lost" describes Satan as having been cast out of Heaven in the time of Adam and Eve, and bases his description on Rev. 12:7-12. But as the Book of Revelation is a prophecy of "Things to Come," and that were all "future" in the Apostle John's day, Satan had not been cast out of heaven up to that time, A. D. 96, and as he has not been cast out since, he must still be at liberty in the heavenlies and on the earth.

III. His Kingdom.

Satan is a King, and has a Kingdom.

"If Satan cast out Satan he is divided against himself; how shall then his 'kingdom' stand." Matt. 12:24-30.

"We wrestle not against flesh and blood, but against Principalities, against Powers, against the Rulers of the Darkness of this World (Age), against Spiritual Wickedness in High Places, (the Heavenlies)." Eph. 6:12.

From this we see that his Kingdom consists of "Principalities," "Powers," "Age Rulers of Darkness," and "Wicked Spirits in the Heavenlies."

These "Principalities" are ruled by "Princes," who control certain nations of our earth, as in the days of Daniel the Prophet, when a heavenly messenger was sent to Daniel, but was hindered "three weeks" from reaching him by the

"Prince of the Kingdom of Persia,"

Satan's ruling "Prince of Persia," until Michael the Archangel came to his rescue. Dan. 10:10-14.

The subjects of Satan's Kingdom are—

1. **Angels.** Not the angels that kept not their first estate and who are reserved in everlasting chains under darkness unto the Judgment of the Great Day, (Jude 6), but angels who are at liberty, and are now with Satan in the heavenlies (Rev. 12:9), and who, with him, are to be cast into the "Lake of Fire" prepared for the Devil and his angels. Matt. 25:41. Rev. 20:10.

2. Demons. There is but one Devil. Where the word "devils" occurs in the New Testament we should substitute the word "demons." These demons are a race or order of "bodiless spirits," supposed by many to be the bodiless spirits of the inhabitants of the Pre-Adamite Earth, who seek to re-embody themselves by taking up their abode in human beings. This we know they can do under certain conditions. Demon possession was common in Christ's day.

These demons are wicked, unclean, vicious, and have power to derange both mind and body. Matt. 12:22; 15:22; Luke 4:35; 8:26-36; 9:42. They are the "Familiar Spirits" and "Wizards" of the Old Testament, and the "Seducing Spirits" of whom Paul warned Timothy. 1 Tim. 4:1.

3. Unregenerated Human Beings. All unregenerated human beings are the subjects of Satan. Jesus called the "Tares" the "Children of the Wicked One," (Matt. 13:38), and He told the Pharisaical Jews that their father was the Devil. John 8:44.

IV. His Methods.

1. He Is the Deceiver of the World.

By the "World" is meant all those who belong to the "Satanic System." All those who are entangled in Satan's mesh.

"And we know that we are of God, and the whole World (the Satanic System), lieth in the Wicked One, (Satan)." 1 John 5:19, R. V.

Satan deceives by "blinding" the eyes of the world.

"If our Gospel is hid, it is hid to them that 'are lost'; in whom the 'God of this World' (Satan), hath blinded the minds of them which believe not, lest the light of the glorious Gospel of Christ, who is the image of God, should shine unto them." 2 Cor. 4:3, 4.

To this end Satan has his preachers who preach "another gospel." Gal. 1:6-9. That gospel is the "doctrine of devils." 1 Tim. 4:1.

He is the instigator of

"The Great Apostasy."

Peter, speaking of the "latter times" says—

"There shall be false teachers among you, who privily shall bring in 'Damnable Heresies,' even denying the Lord that bought them, and bring upon themselves swift destruction. And many shall follow their 'Pernicious Way,' by reason of whom the 'WAY OF TRUTH' shall be evil spoken of." 2 Pet. 2:1, 2.

These "false teachers" are to be seen on every hand. They are those who deny the "Virgin Birth," "Deity," "Bodily Resurrection" and "Personal Premillennial Return" of the Lord Jesus Christ.

Satan is very subtle in his methods, and if it were possible he would deceive the very elect. He knows all the great Scripture subjects that are of universal interest to humanity, and he is too wise to attack them openly, so he adulterates them with false doctrine. He has tried to rob the Church of her "Blessed Hope" of the Lord's return, by mixing with it a lot of false teaching and "time setting" as seen in "Millerism," "Seventh Day Adventism" and "Millennial Dawnism." To prevent mankind from turning to the Lord for healing, he has invented the systems of "Christian Science" and "New Thought."

To satisfy the craving of the human mind to know what is going on in the Spirit World, Satan invented "Spiritualism." And when interest in it began to wane he revived it under the name of "Psychical Research." This system has existed from the earliest ages and has the unqualified condemnation of the Scriptures.

"There shall not be found among you any one that . . . . useth divination, or an observer of times, or an enchanter, or a witch, or a charmer, or a

Consulter With Familiar Spirits,

or a wizard, or a necromancer. For all that do these things are an abomination unto the Lord." Deu. 18:10-12.

Spiritualism is only another name for "Demonism," and all professed impersonations are either counterfeit, or demonic. Christian Science teaches that there is such a thing as "Malicious Animal Magnetism" by which one person may afflict another. It is only another name for "Diabolism." Those who dabble in "Spiritualism" or "Psychical Research," are liable to have their "understanding darkened" and come under the power of demons.

Satan seeing that he could not stamp out the Church by violence and persecution, has changed his tactics and is now trying to seduce her into conformity to the world, and to try to better an "Age" that God has doomed to destruction. His present purpose is to build up a "magnificent civilization," and he has deceived the Church into believing that it can bring in the "Millennium," without Christ, by the Betterment of Society.

His hope is that the "Gospel of Social Service" will take the place of the "Gospel of Grace," and by diverting the attention of Christian people to "secondary" things, they will neglect the primary work of soul saving, and thus delay the evangelization of the world, and postpone the Return of the Lord, and his own confinement in the Bottomless Pit.

2. He Is the Adversary of God's People.

The warfare between "Good" and "Evil," as recorded in the Bible from Gen. 3:15 to Rev. 20:10, is most intensely interesting reading. Satan tempts Eve. She eats, and Adam with her. They are both cast out of the Garden. First victory scored by Satan. Satan enters Cain. The result Abel is murdered. Victory number two for Satan. The "Sons of God" at Satan's instigation marry the "daughters of men." Result the Flood. Victory number three for Satan. Noah delivered from the Flood is tempted to drink, yields, and a curse falls on Ham. Victory number four for Satan. The people multiply and Satan fills their hearts with pride and presumption. The Tower of Babel is built, the result the "Confusion of Tongues," and the unity of the race broken up. Victory number five for Satan.

Then God calls Abraham through whom the promised "Seed of the Woman," the Second Adam, should come who was to bruise Satan's head. Now the fight begins in earnest. We have only space to indicate it. First Satan closes Sarah's womb. Then when Isaac is born he seeks to have him slain by his father's hand on Mt. Moriah. He makes enmity between Esau and Jacob, hoping that the tragedy of Cain and Abel would be repeated. Then he causes Potiphar's wife to tempt Joseph, seeking to get him out of the way. When the time came for Moses, the deliverer of the Children of Israel, to be born, he puts it in the heart of Pharaoh to order that all male Hebrew children shall be destroyed at birth.

But the story is too long. The sin of David was Satan's work, and at one time the "seed royal" was narrowed down to one child. 2 Chron. 2:4-17; 22:10-12.

When the time came that Christ was born, it was Satan who prompted Herod to destroy all the male children at Bethlehem under two years of age. It was Satan who tried to overcome Christ when weakened by fasting in the Wilderness, and who suggested that Christ throw Himself down from the Pinnacle of the Temple. The attempt of the people to throw Him from the hilltop at Nazareth, and the two storms on Galilee were all attempts of Satan to destroy Christ. And when foiled in these Satan renewed the fight through Priests and Pharisees, and succeeded at last in getting Judas to sell his Master.

Then amid the shades of Gethsemane he sought to kill Christ by physical weakness before He could reach the Cross. When Christ was crucified Satan thought he had conquered, but when Christ rose from the dead Satan's rage knew no bounds. In all probability Satan and his angels contested the Ascension of Christ, and the history of the Christian Church is but one long story of the "Irrepressible Conflict" between Satan and God's people. Paul writing to the Thessalonians said:

> "We would have come unto you, even I Paul, once and again, but **SATAN hindered us.**" 1 Thess. 2:18.

Even Paul's "thorn in the flesh" was the "Messenger of Satan" to buffet him.

V. His Expulsion From the Heavenlies.

As we have seen Satan still has his abode in the "Heavenlies" and has access to God. But the time is coming when he shall be cast out of the "Heavenlies." It is described in Rev. 12:7-17.

> "And there was war in Heaven. Michael and his angels fought against the 'Dragon,' and the 'Dragon' fought and his angels, and prevailed not; neither was their place found any more in Heaven. And the '**Great Dragon**' was cast out, that old '**Serpent,**' called the '**Devil,**' and '**Satan,**' which deceiveth the whole world: he was cast out **Into the Earth** and his angels were cast out with him.
>
> "And I heard a loud voice saying in heaven, **now is come Salvation,** and **Strength,** and the **Kingdom of God,** and the **Power of His Christ; for the Accuser of Our Brethren IS CAST DOWN,** which accused them before our God day and night."

While Satan has been the "Accuser of the Brethren" in all **Ages,** the context shows that reference is here made to the "Jewish Remnant," (the brethren of Christ), who during the first three and one-half years of the "Tribulation Period" (for Satan is cast out in the Middle of the "Last Week," or Tribulation Period), pass through great persecution, and die as "martyrs." They are referred to in Rev. 6:9-11 as the "souls of them that were slain for the Word of God," and we are here told (Rev. 12:11) that they overcame by the "Blood of the Lamb," and the "word of their testimony," and died as "martyrs," for they "loved not their lives unto the death."

As they overcame by the **"Blood of the Lamb,"** then the **Time** of their overcoming must be subsequent to the shedding of Christ's blood on Calvary, that is, Satan, according to this account, could not have been cast out of the "Heavenlies" prior to the Crucifixion of Christ. When Jesus said—"I beheld Satan as lightning **fall from heaven,"** (Luke 10:18), He was not referring to some past fall of Satan, but it was a prophetic utterance, by way of anticipation, of his **future fall,** when he shall be cast out of Heaven by Michael the Archangel. As further evidence as to the "Time" of Satan's casting out, Daniel the Prophet tells us that it will be at the "Time of Trouble," (The Great Tribulation), that is to come upon Daniel's people, the Jews, for it is at that time that Michael the Great Prince is to stand up and they shall be delivered. Dan 12:1.

As still further evidence that the casting out of Satan did not happen "before" the Fall in Eden, we are told that it "follows" the birth and catching out of the "Man Child," (Christ), (Rev. 12:5), that the earth shall be full of inhabitants, that is, thickly populated, and that Satan shall be full of wrath, because he knoweth that he has but a "short time" (3½ years), in which to finish his devilish work. (Rev. 12:12.)

VI. His Incarnation.

When Satan is cast out of the Heavenlies on to the earth, he is going to "incarnate" himself in the Antichrist. See the Chapter on "The Antichrist."

VII. His Doom.

When Christ shall return to the Mt. of Olives at the close of the "Tribulation Period," the "Beast" and the "False Prophet" shall be cast "alive" into the "Lake of Fire," and an angel from Heaven will seize Satan and bind him with a great chain, already forged, and cast him into the "Bottomless Pit," where he shall remain for 1000 years. Rev. 20:1-3. At the close of which time he shall be loosed for a season, and then with his angels, demons, and the human beings who have fallen under his power, he shall be cast into the "Lake of Fire" prepared for him in the long ago. Rev. 20:7-10; Matt. 25:41.

XIX
THE ANTICHRIST

In our study of prophecy we lay much stress on the "Second Coming of Christ," forgetting that there are two other comings of "individuals" that are just as momentous as Christ's coming. The first is that of Antichrist, and the other is that of Satan.

In both the Old and New Testament we are told of a

Mysterious and Terrible Personage

that shall be revealed in the "Last Times." He is described under different names and aliases, and it is only by a careful examination and comparison of these names, and the Person they describe that we see that they refer to one and the same individual. These names are—

In the Old Testament.	In the New Testament.
Isaiah	Paul 2 Thess. 2: 3-8
14: 4—"King of Babylon."	"The Man of Sin."
14: 12—"Lucifer."	"Son of Perdition."
Daniel	"That Wicked."
7: 8, 8: 9—"The Little Horn."	John
8: 23—"A King of Fierce Countenance."	1 John 2: 18—"Antichrist."
9: 26—"The Prince that Shall Come."	Rev. 13: 1—"The Beast."
11: 36—"The Wilful King."	

Jesus also made a prophetic reference to him.

"I am come in my **Father's name**, and ye receive me not; if another shall come in **his own name**, him ye will receive." John 5: 43.

The Jews rejected Jesus as their Messiah, when the Antichrist comes they will accept him.

I. His Personality.

The Apostolic Church believed that Antichrist was to be a "person," the embodiment of human blasphemy and wickedness, but toward the close of the Twelfth Century many began to look upon the Pope as Antichrist, and this view has been largely advocated by Protestant commentators. The arguments in favor of this view are ingenious and plausible, but they are hard to reconcile with the Word of God. This view makes Antichrist a "System" rather than a Person, and would see in the "Papal System" the Antichrist. But this is disproved by the Word of God.

1. The Apostle John says—

"Who is a liar, but he that **denieth** that Jesus is the Christ? He is **Antichrist, that denieth the Father and the Son.**" 1 John 2: 22.

"Every spirit that **confesseth not** that Jesus Christ **is come in THE FLESH** (His Deity) is not of God; and this is that **spirit of Antichrist.**" 1 John 4: 3.

Judaism has denied that "**Jesus is the Christ,**" and Unitarianism that He has "**come in the flesh,**" but the Papacy never. The Church of Rome has always confessed—"I believe in God the Father Almighty, maker of heaven and earth, and in Jesus Christ, His only Son, our Lord."

2. All Protestant commentators insist that the "Papal System" is described in Rev. 17: 4, 5, under the figure of a "Woman" arrayed in "purple and scarlet color," and decked with "gold and precious stones and pearls." This is undoubtedly true, but this "Woman," the "Mother of Harlots," is represented as riding upon a "Beast," universally admitted to be the Antichrist. If the "Beast" is the Antichrist, the "Woman" cannot be, and that they are separate and do not signify the same thing is clear.

3. Again Antichrist, as the "Man of Sin" is to—

"Exalt himself and magnify himself above every god." Dan. 11: 36, 37. "So that he **AS GOD sitteth in the Temple of God** showing himself that he **IS GOD.**" 2 Thess. 2: 4.

However false and impious the claims of the Papacy, it always recognizes its subordination to God, and the Pope's highest claim is that he is the "Vicar of Christ."

4. "All the world wondered after the Beast (the Antichrist), and they **worshipped the Dragon** (the Devil), which gave power unto the Beast." Rev. 13: 3, 4.

The "Papal System" worships the "Virgin" and the "Saints," but it is not true that it worships the Devil.

5. "If any man **worship the Beast and His Image**, and receive his mark in his forehead, or in his hand, the same shall **drink of the wine of the Wrath of God**, . . . and he shall **be tormented with fire and brimstone**; . . . and the **smoke of their torment ascendeth up forever and ever**; and they have no rest day nor night, who worship the Beast and His Image, and whosoever receiveth the mark of his name." Rev. 14: 9-11.

If the "Papal System" is the Antichrist, it follows from the above that all its worshippers, instead of being saved, are doomed to eternal torment.

Again, the Lord, who destroys Antichrist "at His Coming," comes to Jerusalem, not to Rome, the seat of the "Papal System."

While there are many things in the history of the Church of Rome, and in the conduct of her Popes that "foreshadow" the Antichrist, yet it is clear from the preceding scriptures that the "Papal System" is not the Antichrist, and that these scriptures can only be fulfilled in the person of some "Individual" yet to appear.

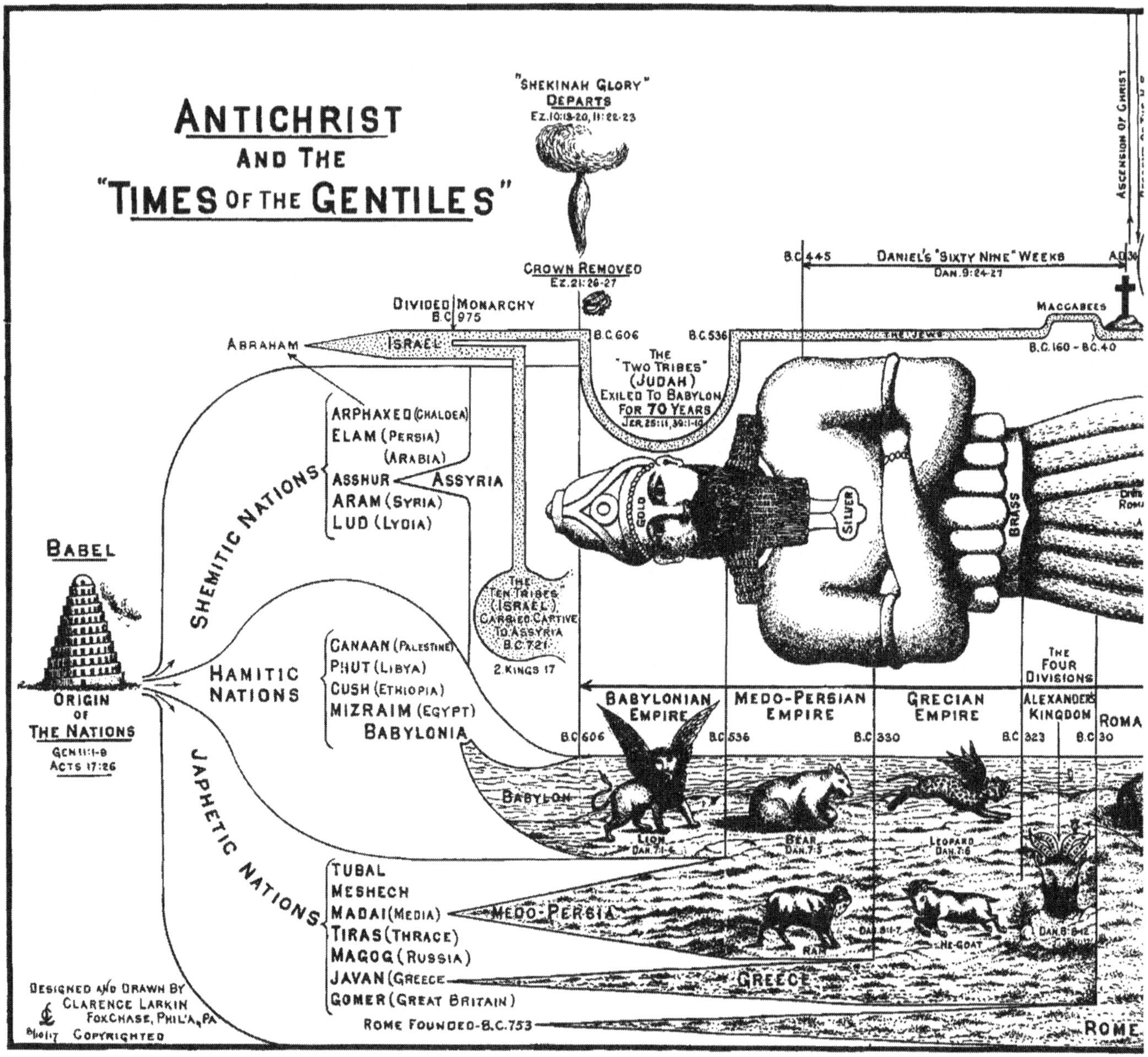

ANTICHRIST
AND THE
"TIMES OF THE GENTILES"
"SHEKINAH GLORY" DEPARTS
EZ.10:18-20, 11:22-23
CROWN REMOVED
EZ.21:26-27
DIVIDED MONARCHY
B.C 975
ABRAHAM
ISRAEL
B.C.606
B.C.536
THE "TWO TRIBES" (JUDAH) EXILED TO BABYLON FOR 70 YEARS
JER.25:11, 39:1-10
B.C 445
DANIEL'S "SIXTY NINE" WEEKS
DAN.9:24-27
AD 30
MACCABEES
B.C.160 - B.C.40
ASCENSION OF CHRIST
GOLD
SILVER
BRASS
ARPHAXED (CHALDEA)
ELAM (PERSIA)
(ARABIA)
ASSHUR
ASSYRIA
ARAM (SYRIA)
LUD (LYDIA)
SHEMITIC NATIONS
THE "TEN TRIBES" (ISRAEL) CARRIED CAPTIVE TO ASSYRIA B.C.721
2.KINGS 17
BABEL
ORIGIN OF THE NATIONS
GEN.11:1-9
ACTS 17:26
HAMITIC NATIONS
CANAAN (PALESTINE)
PHUT (LIBYA)
CUSH (ETHIOPIA)
MIZRAIM (EGYPT)
BABYLONIA
BABYLONIAN EMPIRE
MEDO-PERSIAN EMPIRE
GRECIAN EMPIRE
THE FOUR DIVISIONS
ALEXANDER'S KINGDOM
ROMA
B.C 606
B.C 536
B.C 330
B.C 323
B.C 30
BABYLON
LION
BEAR
LEOPARD
JAPHETIC NATIONS
TUBAL
MESHECH
MADAI (MEDIA)
TIRAS (THRACE)
MAGOG (RUSSIA)
JAVAN (GREECE
GOMER (GREAT BRITAIN)
MEDO-PERSIA
RAM
HE-GOAT
GREECE
ROME FOUNDED-B.C.753
ROME
DESIGNED AND DRAWN BY CLARENCE LARKIN FOXCHASE, PHIL'A, PA
COPYRIGHTED

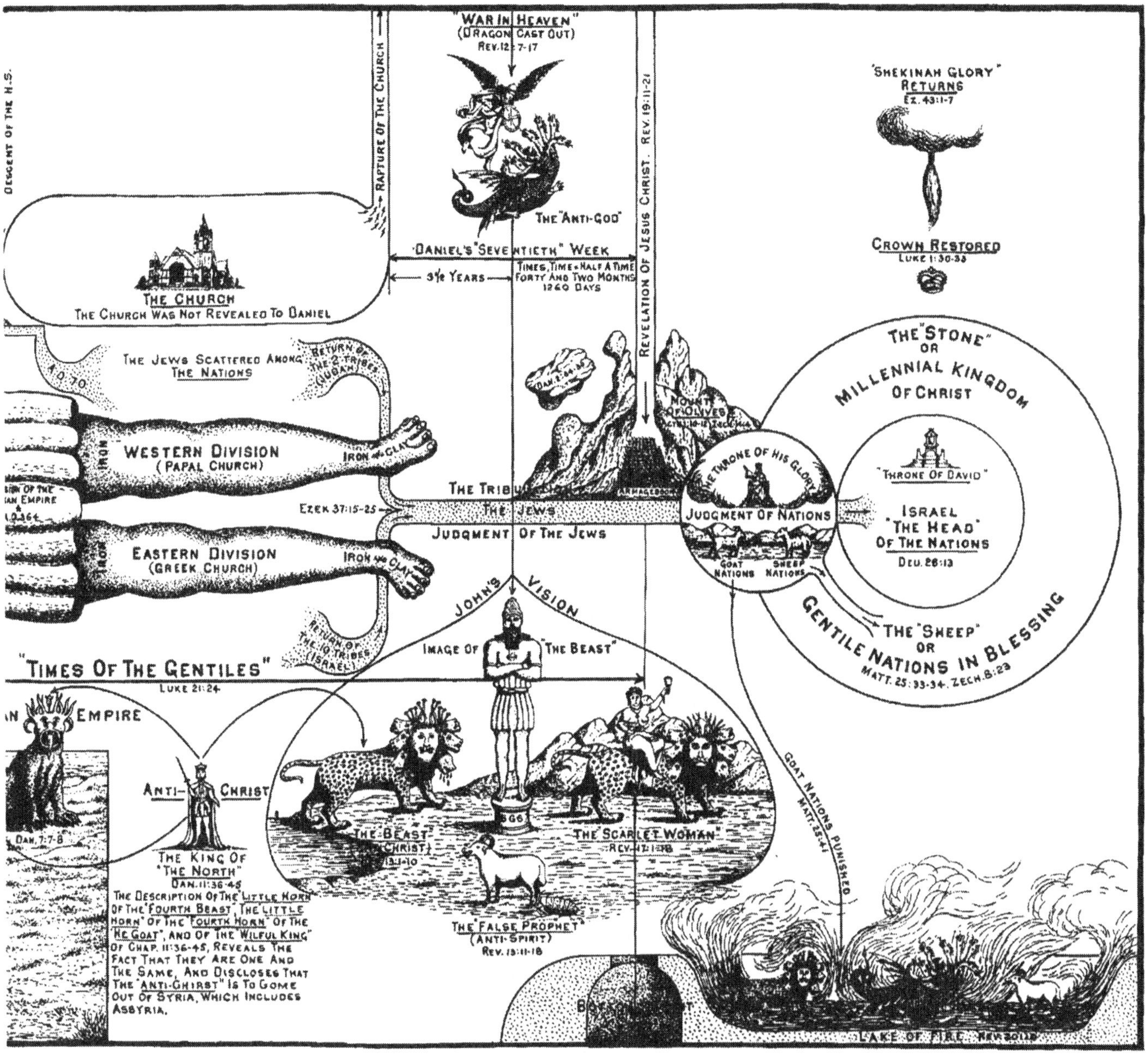

"WAR IN HEAVEN"
(DRAGON CAST OUT)
REV. 12:7-17
DESCENT OF THE H.S.
RAPTURE OF THE CHURCH
REVELATION OF JESUS CHRIST. REV. 19:11-21
"SHEKINAH GLORY" RETURNS
EZ. 43:1-7
THE "ANTI-GOD"
CROWN RESTORED
LUKE 1:30-33
DANIEL'S "SEVENTIETH" WEEK
3½ YEARS
TIMES, TIME & HALF A TIME
FORTY AND TWO MONTHS
1260 DAYS
THE CHURCH
THE CHURCH WAS NOT REVEALED TO DANIEL
THE JEWS SCATTERED AMONG THE NATIONS
RETURN OF THE 2 TRIBES (JUDAH)
A.D. 70
THE "STONE" OR MILLENNIAL KINGDOM OF CHRIST
MOUNT OF OLIVES
IRON
WESTERN DIVISION
(PAPAL CHURCH)
IRON & CLAY
THE TRIBU
THE JEWS
ARMAGEDDON
THE THRONE OF HIS GLORY
"THRONE OF DAVID"
EZEK 37:15-25
JUDGMENT OF NATIONS
JUDGMENT OF THE JEWS
ISRAEL
"THE HEAD"
OF THE NATIONS
DEU. 28:13
IRON
EASTERN DIVISION
(GREEK CHURCH)
IRON & CLAY
GOAT NATIONS
SHEEP NATIONS
JOHN'S VISION
RETURN OF THE 10 TRIBES (ISRAEL)
IMAGE OF "THE BEAST"
THE "SHEEP" OR GENTILE NATIONS IN BLESSING
MATT. 25:33-34. ZECH. 8:23
"TIMES OF THE GENTILES"
LUKE 21:24
EMPIRE
ANTI-CHRIST
666
THE "BEAST"
THE "SCARLET WOMAN"
GOAT NATIONS PUNISHED
MATT. 25:41
DAN. 7:7-8
THE KING OF "THE NORTH"
DAN. 11:36-45
THE DESCRIPTION OF THE "LITTLE HORN" OF THE "FOURTH BEAST", THE "LITTLE HORN" OF THE "FOURTH HORN" OF THE "HE GOAT", AND OF THE "WILFUL KING" OF CHAP. 11:36-45, REVEALS THE FACT THAT THEY ARE ONE AND THE SAME, AND DISCLOSES THAT THE "ANTI-CHRIST" IS TO COME OUT OF SYRIA, WHICH INCLUDES ASSYRIA.
THE "FALSE PROPHET"
(ANTI-SPIRIT)
REV. 13:11-18
LAKE OF FIRE

Antichrist is not a "Rival" or "Counterfeit" Christ, he is an "Opposing" Christ. This is clearly seen when we compare him with Christ in a series of—

Contrasts.

1. **Christ** came from **Above**. John 6:38.
   Antichrist ascends from **The Pit**. Rev. 11:7.
2. Christ came in His **Father's** name. John 5:43.
   Antichrist comes in his **Own** name. John 5:43.
3. Christ **Humbled** Himself. Phil. 2:8.
   Antichrist **Exalts** himself. 2 Thess. 2:4.
4. Christ **Despised**. Isa. 53:3; Luke 23:18.
   Antichrist **Admired**. Rev. 13:3, 4.
5. Christ **Exalted**. Phil. 2:9.
   Antichrist **Cast Down to Hell**. Isa. 14:14, 15; Rev. 19:20.
6. Christ to do His **Father's** will. John 6:38.
   Antichrist to do his **Own** will. Dan. 11:36.
7. Christ came to **Save**. Luke 19:10.
   Antichrist comes to **Destroy**. Dan. 8:24.
8. Christ is the **Good Shepherd**. John 10:4-15.
   Antichrist is the **Idol (evil) Shepherd**. Zech. 11:16, 17.
9. Christ is the "**True Vine**." John 15:1.
   Antichrist is the "**Vine of the Earth**." Rev. 14:18.
10. Christ is the "**Truth**." John 14:6.
    Antichrist is the "**Lie**." 2 Thess. 2:11.
11. Christ is the "**Holy One**." Mark 1:24.
    Antichrist is the "**Lawless One**." 2 Thess. 2:8, R. V.
12. Christ is the "**Man of Sorrows**." Isa. 53:3.
    Antichrist is the "**Man of Sin**." 2 Thess. 2:3.
13. Christ is the "**Son of God**." Luke 1:35.
    Antichrist is the "**Son of Perdition**." 2 Thess. 2:3.
14. Christ, "**The Mystery of Godliness**," is **God** manifest in the flesh. 1 Tim. 3:16.
    Antichrist, "**The Mystery of Iniquity**," will be **Satan** manifest in the flesh. 2 Thess. 2:7.

II. His Origin.

1. Isaiah's Foreview.

In Isa. 11:4—a chapter which is evidently Messianic—we read that among other things which the Messiah will do—

"He shall smite the earth with the 'rod of His mouth,' and with the 'breath of His lips' shall He slay The Wicked."

The word translated "The Wicked," is in the singular number, and cannot refer to wicked persons in general, but to some **one person who is conspicuously wicked**. The expression is strikingly like that of Paul's in 2 Thess. 2:8—

"Then shall that 'Wicked' be revealed, whom the Lord shall consume with the 'Spirit of His Mouth,' and shall destroy with the 'Brightness of His Coming.'"

It is evident that Isaiah and Paul refer to the same individual, who can be no other than the Antichrist.

In Isa. 14:4-17 there is a description of a "King of Babylon" who shall smite the people in his wrath, and rule the nations in anger, and shall in his pride say—

"I will ascend into heaven, I will exalt my throne above the 'Stars of God' (Heavenly Rulers). I will sit also upon the mount of the congregation, in the sides of the north; I will ascend above the heights of the clouds; I will be like the Most High."

This king is called **LUCIFER**, "Son of the Morning," and his "fall" is described. He is cast down to Hell (Sheol, the Grave or Underworld), where his coming creates a great stir among the kings of the earth that have preceded him, and who exclaim when they see him—

"Art thou also become weak as we? Art thou become like unto us?" . . . "Is this the man that made the earth to tremble, that did shake kingdoms; that made the world as a wilderness and destroyed the cities thereof; that opened not the house of his prisoners?"

There has never as yet been such a king of Babylon as is here described. It must therefore refer to some "future ruler" of Babylon when Babylon shall be rebuilt, as it is to be.

Verses 12 to 14 evidently refer to Satan, and are descriptive of him before his fall, but as he is to incarnate himself in the Antichrist, who is to be a future King of Babylon, it explains the source of the pride and presumption of Antichrist, which will lead to his downfall, as it did to Satan's.

DANIEL'S FOURTH WILD BEAST
Dan. 7: 7-8, 19-26

2. Daniel's Foreview.

In the chapter on "The Gentiles" we described how Daniel saw come up among the "Ten Horns" on the head of the Fourth Wild Beast a "Little Horn," and that this "Little Horn" had "eyes like the eyes of a man, and a mouth speaking great things." Dan. 7:7, 8. Daniel was told that this "Little Horn" was a king that should arise, and that he would be a "person" of remarkable intelligence and great oratorical powers, having a "mouth speaking great things." That he would be audacious, arrogant, imperious and persecuting, and change "times and laws" and that the "Saints of the Most High" (Daniel's own people, the Jews) would be given into his hands for a "Time" and "Times" and the "dividing of Time," or 3½ years. Dan. 7:23-26.

Later Daniel had a vision of a Ram and a He-Goat contesting for supremacy. Dan. 8:1-27.

THE RAM **THE HE-GOAT**

Dan. 8: 1-27

The He-Goat had a "notable horn" between his eyes. This "Great Horn" was broken, and in its place "four notable horns" sprang up, and out of one of them sprang forth a "Little Horn"

"which waxed exceedingly great toward the south, and toward the east, and toward the 'Pleasant Land' (Palestine). And it waxed great, even to the 'Host of Heaven,' and it cast down some of the 'Host' and of the 'Stars' (angels) to the ground, and stamped upon them. Yea, He (the Little Horn) magnified himself even to the 'Prince of the Host' (the Lord God, Joshua 5: 13-15, 1 Sam. 17: 45), and by Him (the 'Little Horn'—Antichrist) the daily sacrifice was taken away, and the place of his sanctuary (the Temple) was cast down." Dan. 8: 9-11.

When Daniel asked for the meaning of the vision he was told that the Ram stood for the Medo-Persian Kingdom, and the He-Goat for the Grecian, and that the "Four Horns" that came up in the place of the "Great Horn" stood for "Four Kings" and that the "Little Horn" that came up on one of the "Four Horns" stood for a King of "Fierce Countenance," who in the "latter time" of their kingdom (the Four Worldwide Kingdoms and not the four Kingdoms into which the Grecian Empire was divided, for the "time" will be that when the "transgressors are come to the full"), shall stand up.

This King shall understand "dark sentences," and

"His power shall be mighty, but not by his own power (Satan shall incarnate himself in him), and he shall destroy wonderfully, and shall prosper, and practice and shall destroy the mighty and the Holy People (the Jews). And through his policy also he shall cause craft to prosper in his hand (no one shall be able to buy without the 'mark of the Beast.' Rev. 13: 17), and he shall magnify himself in his heart (2 Thess. 2: 3, 4), and by peace shall destroy many; he shall also stand up against the 'Prince of Princes,' but he shall be broken without hand." Dan. 8: 23-25.

This clearly identifies the "Little Horn" or "King of Fierce Countenance" which came out of one of the "Four Horns" that took the place of the "Notable Horn" on the head of the He-Goat as the Antichrist, for Antiochus Epiphanes (B. C. 175-165) nor any other ruler of the past has ever stood up against JESUS, the **"Prince of Princes."**

Neither was Antiochus Epiphanes "broken without hand;" he died a natural death at Tabae in B. C. 165. But the Antichrist is to be "broken without hand." His Kingdom is to be destroyed by a "stone cut out of the mountain without hands," the "Stone Kingdom" of the Lord Jesus Christ, Dan. 2: 34, 35, 44, 45, and he himself shall be "paralyzed" by the "brightness of the Lord's Coming" (1 Thess. 2: 8), and be cast "alive" into the Lake of Fire. Rev. 19: 20.

Two "good" men, Enoch and Elijah, were translated to Heaven "without dying," and two "bad" men, spoken of officially as the Beast and the False Prophet, shall be cast into the Lake of Fire "without dying."

Those who claim that the "Little Horn" of Dan. 7, and the "Little Horn" of Dan. 8, are not the same, because the "Little Horn" of Dan. 7 arises amid the "Ten Horns," of the Fourth Beast, which represents the Roman Empire, and the "Little Horn" of Dan. 8, arises on one of the Four Horns," that take the place of the "Great Horn" on the head of the He-Goat, which represents the Third Beast, the Grecian Empire, forget that the vision that the Apostle John had of the revived Roman Empire (Rev. 13:1, 2—the Roman Empire in its last stage), reveals the fact that the "last stage" of the Roman Empire will include "all the characteristics" of the whole Four Empires, Babylonian, Medo-Persian, Grecian and old Roman. This is seen in the character of the "Beast" John saw come up out of the sea. It was like unto a Leopard (Greece), with the "feet" of a Bear (Medo-Persian), and the "mouth" of a Lion (Babylon). The fact that the "body" of the Beast was like a Leopard (Greece) reveals the fact that the preponderating feature of the revived Roman Empire will be Grecian, and that therefore the "Ten Federated Kingdoms" will include the Four Kingdoms into which the Grecian Empire was divided, viz., Egypt, Macedon, Thrace and Syria. It follows therefore that the "Little Horn" that arises on the "Fourth Horn" of the He-Goat (Greece) is identical with the "Little Horn" of the Fourth Beast (Rome).

Those who claim that the "Little Horn" that came up on one of the "Four Horns" of the He-Goat was fulfilled in Antiochus Epiphanes (who was a king of Syria) overlook the fact that while Antiochus Epiphanes devastated Palestine and caused an "idol altar" to be erected on the altar of the Temple, on which he offered swine's flesh, which was an abomination to the Jews, he does not fulfill the description of the "Little Horn" of the He-Goat. Dan. 8:9-13. He does not compare with him for Satanic malice.

The "Abomination of Desolation" that Daniel refers to (Dan. 9:27) is to occur in the "last half" of "Daniel's Seventieth Week," and as Jesus spoke of it as still unfulfilled in His day (Matt. 24:15), it is clear that Antiochus Epiphanes was not the fulfillment of the "Little Horn" of Dan. 8:9-13.

While it was revealed to Daniel that the "Little Horn," or Antichrist, should come out of one of the "Four Horns" that took the place of the "Great Horn" on the head of the He-Goat, he needed further light as to which one.

We now know from history that the "Great Horn" represented Alexander the Great, and that the "Four Notable Horns" that took the place of the "Great Horn" at the death of Alexander the Great represented the Four Kingdoms into which his Kingdom was divided, visible, Egypt, Macedon, Thrace and Syria, which included Assyria. These Four Kingdoms were in time all absorbed into the "Fourth World Kingdom," the Roman Empire, the last to lose its identity being Egypt, which succumbed in B. C. 30.

That Daniel might know in which one of these Four Kingdoms the "Little Horn," or Antichrist, should arise, 15 years after his vision of the "Ram and He-Goat" the Lord gave him a third vision, that of two kings, the "King of the North" and the "King of the South." Dan. 11:1-45.

The "King of the North" was the King of Syria, and as his character and conduct is described (Dan. 11:36-38) as similar to that of the "Little Horn" that came out of one of the "Four Horns" it is clear that the Antichrist is to come from Syria.

That the "King of the North" spoken of in Dan. 11:21-31 was Antiochus Epiphanes there can be no question, but that he was not the "Little Horn," or the Antichrist, who is to come out of Syria in the "latter days" is clear from the remainder of the chapter from the 35th verse, which describes the conduct of the future Antichrist.

The intervening verses, the 32d to the 35th inclusive, fill in the gap between the time of Antiochus Epiphanes and the appearance of the Antichrist.

There is no intimation that Antiochus Epiphanes is even to be regarded as a "type" of Antichrist. They are distinct historical personages, each dealt with in his own place, and though they resemble each other in some respects, yet they must not be confounded with each other.

The terms "North" and "South" are applied to Syria and Egypt because of their geographic relation to Palestine (the Pleasant or Glorious Land. Dan. 8:9; 11:16, 41). In the thought of Jehovah Jerusalem is at once the geographic and moral centre of the earth. We are to understand therefore by the "King of the North" the King of Syria, which also included Assyria. This fixes the locality from which the Antichrist shall come, for we read in Isa. 10:12—

"That when the Lord hath performed His whole work upon Mount Zion and on Jerusalem (which will not be until Christ comes back), I will punish the fruit of the stout heart of the King of Assyria (Antichrist) and the glory of his 'high looks.'"

And we read in Isa. 14:25—

"I will break the Assyrian (the Antichrist) in my land (Palestine), and upon my mountains 'tread him under foot;' then shall his yoke depart from off them (Israel), and his burden depart from off their shoulders."

The context shows that this prophecy is connected with the restoration of Israel to their own land and the time of the downfall of Antichrist.

To recapitulate, we see from the three visions of Daniel that—

1. He learned from the "Little Horn" of the Fourth Wild Beast, that a **Mysterious and Terrible Personage** was to arise in the "**Latter Days.**"

2. He learned from the "Little Horn" that came up on one of the "Four Notable Horns" that took the place of the "Great Horn" on the He-Goat, that that "Terrible Personage" was to come out of one of the Kingdoms into which the Grecian Empire was divided at the death of Alexander the Great.

3. He learned from the vision of the "King of the North" that that "Terrible Personage" would come out of the Syrian division of Alexander's Kingdom.

The Antichrist, therefore, in all probability will be a Syrian Jew, for it is not likely that the Jews will accept as their Messiah one who is not a Jew, unless the claimant by false pretence makes them believe he is one. This, however, does not prevent the Antichrist being a Roman citizen, and a king of the revived Roman Empire, for Saul of Tarsus was both a Jew and a Roman citizen.

3. Paul's Foreview.

Writing to the Thessalonians, Paul says—

"Let no man deceive you by any means; for 'that day' (the Day of the Lord) shall not come except there come a 'falling away first,' and that '**MAN OF SIN**' be revealed, the '**Son of Perdition,**' who opposeth and exalteth himself above all that is called God, or that is worshipped; so that he **As God** sitteth in the Temple of God (the rebuilt Temple at Jerusalem), showing himself that he is God. . . . For the '**MYSTERY OF INIQUITY**' doth already work (in Paul's day); only He (the Holy Spirit) who now letteth (restraineth R. V.) will let (restrain), until He be taken out of the way.

And then shall 'THAT WICKED' be revealed, whom the Lord shall consume with the spirit (breath) of His mouth, and shall destroy with the brightness (manifestation R. V.) of His Coming. Even him, whose coming is after the 'working of Satan' with all 'power' and 'signs' and 'lying wonders,' and with all 'deceivableness of unrighteousness' in them that perish; because they received not the love of the truth, that they might be saved." 2 Thess. 2:3-10.

PAUL'S MAN OF SIN

In the American Standard Edition of the Bible the Antichrist is called the "MYSTERY OF LAWLESSNESS" or the "LAWLESS ONE." As such he is not the cause of "Lawlessness," he is the result or fruit of it, for he will arise out of the seething cauldron of "Lawlessness" that is now becoming pronounced and manifest in the world.

The name that the Apostle Paul gives the Antichrist, the—"SON OF PERDITION," is not without significance. The name is used but twice in the Scripture. It is first used by Christ of JUDAS (John 17:12), and then here of ANTICHRIST. The Apostle also calls the Antichrist in this passage the "MYSTERY OF INIQUITY." What does that mean? In 1 Tim. 3:16, Christ is spoken of as the "MYSTERY OF GODLINESS." That is, that He was GOD MANIFEST IN THE FLESH. How did He become "manifest in the flesh"? By being born of the Virgin Mary by the Holy Spirit. Thus it was that Jesus became the "SON OF GOD." Luke 1:35. Now as iniquity is the opposite of Godliness, then the "MYSTERY OF INIQUITY" must be the opposite of the "MYSTERY OF GODLINESS." That is, if Christ is the "MYSTERY OF GODLINESS," Antichrist must be the "MYSTERY OF INIQUITY," and as Christ was the "SON OF GOD," then Antichrist must be the "SON OF PERDITION," that is of SATAN. And as Christ was born of a virgin by the Holy Spirit, so Antichrist will be born of a WOMAN (not necessarily a virgin) by Satan. This is no new view for it has been held by many of God's spiritually minded children since the days of the Apostle John, and there is some warrant for it in the Scriptures. In Gen. 3:15, God said to the Serpent (Satan), "I will put enmity between thee and the woman, and between 'THY SEED' and 'HER SEED'." Now the Woman's SEED was CHRIST, then the Serpent's SEED must be ANTICHRIST. In John 8:44 Jesus said to the Jews—"Ye are of your father THE DEVIL . . . When he speaketh a lie, he speaketh of his own; for he is a liar, and the father of IT." In the Greek there is the definite article before "lie," and it should read "THE LIE," so when the Devil speaks of "THE LIE," he is speaking of his own (child), for he is a liar, and the FATHER OF "IT"—"THE LIE." And it is worthy of note that in the verse (vs. 11) that follows the passage we are considering that the Apostle says—"And for this cause God shall send them strong delusion that they should believe a lie." Here again the definite article is found in the Greek, and it should read "The LIE," the "SON OF PERDITION," the ANTICHRIST.

But why was Judas called the "SON OF PERDITION"? Was he a child of Satan by some woman, or was he simply indwelt by Satan? Here we must let the Scriptures speak for themselves. In John 6:70-71 we read that Jesus said "Have not I chosen you Twelve, and one of you is a DEVIL? He spake of Judas Iscariot the son of Simon; for he it was that should betray Him, being one of the Twelve." In no other passage than this is the word "Devil" applied to anyone but to Satan himself. Here the word is "diabolus," the definite article is employed, and it should read—"and one of you is THE DEVIL." This would make Judas the Devil incarnate, or the "MYSTERY OF INIQUITY," and explains why Jesus in John 17:12, calls him the "SON OF PERDITION."

This is the only place in the Scriptures where the word "diabolus" is applied to a human being, and it implies an incarnation.

While "Perdition" is a PLACE (Rev. 17:8, 11), it is also a "condition" into which men may fall (1 Tim. 6:9; Heb. 10:39), and while men who have committed the "Unpardonable Sin" are "sons of perdition," because they are destined to the place of the irrevocably lost, yet Judas and Antichrist are the "SONS OF PERDITION" in a special sense, for they are the SONS of the author of "Perdition"—THE DEVIL. That is they are not merely "obsessed" or controlled by the Devil, the Devil has incarnated himself in them, and for the time being, to all practical purposes, they are the very Devil himself.

The next question that arises is, "If Judas and the Antichrist are both called the 'SON OF PERDITION,' are they one and the same, or are there two 'Sons of Perdition'?" Here we must anticipate. Turning to Rev. 11:7, we read that the "Beast" that slays the "Two Witnesses" ascends out of the "Bottomless Pit" (ABYSS), and that "Beast" is the ANTICHRIST. Now how did he get into the "ABYSS"? Well, if there is only one "SON OF PERDITION," and Judas and Antichrist are one and the same, then he got in the ABYSS when Judas went to his "Own Place" (the ABYSS). Acts 1:25. Of no other person is it said anywhere in the Scriptures that he went "to his own place." Again in Rev. 17:8 it is said—"The 'Beast' that thou sawest was, and is not: and shall ascend out of the 'Bottomless Pit' (Abyss), and go into PERDITION." As this "Beast" is the same that slays the "Two Witnesses" he is the ANTICHRIST. Now there are four things said of him. First, he "WAS." Second, he "IS NOT." Third, he shall "ASCEND OUT OF THE BOTTOMLESS PIT." Fourth, he shall "GO INTO PERDITION." From this we learn that in John's day the "Beast" "Was Not," but that he had been before on the earth, and was to come again, that he was to

ASCEND FROM THE BOTTOMLESS PIT. This is positive proof that the ANTICHRIST has been on the earth before, and that when he comes in the future he will come from the "ABYSS."

The question then arises, when was "Antichrist" on the earth before? If Judas and Antichrist are one and the same the enigma is solved. When Judas was on the earth, he WAS; when Judas went to his "Own Place" he "WAS NOT"; when Judas comes back from the "Abyss" he will be—THE ANTICHRIST. The Author does not insist on this view of Judas and Antichrist being correct, but with open mind he accepts it, because it seems to be the only logical solution of both Judas and Antichrist being called the "SON OF PERDITION."

When we compare these "Foreviews," and note the similarity of conduct of Daniel's "LITTLE HORN," Paul's "MAN OF SIN," and John's "BEAST," and that Daniel's "LITTLE HORN" and John's "BEAST" are to continue for the same length of time—"Forty and Two Months," or 3½ years, and that Daniel's "LITTLE HORN," Paul's "MAN OF SIN," and John's "BEAST," are all to be destroyed in the same manner at Christ's "Second Coming," we see that they all prefigure the same "Evil Power" which is after the "Working of Satan," and which John in 1 John 2:18, calls THE ANTICHRIST. In other words when we find in prophecy "Three Symbolic Personages" that come upon the stage of action at the same time, occupy the same territory, exhibit the same character, do the same work, exist the same length of time, and meet the same fate, they must symbolize the SAME THING.

JOHN'S BEAST

4. John's Foreview.

On the Isle of Patmos the Apostle John had his vision of the Antichrist.

"And I stood upon the sand of the sea, and saw a Beast rise up out of the sea (Mediterranean Sea), having 'Seven Heads' and 'Ten Horns' and upon his heads the 'name of blasphemy.' And the Beast which I saw was like unto a Leopard, and his 'feet' were as the feet of a Bear, and his 'mouth' as the mouth of a Lion; and THE DRAGON gave him his power, and his seat, and great authority. And I saw one of his heads as it were 'wounded to death;' and his deadly wound 'was healed;' and all the world wondered after THE BEAST.

"And they worshipped THE DRAGON which gave power unto the Beast; and they worshipped THE BEAST, saying, Who is like unto the Beast? Who is able to make war with him? And there was given unto him A Mouth Speaking Great Things and Blasphemies; and power was given unto him to continue Forty and Two Months. And he opened his mouth In Blasphemy Against God, to Blaspheme His Name, and His Tabernacle and Them That Dwell in Heaven. And it was given unto him to make War With the Saints (not the saints of the Church; they were already in glory) and to overcome them; and Power Was Given Him Over All Kindreds and Tongues and Nations. And all that dwell upon the earth shall worship him, whose names are not written in the Book of Life of the Lamb slain from the foundation of the world." Rev. 13:1-8.

Daniel's Fourth Wild Beast
Dan. 7:7, 8, 19, 20, 23-25.

"After this I saw in the night visions, and behold a FOURTH BEAST, dreadful and terrible, and strong exceedingly; and it had great iron teeth; it devoured and brake in pieces, and stamped the residue (the 3 preceding Beasts) with the feet of it; and it was diverse from all the Beasts that were before it; and it had TEN HORNS. I considered the HORNS, and, behold, there came up among them another LITTLE HORN, before whom there were THREE of the FIRST HORNS plucked up by the roots; and, behold, in THIS HORN were eyes like the eyes of a MAN, and a mouth speaking great things."

"Then I would know the truth of the FOURTH BEAST, which was diverse from all the others, exceeding dreadful, whose teeth were of iron, and his nails of brass; which devoured, brake in pieces, and stamped the residue with his feet; and of the TEN HORNS that were in his head, and of the OTHER which came up, and before whom three fell; even of THAT HORN that had eyes, and a mouth that spake very great things, whose look was more stout than his fellows."

"Thus he said, the FOURTH BEAST shall be the FOURTH KINGDOM upon earth, which shall be diverse from all kingdoms, and shall devour the whole earth, and shall tread it down and break it in pieces. And the TEN HORNS out of this Kingdom are TEN KINGS that shall arise; and another (King) shall rise after them; and he shall be diverse from the first, and he shall subdue THREE KINGS. And he shall speak great words against the Most High, and shall wear out the saints of the Most High, and think to change times and laws; and they shall be given into his hand until a TIME and TIMES and the DIVIDING OF TIME."

John's Beast Out Of The Sea
Rev. 13:1-7

"I saw a BEAST rise up out of the SEA, having SEVEN HEADS and TEN HORNS, and upon his horns TEN CROWNS, and upon his heads the NAMES OF BLASPHEMY. And the BEAST which I saw was like unto a LEOPARD, and his feet were as the feet of a BEAR, and his mouth as the mouth of a LION; and the Dragon gave him his power, and his seat, and great authority. And I saw one of his HEADS as it were wounded to death; and his deadly wound was healed; and all the world wondered after the BEAST. . . . And there was given unto him a mouth speaking great things and blasphemies; and power was given unto him to continue FORTY AND TWO MONTHS. And he opened his mouth in blasphemy against God, to blaspheme His Name, and His Tabernacle, and them that dwell in Heaven. And it was given unto him to make war with the saints, and to overcome them; and power was given him over all kindreds, and tongues, and nations."

Before we examine in detail John's "BEAST," it would be well for us to compare it with Daniel's "FOURTH WILD BEAST."

In comparing these two "BEASTS" we find that they both come up out of the sea (the nations), and that they are utterly unlike any beast we have ever heard of. Daniel's "Beast" was **dreadful and terrible,** and **strong exceedingly;** and it had **great iron teeth,** and **nails of brass**; while John's "Beast" was like a LEOPARD, with the feet of a BEAR, and the mouth of a LION. As Daniel's "Beast" represented the "FOURTH KINGDOM" upon the earth, the Roman Empire, it is evident that its characteristics describe the old Roman Empire, while the characteristics of John's Beast represent the revived Roman Empire. We know that the Old Roman Empire was "**strong exceedingly**" and its grip and power were like a beast with "**great iron teeth**" and "**nails of brass,**" and from the description of John's "Beast" we learn that the revived Roman Empire shall embody all the characteristics of the Four World Empires, as seen in its LEOPARD like body, its feet of a BEAR, and its mouth of a LION. That both "Beasts" have TEN HORNS reveals the fact that they will be in existence at the time indicated by the **TEN TOES** of the Colossus, with which they correspond, which will be just before the setting up of the "Stone" or Millennial Kingdom of Christ. We are told that the "**TEN HORNS**" of Daniel's "Beast" stand for "**TEN KINGS,**" and the "**TEN HORNS**" of John's "Beast" stand for the same. Rev. 17:12. From this we see that both Daniel and John foresaw that the Roman Empire was to be eventually divided into "Ten Separate but Federated Kingdoms."

While both "Beasts" have TEN HORNS, they differ in that John's had "SEVEN HEADS" while Daniel's had but ONE, and among the "TEN HORNS" on Daniel's "Beast" there came up a "LITTLE HORN," which is not seen amid the "TEN HORNS" of John's Beast. These, as we shall see, are features that refer to the last stage of the "Beast" and show that we cannot understand the last stage of the "Beast" without carefully comparing Daniel's and John's "Beasts," for the "LITTLE HORN" of Daniel's "Beast" plucks up THREE of the "TEN HORNS" and destroys them, or takes their kingdom away, a thing that John omits to tell us. Again the Antichristian character of Daniel's "Beast" is seen in its "LITTLE HORN" whose conduct corresponds with not a part, but the **whole** of John's "Beast," and that for the same length of time— "TIME" and "TIMES" and the "DIVIDING OF TIME" which equals "FORTY AND TWO MONTHS."

It now remains to analyze the "**Beast**" that John saw come up out of the sea, and try to discover the meaning of its various members.

We have two descriptions of this "**Beast.**"

Daniel's "Fourth Wild Beast" as we have seen, represents the Roman Empire as it existed from B. C. 30, until as a nation it shall cease to exist. While it was divided in A. D. 364, as the result of an ecclesiastical schism, into its Eastern and Western Divisions, and lost its national life as a world power, yet it has never lost its religious existence or influence as seen in the continuance of the Greek and Roman Churches, and Roman Law is still a controlling power in our laws. In this sense the Roman Empire in its influence has never ceased to exist. We are now to consider it in its last stage as outlined in John's "Beast."

In the two descriptions of John's Beast as given above it is very important to see that the "Beast" has a "Dual" meaning. It repre-

JOHN'S TWO VISIONS OF THE BEAST

BEAST OUT OF THE SEA
Rev. 13:1-7

"I saw a BEAST rise up out of the SEA, having SEVEN HEADS and TEN HORNS, and upon his horns TEN CROWNS, and upon his heads the NAMES OF BLASPHEMY. And the BEAST which I saw was like unto a LEOPARD, and his feet were as the feet of a BEAR, and his mouth as the mouth of a LION; and the Dragon gave him his power, and his seat, and great authority. And I saw one of his HEADS as it were wounded to death; and his deadly wound was healed; and all the world wondered after the BEAST. . . . And there was given unto him a mouth speaking great things and blasphemies; and power was given unto him to continue FORTY AND TWO MONTHS. And he opened his mouth in blasphemy against God, to blaspheme His Name, and His Tabernacle, and them that dwell in Heaven. And it was given unto him to make war with the saints, and to overcome them; and power was given him over all kindreds, and tongues, and nations."

SCARLET COLORED BEAST
Rev. 17:3, 7-17

"I saw a Woman sit upon a scarlet colored BEAST, full of names of blasphemy, having SEVEN HEADS and TEN HORNS. . . . I will tell thee the mystery of the Woman, and of the BEAST that carried her, which hath the SEVEN HEADS and TEN HORNS. The BEAST that thou sawest WAS, and IS NOT; and shall ascend out of the BOTTOMLESS PIT, and go into perdition. . . . The SEVEN HEADS are SEVEN MOUNTAINS, on which the Woman sitteth. And they (the Seven Heads, R. V.) are SEVEN KINGS; FIVE are fallen, and ONE is, and the OTHER is not yet come; and when he cometh, he must continue a short space. And the BEAST that WAS, and IS NOT, even he is the EIGHTH, and is of the SEVEN, and goeth into perdition. And the TEN HORNS which thou sawest are TEN KINGS, which have received no kingdom as yet; but receive power as kings one hour with the BEAST. These have one mind, and shall give their power and strength unto the BEAST. . . . And the TEN HORNS which thou sawest upon the BEAST, these shall hate the WHORE, and shall make her desolate and naked, and shall eat her flesh, and burn her with fire. For God hath put in their hearts to fulfil His will, and to agree, and give their kingdom unto the BEAST, until the words of God shall be fulfilled."

sents both the revived Roman Empire, and its Imperial Head the Antichrist. As the revived Roman Empire it is seen coming up out of the sea of the nations, as the Antichrist it comes up out of the ABYSS. For instance it cannot be said of the Roman Empire of John's day, that it WAS, and IS NOT, for it was at the height of its power in John's day. Neither can it be said of it that it shall **ascend out of the pit and go into PERDITION**, that could only be said of a **person.** Again we must distinguish between the body of the "Beast" and its **heads** and **horns.** The **body** being that of a LEOPARD, with the feet of a BEAR, and the mouth of a LION is to show that the revived Roman Empire in its last stage will include the characteristics of the first "**Three Wild Beasts**" of Daniel, that is, of the LION (Babylon), the BEAR (Medo-Persia), and the LEOPARD (Greece), and as the largest part of the "Beast," the **body**, is represented by the LEOPARD, the prevailing characteristic of the revived Roman Empire will be GRECIAN.

The "Beast" that comes up out of the sea (Chap. 13) has SEVEN HEADS and TEN HORNS, and the "Horns" are CROWNED. This

THE SCARLET WOMAN

represents the "Beast," or Empire, at the height of its power, when it will have all its "Heads," and when the **TEN KINGS**, the heads of the **TEN KINGDOMS** into which the Empire shall be divided, will have been crowned. The "Beast" that comes up out of the **ABYSS** also has **SEVEN HEADS** and **TEN HORNS**, but they are not crowned, for the **TEN KINGS** represented by the **TEN HORNS**, have not as yet received their kingdom. (Rev. 17:12.) This implies that the "Beast" of Rev. 17, represents the Antichrist at the beginning of the "Week." As confirmation of this view the "**WOMAN**" is seen at this stage riding the "Beast." For while the "**Scarlet Clothed Woman**" is not seen until chapter 17. it is clear that she rides the "Beast" from the **beginning** of the "Week," for she represents the "**PAPAL CHURCH**" that comes into power after the true Church has been caught out. During the wars preceding the rise of Antichrist the nations that will then be found in the geographical limits of the Old Roman Empire will form an "Alliance" for mutual protection. Those nations will be ten in number, represented by the "**TEN HORNS**" of the Beast. No doubt the "Papal Church" will play a prominent part in those proceedings. She will be rewarded by restoration to political power, and this union of Church and State, in which the Church will have control, is shown by the **WOMAN** riding the Beast, thus dominating it. But when the "Ten Kings" shall receive their Kingdoms and be **CROWNED**, they "shall hate the **WHORE**, and shall make her **desolate** and **naked**, and shall eat her flesh, and burn her with fire." (Vs. 16).

While we are told in Rev. 17:9 that the "**SEVEN HEADS**" of the "Beast" represent "**SEVEN MOUNTAINS**" (this is to identify it with the Roman Empire), we are told in the next verse (R. V.) that they (the "Seven Heads") also represent "**SEVEN KINGS**" of whom "Five **are fallen**, and one is, and the other is **not yet come**; and when he cometh he must continue a **short space**." That is, in John's day "Five" of these Kings had fallen, one was the then ruling Emperor, and the "Seventh" was yet to come. Who are meant by the first "Five Kings" that had fallen we do not know. The King that was on the throne in John's day was Domitian, who had banished John to the Isle of Patmos. The last or "**SEVENTH KING**" who is yet to come is undoubtedly the **ANTICHRIST**. We are told in Rev. 13:3, that one of the "**SEVEN HEADS**," or "**KINGS**," received a **deadly wound**. Which one is not stated. The inference is that it is the last, for the Beast has all of his "HEADS" before one of them is wounded. In Rev. 17:11 he is called the Beast that **WAS**, and **IS NOT**, even he is the "**EIGHTH**," and **is of the** "**SEVENTH**," and **goeth into PERDITION**. The only clear explanation of this passage is that the "**SEVENTH HEAD**"—THE ANTICHRIST, is the one who receives the "**deadly wound**," probably at the hand of an assassin, and as his body is lying in state prepared for burial, he rises from **the dead** (Rev. 13:14) and thus becomes the "**EIGHTH**," though he is of the "**SEVENTH**." By this resurrection of the Antichrist, Satan imitates the Resurrection of Christ and makes the world "**wonder after the Beast**" (Rev. 13:3), and this adds to his prestige and power. If this happens at the "Middle of the Week," at the time the Dragon is cast out of Heaven, it will account for the great change that takes place in the Antichrist, for before receiving his "deadly wound" he will be sweet and lovable, but after his resurrection or recovery he becomes Devilish, the result of the Dragon incarnating himself in him. It is at this time that he breaks the Covenant with the Jews and desecrates the Temple by setting up the "Abomination of Desolation" which is an "Idol Image" of himself—the "**DESOLATOR**." As the "**LITTLE HORN**" of Daniel's "Fourth Wild Beast" he will destroy three of the "Ten Kings" and firmly establish himself in the place of power, and as he, as the "**LITTLE HORN**," does not appear until after the "**TEN HORNS**," or "Ten Federated Kingdoms," come into existence, it is clear that the Antichrist does not form the Federation, but is the outgrowth of it.

III. His Character.

He will be a "composite" man. One who embraces in his character the abilities and powers of Nebuchadnezzar, Xerxes, Alexander the Great and Caesar Augustus. He will have the marvellous gift of attracting unregenerate men, and the irresistible fascination of his personality, his versatile attainments, superhuman wisdom, great administrative and executive ability, along with his powers as a consummate flatterer, a brilliant diplomatist, a superb strategist, will make him the most conspicuous and prominent of men. All these gifts will be conferred on him by Satan, whose tool he will be, and who will thus make him the—

SUPERMAN.

He will pose as a great humanitarian, the friend of men, and the especial friend of the Jewish race, whom he will persuade that he has come to usher in the "Golden Age" as pictured by the prophets, and who will receive him as their Messiah.

He will intoxicate men with a strong delusion and his never varying success. And when he shall be slain and rise again he will have lost none of these powers, but will be in addition the embodiment of all kinds of wickedness and blasphemy.

"He shall speak great words against the Most High, and shall wear out the saints of the Most High, and think to change times and laws." Dan. 7:25.

"He shall also stand up against the 'Prince of Princes'" (Jesus). Dan. 8:25.

"He shall do according to his will; and he shall exalt himself and magnify himself above every god, and shall speak marvellous things against the God of Gods." Dan. 11:36.

"Who opposeth and exalteth himself above all that is called God, or that is worshipped; so that he AS GOD sitteth in the Temple of God (at Jerusalem) showing himself that he IS GOD . . . whose coming is after the **Working of Satan** with all **Power and Signs and Lying Wonders.**" 2 Thess. 2:3-9.

There has never as yet appeared on this earth a person who answers the description given in the above Scriptures. Such a character is almost inconceivable. No writer would have invented such a character.

IV. His Reign.

He shall reign for seven years, or during the whole of Daniel's "Seventieth Week."

"And he shall confirm the Covenant with many for ONE WEEK (Daniel's Seventieth week) and in the **midst of the week** he shall cause the sacrifice and the oblation to cease." Dan. 9:27.

After the Church has been caught out the Jews will be gathered back to their own land unconverted. About this time ten of the Nations occupying the territory of the old Roman Empire will enter into a Federation. Among the Ten Kings of those nations will arise the Antichrist. He will soon prove himself to be a **Great Ruler** and will be made **PRESIDENT**. The Government will be a **Democratic Monarchy.**

The President will make a "Covenant" with the Jewish people. It may be a Covenant restoring to them their own land. Whatever its character, the Prophet Isaiah speaks of it as a **"Covenant With Death and Hell."** Isa. 28:15.

For 3½ years the President of the Federation will keep the Covenant. Then he will break it. For the balance of his reign, 3½ years, he will cause an awful persecution of the Jews, called "The Great Tribulation."

It will not, however, be limited to them, for we read in Rev. 13:7, 8, that he shall be given power

"Over all kindreds, and tongues, and nations. And all that dwell upon the earth shall worship him, whose names are not written in the Book of Life."

For a description of this period see the Chapter on "The Great Tribulation."

V. His Doom.

At the end of the seven years the allied armies of the Ten Federated Nations will gather together in the Valley of Megiddo, north of Jerusalem, to besiege that city. Zech. 14:2. The Lord will pour upon the "House of David" (Israel), and the inhabitants of Jerusalem, the "spirit of grace and supplication" (Zech. 12:10). Then the Lord, at the head of the "armies of Heaven," will come to their rescue (Rev. 19:11-16), and the Jews will see Christ descend upon the Mt. of Olives (Zech. 14:4) and the Beast (Antichrist) and the kings of the earth, and their armies will gather together to make war against the Lord, and the Beast and the False Prophet will be taken and cast **alive** into the **"Lake of Fire"** and the remnant of those armies shall be slain with the sword of Him who sits upon the "White Horse," and the fowls of the air will be summoned unto the "Supper of the Great God" and shall feed on the flesh of kings, and captains, and of mighty men. Rev. 19:17-21.

XX
THE SATANIC TRINITY

THE FALSE PROPHET
Rev. 13:11-18

Satan is the "God of this World." (Age.) 2 Cor. 4:4.

As the God of this world (Age), he aims to "ape" God. As God sent His Son (Jesus) into the world, so Satan shall send Antichrist into the world. As God was in Christ, so Satan will incarnate himself in Antichrist.

The "Mystery of Godliness" is God manifest in the "flesh." 1 Tim. 3:16. The "Mystery of Iniquity" will be Satan manifest in the "flesh." 2 Thess. 2:7. Satan will see to it that Antichrist has all that Christ has.

I. Christ has a Church—the "Ecclesia;" Antichrist will have a church, the "Synagogue of Satan." Rev. 2:9; 3:9.

II. Christ will have a Bride, the "Church," Eph. 5:25-27; Antichrist will have a bride, the "Mystic Harlot Church." Rev. 17:1-16.

III. Christ has a Cup, "The Communion Cup," 1 Cor. 10:16; 11:25; Antichrist has a cup, the "Cup of Devils." 1 Cor. 10:21.

IV. Christ's earthly ministry lasted for three and a half years, and Satan shall reign in Antichrist for the same length of time.

V. Christ died at the age of thirty-three years, and for ought we know Antichrist shall be smitten at the same age; the age at which Alexander the Great, the "Great Horn" of the He-Goat, died.

VI. The Godhead is a Trinity, Father, Son and Holy Spirit, and Satan proposes, as the "God of this Age," to manifest himself as a Trinity. In contradistinction to the Divine Trinity we call this manifestation a

SATANIC TRINITY.

The members of it are—

1. **"The Dragon"**—the Anti-GOD."
2. **"The Beast"**—the "Anti-CHRIST."
3. **"The False Prophet"**—the "Anti-SPIRIT."

We have spoken of the first two under the heads of Satan and Antichrist, all that we need to consider in this chapter is—

123

THE FALSE PROPHET

After the Apostle John had seen and described the "Beast" that came up **out of the SEA**, he saw another "Beast" come up **out of the EARTH**. This "Second Beast," while John does not say it **was a lamb**, had "**Two Horns**" "**like a lamb**," that is, it was LAMB-LIKE. Because of this resemblance many claim that the "Second Beast" is the Antichrist, for Antichrist is supposed to imitate Christ. While the LAMB (Christ) is mentioned in the Book of Revelation 22 times, the description given of Him in chapter 5:6, is that of a lamb having "**SEVEN HORNS**" and not "**TWO**." This differentiates Him from the "lamb-like Beast" that comes up out of the earth, who, though he is "**lamb-like in appearance SPEAKS AS A DRAGON**."

The "Second Beast" has a name. He is called the "**FALSE PROPHET**" three times. First in chapter 16:13, then in chapter 19:20, and again in chapter 20:10. Twice he is associated with the "First Beast" (Antichrist) and once with the "Dragon" (Satan) and the "First Beast," and as they are PERSONS so must he be. The fact that he is called the "False Prophet" is proof that he is not the "Antichrist." Jesus had a foreview of him when He said—"There shall arise '**FALSE CHRISTS**' and '**FALSE PROPHETS,**' and shall show **GREAT SIGNS AND WONDERS**: insomuch that, if it were possible they shall deceive the very elect." Matt. 24:24. Here Jesus differentiates between "**FALSE CHRISTS**" and "**FALSE PROPHETS,**" therefore the "**ANTICHRIST**" and the "**FALSE PROPHET**" cannot be the same.

That the "Second Beast" comes up **out of the EARTH** may signify that he will be a **resurrected person**. If, as was hinted at, "Antichrist" was Judas resurrected, why should not the "False Prophet" also be a resurrected person? There will be two persons, as we have seen, who shall come back from Heaven as the "Two Witnesses," Moses and Elijah, why not two persons come up from "The Underworld," brought up by Satan to counteract the work of the "Two Witnesses"? The fact that the "First Beast" (Antichrist) and the "Second Beast" (False Prophet) are cast **ALIVE** into the "Lake of Fire" (Rev. 19:20) is further proof that they are more than ordinary mortals, and that the "First Beast" is **more** than the last ruling Emperor of the revived Roman Empire. He is the **Antichrist**, Satan's **SUPERMAN**.

In the "Dragon," the "Beast," and the "False Prophet," we have the "**SATANIC TRINITY**," Satan's imitation of the "Divine Trinity." In the unseen and invisible "Dragon" we have the **FATHER** (the **ANTI-GOD**). In the "Beast" we have the "**SON OF PERDITION**" (the **ANTI-CHRIST**), **begotten** of the Dragon, who appears on the earth, dies, and is resurrected, and to whom is given a throne by his Father the Dragon. In the "False Prophet" we have the "**ANTI-SPIRIT**," who **proceeds** from the "Dragon Father" and "Dragon Son," and whose speech is like the Dragon's. The "Dragon" then will be the "**ANTI-GOD**," the "Beast" the "**ANTI-CHRIST**," and the "False Prophet" the "**ANTI-SPIRIT**," and the fact that all **three are cast ALIVE** into the "Lake of Fire" (Rev. 20:10) is proof that they together form a "**Triumvirate**" which we may well call—"**THE SATANIC TRINITY**."

Again the "Antichrist" is to be a **KING** and rule over a **KINGDOM**. He will accept the "Kingdoms of this world" that Satan offered Christ, and that Christ refused. Matt. 4:8-10. He will also **EXALT** himself, and claim to be God. 2 Thess. 2:4. But the "False Prophet" is not a King, He does not exalt himself, he exalts the "First Beast" (Antichrist). His relation to the "First Beast" is the same as the Holy Spirit's relation to Christ. He causeth the earth and them which dwell therein to worship the "First Beast." He also has power to give life, and in this he imitates the Holy Spirit. And as the followers of Christ are sealed by the Holy Spirit until the "**Day of Redemption**" (Eph. 4:30); so, the followers of Antichrist shall be sealed by the False Prophet until the "**Day of Perdition**." Rev. 13:16-17.

The False Prophet will be a "Miracle Worker." While Jesus was a "miracle worker," He did all His mighty works in the "**power**" of the Holy Spirit. Acts 10:38. Among the miracles that the False Prophet will perform he will bring down **FIRE FROM HEAVEN**. As we have seen under the work of the "Two Witnesses," Rev. 11:1-14, there will probably be a "**FIRE-TEST**" between Elijah and the False Prophet, and the test as to who is God of Mount Carmel will be repeated. That Satan, who will then energize the False Prophet, can do this is clear from Job 1:16, where Satan, having secured permission from God to touch all that Job had, brought down "**fire from heaven**" and burned up Job's sheep and servants.

The False Prophet then commands the people to make an

"IMAGE OF THE BEAST."

This is further proof that the "First Beast" is the Antichrist. It is a strange weakness of mankind that they must have some **VISIBLE** God to worship, and when the Children of Israel, who had been delivered from Egypt under Moses' leadership, thought he had forsaken them because he did not come down from the Mount, they called Aaron to make them gods which should go before them, and Aaron made for them the "**GOLDEN CALF**." Ex. 32:1-6. So the False Prophet will have the people make for the purpose of worship an "**IMAGE OF THE BEAST**." But the wonderful thing about the "**IMAGE**" is that the False Prophet will have power to give **LIFE** to it, and cause it to **SPEAK**, and to demand that all who will not worship it shall be put to death. In other words the "**IMAGE**" will be a **living, speaking, AUTOMATON**.

This "Image" reminds us of the "**GOLDEN IMAGE**" that Nebuchadnezzar commanded to be made and set up in the "Plain of Dura," in the Province of Babylon (Dan. 3:1-30), before which, at the sounding of musical instruments, the people were commanded to bow down and worship under penalty, for those who disobeyed, of being cast into a "**BURNING FIERY FURNACE**." Doubtless there will be many in the "Day of Antichrist" who will refuse to bow down and worship the "Image of the Beast," and who will not escape as did the "Three Hebrew Children," though God may interpose in a miraculous way to deliver some. And as if this was not enough the False Prophet shall cause—"ALL, both small and great, rich and poor, free and bond, to receive a 'MARK' in their RIGHT HAND, or in their FOREHEAD; and that no man might BUY or SELL, save he that has the 'MARK' or the 'NAME OF THE BEAST,' or the 'NUMBER OF HIS NAME'." This "**MARK**" will be known as the

"BRAND OF HELL."

This is what the world is fast coming to. The time is not far distant when the various "Trusts" and "Combinations of Capital" will be merged into a "**FEDERATION OF TRUSTS**," at the head of which shall be a "**NAPOLEON OF CAPITAL**." Ultimately this "Federation of Trusts" will extend to the whole world, at the head of which shall be **THE ANTICHRIST**, and the **producer** and **consumer** will be powerless in the tentacles of this **OCTOPUS**, and no man shall be able to BUY or SELL who has not the "**MARK OF THE BEAST**" either upon his "**right hand**" or on his "**forehead**." This "**Mark**" will be BRANDED or burnt on. It will probably be the "**NUMBER OF THE BEAST**" or "666." The number "666" is the "**NUMBER OF MAN**," and stops short of the perfect number

SEVEN. Man was created on the **SIXTH** day. Goliath the opposer of God's people, a type of Satan, was 6 cubits in height, he had 6 pieces of armor, and his spearhead weighed 600 shekels. 1 Sam. 17: 4-7. Nebuchadnezzar's Image, a type of the "Image of the Beast," was 60 cubits in height, 6 cubits wide, and 6 instruments of music summoned the worshippers. Dan. 3:1-7.

IMAGE OF THE BEAST

In that day men will doubtless prefer to have the **"MARK"** on the back of their right hand so it can be readily seen in the act of signing checks, drafts, and receipts. There will doubtless be public officials in all public places of business to see that no one buys or sells who has not the **"MARK."** This will apply to women as well as men. No one can shop, or even buy from the huckster at the door, without the **"MARK,"** under **penalty** of **DEATH**. Those will be awful times for those who will not **WORSHIP THE BEAST**. If they can neither buy nor sell without the **"MARK,"** they must beg, or starve or be killed. The instrument of death will be the guillotine (Rev. 20:4), and the daily papers will contain a list of the names of those who were beheaded the day before so as to frighten the people into obedience to the law. The doom of the "Satanic Trinity" will be, that at the close of that awful time of Tribulation the Lord Jesus Christ will return, and the "Dragon," the **"Anti-God,"** will be cast into the **"BOTTOMLESS PIT"** for a thousand years (Rev. 20: 1-3), and the "Beast," the **"Anti-Christ,"** and the "False Prophet," the **"Anti-Spirit,"** will be cast **ALIVE** into the **"LAKE OF FIRE."** Rev. 19:20.

THE COMING OF HIS FEET

In the crimson of the morning, in the whiteness of the noon,
   In the amber glory of the day's retreat,
In the midnight robed in darkness, or the gleaming of the moon,
   I listen for the coming of his feet.

I have heard his weary footsteps on the sands of Galilee,
   On the Temple's marble pavement on the street,
Worn with weight of sorrow falt'ring up the slopes of Calvary,
   The sorrow of the coming of his feet.

Down the minster-aisles of splendor, from betwixt the cherubim,
   Thro' the wond'ring throng with motion strong and fleet,
Sounds his victor tread, with a music far and dim,
   The music of the coming of his feet.

Sandalled not with shoes of silver, girdled not with woven gold,
   Weighted not with shimmering gems and odors sweet,
But white-winged, and shod with glory as in the Tabor light of old,
   The glory of the coming of his feet.

He is coming, oh, my spirit! with his everlasting peace;
   With his blessedness immortal and complete;
He is coming, oh, my spirit! and his coming brings release!
   I am living for the coming of his feet.

                —Selected.

XXI

THE FOUR GOSPELS

The word "Gospel" means "Good News," and is so familiar that its application is supposed to be uniform. When, therefore, we read of

The Gospel of the **KINGDOM**,
The Gospel of the **GRACE OF GOD**,
The **GLORIOUS GOSPEL**, and
The **EVERLASTING GOSPEL**,

it is taken for granted that they all refer to one and the same thing. But this is not true.

1. THE GOSPEL OF "THE KINGDOM."

Matt. 24:14.

This is the "Good News" that God purposes to set up a Kingdom on this earth over which David's Son, **JESUS**, shall reign, as prophesied in Luke 1:32-33. Two preachings of this Gospel are mentioned, one past, beginning with the ministry of John the Baptist, and preached by Jesus and His Disciples, but it ended with the rejection of Jesus as King. This Gospel is to be preached again after the Church is taken out. It will be the fulfillment of Matt. 24:14, where it says: "This Gospel of 'THE KINGDOM' shall be preached in all the world for a WITNESS unto all nations; and then shall the end come." This has no reference to the Gospel that is now being preached to the nations. It is the Gospel of **SALVATION**, but the "Gospel of the Kingdom" is not for "Salvation" but for a **WITNESS**, that is, it is the **announcement that the time has come to SET UP THE KINGDOM**. It will be preached first by Elijah the forerunner (Mal. 4:5-6), and by others who shall be commissioned to bear the news to all nations as a proclamation of the coming of Christ as King to occupy the "Throne of David," and for the purpose of re-gathering Israel to the Promised Land.

2. THE GOSPEL OF "THE GRACE OF GOD."

Acts 20:24.

This is the "Good News" that Jesus Christ, the rejected King, died on the Cross for our **SALVATION**. This form of the Gospel is described in many ways. It is called the **"GOSPEL OF GOD"** (Rom. 1:1), because it has its source in the **LOVE OF GOD**. John 3:16. Its Character is **GRACE**. Acts 20:24. Its Subject is **CHRIST** (Rom. 1:16; 2 Cor. 10:14), and it is the **POWER OF GOD UNTO SALVATION**. And it is the **"GOSPEL OF PEACE,"** because it makes peace between the sinner and God, and brings peace to the soul. Eph. 6:15.

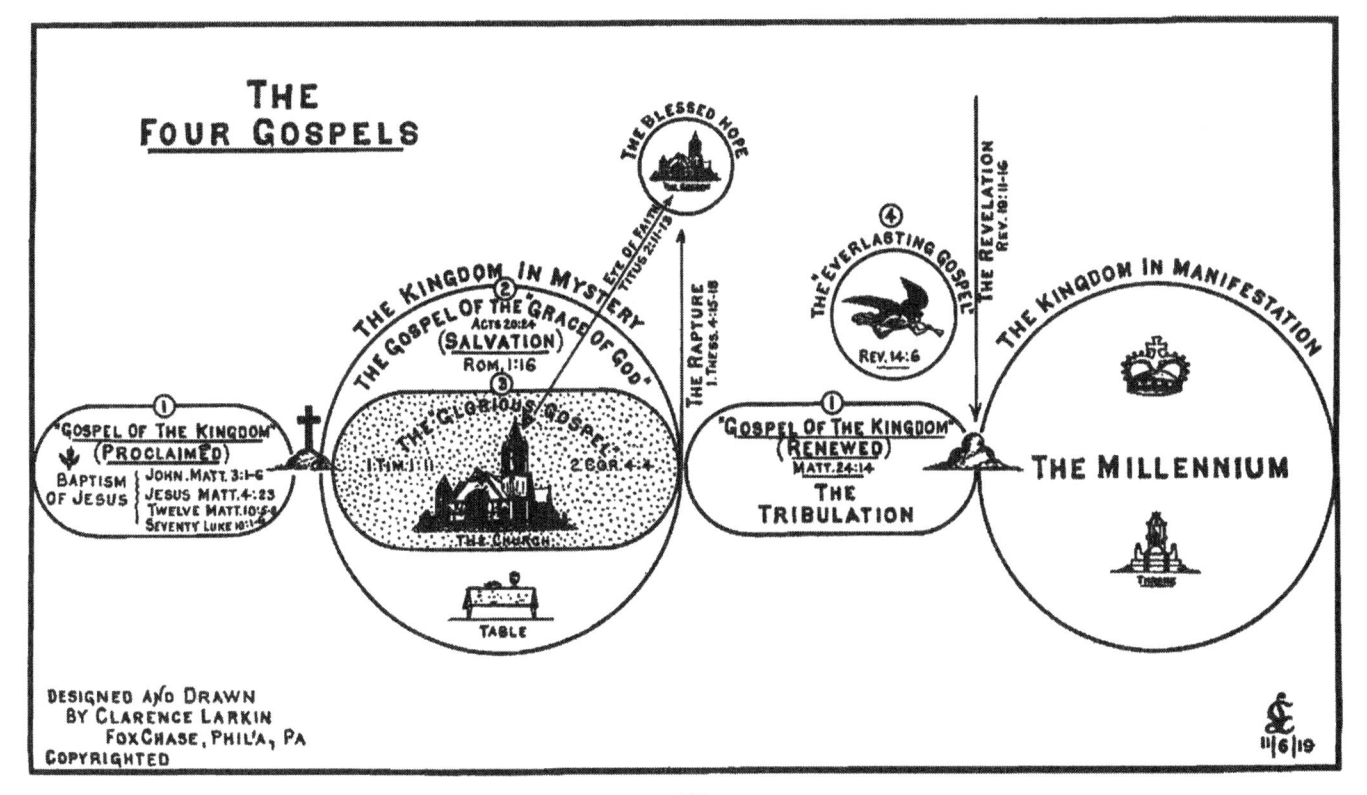

THE FOUR GOSPELS

DESIGNED AND DRAWN BY CLARENCE LARKIN
FOX CHASE, PHIL'A, PA
COPYRIGHTED

3. THE "GLORIOUS" GOSPEL.
2 Cor. 4:4. I Tim. 1:11.

The "GLORIOUS GOSPEL" is that phase of the Gospel of "The Grace of God" that speaks of Him who is in the **GLORY**, and has been **GLORIFIED**, and who is bringing many sons **TO GLORY**. Heb. 2:10. It has special reference to His Second Coming, and is especially comforting to those who are looking for His **GLORIOUS APPEARING** (Titus 2:13), and it is to this Gospel that Satan, the "God of this Age," is particularly anxious to "blind the minds" of those who believe not in the Pre-Millennial coming of the Lord. 2 Cor. 4:3-4.

4. THE EVERLASTING GOSPEL.
Rev. 14:6.

This Gospel will be proclaimed just before the "Vial Judgments," and by an angel. It is the only Gospel committed to an angel. It is neither the Gospel of the "Kingdom," nor of "Grace." Its burden is not **SALVATION** but **JUDGMENT**—"Fear God, and give glory to Him; for the **HOUR OF HIS JUDGMENT IS COME**."

It is "Good News" to Israel, and all who are passing through the "fires of Judgment," because it declares that their troubles will soon end in the Judgment and Destruction of Antichrist and his followers. It calls on men to worship God as "CREATOR," and not as "Saviour" and so it is called in the Revised version—"THE ETERNAL GOSPEL," the Gospel that has been proclaimed from Eden down by Patriarchs and Prophets, and not an "Everlasting Gospel" in the sense that it saves men for all eternity. Its burden is not "Repent," or "do this" or "do that," but—"FEAR GOD, and give GLORY TO HIM; for the HOUR OF HIS JUDGMENT IS COME; and WORSHIP HIM THAT MADE HEAVEN, AND EARTH, AND THE SEA, AND THE FOUNTAINS OF WATERS." From this we see how important it is to distinguish between the various Gospels, not only as to their message, but the period to which they apply, otherwise there will be confusion and false teaching. See Chart, "The Four Gospels."

There is also "ANOTHER GOSPEL" (Gal. 1:6-12, 2 Cor. 11:4), which is not another, and which Paul repudiated. It is a perversion of the true Gospel and has many seductive forms, and in the main teaches that "FAITH" is NOT SUFFICIENT to Salvation, nor able to keep and perfect, and so emphasizes "GOOD WORKS." Col. 2:18-23, Heb. 6:1, 9:14. The Apostle Paul pronounces a fearful "Anathema" upon its preachers and teachers. Gal. 1:8-9.

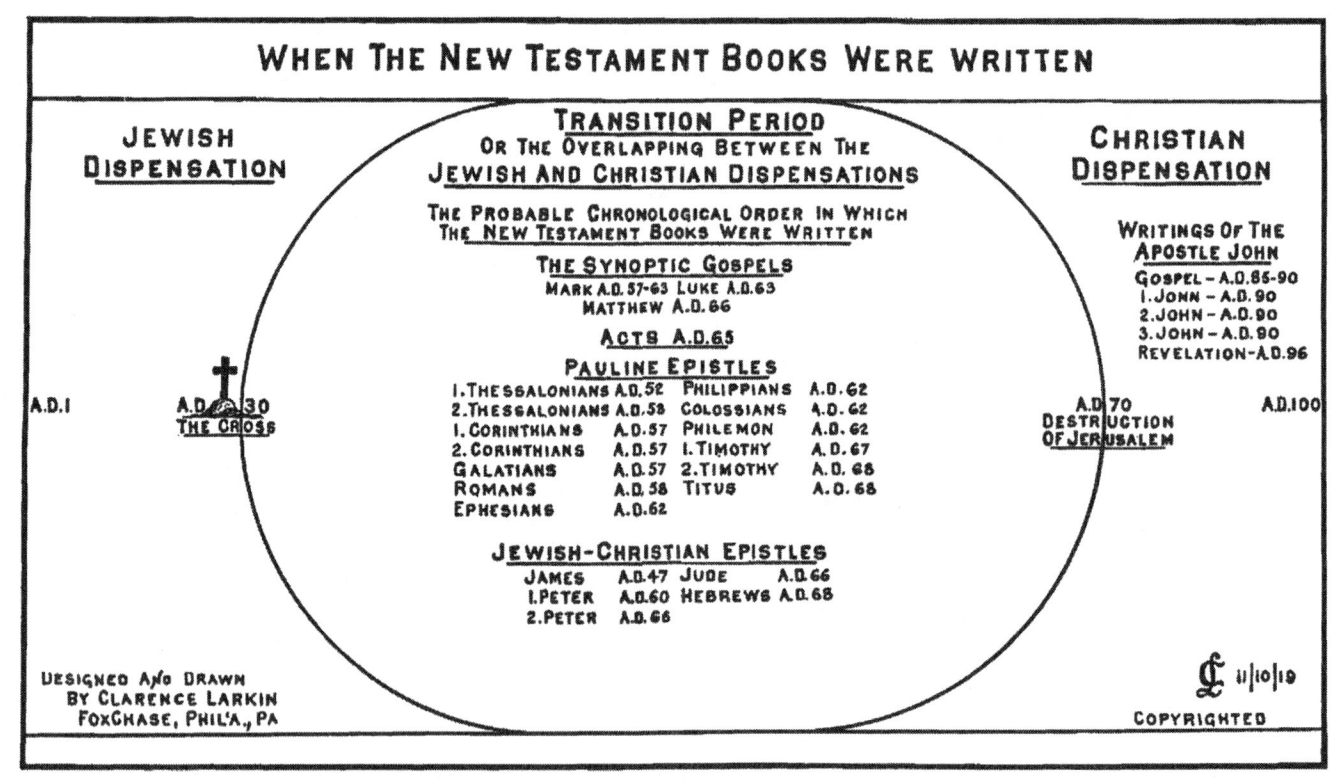

WHEN THE NEW TESTAMENT BOOKS WERE WRITTEN

JEWISH DISPENSATION — A.D. 1 — A.D. 30 THE CROSS

TRANSITION PERIOD
Or The Overlapping Between The Jewish And Christian Dispensations

The Probable Chronological Order In Which The New Testament Books Were Written

THE SYNOPTIC GOSPELS
MARK A.D. 57-63　LUKE A.D. 63
MATTHEW A.D. 66

ACTS A.D. 65

PAULINE EPISTLES
1. THESSALONIANS	A.D. 52	PHILIPPIANS	A.D. 62
2. THESSALONIANS	A.D. 53	COLOSSIANS	A.D. 62
1. CORINTHIANS	A.D. 57	PHILEMON	A.D. 62
2. CORINTHIANS	A.D. 57	1. TIMOTHY	A.D. 67
GALATIANS	A.D. 57	2. TIMOTHY	A.D. 68
ROMANS	A.D. 58	TITUS	A.D. 68
EPHESIANS	A.D. 62		

JEWISH-CHRISTIAN EPISTLES
JAMES	A.D. 47	JUDE	A.D. 66
1. PETER	A.D. 60	HEBREWS	A.D. 68
2. PETER	A.D. 66		

A.D. 70 DESTRUCTION OF JERUSALEM

CHRISTIAN DISPENSATION — A.D. 100

WRITINGS OF THE APOSTLE JOHN
GOSPEL – A.D. 85-90
1. JOHN – A.D. 90
2. JOHN – A.D. 90
3. JOHN – A.D. 90
REVELATION – A.D. 96

Designed And Drawn By Clarence Larkin, Fox Chase, Phil'a., PA
11/10/19　COPYRIGHTED

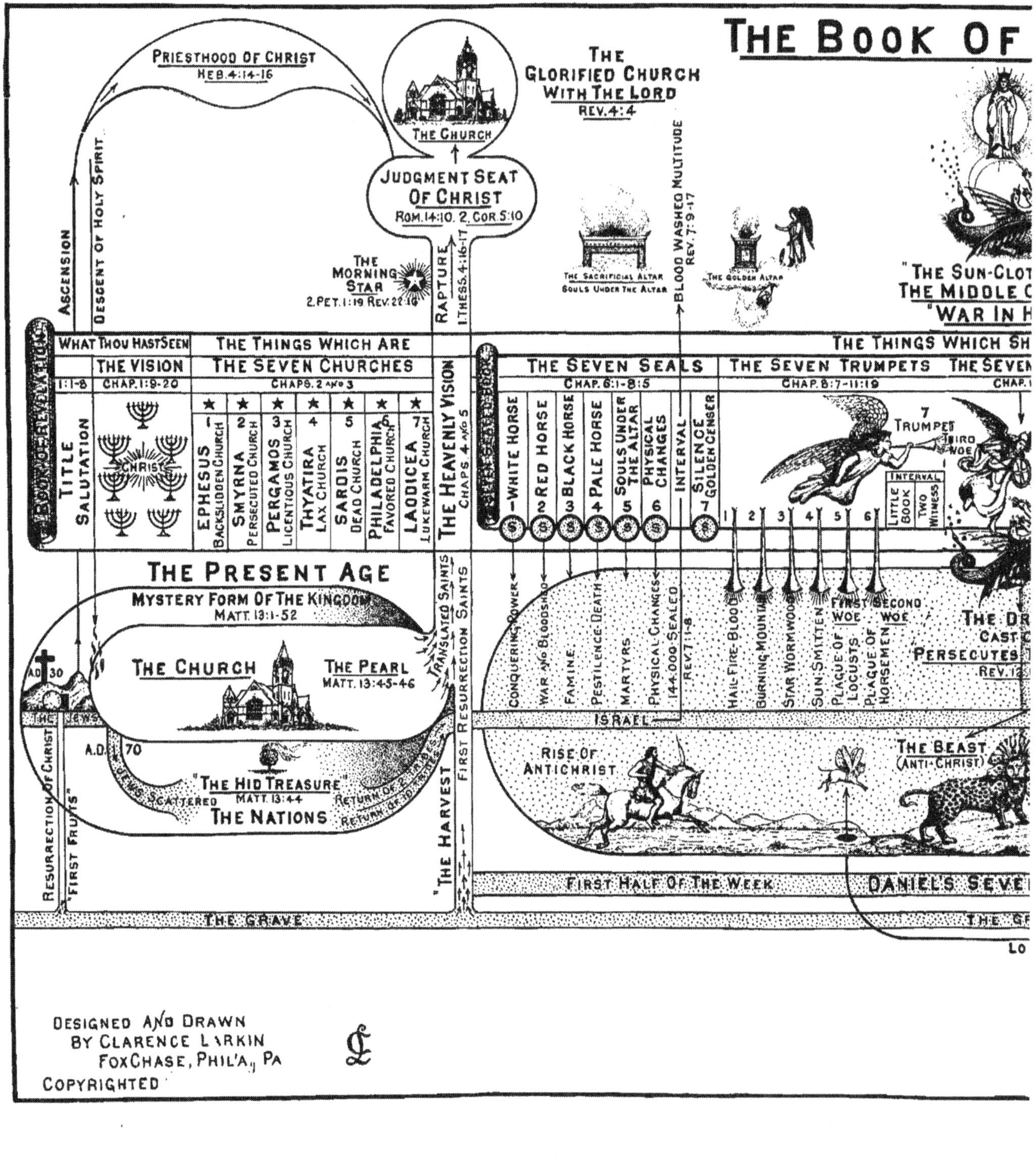
THE BOOK OF
PRIESTHOOD OF CHRIST
HEB. 4:14-16
THE CHURCH
JUDGMENT SEAT OF CHRIST
ROM. 14:10. 2. COR. 5:10
THE GLORIFIED CHURCH WITH THE LORD
REV. 4:4
ASCENSION
DESCENT OF HOLY SPIRIT
THE MORNING STAR
2. PET. 1:19 REV. 22:16
RAPTURE
1. THESS. 4:16-17
THE SACRIFICIAL ALTAR
SOULS UNDER THE ALTAR
BLOOD WASHED MULTITUDE
REV. 7:9-17
THE GOLDEN ALTAR
"THE SUN-CLOT
THE MIDDLE C
"WAR IN H
WHAT THOU HAST SEEN
THE THINGS WHICH ARE
THE THINGS WHICH SH
THE VISION
THE SEVEN CHURCHES
THE SEVEN SEALS
THE SEVEN TRUMPETS
THE SEVEN
1:1-8
CHAP. 1:9-20
CHAPS. 2 AND 3
CHAP. 6:1-8:5
CHAP. 8:7-11:19
TITLE
SALUTATION
CHRIST
1 EPHESUS BACKSLIDDEN CHURCH
2 SMYRNA PERSECUTED CHURCH
3 PERGAMOS LICENTIOUS CHURCH
4 THYATIRA LAX CHURCH
5 SARDIS DEAD CHURCH
6 PHILADELPHIA FAVORED CHURCH
7 LAODICEA LUKEWARM CHURCH
THE HEAVENLY VISION
CHAPS. 4 AND 5
1 WHITE HORSE
2 RED HORSE
3 BLACK HORSE
4 PALE HORSE
5 SOULS UNDER THE ALTAR
6 PHYSICAL CHANGES
INTERVAL
7 SILENCE GOLDEN CENSER
7 TRUMPET
THIRD WOE
INTERVAL
LITTLE BOOK
TWO WITNESS
THE PRESENT AGE
MYSTERY FORM OF THE KINGDOM
MATT. 13:1-52
THE CHURCH
THE PEARL
MATT. 13:45-46
A.D. 30
THE JEWS
A.D. 70
JEWS SCATTERED
"THE HID TREASURE"
MATT. 13:44
THE NATIONS
RETURN OF 2 TRIBES
RETURN OF 10 TRIBES
TRANSLATED SAINTS
FIRST RESURRECTION SAINTS
"THE HARVEST"
RESURRECTION OF CHRIST
"FIRST FRUITS"
CONQUERING POWER
WAR AND BLOODSHED
FAMINE
PESTILENCE-DEATH
MARTYRS
PHYSICAL CHANGES
144,000 SEALED
REV. 7:1-8
HAIL-FIRE-BLOOD
BURNING MOUNTAIN
STAR WORMWOOD
SUN SMITTEN
PLAGUE OF LOCUSTS
PLAGUE OF HORSEMEN
FIRST WOE
SECOND WOE
THE DR
CAST
PERSECUTES T
REV. 12
ISRAEL
RISE OF ANTICHRIST
THE BEAST (ANTI-CHRIST)
FIRST HALF OF THE WEEK
DANIEL'S SEVE
THE GRAVE
THE GR
LO
DESIGNED AND DRAWN
BY CLARENCE LARKIN
FOXCHASE, PHIL'A., PA
COPYRIGHTED

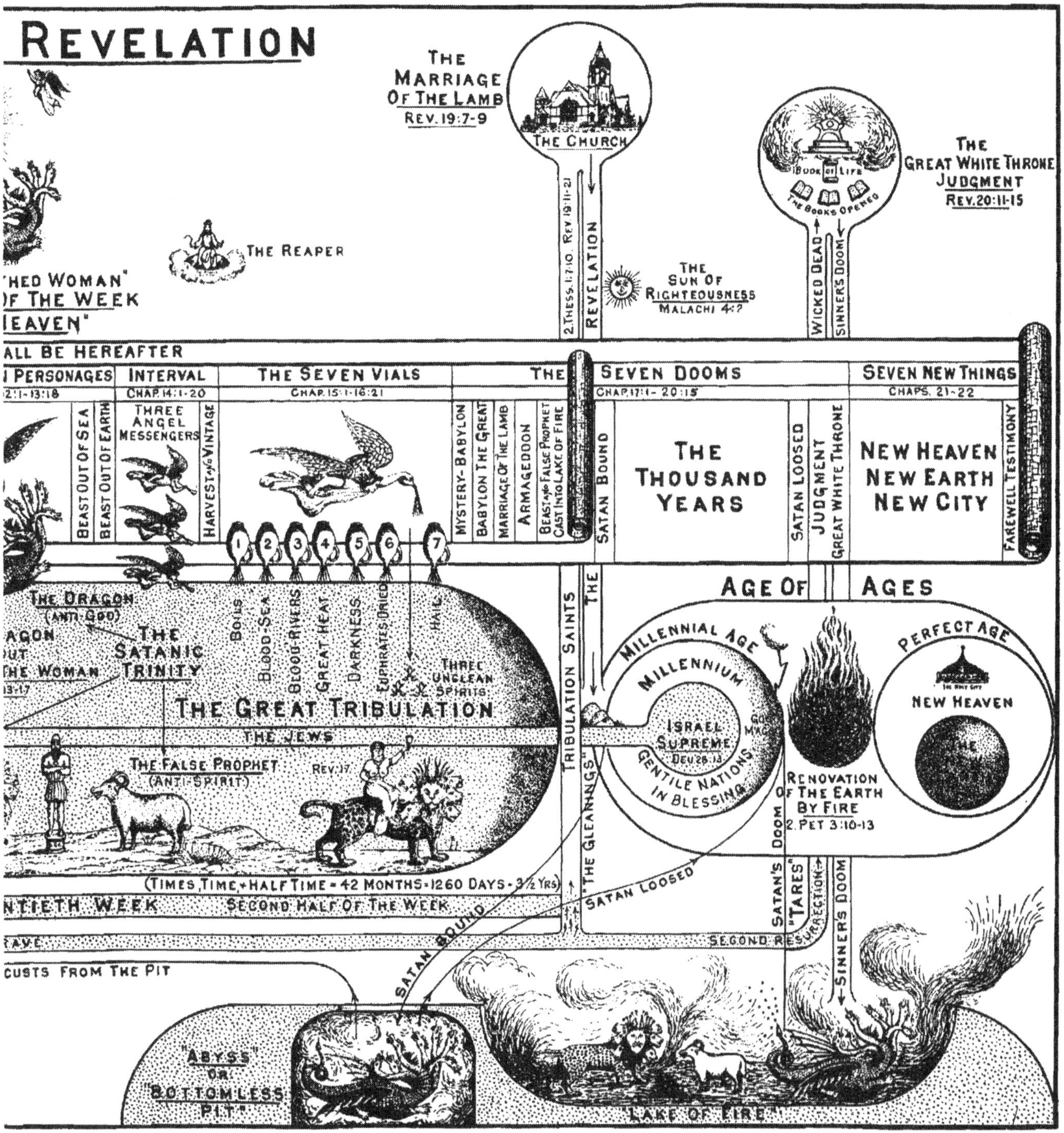
REVELATION
THE MARRIAGE OF THE LAMB
REV. 19:7-9
THE CHURCH
2 THESS. 1:7-10. REV. 19:11-21
REVELATION
THE SUN OF RIGHTEOUSNESS
MALACHI 4:2
BOOK OF LIFE
THE BOOKS OPENED
THE GREAT WHITE THRONE JUDGMENT
REV. 20:11-15
WICKED DEAD
SINNER'S DOOM
THE REAPER
"HED WOMAN"
OF THE WEEK
IEAVEN"
ALL BE HEREAFTER
PERSONAGES
INTERVAL
CHAP. 14:1-20
THE SEVEN VIALS
CHAP. 15:1-16:21
THE SEVEN DOOMS
CHAP. 17:1-20:15
SEVEN NEW THINGS
CHAPS. 21-22
BEAST OUT OF SEA
BEAST OUT OF EARTH
THREE ANGEL MESSENGERS
HARVEST AND VINTAGE
MYSTERY-BABYLON
BABYLON THE GREAT
MARRIAGE OF THE LAMB
ARMAGEDDON
BEAST AND FALSE PROPHET CAST INTO LAKE OF FIRE
SATAN BOUND
THE THOUSAND YEARS
SATAN LOOSED
JUDGMENT
GREAT WHITE THRONE
NEW HEAVEN
NEW EARTH
NEW CITY
FAREWELL TESTIMONY
1 2 3 4 5 6 7
AGE OF AGES
THE DRAGON
(ANTI-GOD)
THE SATANIC TRINITY
THE WOMAN
BOILS
BLOOD-SEA
BLOOD-RIVERS
GREAT HEAT
DARKNESS
EUPHRATES DRIED
HAIL
THREE UNCLEAN SPIRITS
THE GREAT TRIBULATION
THE JEWS
THE FALSE PROPHET
(ANTI-SPIRIT)
REV. 17
TRIBULATION SAINTS
THE "GLEANINGS"
MILLENNIAL AGE
MILLENNIUM
ISRAEL SUPREME
DEU. 28:13
GENTILE NATIONS IN BLESSING
RENOVATION OF THE EARTH BY FIRE
2 PET. 3:10-13
PERFECT AGE
NEW HEAVEN
SATAN'S DOOM
"TARES"
RESURRECTION
SINNER'S DOOM
(TIMES, TIME + HALF TIME = 42 MONTHS = 1260 DAYS = 3½ YRS)
NTIETH WEEK
SECOND HALF OF THE WEEK
SATAN LOOSED
SATAN BOUND
SECOND RESURRECTION
CUSTS FROM THE PIT
"ABYSS" OR "BOTTOMLESS PIT"
"LAKE OF FIRE"

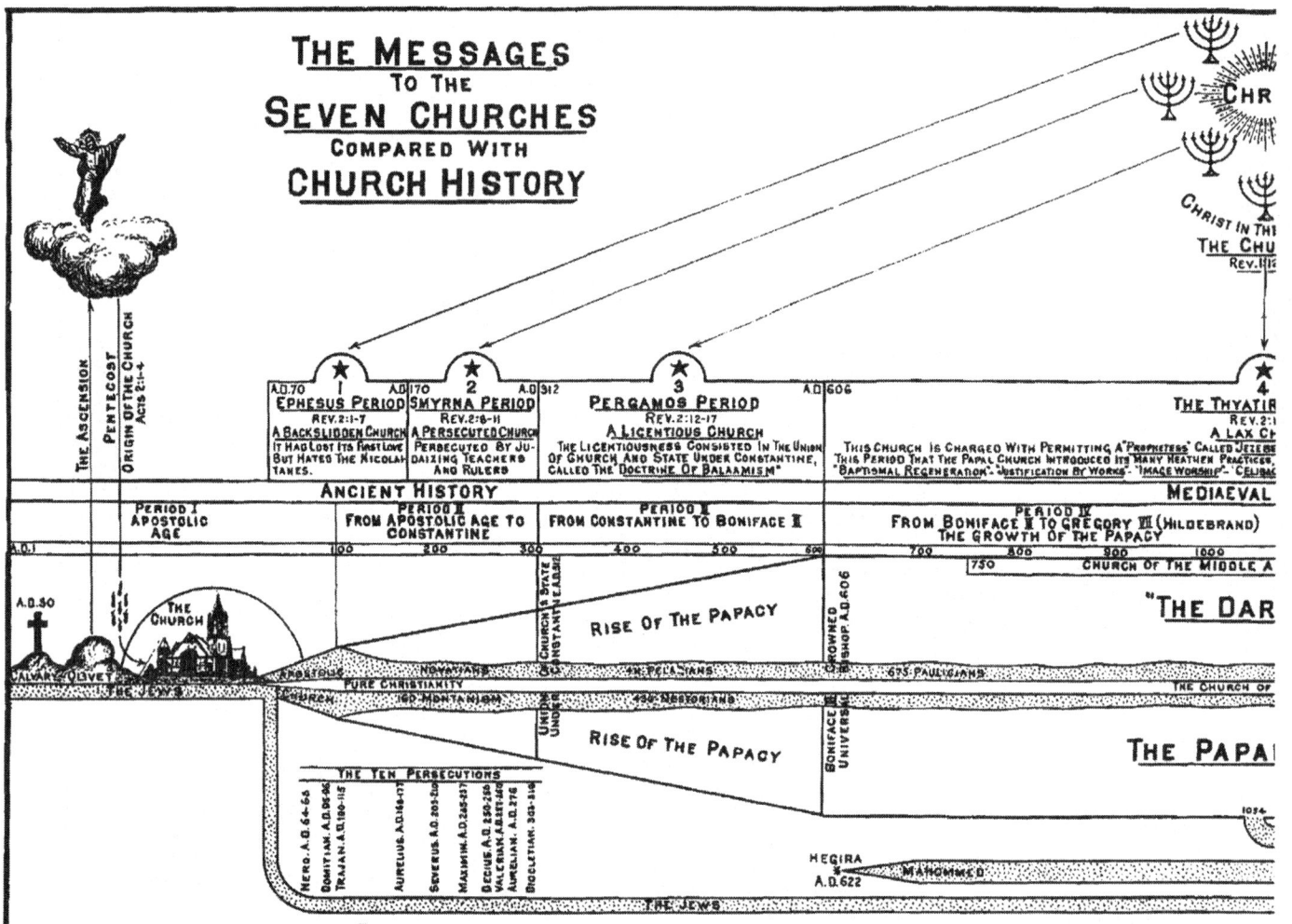

The Messages to the Seven Churches Compared With Church History

1. Ephesus Period (A.D. 70 – A.D. 170)
Rev. 2:1-7
A Backslidden Church
It had lost its first love but hated the Nicolaitanes.

2. Smyrna Period (A.D. 170 – A.D. 312)
Rev. 2:8-11
A Persecuted Church
Persecuted by Judaizing Teachers and Rulers.

3. Pergamos Period (A.D. 312 – A.D. 606)
Rev. 2:12-17
A Licentious Church
The licentiousness consisted in the union of Church and State under Constantine, called the Doctrine of Balaamism.

4. Thyatira Period
Rev. 2:
A Lax Church
This Church is charged with permitting a "Prophetess" called Jezebel. This period that the Papal Church introduced its many heathen practices — "Baptismal Regeneration" — "Justification by Works" — "Image Worship" — "Celibacy"

Christ in the Midst of the Churches — Rev. 1

Ancient History — Mediaeval

- **Period I** — Apostolic Age (A.D. 1–100)
- **Period II** — From Apostolic Age to Constantine (100–312)
- **Period III** — From Constantine to Boniface III (312–606)
- **Period IV** — From Boniface III to Gregory VII (Hildebrand) — The Growth of the Papacy (606–1073)

Church of the Middle Ages — "The Dark"

A.D. 50 — Calvary — Olivet — Pentecost — Origin of the Church — Acts 2:1-4 — The Ascension

The Church — Pure Christianity
Union of Church & State under Constantine
Rise of the Papacy
Novatians — 160 Montanism — 431 Nestorians — 435 Pelagians — 675 Paulicians
Boniface III Universal Bishop A.D. 606 — Crowned Bishop A.D. 606
Rise of the Papacy — The Papa[cy]
1054

The Ten Persecutions
- Nero, A.D. 64-68
- Domitian, A.D. 95-96
- Trajan, A.D. 109-115
- Aurelius, A.D. 161-180
- Severus, A.D. 200-211
- Maximin, A.D. 235-237
- Decius, A.D. 250-253
- Valerian, A.D. 257-260
- Aurelian, A.D. 270
- Diocletian, A.D. 303-310

Hegira A.D. 622 — Mahomet

The Jews

Explanatory

The chart is an attempt to compare the messages to the "Seven Churches" of Asia Minor, with 19 centuries of church history, to see if there is any correspondence between them, and thus prove that the messages to the "Seven Churches" are prophetic of seven periods of church history that were to follow each other in regular order. A careful study of the chart will show a wonderful correspondence between the two. This is brought out in the chapter on "The Messages to the Seven Churches."

The chart shows the Church of the "First-Born" in its course down the centuries and finally taken out, leaving the remainder of the professing church to pass into the "Sea of Apostasy" and be swallowed up by the revived Papal Church. This is seen in the increasing blackness of the stream as the time approaches for the exit of the church. The relation of the Jews and Mohammedans, and various religious cults to the religious history of the age is also shown on the chart.

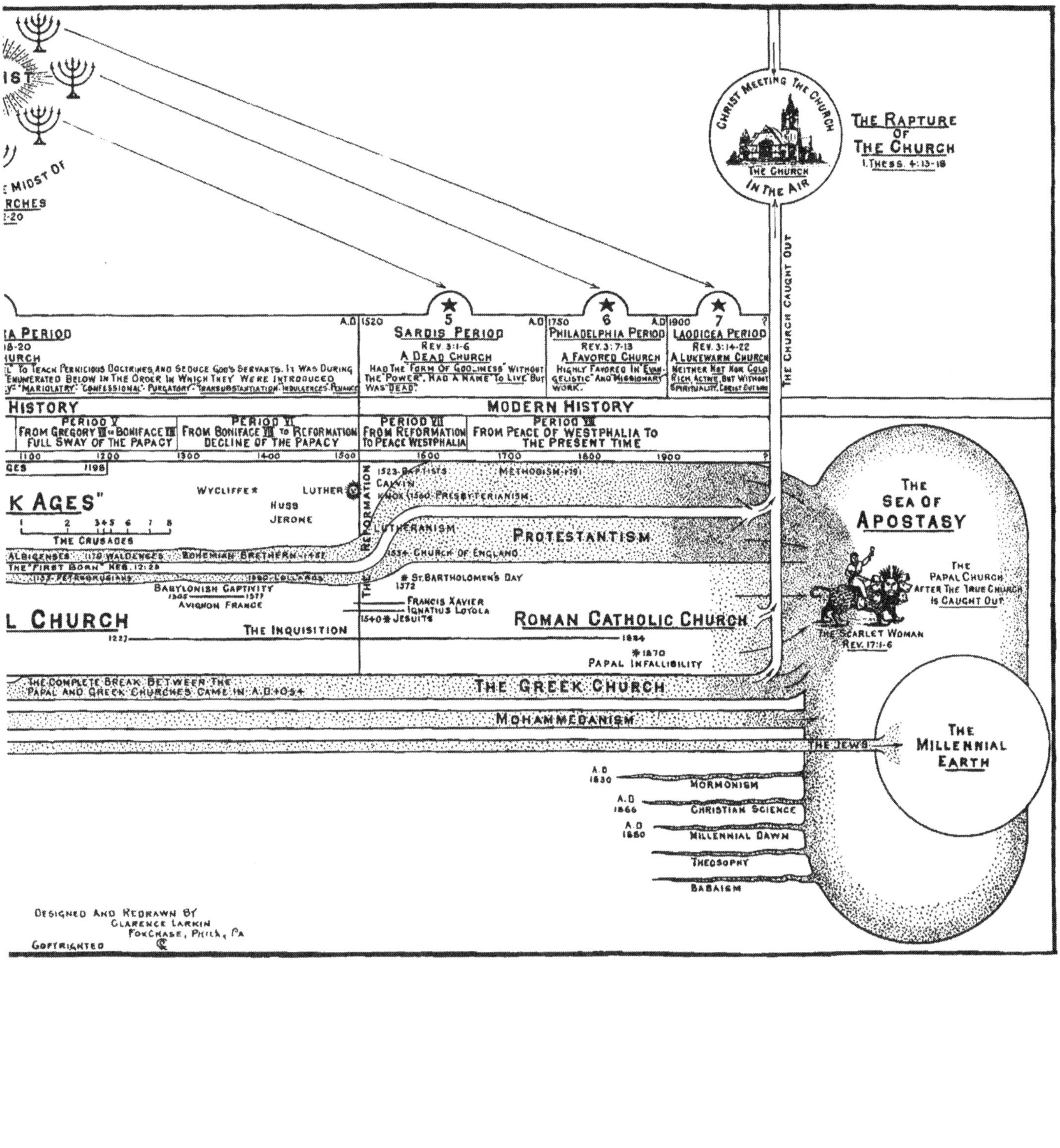

IST
MIDST OF
RCHES
2-20
Christ Meeting The Church
The Church In The Air
The Rapture Of The Church
I. Thess. 4:13-18
The Church Caught Out
A.D. 1520
5
Sardis Period
Rev. 3:1-6
A Dead Church
Had The "Form Of Godliness" Without The "Power", Had A Name To Live But Was "Dead".
A.D. 1750
6
Philadelphia Period
Rev. 3:7-13
A Favored Church
Highly Favored In "Evangelistic" And Missionary Work.
A.D. 1900
7
Laodicea Period
Rev. 3:14-22
A Lukewarm Church
Neither Hot Nor Cold, Rich, Active But Without Spirituality, Christ Outside
A Period
18-20
Church
To Teach Pernicious Doctrines And Seduce God's Servants. It Was During
Enumerated Below In The Order In Which They Were Introduced.
"Mariolatry" "Confessional" "Purgatory" "Transubstantiation" "Indulgences" "Penance"
History
Modern History
Period V
From Gregory VII to Boniface VIII
Full Sway Of The Papacy
Period VI
From Boniface VIII to Reformation
Decline Of The Papacy
Period VII
From Reformation To Peace Westphalia
Period VIII
From Peace Of Westphalia To The Present Time
1100
1200
1300
1400
1500
1600
1700
1800
1900
1198
K Ages"
Wycliffe
Huss
Jerone
Luther
The Reformation
The Crusades
1523 Baptists
Calvin
Knox (1560) Presbyterianism
Methodism 1791
Lutheranism
Protestantism
1534 Church Of England
Albigenses
1170 Waldenses
Bohemian Brethern 1457
The "First Born" Heb. 12:23
1137 Petrobrusians
1380 Lollards
Babylonish Captivity
1305 — 1377
Avignon France
St. Bartholomew's Day
1572
Francis Xavier
Ignatius Loyola
1540 Jesuits
L Church
1227
The Inquisition
Roman Catholic Church
1854
1870
Papal Infallibility
The Complete Break Between The Papal And Greek Churches Came In A.D. 1054
The Greek Church
Mohammedanism
The Jews
The Sea Of Apostasy
The Papal Church After The True Church Is Caught Out
The Scarlet Woman
Rev. 17:1-6
The Millennial Earth
A.D. 1830
Mormonism
A.D. 1866
Christian Science
A.D. 1880
Millennial Dawn
Theosophy
Babaism
Designed And Redrawn By Clarence Larkin
Foxchase, Phila, Pa
Copyrighted

XXII
THE SEVEN CHURCHES

The Book of Revelation was written in A. D. 96. The writer was the Apostle John. He was told to write the things which he "saw" and "heard." The Book therefore is a divinely given book, and is the "Revelation of Jesus Christ" (Rev. 1:1) and not of John. It is the most important and valuable prophetic book in the Bible. All through the Old Testament there are scattered references to things which are to come to pass in the "Last Days." The Book of Revelation reveals

The Divine Program,

or order, in which these events are to happen. It is the Book of Consummation and its proper place in the sacred canon is where it is placed, at the end of the Bible. The Book is full of "action." Earth and heaven are brought near together. The clouds roll away, thrones, elders, and angelic forms are seen; harps, trumpets, cries from disembodied souls, and choruses of song are heard. Earth touches heaven, and alas it touches hell also. There are strong moral contrasts. Good and evil meet. There is no blending, but sharp contrasts, and a long protracted conflict that ends in victory for the good.

The Book is addressed to the "**seven churches which are in Asia.**" By Asia is not meant the great Continent of Asia, or even the whole of Asia Minor, but only its western end. Neither were the seven churches named the only churches in that district, for there were at least three other churches: Colosse, Col. 1:2; Hierapolis, Col. 4:13; and Troas, Acts 20:6, 7. These Seven Churches then must be representative or "typical" churches, chosen for certain characteristics typical of the character of the Church of Christ from the end of the First Century down to the time of Christ's return for His Church, and descriptive of

Seven Church Periods

clearly defined in Church History.

John when he received his message was a prisoner on the Isle of Patmos. He heard behind him a "great voice," as of a trumpet, and when he turned he saw "Seven Golden Candlesticks," and standing in their midst one like unto the "Son of Man," who held in His right hand "Seven Stars." He was told that the "Seven Stars" were the "Angels" (Ministers or Messengers) of the Seven Churches, and the "Seven Candlesticks" represented the Seven Churches. "Lampstand" is a better translation for the word "Candlestick," and is so given in the margin of our Bibles. A "Candlestick" requires a light which is self-consuming, while a "Lampstand" is simply the "Holder" of a lamp whose light is fed from a reservoir of oil, thus typifying the oil of the Holy Spirit. Thus Christ looks upon the churches as not the Light, but simply the "Light Holder." The use of the figures "Lampstands" and "Stars," which are only for service in the night, indicates that we are living in the "Night" of this Age.

The "Key" to the interpretation of the Book of Revelation is its "Threefold Division." Rev. 1:19.

I. Things Past.
"The Things Which Thou Hast SEEN."

The Vision of Christ in the midst of the "Lampstands." Chapter one.

II. Things Present.
"The Things Which ARE."

Obviously the Seven Churches. Chapters two and three. John was not far from 100 years old, and the only remaining Apostle. The Temple and city of Jerusalem had been destroyed, and the Jews dispersed 26 years before, and John's attention was called to the condition of the "Seven" representative churches of Asia.

III. Things Future.
"The Things Which SHALL BE HEREAFTER."

Beginning with the fourth chapter unto the end of the Book. Rev. 4:1.

It is worthy of note that the "Messages to the Seven Churches" are inserted between **Two Visions**, the "**Vision of Christ**" in the midst of the "Seven Lampstands" in chapter one, and the "**Vision of the Four and Twenty Elders**" round about the Throne, in chapter four.

As chapter four is a vision of the "**Glorified Church**" with the Lord, after it has been caught out (1 Thess. 4:13-17), then the Second Division of the Book—

"The Things Which Are,"

and which includes chapters two and three, must be a description or prophetic outline of the "Spiritual History" of the Church from the time when John wrote the Book in A. D. 96, down to the taking out of the Church, or else we have no "prophetic view" of the Church during that period, for she disappears from the earth at the close of chapter three, and is not seen again until she reappears with her Lord in chapter nineteen. This we shall find to be the case.

This interpretation of the "Messages to the Seven Churches" was hidden to the early Church, because time was required for Church History to develop and be written, so a comparison could be made to reveal the correspondence. If it had been clearly revealed that the Seven Churches stood for "Seven Church Periods" that would have to elapse before Christ could come back, the incentive to watch would have been absent.

While the character of these Seven Churches is descriptive of the Church during seven periods of her history, we must not forget that the condition of those churches, as described, were their exact condition in John's day. So we see that at the close of the First Century the leaven of "False Doctrine" was at work in the Churches. The churches are given in the order named, because the peculiar characteristic of that Church applied to the period of Church History to which it is assigned. It also must not be forgotten, that, that which is a distinctive characteristic of each Church Period, does not disappear with that Period, but continues on down through the next Period, and so on until the end, thus increasing the imperfections of the visible Church, until it ends in an open Apostasy, as shown on the chart—"The Messages to the Seven Churches Compared with Church History."

We will now consider each message separately.

1. The Message to the Church at EPHESUS. Rev. 2:1-7.

The complaint that Christ makes against this Church is that it "**had left its First Love.**" Its character is seen in its very name, for Ephesus means to "let go," "to relax." It had become a **Backslidden Church.** Paul, who founded it, warned it of what should happen, in his parting message.

"I know this, that after my departing shall grievous 'wolves' enter in among you, not sparing the flock. Also of your own selves shall men arise, 'speaking perverse things,' to draw away disciples after them." Acts 20:29, 30.

The significance of this warning is seen in the commendation of the Message, vs. 6—"But this thou hast, that thou 'hatest' the deeds of the Nicolaitanes which I also hate." Here Paul's "wolves" are called Nicolaitanes. They were not a sect, but a party in the Church who were trying to establish a "Priestly Order." Probably trying to model

129

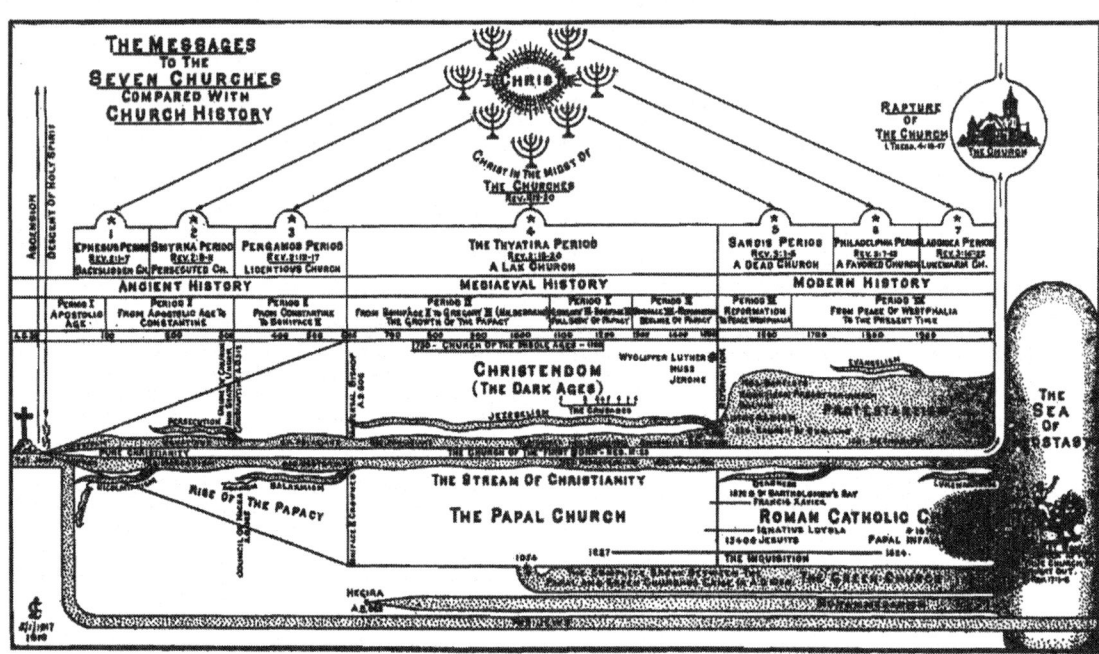

the Church after the Old Testament order of Priests, Levites, and common people. This is seen in the meaning of the word, which is from "Niko" to conquer, to overthrow, and "Laos" the people or laity. The object was to establish a 'Holy Order of Men," and place them over the laity, which was foreign to the New Testament plan, and call them not pastors, but—Clergy, Bishops, Archbishops, Cardinals, Popes. Here we have the origin of the dogma of "Apostolic Succession," and the separation of the Clergy from the Laity, a thing that God "hates." The Church at Ephesus was not deceived, but recognized them as false apostles and liars.

The character of the Church at Ephesus is a fair outline of the Church Period from A. D. 70 to A. D. 170.

II. The Message to the Church at Smyrna. Rev. 2:8-11.

The Church in its "Ephesian Period" having lost its "First Love," the Lord is now about to "chastise" it, so as to cause it to return to Him. Smyrna has for its root meaning "bitterness," and means "Myrrh," an ointment associated with death, and we see in the meaning of the word a prophecy of the persecution and death which was to befall the members of the Smyrna Church. They were told not to "fear" the things that they should be called on to suffer, but to be faithful "unto" death, not "until" death. That is, not until the end of their "natural" life, they were not to "recant" when called upon to face a Martyr's death, but remain faithful until death relieved them of their suffering. The reward would be a "Crown of Life." This is the Martyr's crown.

They were told that the "author" of their suffering would be the Devil, and its duration would be "ten days," which was doubtless a prophetic reference to the "Ten Great Persecutions" under the Roman Emperors, beginning with Nero, A. D. 64, and ending with Diocletian in A. D. 310. Seven of these "Great Persecutions" occurred during this "Smyrna Period" of Church History. Or it may refer to the 10 years of the last and fiercest persecution under Diocletian. This Period extended from A. D. 170 to Constantine A. D. 312.

III. The Message to the Church at Pergamos. Rev. 2:12-17.

In this Message Pergamos is spoken of as "Satan's Seat." When Attalus III, the Priest-King of the Chaldean Hierarchy, fled before the conquering Persians to Pergamos, and settled there, Satan shifted his capital from Babylon to Pergamos. At first he persecuted the followers of Christ, and Antipas was one of the martyrs. But soon he changed his tactics and began to exalt the Church, and through Constantine united the Church and State, and offered all kinds of inducements for worldly people to come into the Church. Constantine's motive was more political than religious. He wished to weld his Christian and Pagan subjects into one people, and so consolidate his Empire. The result of this union was that two false and pernicious doctrines crept into the Church. The first was the "Doctrine of Balaam," and the second the "Doctrine of the Nicolaitanes." The latter we have already considered under the Message to the Church at Ephesus. And the foothold it had secured in the Church was seen in the First Great Council of the Church held at Nicaea, in A. D. 325. The Council was composed of about 1500 delegates, the laymen outnumbering the Bishops 5 to 1. It was a stormy council, full of intrigue and political methods, and from the supremacy of the "Clergy" over the "Laity" it was evident that the "Doctrine of the Nicolaitanes" had secured a strong and permanent foothold.

The "Doctrine of Balaam" is disclosed in the story of Balaam found in the Book of Numbers, chapters 22 to 25 inclusive. When the Children of Israel on their way to Canaan had reached the land of Moab, Balak the king of Moab sent for Balaam the Son of Beor, who lived at Pethor on the river Euphrates, to come and curse them. When the Lord would not permit Balaam to curse Israel, he suggested to Balak that he invite them to the licentious feasts of "Baal-Peor," and thus cause Israel to fall into a snare that would so anger the Lord, that he would Himself destroy them. This Balak did, and the result was that when the men of Israel went to those sensual feasts and saw the "daughters of Moab" they committed whoredoms with them, which so kindled God's anger that He sent a plague that destroyed 42,000 of them. Now the word "Pergamos" means "Marriage," and when the Church entered into a union with the State it was guilty of "Spiritual Fornication" or "Balaamism."

The "Balaam Method" that Constantine employed was to give to the Bishops of the Church a number of imposing buildings called Basilicas for conversion into churches, for whose decoration he was lavish in the gift of money. He also supplied superb vestments for the clergy, and soon the Bishop found himself clad in costly vestments, seated on a lofty throne in the apse of the Basilica, with a marble altar, adorned with gold and gems, on a lower level in front of him. A sensuous form of worship was introduced, the character of the preaching was changed, and the great "Pagan Festivals" were adopted, with but little alteration, to please the Pagan members of the church, and attract Pagans to the church. For illustration, as the Winter Solstice falls on the 21st day of December, which is the shortest day in the year, and it is not until the 25th that the day begins to lengthen, which day was regarded throughout the Heathen world as the "birthday" of the "Sun-God," and was a high festival, which was celebrated at Rome by the "Great Games" of the Circus, it was found advisable to change the Birthday of the Son of God, from April, at which time He was probably born, to December 25th, because as He was the "Sun of Righteousness," what more appropriate birthday could He have than the birthday of the Pagan "Sun-God"?

It was at this time that

"Post-Millennial Views"

had their origin. As the Church had become rich and powerful, it was suggested that by the union of Church and State a condition of affairs would develop that would usher in the Millennium without the return of Christ, and since some scriptural support was needed for such a doctrine, it was claimed that the Jews had been cast off "forever," and that all the prophecies of Israel's future glory were intended for the Church. This "Period" extends from the accession of Constantine, A. D. 312 to A. D. 606, when Boniface III was crowned "Universal Bishop."

IV. The Message to the Church at Thyatira. Rev. 2:18-29.

In His commendation of this Church, Christ lays the emphasis on their "works," as if they depended on them, and claimed they deserved merit for "works" of "Supererogation." But He had a complaint to make against them that was terrible in its awfulness. He charges them not merely with permitting a bad woman, Jezebel, who called herself a "Prophetess," to remain in the Church, but with permitting her to "teach" her pernicious doctrines, and to "seduce" the servants to "commit fornication," and to "eat things sacrificed to idols."

Who this woman was is a question. She was a "pretender," and called herself a "prophetess." Probably she was of noble lineage. She certainly was a woman of commanding influence. Whether her real name was Jezebel or not, she was so like her prototype in the Old Testament, Jezebel the wife of Ahab, that Christ called her by that name. Jezebel, the wife of Ahab, was not by birth a daughter of Abraham, but a princess of idolatrous Tyre, at a time, too, when its royal family was famed for cruel savagery and intense devotion to Baal and

Astarte. Her father, Eth-baal, a priest of the latter deity, murdered the reigning monarch Phales, and succeeded him. Ahab, king of Israel, to strengthen his kingdom, married Jezebel, and she, aided and abetted by Ahab, introduced the licentious worship of Baal into Israel, and killed all the prophets of the Lord she could lay her hands on. And this influence she exercised, not only while her husband was alive, but also during the reign of her two sons, Ahaziah and Jehoram. Moreover, the marriage of her daughter Athaliah to Jehoram, son of Jehoshaphat king of Judah, introduced idolatrous worship into Judah, and it was not long before there was a house of Baal built in Jerusalem, and so Jezebel caused all Israel to sin after the sin of Jeroboam the son of Nebat. 1 Kings 16: 29-33.

There is no question that, whether Jezebel was a real person or not, she typified a "System" and that "System" was the "Papal Church." When the "Papal Church" introduced images and pictures into its churches for the people to bow down to it became idolatrous. And when it set up its claim that the teaching of the Church is superior to the Word of God, it assumed the role of "Prophetess." A careful study of the "Papal System" from A. D. 606 to the Reformation A. D. 1520, with its institution of the "Sacrifice of the Mass" and other Pagan rites, reveals in it the sway of "Jezebelism." It was also a period of "Jezebelistic Persecution," as seen in the wars of the Crusades, and the rise of the Inquisition. A careful comparison of this "Message" with the Parable of "The Leaven," (see the chapter on "The Kingdom"), will reveal the wonderful correspondence between the two, the "Jezebel" of the Church of Thyatira, being the "Woman" of the Parable, who inserted the "Leaven" of "False Doctrine" into the Meal of the Gospel. This Period extended from A. D. 606 to the Reformation A. D. 1520.

V. The Message to the Church at Sardis. Rev. 3: 1-6.

The Church at Sardis was called a "Dead Church" though it had a name to live. That is, it was a "Formalistic Church," a church given over to "formal" or "ritualistic" worship. It had the "Form of Godliness without the power." The meaning of the word "Sardis" is the "escaping one," or those who "come out" and so it is an excellent type of the Church of the

Reformation Period.

By the Reformation we mean that period in the history of the Christian Church when Martin Luther and a number of other reformers protested against the false teaching, tyranny and claims of the Papal Church.

This Period began about A. D. 1500. The condition of affairs in the realm dominated by the Papal Church became intolerable, and came to a crisis when Martin Luther on October 31, 1517 A. D., nailed his 95 Theses on the church door at Wittenberg, Germany. From that date the Reformation set in. But it was more a struggle for political liberty, than a purely Christian or religious movement.

It had the advantage of encouraging and aiding the circulation of the Holy Scriptures, that had hitherto been a sealed book, the revival of the Doctrine of "Justification by Faith," and a reversion to more simple modes of worship; but the multiplication of sects only led to bitter controversial contentions, that, while they threw much light on the Word of God, interfered greatly with the spiritual state of the Church, until it could truthfully be said, "That she had a name to live and was dead."

While the reformers swept away much ritualistic and doctrinal rubbish they failed to recover the promise of the Second Advent. They turned to God from idols, but not to "wait for His Son from the Heavens." The "Sardis Period" extended from A. D. 1520 to about A. D. 1750.

VI. The Message to the Church at Philadelphia. Rev. 3: 7-13.

There is no question about the meaning of the word Philadelphia. It means "Brotherly Love," and well describes the charity and brotherly fellowship that dissipated the bitter personal animosities that characterized the theological disputants of the "Sardis Period," and made possible the evangelistic and missionary labors of the past 150 years.

Three things are said of this Church. 1. It had a "little strength." It was like a person coming back to life who was still very weak. It was the "dead" Sardis Church "revived," and Revivals have been characteristic of the Philadelphia Period. These Revivals began with George Whitefield in A. D. 1739, followed by John Wesley, Charles G. Finney and D. L. Moody.

2. It had set before it an "open door," that no "man" could shut. Note that this promise was made by Him, who "hath the 'Key of David,' He that 'openeth' and no man shutteth; and 'shutteth' and no man openeth." In 1793 William Carey sailed for India, where he found an "open door," and since then the Lord has opened the door into China, Japan, Korea, India, Africa and the isles of the sea, until there is not a country in the world where the missionary cannot go.

3. It was to be kept from the "hour of temptation" (Tribulation), that shall come upon all the world. As the Church at Philadelphia is still in existence, and the only one of the seven that has survived, and while it suffered more or less under the "Ten Persecutions" of the "Smyrna Period," it has never yet suffered in a persecution that was world-wide. This "hour of temptation" then must be still future and refers doubtless to the "Great Tribulation" that is to come upon the "whole world," just before the return of the Lord to set up His Millennial Kingdom, and as the promise is that the "Philadelphia Church" shall **not pass through the Tribulation,** is not this additional proof that the Church shall be "**caught out**" **before the Tribulation?**

The "Philadelphia Period" covers the time between A. D. 1750 and A. D. 1900. We must not forget that the characteristics of all these Periods continue on in the Church down to the end. This is true of the Evangelistic and Missionary movements of the "Philadelphia Period," but they are now more mechanical and based on business methods, and there is less spiritual power, and this will continue until Christ returns.

VII. The Message to the Church at Laodicea. Rev. 3: 14-22.

Christ has no "commendation" for this Church, but much to complain of. He says—

"I know thy works, that thou art **neither cold or hot;** I would thou wert **cold or hot.** So then, because thou art **lukewarm,** and neither cold or hot, I will **spue thee out of my mouth.**"

There is nothing more disgusting or nauseating than "tepid" water. So there is nothing more repugnant to Christ than a "tepid" church. He would rather have a church "frozen" or "boiling." It was the "chilly spiritual atmosphere" of the Church of England that drove John Wesley to start those outside meetings which became so noted for their "religious fervor," and it was the same "chilly atmosphere" of the Methodist Church that drove William Booth in turn to become a "Red-hot" Salvationist.

Our churches today are largely in this "lukewarm" condition. There is very little of warm-hearted spirituality. There is much going on in them, but it is largely mechanical and of a social character. Committees, societies, and clubs are multiplied, but there is an absence of "spiritual heat." Revival meetings are held, but instead of waiting on the Lord for power, evangelists and paid singers are hired and soul winning is made a business.

The cause of this "lukewarmness" is the same as that of the Church of Laodicea—**Self-Deception.**

> "Because thou sayest **I am rich, and increased with goods, and have need of nothing;** and knowest not that thou **art wretched, and miserable, and poor, and blind and naked.**"

They thought they were **rich**, and outwardly they were, but Christ saw the poverty of their heart. There are many such churches in the world today. More so than in any other period in the history of the church. Many of these churches have Cathedral-like buildings, stained glass windows, eloquent preachers, paid singers, large congregations. Some of them have large landed interests and are well endowed, and yet they are poor. Many of the members, if not the majority, are worldly, card playing, dancing, and theatre going Christians. The poor and the saintly are not wanted in such churches because their presence is a rebuke. These churches do not see that they are **wretched, miserable, poor, blind, and naked.**

If we were to visit such churches they would take pride in showing us the building, they would praise the preaching and singing, they would boast of the character of their congregations, the exclusiveness of their membership, and the attractiveness of all their services, but if we suggested a series of meetings for the "deepening of the **Spiritual Life,**" or the **"conversion of the unsaved,"** they would say—"Oh, no, we do not want such meetings, we have **need of nothing.**" The Church at Laodicea was not burdened with **debt**, but it was burdened with **WEALTH.**

The trouble with the church today is that it thinks that nothing can be done without **money**, and that if we only had the money the world would be converted in this generation. The world is not to be converted by money, but by the **Spirit of God.**

The trouble with the Church of Laodicea was that its "Gold" was not of the right kind, and so it was counseled to buy of the Lord **"gold tried in the fire."** What kind of gold is that? It is gold that has no **taint** upon it. Gold that is not **cankered,** or secured by **fraud**, or the withholding of a just wage. What a description we have of these Laodicean days in James 5:1-4.

But the Church of Laodicea was not only poor, though rich, it was blind. Or to put it more accurately—**"Near-Sighted."** They could see their worldly prosperity, but were **"Short-Sighted"** as to heavenly things, so the Lord counseled them to anoint their eyes with **"Eye-Salve."** Their merchants dealt in ointments and herbs of a high degree of healing virtue, but they possessed no salve that would restore **impaired Spiritual Vision**, only the **Unction of the Holy One** could do that.

But the Church was not only poor, and blind, it was **naked.** Their outward garments were doubtless of the finest material and the latest fashionable cut, but not such as should adorn the person of a Child of God. So they were counseled to purchase of Christ **"White Raiment,"** in exchange for the "raven black woolen" garments for which the garment makers of Laodicea were famous.

Then a most startling revelation was made to the Church of Laodicea, Christ said—

"Behold, I Stand at the Door and Knock."

These words are generally quoted as an appeal to sinners, but they are not, they are addressed to a **Church,** and to a Church in whose midst Christ had **once stood,** but now found Himself **excluded** and standing **outside** knocking for admittance.

This is the most startling thing recorded in the New Testament, that it is possible for a church to be outwardly prosperous and yet have no Christ in its midst, and be unconscious of the fact. This is a description of a **Christless Church.** Oh, the

EXCLUDED CHRIST.

Excluded from His own nation, for they **Rejected Him;** excluded from the world, for it **Crucified Him;** excluded from His Church, for He stands outside its door **Knocking for Entrance.**

How did Christ come to be outside the Church? He had been within it once or there never would have been a Church. How did He come to leave? It is clear that they had not **thrust** Him out, for they do not seem to have missed His presence. They continued to worship Him, to sing His praises, and engage in all manner of Christian service, yet He had withdrawn. Why? The reason is summed up in one word—**Worldliness.**

But how is Christ to get back into His Church? Does it require the unanimous vote or invitation of the membership? No. "If any **man** hear my voice, and **open the door,** I will come in to Him, and will **sup with him,** and **he with Me.**" That is, the way to revive a lukewarm church is for the individual members to open their hearts and let Christ **re-enter,** and thus **open the door** for His reappearance.

The character of the Church today is Laodicean, and as the Laodicean Period is to continue until the Church of the "New-Born" is taken out, we cannot hope for any great change until the Lord comes back.

"If Christ should come today,
I'll not be here tomorrow;
He'll take His ransomed ones away
From death and sin and sorrow.
In the midair He'll come
To call His loved ones home,
To take them to the 'place prepared,'
As He, before He left, declared."

XXIII
THE TRIBULATION

The Scriptures speak of a "Great Tribulation" that is coming on the earth. Jesus in His "Olivet Discourse" uttered on the Mt. of Olives on the Tuesday evening before His Crucifixion, said—

"Then shall be **great tribulation**, such as was not since the beginning of the world to this time, no, nor ever shall be. And except those days **should be shortened**, there should no flesh be saved; but for the Elect's Sake (the elect of Israel) those days **shall be shortened**." Matt. 24: 21, 22.

That this Tribulation was not the terrible sufferings that befell the Jewish people at the time of the destruction of Jerusalem in A. D. 70, is clear, because many of the things that are to happen before and after "The Great Tribulation," did not happen at the destruction of Jerusalem.

I. The "FACT of the Tribulation.

Our Lord's prophecy does not stand alone. It is backed up by other prophecies both in the Old and New Testament.

Turning to the Old Testament we find in Jer. 30: 4-7, that it is the time of "Jacob's Trouble," and is compared in its sufferings to the "birth-pangs" of a woman. In Ezek. 20: 34-38 it is spoken of as the time when Israel shall "Pass under the Rod;" and in Ezek. 22: 19-22, we read how that God is going to cast Israel into His "Melting Pot," where they are to be refined as "gold is refined." See also Malachi 3: 1-3, and Zech. 13: 9. Daniel speaks of it as a "Time of Trouble" for his people, the Jews. Dan. 12: 1.

From these references we see that "The Great Tribulation" is something that has to do with the Jewish people, and is a Judgment through which they must pass as a "refining process" to fit them to again be God's chosen people. Indirectly the Gentiles will be affected by it, but the Church will be "caught out" before that "Great and Terrible Day of the Lord."

In the New Testament we have two descriptions of it.

The first is by Jesus in His Olivet Discourse, Matt. 24: 9-22, and the second is in the Book of Revelation, chapters 6: 1 to 19: 21, where in the breaking of the "Seals," the sounding of the "Trumpets" and the pouring out of the "Vials" John sees in vision the things that are to occur during the Tribulation Period.

II. The "TIME" of the Tribulation.

The Old Testament prophets speak of it as "That Day," and the "Latter Days," and the Prophet Joel calls it the "Day of the Lord." Joel 1:15; 2:1; 3:14. The Scriptures speak of "Four Days."

1. **"Man's Day."** That is the present Dispensation in which we are living.

2. **"The Day of Christ."** That is the day when the Lord Jesus will come and take His Church out of the world, and includes the time between the "Rapture" and the "Revelation." On earth it is the "Day of Antichrist."

3. **"The Day of the Lord,"** that is the day of "Vengeance of Our Lord," and includes the period of the "Great Tribulation" and the Millennium that follows.

4. **"The Day of God."** That is the period that begins with the "Renovation of the Earth by Fire" and extends to eternity. See the Chart on the "Days of Scripture."

The time of the Tribulation then is "after" the Church has been "caught out," and during the reign of Antichrist on the earth.

The Prophet Daniel in his Vision of the "Seventy Weeks" (Dan. 9: 20-27) was told that it would be 69 weeks from the going forth of the Edict "to restore and rebuild Jerusalem unto Messiah the Prince." Those were "Prophetic Weeks," in which each week stood for "seven years," and they were literally fulfilled, for it was exactly 483 years of 360 days, from the going forth of that Edict, B. C. 445, until Jesus rode in triumph into Jerusalem, A. D. 30, and was hailed as the promised Son of David. See the chart on "Prophetical Chronology."

Within a week the Jews had Jesus crucified and then "God's Clock" stopped, and the remaining "one" week, the "Seventieth," has still to be fulfilled. In the meantime, in the break between the "sixty-ninth" and "seventieth" week, the Holy Spirit is gathering out the Church, and when it is complete it will be taken away, and then "God's Clock" will begin to tick again, because He will again be dealing with His People the Jews.

It is during this last, or "Seventieth Week" of Daniel's "Seventy Weeks," that the Tribulation is to occur, and as the "weeks" of the already fulfilled "sixty-nine" weeks, were each "seven years" in length, so this last, or "Seventieth Week," must be the same. The length then of the "Tribulation Period" should be "seven years," but Jesus tells us in Matt. 24: 22, that for the "**ELECT'S SAKE**" **Those Days Shall Be Shortened.** Not the "Elect" of the Church, for they are "caught out" before the Tribulation, but the "Elect" of Israel, the 144,000 "Sealed Ones" of Rev. 7: 1-8.

III. The "CHARACTER" of the Tribulation.

While the "Tribulation Period" shall last for about seven years, as to its severity it will be divided into two parts of three and a half years each. The second or last part so far exceeding in its severity the first part as to be known as

"The GREAT TRIBULATION."

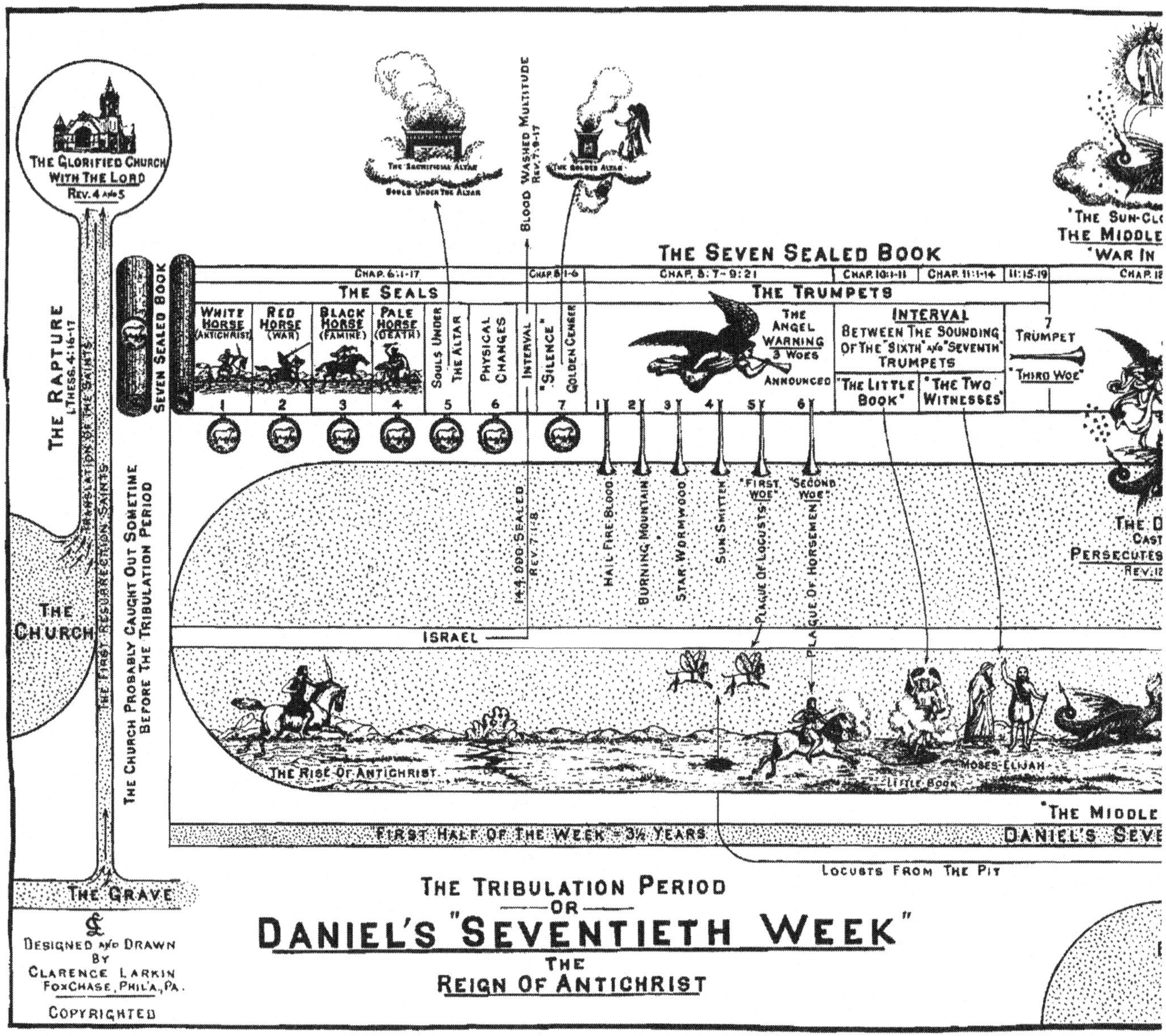

The Glorified Church With The Lord
Rev. 4 and 5
The Rapture
I. Thess. 4:16-17
Translation Of The Saints
The First Resurrection Saints
The Church
The Grave
The Church Probably Caught Out Sometime Before The Tribulation Period
Seven Sealed Book
The Sacrificial Altar
Souls Under The Altar
Blood Washed Multitude
Rev. 7:9-17
The Golden Altar
The Seven Sealed Book
Chap. 6:1-17
Chap. 8:1-6
Chap. 8:7-9:21
Chap. 10:1-11
Chap. 11:1-14
11:15-19
The Seals
White Horse (Antichrist)
Red Horse (War)
Black Horse (Famine)
Pale Horse (Death)
Souls Under The Altar
Physical Changes
Interval
"Silence"
Golden Censer
1
2
3
4
5
6
7
The Trumpets
The Angel Warning 3 Woes Announced
Interval
Between The Sounding Of The "Sixth" and "Seventh" Trumpets
"The Little Book"
"The Two Witnesses"
7
Trumpet
"Third Woe"
144,000 Sealed
Rev. 7:1-8
Hail-Fire-Blood
Burning Mountain
Star Wormwood
Sun Smitten
"First Woe"
Plague Of Locusts
"Second Woe"
Plague Of Horsemen
Israel
The Rise Of Antichrist
Little Book
Moses-Elijah
First Half Of The Week = 3½ Years
Locusts From The Pit
"The Sun-Cl
The Middle
"War In
The D
Cast
Persecutes
Rev. 12
"The Middle
Daniel's Seve
The Tribulation Period
—Or—
Daniel's "Seventieth Week"
The
Reign Of Antichrist
Designed and Drawn By Clarence Larkin Fox Chase, Phil'a, Pa.
Copyrighted

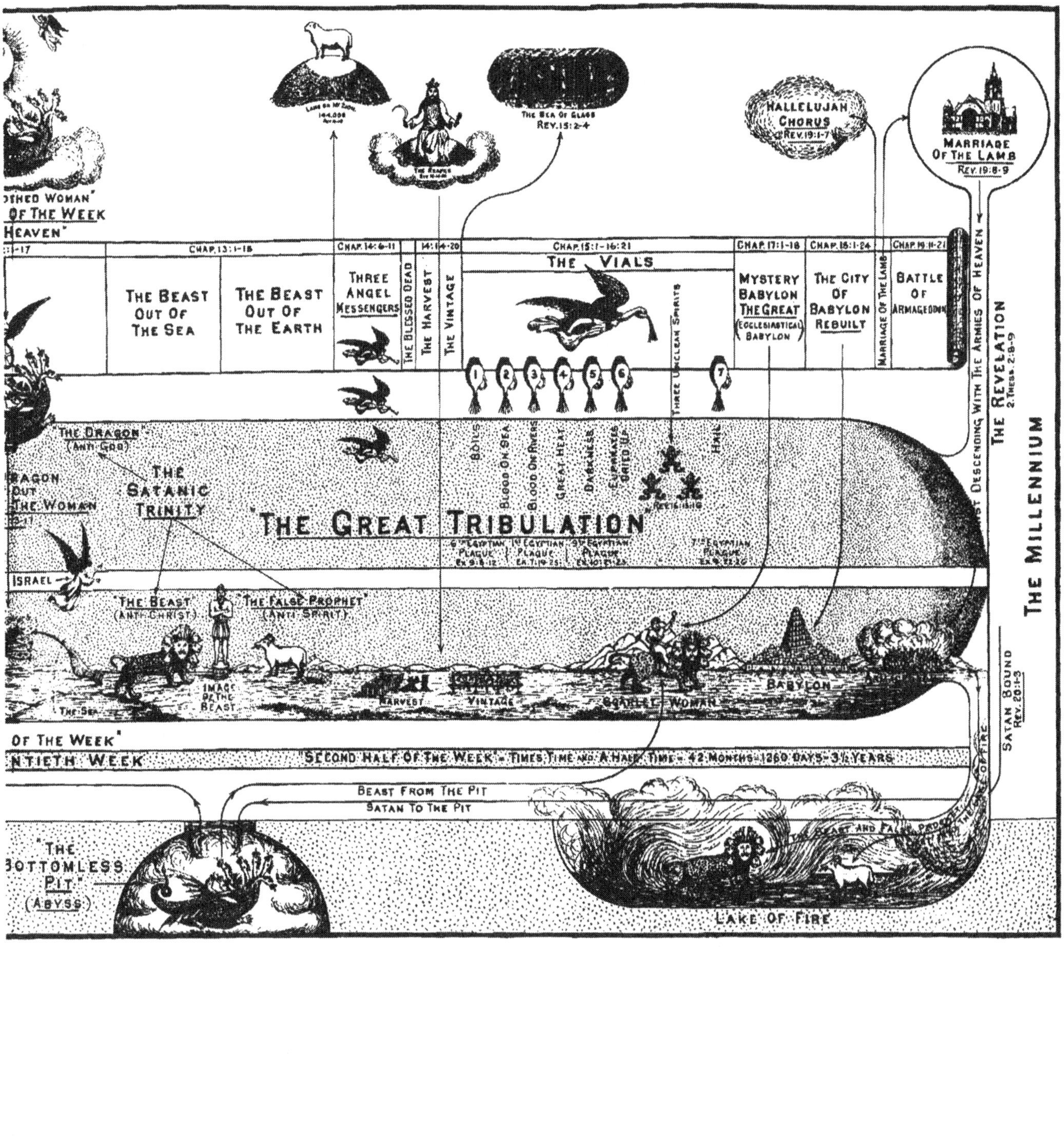
Of The Week
Hallelujah Chorus Rev. 19:1-7
Marriage Of The Lamb Rev. 19:8-9
The Sea Of Glass Rev. 15:2-4
Chap. 13:1-18
Chap. 14:6-11
14:14-20
Chap. 15:1-16:21
Chap. 17:1-18
Chap. 18:1-24
Chap. 19:11-21
The Beast Out Of The Sea
The Beast Out Of The Earth
Three Angel Messengers
The Blessed Dead
The Harvest
The Vintage
The Vials
Mystery Babylon The Great (Ecclesiastical Babylon)
The City Of Babylon Rebuilt
Marriage Of The Lamb
Battle Of Armageddon
Descending With The Armies Of Heaven
The Revelation 2 Thess. 2:8-9
The Millennium
1 2 3 4 5 6 7
Boils
Blood On Sea
Blood On Rivers
Great Heat
Darkness
Euphrates Dried Up
Three Unclean Spirits
Hail
"The Dragon" (Anti-God)
The Satanic Trinity
"The Great Tribulation"
6th Egyptian Plague Ex. 9:8-12
1st Egyptian Plague Ex. 7:19-25
7th Egyptian Plague
Israel
"The Beast" (Anti-Christ)
"The False Prophet" (Anti-Spirit)
Image Of The Beast
The Sea
Harvest
Vintage
Scarlet Woman
Babylon
Of The Week"
"Second Half Of The Week - Times, Time and A Half Time - 42 Months - 1260 Days - 3½ Years"
Beast From The Pit
Satan To The Pit
Satan Bound Rev. 20:1-3
"The Bottomless Pit" (Abyss)
Lake Of Fire

What was to happen during Daniel's "Seventieth Week" was not revealed to Daniel. He received a communication which he did not understand and was told to "seal the Book up until the Time of the End." Dan. 12:4, 8, 9. All Daniel knew was that the contents of the Book had reference to the "Time of Trouble" that should befall his People at the "Time of the End" (of their sorrows), not the "End of Time." What that "Sealed Book" contained is no longer a Mystery, for the Apostle John saw the "seals" of that Book broken, and was told to record what it contained. The "Seven-Sealed Book" of the Book of Revelation is the Book that Daniel was told to seal up.

If we want to know then about what is to happen during the Tribulation, all we have to do is to read and study the Book of Revelation from Rev. 6:1 to 19:21.

As the Dragon is cast out of the Heavenlies in chapter 12, and he is cast out in the "Middle of the Week," it follows that chapters 6 to 11 inclusive cover the "First Half" of the Week, or 3½ years, and chapters 13 to 19 inclusive the "Second Half." See the Charts on "Revelation" and "Daniel's Seventieth Week."

Let us study each half of the Week by itself.

1. **First Half of the Week.**

The "Week" begins with the breaking of the "Seals."

First Seal. Rev. 6:1, 2.

A "White Horse" appears, the Rider of which is uncrowned at first, but is afterward crowned. He has a bow in his hand, and goes forth conquering. This rider is not Christ. Christ as the Lamb, is holding and breaking the "seals" of the Book. He does not appear as a White Horse Rider until chapter 19.

The "Rider" is Antichrist, and pictures him before he is crowned and becomes the Chief Ruler of the "Ten Federated Kingdoms" of the revived Roman Empire. He is the "Prince who is to come," and who shall "confirm the Covenant" with the Jews for "one week." Dan.: 9:26, 27. This proves that Antichrist appears at the "beginning" of the "Week" and not in the "Middle" as some claim.

Second Seal. Rev. 6:3, 4.

A "Red Horse" appears, the Rider of which has power to take peace from the earth. The symbolism is clear. Red, the color of the horse, is a symbol of "blood," and the sword of "war." The time is clearly that prophesied by Christ. Matt. 24:6, 7. The outcome of these wars will probably be the "Ten Kingdom Federation" over which Antichrist shall become the head.

Third Seal. Rev. 6:5, 6.

A "Black Horse" appears, the Rider of which holds a pair of scales in his hand and a voice cries—"A measure of wheat for a penny, and three measures of barley for a penny; and see thou hurt not the oil and the wine." The meaning is clear. When all able-bodied men are drafted for war, the fields remain untilled and "famine" follows, just as Christ prophesied. Matt. 24:7. The olive and the grape do not need cultivation, so their ruthless destruction is forbidden.

Fourth Seal. Rev. 6:7, 8.

A "Pale Horse" appears, the Rider of which is "Death." It is noteworthy that the Riders of the first three horses are not named. They will be recognized when they appear.

Hell (Hades) follows in the wake of "Death" ready to swallow up his victims caused by war and famine.

Fifth Seal. Rev. 6:9-11.

When the Fifth Seal was broken John saw the "souls of martyrs" under the Altar. These Martyrs, whose "souls" John saw are not the Martyrs of "past ages;" they were taken up with the Church, but the Martyrs who will be killed for the "Word of their Testimony, and who love not their lives unto the death" (Rev. 12:11), during the Tribulation. After the Church is caught out the preaching of the "Gospel of the Kingdom" will be resumed. Matt. 24:14. As it is a proclamation that Christ is about to set up an "Earthly Kingdom," it will be exceedingly distasteful to Antichrist and his followers, and a "Great Persecution" will follow. Matt. 24:9-13. It is the "souls" of the martyrs of this Persecution that John saw under the Altar.

They asked that their death should be avenged, but were told to rest for a "little season" until they were joined by their fellow servants and brethren who should die as they did. The promise is fulfilled in Rev. 20:4.

Sixth Seal. Rev. 6:12-17.

When the Sixth Seal is broken great "physical changes" will occur on the earth. Joel 2:30, 31; Matt. 24:29; Isa. 13:9-11. So terrible will these changes be that men will call upon the mountains and rocks to fall and hide them from the wrath of the Lamb. The 24th chapter of Matthew should be compared with Rev. 6:1-17.

Between the breaking of the "Sixth" and "Seventh" Seals there will be a pause or interval, during which 144,000 of the Children of Israel, 12,000 from each of the Twelve Tribes, will be "sealed." As there were 7000 in Ahab's time who would not bow the knee to Baal (I Kings 19:18), so in the Tribulation there shall be 144,000 of Israel who will not bow the knee to Antichrist. They are "sealed" by an angel, and the "Seal" is the imprint of the "Father's Name" on their foreheads. Rev. 14:1; 22:4.

Then John saw a

"Blood Washed Multitude." Rev. 7:9-17.

This introduces us to another class of saved of the "End Time." They are not the Church, for they come out of the "Great Tribulation." They are probably Gentiles who accept Christ as their Saviour after the Church is caught out. They are saved and shall serve God in His Heavenly Temple, and never hunger or thirst any more, but they are not part of the Church and shall not participate in any Millennial blessings on the earth.

Seventh Seal. Rev. 8:1.

At the breaking of the "Seventh Seal" there will be "silence in Heaven" for a limited period. This will be a period of preparation for the greater conflict to follow.

Following the "Silence," Seven Angels in succession sound upon Seven Trumpets.

First Trumpet. Rev. 8:7.

When the "First Trumpet" sounds "hail" and "fire mingled with blood" will be cast upon the earth and a "third part of the trees" and "all green grass" will be "burnt up." This will be a fulfillment of Joel 2:30, 31. This is a repetition of the "Seventh Egyptian Plague." Ex. 9:22-26. That was "literal." Why should not this be?

Second Trumpet. Rev. 8:8, 9.

When the "Second Trumpet" sounds a "burning mountain," probably a Meteor, will fall into the sea (Mediterranean) and will destroy a "third part of the creatures of the sea" and a "third part of the ships," probably some fleets assembled for a naval battle, and the "blood" of the destroyed will discolor a third part of the sea.

Third Trumpet. Rev. 8:10, 11.

When the "Third Trumpet" sounds a "great burning star," called "Wormwood," will fall from the heavens and poison the streams of fresh water. This will probably be another Meteor that in exploding will fill the atmosphere with "noxious gases," that will be absorbed by the rivers and fountains of water, and poison them, so as to cause the death of all who drink of them. Wormwood is used in the manufacture of "Absinthe," an intoxicating beverage much used in France, and poisonous. The Prophet Jeremiah refers to this time. Jer. 9:13-15.

Fourth Trumpet. Rev. 8:12.

When the "Fourth Trumpet" sounds the "third part" of the sun, moon and stars will be smitten and their light diminished a "third." This is one of the "signs" spoken of by Christ. Luke 21:25, 26.

An Angel will then fly through the midst of heaven announcing "Three Woes" that are to follow the sounding of the three Trumpets yet to sound. Rev. 8:13.

Fifth Trumpet. Rev. 9:1-12
"First Woe"
"The Plague of Locusts."

When the "Fifth Trumpet" sounds a "Star" will fall from heaven to the earth with the "key" of the

"Bottomless Pit."

This is not a real star, but an Angel who will look like a Star, for "to him" was given the Key. He will not be a "Fallen Angel," nor Satan himself as some suppose, for God would not entrust the Key of the "Bottomless Pit" to Satan, but he will be the "same Angel" that will bind Satan and cast him into the "Bottomless Pit" for 1000 years. Rev. 20:1-3. When the "Bottomless Pit" is opened a cloud, like smoke, of "locusts" will emerge and cover the earth. They will be a combination of horse, man, woman, lion and scorpion. The "sound of their wings" will be as the sound of chariots of many horses running to battle.

Their size is not given, but they will doubtless be much larger than ordinary locusts, but they will not be like them, for ordinary locusts feed on vegetation, but these locusts will be forbidden to hurt the grass or the trees, or any green thing, and only be permitted to afflict "men," and only those men who have not the "seal of God" in their foreheads, and these they shall not be permitted to "kill," but only "torment."

The meaning of this scourge of "Scorpion Locusts" seems to be that a vast army of "Demons" will be liberated from the "Bottomless Pit," who shall enter into and take possession of the "bodies" of men, and so "torment" them that they shall desire to die and shall not be able, the demons preventing them.

These "Scorpion Locusts" have a king, which ordinary locusts have not. Prov. 30:27. This king's name in the Hebrew is "Abaddon," but in the Greek is "Apollyon." The word means "destroyer." This king is not Satan. Satan is at liberty, while the king of the Bottomless Pit" is confined with his subjects.

Sixth Trumpet. Rev. 9:13-21.
"Second Woe."
"The Plague of Horsemen."

When the "Sixth Trumpet" shall sound a voice from the "Golden Altar" will command the Trumpeter to loose "four angels" which are bound in the great river Euphrates. That they are "Bad Angels" is seen from the fact that they are "bound" and that they are the leaders of an army of 200,000,000 "Infernal Cavalry."

This Cavalry will not be composed of ordinary men and horses. The horses will have the "body" of a Horse, the "head" of a Lion, a "tail" like a serpent, with the "head of a serpent" at its end. Out of their mouths will issue "fire," "smoke" and "brimstone," and by these three the "third part of men will be killed," and the sting of their "serpent tails" will cause great pain. The riders upon these horses will have "breastplates of fire and brimstone" to match the breath of the horses.

Supernatural armies are not unknown to the Scriptures. 2 Kings 6:13-17. When Jesus returns He will be accompanied by the Armies of Heaven, and it stands to reason that Satan has his armies. Awful as this "demon" invasion will be it will not cause men to repent.

According to the Revised Version verse 15 should read: "The four angels were loosed which had been prepared for **the Hour and Day and Month and Year.**" That is, the Four Angels now bound in the Euphrates will be loosed in the **Exact Year, Month, Day** and even **Hour** predetermined by God for the "Demon Invasion," and not, as some think, to slay for a year, month and day, or 391 days. These two invasions of "Scorpion Locusts and Infernal Cavalry" warn us that in the days after the Church is caught out, Satan and his "Demon Forces" will be increasingly active and do all they can to torment and destroy mankind.

The Interval

Between the sounding of the "Sixth" and "Seventh Trumpets" there will be an "Interval," just as there was between the breaking of the "Sixth" and "Seventh Seals." During this "Interval" a "Mighty Angel" will come down from Heaven having a "Little Book" (open) in his hand. This "Mighty Angel" will be Christ Himself, for the description of Him corresponds with chapter 1:12-15, and as His "voice" is like that of a Lion, this identifies Him as the "Lion of the Tribe of Judah" of chapter 5:5; and in chapter 11:3, He speaks of the "Two Witnesses" as "My Witnesses." When the "Mighty Angel" shall set His "Right Foot" on the "sea," and His "Left Foot" on the "earth," and lift up His hand to Heaven, and swear that there shall be "Time no longer" He shall take formal possession of the Earth. The expression, "Time no longer," should read, as in the Revised Version (margin), "No longer delay," for Time does not end until the close of the "Perfect Age." While Christ at this time will take formal possession of the earth, actual possession will not be secured until He comes again to the Mt. of Olives, at the close of the Tribulation.

The Two Witnesses.

In chapter 11:1-14 we are given a description of "Two Witnesses" who are to prophesy during the greater part of the last half of the Week. Who they will be is very clear. One has "power to shut heaven that it rain not in the days of their prophecy." This can be no other than Elijah who was translated that he might come again before the "Great and Terrible Day of the Lord" (Malachi 4:5, 6), and who will shut up the heavens for 42 months, or 3½ years, which is exactly the length of time he did it in the days of Ahab. The other Witness will "have power over waters to turn them to blood, and to smite the earth with all plagues as often as he will." This identifies him as Moses, for he is the only person mentioned in the Scriptures who had such power, and it was for this purpose that he was raised from the dead. Jude 9. As Moses and Elijah appeared together on the Mount of Transfiguration with Christ and as they probably were the two "men" in "white apparel" (angel-like) that testified at the Ascension to Christ's coming again (Acts 1:10, 11), what more probable than that they are the "Two Witnesses" who will return to the earth to announce that Coming? During their "witnessing" they will have power to destroy their enemies with "fire" that shall issue from their mouths, but at the end of 1260 days they will be slain and their bodies lay exposed in the streets of the city of Jerusalem for 3½ days, when they shall rise and ascend to Heaven, to the amazement of those who see them go. Their ascent will be followed by a destructive earthquake, which completes the "Second Woe."

Seventh Trumpet. Rev. 11:15-19.

"Third Woe."

The "Seventh Trumpet" includes all that follows down to the end of chapter nineteen. We must not forget in our study of the Book of Revelation that the "Seventh Seal" includes the "Seven Trumpets" and the "Seven Vials," and that the "Seventh Trumpet" includes the "Seven Vials," for the "Seventh Seal," and the "Seventh Trumpet," and the "Seventh Vial" all end alike with "voices," "thunderings," "lightnings" and an "earthquake." Rev. 8:5, 11:19; 16:18.

2. Middle of the Week. Rev. 12:1-17.

In the "Middle of the Week" two "Wonders" shall appear in Heaven. The Revised Version calls them "signs," that is, they are "symbols" of something. The first will be a

"Sun-Clothed Woman."

This "Woman" is neither the Virgin Mary, nor the Church, she is Israel. We have only to be reminded of Joseph's Dream of the "sun" and "moon," and the "eleven stars" (Gen. 37:9), to see that this "Sun-Clothed Woman," with the "moon" under her feet and upon her head a crown of "Twelve Stars," is Jewish in character. Joseph was the twelfth star. Israel is again and again compared to a "married" woman in the Old Testament, but the Church is a "virgin," and only an "espoused virgin" at that. 2 Cor. 11:2. This "Woman" is described as being "with child" and "travailing to be delivered." When was the Church in such a condition? Paul says of Israel, "Of whom as concerning the flesh Christ Came." Rom. 9:4, 5. And Israel looked forward to the time when she could say—"Unto us a **Child Is Born**, unto us a Son is given." Isa. 9:6, 7. But before that could happen Israel had to pass through many sore afflictions and judgments. These were her **"Travail Time."**

As the result of her "travail" the Woman brought forth a "Man-Child" who was to rule the nations with a "Rod of Iron." There can be no question as to who is meant by the "Man-Child." The 2d Psalm settles that. He is Christ, who at His Ascension was caught up and seated on His Father's Throne.

After her child is delivered the Woman "flees into the Wilderness" where she hath a place prepared of God, and where she is fed for 1260 days. Here is where many interpreters make a mistake. They overlook the fact that between the "fifth" and "sixth" verses of this chapter the present "Church Period" comes in. Here is the "gap" between the "Sixty-ninth" and "Seventieth" Weeks of Daniel's "Seventy Weeks." John jumps over this "gap," from the Ascension of Christ to the casting out of Satan, because he is not dealing in these Tribulation chapters with the Church but with Israel, and wishes to continue her history without a break. Here is further evidence that the "Woman" is not the Virgin Mary, for she does not flee into Egypt, but into the Wilderness, neither does she flee "with" her child, for that was caught up to the Throne of God; neither does she flee for her child's "protection," but for her own.

The Dragon.

The second "Wonder" that will appear in Heaven will be a

"Great Red Dragon."

We are not left in doubt as to who is meant, for in verse 9 he is called that "Old Serpent," "The Devil," and "Satan." His color is "red," the color of "blood," for he was a murderer from the beginning. John 8:44. The "Stars of Heaven" attached to his "tail" reveal the fact that Satan will lead astray a third of the Angels, for the Angels are spoken of as "Stars" in the Old Testament. Job. 38:7. They will be cast to the earth with him. The casting out of the Dragon is described in verses 7 to 12. His expulsion will start a War in Heaven.

That the Dragon has not yet been cast out of Heaven is clear. He had access to God in the days of Job, 2000 years before Christ. Job 1:1-2:8. He tried to destroy the "Man-Child" (Christ) at the hand of Herod when He was born. Matt. 2:16-18. He was at liberty to tempt Christ in the Wilderness, and to sift Peter. He is today the "Prince of the Powers of the Air," Eph. 2:2, and the "God of this World" (age). 2 Cor. 4:14. When the "Dragon" is cast out of the Heavenlies there will be great rejoicing in Heaven because the "Accuser" of Christ's "Brethren" (the Jews) is cast down, but there will be "woe" for the "inhabitants of the earth," for the "Dragon" will be filled with "great wrath" because he knows that he will have but a "short time" (3½ years) to vent his wrath on the inhabitants of the earth before he is chained and cast into the Bottomless Pit.

When the "Dragon" is cast out, knowing that his defeat has been brought about by the elevation of the "Man-Child" to the place of power, he will concentrate his hatred and malice on the "Woman" (Israel) who gave Him birth. To the "Woman" will be given the "wings of a great eagle," that she may fly into the "Wilderness," into "her place," where she shall be nourished for a "Time, Times, and Half a Time," or 3½ years. This takes us back to the flight of Israel from Egypt, of which God said—"Ye have seen what I did unto the Egyptians, and how I bare you on 'Eagle's Wings,' and brought you unto myself." Ex. 19:4. As the "Woman" and the "Dragon" are symbols, so are the "Eagle's Wings." They speak of the rapid and safe flight of the "Woman" (Israel) into the "Wilderness," where she shall be safely kept and nourished for 3½ years until the "Dragon" is bound.

The Cities of Refuge.

The "Cities of Refuge" of Old Testament times are a type of this "Wilderness Refuge" of the Children of Israel.

The "Cities of Refuge" were designated cities, 3 on each side the river Jordan, where the "Man-Slayer" could flee for safety from the "Avenger of Blood." If it was proved after trial that he had slain a man "wilfully," he was turned over to the "Avenger of Blood," but if he did it unwittingly, his life was spared, but he had to remain in the city until the death of the High Priest. If there were no "Man-Slayer" there would be no "Avenger of Blood," and therefore no need for a "City of Refuge."

Now if I find in the New Testament that a certain class of people are called upon to flee to a "Place of Refuge" for the protection of their lives, then I must believe that they flee because an "Avenger of Blood" is after them, and that they flee because they are guilty of "Manslaughter."

Such a class of people I find in the Jewish Race. They were the cause of the death of Christ, and though He was crucified by the Roman authorities they assumed the guilt for they cried—"His blood be on **Us**, and on **Our Children**." Matt. 27:25. At first sight it looks like "wilful" murder, yet from the prayer of Jesus on the Cross— "Father, forgive them for they **know not what they do**," it is clear that Jesus' death was not so much a premeditated murder as it was a murder committed in a blind religious frenzy. Paul says—"had they known they would not have crucified the Lord of Glory." 1 Cor. 2:8.

It is clear then that the Jewish race is only guilty of "Manslaughter." As the "Man-Slayer" of Jesus they have been for over 1800 years running for a "City of Refuge" and have not as yet reached it. The "Avenger of Blood" has been on their track and has hounded them from nation to nation, and the epithet of

"The Wandering Jew"

has followed them down the centuries, and the prophecy of Moses is being fulfilled that they should find no rest for the sole of their foot. Deut. 28:64-67.

If the Jews are the "Man-Slayer" who is the "Avenger of Blood?" Antichrist. If the "Avenger of Blood" must be a "Kinsman" of the man slain, that means that he must be of the same "Race," and the nearest kinsman alive at the time vengeance is sought. While Jesus was the "first born" of the Virgin Mary, he was not the only child she had. She afterwards had by Joseph four sons, James, Joseph, Judas and Simon, and there were daughters. Two of these brothers of Jesus filled a large place in the Church in the first century. James was pastor of the church at Jerusalem, and Judas wrote the Epistle of Jude. The kinsfolk of Jesus occupied a place by themselves for a long time after Jesus passed away, and could be traced as late as A. D. 324. Somewhere in the world today, without doubt, are living some of the "Kinsfolk" of the Lord Jesus. They may not be able to trace their descent back to Jesus, but God knows where they are, and who they are, and who dare deny that when the time comes for the manifestation of the Antichrist, that the "Avenger of Blood" shall be a Jew, who is a lineal descendant of the family of Jesus.

And now as to the "City of Refuge" that God will provide for Israel when the "Avenger of Blood" (Antichrist), who shall then be indwelt by the Dragon, is on her track. In Isa. 26:20 we read—

"Come, my people (Israel), enter thou into my 'chambers,' and shut thy doors about thee; hide thyself as it were for a 'little moment,' until the 'indignation' be overpast.'"

The context shows that this refers to the time when Antichrist, the "Avenger of Blood," will seek to destroy the Jewish people, and is the time referred to by Christ in Matt. 24: 15-22.

When the Lord God brought the Children of Israel out of Egypt they journeyed from the Red Sea, tarrying for a while at Mt. Sinai to receive the Law and build the Tabernacle, until they came, one year, after leaving Egypt, to Kadesh Barnea. There they sent up spies to spy out the land of Canaan, but refused to go up and take possession of the land, and were compelled to wander in the Wilderness south of the Dead Sea. There God took care of them and fed them for 40 years. Now it is in the same Wilderness that God is going to provide for them a place of "Refuge" in the day when the "Avenger of Blood" shall seek to destroy them.

Speaking of the Antichrist, the Prophet Daniel says—

"He shall enter also into the Glorious Land (Palestine) and many countries shall be overthrown; but these shall **escape** out of his hand, even **Edom** and **Moab** and the chief of the **Children of Ammon**." Dan. 11:41.

Now Edom takes in the Wilderness where Israel wandered for 40 years. And it is here in Edom that the "City of Refuge" that God has provided for Israel is located, and is known today as Petra. It was a great commercial centre in the days of King Solomon. In A. D. 105 the Romans conquered the country and called the province Arabia Petra. When the power of Rome waned **Petra** gradually fell into the hands of the Arabs and became completely lost to the civilized world in the seventh century, and remained so until it was rediscovered by Burckhardt in 1812.

It is located in the mountains like as in the crater of a volcano. It has but one entrance, and that is through a narrow winding defile or canyon from 12 to 40 feet wide, the sides of which are precipitous and at times so close together as to almost shut out the blue sky above and make you think you are passing through a subterranean passageway. The height of the sides varies from 200 to 1000 feet, and the length of the canyon is about two miles. No other city in the world has such a wonderful gateway. The sides of the canyon are lined with wonderful monuments and temples carved out of the rocky sandstone of the sides. Once inside the rocky enclosure of the city we find the ruins of magnificent buildings, tombs and monuments. The cliffs that surround the city are carved and honeycombed with excavations to a height of 300 feet above the floor of the valley, and the excavations cut as they are out of different colored strata of the rock, such as red, purple, blue, black, white and yellow, lend a beauty to their appearance that is indescribable and overpowering to the beholder.

When the time comes for the "Man-Slayer" (Israel), to escape from the hands of the "Avenger of Blood" (Antichrist), the rocky fastness of the ancient city of Petra will be her "City of Refuge." We read that when the "Woman" (Israel) shall flee into the Wilderness that the "Serpent" (Antichrist, indwelt by Satan) shall cast a flood of water out of his mouth after her to destroy her, but that the earth shall open her mouth and swallow the flood. That is, Antichrist will send his army after the fleeing Israelites, and it will probably be swallowed up in a "Sand storm" of the desert, and Israel shall safely reach her place of refuge, where she shall be safe, not until the death of the High Priest, but until the return of "The High Priest" (Jesus), from Heaven, who as "King-Priest" of the Armies of Heaven will deliver her and allow her to leave her place of refuge.

3. Last Half of the Week.

Filled with wrath at the escape of the "Sun-Clothed Woman," the Dragon will turn his attention to the "remnant of her seed," and to the better carry out his plans he will give to the "Beast" (Antichrist) his "Power" and his "Seat," and "Great Authority." Rev. 13:2. While Antichrist, as Antichrist, exists from the "beginning" of the "Week," for at that time he makes a "covenant for one week," (Dan. 9:27); in the "Middle of the Week" he will break "the Covenant," and for the "last half of the week" his reign will be terrible, and the change in his character, and the character of his reign, can only be accounted for on the basis that the Dragon has incarnated himself in him. It is this phase of the reign of "Antichrist" that is brought out in the 13th chapter of the Book of Revelation.

John tells us that he saw two Beasts. The first came up out of the sea. This represents "Antichrist" after his incarnation by the "Dragon." The second came up out of the earth and is called the "False Prophet."

For a full description of these Beasts read the chapters on "The Antichrist and the Satanic Trinity." Suffice it to say that for the balance of the "Week," no man can buy or sell unless he has the "**Brand of Hell**," and "**Mark of the Beast**," on his **Right Hand**, or in his **Forehead**.

At this time three "Angel Messengers" will be sent forth. The first will be a preacher of the Gospel. This is the first time an angel is commissioned to preach the Gospel. But it will not be the Gospel of the "**Grace of God**," (Acts 20:24), nor the Gospel of "**The Kingdom**," (Matt. 24:14), but a new Gospel, called the "**Everlasting Gospel**." Its burden is "**Judgment**" not "**Salvation**," and it will be "**Good News**" to all those passing through the "fiery trials" of those days, for it will be the announcement that the **"Hour of Judgment"** is come for all that do wickedly.

The second "Angel Messenger" will announce the "Fall of Babylon." This is by way of anticipation, for the City of Babylon is not destroyed until after the pouring out of the "Vials."

The third "Angel Messenger" will utter an awful warning to those who are tempted to worship the Beast. Declaring that if they do, they shall drink of the wine of the"**"Wrath of God,"** and shall be tormented with **"fire"** and **"brimstone" Forever and Ever.**

At this time preparation will be made in Heaven for the

Harvest and Vintage

of the earth. This is not the Harvest of the Church, that took place before the beginning of the "Week." This is the Harvest of the Gentile nations. It begins with the pouring out of the "Vials," and ends with the Battle of Armageddon.

First Vial. Rev. 16:1, 2.

When the "First Vial" is poured out a "noisome and grievous sore" will fall upon the men who have the "Mark of the Beast," and who "worship his Image." This is a repetition of the "Sixth Egyptian Plague." Ex. 9:8-12. If that was literal why should not this be? The "literalness" of these "Vial Judgments" is the key to the literalness of the whole Book of Revelation.

Second Vial. Rev. 16:3.

When the "Second Vial" is poured out, the sea (Mediterranean) will become as the "blood of a dead man," and every "living soul"(creature, for creatures have souls) in the sea will die. Something similar, though not so great in extent, happened when the "Second Trumpet" sounded. Rev. 8:8, 9.

Third Vial. Rev. 16:4-7.

When the "Third Vial" is poured out the "rivers" and "fountains of water" will become "blood." This is a repetition of the "First Egyptian Plague." Ex. 7:19-24. Those will be awful times when there will be nothing to quench the thirst but "blood."

Fourth Vial. Rev. 16:8, 9.

When the "Fourth Vial" is poured out men will be "scorched with great heat." This is the only plague for which there is no Egyptian parallel, and as the others are literal so must it be. The Prophet Malachi refers to it. Malachi 4:1. The effect of this plague will be not to make men repent, but to cause them to **Blaspheme the Name of God.**

Fifth Vial. Rev. 16:10, 11.

When the "Fifth Vial" is poured out there will be "darkness" over the whole kingdom of the "Beast," and men will gnaw their tongues for pain." This will be a repetition of the "Ninth Egyptian Plague." Ex. 10:21-23. Notice that this Plague follows the Plague of "Scorching Heat," as if God will hide the sun whose heat was so hard to bear. The effect of the "Darkness" will be to make men "gnaw their tongues" for pain, and for their sores, showing that these "Vial Plagues," overlap or follow each other rapidly.

Sixth Vial. Rev. 16:12.

When the "Sixth Vial" is poured out the river Euphrates will be dried up so the kings of the East (India, China, Japan) and their armies may cross over and gather for the great Battle of Armageddon. This will be a repetition of the opening of the Red Sea and of the river Jordan. The Prophet Isaiah foretells this—

"The Lord shall utterly destroy the tongue of the Egyptian (Red) **Sea, and . . . shake His hand over the River** (Euphrates), and smite its seven streams, so men can go over **Dry-Shod."** Isa. 11:15, 16.

These nations will be gathered by "Three Unclean Spirits" like frogs, that shall come out of the mouth of the "Dragon," and the "Beast," and the "False Prophet." Rev. 16:13-16. They will be the "Spirits of Demons," the "Seducing Spirits" of those days. 1 Tim. 4:1. It was such a "Lying Spirit" that deceived King Ahab and led him to his death. 1 Kings 22:20-38.

Seventh Vial. Rev. 16:17-21.

When the "Seventh Vial" is poured out a "great voice," probably the voice of the One who cried on the Cross—"It is Finished," will cry—"It is Done," and there will be a "Great Earthquake" that will divide into three parts the "Great City" and the cities of the Nations (the 10 Federated Nations), London, Rome, Paris, etc., and "Great Babylon" that shall be rebuilt by that time, and whose destruction by an earthquake is foretold in chapter eighteen, will fall. This earthquake is foretold by the Prophet Zechariah. Zech. 14:4, 5.

In the "Great Hail," every stone of which shall weigh a 100 pounds, that will fall on men, we have a repetition of the "Seventh Egyptian Plague." Ex. 9:13-35. Hail has been one of God's engines of war. He used it to discomfit the enemies of Israel at Beth-horon in the days of Joshua. Joshua 10:11. The Law required that the "blasphemer" should be "stoned" (Lev. 24:16), and the **"Blasphemers"** of the **"End Time"** shall be stoned from **HEAVEN.**

In the Book of Revelation, between the pouring out of the Vials and the "Battle of Armageddon," which ends the "Tribulation Period," in chapters seventeen and eighteen, there is an account of the destruction of a "System" called

"Mystery, Babylon the Great,"

and a city called Babylon.

They are mentioned at that place in the book, not because they did not exist until that time, but because at that time they are both destroyed. For the meaning of these two chapters, see the Chapter on Babylon the Great.

Battle of Armageddon.
Rev. 19:11-21.

The "Tribulation Period" will close with the great "Battle of Armageddon." As we have seen the armies of the East and the West will be assembled in the Holy Land by the "Demon Spirits" that shall be sent forth from the mouths of the "Satanic Trinity." The field of battle will be the "Valley of Megiddo," located in the heart of Palestine, the battlefield of the great battles of the Old Testament. The forces engaged will be the "Allied Armies" of Antichrist on the one side, and the "Heavenly Army" of Christ on the other. The "time" will be when the **"Harvest of the Earth" IS RIPE,** (Rev. 14:15), and at the "Psychological Moment" when the "Allied Armies" of Antichrist are about to take the city of Jerusalem.

The Prophet Zechariah says—

"Behold the **'Day of the Lord'** cometh." (The "Day of the Lord" is the Millennial Day.) When—"I will **Gather All Nations Against Jerusalem to Battle . . . Then shall the Lord Go Forth and Fight Against Those Nations."** Zech. 14:1-3.

This "going forth" is graphically described in Rev. 19:11-21. When He came the first time to Jerusalem as King, He rode on a "colt," the foal of an ass, (Matt. 21:1-11), this time He shall come on a "White Horse." His eyes will be as a "flame of fire" and on His head shall be "many crowns," and He shall be clothed in a vesture "dipped in blood." Not His own blood but the blood of His enemies. The Prophet Isaiah foresaw that day—

"Who is this that cometh from Edom, with **dyed garments from Bozrah**? this that is glorious in his apparel, travelling in the greatness of his strength?" And the answer comes back—"I that speak in righteousness, mighty to save." Then the Prophet asks, "Wherefore art thou **red** in thine apparel, and thy garments like him that treadeth in the Winefat?" And the response is—"I have trodden the wine-press **alone**; and of the people there was none with me; for I will tread them in mine anger, and trample them in my fury; and their blood shall be sprinkled upon my **garments**, and I will **stain all My Raiment.**" Isa. 63:1-6.

That this does not refer to Christ's atonement on the Cross is clear, for the Prophet adds—

"For the '**Day of Vengeance**' is in mine heart, and the year of my redeemed is come."

There was no "vengeance" in Christ's heart on the Cross. It was "Father 'forgive them' for they know not what they do." The time the Prophet foretells, is the "Day of Christ's Vengeance" on His enemies, and the day when He shall redeem His chosen people the Jews from the power of Antichrist. It is the time when He shall tread—

"THE 'WINEPRESS'
Of the Fierceness and Wrath of
Almighty God."

The Apostle John had a vision of this "Winepress" in chapter fourteen, verses 14 to 20. That was before the pouring out of the "Vials," and was a prophetic foreview of what should happen in chapter nineteen.

In verses 18 to 20, an angel with a "sharp sickle" is told to—

"Thrust in thy **Sharp Sickle**, and gather the clusters of the '**Vine of the Earth**,' for her grapes are **fully ripe**." And the angel thrust in his Sickle into the earth, and gathered of the '**Vine of the Earth**,' and cast it into the **Great Winepress** of the wrath of God." And we read that "The Winepress was trodden **Without the City**, and blood, (not wine), came out of the Winepress, even unto the **horses' bridles**, by the space of **a Thousand and Six Hundred Furlongs.**"

From this we see that the "Allied Armies" of Antichrist will cover the whole of Palestine, and so great shall be the slaughter, that, in the valleys and hollows, all over the whole of Palestine, for the length of Palestine as far south as Bozrah is 1600 furlongs or 200 miles, the blood shall be up to the **horses' bridles**.

It will be the time of which Isaiah speaks, when the land shall be "**Soaked With Blood.**" Isa. 34:1-8.

So great will be the carnage, God will prepare for it in advance.

"And I saw an angel standing in the sun; and he cried with a loud voice, saying to all the **fowls that fly in the midst of Heaven,** (Buzzards, Vultures, Eagles, etc.), Come and gather yourselves together unto the

SUPPER OF THE GREAT GOD,

that ye may eat the **flesh** of **Kings** . . . **Captains** . . . **Mighty Men**, and the **flesh** of **horses** and of them that **sit on them**, (common soldiers), and the **flesh** of **all men**, both **free and bond**, both **small and great**." Rev. 19:17, 18.

This "Feast" is described in the Old Testament.

"And, thou son of man, thus saith the Lord God, Speak unto every **feathered fowl**, and to every **beast of the field**, Assemble yourselves, and come, gather yourselves on every side to **My Sacrifice**, that I do sacrifice for you, even a great sacrifice upon the **Mountains of Israel**, that ye may eat flesh, and drink blood. Ye shall eat the **flesh of the Mighty**, and **drink the blood of the Princes of the Earth**, of rams, of lambs, and of **goats**, of **bullocks**, all of them fatlings of Bashan. And ye shall eat fat till ye be full, and drink blood till ye be drunken. . . . Thus ye shall be filled 'at My Table,' with **horses** and **chariots** (their occupants), with **Mighty Men**, and with all **Men of War**, saith the Lord God." Ez. 39:1-22.

And in the same chapter we are told that the "**House of Israel**," the occupants of Palestine in that day, shall be **seven months** burying the **bones** of the dead, the flesh having been eaten by the birds and beasts of prey, and the wood from the weapons of warfare, army wagons, spears, etc., shall last the inhabitants of the land for fuel **seven years**, so that they will not have to take wood out of the field, nor cut down any out of the forests.

The words in Rev. 19:21, "and all the **fowls were filled with their flesh**," declare that those "**Fowl Guests**" will be GORGED WITH CARRION.

Then will be fulfilled the words of Jesus—"For wheresoever the **carcase** is, there will the **Eagles** (birds of prey) be gathered together." Matt. 24:27, 28. The eagle feeds mainly on fresh meat. The Hebrews classed the eagle among the birds of prey, such as the vulture.

The destruction of this great army will be brought about by the "sword" of Him who will head the Armies of Heaven. The "sword" that proceedeth out of the mouth of the "White Horse Rider," is not the "Sword of the Spirit," for that bringeth "Salvation," not destruction. The "sword" stands for some supernatural means of destruction, and as there is to be a "Great Hail" to fall from Heaven upon the enemies of God at this time, that may be the means God will use, for it was in that way that the enemies of Israel were destroyed on the same battlefield in the "Battle of Beth-Horon" in the days of Joshua. Joshua 10:1-11.

The issue of the "Battle of Armageddon" will never be in doubt. The previous summoning of the birds and beasts of prey, prove this. Before the destruction of the army of Antichrist, he and the False Prophet will be cast "alive" into the "Lake of Fire." This shows that they are not "Systems" but "Persons," and as Enoch and Elijah were taken to Heaven **without dying**, so Antichrist and the False Prophet will be cast into the "Lake of Fire" **without dying**, and will be still there and alive when Satan is cast in a 1000 years later.

Before Antichrist is seized and cast into the "Lake of Fire," Satan will make his exit from his person, and after the battle is over, Satan will be bound and cast into the "Bottomless Pit," where he will be "sealed up" for 1000 years. This is the culminating act of the "Tribulation Period."

NOTE—For a full description of "Daniel's Seventieth Week" or the "Tribulation Period," see the author's book on the Book of Revelation.

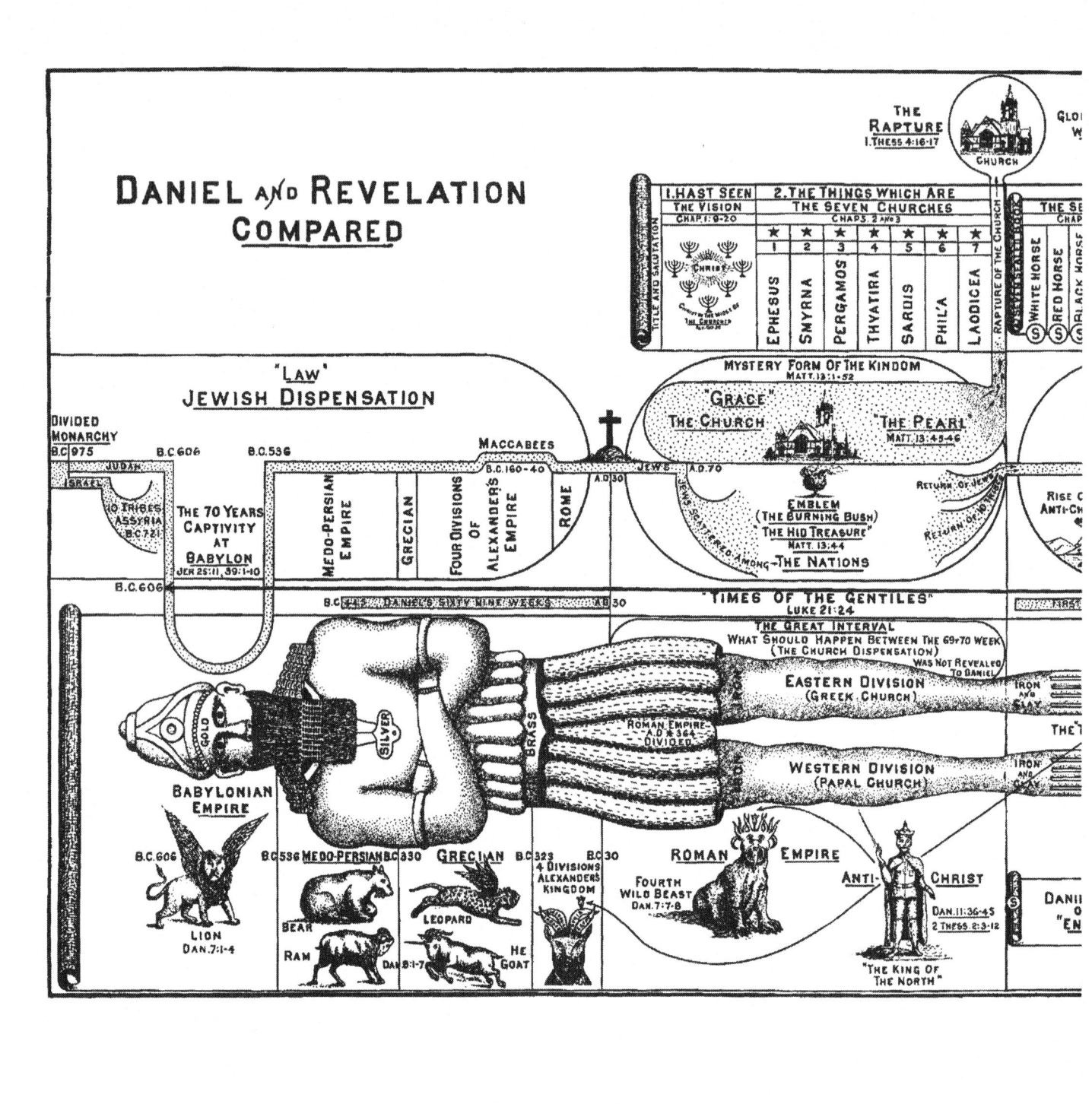

Daniel and Revelation Compared

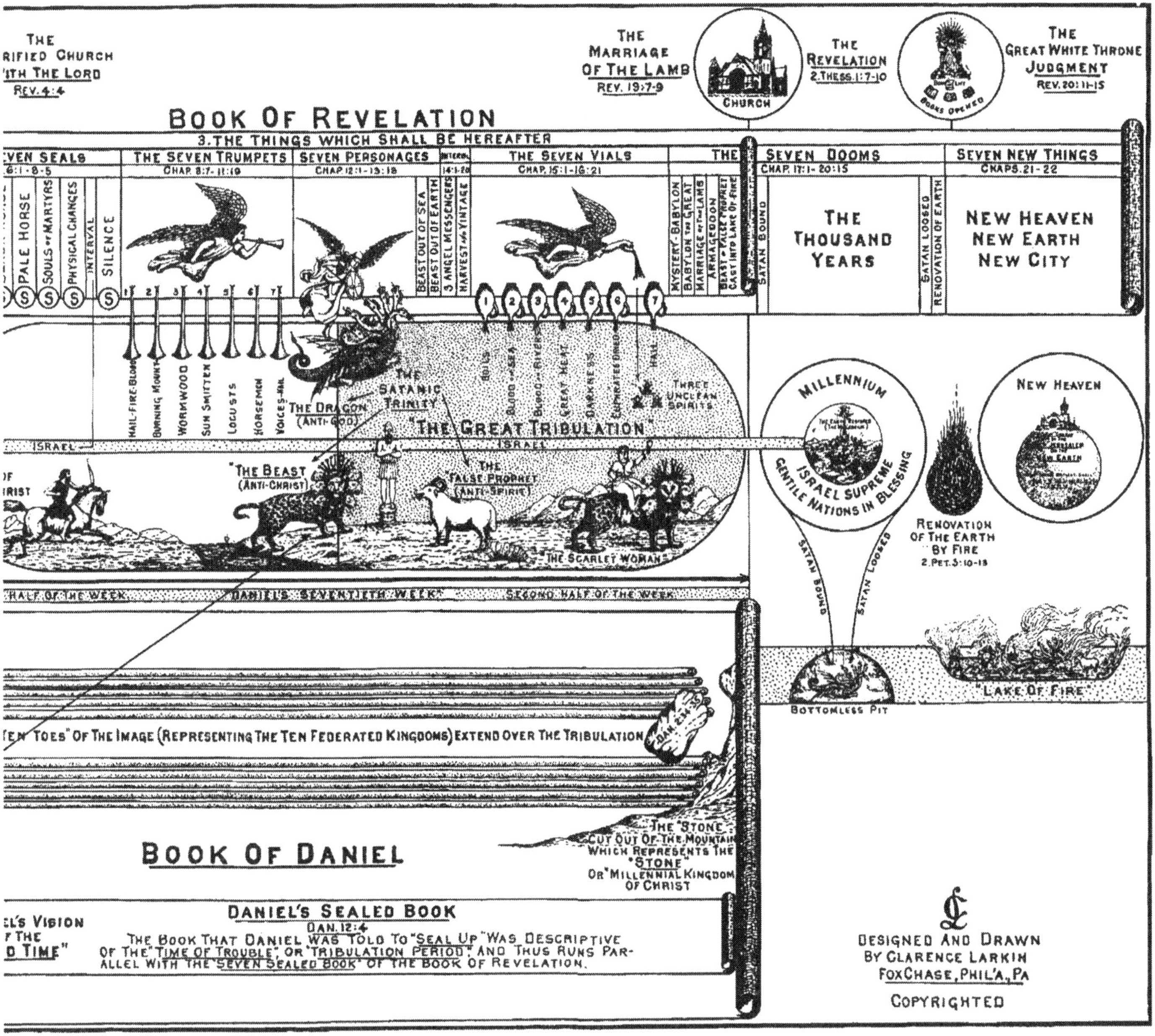

THE
RIFIED CHURCH
'ITH THE LORD
REV. 4:4
THE MARRIAGE OF THE LAMB
REV. 19:7-9
CHURCH
THE REVELATION
2 THESS. 1:7-10
THE GREAT WHITE THRONE JUDGMENT
REV. 20:11-15
BOOKS OPENED
BOOK OF REVELATION
3. THE THINGS WHICH SHALL BE HEREAFTER
EVEN SEALS
6:1-8:5
THE SEVEN TRUMPETS
CHAP. 8:7-11:19
SEVEN PERSONAGES
CHAP. 12:1-13:18
INTERL.
14:1-20
THE SEVEN VIALS
CHAP. 15:1-16:21
THE
SEVEN DOOMS
CHAP. 17:1-20:15
SEVEN NEW THINGS
CHAPS. 21-22
PALE HORSE
SOULS OF MARTYRS
PHYSICAL CHANGES
INTERVAL
SILENCE
BEAST OUT OF SEA
BEAST OUT OF EARTH
3 ANGEL MESSENGERS
HARVEST AND VINTAGE
MYSTERY-BABYLON
BABYLON THE GREAT
MARRIAGE OF THE LAMB
ARMAGEDDON
BEAST & FALSE PROPHET CAST INTO LAKE OF FIRE
SATAN BOUND
THE THOUSAND YEARS
SATAN LOOSED
RENOVATION OF EARTH
NEW HEAVEN
NEW EARTH
NEW CITY
HAIL-FIRE-BLOOD
BURNING MOUNT
WORMWOOD
SUN SMITTEN
LOCUSTS
HORSEMEN
VOICES-HAIL
BOILS
BLOOD-SEA
BLOOD-RIVERS
GREAT HEAT
DARKNESS
EUPHRATES DRIED
HAIL
THE SATANIC TRINITY
THE DRAGON
(ANTI-GOD)
THREE UNCLEAN SPIRITS
"THE GREAT TRIBULATION"
ISRAEL
ISRAEL
"THE BEAST"
(ANTI-CHRIST)
THE "FALSE PROPHET"
(ANTI-SPIRIT)
THE SCARLET WOMAN
MILLENNIUM
ISRAEL SUPREME
GENTILE NATIONS IN BLESSING
SATAN BOUND
SATAN LOOSED
NEW HEAVEN
RENOVATION OF THE EARTH BY FIRE
2 PET. 3:10-13
HALF OF THE WEEK
"DANIEL'S SEVENTIETH WEEK"
SECOND HALF OF THE WEEK
BOTTOMLESS PIT
"LAKE OF FIRE"
"TEN TOES" OF THE IMAGE (REPRESENTING THE TEN FEDERATED KINGDOMS) EXTEND OVER THE TRIBULATION
DAN. 2:34-35
THE "STONE" CUT OUT OF THE MOUNTAIN WHICH REPRESENTS THE "STONE" OR "MILLENNIAL KINGDOM OF CHRIST"
BOOK OF DANIEL
EL'S VISION
F THE
D TIME"
DANIEL'S SEALED BOOK
DAN. 12:4
THE BOOK THAT DANIEL WAS TOLD TO "SEAL UP" WAS DESCRIPTIVE OF THE "TIME OF TROUBLE", OR "TRIBULATION PERIOD", AND THUS RUNS PARALLEL WITH THE "SEVEN SEALED BOOK" OF THE BOOK OF REVELATION.
DESIGNED AND DRAWN
BY CLARENCE LARKIN
FOXCHASE, PHIL'A, PA
COPYRIGHTED

XXIV
BABYLON THE GREAT

1. Ecclesiastical Babylon
"MYSTERY,"
Babylon the Great.
Rev. 17:1-18.

That the ancient city of Babylon restored is to play an important part in the startling events of the last days of this Dispensation, is very clear. This is seen from what is said of it in the seventeenth and eighteenth chapters of the Book of Revelation. At first sight the two chapters, which contain some things in common, are difficult to reconcile, but when we get the "**Key**" the reconciliation is easy.

The seventeenth chapter speaks of a "**Woman**," and this "**Woman**" is called

"MYSTERY,"
Babylon the Great,
The Mother of Harlots
And
Abominations of the Earth."

The eighteenth chapter speaks of a "City," a literal city, called "Babylon the Great." That the "**Woman**" and the "**City**" do not symbolize the same thing is clear, for what is said of the "Woman" does not apply to a city, and what is said of the "City" does not apply to a woman. The "Woman" is destroyed by the "**Ten Kings**," while the "Kings of the Earth" in the next chapter, "**bewail and lament**" the destruction of the "City," which is not destroyed by them, but by a mighty earthquake and fire. Again the "Woman" is destroyed **Three and a Half Years BEFORE THE CITY**; and the fact that the first verse of chapter eighteen says—"**after these things**," that is after the destruction of the "Woman" what happens to the "City" occurs, shows that the "Woman" and the "City" are not one and the same.

The "Woman's" name is—

"MYSTERY, Babylon the Great."

"**Mystery!**" Where have we heard that word before, and in what connection? Paul calls the Church a "Mystery" because it was not known to the Old Testament Patriarchs and Prophets. Eph. 3:1-21. That Christ was to have a "Bride" was first revealed to Paul (Eph. 5:23-32), and the "Mystery" that Antichrist is to have a "bride" was first revealed to John on the Isle of Patmos. The name of Antichrist's "bride" is "Babylon the Great." Some one may ask why give to a "bride" the name of a "City"? The answer is that it is not unusual in the Scriptures. When the same angel that showed John in this chapter "Mystery, Babylon the Great," came to him in chapter 21:9-10 and said—"Come hither, I will shew thee the Bride—'**The Lamb's Wife,**'" he showed John, instead of a woman, that great City, the "**Holy Jerusalem**" descending out of Heaven from God. Here we see that a "city" is called a "bride" because its **inhabitants**, and not the city itself, are the **bride**. "Mystery, Babylon the Great," the "bride" of Antichrist, then, is not a literal city, but a "**System**," a religious and apostate "System." As the Church, the Bride of Christ, is composed of regenerated followers of Christ, so "Mystery, Babylon the Great," the bride of Antichrist, will be composed of the followers of all **False Religions**.

The river Euphrates, on which the city of Babylon was built, was one of the four branches into which the river that flowed through the Garden of Eden was divided, and Satan doubtless chose the site of Babylon as his headquarters from which to sally forth to tempt Adam and Eve. It was doubtless here that the Antediluvian Apostasy had its source that ended in the Flood. To this centre the "forces of Evil" gravitated after the Flood, and "**Babel**" was the result. This was the origin of nations, but the nations were not scattered abroad over the earth until Satan had implanted in them the "**Virus**" of a doctrine that has been the **source** of every false religion the world has ever known.

Babel, or Babylon, was built by Nimrod. Gen. 10:8-10. It was the seat of the first great Apostasy. Here the "**Babylonian Cult**" was invented, a system claiming to possess the highest wisdom and to reveal the divinest secrets. Before a member could be initiated he had to "confess" to the Priest. The Priest then had him in his power. This is the secret of the power of the Priests of the Roman Catholic Church today.

Once admitted into this order men were no longer Babylonians, Assyrians, or Egyptians, but members of a

Mystical Brotherhood,

over whom was placed a Pontiff or "High Priest," whose word was law. The city of Babylon continued to be the seat of Satan until the fall of the Babylonian and Medo-Persian Empires, when he shifted his Capital to Pergamos in Asia Minor, where it was in John's day. Rev. 2:12, 13.

When Attalus, the Pontiff and King of Pergamos, died in B. C. 133, he bequeathed the Headship of the "Babylonian Priesthood" to Rome. When the Etruscans came to Italy from Lydia (the region of Pergamos), they brought with them the Babylonian religion and rites. They set up a Pontiff who was head of the Priesthood. Later the Romans accepted this Pontiff as their civil ruler. Julius Caesar was made Pontiff of the Etruscan Order in B. C. 74. In B. C. 63 he was made "Supreme Pontiff" of the "Babylonian Order," thus becoming heir to the rights and titles of Attalus, Pontiff of Pergamos, who had made Rome his heir by will. Thus the first Roman Emperor became the Head of the "Babylonian Priesthood," and Rome the successor of Babylon. The Emperors of Rome continued to exercise the office of "Supreme Pontiff" until A. D. 376, when the Emperor Gratian, for Christian reasons, refused it. The Bishop of the Church at Rome, Damasus, was elected to the position. He had been Bishop 12 years, having been made Bishop in A. D. 366, through the influence of the monks of Mt. Carmel, a college of Babylonian religion originally founded by the priests of Jezebel. So in A. D. 378 the Head of the "Babylonian Order" became the Ruler of the "Roman Church." Thus Satan united

Rome and Babylon
In One Religious System.

Soon after Damasus was made "Supreme Pontiff" the "rites" of Babylon began to come to the front. The worship of the Virgin Mary was set up in A. D. 381. All the outstanding festivals of the Roman Catholic Church are of Babylonian origin. Easter is not a Christian name. It means "Ishtar," one of the titles of the Babylonian Queen of Heaven, whose worship by the Children of Israel was such an abomination in the sight of God. The decree for the observance of Easter and Lent was given in A. D. 519. The "Rosary" is of Pagan origin. There is no warrant in the Word of God for the use of the "Sign of the Cross." It had its origin in the mystic "Tau" of the Chaldeans and Egyptians. It came from the letter "T," the initial name of "**Tammuz**," and was used in the "Babylonian Mysteries" for the same magic purposes as the Romish Church now employs it. **Celibacy**, the **Tonsure**, and the **Order of Monks** and **Nuns**, have no warrant or authority from Scripture. The Nuns are nothing more than an imitation of the "**Vestal Virgins**" of Pagan Rome.

As to the word **"Mystery,"** the Papal Church has always shrouded herself in **mystery**. The mystery of **"Baptismal Regeneration;"** the mystery of **"Miracle and Magic"** whereby the simple memorials of the Lord's Supper are changed by the mysterious word **"Transubstantiation,"** from simple bread and wine into the literal Body and Blood of Christ; the mystery of the **"Holy Water;"** the mystery of **"Lights on the Altar,"** the **"Mystery Plays,"** and other superstitious rites and ceremonies mumbled in a language that tends to mystery, and tends to confusion which is the meaning of the word Babylon.

All this was a "Mystery" in John's day, because the "Papal Church" had not as yet developed; though the **"Mystery of Iniquity"** was already at work (2 Thess. 2:7), but it is no longer a "Mystery" for it is now easy to identify the **"Woman"—Mystery, Babylon the Great,"** which John described as the **"Papal Church."**

In Rev. 17:4 we read that the "Woman" **"was arrayed in purple and scarlet color, and decked with gold and precious stones and pearls, having a 'Golden Cup' in her hand full of abominations and filthiness of her fornications."**

Now who does not know that **scarlet** and **purple** are the colors of the Papacy? Of the different articles of attire specified for the Pope to wear when he is installed into office **five** are scarlet. A vest covered with **pearls**, and a mitre, adorned with gold and **precious stones** was also to be worn. How completely this answers the description of the Woman's dress as she sits upon the **Scarlet Colored Beast.**

We are also told that the Woman was **"drunken with the blood of the Saints, and with the blood of the Martyrs of Jesus."** While this refers more particularly to the martyrs of the time of Antichrist, yet who does not know, who has studied the history of the Christian Church for the past nineteen centuries, that this is true of the Papal Church during those centuries? One has only to read the history of the persecutions of the early Christians and more particularly the story of the "Inquisition" in Papal lands, to see that the Papal Church has been "drunk" with the **blood of the Saints.**

The fact that the Woman sits on a "Scarlet Colored Beast" reveals the fact that at that time the Beast (Antichrist) will support the Woman in her ecclesiastical pretensions, or in other words, the Woman, as a "State Church," will control and rule the State, and her long dream of world-wide Ecclesiastical Supremacy will at last be realized, for John tells us that "the waters which thou sawest, where the **'Whore' sitteth, are Peoples, and Multitudes, and Nations and Tongues."** That means that after the **"True Church"** (the Bride of Christ) is taken out of the world the **"False"** or **"Papal Church"** (the bride of Antichrist) will remain, and the professing body of Christians (having the "form of Godliness without the power") left behind, will largely enter the Papal Church, and it will become the **Universal Church.** But this will continue for only a short time for the "Ten Kings" of the "Federated Kingdom," finding their power curtailed by the "Papal System" will **"hate The Whore,"** and strip her of her gorgeous apparel, confiscate her wealth (eat her flesh) and burn her churches and cathedrals with fire. Rev. 17:16.

This will occur at the time the worship of the Beast is set up, for Antichrist in his jealous hate will not permit any worship that does not centre in himself.

The Beast upon which the Woman sits is introduced to show from whom the Woman (the Papal Church) gets her power and support after the True Church has been "caught out," and also to show that the Beast (Antichrist) and the Woman (the Papal Church) are not one and the same, but separate. Therefore the Papacy is not Antichrist. For a description of the "Scarlet Colored Beast" see the Chapter on The Antichrist.

From this foreview of the Papacy we see that the Papal Church is not a dying **"System."** That she is to be revived and become a **"Universal Church,"** and in doing so is to commit fornication with the kings of the earth, and that she shall again be "drunk with the blood" of the martyrs of the Tribulation Period. The meaning of chapter seventeen of the Book of Revelation is no longer a Mystery; the prophetic portrait of the Woman there given corresponds too closely with the history of the Papal Church to be a mere coincidence.

2. Commercial Babylon.
Rev. 18:1-24.

This chapter begins with the words **"after these things."** What things? The things recorded in the previous chapter, the **destruction of "Mystical Babylon."**

If "Mystical Babylon" was destroyed in the previous chapter then she cannot appear in this chapter, and the "City" here described must be a literal city called Babylon, and as there is no city of that name on the earth today, nor has been since the ancient city of Babylon was destroyed, it must refer to some future city of Babylon. That the two chapters refer to different things is further verified by the fact that they are announced by different angels. The events of chapter seventeen are announced by one of the "Vial" Angels, while those of the eighteenth are announced by "another" angel; probably the "Second Angel Messenger," who by way of anticipation, announced in chapter 14:8, the "Fall of Babylon," that is there called—**"That Great City."**

The ancient city of Babylon from the days of Nimrod (Gen. 10:10), grew in size and importance century after century until it reached its greatest glory in the reign of Nebuchadnezzar B. C. 604-562. As described by Herodotus it was an exact square of 15 miles on a side, or 60 miles around, and was surrounded by a brick wall 87 feet thick, and 350 feet high, though probably that is a mistake, 100 feet being nearer the height. On the wall were 250 towers, and the top of the wall was wide enough to allow 6 chariots to drive abreast. Outside this wall was a vast ditch surrounding the city, kept filled with water from the river Euphrates; and inside the wall, and not far from it, was another wall, not much inferior, but narrower, extending around the city.

Twenty-five magnificent avenues, 150 feet wide, ran across the city from North to South, and the same number crossed them at right angles from East to West, making 676 great squares, each nearly three-fifths of a mile on a side, and the city was divided into two equal parts by the river Euphrates, that flowed diagonally through it, and whose banks, within the city, were walled up, and pierced with brazen gates, with steps leading down to the river. At the ends of the main avenues, on each side of the city, were gates, whose leaves were of brass, and that shone as they were opened or closed in the rising or setting sun, like "leaves of flame."

The Euphrates within the city was spanned by a bridge, at each end of which was a palace, and these palaces were connected by a subterranean passageway, or tube, underneath the bed of the river, in which at different points were located sumptuous banqueting rooms constructed entirely of brass.

Near one of these palaces stood the

"Tower of Bel,"

or Babel, consisting of 8 towers, each 75 feet high, rising one upon the other, with an outside winding stairway to its summit, which towers, with the Chapel on the top, made a height of 660 feet. This Chapel contained the most expensive furniture of any place of worship in the world. One golden image alone, 45 feet high, was valued at $17,500,-

000, and the whole of the sacred utensils were reckoned to be worth $200,000,000.

Babylon also contained one of the "Seven Wonders" of the world, the famous Hanging Gardens.

These Gardens were 400 feet square, and were raised in terraces one above the other to the height of 350 feet, and were reached by stairways 10 feet wide. The top of each terrace was covered with large stones, on which was laid a bed of rushes, then a thick layer of asphalt, next two courses of brick, cemented together, and finally plates of lead to prevent leakage; the whole was then covered with earth and planted with shrubbery and large trees. The whole had the appearance from a distance of a forest-covered mountain, which would be a remarkable sight in the level plain of the Euphrates. These Gardens were built by Nebuchadnezzar simply to please his wife, who came from the mountainous country of Media, and who was thus made contented with her surroundings. The rest of the city was, in its glory and magnificence, in keeping with these palaces, towers, and "Hanging Gardens." The character of its inhabitants and of its official life is seen in the description of "Belshazzar's Feast" in Dan. 5: 1-31.

Babylon was probably the most magnificent city the world has ever seen and its fall reveals what a city may become when it forsakes God and He sends His judgment upon it. It is so intimately connected with the history of God's people that the Scriptures have much to say about it. A large part of the Book of Daniel and of the prophecy of Jeremiah relate to it, and it is mentioned in 11 other books of the Old Testament, and in 4 of the New Testament. And that the Book of Revelation is a continuation of the Book of Daniel is further proven by the fact that the city of Babylon is again spoken of in it, and its prominence in the affairs of the world at the "End Time" disclosed, and its final destruction foretold.

That the ancient city of Babylon was destroyed there can be no question, but when we affirm that it is to be rebuilt and again destroyed we are met with two objections.

1. That all the Old Testament prophecies in reference to its destruction have been literally fulfilled, and that it cannot be rebuilt.

2. As there is no city of Babylon now in existence the references in the Book of Revelation to the destruction of such a city must be symbolical and not refer to a literal city.

Let us take up the first objection. For a description of Babylon and her destruction we must turn to Isaiah, chapters 13 and 14, and Jeremiah, chapters 50 and 51. In these two prophecies we find much that has not as yet been fulfilled in regard to the city of Babylon.

The city of Babylon was captured in B. C. 541 by Cyrus, who was mentioned "by name" in prophecy 125 years before he was born. Isa. 44: 28-45: 4, B. C. 712. So quietly and quickly was the city taken on the night of Belshazzar's Feast by draining the river that flowed through the city, and entering by the river bed, and the gates that surmounted its banks, that the Babylonian guards had forgotten to lock that night, that some of the inhabitants did not know until the "third" day that the king had been slain and the city taken. There was no destruction of the city at that time.

Some years after it revolted against Darius Hystaspis, and after a fruitless siege of nearly 20 months was taken by strategy. This was in B. C. 516. About B. C. 478 Xerxes, on his return from Greece plundered and injured, if he did not destroy, the great "Temple of Bel."

In B. C. 331 Alexander the Great approached the city which was .hen so powerful and flourishing that he made preparation for bringing all his forces into action in case it should offer resistance, but the citizens threw open the gates and received him with acclamations. After sacrificing to "Bel," he gave out that he would rebuild the vast Temple of that god, and for weeks he kept 10,000 men employed in clearing away the ruins from the foundations, doubtless intending to revive the glory of Babylon and make it his capital, when his purpose was defeated by his sudden death of marsh-fever and intemperance in his thirty-third year.

During the subsequent wars of his generals Babylon suffered much and finally came under the power of Seleucus, who, prompted by ambition to build a Capital for himself, founded Seleucia in its neighborhood about B. C. 293. This rival city gradually drew off the inhabitants of Babylon, so that Strabo, who died in A. D. 25, speaks of the latter as being to a great extent deserted. Nevertheless the Jews left from the Captivity still resided there in large numbers, and in A. D. 60 we find the Apostle Peter working among them, for it was from Babylon that Peter wrote his Epistle (I Pet. 5: 13), addressed "to the strangers scattered throughout Pontus, Galatia, Cappadocia, Asia and Bithynia."

About the middle of the 5th century Theodoret speaks of Babylon as being inhabited only by Jews, who had still three Jewish Universities, and in the last year of the same century the "Babylonian Talmud" was issued, and recognized as authoritative by the Jews of the whole world.

In A. D. 917 Ibu Hankel mentions Babylon as an insignificant village, but still in existence. About A. D. 1100 it seems to have again grown into a town of some importance, for it was then known as the "Two Mosques." Shortly afterwards it was enlarged and fortified and received the name of Hillah, or "Rest." In A. D. 1898 Hillah contained about 10,000 inhabitants, and was surrounded by fertile lands, and abundant date groves stretched along the banks of the Euphrates. Certainly it has never been true that "neither shall the Arabian pitch tent there, neither shall the shepherds make their fold there." Isa. 13: 20. Nor can it be said of Babylon—"Her cities are a desolation, a dry land, and a wilderness, a land wherein no man dwelleth, neither doth any son of man pass thereby." Jer. 51: 43. Nor can it be said—"And they shall not take of thee a stone for a corner, nor a stone for foundations, but thou shalt be desolate forever, saith the Lord" (Jer. 51: 26), for many towns and cities have been built from the ruins of Babylon, among them Four Capital Cities, Seleucia, built by the Greeks; Ctesiphon, by the Parthians, Al Maiden, by the Persians; and Kufa, by the Caliphs. Hillah was entirely constructed from the debris, and even in the houses of Bagdad, Babylonian stamped bricks may be frequently noticed.

But Isaiah is still more specific for he locates the Time when his prophecy will be fulfilled. He ca!ls it the "Day of the Lord." Isa. 13: 9. That is the Millennium. And he locates it at the beginning of the Millennium, or during the events that usher in the Millennium, for he says—

"The stars of heaven and the constellations thereof shall not give their light; the sun shall be darkened in his going forth, and the moon shall not cause her light to shine." Isa. 13: 10 (Luke 21: 25-27).

Surely nothing like this happened when Babylon was taken by Cyrus.

In the description of the destruction of the city of Babylon given in Rev. 18, we read that her judgment will come in one hour (vs. 10), and that in one hour she shall be made desolate (vs. 19), and as an illustration of the suddenness and completeness of her destruction, a mighty angel took up a stone like a Great Millstone, and cast it into the sea, saying—"Thus with Violence shall that great city Babylon be thrown down and shall be found no more at all." Rev. 18: 21.

We are also told in the same chapter that she is to be destroyed by FIRE (Rev. 18: 8, 9, 18), and this is in exact harmony with the words of Isa. 13: 19.

"And Babylon, the glory of kingdoms, the beauty of the Chaldeees' excellency, shall be as when God overthrew

Sodom and Gomorrah;"

and the Prophet Jeremiah makes the same statement. Jer. 50: 40.

The destruction of Sodom and Gomorrah was not protracted through many centuries, their glory disappeared in a few hours (Gen. 19:24-28), and as ancient Babylon was not thus destroyed, the prophecies of Isaiah and Jeremiah cannot be fulfilled unless there is to be a Future Babylon that shall be thus destroyed.

In Rev. 16: 17-19, we are told that Babylon shall be destroyed by an Earthquake, attended with most vivid and incessant lightning and awful thunder. It would appear then, that as Sodom and Gomorrah were first set on fire and then swallowed up by an earthquake, that the rebuilt city of Babylon will be set on fire, and as the site of ancient Babylon is underlaid with **Bitumen** (Asphalt), that an earthquake will break up the crust of the earth, and precipitate the burning city into a **"Lake of Fire,"** and the city like a **"Millstone"** (Rev. 18:21) sink below the surface of the earth as into the sea, and be swallowed up so that it will be impossible to ever take of her stones for building purposes, and the land shall become a **Wilderness** where no man shall ever dwell.

As to the probability of the ancient city of Babylon being rebuilt we have only to consider the events that in recent years have been happening in that part of the world looking to just such a thing.

In the Department of War of France, at Paris, there is to be seen the records of valuable surveys and maps made by order of Napoleon I, in Babylonia, and among them is a plan for a **New City of Babylon**, thus showing that the vast schemes of Napoleon comprehended the **Rebuilding of the Ancient City of Babylon**, and the making it his Capital, as his ambition was to conquer the whole of Europe and Asia, and he recognized to that end the strategical position of ancient Babylon as a governmental and commercial centre.

It is a fact that the whole country of Mesopotamia, Assyria and Babylonia, only needs a system of irrigation to make it again the most fertile country in the world, and steps have already been taken in that direction. In 1850 the British Government sent out a military officer with his command to survey and explore the river Euphrates at a cost of $150,000, and when the European war broke out, the great English Engineer who built the Assouam dam in Egypt, was engaged in making surveys in the Euphratean valley for the purpose of constructing a series of irrigation canals that would restore the country and make it again the great grain producing country it once was. As a result towns and cities would spring up and railroads would be built. What is needed in that part of the world is a **"Trans-European-Asiatic-Indian Air Line"** that will connect Europe with India, and China. Such a line has been the dream of Emperor William of Germany. It was that desire that made him and Abdul Hamid, of Turkey, the closest of political friends, and he secured from Abdul Hamid a concession to build a railway from the Asiatic side of the Bosphorus, by way of Aleppo, to the Tigris river, and from there to Bagdad, and from Bagdad via **Babylon** (via Babylon, mark that) to Koweit on the Persian Gulf, and most of the road has been built to Bagdad.

With these facts in mind it can readily be seen that it is the purpose of European capitalists to revive the country of Babylonia and rebuild its cities, and when once the time comes the city of Babylon will be rebuilt almost in a night and on a scale of magnificence such as the world has never seen.

But I hear a protest. How you say can we be expecting Jesus to come at "any moment," if the city of Babylon must be rebuilt before He can come? There is not a word in Scripture that says that Jesus cannot come and take away His Church, until Babylon is rebuilt. The Church may be taken out of the world 25 or even 50 years before that.

Babylon the Great will be an immense city, the greatest in every respect the world has ever seen. It will be a typical city, the London, the Paris, the Berlin, the Petrograd, the New York, the Chicago of its day. It will be the greatest commercial city of the world. Its merchandise will be of gold and silver, and precious stones and pearls, of purple, and silk, and scarlet and costly wools. Its fashionable society will be clothed in the most costly raiment and decked with the most costly jewels. Their homes will be filled with the most costly furniture of precious woods, brass, iron and marble, with the richest of draperies, mats and rugs. They will use the most costly of perfumes, cinnamon, fragrant odors, ointments and frankincense. Their banquets will be supplied with the sweetest of wines, the richest of pastry, and the most delicious of meats. They will have horses and chariots and the swiftest of fast moving vehicles on earth and in the air. They will have their slaves, and they will traffic in the **"souls of men."** That is, women will sell their bodies, and men their souls, to gratify their lusts.

The markets will be crowded with cattle, sheep and horses. The wharves will be piled with goods from all climes. The manufactories will turn out the richest of fabrics, and all that genius can invent for the comfort and convenience of men will be found on the market. It will be a city given over to pleasure and business. Business men and promoters will give their days and nights to scheming how to make money fast, and the pleasure loving will be constantly planning new pleasures. There will be riotous joy and ceaseless feasting. As it was in the days of Noah and of Lot, they will be marrying and giving in marriage, buying and selling, building and planting.

The blood will run hot in their veins. Money will be their god, pleasure their high-priest, and unbridled passion the ritual of their worship.

It will be a city of music. Amid the noise and bustle of its commercial life will be heard the music of its pleasure resorts and theatres. There will be the sound of "harpers and musicians, of pipers and trumpeters" (vs. 22). The world's best singers and players will be there. Its theatres and places of music will be going day and night. In fact there will be no night, for the electric illumination of the city by night will make the night as bright and shadowless as the day, and its stores and places of business will never close, night or day, or Sunday, for the mad whirl of pleasure and the absorbing desire for riches will keep the wheels of business constantly moving. And all this will be easy because the "God of this World"—**Satan**, will possess the minds and **bodies** of men, for we read in verse 2, that Babylon at that time will be the **"Habitation of Devils**, and the Hold of Every Foul Spirit, and the **Cage of Every Unclean and Hateful Bird."** The city will be the seat of the most imposing **"OCCULTISM,"** and mediums, and those desiring to communicate with the other world, will then go to Babylon, as men and women now go to Paris for fashions and sensuous pleasures. In that day demons, disembodied souls, and unclean spirits will find at Babylon the opportunity of their lives to materialize themselves in human bodies, and from the atmospheric heavens above, and from the Abyss below they will come in countless legions until Babylon shall be full of demon possesssed men and women, and at the height of its glory, and just before its fall, Babylon will be ruled by **SATAN HIMSELF**, incarnate in the "Beast"—**ANTICHRIST**.

But before its destruction God will mercifully deliver His own people, for a voice from heaven will cry—

"Come Out of Her, My People, That Ye be Not Partakers of Her Sins, and that Ye Receive Not of Her Plagues." vs. 4.

As Sodom and Gomorrah could not be destroyed until righteous Lot had escaped, so Babylon cannot be destroyed until all the righteous people in it have fled.

The destruction of the city will be sudden and without warning. A fearful storm will sweep over the city. The lightning and thunder will be incessant. The city will be set on fire and a great earthquake will shake it from centre to circumference. The tall office buildings, the "Hanging Gardens" and the great towers will totter and fall, the crust of the earth will crack and open, and the whole city with its inhabitants will sink like a "**Millstone**," (vs. 21), into a lake of burning bitumen, and the smoke will ascend as of a burning fiery furnace, and the horror of the scene will be intensified by vast clouds of steam, generated by the waters of the Euphrates pouring into that lake of fiery asphalt, and when night comes on those clouds of steam will reflect the light of the burning city so it can be seen for miles in all directions in that level country. And the kings of the earth, and the merchants, and the shipmasters, and sailors, and all who have profited by her merchandise, will stand afar off and cry, and wail because of her destruction, but the heavens will rejoice for God will have rewarded her **Double** according to her works, and **BABYLON WILL BE NO MORE**.

XXV
RENOVATION OF THE EARTH

Immediately after the destruction of Satan and his armies, John says,

"I saw a **'Great White Throne'** and Him that sat on it, from whose face the **Earth** and the **Heaven** (atmosphere of the earth) **fled away**; and there was no place for them." Rev. 20:11.

John then describes the Judgment of the "Great White Throne," and then adds—

"I saw a **New Heaven**; and a **New Earth**; for the first heaven and the first earth were passed away; and there was **no more sea**." Rev. 21:1.

Of such a change in this earth we are not ignorant, but John does not tell us how it is to come to pass. But the Apostle Peter does.

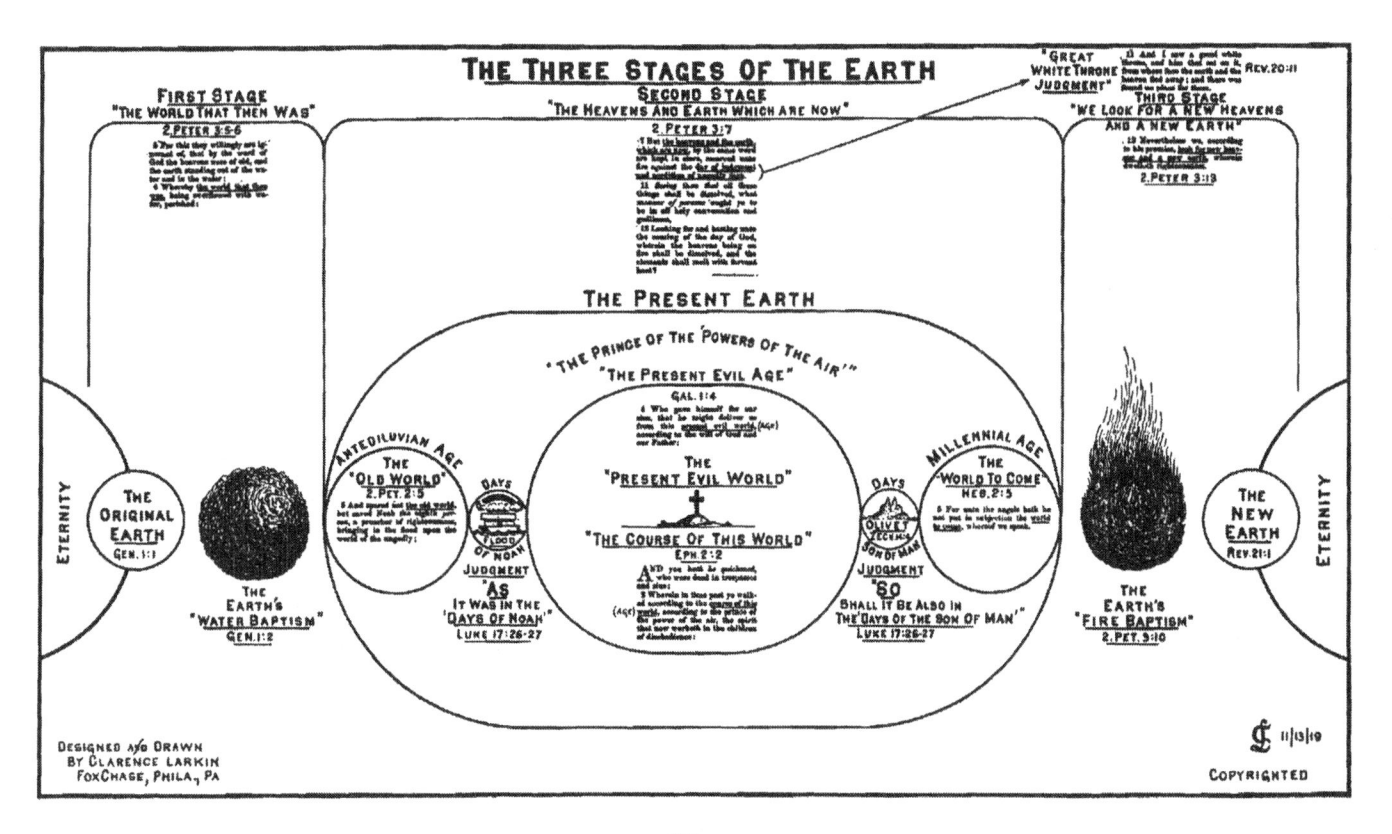

GREAT WHITE THRONE
JUDGMENT Rev. 20:11-15
"RENOVATION OF THE EARTH BY FIRE"
2 Pet. 3:10-13 Rev. 21:1-4

PARENTHETICAL DISPENSATION
BETWEEN
THE MILLENNIUM AND THE NEW EARTH

"But the heavens and the earth which are now, by the same word are kept in store, **RESERVED UNTO FIRE** against the Day of Judgment and Perdition of Ungodly Men. (The Great White Throne Judgment)— The 'Day of the Lord' will come as a thief in the night; in the which the **Heavens Shall Pass Away With a Great Noise, and the Elements Shall Melt With Fervent Heat, the Earth Also and the Works That Are Therein Shall be Burned Up.**

"Nevertheless we, according to His **Promise**, (Isa. 65:17; 66:22) look for a **New Heavens** and a **New Earth**, wherein dwelleth righteousness." 2 Pet. 3:7-13.

It is clear that Peter is referring to the same event as John, for he says it is to be at the **"Day of Judgment and Perdition of Ungodly Men,"** and that is the **"Great White Throne Judgment"** of the Wicked Dead.

A surface reading of the above passage would lead one to believe that the earth as a planet, and the sidereal heavens, are to be **destroyed by fire and pass away**. But a careful study of the Scriptures will show us that this is not so, that what is to happen is, that this present earth, and the atmosphere surrounding it, is to be **Renovated by Fire**, so that its **exterior surface shall be completely changed**, and all that sin has brought into existence, such as thorns and thistles, disease germs, insect pests, etc., shall be destroyed, and the atmosphere purified and forever freed from evil spirits and destructive agencies.

That this is the correct view of the passage is clear from Peter's words in verses 5 and 6.

"By the word of God the heavens were of old, and the earth standing out of the water and in the water; whereby the world that **then was, being overflowed with water, PERISHED.**"

The world that the Apostle is referring to here, was not the "Antediluvian World" that was changed by the "Flood," but to the "Primeval World," mentioned in Gen. 1:1, and which was made **waste and void** by a **Flood** that completely submerged it. Gen. 1:2. See the Chapter on "Rightly Dividing the Word."

The Apostle Peter divides the history of the earth into three periods. The period before the earth was made "formless and void," or the "Primeval Earth," which he calls "the world that **Then Was**;" the present period which he calls "the heavens and the earth which **Are Now**," and in which there has been no great change since the **restoration** of the earth, described in Gen. 1:3-2:1; and the **New Heaven and Earth** which is yet future. 2 Pet. 3:5-7, 13.

Now as the **Framework** of the "Primeval Earth" was not destroyed by its **"Watery Bath,"** so the **Framework** of the "Present Earth" is not to be destroyed by its **"Baptism of Fire."**

This is confirmed by the Apostle's use of the Greek word **"Cosmos,"** which means the **"land surface, the inhabitableness of the earth,** and not the earth as a planet. It is the **exterior surface** of the earth then that is to **"Melt With Fervent Heat"** and the **"Works Therein Burnt Up."** The intense heat will cause the gases in the atmosphere to explode, which the Apostle describes as the "heavens (the atmosphere) passing away with a **great noise.**" The result will be the destruction of all animal and vegetable life, and the alteration of the earth's surface.

The Greek work **"Parerchomai,"** translated **"pass away,"** does not mean **"termination of existence"** or **"annihilation,"** but means to pass from **"one condition of existence to another."** The Apostle Paul in his letter to Titus, (Titus 3:5), speaking of the **"Regeneration"** of men, uses the same word that Jesus used when, in Matt. 19:28, He promised His Disciples that in the **"Regeneration,"** that is in the **"New Earth,"** they should sit on **"Twelve Thrones"** judging the **"Twelve Tribes"** of Israel. Now no one supposes that the Regeneration of a man is his **Annihilation."** It is simply a **Renewing Process** by which he is brought back to the condition of man spiritually as before the Fall. The word **"Restitution"** in Acts 3:21, means the same thing. The **"Dissolving"** of which Peter speaks, (2 Pet. 3:11), is the same word Jesus used when He said of the colt—**"Loose him and let him go."** The teaching of the Scriptures is, that "Creation" is at present in a **"State of Captivity,"** waiting to be **Loosed from the Bondage** that sin has caused. Rom. 8:19-23.

As to the **"Departing as a Scroll"** of the heavens, and the **"Flying Away"** of the earth and heavens, of which John speaks, (Rev. 6:14; 20:11), a total disappearance of all the material worlds is not at all the idea, for he tells us that **afterwards** he saw—the New Jerusalem coming down out of **Heaven**, and **nations living and walking in the Light**

145

of it on the earth, and the **Kings of the Earth bringing their Glory and Honor Into It.**" Rev. 21:2, 24.

The Holy Spirit by Solomon said,

"One generation passeth away, and another generation cometh, but the **Earth Abideth Forever.**" Ecc. 1:4.

It is specifically promised that "the **Meek** shall **Inherit the Earth,**" (Matt. 5:5), and that the Children of Israel shall dwell in it **forever,** (Isa. 60:21; 66:22), and if God's people are to inhabit it **forever,** it must **EXIST FOREVER.** It is clear then that this earth as a planet is not to be annihilated, but that it is to be **Cleaned and Purified by Fire** and made fit for the home of those peoples and nations that are to occupy it after its renovation.

This earth that has been consecrated by the **Presence of the Son of God,** where the costliest sacrifice that the Universe could furnish was offered up on Calvary to redeem a race, for which God has a great future, is too sacred a place to ever be blotted out or cease to exist, for it is the most cherished orb in the mind of God of all His great creation.

The New Heaven and the New Earth.

With the "Renovation of the Earth by Fire," Time does not end and Eternity begin, for we read in the New Testament of a

"Perfect Kingdom"

that Christ shall surrender to the Father, so that God may be "**All in All.**" 1 Cor. 15:24-28. A Kingdom in which—

"At the name of Jesus **every knee shall bow,** of things in **Heaven,** and things in **Earth,** and things **Under the Earth,** and that **every tongue shall confess** that **Jesus Christ IS LORD.**" Phil. 2:9-11.

This describes a Kingdom in which all things **Celestial, Terrestrial and Infernal** are to be subject to the **SON OF MAN.**

Now this "Perfect Kingdom" cannot be the "Millennial Kingdom," for that, as we have seen, ends in **Apostasy** and **Rebellion.** It must therefore mean another Kingdom on the **Other Side of the Millennial Kingdom,**" and as there is to be no other Kingdom between the "Millennial Kingdom" and the "Renovation of the Earth by Fire," it must mean a Kingdom that is to **follow** the "Renovation of the Earth by Fire," and that Kingdom is the Kingdom of the "**New Heaven and the New Earth,**" which we call on the "Rightly Dividing the Word" Chart, the "**Perfect Kingdom.**"

If, as some hold, the "Seventh Day" of the "Creative Week" corresponds to the Millennium, then we have a prophecy of the Dispensation that follows the "Renovation of the Earth" in the "**Morrow After the Sabbath.**" Lev. 23:36.

The Seventh day of Genesis had to do with the "Old Creation," which was imperfect, but the "**Eighth Day**" has to do with the "**New Creation,**" which is perfect, for it was on the "**Eighth Day,**" or the "First Day of the week," that our Lord arose from the dead, and 50 days later, on the "**Eighth Day,**" that the Holy Spirit was given at Pentecost. The "Eighth Day" cannot point to the Millennium, for that is represented by the "Seventh Day," neither can it point to Eternity, for a day is a **Period of Time,** while Eternity is **Timeless.** The "Eighth Day" must then point to a "period of time" **between** the "Renovation of the Earth" and Eternity, or what we are pleased to call the "**Perfect Age.**"

It is also a Dispensation, called in Eph. 1:10—

"The Dispensation of the Fulness of Times."

That is, a "**Full-Time Dispensation.**" The intimation is, that all the previous Dispensations were not "Full-Time" Dispensations, that God had to cut them short on account of sin.

As to the duration of this Dispensation of the "Fulness of Times" we are not in the dark. Israel is to have a large place in that Dispensation.

"For as the New Heavens and the New Earth, which I will make shall remain before me, saith the Lord, so shall your (Israel's) **Seed** and your **Name REMAIN.**" Isa. 66:22.

And as the duration of God's Covenant with Israel was extended in Deu. 7:9 to a "Thousand Generations" or 33,000 years, we have an intimation that the "Dispensation of the Fulness of Times" will last for at least that length of time.

Let us look at some of the characteristics of that Age or Dispensation.

There Will Be No Sin.

All the powers of Evil will have been expelled from the earth and imprisoned in the "Lake of Fire" forever.

The atmosphere of the New Earth will afford no lurking place for disease germs, for there shall be no more sickness or death, and health will be preserved by the use of the leaves of the "Tree of Life." The heavens shall not robe themselves in angry tempests and sombre blackness, nor flash with the thunderbolts of Divine wrath, nor cast plagues of hail on the earth, nor cause devouring floods of water or destructive wind storms. It may be that in that day, "a **Mist** shall go up from the earth and water the whole face of the ground" as in Eden, for we read that there shall be—"**No More Sea,**" not that there shall not be large bodies of water, for the river that flows through the street of the New City must have an outlet, but that there shall be no great oceans.

The earth shall also put on its Edenic beauty and glory. There shall no longer be thorns and thistles, no parasites or destructive insects, and labor shall be a delight. No serpents shall hiss among its flowers, nor savage beasts lie in ambush to destroy and devour. Its sod shall not be heaped over newly made graves, nor its soil moistened with tears of sorrow and shame, or saturated with human blood in fratricidal strife. The meek shall inherit the earth, and from north to south, and from east to west, it shall blossom like the rose and be clothed with the verdure of Paradise Restored.

But there is not only to be a New Heaven and a New Earth, there is to be a **New City.** This City is the place Jesus said He was going back to Heaven to prepare for His Bride the Church. John 14:2-4. It is just such a place as we would expect the Divine Architect to design and build. The description of it is surpassingly grand. It is of Celestial origin. It is not Heaven itself, for it comes down "out of Heaven." No mortal hands are employed in its construction. It will take up its abode on the New Earth, and we see in this why this present Earth will have to be renovated by fire, and why there shall be "no more sea," for the New City is 12,000 furlongs, or 1500 miles square, and would reach from Maine to Florida, and from the Atlantic Seaboard 600 miles to the west of the Mississippi River. In other words would occupy more than one-half of the United States.

We are told that the length and breadth and the height of it **are equal.** This does not necessarily imply that it is a Cube, for there is another geometrical figure that has equal dimensions, and that is a—**Pyramid.** This is its probable form, for a wall 144 cubits, or 216 feet thick, could not support a wall 1500 miles high, and a wall that high would hide the pyramidal part of the City from view.

The 144 cubits (Rev. 21:17) then must refer to the "height" of the wall. In this wall are 12 gates, 3 on each side, each gate of one Pearl, and these gates are never closed.

The wall itself is of Jasper, and the foundations are garnished with all manner of precious stones. The foundations contain the names of the Twelve Apostles of the Lamb, and over the gates are the names of the Twelve Tribes of Israel.

What a magnificent spectacle such a city must present from a distance with its pyramidal top surmounted by the light of the

"Glory of God."

"For the city had no need of the sun, neither of the moon, to shine in it, for the '**Glory of God** did lighten it, and **THE LAMB** is **The LIGHT THEREOF.**" Rev. 21:23.

"And the gates of it shall not be shut at all by day, for there shall be **No Night There.**" Rev. 21:25.

This refers to the City only, and not to the outlying parts of the New Earth, for there will be day and night wherever the light of the City does not reach.

The Pyramidal part of the City will doubtless be in the centre of the City, and probably not occupy over one-half of the surface area, leaving the remainder to be divided up into boulevards and broad avenues, with numerous parks and residential sections. We are told that the City itself is of **Pure Gold, Like Unto Clear Glass.** Rev. 21:18. If this refers to the houses and homes of the inhabitants, then the redeemed are to live in palaces of **Transparent Gold**, and the streets are to be of the same material. Rev. 21:18, 21. We cannot imagine a city with such dwellings and streets to be unclean or lack beauty.

The streets are to be lined with trees, as are also the banks of a wonderful river. These trees are not mere shade trees, but beautiful **Fruit Trees**, called the **"TREE OF LIFE,"** that bear **Twelve Kind of Fruit**, a different kind each month. The fruit of these trees is for **Overcomers Only.**

"To him that **overcometh** will I give to eat of the '**Tree of Life**' which is in the midst of the Paradise of God." Rev. 2:7.

The leaves of the trees are for the **Healing of the Nations that shall occupy the New Earth.** Not that there will be any sickness, but to preserve them in health, as Adam would have been preserved in health if he had eaten of the Tree of Life in the Garden of Eden. Gen. 3:22-24.

The wonderful river is called the River of the "Water of Life," because of its "life giving" properties. Earthly streams have their source in some mountain spring, but the "River of Life" has its source in the Throne of God. Rev. 22:1.

Somewhere on that "Pyramidal Mountain" in the centre of the City, probably on its summit, will rest

"The Throne of God,"

from under the seat of which shall flow down in cascades, from terrace to terrace, the crystal stream that shall feed that wonderful "River of Life."

Whoever heard of an earthly city without some place of worship, be it heathen or Christian, but the wonderful thing about the New Jerusalem is, that it has no **Temple.** Why need a Temple when the object of worship is present, for **"The Lord God Almighty and the Lamb Are the Temple of It."** In fact the whole City itself will be a Temple.

"Then the '**Tabernacle of God**' shall be with men, and He will **dwell with them**, and they shall be His People, and God Himself shall be with them, and be their God. And God shall wipe away all tears from their eyes; and there shall be no **more death**, neither sorrow, nor crying, neither shall there be any more pain; for the **FORMER THINGS ARE PASSED AWAY.**" Rev. 21:3, 4.

This means that Heaven shall have come down to Earth, and that this earth will become the **RESIDENCE OF GOD.**

Outside the walls of this beautiful City, spread over the surface of the "New Earth," nations shall dwell, whose kings shall bring their glory and honor into it, but nothing that will defile or work abomination shall ever enter in through those "Gates of Pearl," for there will be no sin on that New Earth. Rev. 21:24-27.

Who Are to Be the Happy Inhabitants of This New Earth?

Where did the people who inhabited the earth **after the Flood** come from? They were the lineal descendants of Noah, how did they escape the Flood? They were saved in an Ark which **God Provided**. Gen. 6:13-16. Shall not God then during the "Renovation of the Earth by Fire," in some manner, not as yet revealed, take off righteous representatives of the Millennial nations that He purposes to save, and when the earth is again fit to be the abode of men, place them back on the New Earth, that they may increase and multiply and **replenish** it, as Adam (Gen. 1:27, 28), and Noah (Gen. 9:1), were told to **multiply and replenish** the present earth.

If God could take off Elijah for the purpose of sending him back again to herald the Second Coming of the Lord, surely God can take off representative men from the nations and put them back again on the New Earth to **repopulate it.** If this is not God's plan then we have one type in the Scriptures that has no antitype, for Noah's Ark, which is a type, has no antitype unless it be this.

It is clear from the Scriptures that God does not purpose to create a new race for the New Earth. His promise as to Israel is that the descendants of Abraham shall inherit this earth for a "thousand generations," or 33,000 years; now this is not possible unless they are transplanted to the New Earth. And this is just what God has promised.

"For as the New Heavens and the New Earth, which I will make, shall **remain before Me**, saith the Lord, so shall Your 'Seed' and Your 'Name' REMAIN." Isa. 66:22.

It seems clear from the presence of the Tree of Life in the Garden of Eden, that God intended the human race to populate the Earth, and when it became too thickly populated, to use the surplus population to colonize other spheres. Our "Solar System" is only in its infancy. The Earth is the only one of its planets as yet habitable. Where are the inhabitants for the other planets to come from? Think you that the planets of our Solar System, and the planets of other solar systems, of which the stars are the suns, were made simply to adorn the heavens for our little earth? God does not plan things on a **Small Scale**, and it magnifies His power and wisdom to believe that He created man in His own likeness, a created being higher than the angels, and gifted with the power of **Procreation**, that He might by means of him populate the Universe. This magnifies the Scheme of Redemption. Think you that God gave His Son to die on Calvary just to redeem a **few** millions of the human race? Why He could have blotted them out, as He probably did the Preadamite race, and created a new race, and Satan would have laughed because he had the second time blocked God's plan for the peopling of this earth.

No, God will not permit Satan to block His plan for peopling this earth with a **Sinless Human Race.** The death of Christ was not merely to redeem a few millions of the human race, but to redeem the **Earth**, and the **Race Itself** from the curse of sin, and the dominion of Satan.

The Apostle James tells us that we are only the "**First Fruits**" of His **Creatures.**" James 1:18. What then must the **HARVEST BE?**

THE HOLY CITY
REV. 21:1-22:6.

The Universe is young yet. We are only in the beginning of things, for

"Of the increase of His government and peace **THERE SHALL BE NO END.**" Isa. 9:7.

When this Earth shall have gone through its "Baptism of Fire," and shall be again fit for the occupancy of man, the representatives of the "Saved Nations" (Rev. 21:24) will be men and women in whom no taint of sin will remain, and who cannot therefore impart it to their offspring, who will be like the offspring of Adam and Eve would have been if they had not sinned. This magnifies the whole scheme of redemption, and justifies God in the creation of the human race.

The Great Abdication.

The "**Millennial Age**" and the "**Perfect Age**," between which the Earth is Renovated by Fire, make up the "**Age of Ages**," which period is called the **KINGDOM OF THE SON OF MAN**.

At the close of the "Age of Ages" when Christ "shall have put down all rule and all authority and power. For He must reign till He hath put all enemies under his feet," then Christ as the Son of Man, shall surrender the Kingdom to God, that God may be **ALL IN ALL**. 1 Cor. 15:24-28. This is known as **The Great Abdication**.

There have been many abdications of thrones in the world's history, but none like this. Thrones have been abdicated for various reasons. Some have been forced, others voluntary. Some on account of physical infirmity, or to secure some particular successor. But Christ will not abdicate for any of these reasons. He will abdicate because He has **Finished the Work That Was Given Him to Do as the Son of Man**. He will not surrender His Human Nature, but His title "**Son of Man**" will merge back into that of "**Son of God**" so that the Divine **Godhead** shall thereafter act in its **Unity**, and God shall be "**ALL IN ALL**." This will end what we understand by **Time**. Then **Eternity** will begin, which will be divided up into the **Ages of the Ages**. Of its end there is no hint.

XXVI
THE COVENANTS

A Covenant is an agreement or contract between men, or between men and God. Generally it is based on certain conditions agreed upon. Sometimes, as between God and man, it is unconditional. God's covenants with man originate with Him, and generally consist of a promise based on the fulfilment of certain conditions. God has made eight Covenants with man. They all relate to the earth. Each one introduces a New Dispensation. Six of them were given to individual and representative men, as Adam, Noah and Abraham, and went into effect during their lives except the one given to David, which took effect at the birth of Jesus. Each one has a time element and expires at a certain time. Four of them are distinguished by a "Sign." See the Chart on The Covenants.

I. The Edenic Covenant.
Gen. 1:28-30; 2:15-17.

This Covenant was given to Adam and Eve, in the Garden of Eden, before the Fall of Man. It ushered in the "Dispensation of Innocence" which was conditioned on obedience.

The Seven Conditions of this Covenant were.

1. To **Replenish the Earth** with an earthly race of people, the first or Pre-Adamite Race having become extinct, through the earth having been thrown into a chaotic condition. Gen. 1:2.

2. To **Subdue the Earth** to the needs of the human race. What this means is not clear, unless it means to so control the forces of light, heat, electricity, gravitation, etc., as to enable man to use them to supply his needs.

3. To have **Dominion Over the Animal Creation.** Not over the domestic animals only, but over wild creatures as well. This is beautifully described in Psa. 8:3-9.

4. To **Restrict Themselves to a "Vegetable Diet."** And from verse 30 it would appear that the animal creation, before the Fall, was limited to a vegetable diet.

5. To **Till the Garden** in which God had placed him. This was doubtless a pleasure and not a task. There was no curse upon the earth at that time. It was not until after the Fall that "thorns" and "thistles" and "weeds" made the cultivation of the soil laborious. Gen. 3:17-19.

6. To **Abstain From Eating of the "Tree of the Knowledge of Good and Evil."** Man was created innocent like the infant. He did not know what sin is. His environment was such that he would have remained innocent if he had obeyed God, and refused to eat of the "Tree" which **opened his eyes.** The moment he ate of that "Tree" he broke the Covenant and knew the difference between good and evil.

7. The punishment of disobedience was **Physical Death.** And this would have happened to both Adam and Eve at once if God in His Grace had not intervened and instituted a new covenant, known as the **"Adamic Covenant."**

II. The "Adamic" Covenant.
Gen. 3:14-19.

This Covenant, like the first, was given to Adam and Eve in the Garden of Eden before their expulsion. It ushered in the "Dispensation of Conscience." It was without conditions, and embodied a "Curse" and a "Promise."

1. The "Curse."

The Curse was fourfold.

a. As to the Serpent.

The Serpent was Satan's tool, and from being a most beautiful and attractive creature became a loathsome reptile. It still retains traces of its former beauty and grace. It was condemned to crawl upon its belly and eat dust.

b. As to the Woman.

Her state was changed in three particulars.

(1)—**Multiplied Conception.** If Adam and Eve had any children before the "Fall" it is not revealed. It is certain Cain was not conceived until after their expulsion from the Garden. Gen. 4:1. By "Multiplied Conception" is probably meant that there would be several children born at a time. This would be necessary to rapidly replenish the earth. As a matter of necessity the children of the same parents intermarried, as there were no other human beings on the earth at that time.

THE COV

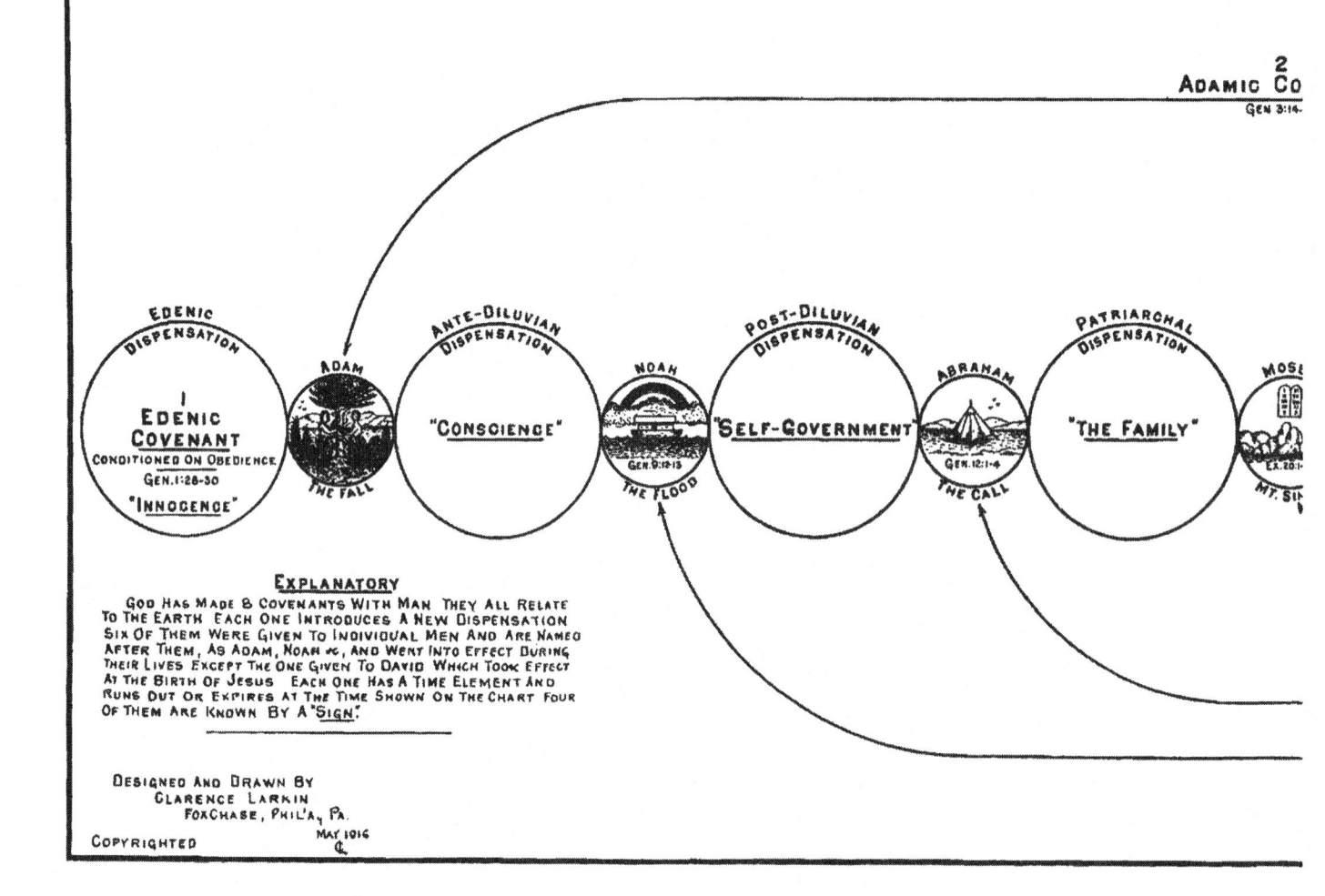

2
ADAMIC CO
GEN 3:14

EDENIC DISPENSATION

1 EDENIC COVENANT
CONDITIONED ON OBEDIENCE.
GEN. 1:28-30
"INNOCENCE"

ADAM
THE FALL

ANTE-DILUVIAN DISPENSATION
"CONSCIENCE"

NOAH
GEN. 9:12-13
THE FLOOD

POST-DILUVIAN DISPENSATION
"SELF-GOVERNMENT"

ABRAHAM
GEN. 12:1-4
THE CALL

PATRIARCHAL DISPENSATION
"THE FAMILY"

MOSES
EX. 20:1-
MT. SI

Explanatory

God has made 8 covenants with man. They all relate to the earth. Each one introduces a new dispensation. Six of them were given to individual men and are named after them, as Adam, Noah &c, and went into effect during their lives except the one given to David which took effect at the birth of Jesus. Each one has a time element and runs out or expires at the time shown on the chart. Four of them are known by a "Sign".

Designed and Drawn by
Clarence Larkin
FoxChase, Phil'a, Pa.
May 1916
COPYRIGHTED

ENANTS

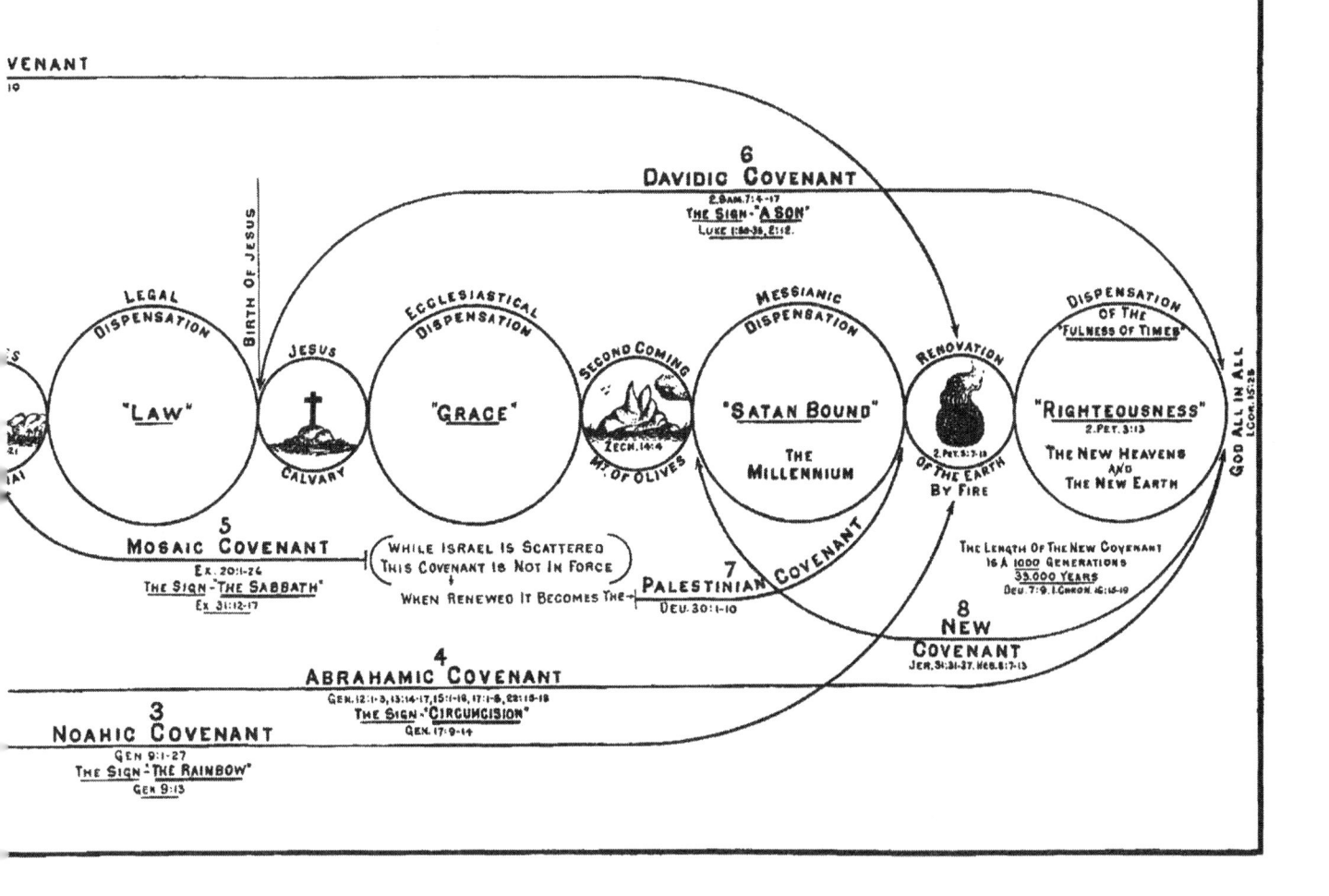

6 Davidic Covenant
2 Sam. 7:4-17
The Sign - "A Son"
Luke 1:30-35, 2:11

VENANT

Birth of Jesus

Legal Dispensation
"LAW"

Jesus Calvary

Ecclesiastical Dispensation
"GRACE"

Second Coming Mt. of Olives
Zech. 14:4

Messianic Dispensation
"Satan Bound"
The Millennium

Renovation of the Earth by Fire
2 Pet. 3:7-13

Dispensation of the "Fulness of Times"
"Righteousness"
2 Pet. 3:13
The New Heavens and The New Earth

God All in All
1 Cor. 15:28

5 Mosaic Covenant
Ex. 20:1-26
The Sign - "The Sabbath"
Ex. 31:12-17

While Israel is Scattered This Covenant is Not in Force → When Renewed It Becomes The →

7 Palestinian Covenant
Deu. 30:1-10

The Length of the New Covenant is a 1000 Generations
35,000 Years
Deu. 7:9, 1 Chron. 16:15-19

4 Abrahamic Covenant
Gen. 12:1-3, 13:14-17, 15:1-18, 17:1-8, 22:15-18
The Sign - "Circumcision"
Gen. 17:9-14

8 New Covenant
Jer. 31:31-37, Heb. 8:7-13

3 Noahic Covenant
Gen. 9:1-27
The Sign - "The Rainbow"
Gen. 9:13

(2)—**Sorrowful Motherhood.** That is, child-birth was to be accompanied with much pain and anguish. If sin had not entered, child-birth would doubtless have been painless, and motherhood a pleasure and children a delight.

(3)—**Headship of Man.** Woman was created the equal of man, but because she caused his fall she lost her equality and man was given the Headship over her. Gen. 3:16.

c. **As to the Man.** The ground was cursed for his sake, and whereas it had been a pleasure to look after the Garden, now he would have to secure a living from the soil by hard labor and the "sweat of his face," which would wear out his system and end in physical death.

d. **As to the Ground.** Henceforth it was to be cursed with "thorns" and "thistles." That is, with everything that would make the cultivation of the earth difficult.

2. **The "Promise."** The Promise was that the **"Seed"** of the Woman (Christ) should bruise the "Serpent's" head, while his "seed" should bruise Christ's heel. Here is the Promise that Christ shall redeem the world from the power of Satan, and restore the human race and the Earth to their condition before the "Fall." This Covenant reaches until the Renovation of the Earth by Fire."

III. The "Noahic" Covenant.
Gen. 8:20-9:17.

Man having proved himself a failure under the "Dispensation of Conscience," God sent a Flood to destroy the race from off the earth, sparing only Noah and his family. After the Flood Noah offered a "sacrifice" which was well pleasing to God, and God made an **unconditional** Covenant with Noah. It ushered in the "Dispensation of Human Government." It contained the following provisions.

1. That God would not **curse the ground** any more, nor destroy all the living. And that the "day" and the "night" and the "seasons" should not cease.

2. That Noah and his descendants were to be **fruitful and multiply, and replenish the earth.**

3. That they should have **dominion over the animal creation** as before.

4. That from that time they were not to be restricted to a "vegetable" diet, but could eat meat if they drained the **blood** from it. Vs. 3-4.

5. The law of **"Capital Punishment"** was established. Vs. 6. This has never been abrogated, though the manner of enforcing it has been more clearly laid down in the account of the Cities of Refuge. Num. 35:1-34.

6. That the earth shall never be destroyed again by the "waters of a Flood."

The "Sign" of this Covenant is the **Rainbow,** and the Covenant reaches until the "Renovation of the Earth by Fire," of which it is the Type.

IV. The "Abrahamic" Covenant.
Gen. 12:1-3.

The Tower of Babel episode was a turning point in human history. (Gen. 11:1-9). Up to that time the human race was a unit. There was neither Jew nor Gentile. The race had become idolatrous. To remedy this God decided to call out an individual of the seed of Shem, and of him form a separated people and nation. The man selected was Abraham. The "Call" came to him while dwelling at Ur of the Chaldees, in Mesopotamia. He obeyed. The Covenant then made with him was afterwards enlarged and confirmed to his son, Isaac, (Gen. 26:1-5), and in turn to his grandson Jacob (Israel), Gen. 28:10-15. The Covenant was unconditional and ushered in the Dispensation of the Family. It contained seven promises.

1. **"I Will Make of Thee a Great Nation."** This was to be fulfilled in a twofold way.

a. **Natural Posterity.** "As the dust of the earth." This has been fulfilled through Isaac and through Ishmael. Gen. 17:20.

b. **Spiritual Posterity.** "As the stars of heaven." Gal. 3:6, 7, 29.

2. **"I Will Bless Thee."** This was fulfilled temporally in flocks and herds and lands. Gen. 13:14-18; 15:18-21; 24:34, 35. Abraham was also blessed **spiritually.** Gen. 15:6.

3. **"And Make Thy Name Great."** Abraham, next to Christ, is the outstanding name in the Scriptures.

4. **"And Thou Shalt Be a Blessing."** Abraham was a blessing to the people of his own time and to the world, as through him came the chosen seed. Gal. 3:14.

5. **"I Will Bless Them That Bless Thee."**

6. **"And Curse Him That Curseth Thee."** These last two have been wonderfully fulfilled in the past history of the Jewish people and will be more wonderfully fulfilled in the future. Every nation that has treated them well has been blessed and every nation that has mistreated them has suffered.

7. **"In Thee Shall All the Families of the Earth Be Blessed."** This promise is fulfilled in Christ spiritually and shall be fulfilled temporally in the Millennium when the Gentile nations shall be blessed through Israel. Deu. 28:8-14; Isa. 60:3-5, 11, 16.

After Abraham's faith had been tested in the offering up of Isaac this Covenant was reaffirmed and confirmed. Gen. 22:15-18. It was an **Everlasting** Covenant. Gen. 17:1-8.

The "Sign" of this Covenant is **"Circumcision"** (Gen. 17:9-14), and the Covenant extends to the "End of Time," taking in the New Earth.

We must not forget that the "Adamic" and "Noahic" Covenants were not done away with or superseded by the "Abrahamic" Covenant. The "Abrahamic" Covenant is confined to the Hebrew Race, while the others cover the whole Gentile world. The Dispensations of "Conscience" and "Human Government" still continue as to the Gentiles.

V. The "Mosaic" Covenant.

The "Mosaic Covenant" was given to Moses on Mt. Sinai, shortly after the Exodus from Egypt. It ushered in the "Dispensation of Law." It was conditioned on obedience, and may be divided into three parts.

1. **The Moral Law.** Ex. 20:1-26. This consists of the Ten Commandments.

2. **The Civil Law.** Ex. 21:1-24:18.

3. **The Ceremonial Law.** Ex. 25:1-40:38. This includes the Tabernacle, the Priesthood, and the order of service. See Chart of Book of Leviticus. The "Sign" of this Covenant is **the Sabbath.** Ex. 31:12-18.

This Covenant continued in force until the Jews were scattered at the destruction of Jerusalem in A. D. 70. It will be renewed when Israel is converted and restored to their own land, and will then be known as the "Palestinian Covenant," which Covenant ends with the "Renovation of the Earth by Fire."

VI. The "Davidic" Covenant.
2 Sam. 7:4-17.

This Covenant was given to King David, through Nathan the Prophet, at Jerusalem. It ushered in the "Dispensation of Grace." It has but one condition, based on disobedience, this would lead to chastisement and postponement of the promise, but not its abrogation. The Covenant contains four promises.

1. **A Davidic House.** Vs. 13. That is the posterity of David shall never be destroyed.

2. **A Davidic Throne.** Vs. 13. The Kingdom of David shall never be destroyed. At present it is in abeyance, but it will be set up again. Since the "Captivity" but one King of the Davidic family has been crowned and He with **"thorns"** (Matt. 27:29), but He will receive the Kingdom and return when Israel's chastisement is over, and the time comes to restore the Kingdom to David's **Son.** Luke 1:30-33.

3. **A Davidic Kingdom.** David's Son is to have an earthly "sphere of rule." It will be over the Millennial Earth. "He shall have dominion also from sea to sea, and from the river unto the ends of the earth." Psa. 72:1-20.

4. **It Shall Be Unending.**

"Thine **House** and thy **Kingdom** shall be established **Forever**; thy **Throne** shall be established **Forever**." Vs. 16.

The "**Sign**" of this Covenant is a Son. Luke 1:30-33; 2:12. This Covenant extends to the "End of Time."

VII. The "Palestinian" Covenant.
Deu. 30:1-10.

This Covenant was given to Israel through Moses, and is conditioned on the repentance of Israel. It will go into effect after their return to Palestine and their repentance. It ushers in the "Millennial Dispensation" and ends with it.

VIII. The "New" Covenant.
Heb. 8:7-13.

This Covenant has not yet been made. It is to be made with Israel after they get back to their own land. It is promised in Jer. 31:31-37. It is unconditional, and will cover the Millennium and the New Heaven and New Earth. It is based on the finished work of Christ. Matt. 26:28. It has nothing to do with the Church and does not belong to this Dispensation. It is the "Eighth Covenant," and speaks of **Resurrection** and **Eternal Completeness.**

XXVII
THE MYSTERIES

Writing to the Corinthians Paul says—"Let a man so account of us as of the ministers of Christ, and stewards of the—'**Mysteries of God**'." 1 Cor. 4:1.

In Rom. 16:25, 26, Paul speaks of what he calls "My Gospel," which he calls the "Revelation of the Mystery," which was kept "Secret" since the world began, but now is made "manifest." It was the "revelation" that was promised to Paul at his conversion (Acts 26:16-18), and which comprises the "Mysteries of God."

The "Mysteries" are eleven in number, eight of which were revealed to Paul. Of the remaining three, one was revealed by Christ, and two were revealed to the Apostle John.

A "Mystery" in the New Testament sense is not something that cannot be understood, but is some plan or purpose of God that has been known to Him from the beginning, but which He has withheld from the knowledge of men until the time came for Him to reveal it. Let us examine these "Mysteries" in the order in which they are fulfilled.

I. The Mystery of the "Incarnation."

"Without controversy great is the

'**Mystery of Godliness**';

God was manifest in the flesh, justified in the Spirit, seen of angels, preached unto the Gentiles, believed on in the world, received up into glory." 1 Tim. 3:16.

It is no mystery that God should reveal Himself by speaking from the Heavens, as on Mt. Sinai, but that He should take on the "Human Form" and "tabernacle" among us that was a great mystery. This He did in the person of Christ. John 1:1-14. So Jesus could say, "He that hath seen Me hath seen the Father." John 14:9.

II. The Mystery of the "Divine Indwelling."

In Col. 1:26-28, Paul speaks of another "Mystery" which had been hid from "Ages" and from "Generations," but was then made manifest to the saints. He calls it the Mystery of "**Christ in You**." This is a great mystery because it is the mystery of the "**New Birth.**" A mystery that brought from Nicodemus the exclamation—"How can a man be born when he is old?" John 3:4. The New Birth is wonderful, but it is a wonderful fact. It is the union of the Divine Nature and ours. So that just as Jesus became one with us by His taking our human nature, so we become one with Him by taking on the Divine Nature. The mystery of this union is, that it is a union of "identity." We are just as much a part of Christ as the members of the body are a part of the body. 1 Cor. 12:12. It is for Christ to **live in us**. Gal. 2:20.

III. The **Mystery** of the "Union of Jews and Gentiles in One Body Called the Church."

In his letter to the saints at Ephesus (Eph. 3:1-11), Paul says, that God by revelation made known to him the "Mystery," which in

The Mysteries

1 Mystery — The Incarnation

1 TIM. 3:16
16 And without controversy great is the mystery of godliness: God was manifested in the flesh, justified in the Spirit, seen of angels, preached unto the Gentiles, believed on in the world, received up into glory.

JOHN 1:1,14
In the beginning was the Word, and the Word was with God, and the Word was God. 14 And the Word was made flesh, and dwelt among us, (and we beheld his glory, the glory as of the only begotten of the Father,) full of grace and truth.

CALVARY

2 Mystery — The Divine Indwelling

COL. 1:26-27
26 Even the mystery which hath been hid from ages and from generations, but now is made manifest to his saints:
27 To whom God would make known what is the riches of the glory of this mystery among the Gentiles; which is Christ in you, the hope of glory:

GAL. 2:20
20 I am crucified with Christ: nevertheless I live; yet not I, but Christ liveth in me: and the life which I now live in the flesh I live by the faith of the Son of God, who loved me, and gave himself for me.

THE GENTILE → **3 Mystery — The Union Of "Jews" And "Gentiles" In The Church "The Body" Of Christ**

THE JEW →

EPH. 3:3-6
3 How that by revelation he made known unto me the mystery; (as I wrote afore in few words,
4 Whereby, when ye read, ye may understand my knowledge in the mystery of Christ,)
5 Which in other ages was not made known unto the sons of men, as it is now revealed unto his holy apostles and prophets by the Spirit;
6 That the Gentiles should be fellowheirs, and of the same body, and partakers of his promise in Christ by the gospel.

4 Mystery — The 7 Stars And Candlesticks

CHRISTENDOM
- ☆ Ephesus
- ☆ Smyrna
- ☆ Pergamos
- ☆ Thyatira
- ☆ Sardis
- ☆ Philadelphia
- ☆ Laodicea

The 7 Churches Correspond With The 7 Parables Of Matthew 13

REV. 1:12-20
20 The mystery of the seven stars which thou sawest in my right hand, and the seven golden candlesticks. The seven stars are the angels of the seven churches: and the seven candlesticks which thou sawest are the seven churches.

5 Mystery — The Kingdom Of Heaven

MATT. 13:1-52
10 And the disciples came, and said unto him, Why speakest thou unto them in parables?
11 He answered and said unto them, Because it is given unto you to know the mysteries of the kingdom of heaven, but to them it is not given.

1. The Sower
2. The Wheat and Tares
3. The Mustard Seed
4. The Leaven
5. The Hid Treasure
6. The Pearl
7. The Drag Net

SEE THE AUTHOR'S CHART ON THE "KINGDOM OF HEAVEN PARABLES"

CHRISTENDOM

The Translation — The Rapture

1 COR. 15:51
51 Behold, I shew you a mystery; We shall not all sleep, but we shall all be changed,
52 In a moment, in the twinkling of an eye, at the last trump: for the trumpet shall sound, and the dead shall be raised incorruptible, and we shall be changed.

6
MYSTERY
...ION OF THE SAINTS

1. THESS. 4:16-17

16 For the Lord himself shall descend from heaven with a shout, with the voice of the archangel, and with the trump of God; and the dead in Christ shall rise first:

17 Then we which are alive and remain shall be caught up together with them in the clouds, to meet the Lord in the air: and so shall we ever be with the Lord.

The Church Caught Out

EPH. 5:25-32

25 Husbands, love your wives, even as Christ also loved the church, and gave himself for it;

26 That he might sanctify and cleanse it with the washing of water by the word,

27 That he might present it to himself a glorious church, not having spot, or wrinkle, or any such thing; but that it should be holy and without blemish.

32 This is a great mystery: but I speak concerning Christ and the church.

10
MYSTERY
THE CHURCH—THE BRIDE OF CHRIST

THE HOLY CITY
NEW JERUSALEM

REV. 21:9-10

Come hither, I will shew thee the bride, the Lamb's wife.

10 And he carried me away in the spirit to a great and high mountain, and shewed me that great city, the holy Jerusalem, descending out of heaven from God.

REV. 19:7-9

7 Let us be glad and rejoice, and give honour to him: for the marriage of the Lamb is come, and his wife hath made herself ready.

8 And to her was granted that she should be arrayed in fine linen, clean and white: for the fine linen is the righteousness of saints.

9 And he saith unto me, Write, Blessed are they which are called unto the marriage supper of the Lamb.

The Revelation

7
MYSTERY
ISRAEL'S BLINDNESS

GOOD OLIVE — WILD OLIVE
NATURAL BRANCH

ROM. 11:25

25 For I would not, brethren, that ye should be ignorant of this mystery, lest ye should be wise in your own conceits; that blindness in part is happened to Israel, until the fulness of the Gentiles be come in.

8
MYSTERY
OF INIQUITY

ANTICHRIST
REV. 6:1-2

2. THESS. 2:7-9

7 For the mystery of iniquity doth already work: only he who now letteth will let, until he be taken out of the way.

8 And then shall that Wicked be revealed, whom the Lord shall consume with the spirit of his mouth, and shall destroy with the brightness of his coming:

9 Even him, whose coming is after the working of Satan with all power and signs and lying wonders,

9
MYSTERY
BABYLON THE GREAT

REV. 17:3-5

3 So he carried me away in the spirit into the wilderness: and I saw a woman sit upon a scarlet coloured beast, full of names of blasphemy, having seven heads and ten horns.

4 And the woman was arrayed in purple and scarlet colour, and decked with gold and precious stones and pearls, having a golden cup in her hand full of abominations and filthiness of her fornication:

5 And upon her forehead was a name written, MYSTERY, BABYLON THE GREAT, THE MOTHER OF HARLOTS AND ABOMINATIONS OF THE EARTH.

OLIVET
ZECH.14:4
ACTS 1:9-12

11
MYSTERY
THE RESTORATION OF ALL THINGS

ACTS 3:19-21

19 ¶ Repent ye therefore, and be converted, that your sins may be blotted out, when the times of refreshing shall come from the presence of the Lord;

20 And he shall send Jesus Christ, which before was preached unto you:

21 Whom the heaven must receive until the times of restitution of all things, which God hath spoken by the mouth of all his holy prophets since the world began.

EPH. 1:9-10

1. COR. 15:24-28

MILLENNIAL AGE
MICAH 4:1-4

"RENOVATION OF THE EARTH BY FIRE"
2. PET. 3:7-13

KINGDOM OF "SON OF MAN"
THRONE
DAN. 7:13-14
LUKE 1:30-33

HOLY CITY

"THE NATIONS SHALL WALK IN THE LIGHT OF IT." REV. 21:24

THE NEW HEAVENS

THE NEW EARTH

REV. 21:1-2

DESIGNED AND DRAWN BY
CLARENCE LARKIN
FOXCHASE, PHIL'A, PA
5/5/1916 COPYRIGHTED

other Ages had not been made known unto the sons of men, "That the Gentiles should be 'Fellow Heirs,' and of the 'Same Body,' and partakers of His promise in Christ by the Gospel."

It is almost impossible to overestimate the bitter "Race Hatred" which existed in Christ's day between Jew and Gentile. It was a lofty "middle wall or partition" between them. The Jews looked upon the Gentiles as "dogs," and the Gentiles despised the Jews. It was worse than the caste spirit of India. It was therefore to them a revelation that God was going in this Dispensation to take some Jews and some Gentiles and form of them a "New Body" called the Church. In Christ all race and class distinctions disappear, and it is only in the Church that such a "Holy Brotherhood" can be found as the world is seeking.

IV. The Mystery of the "Seven Stars" and the "Seven Candlesticks."

To the Apostle John was revealed the Mystery of the "Seven Stars," and the "Seven Candlesticks." Rev. 1:12-20. He was told that the "Seven Stars" stood for the Angels or Messengers of the Seven Churches that were in Asia Minor, and the Seven Candlesticks stood for the Seven Churches themselves. The Mystery of these Candlesticks lay in the fact that the Seven Churches mentioned were representative Churches, whose history was typical of the history of the Christian Church for the past 1900 years, and the Mystery could not be understood until the present time, or until the correspondence between the character of those Churches and Church history should be revealed. For a full discussion of this see the Chapter on "The Seven Churches."

V. The Mystery of the "Kingdom of Heaven."

When the Jews rejected Christ, and thus prevented the setting up of the Kingdom, the Kingdom took on another form, the "Mystery Form." To show the character of this "Mystery Form" of the Kingdom, Jesus resorted to parables. These parables are 12 in number and are found in Matthew's Gospel only. For a full description of them see the Chapter on "The Kingdom," part two, "The Kingdom In Mystery."

VI. The Mystery of the "Translation of the Living Saints."

In 1 Cor. 15:51-55, Paul says—

"Behold, I show you a '**Mystery**'; we shall not all sleep, but we shall all be changed, in a moment, in the twinkling of an eye, at the last trump."

This is the greatest of all mysteries, because it reveals something that reason never dreamed of. According to reason the common lot of man is to die, but to be taken off this earth and translated to heaven without dying was never thought of until revealed to Paul. For a full description of this Mystery see the Chapter on "The Church."

VII. The Mystery of "Israel's Blindness."

Writing to the Romans (Rom. 11:25) Paul says—

"I would not, brethren, that ye should be ignorant of **This Mystery,** lest ye should be wise in your own conceits, that **Blindness in Part** is happened to Israel, until, the 'Fulness of the Gentiles' be come in."

This is not so much spiritual blindness as **Judicial** blindness caused by their rejection of Christ. This blindness is national and not individual, for we must not forget that the bulk of believers in the Apostles' day were Jews, and quite a few Jews have embraced Christianity since. The revelation of this Mystery to Paul was to account for what otherwise would remain a Mystery, the survival of the Jewish people as a race while scattered among the nations. See the Chapter on "The Jews."

VIII. The Mystery of "Iniquity."

In 2 Thess. 2:1-12, Paul, speaking of the "Man of Sin" or Antichrist, calls his teaching and claims the

"Mystery of Iniquity,"

which was already at work in Paul's day. The "Mystery of Godliness" is **God** manifest in the flesh, and the "Mystery of Iniquity" is **Satan** manifest in the flesh. This Mystery is fully explained in the Chapter on "The Antichrist."

IX. The Mystery of "Babylon the Great."

This Mystery is revealed in the seventeenth chapter of the Book of Revelation and is fully described in the Chapter on "Babylon the Great."

X. The Mystery of the Church As the "Bride of Christ."

This was revealed to Paul, and is disclosed in Eph. 5:22-33, under the figure of the relation of man and wife. "This is a '**Great Mystery**'; but I speak concerning Christ and the Church." The first Adam had a bride, Eve; and the second, or Last Adam must have a Bride, the Church. This is a "Great Mystery" because it explains why there should be a "Parenthetical Dispensation" between the First and Second Comings of Christ, in which, by grace, a chosen people should be "called out" to form the Church, the Bride of Christ. This is fully described in the Chapter on "The Church."

XI. The Mystery of the "Restoration of All Things."

This is spoken of by Paul in his letter to the Ephesians (Eph. 1:9-10), as the

"Mystery of His Will,"

and reveals how that in the "Dispensation of the Fulness of Times," it is God's purpose to undo all that sin has done, and restore "All Things" as they were before the "Rebellion of Satan" and the "Fall of Man." How this is to be done is described in the Chapter on the "Renovation of the Earth."

XXVIII
TYPES AND ANTI-TYPES

Jesus summed up His Discourse on the "Kingdom of Heaven" Parables of Matt. 13:1-52, with these words.

"**Therefore** (and we must note the "Therefores" of Scripture) every scribe (Bible Teacher) who is instructed unto the 'Kingdom of Heaven' is like unto a Householder, who bringeth forth out of his **Treasure** things NEW and OLD."

The "**OLD**" things are the "**TYPES**" of the Old Testament, and the NEW things what they stand for in the New Testament. The New Testament is "enfolded" in the Old Testament, and the Old Testament is "unfolded" in the New. Or as St. Augustine puts it—

"The New is in the Old **contained**;
The Old is by the New **explained**."

You cannot understand Leviticus without Hebrews, or Daniel without Revelation, or the Passover, or Isaiah 53 without the Gospel account of the Crucifixion. The value of the study of the "Types" and "Antitypes" is the proof they furnish of the Inspiration of the Scriptures. Their study proves beyond question that the Scriptures had but one Author—the **HOLY SPIRIT**.

The "Typology" of the Old Testament is the "**PICTURE LANGUAGE**" in which the Doctrines of the New Testament, such as the Atonement, are prefigured. For illustration the "Brazen Serpent" and the "Cross." John 3:14-15. Therefore no preacher or Bible Teacher is competent to preach the doctrines of the New Testament who is not acquainted with the "Typology" of the Old Testament.

What do we mean by "Types?" The Apostle Paul gives the answer in 1 Cor. 10:1-11. In verse 11 he says—

"Now all these things happened unto them for **ENSAMPLES** (examples, see verse 6): and they are written for our **ADMONITION** (instruction), upon whom the ends of the world (Age) are come."

Of "whom" and of what "things" is the Apostle speaking? Of the Children of Israel, and the "things" that happened to them from the time of their "Egyptian Bondage" until they reached the "Land of Promise." So we see that while the Old Testament is a record of the History of the Children of Israel, the events of that "History" are more than mere events; they are "**TYPICAL**" of the "Plan of Salvation" as revealed in the New Testament, and are neither "mythical" nor "allegorical," but really happened to Israel and were recorded for our instruction.

The writer to the Hebrews tells us that the "Types" are but the **SHADOW OF GOOD THINGS TO COME, AND NOT THE VERY IMAGE OF THE THING.**" Heb. 10:1. That is, the Old Testament "Types" are but "**SHADOWS**." But there cannot be a "shadow" without some "**REAL THING**" to make it. And a "shadow" is not the "**very image of the thing**," for a shadow is out of proportion, and is an imperfect representation of the thing it reveals. So the Old Testament Types are "**shadows**" in the sense that they are not the "**Real Thing**," and are but imperfect revelations of it.

A "Type" then is some "person," or "event," or "ceremony" that is recorded to "foreshadow" some future "person," or "event," or "ceremony." For illustration—

1. **TYPICAL PERSONS**, like Adam, Cain, Abel, Melchizedek, Abraham, Isaac, Joseph, Moses, Joshua, David, Jonah.

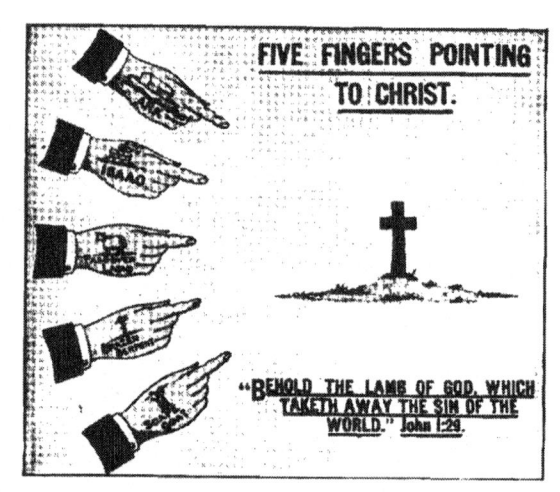

2. **TYPICAL EVENTS**, like the "Flood," the "Plagues of Egypt," the "Passover," the "Brazen Serpent," "Crossing the Jordan," "Cities of Refuge."

3. **TYPICAL CEREMONIES**, like the "Offerings," "Ceremonial Cleansing," "Feasts," "Year of Jubilee," "Day of Atonement."

To which might be added—"**Typical Structures**," like the "Ark," the "Tabernacle," the "Temple." "**Typical Furniture**," like the "Brazen Altar," the "Laver," the "Seven Branched Candlestick," the "Table of Shewbread," the "Altar of Incense," and the "Ark of the Covenant" with its "Mercy Seat." "**Typical Colors**," like "Blue," "Red," "White," "Purple," "Scarlet," "Green." "**Typical Numbers**," like "one," "three," "four," "seven," "twelve," "forty."

In studying the "Types" the two comparative words "**AS**" and "**SO**" are forcibly called to our attention. The word "**AS**" is used for the "Type," and the word "**SO**" for the Antitype. The first is **historic**; the second is **prophetic**.

"**AS** in Adam all die, even **SO** in Christ shall all be made alive." 1 Cor. 15:22.

"**AS** the days of Noah were, **SO** shall also the coming of the Son of Man be." Matt. 24:37.

"**AS** Moses lifted up the serpent in the Wilderness, even **SO** must the Son of Man be lifted up." John 3:14.

"**AS** Jonah was three days and three nights in the Whale's belly; **SO** shall the Son of Man be three days and three nights in the heart of the earth." Matt. 12:40.

The above "Types" with their "Antitype" stand out so prominently in Scripture that their meaning is clear to the most superficial reader. But there are "Types" in the Old Testament whose "Dispensational Teaching" does not lie on the surface, and is never seen by the superficial reader. For illustration take the story of—

ISAAC AND REBEKAH
Gen. 24:1-67.

In this story—

I. **ABRAHAM IS A TYPE OF "GOD."**

II. **ISAAC A TYPE OF "CHRIST."**

1. Both Isaac and Christ were **CHILDREN OF PROMISE**. Gen. 15:4. Isa. 7:14.

The Types and Anti-Types of Scripture

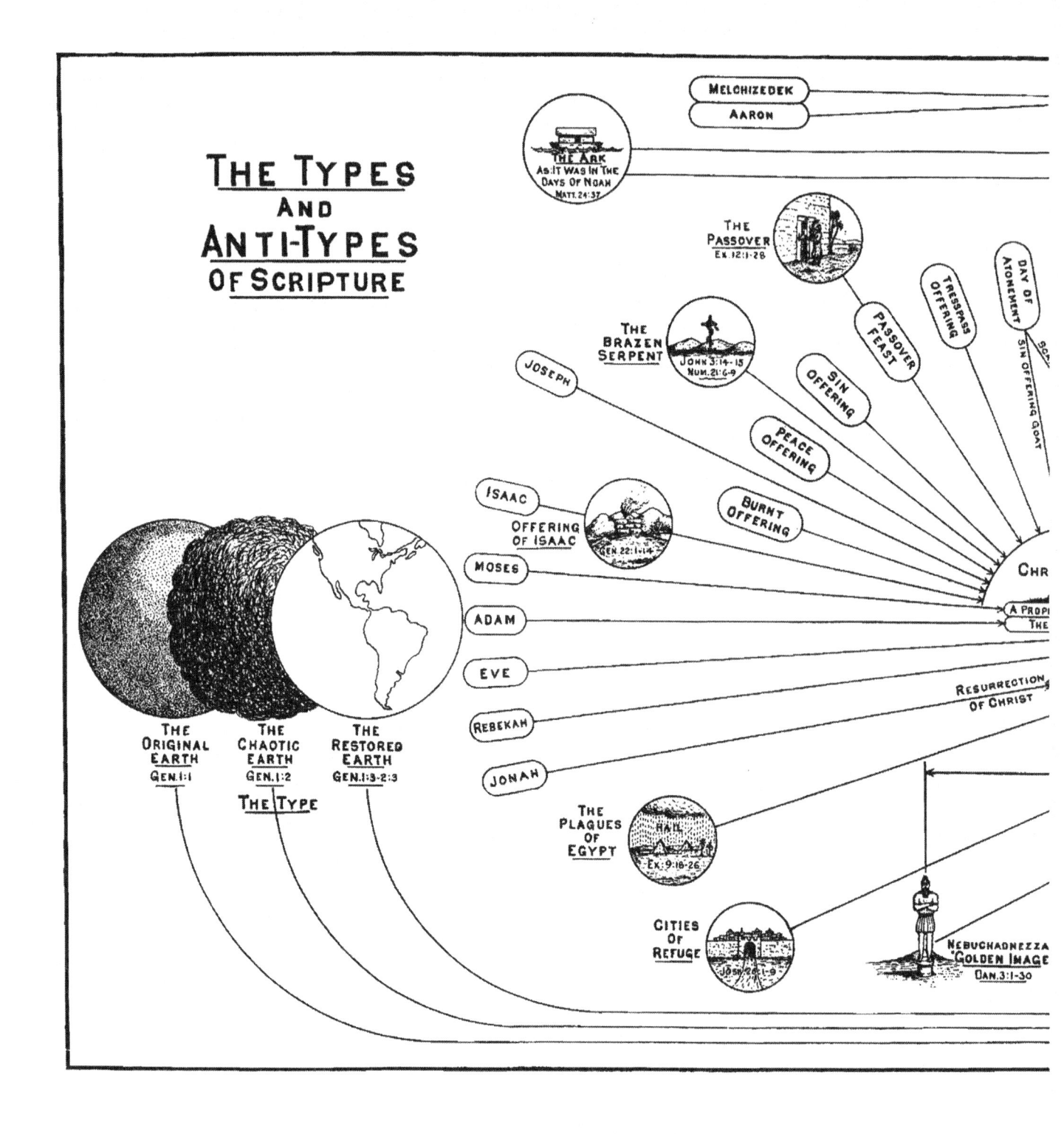

The Type

- The Original Earth — Gen. 1:1
- The Chaotic Earth — Gen. 1:2
- The Restored Earth — Gen. 1:3–2:3

Melchizedek
Aaron
The Ark — As It Was In The Days Of Noah — Matt. 24:37
The Passover — Ex. 12:1-28
Passover Feast
Trespass Offering
Day of Atonement — Sin Offering Goat
The Brazen Serpent — John 3:14-15; Num. 21:6-9
Sin Offering
Peace Offering
Joseph
Isaac
Offering of Isaac — Gen. 22:1-14
Burnt Offering
Moses
Adam
Eve
Rebekah
Jonah
The Plagues of Egypt — Ex. 9:16-26
Cities of Refuge — Josh. 20:1-9
Nebuchadnezzar's Golden Image — Dan. 3:1-30

Christ
A Prophet
The ...
Resurrection Of Christ

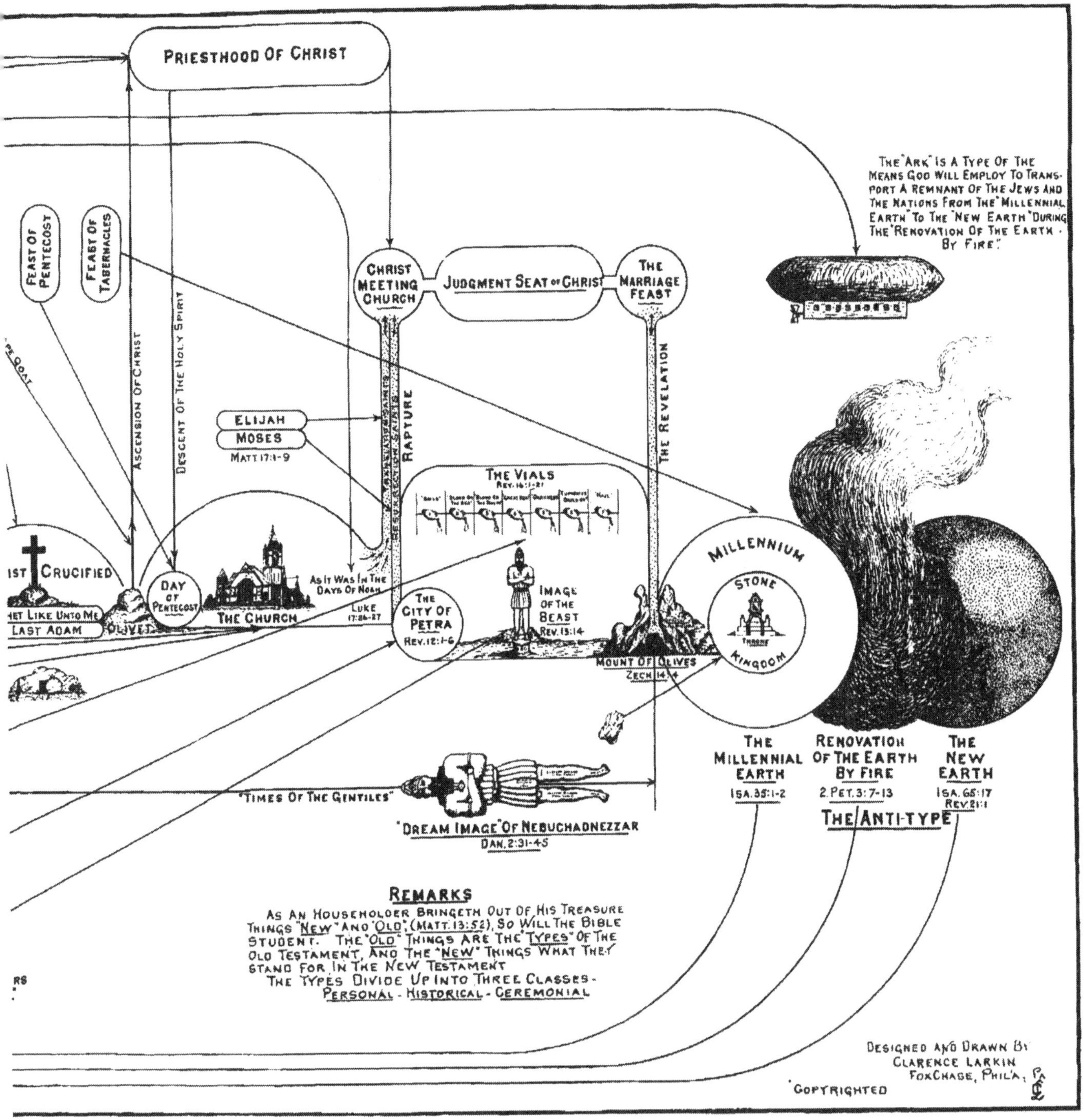
PRIESTHOOD OF CHRIST
THE "ARK" IS A TYPE OF THE MEANS GOD WILL EMPLOY TO TRANSPORT A REMNANT OF THE JEWS AND THE NATIONS FROM THE "MILLENNIAL EARTH" TO THE "NEW EARTH" DURING THE "RENOVATION OF THE EARTH BY FIRE".
FEAST OF PENTECOST
FEAST OF TABERNACLES
CHRIST MEETING CHURCH
JUDGMENT SEAT OF CHRIST
THE MARRIAGE FEAST
ASCENSION OF CHRIST
DESCENT OF THE HOLY SPIRIT
RAPTURE
THE REVELATION
ELIJAH
MOSES
MATT 17:1-9
THE VIALS
REV. 16:1-21
CRUCIFIED
DAY OF PENTECOST
THE CHURCH
OLIVET
LAST ADAM
AS IT WAS IN THE DAYS OF NOAH
LUKE 17:26-27
THE CITY OF PETRA
REV. 12:1-6
IMAGE OF THE BEAST
REV. 13:14
MOUNT OF OLIVES
ZECH. 14:4
MILLENNIUM
STONE
THRONE
KINGDOM
THE MILLENNIAL EARTH
ISA. 35:1-2
RENOVATION OF THE EARTH BY FIRE
2 PET. 3:7-13
THE NEW EARTH
ISA. 65:17
REV. 21:1
THE ANTI-TYPE
"TIMES OF THE GENTILES"
"DREAM IMAGE" OF NEBUCHADNEZZAR
DAN. 2:31-45
REMARKS
AS AN HOUSEHOLDER BRINGETH OUT OF HIS TREASURE THINGS "NEW" AND "OLD", (MATT. 13:52), SO WILL THE BIBLE STUDENT. THE "OLD" THINGS ARE THE "TYPES" OF THE OLD TESTAMENT, AND THE "NEW" THINGS WHAT THEY STAND FOR IN THE NEW TESTAMENT.
THE TYPES DIVIDE UP INTO THREE CLASSES - PERSONAL - HISTORICAL - CEREMONIAL
DESIGNED AND DRAWN BY CLARENCE LARKIN FOXCHASE, PHIL'A, PA.
COPYRIGHTED

JOHN 3:14.

AS Moses lifted up the SERPENT in the wilderness,

SO must the SON OF MAN be lifted UP.

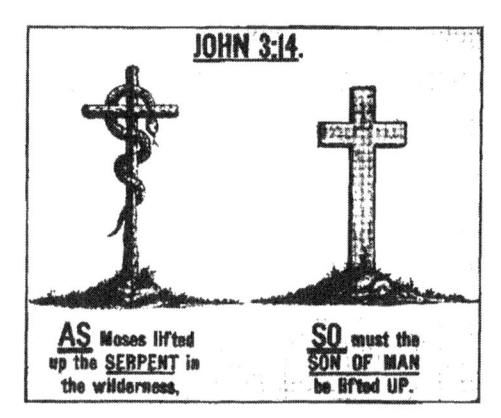

2. The birth of both was **PRE-ANNOUNCED**. Gen. 18:10. Luke 1:30-31.
3. Both were **NAMED BEFORE THEIR BIRTH**. Isaac—Gen. 17:19. Jesus—Luke 1:31.
4. The birth of both was

CONTRARY TO NATURE

Sarah was **barren**. Gen. 11:30.
Mary was a **virgin**. Matt. 1:18-20.

5. Both are called an **ONLY SON**. Gen. 22:2 (Heb. 11:17). John 3:16.
6. Both **mocked** and **persecuted** by their **OWN KINDRED**. Gen. 21:9-10. Gal. 4:28-29. Matt. 27:29.
7. Neither Isaac nor Christ had **BROKEN THE LAW** that they should be offered up. Gen. 22:2. Matt. 27:24.
8. As Isaac **carried the wood** on which he was to die, so Christ carried His **OWN CROSS**. Gen. 22:6. John 19:17.
9. As Isaac went willingly to the "altar," so Christ went willingly to the "**CROSS**." Gen. 22:9. John 10:17.
10. Both apparently given up or **FORSAKEN BY HIS FATHER**. Gen. 22:12. Matt. 27:46.
11. Both rose from the place of death in **RESURRECTION**. Heb. 11:17-19. Matt. 28:6.

In both cases **GOD** interposed.

III. ELIEZER A TYPE OF THE "HOLY SPIRIT."

1. As Eliezer was a servant of Abraham, so the Holy Spirit is a "**Servant of God**."
2. As Eliezer's mission was to go to Haran and get a **bride for Isaac**, so the Holy Spirit has been sent from Heaven to get a **BRIDE FOR CHRIST**.
3. As Eliezer was not sent to get a bride for Isaac until **after he was typically offered up**, so the Holy Spirit was not sent to get a Bride for Christ until **AFTER HIS DEATH AND RESURRECTION**.
4. As Eliezer did not talk **about himself**, but about his **Master's son**, so the Holy Spirit does not talk about **HIMSELF, BUT ABOUT CHRIST**.
5. As Eliezer was **urgent**, so the Holy Spirit is **URGENT**. Gen. 24:53-56. 2 Cor. 6:2.
6. As Eliezer by the precious gifts he gave Rebekah revealed the wealth of his Master Isaac, so the Holy Spirit by His Gifts gives us a foretaste of what is in store for the Bride of Christ, the Church.
7. When Eliezer got Rebekah's consent to be the bride of Isaac **he himself took her back**; he did not send her back while he remained with her kinsfolk. So when the Bride, the Church, is ready the **HOLY SPIRIT WILL GO BACK TO HEAVEN WITH HER**.

IV. REBEKAH A TYPE OF THE "BRIDE OF CHRIST."

1. As Rebekah believed and yielded to the pleadings of **Eliezer**, so the Church believes and yields to the pleadings of the **HOLY SPIRIT**.
2. As Rebekah was willing to separate herself from her kinsfolk for **Isaac's sake**, so the Believer is willing to separate himself from his kinsfolk for **JESUS' SAKE**.
3. As Eliezer on the way to Isaac told Rebekah all about his Master Isaac, and what was in store for her, so the Holy Spirit as we journey on our earthly pilgrimage tells us what is in store for us when we shall meet our Isaac—**JESUS**.
4. As Rebekah was a **Gentile** bride, so the Church of Christ is a **GENTILE** Bride.

   While Rebekah was a kinswoman of Isaac, she was a Gentile, for while Abraham was the first Hebrew, his kinspeople were Gentiles, for the Jews are the descendants of Judah, the fourth son of Abraham's grandson Jacob.
5. As Rebekah did not have to pass through any **tribulation** before she left her home to go to Isaac, so the Church will not have to pass through **THE TRIBULATION** before meeting Jesus.
6. As Isaac left his home and went **out into the field** to meet Rebekah, so Jesus will **DESCEND FROM HEAVEN TO MEET HIS BRIDE, THE CHURCH, IN THE AIR**.
7. As it was "eventide" when Isaac met Rebekah, so it will be the **EVENTIDE OF THIS DISPENSATION WHEN JESUS MEETS HIS CHURCH**.

Some "Types" have a double application. Take the Prophet Jonah. Jesus uses the swallowing of Jonah by a "great fish," and after 3 days being vomited up alive, as a "Type" of His own Resurrection from the Tomb of Joseph of Arimathea. Matt. 12:40. But Jonah is also a "Type of the Jewish Nation."

1. Jonah was called and sent to preach to a heathen city—Nineveh, so the Jews were called and sent to preach to the heathen nations.
2. Jonah disobeys and flees to Tarshish, so the Jews fail in their mission to the heathen.
3. Jonah for his disobedience was cast overboard, so the Jews have been scattered among the nations.
4. Jonah was miraculously preserved in the stomach of the fish, so the Jews have remained undigested by the nations.
5. Jonah repented in his "grave" in the stomach of the fish, so the Jews will mourn their lost condition in the "graveyard of the nations."

6. Jonah was restored to the land, so the Jews will be restored to their own land.
7. Jonah received a "Second Call" and obeyed, so the Jews will have a second opportunity to witness to the nations and will obey.

Take one more "Typical Person."

JOSEPH A TYPE OF CHRIST

1. Joseph was "beloved" of his father, so was Jesus.
2. Joseph was sent unto his brethren, so was Jesus.
3. Joseph's brethren refused to receive him, so did the brethren of Jesus.
4. Joseph was sold by his brethren, so was Jesus.
5. Joseph was unjustly accused and condemned, so was Jesus.
6. Joseph was buried in prison, so was Jesus in the Tomb of Joseph.
7. Joseph was resurrected from prison and exalted to sit with Pharaoh on his throne, so Jesus was resurrected and exalted to sit on His Father's Throne.
8. Joseph on the throne became the dispenser of bread to starving Egypt, so Jesus on His Father's Throne is the "Bread of Life" for a perishing world.
9. After Joseph was exalted he got a Gentile bride, so Jesus will get a Gentile Bride—**THE CHURCH.**
10. After Joseph got his bride his brethren suffered famine and came to him for corn, so after Jesus gets His Bride, His brethren, the Jews, will turn to Him, during the time of "Jacob's Trouble," the "Great Tribulation," for relief.
11. Joseph knew his brethren the first time, but they did not know him, so Jesus knew His brethren when He came the first time but they knew him not.
12. Joseph made himself known to his brethren when they came the "Second time," so Jesus will be recognized by the Jews when He comes the **SECOND TIME.**
13. After Joseph's revelation of himself to his brethren, they go forth to proclaim that he is alive and the "saviour of the world," so when Jesus reveals Himself to His brethren the Jews they will proclaim Him alive and the **SAVIOUR OF MANKIND.**
14. Joseph then establishes his brethren and their families in the "**land of Goshen,**" so Jesus will re-establish the Jews in the **LAND OF PALESTINE.**

If the "Type" and the "Antitype" have both appeared, as the "Brazen Serpent" and the "Uplifted Christ," then the Type has been fulfilled. If the Antitype has not yet appeared then the fulfilment is future. For instance Noah's Ark is not a type of Christ, but is a type of the provision God is going to make to transport the saved of the nations of the "Millennial Earth," over on to the "New Earth." The "Plagues of Egypt" are a type of the Plagues of the Great Tribulation. The "Cities of Refuge" are a type of the "Refuge" God will provide for the "Jewish Remnant" during the time of "Jacob's Trouble." The "Golden Image" that Nebuchadnezzar erected on the Plain of Dura is a type of the "Image of the Antichrist" that the False Prophet shall command to be made. Rev. 13:14-15. For the Typical teaching of the "Feasts" and the "Offerings," see the chapters and charts on those subjects. From what has been said we can see that no Bible Teacher can be fully instructed in the "Things of God," **unless he is a student of Typology.**

XXIX

THE THREE TREES TO WHICH ISRAEL IS COMPARED IN THE SCRIPTURES

"THE VINE"—"THE FIG-TREE"—"THE OLIVE."

These three trees are particularly fit symbols of Israel, for in Palestine the "**Vine,**" the "**Fig-tree,**" and the "**Olive,**" stand for the fruitfulness of the land. And the "Vine" and "Fig-tree" prefigure the Millennial days when every man shall sit under his own "Vine" and "Fig-tree." Micah 4:3-4. When Jacob (Israel) was about to die he summoned his sons, and prophesied their future. Of Judah he said that his portion of Canaan should be so full of vineyards that asses should be tethered to the vines, and that the juice should be so plentiful that they would wash their clothes in it as in water. Gen. 49:9-12.

THE VINE is a symbol of Israel's **Spiritual** privileges.

THE FIG-TREE is a symbol of Israel's **National** privileges.

THE OLIVE TREE is a symbol of Israel's **Religious** privileges.

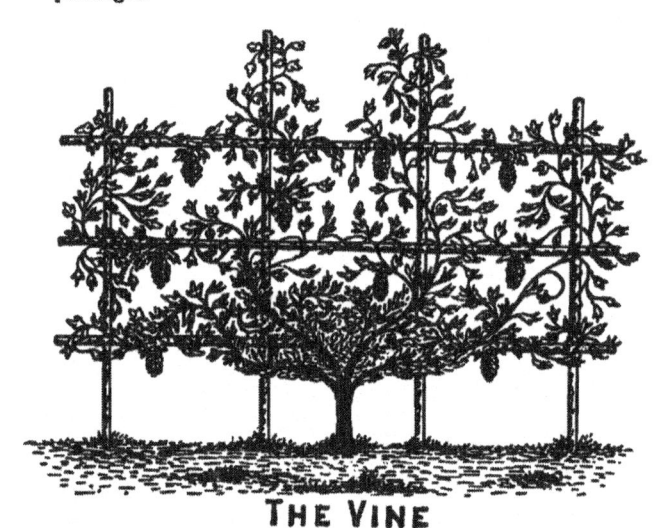

THE VINE

In Psalm 80:8-11, we read—

"Thou hast brought a '**VINE**' out of Egypt: Thou hast **cast out the heathen** (the Canaanites), and planted it. Thou preparedst room before it, and didst cause it to take deep root, and it **filled the land.** The hills were covered with the shadow of it, and the boughs thereof were like goodly cedars. She sent out her boughs unto the sea (Mediterranean), and her branches unto the river (Euphrates)."

In these words the Psalmist graphically pictures the taking of Israel from the uncongenial soil of Egypt, and the planting of them in the land of Canaan.

It was the Almighty with His "outstretched arm" that did it, for without His Divine help they never could have escaped from the Land of Pharaoh. He was the "Divine Husbandman" who transplanted them. And it was all of grace, for the moral and spiritual condition of Israel in Egypt was that of a degenerate vine. And it was the Almighty who cast out the heathen nations of Canaan in order to "clear the ground" for their transplanting, for it was a land of "walled cities" and "giants." Num. 13:26-33.

Once the "Vine" was transplanted it began to grow and spread over the land, until in the words of the Psalm it sent out its boughs unto the Mediterranean Sea, and its branches unto the Euphrates river, as in the reign of King Solomon. Deu. 11:24. This is to be completely fulfilled during the Millennium. The prophet Isaiah beautifully describes this "Vineyard."

"Now will I sing to my Well-Beloved a song of my Beloved touching His Vineyard. My Well-Beloved hath a **VINEYARD** in a very fruitful hill (Canaan): and He fenced it, and gathered out the stones thereof, and planted it with the **CHOICEST VINE**, and built a Tower in the midst of it, and also made a Winepress therein." Isa. 5:1-2.

No nation was ever more greatly favored than Israel, and God could truthfully say—"What could have been done more for my 'Vineyard,' that I have not done in it?" Vs. 4. Great therefore was the disappointment of God when he looked for Israel to bring forth grapes proportionate with her advantages, but found them to be "**WILD GRAPES.**" The Prophet Jeremiah records God's complaint of Israel's failure in these words—"I had planted thee a '**NOBLE VINE,**' wholly a **right seed**: how then art thou turned into the **DEGENERATE PLANT OF A STRANGE VINE** unto me?" Jer. 2:21.

What was God to do to His Vineyard for its miscarriage? Note the punishment: "And now go to; I will tell you what I will do to my Vineyard: I will **TAKE AWAY THE HEDGE THEREOF**, and it (the Vine) shall be **eaten up**; and **BREAK DOWN THE WALL THEREOF**, and it (the Vineyard) shall be **trodden down**; and I will lay it **WASTE**: it shall not be **pruned**, nor **digged**; but there shall come up **briers** and **thorns**: I will also command the clouds that they **rain no rain** upon it." And now, that there may be no mistake as to what is meant by the "Vineyard" and the "Vine," God adds—"For the '**Vineyard**' of the Lord of Hosts is the '**HOUSE OF ISRAEL,**' and the men of Judah (Jews) His '**PLEASANT PLANT**' (Vine)." Isa. 5:5-7.

How faithfully this punishment has been meted out to Israel is seen when we consider the physical condition of Palestine (The Vineyard) today, and the uprooted members of Israel (The Vine) scattered throughout the world. The Lord told Israel through the Prophet Ezekiel, that a vine, unless it bear fruit, is fit for nothing but fuel. "What is the 'vine tree' more than any tree, or than a branch which is among the trees of the forest? Shall wood be taken thereof to do any work? or will men take a pin of it to hang any vessel thereon? Behold, it is cast into the fire for fuel. . . . As the vine tree among the trees of the forest, which I have given to the fire for fuel, so will I give the inhabitants of Jerusalem," etc. Ezekiel 15:1-8. The Emblem of Israel is a bush, burning and unconsumed. Ex. 3:1-3. Israel is now passing through the "fires of persecution." As she is not bearing fruit, she is only fit for fuel. But it is only the stem that is being consumed, the "**root**" is alive,

and the "Vine" will again spring up, and the "Vineyard" (Palestine) again be fruitful in Millennial days.

In the New Testament Jesus, in the "Parable of the Vineyard," (Matt. 21:33-41) reveals why the husbandmen or keepers of the Vineyard, the Jewish nation, have been cast out of the Vineyard (Palestine). It was because they took the **HEIR** (Jesus) and crucified Him, and so they were cast out of the Vineyard, and it has been let to other husbandmen, the Gentiles. The "Vine" then is a symbol of Israel's **SPIRITUAL** Privileges.

FIG TREE

The "Fig-tree" is a New Testament symbol or figure of Israel and was used by Jesus Himself. As Jesus sat upon the Mount of Olives, on the Tuesday evening preceding His Crucifixion, His Disciples came to Him and asked a threefold question—"Tell us, when shall these things be (the destruction of the Temple)? and what shall be the **SIGN** of Thy Coming, and of the end of the world (Age)?" Matt. 24:3. These three questions Jesus answered in His "Olivet Discourse" which followed. In His answer to the question—"What shall be the **SIGN** of Thy Coming?" Jesus mentioned three signs.

1. The appearance of the "**ABOMINATION OF DESOLATION**" (the "**DESOLATOR**"—Antichrist), spoken of by Daniel the prophet (Dan. 9:27) in the Holy Place of the rebuilt Temple at Jerusalem, as foretold by Paul in his Second Letter to the Thessalonians. 2 Thess. 2:1-4.

2. The "**SIGN OF THE SON OF MAN,**" which is a "**CLOUD,**" such as He disappeared in when He ascended. Acts. 1:9. Matt. 24:30.

3. The "**FIG-TREE SIGN,**" or the re-gathering of the Jews back to their own land. In connection with this "Sign" Jesus said—

"Now learn a Parable of the '**FIG-TREE.**' When his branch is yet tender, and putteth forth **LEAVES**, ye know that **summer is nigh**: so likewise ye, when ye shall see all these things, know that it (He, R.V.), is near, even at the doors. Verily I say unto you, This **GENERATION** (the word means '**Race**'—JEWISH RACE) shall not pass, till all these things be fulfilled. Heaven and earth shall pass away, but my words shall not pass away." Matt. 24:32-35.

The "Fig-tree" is a fit emblem of Israel. Its peculiarity is that the blossoms of the fruit appear **before** the leaves. Naturally, therefore, we should look for fruit on a tree in full leaf. This accounts for why Jesus cursed the Fig-tree that had on it **nothing but leaves**. Matt. 21:18-20. The presence of the leaves led Him to expect fruit, and when He found none He cursed the tree for its fruitlessness. Mark gives us another version of the incident. Mark 11:12-14. He says that Jesus found nothing but leaves, "for the **time of figs was NOT YET**." Why then curse the tree? This is easily explained. The early fruit, or blossoms, appear in spring before the leaves open, on branches of the last year's growth, and the first ripe fruit is ready in June or earlier. The late figs grow on the new wood, keep appearing during the season, and are ripe from August onward. The unripe fruit of autumn often survives the winter and ripens when vegetation revives in the spring. Now it was about the first of April that Jesus cursed the Fig-tree, and the time of figs was **not yet**, because they did not ripen before June. But fig-trees which have retained their leaves through the winter usually have some of the last year's figs also, and as April was too early for new leaves or fruit, Jesus knowing this, and seeing leaves on the tree, naturally expected to find some of last year's fruit, and when He found none He cursed the tree because of its deceptive character.

The application of this incident to Israel is simple. Naturally Jesus from their "leafy profession" would expect to find fruit on the tree of their National life, and when He found none He cursed them for their **HYPOCRISY**. Matt. 23:1-33.

In the Parable of the "Barren Fig-tree" (Luke 13:6-9) we have another picture of Israel. The "Fig-tree" is the Jewish nation. The "Fig-tree" was planted in a "Vineyard," which we have seen stands for the land of Palestine. The owner of the Vineyard and of the Fig-tree was God. He came in the person of His Son Jesus, and for three years of Jesus' ministry He had sought for fruit from the Jewish nation and found none. He therefore decided to cut down the tree, that is, remove the nation from the Vineyard.

But the tree was not destroyed immediately, for intercession was made for it, and the day of grace was lengthened out for forty years, and then the "axe-man" Titus, at the head of the Roman Army besieged Jerusalem in A.D. 70, and Israel, the Fig-tree, was cut down and cast out of the Vineyard into the field of the world.

But while the "Fig-tree" (Israel) was cut down and cast out of the "Vineyard" (Palestine), its root was not destroyed, the axe was only laid at the **root** of the "Tree" (Luke 3:7-9), the root itself was not killed or removed from the soil. It is clear then from the "Parable of the Fig-tree," (Matt. 24:32-34), that a new tree will spring from the root, that is, the nation of Israel will revive, and when it shall reach the point where it shall "put forth leaves" then we shall have the **"FIG-TREE SIGN"** that Christ's return is not far away. In this case the "Fig-tree" will bear leaves before it bears fruit, for Israel is to be revived nationally before she is converted. See my chapter on the Jews.

The "Signs of the Times" clearly point to the revival of the "Fig-tree;" and in **"ZIONISM"** and **"ANTI-SEMITISM"** we see the "putting forth of leaves." **"ZIONISM"** is the longing of the Jews to return to their own land and the establishment of a "Jewish State" there. There are three phases of it, **"Religious," "Economic,"** and **"Political"** Zionism. The "Religious" phase is the revival of faith in the fulfilment of the Old Testament prophecies of the restoration of Jewish worship in a rebuilt Temple in the Holy Land. The "Economic" phase is the desire of Israel to escape from their condition of servitude in Russia, and other lands where they are persecuted, and by colonization in Palestine secure a home in the land associated with the most sacred memories of their race, where they can dwell safely under their own vine and fig-tree. The "Political" phase is the revival of their "national Hope" of a restored nation under the leadership of the promised and long-hoped-for Messiah.

"ANTI-SEMITISM" is the desire on the part of the nations to drive the Jews out of the countries where their number and habits have become a menace. It is a revival of Egyptian Bondage. Pharaoh did not want to part with Israel, he needed their service in the construction of public works and in the raising of cattle. All he purposed to do was by hard bondage to prevent their increase. Ex. 1:7-22. Israel's experience in Egypt is a type of the time that the Prophet Jeremiah speaks of as the time of **"JACOB'S TROUBLE,"** when God will break the **"YOKE"** from off their neck, and burst their **"BONDS,"** and strangers shall no more **serve themselves of them**. Jer. 30:4-9.

These two "Signs," Zionism and Anti-Semitism, which are becoming more and more marked, are evidence, like the budding of a tree in the springtime that it is about to send forth leaves, that **"SUMMER IS NIGH,"** and that the return of the Lord is not far off. Matt. 24:33-35. The "Fig-tree" then is a symbol of Israel's **NATIONAL** Privileges.

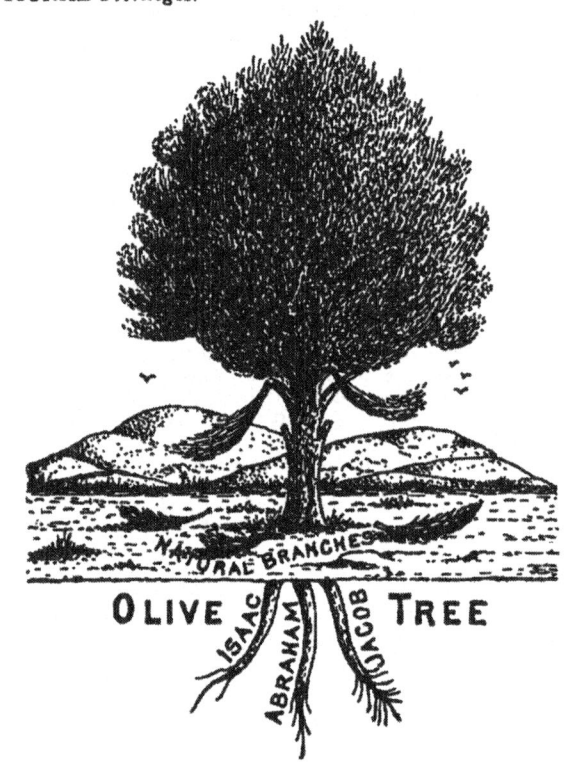

In Jer. 11:16-17, Israel is called a **"GREEN OLIVE TREE,"** fair, and of goodly fruit, but is warned that for its idolatry its branches shall be broken off. In Rom. 11:17-27 we have the Parable of the

"TWO OLIVE TREES."

One is called a **GOOD** Olive Tree, the other a **WILD** Olive Tree. The **GOOD** Olive Tree represents Israel, the **WILD** Olive Tree the Gentiles. The root of the Good Olive Tree is **THREEFOLD**. The main root is Abraham, the other two are Isaac and Jacob. "And God said moreover unto Moses, Thus shalt thou say unto the Children of Israel, The Lord God of your fathers, the God of **ABRAHAM**, the God of **ISAAC**, and the God of **JACOB**, hath sent me unto you: this is my name forever, and this is my memorial unto all generations." Ex. 3:15. Why should God speak of Himself in this "threefold" manner? Because He wished to reveal Himself in His **"TRI-UNITY."** Abraham is a type of God the Father, Isaac is a type of God the Son, and the Holy Spirit is seen in the guidance of Jacob.

The "Threefold root" of the Good Olive Tree was **HOLY** because separated, and as the "Root" was holy so were the "**branches.**" We next read that "**some,**" not all, of the branches were broken off. They were not broken off that the Gentiles might be grafted in, but they were broken off because of "**UNBELIEF,**" and the Gentiles were not grafted in that they might **supplant**, or take the place of the branches that had been broken off, but that they, as branches of a "**WILD** Olive Tree," might be **PARTAKER** of the "**root**" and "**fatness**" of the **GOOD** Olive Tree. We see from this that the "**GOOD** Olive Tree" is not **rooted up and destroyed** and a "**WILD** Olive Tree" **planted in its place**, but it still remains alive and gives life to both the "**Good**" and "**Wild**" Olive branches. So we see that those who claim that the "Wild Olive Branches" that are grafted in represent the Church, and that the Church has taken the place of Israel, are in error, for the "Wild Olive Branches" do not remain on the "Good Olive Tree," but will be broken off that the original branches may be grafted back again. Jewish and Gentile believers in Christ are alike Abraham's **spiritual** children, and are joint partakers of the "**root**" and "**fatness**" of the "Good Olive Tree," for Christ was of the seed of Abraham. Those Jews who rejected Christ and thus broke away from the religion of Abraham, are the branches, who, through **unbelief**, are broken off.

In grafting the practice is to graft the "**Good**" Olive on the "**Wild**" Olive so as to improve the fruit of the "Wild" Olive. If the "Wild" Olive is grafted on the "Good" Olive the effect is the reverse, and the "Good" Olive will run to **wildness.** So Paul knew what he was talking about when he said that the grafting of the "Wild" Olive on the "Good" Olive Tree was **"CONTRARY TO NATURE."** From this we see that the injection of Gentilism into Judaism is not beneficial to Judaism. That Judaism is of purer stock than Gentilism, and for the purification of Judaism, Gentilism, or the "Wild" Olive branches, must be removed, or cut off, from the "Good" Olive Tree, and be replaced by the grafting back again of the "**Natural Branches.**" Rom. 11:24. By Gentilism we mean that part of the Gentile world known as Christendom, or the professing Church, as described in the Kingdom of Heaven parables of Matt. 13. And it is only the Laodicean part of it that God says He will **"SPUE OUT OF HIS MOUTH"** (Rev. 3:16), that as "Wild" Olive branches God will remove from the "Good" Olive Tree, for all true believers who have been regenerated by the Holy Spirit, and that make up the true Church the "Body of Christ," and belong to the "Spiritual Israel" of God cannot be displaced.

The Parable of the "Two Olive Trees" teaches three things, and what is very important, the order in which these three things take place.

1. "Blindness **in part** is happened to Israel until the '**FULNESS OF THE GENTILES BE COME IN.**'"

By the **"FULNESS OF THE GENTILES"** is not meant the "Times of the Gentiles," but those Gentiles who shall be saved through the Gospel. And when the last Gentile shall be thus saved the **FULL NUMBER** of saved Gentiles will be complete.

2. That the "Wild Olive Branches" that are grafted in do not take the place of the branches that were broken off, and because they shall not "**continue in God's goodness**" they shall be broken off again.

3. That God has not "**Cast Away**" His people Israel, and that He will revive the broken off branches and graft them back again.

Today we are witnessing the Apostasy of the "Wild Olive Branches," the professing Church. Soon they will be "cut off," and then the **BLINDNESS** shall be removed from Israel, and the "Natural Branches" will be grafted back again.

This Parable teaches us that we are not to look upon the unbelieving Jew as a cast-off and withered branch only fit for fire-wood, but we are to consider that his "**casting away**" as well as his "**blindness**" is only temporary, and that he will again take up his position among the nations of the earth.

The "Olive Tree" then is a symbol of Israel's **RELIGIOUS** Privileges, and it is worthy of note that while Israel is compared to **trees**, their oppressors, the Gentile Nations, are spoken of in the Scriptures as **WILD BEASTS.** Dan. 7:1-28.

XXX
THE FEASTS OF THE LORD

The 23d chapter of the Book of Leviticus gives us an account of the "Seven Great Feasts" of the Lord. They were a prophecy and foreshadowing of future events, part of which have been fulfilled, and part are yet to be. They are the "shadow of things to come," of which Christ is the "body" or substance. Col. 2:16, 17. They were "Holy Convocations" of the people. They were instituted by the Lord. The people had no voice in the matter. God promised that if the males went up at the "set time" **to Jerusalem** to keep these Feasts, He would look after their families. When the people became formal and indifferent, the Lord said, **"Your** new moons and **Your** appointed Feasts My soul **Hateth;** they are a **Trouble** unto Me; I am weary to bear them." Isa. 1:14. Therefore Jesus called them the "Feasts of the **Jews,"** rather than the "Feasts of the Lord."

The "Feasts of the Lord" are seven in number. If we include the Sabbath there are eight. But the Sabbath stands by itself. It was to be observed "weekly," the other Feasts "annually." The Sabbath was to be observed at "home," the other Feasts at "Jerusalem."

The "Seven Feasts" may be divided into two sections of "four" and "three." The first section includes the "Passover," the Feasts of "Unleavened Bread," of "First-Fruits" and "Pentecost." Then there was an interval of four months, followed **by the Feasts of "Trumpets,"** "Day of Atonement," and "Tabernacles." The "Three Great Festivals" were the "Passover," "Pentecost," and "Tabernacles." They extended from the 14th day of the First Month to the 22d day of the Seventh Month.

The First Four Feasts foreshadow truths connected with this present Gospel Dispensation and those who form the "heavenly" people of the Lord, the Church; while the Last Three Feasts foreshadow the blessings in store for God's "earthly" people, the Jews.

1. The Passover Feast.

The Passover Feast had its origin in Egypt. It was the memorial of the redemption and deliverance of the Children of Israel from Egypt. It was to them the "beginning of months," and their birthday as a Nation. Ex. 12:2. It consisted of the taking of a male lamb, without blemish, of the first year, a lamb for a family, and killing it on the 14th day of the month in the evening, and sprinkling its blood, with a bunch of hyssop, on the two side posts and upper lintel of the door of their houses, so that when the Lord passed through Egypt that night and saw the blood on the doorposts, He would spare the first born sheltered within. The flesh of the lamb was to be roasted, and eaten with unleavened bread and bitter herbs, and none of it left until the morning. Those who ate of it were to do so with their loins girded, their shoes on their feet, and their staff in their hand, ready to leave Egypt.

The Passover Feast was to be to them as a "Memorial," and they were to keep it as a Feast throughout their generations, and as an ordinance **Forever.** Ex. 12:14.

The Passover Lamb was intended as a "type" of Jesus, the

"Lamb of God."

The shedding of His blood on Calvary, and our applying it to our hearts by faith, has the same effect as to our salvation, as the applying of the Passover Lamb's blood to the doorposts of those Egyptian houses had to the safety of those who were sheltered within. As that night was the "beginning of months" to them, so the moment a soul accepts Jesus Christ as its Saviour, that moment it is "born again," and a new life begins, for Christ **Our Passover** was sacrificed for us. 1 Cor. 5:7.

The first time the Children of Israel observed the Passover Feast it was amid the terrors of God's judgment plagues in the land of Egypt, a type of the world. Thereafter its yearly observance was as a joyful Memorial of their deliverance from Egypt. While they still observe the Passover Feast no "lamb" is slain, and no "blood" used, but when they get back to their own land they will again keep the Passover. The Christian Church does not observe the Passover, but they do observe as a Memorial the ordinance of the Lord's Supper that Christ instituted in its place.

2. The Feast of Unleavened Bread.

The Feast of Unleavened Bread began on the day after the Passover, and continued for seven days. Lev. 23:6-8. The lamb was slain on the 14th day at sunset, which ended the day. The Feast of Unleavened Bread began immediately after sunset, which was the beginning of the 15th day. Thus there was no interval between them. As the Passover is a type of the death of Christ, so the Feast of Unleavened Bread is a type of the "Walk" of the Believer, and there should be no interval between the salvation of a soul and its entrance on a holy life and walk. The "seven days" point to the whole course of the Believer's life after conversion.

Leaven in the Scriptures is a type of evil, so the Feast was to be kept with "unleavened" bread. Ex. 13:7. Paul speaks of "malice" and "wickedness" as leaven. "Purge out therefore the 'old leaven' that ye may be a 'new lump,' as ye are unleavened. For even Christ our Passover is sacrificed for us. Therefore let us keep the Feast, not with 'old leaven,' neither with the 'leaven of malice and wickedness,' but with the 'unleavened bread of sincerity and truth.'" 1 Cor. 5:7, 8.

The typical teaching then of the Feast of Unleavened Bread is that, having been saved by the shed blood of Christ our Passover, we are to "walk" in newness of life, purging out the leaven of wordliness, and doing no "servile work," or work that is done to earn salvation.

3. The Feast of First-Fruits.

The Passover took place on the 14th day of the month, the Feast of Unleavened Bread on the next day, which was the Sabbath, and the following day, which was the "morrow after the Sabbath," the Feast of First Fruits was to be celebrated. This however could not be done until after the Children of Israel had entered Canaan, therefore the Feast of First Fruits was not observed during the Wilderness Wanderings. The Offering was a sheaf reaped from the waving fields of the ripened harvest, and carried to the priest to be waved before the Lord for acceptance, and was to be followed by a Burnt, Meat and Drink-Offering, but no Sin-Offering. The Burnt-Offering was to be a male lamb without blemish of the first year.

The Feast of First-Fruits was a type and foreshadowing of the

Resurrection of Christ.

He arose on the "morning after the Sabbath," and His resurrection is spoken of by Paul, as the "First-Fruits" of the resurrection of the dead. As the "Corn of Wheat" (John 12:24) He was buried in Joseph's Tomb, and His resurrection was the "First-Fruits" of the Harvest of those who will be Christ's at His coming. 1 Cor. 15:23.

When the Priest on the day of Christ's resurrection waved the sheaf of "First-Fruits" in the Temple, it was before a "rent veil," and was but an empty form, for the Substance had come and the shadow

THE FEASTS

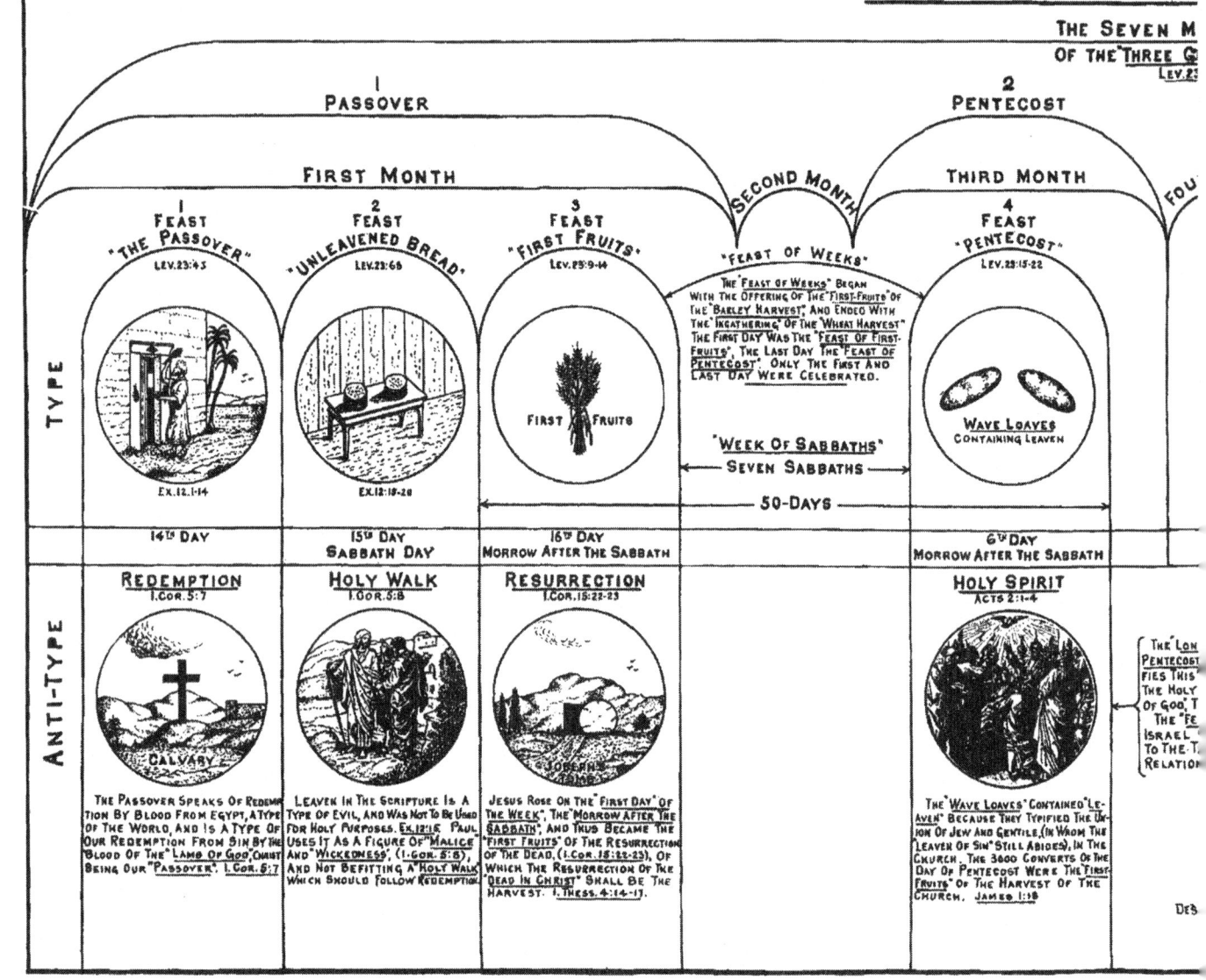

THE SEVEN M[...]
OF THE "THREE G[...]
LEV. 23[...]

1 PASSOVER — FIRST MONTH

2 PENTECOST — SECOND MONTH / THIRD MONTH

TYPE

1 FEAST "THE PASSOVER" — Lev. 23:4-5 — Ex. 12:1-14 — 14th Day

2 FEAST "UNLEAVENED BREAD" — Lev. 23:6-8 — Ex. 12:15-20 — 15th Day, Sabbath Day

3 FEAST "FIRST FRUITS" — Lev. 23:9-14 — 16th Day, Morrow After The Sabbath

"Feast Of Weeks" — The "Feast Of Weeks" Began With The Offering Of The "First-Fruits" Of The "Barley Harvest", And Ended With The "Ingathering" Of The "Wheat Harvest". The First Day Was The "Feast Of First-Fruits", The Last Day The Feast Of Pentecost. Only The First And Last Day Were Celebrated.

"Week Of Sabbaths" — Seven Sabbaths — 50-Days

4 FEAST "PENTECOST" — Lev. 23:15-22 — Wave Loaves Containing Leaven — 6th Day, Morrow After The Sabbath

ANTI-TYPE

REDEMPTION — 1. Cor. 5:7 — Calvary

The Passover Speaks Of Redemption By Blood From Egypt, A Type Of The World, And Is A Type Of Our Redemption From Sin By The Blood Of The "Lamb Of God", Christ Being Our "Passover". 1. Cor. 5:7.

HOLY WALK — 1. Cor. 5:8

Leaven In The Scripture Is A Type Of Evil, And Was Not To Be Used For Holy Purposes. Ex. 12:15. Paul Uses It As A Figure Of "Malice And Wickedness", (1. Cor. 5:8), And Not Befitting A Holy Walk Which Should Follow Redemption.

RESURRECTION — 1. Cor. 15:22-23

Jesus Rose On The "First Day" Of The Week", The "Morrow After The Sabbath", And Thus Became The "First Fruits" Of The Resurrection Of The Dead, (1. Cor. 15:22-23), Of Which The Resurrection Of The "Dead In Christ" Shall Be The Harvest. 1. Thess. 4:14-17.

HOLY SPIRIT — Acts 2:1-4

The "Wave Loaves" Contained "Leaven" Because They Typified The Union Of Jew And Gentile, (In Whom The "Leaven Of Sin" Still Abides), In The Church. The 3000 Converts Of The Day Of Pentecost Were The "First Fruits" Of The Harvest Of The Church. James 1:18.

The "Lon[...] Pentecost [...] fies This [...] The Holy [...] Of God", T[...] The "Fe[...] Israel [...] To The T[...] Relation[...]

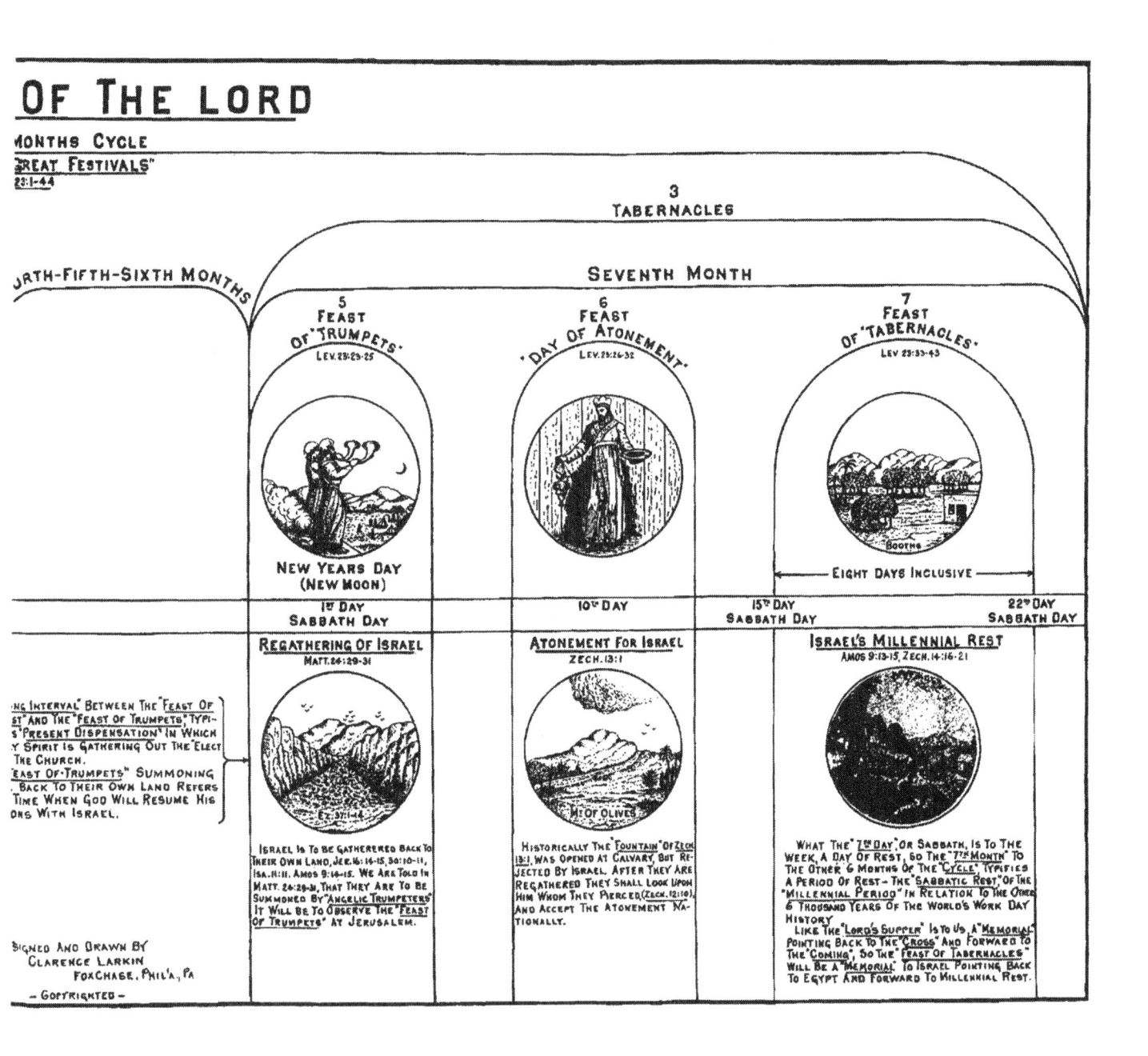

OF THE LORD

MONTHS CYCLE
"GREAT FESTIVALS"
23:1-44

3 TABERNACLES

FOURTH-FIFTH-SIXTH MONTHS | SEVENTH MONTH

5 FEAST OF "TRUMPETS"
LEV. 23:23-25

NEW YEAR'S DAY (NEW MOON)

1ST DAY SABBATH DAY

6 FEAST "DAY OF ATONEMENT"
LEV. 23:26-32

10TH DAY

7 FEAST OF "TABERNACLES"
LEV. 23:33-43

BOOTHS

EIGHT DAYS INCLUSIVE

15TH DAY SABBATH DAY — 22ND DAY SABBATH DAY

REGATHERING OF ISRAEL
MATT. 24:29-31

ATONEMENT FOR ISRAEL
ZECH. 13:1

M. OF OLIVES

ISRAEL'S MILLENNIAL REST
AMOS 9:13-15, ZECH. 14:16-21

LONG "INTERVAL" BETWEEN THE "FEAST OF PENTECOST" AND THE "FEAST OF TRUMPETS" TYPIFIES THE "PRESENT DISPENSATION" IN WHICH THE HOLY SPIRIT IS GATHERING OUT THE ELECT OF THE CHURCH.
THE "FEAST OF TRUMPETS" SUMMONING ISRAEL BACK TO THEIR OWN LAND REFERS TO THE TIME WHEN GOD WILL RESUME HIS DEALINGS WITH ISRAEL.

SIGNED AND DRAWN BY
CLARENCE LARKIN
FOX CHASE, PHIL'A, PA
— COPYRIGHTED —

ISRAEL IS TO BE GATHERED BACK TO THEIR OWN LAND, JER. 16:14-15, 30:10-11, ISA. 11:11, AMOS 9:14-15. WE ARE TOLD IN MATT. 24:29-31, THAT THEY ARE TO BE SUMMONED BY "ANGELIC TRUMPETERS". IT WILL BE TO OBSERVE THE "FEAST OF TRUMPETS" AT JERUSALEM.

HISTORICALLY THE "FOUNTAIN" OF ZECH. 13:1, WAS OPENED AT CALVARY, BUT REJECTED BY ISRAEL. AFTER THEY ARE REGATHERED THEY SHALL LOOK UPON HIM WHOM THEY PIERCED (ZECH. 12:10), AND ACCEPT THE ATONEMENT NATIONALLY.

WHAT THE "7TH DAY" OR SABBATH, IS TO THE WEEK, A DAY OF REST, SO THE "7TH MONTH" TO THE OTHER 6 MONTHS OF THE "CYCLE", TYPIFIES A PERIOD OF REST — THE "SABBATIC REST" OF THE "MILLENNIAL PERIOD" IN RELATION TO THE OTHER 6 THOUSAND YEARS OF THE WORLD'S WORK DAY HISTORY.
LIKE THE "LORD'S SUPPER" IS TO US A "MEMORIAL" POINTING BACK TO THE "CROSS" AND FORWARD TO THE "COMING", SO THE "FEAST OF TABERNACLES" WILL BE A MEMORIAL TO ISRAEL POINTING BACK TO EGYPT AND FORWARD TO MILLENNIAL REST.

The Tabernacle

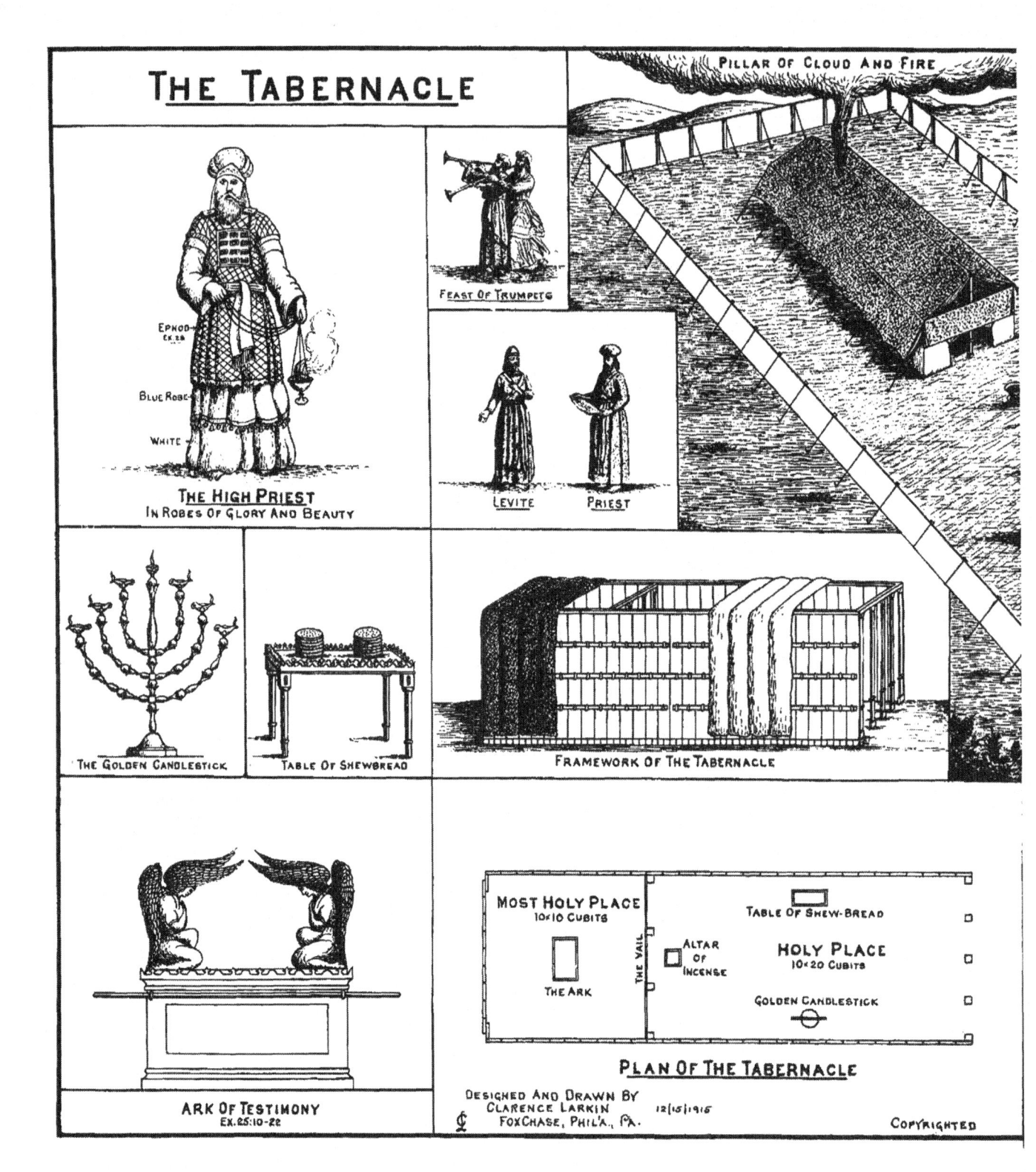

The High Priest — In Robes Of Glory And Beauty
- Ephod Ex. 28
- Blue Robe
- White

Feast Of Trumpets

Levite   **Priest**

Pillar Of Cloud And Fire

The Golden Candlestick

Table Of Shewbread

Framework Of The Tabernacle

Ark Of Testimony Ex. 25:10-22

Plan Of The Tabernacle
- Most Holy Place 10×10 Cubits
- The Ark
- The Vail
- Altar Of Incense
- Table Of Shew-Bread
- Holy Place 10×20 Cubits
- Golden Candlestick

Designed And Drawn By Clarence Larkin, Fox Chase, Phil'a, Pa.   12/15/1915   Copyrighted

The High Priest (The Day Of Atonement)

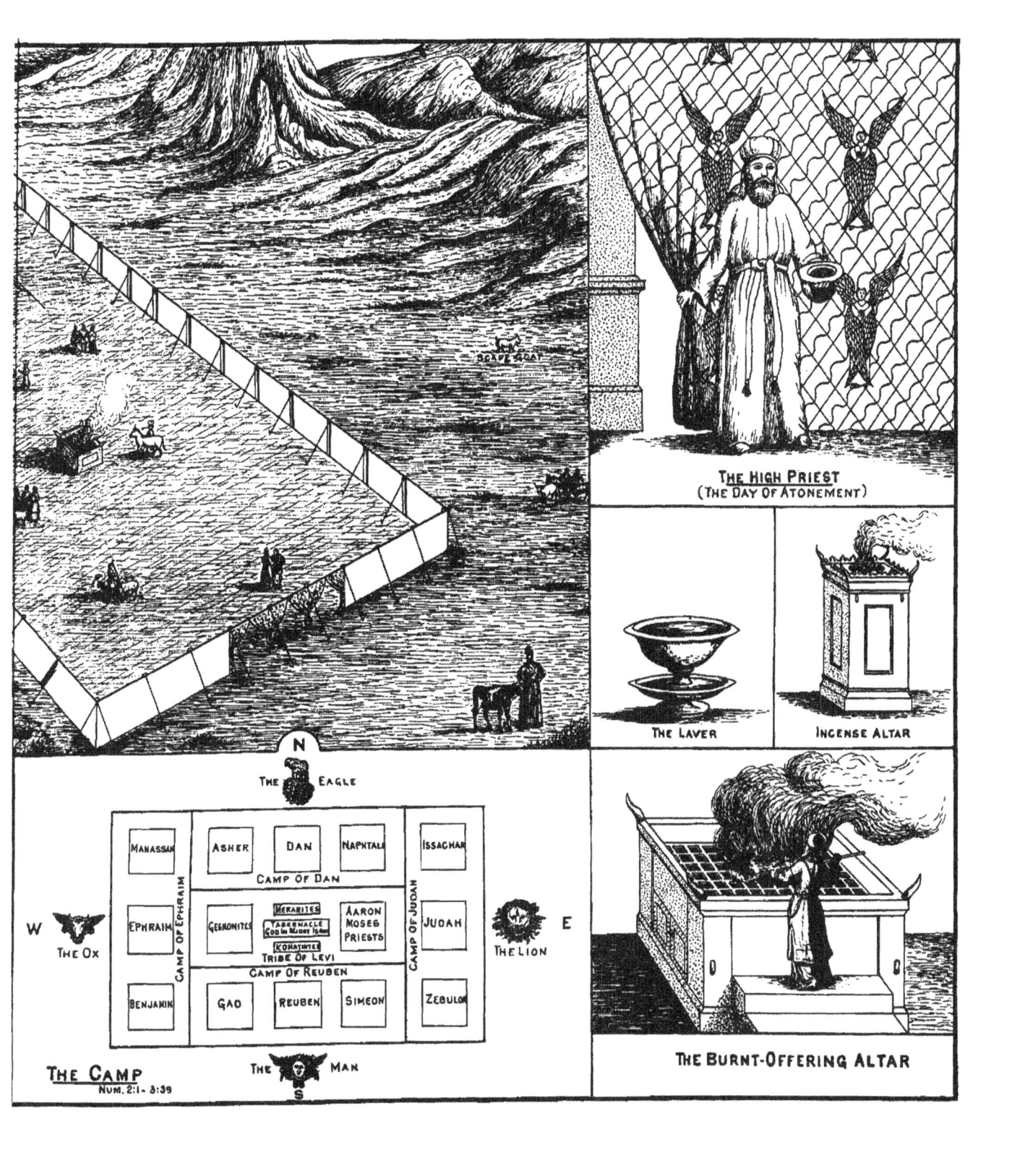

The Laver

Incense Altar

The Burnt-Offering Altar

The Camp
Num. 2:1 - 3:39

N — The Eagle
W — The Ox
E — The Lion
S — The Man

Manasseh	Asher	Dan	Naphtali	Issachar
Ephraim	Gershonites	Merarites / Tabernacle / Kohathites — Tribe of Levi	Aaron Moses Priests	Judah
Benjamin	Gad	Reuben	Simeon	Zebulun

Camp of Ephraim — Camp of Dan — Camp of Reuben — Camp of Judah

had passed away, and the empty tomb of Joseph proclaimed that the "Great First-Fruits' Sheaf" had been reaped and waved in the Heavenly Temple. There will be no Feast of First Fruits in the Millennium, it has been fulfilled in Christ.

4. The Feast of Pentecost.

Fifty days after the Feast of First-Fruits, the Feast of Pentecost was observed. The space between the two Feasts, which included Seven Sabbaths, was called the "Feast of Weeks." It began with the offering of the First-Fruits of the Barley Harvest, and ended with the ingathering of the Wheat Harvest. The First Day was the Feast of the First-Fruits, the Last Day was the Feast of Pentecost. Only the First and Last day were celebrated. See Chart of the Feasts of the Lord.

At the Feast of Pentecost a New Meat Offering was to be offered before the Lord. It was called "new" because it must be of grain from the "new" harvest. At the Feast of First-Fruits "stalks of grain" were to be offered and waved, but at the Feast of Pentecost the grain was to be ground and made into flour, from which two loaves were to be baked with leaven. The "two loaves" represent the two classes of people that were to form the Church, the Jews and Gentiles, and as believers are not perfect, even though saved, that imperfection is represented by the leaven.

A "Burnt Offering" of seven lambs without blemish of the first year, one young bullock, and two rams, was to be offered with the "Wave Loaves," as was also "Meat" and "Drink" Offerings for a sweet savor unto the Lord. These were to be followed by a "Sin Offering" of a kid of the goats, and two lambs of the first year for a "Peace Offering." The "Wave Loaves" were to be waved before the Lord. Note that it is now "loaves," not loose stalks of grain. The "loaves" represent the homogeneousness of the Church.

The Feast of Pentecost had its fulfilment on the Day of Pentecost, when the disciples of the Lord were baptized into one body by the Holy Spirit. 1 Cor. 12:13.

The Interval.

Between the Feast of Pentecost and the Feast of Trumpets there was an interval of four months during which the Harvest and Vintage were gathered in. There was no convocation of the people during those busy months. This long "Interval" typifies the "Present Dispensation" in which the Holy Spirit is gathering out the elect of the Church, and during which Israel is scattered among the Nations. When the Present Dispensation has run its course, and the "Fulness of the Gentiles" has been gathered in (Rom. 11:25) along with the "remnant according to the election of grace" of Israel (Rom. 11:5), then this "Dispensation of Grace" will end, and the elect of Israel will be gathered back from the four quarters of the earth to keep the Feast of Trumpets at Jerusalem. Matt. 24:31.

5. The Feast of Trumpets.

The Feast of Trumpets, which was observed on the first day of the Seventh month, ushered in the second series of the "set feasts." It fell on a Sabbath day, at the time of the New Moon, and ushered in the Jewish New Year. It was followed by the "Day of Atonement" on the 10th day of the month, and by the "Feast of Tabernacles" which began on the 15th day of the month, a Sabbath day, and ended on the 22d day of the month, which was also a Sabbath day. It was ushered in with the blowing of Trumpets. During the Wilderness Wandering two silver Trumpets, made of the atonement money of the people, were blown for the "calling of the Assembly," and for the "journeyings of the Camps." Num. 10:1-10.

The fact that the Feast of Trumpets comes immediately at the close of the "Interval" between the two series of "set feasts" is not without significance. As we have seen the "Interval" represents this "Dispensation of Grace," and we know that two things are to happen at the close of this Dispensation. First the Church is to be caught out, and secondly Israel is to be gathered back to their own land. When the Church is caught out—"The Lord Himself shall descend from Heaven with a shout, with the voice of the Archangel, and with the **Trump** of God" (1 Thess. 4:16), and "We shall not all sleep (die), but we (who are then alive) shall all be changed, in a moment, in the twinkling of an eye, at the

Last Trump;

for the **Trumpet** shall sound, and the dead shall be raised incorruptible, and we shall be changed." 1 Cor. 15:51, 52.

This "last trump" is not the last of the "Seven Trumpets" that sound in the Book of Revelation, for it does not sound until the "Middle of the Week," while the Church is caught out "before" the beginning of the "Week." We probably are to understand by the "last trump" the last of the Two Trumpets used by Israel, the first, for the "calling of the Assembly," will call out the dead in Christ from their graves, and the second or "last," for the "journeying of the camps," will be the signal for the upward journey of the risen and transformed saints to meet the Lord in the air.

Then we read in Matt. 24:31, that the Son of Man, when He comes in the clouds of heaven with power and great glory at His Revelation of Himself, shall send His angels with a great sound of a **Trumpet**, and they shall gather together His "elect" (not of the Church but of Israel) from the four winds, from one end of heaven to the other." From this we see that the "Feast of Trumpets" has a typical relation to the "catching out" of the Church, and the regathering of Israel at the Second Coming of Christ. This has led some to believe that as Jesus was crucified at the time of the Passover, and the Holy Spirit was given at Pentecost, that when He comes back the "Rapture" will take place at the Feast of Tabernacles, and the "Revelation" seven years later at the time of the same Feast. Time alone will reveal the correctness of this view.

6. The Day of Atonement.

The "Day of Atonement" was Israel's annual cleansing from sin. For a full account of the day and its services read Lev. 16:1-34. Its typical meaning was fulfilled in Christ. He is our Great High Priest, who instead of offering a "Sin-Offering" for Himself, offered Himself as a "Sin-Offering" for us. Heb. 9:11-14. But the fact that the "Day of Atonement" is placed between the "Feast of Trumpets," which we have seen will have its typical fulfilment at the Second Coming of Christ, and the "Feast of Tabernacles," which is a type of Israel's "Millennial Rest," implies that it has some typical significance between those two events. It must therefore refer to the time when a "Fountain will be opened to the

House of David

and to the inhabitants of Jerusalem for sin and for uncleanness." Zech. 13:1. That is, there will be a National "Day of Atonement" for Israel after they have been gathered back to their own land unconverted, and shall repent and turn to God. Zech. 12:9-14.

7. The Feast of Tabernacles.

This was the last of the Seven Set Feasts. It was a "Harvest Home" celebration to be observed at the end of the harvest, and was to continue seven days. Deu. 16:13. The people during the Feast were to dwell in booths (arbors) made of the branches of palm trees and willows from the brook, which would remind them of the palm trees of Elim, and the "Willows" of Babylon. Psa. 137:1-9. The Antitype of this Feast has not as yet appeared though Peter anticipated it, when on the Mt. of Transfiguration, he said—"Lord, it is good for us to be here; if thou wilt, let us make here three Tabernacles; one for Thee, and one for Moses, and one for Elias." Matt. 17:4. What Peter desired, the dwelling of heavenly with earthly people on the earth, was not possible then, but will come to pass in Millennial Days, when Heaven and Earth shall be in closer union. The Feast of Tabernacles points forward to Israel's "Millennial Rest."

What the "Seventh Day," or Sabbath, is to the week, a day of rest; so the "Seventh Month" to the other six months of the "Seven Month Cycle," typifies a period of rest—the

"Sabbatic Rest"

of the "Millennial Age," or 1000 years, in relation to the other six thousand years of the world's work day history. Like the Lord's Supper is to us, a "Memorial" pointing back to the "Cross" and forward to the "Coming," so the "Feast of Tabernacles" will be a "Memorial" to Israel, pointing back to Egypt and forward to Millennial Rest.

While the Feast of Tabernacles began on the Sabbath and continued seven days, it was to be followed by a Sabbath. Lev. 23:39. This Sabbath on the "Eighth Day" points to the New Heaven and Earth that follow the Millennium, and to the "Eighth Dispensation," the Dispensation of the "Fulness of Times" as shown on the Chart "Rightly Dividing the Word of Truth."

XXXI
THE OFFERINGS

The third Book in the Old Testament is called Leviticus. It is called Leviticus because it treats of the duties of the priests, the sons of Levi. It is the

Book of Sacrifice.

The Keyword is "Atonement." Lev. 16:34. The Book contains the **Very Words of God Himself** dictated to Moses B.C. 1490, from the newly set up Tabernacle, except the last three chapters given from Mt. Sinai. The time occupied in giving it was about 30 days. Over 50 times, in its 27 chapters, it declares that its words are the words of God.

Critical scholars of today claim that it was not written by Moses, but is "a priestly forgery of the times following the Babylonian Captivity," nearly a 1000 years after Moses, and that it is a compilation of certain Jewish priests who wished to magnify their office, and to give it authority they assigned it to Moses.

But this is an absurd claim. How could the priests of the Captivity persuade the people that a book they had just written had been in existence for 1000 years?

Then we have the testimony of Christ that the Book of Leviticus was written by Moses. If Moses did not write it, then Christ was mistaken, or guilty of misrepresentation. Neither of which we can believe and claim that Jesus in His teaching was divine and inerrant.

The Book of Leviticus is little read in these days, and is considered by many to be obsolete and only fit for the shelves of a religious antiquarian, because it treats of a system of worship which they claim has been done away with.

The fact is, we cannot understand the Office and Work of Christ without studying the Book of Leviticus in the light of its exposition in the Epistle to the Hebrews. And the Book is of value because it contains the laws of the Priesthood, that are to be again in force when the Children of Israel are gathered back into their own land in the Millennial days, and the Temple of Ezekiel shall be built and the Mosaic order of worship re-established.

But the Book of Leviticus has a value beside that of throwing light on the High Priestly Work and Office of Christ. It is not only a "Ritual," it is more. It contains a body of

Civil Laws.

Laws as to Marriage and Divorce, as to Capital and Labor, as to the Social Evil, as to the Accumulation of Property, as to Capital Punishment, as to the Observance of the Sabbath, as to the use of the Quarantine.

If the statesmen of today desire to make laws in conformity with the will of God, laws that will conserve the public health, and minister to the well-being of mankind, let them study the "Civil Laws" of the Book of Leviticus, and they will find that they throw a flood of light on these subjects.

The two main divisions of the Book are

1. The "Way to God" by SACRIFICE.
   Chapters 1-16.
2. The "Walk With God" by SANCTIFICATION AND SEPARATION
   Chapters 17-27.

The main teaching of the Book is—

HOW SIN MAY BE PUT AWAY.

The two great commandments of the Book are, be **Holy**, be **Clean**. The word "blood" occurs 87 times.

THE OFFERINGS

The Offerings were 5 in number—

1. The Burnt Offering.
2. The Meat Offering.
3. The Peace Offering.
4. The Sin Offering.
5. The Trespass Offering.

These Offerings were divided into two classes. The first three were

"Sweet Savor Offerings,"

the last two were

"Sin Offerings."

I. The Burnt Offering.
Lev. 1:1-17.

The "Burnt" Offering was of three grades according to the ability of the offerer. If the offerer was well to do he brought an offering from the herd. If he was in moderate circumstances he brought an offering from the flock. If he was poor, he brought a fowl, either a turtle dove or a young pigeon.

Only clean animals or fowls could be offered. That which lived by the death of others, or fed on carrion, was unfit to offer as a type

LEVITICUS
THE BOOK OF...

THE WAY TO GOD THROUGH SACRIFICE

THE OFFERINGS					THE PRIESTHOOD	LAWS OF PURITY
SWEET SAVOUR OFFERINGS		SIN OFFERINGS		LAW OF THE OFFERINGS		AS TO THE PEOPLE
CHAP. 1:1 – 3:17		CHAP. 4:1 – 6:7		CHAP. 6:8 – 7:38	8:1-36 / 9:1-24 / 10:1-20	11:1-47 / 12:1-8 / 13:1-14:57 / 15:1-33 / CHAP.

1 BURNT OFFERING	2 MEAL OFFERING	3 PEACE OFFERING	4 SIN OFFERING	5 TRESPASS OFFERING	BURNT OFFERING	MEAL OFFERING	SIN OFFERING	TRESPASS OFFERING	PEACE OFFERING	CONSECRATION OF AARON AND HIS SONS	WORK OF THE PRIEST	PUNISHMENT OF PRIESTS	AS TO FOOD	AS TO MOTHERHOOD	AS TO LEPROSY	AS TO UNCLEANNESS	THE DAY OF ATONE...
THESE OFFERINGS ARE DESCRIBED BELOW																	

THE LEVITICAL OFFERINGS

OFFERINGS	THE OFFERING	THE OFFERER'S WORK	THE PRIEST'S WORK	GOD'S PORTION	THE PRIEST'S PORTION	THE OFFERER'S PORTION	SYMBOLISM
BURNT OFFERING	A BULLOCK, OR A SHEEP, OR A GOAT, OR TURTLE DOVES OR YOUNG PIGEONS, ACCORDING TO THE ABILITY OF THE OFFERER. IF OF THE HERD OR FLOCK, A YEAR OLD AND WITHOUT BLEMISH.	HE LED IT TO THE DOOR OF THE TABERNACLE, LAID HIS HAND ON IT, SLEW, SKINNED, CUT IN PIECES, WASHED THE PARTS AND GAVE TO PRIEST. WHEN A FOWL HE HANDED IT TO THE PRIEST. LEV. 1:14-17	HE CAUGHT THE BLOOD, SPRINKLED IT AROUND THE ALTAR AND PLACED THE PARTS IN ORDER ON THE ALTAR. THUS IT WAS CALLED A "WHOLE" BURNT OFFERING.	ALL THAT WAS BURNED	THE SKIN. LEV. 7:8	NOTHING	COMPLETE CONSECRATION OF THE OFFERER TO GOD. ROM. 12:1
MEAL OFFERING	UNBAKED FLOUR GROUND FINE, OR BAKED CAKES, OR GREEN EARS OF CORN, PARCHED OR ROASTED. IT WAS TO BE MIXED WITH OIL, SEASONED WITH SALT, SPRINKLED WITH FRANKINCENSE, CONTAIN NO LEAVEN OR HONEY.	HE SIMPLY BROUGHT THE OFFERING TO THE PRIEST.	HE THREW A HANDFUL OF THE OFFERING, AND ALL THE FRANKINCENSE, ON THE ALTAR FIRE.	THE HANDFUL OF THE OFFERING AND THE FRANKINCENSE.	THE REMAINDER OF THE OFFERING. LEV. 6:14-18	NOTHING	THE CONSECRATION OFFERER'S TOIL AND POSSESSIONS TO GOD.
PEACE OFFERING	A BULLOCK, OR LAMB, OR GOAT. MALE OR FEMALE.	HE LED THE OFFERING TO THE DOOR OF THE TABERNACLE, LAID HIS HAND UPON IT, KILLED IT, OPENED IT, TOOK OUT FAT, CAUL, AND KIDNEYS AND GAVE TO THE PRIEST TO BE BURNED.	THE PRIEST CAUGHT THE BLOOD, SPRINKLED IT AROUND THE ALTAR, AND WAVED THE "BREAST" AND "RIGHT SHOULDER" BEFORE THE LORD.	ALL THAT WAS BURNED.	THE "WAVE BREAST" AND "HEAVE SHOULDER".	THE REMAINDER OF THE OFFERING WHICH HE MUST EAT WITH HIS FAMILY OR FRIENDS IN THE COURT OF THE TABERNACLE. LEV. 12:3-12	THE "RECONCILIATION" THE OFFERER WITH G...
SIN OFFERING	A BULLOCK, OR GOAT, (MALE OR FEMALE), OR LAMB ACCORDING TO THE POSITION OF THE OFFERER.	HE BROUGHT THE OFFERING TO THE DOOR OF THE TABERNACLE, LAID HIS HAND ON IT, SLEW IT, REMOVED THE FAT, KIDNEYS AND CAUL AND GAVE TO PRIEST TO BE BURNED ON THE ALTAR.	IF FOR HIMSELF OR CONGREGATION, TOOK OF THE BLOOD AND SPRINKLED IT 7 TIMES BEFORE THE VEIL, PUT OF IT ON THE HORNS OF THE "INCENSE ALTAR" AND POURED THE BALANCE AT THE FOOT OF BURNT OFFERING ALTAR. IF FOR OTHERS THE BLOOD IS PUT ON THE HORNS AND POURED OUT AT THE FOOT OF THE BURNT OFFERING ALTAR. SHALL DO AS HE DID WITH THE "SIN-OFFERING" OF THE COMMON PEOPLE.	ALL OF PRIESTS AND CONGREGATION'S OFFERING THAT WAS NOT CONSUMED ON THE ALTAR, WAS BURNED WITHOUT THE CAMP.	ALL OF THE OFFERING OF THE RULER OR COMMON PEOPLE, THAT WAS NOT BURNED ON THE ALTAR, BELONGED TO THE PRIESTS, AND WAS TO BE BOILED AND ATE IN THE COURT OF THE TABERNACLE. LEV. 6:24-29.	NOTHING	THE EXPIATION OF THE SIN OF THE OFFERER.
TRESPASS OFFERING	FEMALE LAMB OR KID, TWO TURTLE DOVES, OR TWO YOUNG PIGEONS, OR 1/10 PART OF EPHAH OF FLOUR. IT MUST CONTAIN NO OIL OR FRANKINCENSE.	SHALL DO AS HE DID WITH THE "SIN-OFFERING".		ALL THAT WAS BURNED ON THE ALTAR.	WHAT WAS NOT BURNED ON THE ALTAR BELONGED TO THE PRIEST.	NOTHING	WAS TO MAKE REPARATION AND RESTITUTION FOR THE TRESPASS OF THE OFFERER.

LEVITICUS
"The Book of Sacrifice"

The Walk With God Through Separation

Laws Of Holiness			The Feasts	Civil Laws	
As To The People (Chap. 17:1-20:27)	As To The Priests (Chap. 21:1-22:16)	As To The Offerings (22:17-33)	Chap. 23:4-44	Chap. 24:10-25:55	26:1-27:34

Laws As To The People (6:1-34):
- Place Of Sacrifice
- As To Blood
- Unholy Relationships And Vile Practices
- As To Social Morality
- The Punishment For Idolatry And Immorality

As To The Priests:
- As To The Dead
- As To The Hair And Beard
- As To Marriage
- As To Physical Disqualification
- As To Uncleanness
- As To Who Shall Eat Of The Holy Things

As To The Offerings:
- One Year Old And Without Blemish
- The Sabbath Is Here Mentioned To Separate It From The Feasts

The Feasts (23:1-3):
1. Passover
2. Unleavened Bread
3. First Fruits
4. Pentecost
5. Trumpets
6. Day Of Atonement
7. Tabernacles

Civil Laws (24:1-9):
- Oil For The Light
- The Shewbread
- As To Blasphemy
- As To Taking Life
- The Sabbatic Year
- Year Of Jubilee
- Redemption Of The Inheritance
- Treatment Of A Poor Brother
- Redemption Of A Poor Brother
- Blessings And Cursings
- The Law Of The Vow And Dedicated Things

Typical Teaching

- Christ Giving Himself As A "Whole" Burnt Offering On The Altar Of The Cross. Eph. 5:2. Heb. 9:14
- Christ Was The "Corn Of Wheat" (John 12:24) Bruised In The Mill Of Calvary, And Offered As The "Bread Of Life" To His People.
- Christ Is Our "Peace Offering". Rom. 5:1 Col. 1:20
- Christ Is Our "Sin Offering". 2 Cor. 5:21 1 Pet. 2:24
- Christ Is Our "Trespass Offering". Col. 2:13-14. 2 Cor. 5:19

Christ — The One To Whom The Offerings And Feasts Point

Designed And Drawn By Clarence Larkin, Fox Chase, Phil'a, Pa.
Copyrighted

The Feasts Of The Lord

1 Passover	2 Unleavened Bread	3 First-Fruits	4 Pentecost	5 Trumpets	6 Day Of Atonement	7 Tabernacles
14th Day	First Month 15th Day	16th Day	Third Month 6th Day	1st Day	Seventh Month 10th Day	15th to 22nd Day

See My Chart On The Feasts

The Day Of Atonement

The High Priest Washed His Person, Put On Linen Clothes, And Presented His Bullock, And The 2 Goats Presented By The Congregation, Before The Door Of The Tabernacle, And Cast Lots Upon The 2 Goats For Which Should Be The "Scape Goat". Then He Killed His Bullock, Took Of Its Blood, And A Censer Full Of Burning Coals From Off The "Brazen Altar", With Incense, And Entered Within The Veil, And Threw The Incense On The Live Coals Of The Censer To Fill The "Most Holy Place" With Incense, He Sprinkled Of The Blood Of His Bullock On The "Mercy Seat", And 7 Times Before It. Then He Went Out And Killed The Goat Of The "Sin Offering" And Did The Same With Its Blood. In Like Manner He Made Atonement For The Holy Place And The "Brazen Altar". No Other Person Than The High Priest Was Permitted In The Tabernacle At The Time. He Then Laid Both Of His Hands On The Head Of The "Scape-Goat" And Confessed The Sins Of The People, And Then Sent The "Scape-Goat" Into The Wilderness By A Fit Man Who Left Him There. The High Priest Then Returned To The Holy Place Of The Tabernacle, Put Off His Linen Clothes, Washed Himself, And Put On His Garments Of "Glory And Beauty", And Came Out. The Bodies Of The Slain Bullock And Goat Were Then Wrapped In Their Skins And Carried Outside The Camp And Burned.

The Typical Meaning.

Christ As Our "Great High Priest" Had No Occasion To Offer A Bullock For Himself, For He Was Sinless. The 2 Goats Represent His Two-Fold Office. One His Death As Our "Sin-Offering", The "Scape-Goat", His Carrying Of Our Sins Away. He Carried His Own Blood Within The "Heavenly Veil", And, Having Made Atonement For Sin, He Tarries Within The "Heavenly Tabernacle" Making Intercession. When He Comes Out His High Priestly Work Will End.

of the "Holy Victim" (Christ), who was prefigured in the Offering. Israel was not to offer as the "food of God" that which they themselves were forbidden to eat.

And even among clean animals, only "domestic" animals were permitted to be used, for it was fitting that only that should be offered that had cost something and was more or less endeared to the offerer. Then domestic animals are "tame," and easily led, and are a fit type of Him who was led as a sheep to the slaughter. Isa. 53:7.

Not only must it be a "domestic" animal either from the herd or the flock, but it must be a "male," and a male without "blemish," that is, ideally perfect. The Israelite was taught to give the "best" that he had, not for unselfish reasons, but because only the animal "without blemish" could typify the Spotless Son of God.

The fault that God found with the Children of Israel in Malachi's day was, that they "brought that which was torn, and the lame, and the sick." Mal. 1:8.

The offerer having brought his offering into the Court of the Tabernacle, the officiating priest approached him and led him and his offering to the North side of the Altar of Burnt Offering, facing the Door of the Tabernacle. The Offerer then laid his hand heavily upon the "head" of the Offering, thus symbolizing the "identity" of the Offerer with his Offering, and confessing by the act that he deserved the death which the animal was to suffer.

The Offerer then with his own hands slew the Offering, if it was of the herd or of the flock, but if it was a fowl the priest himself wrung off its head.

When the Offerer slew his Offering, whether bullock, sheep, or goat, the priest caught the streaming blood in a basin and sprinkled it round about the Altar of Burnt Offering.

The animal was then skinned, the skin becoming the property of the priest, probably as compensation for his work.

The body of the Offering was then cut in pieces, every joint being separated. The legs and intestines were washed in water, and the whole was then rearranged in order upon the Altar and completely consumed with fire. For this reason it was spoken of as a "**Whole Burnt Offering.**"

The animal was dissected before being burnt to see that it was perfect and without blemish in any of its parts.

When the Offering was a fowl all the Offerer did was to bring it to the priest. The priest took it, wrung off its head, permitted the blood to squirt out at the side of the Altar, and then cleaved it open between the wings without separating the two halves, removed the crop and intestines and cast them on the pile of ashes beside the Altar and then burnt the body of the fowl on the Altar.

Now what is the typical meaning of the "Burnt Offering?" It is clearly not an offering for "sin," for that is made in the "Sin Offerings."

The meaning is plain. It typifies the

Consecration

of the Offerer to the Lord. The purpose is beautifully expressed in Paul's Letter to the Romans—

"I beseech you therefore, brethren, by the mercies of God, that ye

Present Your 'BODIES' a 'LIVING SACRIFICE,'

holy (without blemish), acceptable unto God, which is your reasonable service." Rom. 12:1.

God wants us to present ourselves (as a man volunteers for service), a **Living Sacrifice**. He wants us in the full vigor and strength of our lives, not when we are more dead than alive and unfit for service.

The Burnt Offering was also a type of Christ, of whom the Apostle writing to the Ephesians said—

"Christ also hath loved us, and hath given **HIMSELF** for us an **Offering** and a **Sacrifice** to God for a **SWEET-SMELLING SAVOR.**" Eph. 5:2.

This verse exhibits the surrender of Christ to God as a "whole burnt offering." On the "Altar of the Cross" Christ was our **BURNT OFFERING.**

By our accepting Him as our "Burnt Offering" we identify ourselves with Him, and confess that He died as our substitute. As a substitute He is the ideal of consecrated service, for His will was always in complete submission to the Father's. Of Him the Father could say, "This is my beloved son in whom I am well pleased."

Thus he was an Offering of a "sweet smelling savor," such as was the Burnt Offering.

But while individual Offerers at different times brought their offerings to the Lord, there was a "daily" Burnt Offering for the whole congregation of Israel. Ex. 29:42.

This consisted of two lambs, one offered at the time of the morning sacrifice, and the other at the time of the evening sacrifice.

In the morning the officiating priest laid off his ordinary garments, and putting on his "linen garments," overhauled the fire that had been burning on the Altar all night, and removed the ashes and laid them by the side of the Altar. He then put off his "linen garments," and replacing them with his ordinary garments he carried forth the ashes and deposited them in a clean place outside the camp. Returning he put on his "linen garments" again and offered the lamb of the morning Burnt Offering. This he repeated in the afternoon, and from day to day, as a "continual" Burnt Offering, thus typifying the fact that Christ is a "continual" Burnt Offering for His people, and that the believer should offer himself, not merely once for all, but continually in consecration service.

II. The Meat Offering.
Lev. 2:1-16.

The term **"Meat"** Offering should read **"Meal"** Offering, as there is no "meat" in it.

When the King James' version of the Bible was printed in A. D. 1611, the word "Meat" meant all kinds of food, and not "flesh" merely.

The "Meal" Offering was of three kinds.

1. **Unbaked** flour ground fine.
2. **Baked** loaves or cakes, baked in a pan.
3. **Green Ears** of corn parched or roasted.

By "corn" we are to understand "wheat," as what we know as corn was unknown in Bible Lands in Bible times.

The "Meal" Offering was to be mixed with **Oil**, seasoned with **Salt**, sprinkled with **Frankincense**, and was not to contain any **Leaven** or **Honey**.

The Offerer was to bring his "Meal" Offering to the officiating priest, who was to take a "handful" of it and throw it upon the sacrifice upon the Altar of Burnt Offering as the "Meal" Offering was never offered by itself but always in connection with a burnt sacrifice.

The remainder of the "Meal" Offering was to be eaten by the priests. The Offerer did not eat of it. In the preparation of the "Meal" Offering we must note the ingredients "commanded," and the ingredients "forbidden." "Oil," "Salt" and "Frankincense" were to be used and "Leaven" and "Honey" omitted.

"Olive Oil" was largely used for food by the inhabitants of Bible lands, and is a type in the Bible of the life-giving power of the Holy Spirit.

"Salt" is an antiseptic and a preventive of putrefaction, and was used for its preserving qualities.

"Frankincense" was a resinous gum that exuded from a tree, and that when dried and beaten fine and thrown on a fire, gave out a sweet fragrance. The Frankincense was not mixed with the "Meal" Offering but sprinkled only upon the handful that was thrown upon the sacrifice on the Altar to be burnt, to make the sacrifice of a sweet smelling savor. All the Frankincense was burnt.

"Leaven" was forbidden because it has fermenting qualities, and "Honey," because Honey is spoiled by heat and would make the batch sour.

What is the meaning of the "Meal" Offering?

The "Meal" Offering was to be of "Wheat," the best and most valued of all grains for food, and it was to be of the "finest of the wheat." Now wheat does not grow spontaneously like weeds, it has to be planted after the soil has been laboriously prepared for its reception. Wheat then represents the outcome of man's labor and toil. It was also a common article of food of both rich and poor, as was the olive from which the oil was extracted, and so obtainable by all.

But the "wheat" was not to be presented to the Lord as grain, it was to be ground and sifted; and where the Offerer had an oven and could prepare the wheat as cakes for food for the priests, he was to do so, and where he could not grind or bake it he was to parch it and present it in that form.

The meaning of the "Meal" Offering therefore is plain. It was to be offered with the Burnt Offering; and as we saw that the meaning of the Burnt Offering was the consecration of the **Body** of the Offerer, it follows then that the "Meal" Offering which is the fruit of a man's "labor," means that we are not only to consecrate our "bodies" a living sacrifice to God, but we are to consecrate the **Fruit of Our Toil**.

This not only means the fruit of our "physical" toil, but all our "spiritual" work in the Lord's Harvest Field.

The fact that only a "handful" of the "Meal" Offering was consumed on the Altar, and the rest was eaten by the priests, is not without its significance. It means that the bulk of our gifts should go to the support of the Gospel.

How beautifully the "Meal" Offering represents Christ the great anti-typical "Meal" Offering.

He was the "corn of wheat," bruised in the "Mill of Calvary," that was mixed with the "Oil of the Holy Spirit," seasoned with the "Salt of Incorruption," and offered with the "Frankincense of a Holy Life." In Him was no corrupting Leaven or Sour Honey and He, when offered, became the **Bread of Life**.

III. The Peace Offering.
Lev. 3:1-17,

The "Peace" Offering was of two kinds, of the herd or of the flock, and was different from the Burnt Offering in that a male or female could be offered. The Offering was however to be without blemish.

The Offerer brought his Offering, either a bullock, lamb or goat, into the Court of the Tabernacle to the Altar of Burnt Offering, and there, before the Lord, he laid his hand upon its head and then killed it the officiating priest catching the blood in a basin and sprinkling it around the Altar.

The animal was then opened and the fat and kidneys and rump were burned upon the Altar. The remainder of the animal was to be eaten by the Priests and the Offerer and his family and friends.

The "breast" was "waved" to and fro before the Lord and given to the High Priest and his sons. The "right shoulder" was heaved up and down before the Lord and given to the officiating priest; the remainder of the animal belonged to the Offerer.

There were two kinds of "Peace" Offerings. Lev. 7:11-21. The "Offering of Thanksgiving," and the Offering in fulfillment of a "Vow."

The flesh of the "Peace Offering of Thanksgiving" was to be eaten the same day that it was offered, but the flesh of a "Vow" Offering could be kept over until the next day; but if any of it remained over until the third day it was considered corrupt and must be burnt.

If the Offerer ate of it on the third day his Offering was not accepted, and he, and any who ate of it, were guilty of committing an abomination before the Lord and would have to bear their iniquity.

If the flesh of the Offering touched an unclean thing it was not to be eaten, and if any person ate of the Offering while unclean that person was to be cut off from his people.

The Offerer did not have to eat of his Offering alone. He had the privilege of inviting his sons and daughters, his menservants and maidservants and the Levites within the gates to feast with him, Deut. 12:5-12, but the feasting must be "before the Lord" in the Court of the Tabernacle, and nowhere else.

The "Peace" Offering was an Offering of **Reconciliation**. Not for the purpose of reconciling the Offerer, for it was not made by God, but by the Offerer, but to show that the Offerer "had been" reconciled to God.

While Christ is our **"PEACE OFFERING"** by whom we have been reconciled to God, yet He is more, He is the One upon whom we are to "feast," for He said, "my Flesh is meat indeed, and my blood is drink indeed." John 6:53-56; Matt. 26:26-29; 1 Cor. 11:23-26.

We see then that the "Peace" Offering has an antitypical fulfillment in the **"Lord's Supper"** where we feast before the Lord by faith, on His broken body and shed blood.

IV. The Sin Offering.
Lev. 4:1-35.

We now come to the second class of Offerings. The first class, the "Burnt," the "Meal" and the "Peace" Offerings, were voluntary and therefore "sweet savor" Offerings, the second class, the "Sin" and "Trespass" Offerings are compulsory, and because they were for sins committed there was no "sweet savor" in them.

Once a year on the

"Day of Atonement,"

atonement was made by the High Priest for his own sin, and the sin of the people, but the "Sin Offering" we are now about to consider is the Offering for sin made from time to time during the year.

These Offerings were for four classes of persons, namely, the anointed Priest, the whole Congregation, a Ruler, and an individual member of the congregation.

In each case the animal offered was to be without blemish and was to be slain at the door of the Tabernacle before the Lord.

The anointed Priest who sinned was to bring a "young bullock," and lay his hand upon its head and then kill it. When the Congregation had sinned they brought a "young bullock," and the Elders of the Congregation laid their hands upon its head and it was killed. When a Ruler sinned he brought a "male kid" and laid his hand upon its head and killed it. When one of the common people sinned he brought a "female kid" and laid his hand upon its head and killed it.

The difference between the Offerings is seen in the **Treatment of the Blood** and in the **Disposition** of the bodies.

The blood of the Offering for the Anointed Priest and the Congregation was taken by the Priest into the Holy Place of the Tabernacle, and he dipped his finger in the blood and sprinkled it seven times before the "Veil" of the Tabernacle, and put some of it on the Horns of the Altar of Incense, and coming out he poured the remainder of the blood at the bottom of the Altar of Burnt Offering.

But the blood of the Offering of a Ruler or of one of the common people was not taken into the Tabernacle, but the officiating priest took of it and put some of it on the Horns of the Altar of Burnt Offering, and the remainder he poured out at the bottom of the Altar.

In the disposition of the body of the victim the Offering of the Priest and of the Congregation was skinned, and all the fat, and the fat upon the kidneys, and the kidneys and the rump were burned on the Altar of Burnt Offering, and the rest of the bullock, its skin, its head, its legs and all its flesh and inwards were carried forth outside the camp unto a clean place, where the ashes were poured out, and burnt.

But in the disposition of the body of the Offering of a Ruler, or of the common people, while the fat was removed and burnt upon the Altar, the body of the Offering was not carried without the camp and burnt, but was given to the priests who boiled it and ate it in the Court of the Tabernacle. The flesh was considered holy, and any garment on which its blood was sprinkled had to be washed in the Holy Place, and the earthen vessel in which it was boiled was to be broken, and if it was boiled in a brazen pot, the pot was to be scoured and washed with water. Lev. 6:24-29.

The two distinguishing features of the "Sin" Offering are the taking of the "blood" **Into the Tabernacle**, and sprinkling it before the "Veil," and the carrying of the "body" **Outside the Camp**.

In these two features we see the meaning of the "Sin" Offering. It speaks of Him who shed His blood on Calvary **Outside the City** to make **Expiation for Sin**.

V. The Trespass Offering.
Lev. 5:1-6:7.

The difference between the "Sin" Offering and the "Trespass" Offering seems to be that the first was to be made for sins against **God**, the second for sins against **Man** or **Holy Things**. The Offerer was to bring a "Trespass" Offering if he "overheard swearing and kept silent," if he "touched any unclean thing," if he "sinned ignorantly in the things of the Lord," if he "lied to his neighbor," if he "found and kept lost property and lied about it," etc.

There were three kinds of Offering he could bring according to his ability, a "female lamb or kid;" "two turtle doves, or young pigeons," one of which was to be offered for a **Sin** Offering, the other for a **Burnt** Offering; or the "tenth part of an ephah of fine flour" for a "Sin" Offering, that should contain no oil or frankincense.

If his trespass was against "holy things," or against the "property of his neighbor," he was to make "restitution" and add thereto one-fifth of the value in silver money. The meaning of the "Trespass" Offering is, that if I have done anything that has caused injury to any one else, I should seek to make all the reparation I can, and where necessary, make restitution. See Chart of Leviticus.

XXXII
DISPENSATIONAL TEACHING OF THE GREAT PYRAMID

In the midst of Egypt, on the west side of the River Nile, almost opposite Cairo, and a short distance north of ancient Memphis, stands the only remaining one of the "Seven Wonders of the World"—**"THE GREAT PYRAMID."** Of the many pyramids of Egypt it was the first built, and the largest of them all, and served as a pattern for the others. It was not built for a Tomb, as were the others, but embodies in its construction such a wonderful knowledge of mathematics, astronomy, and Scriptural information as to clearly show that the Architect and Builder was especially endowed with Divine wisdom.

The Great Pyramid, as originally constructed, was built of granite overlaid with white limestone, and its exterior surface was smooth and unmountable, and it appeared like a building let down from Heaven. But it has been robbed of its white casing stones for building material, and you can mount on the layers of stone, as on steps, to the summit, from which the top stone is missing. Up to the year A. D. 825 its interior was a mystery, its entrance being closed by an accurately-fitted, pivot-working stone whose location was unknown.

At that time the Mohammedan Caliph, Ali Mamoun, came to Cairo to reside. He was so wrought upon by the stories that reached his ears of the fabulous wealth that was locked up in the Pyramid that he decided to break into its interior. According to tradition the entrance was on the North side, and naturally supposing that it was in the centre of the North side, Ali Mamoun set his laborers to work at that point; but it was afterward discovered that for Astronomical reasons the entrance was 24 feet to the East of the centre line. Ali Mamoun's workmen started in about 30 feet above the ground. The tunnel was driven in about 100 feet with no signs of a hollow interior, when, as the workmen, discouraged, were about to give up the undertaking, a sound was heard in the interior, and not far away, as of a stone falling. This fired them with new zeal, and shortly they came to a passageway on the floor of which they found a beautifully-chiseled prismatic stone, which evidently had fallen from above and disclosed an upward passage, whose entrance, however, was closed by an immense granite "Port-cullis," with a hole bored through it, but the hole was filled with wedge-shaped granite blocks impossible to remove. To overcome this obstacle the workmen tunneled around the granite "Port-cullis" in the softer stone, only to find another stone filling the passageway. After this was removed, and several others that came sliding down, the passageway was clear for an upward ascent, which let them into the passageways and chambers of the interior of the Pyramid. But to the disgust of Ali Mamoun the interior contained no riches, no furniture of any kind, except an empty "Coffer," and there were no inscriptions or hieroglyphics on the walls to bear witness to its being a tomb.

Diagram "A"

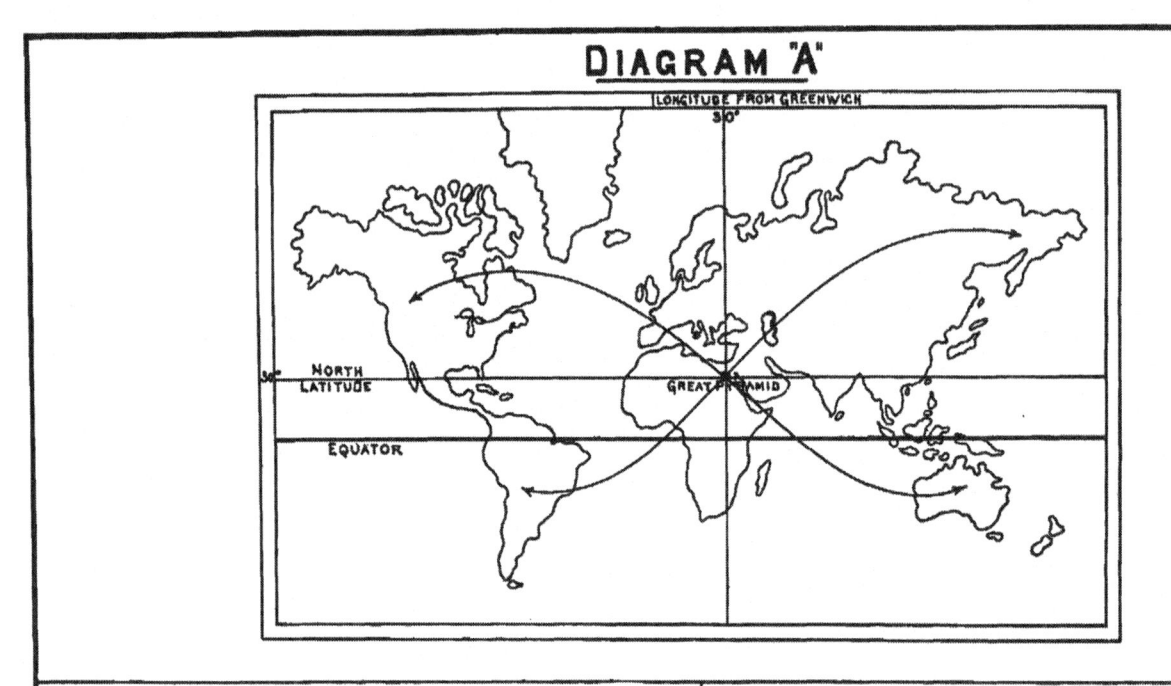

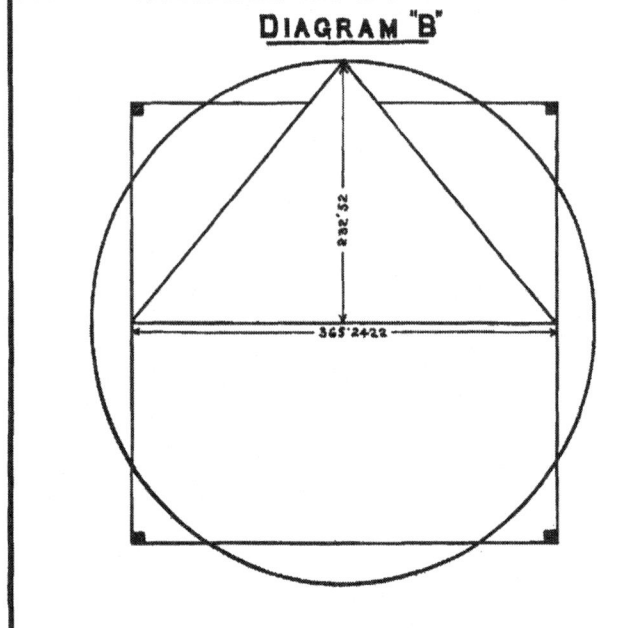

LONGITUDE FROM GREENWICH
30°

NORTH LATITUDE

GREAT PYRAMID

EQUATOR

Diagram "B"

282.52
365.2422

Diagram "D"

MEDITERRANEAN SEA

Rosetta
Damietta
Port Said

LOWER EGYPT
THE DELTA

EGYPT

SUEZ CANAL

Great Pyramid • Cairo
Ancient Memphis
RIVER NILE
SUEZ
GULF OF SUEZ

UPPER EGYPT

166

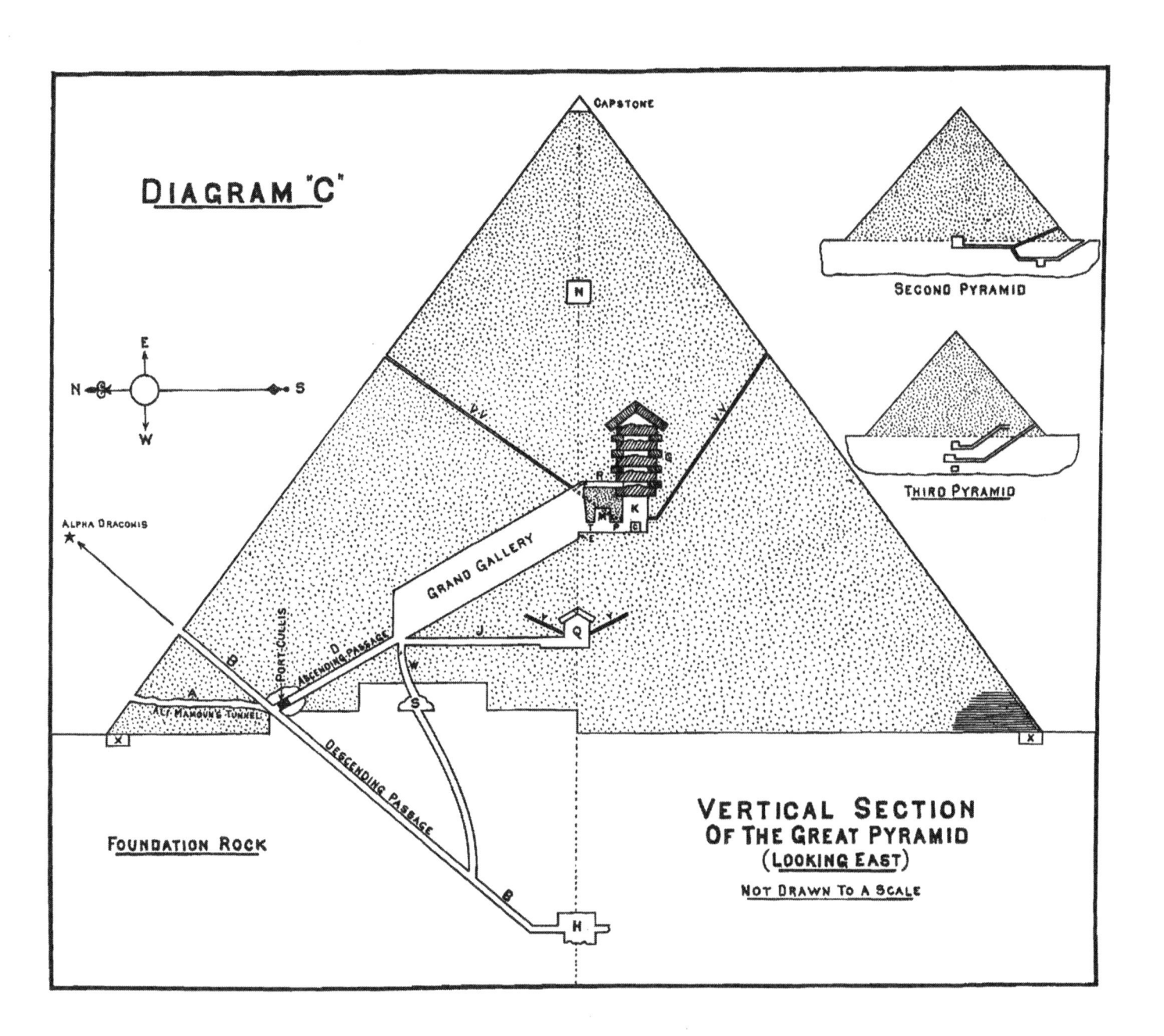

For over 10 centuries the Great Pyramid remained as to its construction comparatively unknown. In A. D. 1865, Prof. Piazzi Smyth, Astronomer Royal of Scotland, with his wife, encamped on the site of the Great Pyramid and began to make exterior and interior measurements. He found that the Pyramid was located on the 30th degree of North Latitude, and that its triangular sides faced exactly the four points of the compass. The Pyramid covers 13 acres of ground, equal to about 4 city squares, and is located in about the land centre of the earth. See Diagram "A."

DESCRIPTION OF THE GREAT PYRAMID

The Great Pyramid is built on the solid rock. The rock was leveled around the base lines, and cornerstones (X), sunk 8 inches in the rock, were placed in position. The cubit of measurement is the Hebrew cubit of 25·025 inches. The length of each side of the base is 365·2422 cubits, the exact number of days in the **SOLAR** year, including the extra day every 4 years, and also allowing for the periodical dropping of a leap year at intervals. The slope of the sides of the Pyramid is of such an angle that they meet at the apex at the predetermined height of 232·52 cubits. Why this fraction of a cubit? So that if twice the length of a side at the base, be divided by the height of the Pyramid, we shall have the figures 3·14159, (365·242×2÷232·52=3·14159), which, when multiplied by the diameter of a circle, gives its circumference. Now the perimeter of the base of the Pyramid (365·242×4=14609·68) is exactly equal to the circumference of a circle whose diameter is twice the height of the Pyramid (232·52×2×3·1416=14609·68). So we see in the equality of these figures the solution of the mathematical problem of how to **SQUARE THE CIRCLE**. See Diagram "B."

The angle of the slope of the sides is as 10 to 9. That is, for every 10 feet you ascend up the slope of the Pyramid you rise in altitude 9 feet, and if you multiply the altitude of the Pyramid by 10 raised to the 9th power, you have 91,840,000, which in miles, gives the exact distance of the sun from the earth.

There is a twofold year, the "Sidereal," or year of the stars, and the "Equinoctial," or year of the seasons. They differ by about 50 seconds each year. That is, the stars in their rising and setting are retarded about 50 seconds a year, so that for the "Sidereal" and "Equinoctial" years to come around and again coincide, will take 25,827 years, which is known as a "**CYCLE**," and when we add together the diagonals of the Pyramid's base, in Pyramid inches, we have 25,827 inches, or as many inches as the Cycle has years.

In 1839 Sir John Herschel, assuming that the long, narrow, polished, descending passage, marked B B on Diagram "C," was meant to be levelled at the "Polar Star" of the date of the construction of the Pyramid, made a calculation and found that such was the case. That star has since been proven to be "**ALPHA DRACONIS**," the Polar Star of the year B. C. 2170. But "Alpha Draconis" by itself does not fix the date, but its combination with another star does. For a long time it was supposed that the sun of our Solar System was stationary, and that the planets and comets circled around it. But now we know that it is not stationary, but that it is circling, with all the members of our Solar System, around some central point in the Universe. This central point is now believed to be the Star "**ALCYONE**," the central star of the Pleiades. And it was to this star that the apex of the Pyramid pointed on the meridian at midnight of the year B. C. 2170. This combination of these two stars ("Alpha Draconis" and "Alcyone") will not occur again until the "**PRECESSION OF THE EQUINOXES**," or until 25827 years have rolled around.

But as at the time of the date of the building of the Pyramid (B. C. 2170) the "Polar Star" was a trifle to the East of the centre of the North side of the Pyramid, it was necessary to put the entrance passage at that point, and that accounts for why the tunnel driven in from the centre of the North side by the workmen of Ali Mamoun failed to hit the descending passage.

Entering the Pyramid we find that the descending entrance passage leads in a straight line down to a chamber marked "H" (Diagram "C"), which has been cut out of the solid rock, and is about 100 feet below the base of the Pyramid. This chamber appears to be unfinished, as it has a passageway leading out from the opposite side that stops short, and the bottom of the chamber is rough and unfinished.

The entrance passage is not quite 4 feet high, and a trifle over 3 feet 5 inches wide.

Descending this entrance passage, about 985 inches from the entrance an upward passage of the same size (D), leads upward at about the same angle as the descending passage, a distance of 1542 inches, when it opens out into a Grand Gallery 1882 inches long, that is 28 feet high, 6 feet wide at the bottom and narrows toward the top, the narrowing above the base sides being produced by 7 courses of stones, each course overhanging the one below.

About 3 feet from the entrance to the "Grand Gallery," on the West side, is a torn and ragged opening that leads into a well (W), that passes through the masonry of the Pyramid and solid rock in a serpentine manner, down to the chamber marked "H." Midway of this well is a cavern-shaped opening (S) made in the solid rock.

Just above the mouth of this well a horizontal passageway (J) leads to a chamber (Q) called the Queen's Chamber. This chamber is 205 inches wide, 226 inches long, and has a triangular-shaped ceiling, and a vertical line let fall from the apex of the Pyramid passes through its centre.

At the top of the sloping floor of the "Grand Gallery" there is a vertical step (E) 3 feet high, the top of which leads to a low passageway (T) that opens into an "Ante-Chamber" (M), from which, by another low passageway (P), entrance is had into a large chamber (K), twice the size of the "Queen's Chamber." This chamber, called the "King's Chamber," is constructed of polished red granite, and is 412 inches long, 206 inches wide, and 230 inches high. It contains the only piece of furniture in the Pyramid, a stone "Coffer" (C), lidless and empty and cut from a solid block of red granite, polished within and without. It is an oblong rectangular trough, without inscription or ornament, and of a size that it could not possibly have been taken in or out of its place since the Pyramid was built. The King's Chamber has two ventilating tubes (VV), that connect with openings on the outside of the Pyramid, and keep the Chamber at the standard temperature of 68° Fahrenheit all the year round. The roof of the King's Chamber is composed of 9 heavy blocks of granite supported on the side walls, and above the roof are 5 hollow spaces (G), covered with massive stones, and so arranged as to carry the weight of the superincumbent mass of masonry. The "King's Chamber" is on the 50th layer of masonry, and the "Queen's Chamber" on the 25th. That the so-called King's and Queen's Chambers were not intended as Mortuary Chambers is seen when we examine the Second and Third Pyramids (Diagram "C"), for in those pyramids, built for tombs, the Mortuary Chambers are built in the foundation of the Pyramid, as if those who built them knew nothing about the chambers and passageways in the centre of the Great Pyramid.

Now why all this interior arrangement of passageways and chambers? There was no architectural need for them unless the Great Pyramid was intended for a storehouse of historical or material treasure, or a mausoleum of the dead, of which it gives no evidence, for there are no interior decorations or hieroglyphics upon its walls or passageways, which are to be found in all the other pyramids that were built for tombs. It will not do to say that it had not reached the stage in its construction for ornamentation, for it was completely finished on the outside, and then sealed up and left, the purpose of its construction evidently having been completed. Could it be that the Great Pyramid was built for the purpose of embodying in its construction not only mathematical and astronomical knowledge, but also chronological and Scriptural knowledge? Let us see: In Isaiah 19:19-20 there is a remarkable prophecy that most commentators fail to notice:

"In THAT DAY shall there be an ALTAR to the Lord in the MIDST of the Land of Egypt, and a PILLAR at the BORDER thereof to the Lord. And it shall be for a SIGN and for a WITNESS unto the Lord of Hosts in the Land of Egypt."

That this prophecy has not as yet been fulfilled is clear from the date mentioned—"THAT DAY," which is 3 times repeated in the context (verses 21, 23, 24), and which refers to the "Day of Lord" which is still future.

The prophecy declares that in "That Day" there shall be an "ALTAR" and a "PILLAR" in the MIDST of the LAND OF EGYPT (not Palestine), and at the BORDER thereof, and "IT" shall be for a SIGN and a WITNESS. The word "IT" conveys the idea that the "ALTAR" and "PILLAR" are not two objects but are one and the same. While the word "Altar" in the Hebrew means the "Lion of God," and could refer to the "Sphinx," which is nearby, the "Great Pyramid" is pre-eminently the "lion" in massiveness and strength among buildings, and its shape also answers to the description of a "PILLAR," or mammoth pyramidal obelisk.

Then the position of the "Great Pyramid" harmonizes with the location of the "Altar and Pillar," which was to be in the MIDST of Egypt and at the BORDER thereof. In 1868 Professor H. Mitchell, of the United States Survey, was sent by the Government to report on the progress of the Suez Canal. Struck with the peculiar curvature of the shore line of the Delta of the Nile, he took a good map and drew a curved line touching all the prominent points of the coast, and found that it formed an arc of a sector whose centre was located at the site of the Great Pyramid. See Diagram "D." Thus, without any knowledge of the Biblical prophecy, he confirmed the fact that the Great Pyramid was located at the centre or in the MIDST of Egypt, and as the Delta, or Lower Egypt, comprised the section of Egypt included in the sector, and the Great Pyramid stands on the BORDER between Upper and Lower Egypt, therefore the Great Pramid is both in the MIDST of Egypt, and on its BORDER. It would seem then that beyond question the Great Pyramid is the "Altar and Pillar" that the Prophet Isaiah declared should in the last days of this Dispensation be a "SIGN" and a "WITNESS" unto the Lord. If this be true then it becomes us to prayerfully, and with the help of the Holy Spirit, who spake through the Prophet, try to discover what the Great Pyramid as a "WITNESS" has to reveal to us.

THE GREAT PYRAMID AND CHRIST

In a remarkable passage in Job the earth is compared to a building. The question is asked Job—

"Where wast thou when I laid the FOUNDATIONS of the earth? Declare, if thou hast understanding. Who hath laid the MEASURES thereof, if thou knowest? Or who hath stretched the LINE upon it? Whereupon are the FOUNDATIONS thereof fastened? Or who laid the

'CORNER-STONE'

thereof; when the 'Morning Stars' sang together, and all the 'SONS OF GOD'

SHOUTED FOR JOY?"
Job 38:4-7.

Now we know that the earth has no foundations, for it is a sphere and hung upon nothing, as Job well knew. Job 26:7. The building referred to in the above passage must therefore be one with which Job was familiar. And to what can it better refer than to the Great Pyramid of which, as we shall see, Job was the probable builder, for what other form of building is there that has FOUR FOUNDATION STONES, and a CAPSTONE, or HEAD CORNER-STONE, but a pyramid? In the above passage the "Foundations" are distinct from the "Corner-Stone," and it was not until the building was completed by the laying of the chief "CORNER" or "CAPSTONE," that the "SONS OF GOD," the angels, shouted for joy, as doubtless did the builders of the "Great Pyramid" when it was finished and dedicated.

The Great Pyramid is the only form of building that conforms to the symbolic description of the "SPIRITUAL BUILDING," spoken of in Scripture, of which Christ is said to be the "CHIEF CORNER-STONE."

"Ye are built upon the FOUNDATION OF THE APOSTLES AND PROPHETS, Jesus Christ Himself being the

'CHIEF CORNER-STONE';

in whom all the building fitly framed together groweth unto an 'HOLY TEMPLE' in the Lord; in whom ye also are builded together, for an

'HABITATION OF GOD'

through the Spirit." Eph. 2:21-22.

There is no "CHIEF CORNER-STONE" in architectural construction but in a building of Pyramidal form, and in shape it is exactly like the building it tops out. To its angles is "ALL THE BUILDING FITLY FRAMED TOGETHER." Being five-sided there is no place for it in the building until the finishing touch is given, and therefore the builders rejected it until needed. So we read of Christ—"The stone, which the builders DISALLOWED (REFUSED Psa. 118:22), the same is made the HEAD OF THE CORNER ("Chief Corner-Stone" Verse 6), and a 'STONE OF

STUMBLING,' and a 'ROCK OF OFFENCE.'" 1 Pet. 2:7-8. Rom. 9:32-33. The "Capstone" of a pyramid until needed would be in the way, and a "Stone of Stumbling," and "Rock of Offence" to the workmen. So with Christ. Paul says—"We preach Christ crucified, unto the Jews a 'STUMBLING BLOCK,' and unto the Greeks 'FOOLISHNESS,'" or a "Rock of Offence." 1 Cor. 1:23.

The "Capstone" of a pyramid is 5 sided and 5 pointed, with one sharp point always sticking up. Anyone falling on it would be "broken" or injured, and when on its way to its lofty position, were it to fall on anyone, it would "GRIND HIM TO POWDER." Matt. 21:42-44. From what has been said we see that the Great Pyramid is symbolic of the Spiritual Building of which Christ is the "Chief Capstone."

THE GREAT PYRAMID AND DISPENSATIONAL TRUTH

Here we must tread softly lest we be charged with "Time Setting" and subject ourselves and our subject to ridicule. The interior measurements, while carefully and accurately made, can only be used approximately, for there are other things to be taken into account in drawing conclusions from them. All we shall essay to do is in broad outlines to suggest what the interior arrangement of passageways and chambers may be intended to teach Dispensationally, leaving to others who may come after to verify them.

As the polished descending passageway (B B) pointed in B. C. 2170, the date of the building of the Pyramid, to "ALPHA DRACONIS," the "chief star" in the Constellation of the "DRAGON" or "GREAT SERPENT," we see that the Pyramid reveals the existence of the "DEVIL," and as the passageway continues downward to an unfinished Chamber (H), which may be intended to represent "Hell," we see that mankind, marching down that passage, would be under the sign and dominion of the Dragon with "Hell" as their destination.

About quarter way down the descending passageway we come to an ascending passage (D). This seems to indicate an upward trend of a part of the human race, and is believed by many to represent the period from the Exodus to the Birth of Christ.

The "Grand Gallery" is supposed to represent the Dispensation from the Birth of Christ to the Rapture of the Church. Measured in Pyramid inches the length of the Grand Gallery is 1882 inches, and if each inch stood for a year, that would make this Dispensation 1882 years long. But it is already 1920+ years long, and this shows us that we have not yet discovered the unit of measurement if we are going to use the measurements of the interior passageways and chambers to set dates. There are, however, several striking things connected with the "Grand Gallery." If the commencement of the "Grand Gallery" indicates the Birth of Christ, we have to measure but about 30 inches before we come to the mouth of an open well, that leads downward by a serpentine passage to the chamber "H." At "S" this well opens into a wide cavern.

The edges of the mouth of the well are ragged, as if its cover had been violently forced upward from below. The well then may represent the grave, and the open and ragged mouth the Resurrection of Christ, who could not be "holden of death," and the cavern ("S") the "UNDERWORLD," where His soul and spirit went to meet the penitent thief in its Paradise compartment. See the chapter on "The Spirit World." The seven overhanging courses of stone that form the sides of the "Grand Gallery" may represent the "Seven Church Periods." If the "Grand Gallery" represents the present Dispensation, and the low horizontal passageway ("T"), in which it ends, represents the "Tribulation," then we would naturally expect some outlet from the "Grand Gallery" for the "Rapture of the Church." Upon investigation, such an opening was found in a corner of the ceiling leading into the open spaces over the ceiling of the "King's Chamber." See ("R"). This opening was filled with the remains of bats, showing that only winged beings could find an exit there.

The end wall of the "Grand Gallery" at this point leans inward as if to indicate that the Rapture of the Church will precede by some years the "Tribulation Period." That the "Grand Gallery" was constructed with such grand proportions, out of all harmony with the "Tomb Theory," seems to indicate that it was constructed with special reference to the Present Dispensation.

If the low passageway ("T") represents the "Tribulation," and the "Ante-Room" ("M"), the "Millennium," the low passageway ("P"), represents the Apostasy of Gog and Magog at the close of the Millennium, and the "King's Chamber" ("K") the New Heavens and the New Earth, or the Eternal State.

The "King's Chamber" is so called because it was supposed to have been built to contain the body of the King, and the "Queen's Chamber" to hold the body of the Queen. But as we have seen the Great Pyramid was not constructed for a tomb. In the "King's Chamber" we find the only article of furniture in the Pyramid, a "COFFER." It is a lidless, empty box, cut from a solid block of red granite, and polished within and without, but without ornamentation or inscription. Its inside length and width is large enough to receive the Sarcophagus of a man 6 feet tall, but there is no indication of its ever being used for that purpose. The remarkable thing about it is, that its interior capacity is exactly equal to that of the Ark of the Covenant of the Tabernacle, or one-fiftieth of Solomon's molten sea. Here again we note an agreement between the Pyramid and the Scriptures, as if the "Coffer" and the "Ark of the Covenant" were designed by the same Divine Architect.

Says Dr. Seiss, "If the Pyramid was built to symbolize spiritual things, we should naturally look for some chamber or room representing the 'NEW JERUSALEM'." No such chamber has as yet been found, though there is evidence of the existence of an as yet undiscovered chamber. Among the debris of building material fragments of a green and white "DIORITE" stone have been found, and no stone of that kind has as yet been found anywhere in the Pyramid. If such a chamber exists it will probably be found on the 100th layer of masonry, on the vertical line of the Pyramid ("N"), and cubical in form with 3 entrances on a side.

From the mouth of the well ("W") a horizontal passageway ("J") leads to the chamber ("Q"), called the "Queen's Chamber." One-seventh of the way from the "Queen's Chamber" it drops to a lower level and forms the unfinished floor of the "Queen's Chamber." This horizontal passageway is supposed to represent the Jews in their present dispersed condition, and the beginning of the passageway about 70 inches from the commencement of the "Grand Gallery," the date of their dispersion, A. D. 70. The fact that this low horizontal passageway terminates in the "Queen's Chamber" seems to confirm the teaching of Scripture that the Jews will again become a great and leading nation.

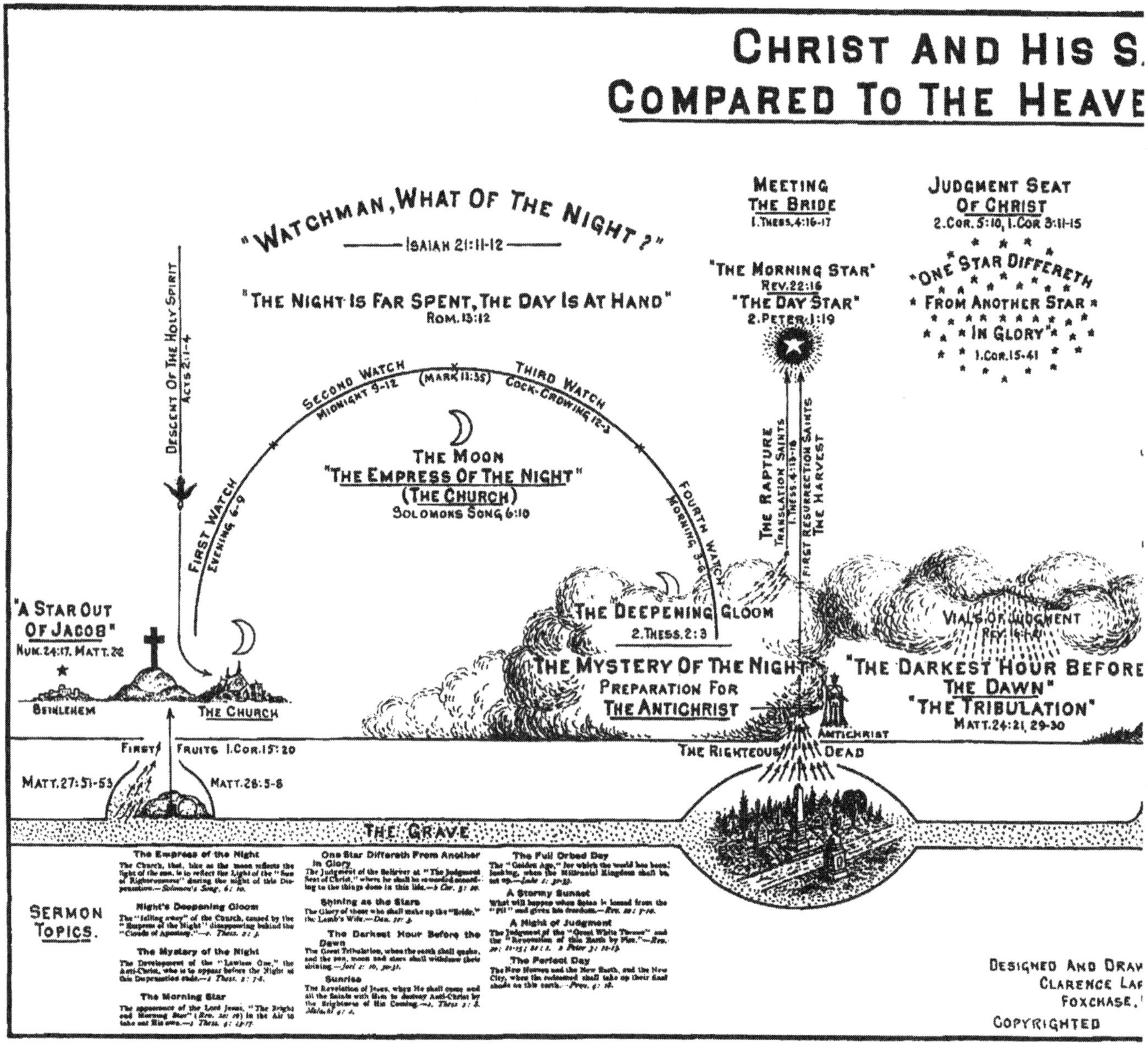

CHRIST AND HIS S.
COMPARED TO THE HEAVE
"WATCHMAN, WHAT OF THE NIGHT?"
ISAIAH 21:11-12
"THE NIGHT IS FAR SPENT, THE DAY IS AT HAND"
ROM. 13:12
MEETING THE BRIDE
I. THESS. 4:16-17
"THE MORNING STAR"
REV. 22:16
"THE DAY STAR"
2. PETER 1:19
JUDGMENT SEAT OF CHRIST
2. COR. 5:10, I. COR 3:11-15
"ONE STAR DIFFERETH FROM ANOTHER STAR IN GLORY"
I. COR. 15-41
DESCENT OF THE HOLY SPIRIT
ACTS 2:1-4
SECOND WATCH
MIDNIGHT 9-12
(MARK 13:35)
THIRD WATCH
COCK-CROWING 12-3
FIRST WATCH
EVENING 6-9
FOURTH WATCH
MORNING 3-6
THE MOON
"THE EMPRESS OF THE NIGHT"
(THE CHURCH)
SOLOMONS SONG 6:10
THE RAPTURE
TRANSLATION SAINTS
I. THESS. 4:13-16
FIRST RESURRECTION SAINTS
THE HARVEST
"A STAR OUT OF JACOB"
NUM. 24:17. MATT. 2:2
BETHLEHEM
THE CHURCH
THE DEEPENING GLOOM
2. THESS. 2:3
THE MYSTERY OF THE NIGHT
PREPARATION FOR THE ANTICHRIST
VIALS OF JUDGMENT
"THE DARKEST HOUR BEFORE THE DAWN"
"THE TRIBULATION"
MATT. 24:21, 29-30
ANTICHRIST
FIRST FRUITS I. COR. 15:20
THE RIGHTEOUS DEAD
MATT. 27:51-53
MATT. 28:5-6
THE GRAVE
SERMON TOPICS.
The Empress of the Night
Night's Deepening Gloom
The Mystery of the Night
The Morning Star
One Star Differeth From Another in Glory
Shining as the Stars
The Darkest Hour Before the Dawn
Sunrise
The Full Orbed Day
A Stormy Sunset
A Night of Judgment
The Perfect Day
DESIGNED AND DRAW
CLARENCE LAR
FOXCHASE,
COPYRIGHTED

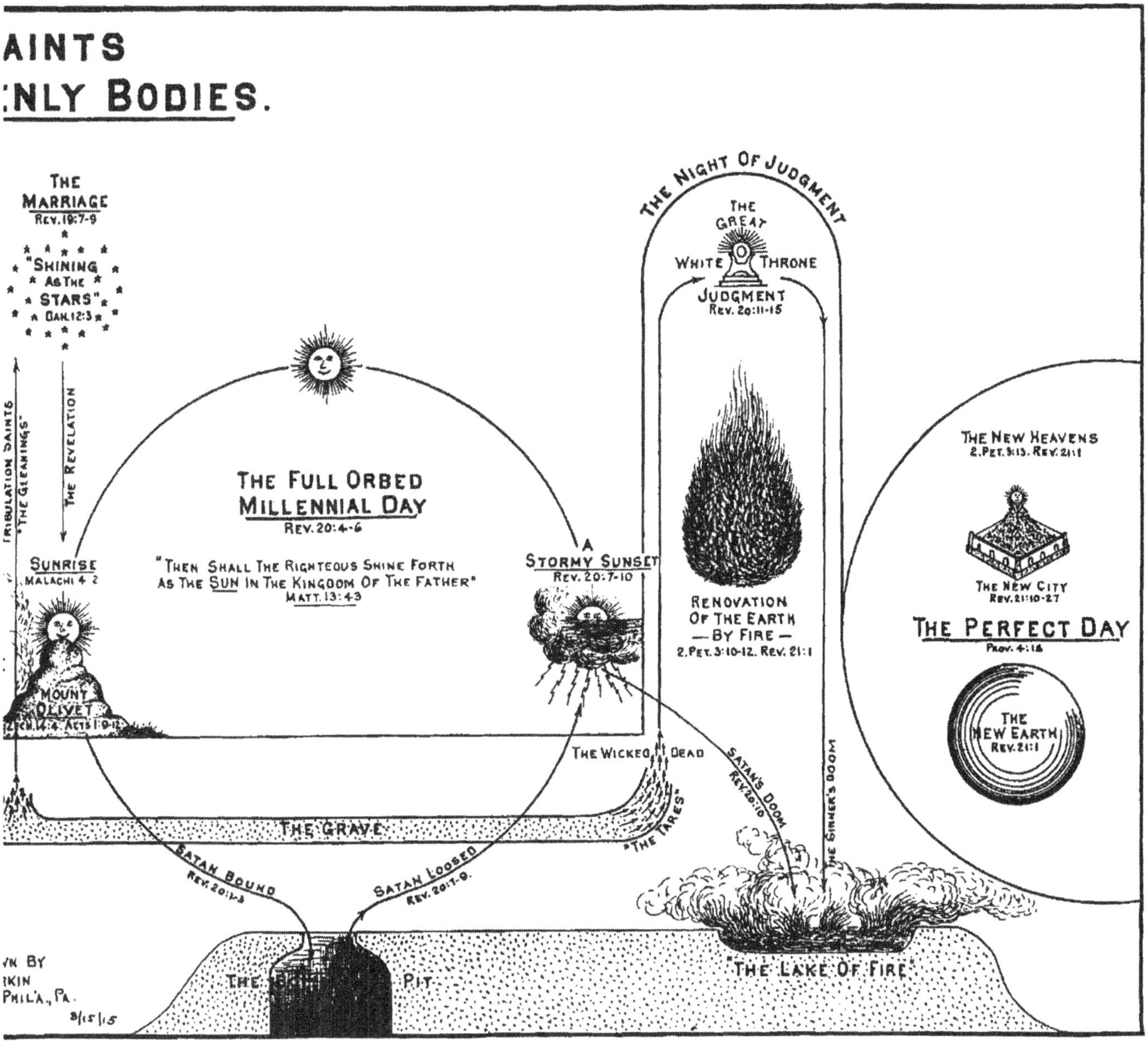
AINTS
NLY BODIES.
THE MARRIAGE
REV. 19:7-9
"SHINING AS THE STARS"
DAN. 12:3
TRIBULATION SAINTS
"THE GLEANINGS"
THE REVELATION
SUNRISE
MALACHI 4:2
MOUNT OLIVET
ZECH. 14:4 ACTS 1:9-12
THE FULL ORBED MILLENNIAL DAY
REV. 20:4-6
"THEN SHALL THE RIGHTEOUS SHINE FORTH AS THE SUN IN THE KINGDOM OF THE FATHER"
MATT. 13:43
A STORMY SUNSET
REV. 20:7-10
THE NIGHT OF JUDGMENT
THE GREAT WHITE THRONE
JUDGMENT
REV. 20:11-15
RENOVATION OF THE EARTH
— BY FIRE —
2. PET. 3:10-12. REV. 21:1
THE NEW HEAVENS
2. PET. 3:13. REV. 21:1
THE NEW CITY
REV. 21:10-27
THE PERFECT DAY
PROV. 4:18
THE NEW EARTH
REV. 21:1
THE WICKED DEAD
"THE TARES"
THE GRAVE
SATAN BOUND
REV. 20:1-3
SATAN LOOSED
REV. 20:7-8
SATAN'S DOOM
REV. 20:10
THE SINNER'S DOOM
"THE LAKE OF FIRE"
THE
PIT
WN BY
RKIN
PHIL'A, PA.
8/15/15

Paul tells us in Rom. 11:25, that **"BLINDNESS IN PART** is happened to Israel, until the fullness of the Gentiles be come in," and a remarkable thing, connected with the "Queen's Chamber," is that it was noted for its foul air and noisome smell for lack of ventilation, but in the year 1872 a visitor to the Pyramid noticed in the south wall of the Queen's Chamber a crack, into which he inserted a piece of wire that met no obstruction. A workman was sent for who, with a hammer and chisel, cut into the wall and disclosed an air tube (Y), evidently purposely made, and extending back about 7 feet, and then turning upward. The mouth of this tube, for 5 inches back from the side of the chamber, for some mysterious reason, had been filled up, and the existence of the tube left unknown. At the same location, on the opposite wall of the Chamber, a similar tube was discovered hidden behind the surface of the wall. Why were these tubes thus hidden if it were not with some symbolic intent? How beautifully then do they symbolize the blindness of the Jews that is to remain as **Scales** upon their eyes until they are converted, and as their conversion is not to be until after they have been restored to their land, symbolized by the "Queen's Chamber," we see how the removal of the scales from the mouth of the tubes beautifully symbolizes the removal of Israel's blindness. The "Queen's Chamber" might therefore well be called the **"JEWS' CHAMBER."**

The position of the "Queen's Chamber," almost directly under the ending of the "Grand Gallery," would seem to teach that the gathering back of the Jews would begin about the time of the ending of this Present Dispensation, which harmonizes with the teaching of the Scriptures.

The strange thing about the "Great Pyramid" is, that, if it were simply built for the sepulchre of a king and his wife, why does it record so many mathematical and astronomical facts, and why were the interior passageways and chambers so constructed and arranged as to harmonize with the prophetic teachings of the Scriptures?

WHO BUILT THE GREAT PYRAMID?

The "Great Pyramid" was built during the reign of Cheops, and Herodotus tells us that it took the labor of 100,000 men 20 years to build it, and that during its building the idol temples of Egypt were closed. Manetho, an Egyptian priest, records how at that time—"the Deity was displeased with us; and there came up from the East in a strange manner, men of an ignoble race, who had the confidence to invade our country and easily subdued it by their power without a battle. And when they had our rulers in their hands they demolished the temples of the gods." This state of things continued during the reign of Cheops and his successor, but when Mycerius, or Mencheres, began to reign, he re-opened the temples, and restored the worship of the gods. Manetho styled these kings, **"HYKSOS"** or "Shepherd Kings," who were reputed to be Arabians, that afterward left Egypt in large numbers and went up to Judea and built a city named Jerusalem.

Herodotus tells us that they called the pyramids after **"PHILITION,"** a shepherd who at that time fed his flocks about the place. This **"PHILITION,"** or **"PHILITIS,"** appears to have been the Architect of the Great Pyramid. He was an Arabian, but went up to Philistia in Judea with those who went up, and was known in Manetho's time as **"PHILITION,"** the Philistine. Who then was **"PHILITION"**? Some have identified him with Shem, others with Melchisedec, but the writer believes he was **"JOB."** Job was the greatest man in the East, or Arabia. Job. 1:3. His age (he lived to be nearly 250 years old) places him back before the days of Abraham (B. C. 2000), who lived to the age of 175 years, and locates him as living at the time when the Great Pyramid was built. And in the 38th chapter of Job, the Almighty speaks to Job as if he was the identical person who built the Great Pyramid, laying its foundations, and placing its "Capstone" in position, while the people shouted for joy. That Job had great meteorological and astronomical knowledge is clear from the way God spoke to him about the snow (vs. 22), and the rain vs. 25-28), and the ice (vs. 29-30), and the heavenly bodies (vs. 31-32), and the weather probabilities (vs. 33-34), and electricity (vs. 35), and there can be no question but what God would impart to such a man as Job, who was so God-fearing and spiritual, that he was both a prince and a priest, all the Scriptural and prophetical knowledge that is embodied in the arrangement of the passageways and chambers of the Great Pyramid. It does not follow, however, that Job knew the symbolic meaning of the construction of the Great Pyramid any more than the Prophets understood their prophecies. 1 Pet. 1:10-12. The Almighty may have given to Job the plan of the Great Pyramid, as Moses was given the plan of the Tabernacle and its furnishings on Mount Sinai.

There is no question but what the people of Job's day were well versed in the mechanic arts. It was not long after the Flood, and the skill of the artizans of Noah's day, and of the Babel builders had not been lost. This is evident from the Temples and Palaces of Egypt that were built in those days. But the Great Pyramid was unlike any of them. It was a new kind of Architecture, the first of its kind, and such as the world had never seen before. The plainness of its outlines, and the slope and smoothness of its sides, and the absence of all ornamentation, was a striking contrast to the Egyptian style of Architecture. Whence came it? It must have come from some source not Egyptian. Why? Because there was a purpose in its building. It was built to record mathematical, astronomical, and Scriptural knowledge, that should bear witness to the inspiration of the Scriptures in these last days. That accounts for its peculiar architectural shape, and the character of its interior construction. To that end it was sealed up that in the closing days of this Dispensation it might disclose its message to an unbelieving world.

XXXIII
SCRIPTURE NUMERICS

Every careful reader of the Holy Scriptures has had his attention called to the frequent use of certain numbers as **four, seven, ten, twelve, forty** and **seventy.** These numbers occur with more or less frequency in both the Old and New Testament and indicate that the Scriptures have a "**Numerical Structure**" that is based on the "**Symbolic significance of these numbers.**"

God has been called "**The Great Geometrician,**" and is said to do everything after a plan and by **number, weight** and **measure.** If God is the Author of the Scriptures and the Creator of the world, then the "**Word of God**" and the "**Works of God**" should harmonize.

The Scriptures reveal a "Time System" known as the "**Weeks of Scripture.**" They are "seven in number.

1. The Week of "**Days.**"
2. The Week of "**Weeks.**"
3. The Week of "**Months.**"
4. The Week of "**Years.**"
5. The Week of "**Weeks of Years.**"
6. The Week of "**Millenniums.**"
7. The Week of "**Ages.**"

See the Chart on the "Weeks of Scripture."

Now this "Scale of Weeks" is common in nature. The hen sits 3 weeks, the pigeon 2, after having laid eggs for 2 weeks. The ova of salmon is hatched in 20 weeks. Of 129 species of Mammalia the majority have a period from conception to birth of an exact number of weeks. The same is true of the human race. Fevers, and intermittent attacks of gout, ague and similar complaints have a "**Septiform Periodicity,**" and the **Seventh, Fourteenth** and **Twenty-first** days in certain diseases are known as "critical" days. Then there are 7 notes in the musical scale, 7 colors in the rainbow, 7 rays in prismatic light, and the leaves of plants are largely governed in their forms by the same Law of Sevens.

This agreement of Nature with the Scriptures cannot be a mere coincidence. It reveals the fact that they are both built on a "**Divine Plan.**"

ONE
The Number of "Unity."

It symbolizes the Unity of God. Mark 12:32. John 10:30. In Eph. 4:4-6 we have seven distinct "Unities," **One Body, One Spirit, One Hope, One Lord, One Faith, One Baptism, One God.**

TWO
The Number of "Union."

The Union of Marriage, and "they shall be one flesh." Gen. 2:23, 24. The Union of Christ and the Church. Eph. 5:31, 32. The Union of the "Two Natures" in Jesus. Luke 1:35. The Union of death and life in the Atonement of Christ, as seen in the "Two Birds" (Lev. 14:4-7), and the "Two Goats." Lev. 16:5-22. The Disciples were named in Pairs (Matt. 10:2-4) and were sent out Two by Two. Mark 6:7. There were "Two Tables" of Testimony, and "Two Witnesses" were necessary to a fair trial, and "Two Witnesses" will testify during the Tribulation. Rev. 11:3.

THREE
The Number of "Divinity."

It is called the "Divine Number" because it is mentioned so often in connection with Holy Things. It speaks of the Trinity of God—Father, Son and Holy Spirit; and the Trinity of Man—Body, Soul and Spirit; of the Three Great Feasts, the Passover, Pentecost and Tabernacles; the Threefold character of the Baptismal Formula (Matt. 28:19); of the Apostolic Benediction (2 Cor. 13:14); the Three Temptations of Christ, and His Three Prayers in Gethsemane; the Three Denials of Peter and the Lord's Threefold Question and Charge, and the Threefold Vision of the Sheet. The number Three is also associated with the Restoration of Israel (Hosea 6:1, 2), the Resurrection of Jonah, and the Resurrection of Christ. Matt. 12:38-40. The number Three is very prominent in the Threefold ascriptions in the Book of Revelation. Jesus Christ is spoken of as He which **is and was and is to come**; as the "**Faithful Witness,**" the "**First Begotten From the Dead,**" and the "**Prince of the Kings of the Earth.**" The four "Living Creatures" chant "Holy, Holy, Holy" unto the Almighty, and give Him "Glory," and "Honor" and "Thanks." The Book is divided into "Three Parts." There are Three "Woe Trumpets," and Three "Froglike Spirits" issue from the mouth of the Dragon, the mouth of the Beast, and the mouth of the False Prophet. Rev. 16:13, 14.

Three plagues are to come upon Babylon, "Death," "Mourning" and "Famine" (Rev. 18:8), and "three classes" of persons shall bewail her downfall, "Kings," "Merchants" and "Seamen." These are but a few specimens of the use of the number Three in the Scriptures.

The number Three is also prominent in nature. The primary colors of "Solar Light" are Blue, Yellow and Red; and the Sun itself is a Trinity whose manifestations are Light, Heat and Chemical Rays. In nature there are Three Kingdoms, Animal, Vegetable and Mineral. Matter exists in Three forms, Gaseous, Liquid and Solid, and the great forces of nature are Gravitation, Light and Electricity. The history of the Earth between the Fall of Man and the Renovation of the Earth by Fire is divided into Three Ages, the Antediluvian, Present, and the Millennial Age, all bounded by great climatic changes.

FOUR
The Number of the "World."

The Four Seasons, Winter, Spring, Summer and Autumn. The Four points of the Compass, North, East, South and West. The Four Elements, Earth, Air, Fire and Water. The River that flowed out from the "Garden of Eden" was divided into Four Parts. Gen. 2:10-14. Ezekiel had a vision of the Cherubim. They were Four in number and each had Four Faces and Four Wings. The first face was that of a Man. The second that of a Lion, the third that of an Ox, and the fourth that of an Eagle, all of them "earthly" creatures. The great "World Powers" as revealed to the Prophet Daniel were Four in number, Babylon, Medo-Persia, Greece and Rome. The Four World Judgments to come upon the Nations are War, Famine, Pestilence and Earthquakes. Matt. 24:6, 7. Four divisions of the human race are Nations, Kindred, Peoples and Tongues. There are Four Portraits of Christ in the Four Gospels. God's Four "Sore Judgments" upon Jerusalem are the Sword, Famine, Noisome Beast and the Pestilence. The Brazen Altar had Four Sides and Four Horns, and the New Jerusalem is Foursquare.

FIVE
The Number of "Division."

This number is not of frequent occurrence. There were Five Wise and Five Foolish Virgins. Jesus fed the Multitude (Five Thousand

The Weeks Of Scripture

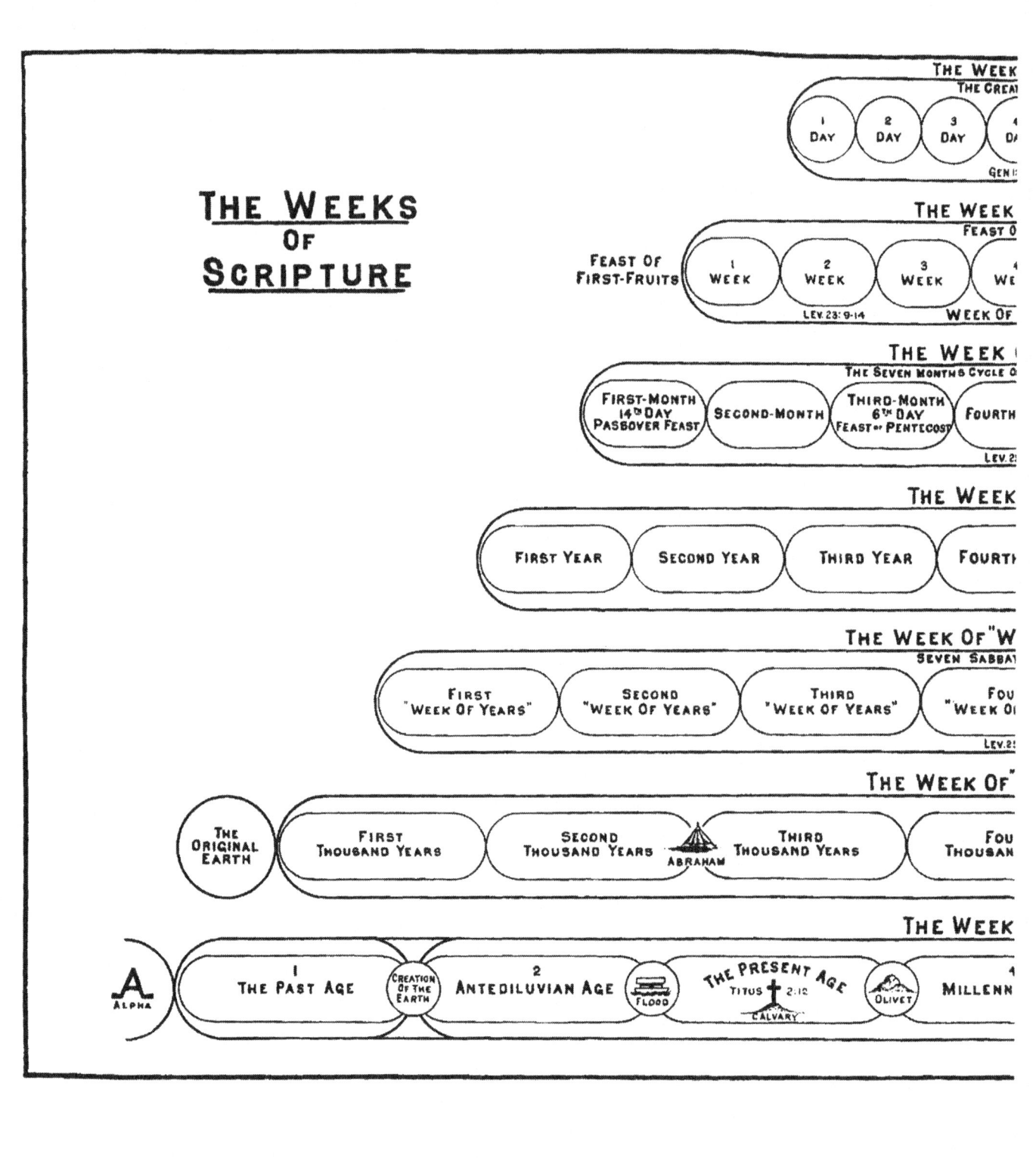

THE WEEK
THE CREA[TION]
| 1 Day | 2 Day | 3 Day | 4 DA[Y] |
GEN 1[:...]

THE WEEK
FEAST O[F]
| Feast Of First-Fruits | 1 Week | 2 Week | 3 Week | 4 We[ek] |
LEV. 23:9-14
WEEK OF

THE WEEK
THE SEVEN MONTHS CYCLE O[F]
| First-Month 14th Day Passover Feast | Second-Month | Third-Month 6th Day Feast of Pentecost | Fourth |
LEV. 2[3]

THE WEEK
| First Year | Second Year | Third Year | Fourth |

THE WEEK OF "W[EEKS]"
SEVEN SABBAT[HS]
| First "Week Of Years" | Second "Week Of Years" | Third "Week Of Years" | Fou[rth] "Week O[f Years]" |
LEV. 2[5]

THE WEEK OF
| The Original Earth | First Thousand Years | Second Thousand Years — Abraham | Third Thousand Years | Fou[rth] Thousan[d] |

THE WEEK
| A Alpha | 1 The Past Age | Creation Of The Earth | 2 Antediluvian Age | Flood | The Present Age Titus 2:12 — Calvary | Olivet | 4 Millenn[ium] |

OF "DAYS"

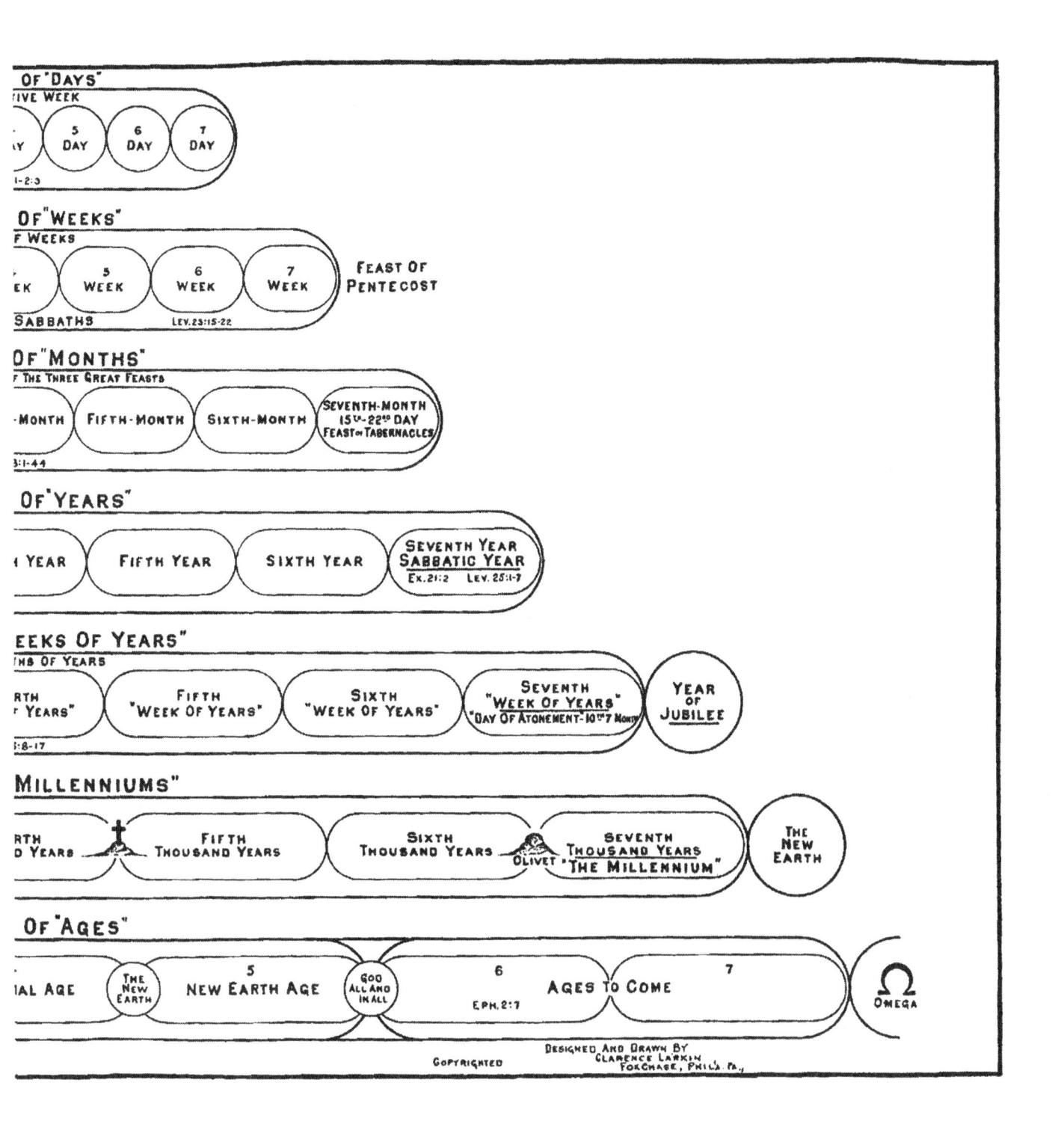

| | 5 DAY | 6 DAY | 7 DAY |

OF "WEEKS"

| 5 WEEK | 6 WEEK | 7 WEEK | FEAST OF PENTECOST

SABBATHS LEV. 23:15-22

OF "MONTHS"

| -MONTH | FIFTH-MONTH | SIXTH-MONTH | SEVENTH-MONTH 15TH-22ND DAY FEAST OF TABERNACLES |

OF "YEARS"

| YEAR | FIFTH YEAR | SIXTH YEAR | SEVENTH YEAR SABBATIC YEAR Ex. 21:2 Lev. 25:1-7 |

"WEEKS OF YEARS"

| "FIFTH WEEK OF YEARS" | SIXTH "WEEK OF YEARS" | SEVENTH "WEEK OF YEARS" "DAY OF ATONEMENT - 10TH 7 MONTH" | YEAR OF JUBILEE |

"MILLENNIUMS"

| FIFTH THOUSAND YEARS | SIXTH THOUSAND YEARS | Olivet SEVENTH THOUSAND YEARS "THE MILLENNIUM" | THE NEW EARTH |

OF "AGES"

| IAL AGE | THE NEW EARTH | 5 NEW EARTH AGE | GOD ALL AND IN ALL | 6 AGES TO COME EPH. 2:7 | 7 | Ω OMEGA |

COPYRIGHTED   DESIGNED AND DRAWN BY CLARENCE LARKIN FOX CHASE, PHIL'A. PA.

men), with Five loaves. David took Five smooth stones from the brook. There are Five digits on each hand and foot. The books of Moses are Five in number. There are Five senses.

SIX
The Number of "Man."

Man was made on the Sixth day. His appointed days of labor are Six. The Hebrew slave was to serve Six years. For Six years the land was to be sown and to rest during the seventh. The kingdoms of this world are to last for Six Thousand Years. Moses was compelled to wait for Six days on the Mount before God revealed Himself unto him. Ex. 24:15-18. Six days the Children of Israel compassed the city of Jericho before its walls fell on the seventh. Joshua 6:1-20. There were Six steps to Solomon's Throne. 1 Kings 10:19. It was Six days after Jesus foretold of His coming glory before He took His Disciples to the Mount where He was transfigured before them. Matt. 16:28-17:2. Nebuchadnezzar, a type of those who want to "deify" man, erected a "Golden Image," typical of himself, in the Plain of Dura, and commanded the rulers and people of his provinces to fall down before it and worship it under penalty of being thrown into a burning fiery furnace. Dan. 3:1-30. The dimensions of the "Image" are worthy of note. It was Sixty cubits high and Six cubits broad. It was prophetic of the "Image of the Beast" that the False Prophet will command the people to make in the day of the Beast (Antichrist) (Rev. 13:13-18), and it is significant that the "Number" of the Beast is **666**. This is the day when men are seeking the

"Deification of Man,"

and his powers, and dethroning the "Son of Man," and they will reach the consummation of their desire when they for **Commercial Reasons** (Rev. 13:15-17) will worship the Beast. This is **"Man's Day,"** and its symbol is Six, which stops short of seven.

SEVEN
The Number of "Perfection" or "Dispensational Fulness."

It is made up of the sum of 3+4=7. That is of the Divine number and the World number. It is more frequently used in the Scriptures than any other numeral. It stands for the Seventh Day of the "Creative Week," and speaks of the Millennial Rest Day.

The Sabbath was the Seventh day. Enoch was the Seventh from Adam. There were Seven days of grace after Noah entered into the Ark. Jacob served Seven years for Rachel. There were Seven years of plenty, and Seven years of famine in Egypt. At the taking of Jericho, Seven **Priests,** with Seven Trumpets, marched at the head of the people Seven times around the city. There was a Seven-Branched Candlestick in the Tabernacle. The land was to rest in the Seventh year. Solomon was Seven years in building the Temple and kept the feast for Seven days. Job had Seven sons. When his friends came to visit him they sat Seven days and Seven nights in silence, and afterward they were required to offer a Burnt Offering of Seven bullocks and Seven rams. Naaman washed Seven times in the Jordan. The blood was to be sprinkled Seven times before the Mercy Seat. Lev. 16:14. There were Seven Feasts of Jehovah, some of which lasted Seven days. The Saviour spake Seven words from the cross. Seven men of honest report were chosen to administer the alms of the Church. But it is not until we come to the Book of Revelation that we see the significance of the number Seven.

The Book is addressed to the Seven Churches of Asia by Him who stands in the midst of the Seven Golden Candlesticks, and from the Seven Spirits before His Throne, and was to be sent to the Seven Stars, or ministers of those churches. There is a Seven-Sealed Book, which is opened by a Lamb having Seven horns and Seven eyes. Seven Seals are broken. Seven Angels sound Seven Trumpets and Seven Angels pour out Seven Golden Vials containing the Seven last Plagues. There is a Beast with Seven Heads, and a Dragon with Seven Heads and Seven Crowns on the Heads. There are Seven Mountains, and in all the number Seven is mentioned upward of 50 times in the Book of Revelation. It is the Book of Sevens because it is the Book of the Consummation of all the Seven Dispensations of God's Plan and Purpose of the Ages, and ushers in the New Heaven and the New Earth, and the New City.

EIGHT
The Number of the "New Order of Things."

The Eighth Day is the beginning of a New Week. The Jewish Sabbath was on the last or Seventh Day of the week, Jesus rose on the First day of a new week or the Eighth day. His Resurrection introduced a **New Order of Things,** the Christian Sabbath and the "New Creation," or Regeneration of the Soul, and points to the New Heaven and the New Earth, which will be the Eighth Dispensation, following the Seventh or Millennial Dispensation.

God commanded Abraham to "circumcise" every male child on the Eighth day. Gen. 17:11-14. Any who were not "circumcised" were to be "cut off" from the people—the Hebrew Nation. Isaac was "circumcised" on the Eighth day. What did Circumcision symbolize? It symbolized that Abraham and his descendants were a New Race, who by Circumcision were "cut off" from the old Adamic Headship, and entered into a new relationship with God.

Noah was the Eighth person (2 Pet. 2:5), and his family consisted of Eight persons (1 Pet. 3:20), and they populated the new earth after the Flood. David was the Eighth son of Jesse, and he introduced a new order in Israel. 1 Sam. 16:10, 11. The leper was cleansed on the Eighth day from his leprosy, thus proclaiming a new man. Lev. 14:10, 23. The sheaf of "First Fruits" was to be waved before the Lord on the Eighth day, or the **"Morrow After the Sabbath"** (Lev. 23:11), and 50 days later, on the same day of the week the Feast of Pentecost was observed, which typified the sending of the Holy Spirit, Who inaugurated the new Gospel Dispensation. Lev. 23:16.

The Feast of Tabernacles lasted for seven days, but on the Eighth day a "Holy Convocation" was to be held. Lev. 23:36. The Feast of Tabernacles was the last of the three great Festivals, and came at the close of the harvest, and during it the Children of Israel dwelt in booths. It is typical of God's eternal rest.

TEN
The Number of "Worldly Completion."

It is made up of the sum of the World number 4 and 6 the Number of Man. It is probably based on the decimal system, suggested by the 10 digits of hands or feet. It was looked upon as a complete number, and was used as such in the Ten Commandments. In the parable of the Ten Virgins it gives the legal number necessary for a Jewish function. In the Ten Toes of Nebuchadnezzar's Image, and the Ten Horns of Daniel's "Fourth Beast," that point to the Ten Kings, or Kingdoms, typified by the Ten Horns of John's "Beast" (Rev. 17:3, 12), we see the summing up of Gentile power in Ten Federated Kingdoms, which will be the completion of worldly Gentile rule, and which will be destroyed by the "Stone Kingdom" of Christ. Then we have the Ten "pieces of silver" (Luke 15:8), and the Ten servants to whom were entrusted Ten pounds and one rewarded by being given authority over Ten cities (Luke 19:13, 17) and the Ten plagues of Egypt, and other uses of the number Ten scattered through the Scriptures.

TWELVE
The Number of "Eternal Perfection."

It is the product of the Divine number 3, and 4 the World number, There were Twelve Tribes of Israel; Twelve stones in the High Priest's Breastplate; Twelve cakes of Shewbread; Twelve wells of water at Elim; Twelve spies were sent into Canaan; Joshua placed Twelve stones in the bed of Jordan; Elijah built an altar of Twelve stones; Solomon's "Molten Sea" stood on Twelve brass oxen. In the New Testament we read that at Twelve years of age Jesus visited the Temple; that He chose Twelve Apostles, and that His Father would send at His request Twelve Legions of Angels. Then there was the woman who was diseased for Twelve years, and the Twelve-year-old daughter of Jairus.

In the Book of Revelation we read of the woman with a crown of Twelve stars, and that the New Jerusalem has Twelve gates and at the gates Twelve angels; that it has Twelve foundations, and in them the names of the Twelve Apostles of the Lamb; that its trees bear Twelve manner of fruits; that it lieth foursquare and measures Twelve thousand furlongs on a side, and that the height of the wall is 144 cubits, or 12×12. We are also told that in the "Regeneration" the Twelve Apostles shall sit on Twelve Thrones judging the Twelve Tribes of Israel. Matt. 19:28. Thus it is clear that in the final consummation of all things Israel and the Church shall have their place in the New Earth and the New City.

FORTY
The Number of "Probation."

At the Flood it rained Forty days and Forty nights. Moses was on probation Forty years in Egypt, Forty years in the desert, and Forty years with Israel in the Wilderness. The Spies were Forty days spying out the land and Israel wandered Forty years in the Wilderness. The reigns of Saul, David and Solomon each lasted Forty years. Goliath defied Israel for Forty days. Nineveh was given Forty days to repent. Elijah fasted Forty days and Forty nights. Jesus was tempted Forty days and appeared eleven times during Forty days after His Resurrection. Punishment by flogging was limited to Forty stripes save one. All these instances show that God was not hasty in His judgments, but gave man ample time for a fair trial.

There are other numbers mentioned in Scripture as **Seventy, One Hundred and Twenty, "One Hundred and Forty-four,"** etc., but it is not necessary to pursue the subject further as we have seen that there is a symbolism attached to the numbers of Scripture.

XXXIV
THE SIGNS OF THE TIMES

While we cannot name the exact date of the Lord's Return its nearness may be known by the **character** of the Times. As to this the New Testament gives no uncertain sound. In Dan. 12:4, 9-10, we read, "But thou, O Daniel, shut up the words, and seal the Book, even to the **'TIME OF THE END'**: many shall run to and fro, and knowledge shall be increased. . . . Go thy way, Daniel: for the words are closed up and sealed till the **'TIME OF THE END.'** Many shall be purified, and made white, and tried; but the wicked shall do wickedly; and none of the wicked shall understand; but the **WISE SHALL UNDERSTAND."** These words declare that the prophecies of Daniel were to be **"shut up"** and **"sealed"** until the **"TIME OF THE END."** This expression does not mean the **"end of Time,"** but is the angelic messenger's way of referring to the "Last Days" of the "Times of the Gentiles." At which time he declares that the Book will be **"unsealed,"** and **"knowledge shall be increased."** What is here meant is **"prophetic knowledge"** of the things recorded in the Book of Daniel and other prophetic writings of the Scriptures. This is made clear by the statement that only the **"wise"** shall understand. That is, those who are enlightened by the Holy Spirit, and not those who merely have intellectual knowledge, for the wicked **SHALL NOT UNDERSTAND.** How wonderfully this is true of these days. The Higher Critics have labored hard to discredit the Book of Daniel, but without avail, for the Book is more studied than ever, and is being **"unsealed"** by Holy Spirit enlightened students of the Word of God, who clearly see that we have reached the "Time of the End," and are living in the closing days of the "Times of the Gentiles."

The "unsealing" began about 100 years ago, when the **"Midnight Cry," "Behold, the Bridegroom Cometh,"** was heard in the "Revival of Premillennial Truth." For centuries while the Bridegroom tarried the Wise and Foolish virgins **"ALL slumbered and slept,"** and the Church lapsed into a condition of spiritual apathy, and "The Blessed Hope" was eclipsed. But now all over the world the Blessed Hope has emerged from the shadow, and the virgins are "trimming their lamps" preparatory to going out to meet their Lord, but only the "wise" have oil in their vessels and in their lamps. We are now living in the "Fourth Watch of the Night," soon the **"MORNING STAR"** (Christ. Rev. 22:16) will appear and we shall be caught out at the Rapture to meet Him and go into the Marriage Feast.

Let us take a hasty glance at the "Signs of the Times." A careful study of the Chart will reveal "Ten Signs."

1. POST-MILLENNIAL SCOFFERS.

In 2 Pet. 3:3-4 we read: "That there shall come in the **'Last Days'** SCOFFERS, walking after their own lusts, and saying, Where is the **promise of HIS COMING?** for since the fathers fell asleep, all things continue as they were from the beginning of the creation." How true this is of the present day. The Doctrine of the Second Coming is "scoffed" at, and those who hold it are looked upon as deluded fanatics, and sad to say, this opposition comes from prominent religious leaders of the Day.

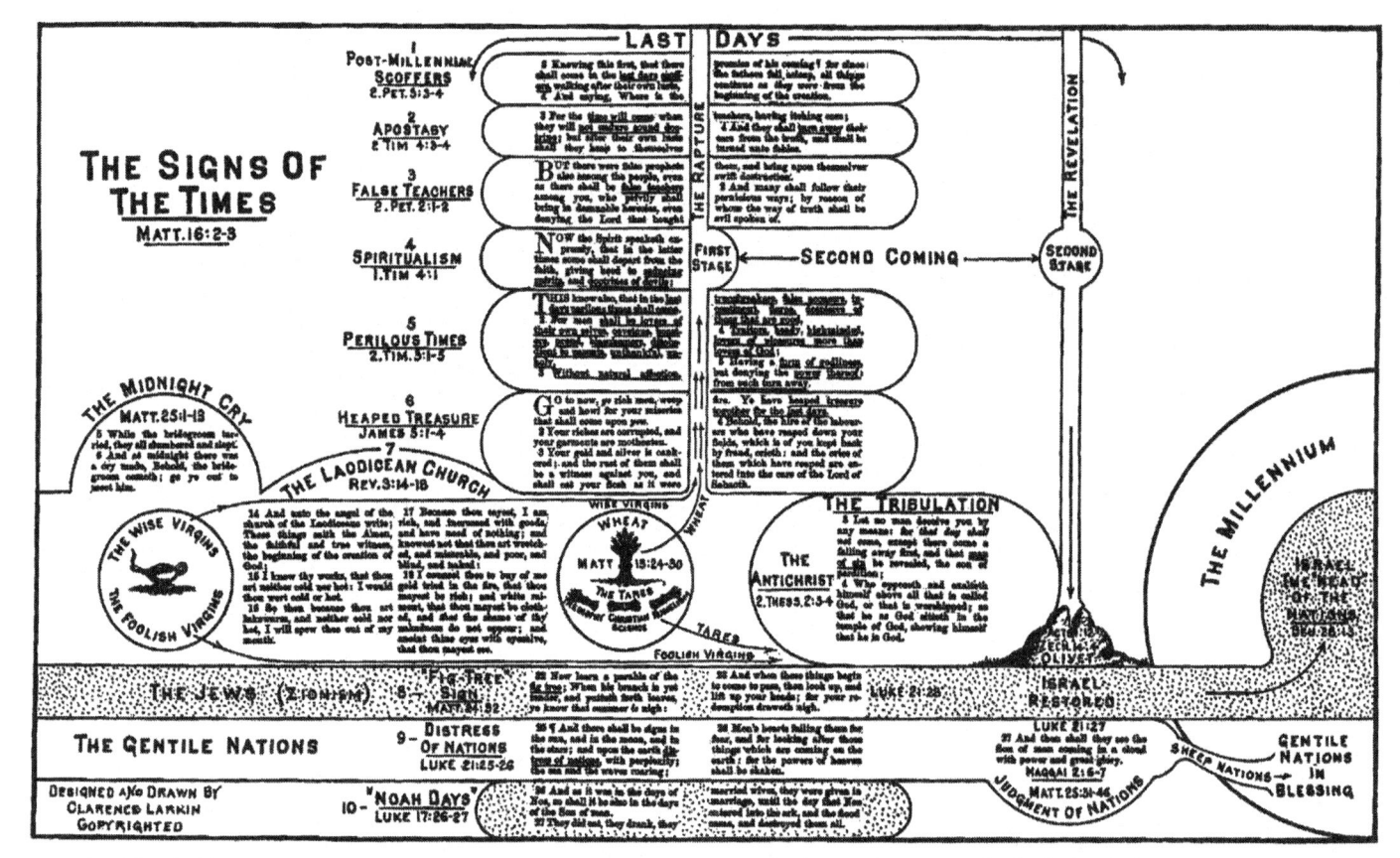

2. APOSTASY.

In 2 Thess. 2:3, we are told that **"THAT DAY** (the Day of the Lord) shall not come, except there come a **'FALLING AWAY'** first." This **"Falling Away"** is evidenced on every hand.

3. FALSE TEACHERS.

In 2 Peter 2:1-2 we are warned against "False Teachers" who shall privately bring in **"damnable heresies,"** even denying the Lord that bought them, such as Christian Scientists and Russelites, and that many shall follow their **"pernicious ways,"** and sad to relate these "followers" are recruited from the orthodox church members, of whom the Apostle Paul wrote to Timothy (2 Tim. 4:3-4), saying: "The time will come when they **will not endure sound doctrine**; but after their own lusts shall they heap to themselves teachers, having **itching ears**: and they shall turn away their ears **from the truth**, and shall be turned unto **FABLES."** This "turning away" is evidenced on every hand. There is a "turning away" in doctrinal standards, in the demand for a regenerated church membership, in church and Sunday school attendance, and in Sabbath observance. Many churchgoers will not endure "sound doctrine." They will not go to hear those who preach the "total depravity" of man, the necessity of the "New Birth," and the conscious and endless torment of those who reject Christ as a personal Saviour. They demand teachers who will **"itch"** (tickle) their ears with pleasing, novel and sensational doctrines.

4. SPIRITUALISM.

In 1 Tim. 4:1 we are warned of a departure from the faith. That in the **"Latter Times"** (the Last Days of this Dispensation), some shall **"depart from the faith, giving heed to seducing spirits and doctrines of devils."** This is being fulfilled in the increasing number of those who are forsaking their Christian belief to become followers of Spiritualistic Mediums and to dabble in Psychical Research.

5. PERILOUS TIMES.

Of these times Paul told Timothy. "This know also, that in the **'LAST DAYS'** Perilous Times shall come. For men shall be

174

lovers of their own selves, covetous, boasters, proud, blasphemers, disobedient to parents, unthankful, unholy, without natural affection (for their own offspring), truce breakers, false accusers, incontinent, fierce, despisers of those who are good, traitors, heady, highminded, lovers of pleasures more than lovers of God; having a **FORM of godliness,** but denying the **POWER thereof.**" 2 Tim. 3:1-5. We have neither time nor space to enlarge upon the above, but what a catalogue we have here of the "perilous conditions" of the times in which we live.

6. HEAPED UP TREASURE.

In James 5:1-6, we are told that in the **"LAST DAYS"** there shall be a class of "rich men," who shall have **"HEAPED treasure together,"** and that by **"FRAUD,"** and who shall use their ill-gotten gain in the pursuit of "pleasure" and "wantonness," and that God will hear the cry of those who have been cheated of their just share of the profits, and will send a sore judgment upon the guilty. What a description we have here of the unprincipled, speculative and profiteering spirit of the days in which we live, when men become millionaires, and multi-millionaires, in a few years. Truly we are living in the "Last Days" of this Dispensation.

7. A LAODICEAN CHURCH.

In the Message to the Church of Laodicea (Rev. 3:14-22) we have a description of the last stage of the professing Church on earth. It is described as neither "hot" nor "cold," but nauseatingly lukewarm, so that Christ says He will "spue it out of His mouth." It boastingly will claim to be "rich" and "increased with goods," and to have "need of nothing," not even of Christ, for He will be excluded and will have to knock for admittance, and it will be ignorant of its true condition, that it is **wretched,** and **miserable,** and **poor,** and **blind** and **naked.** Unspeakably sad it is that this is the condition to a large extent of the professing Church of today.

8. THE FIG-TREE SIGN.

When Jesus' Disciples asked Him, after He had foretold the destruction of the Temple: "Tell us, when shall these things be? and what shall be the **SIGN of THY COMING,** and of the end of the world (Age)?" (Matt. 24:1-3), Jesus gave as a "Sign" of His Coming the "Fig-Tree Sign." The "Fig-Tree" symbolizes the nation of Israel, and its "budding" the revival of Israel as a nation. Here again we have evidence of the nearness of the Lord's Return for the revival of Zionism, and the passing of the Land of Palestine into the hands of a Christian nation, opens the way for the restoration of the Jews to their own land, and the fulfillment of the Fig-Tree Sign. The fact that the City of Jerusalem surrendered without the firing of a shot is significant. Jesus said that Jerusalem was to be trodden down of the Gentiles until "The Times of the Gentiles" should be fulfilled (Luke 21:24), and the taking of Jerusalem at this time may signify that "The Times of the Gentiles" is drawing to a close.

9. THE DISTRESS OF NATIONS.

In Luke 21:24-27 Jesus tells us that as the "Times of the Gentiles" come to a close, "there shall be signs in the sun, and in the moon, and in the stars; and upon the earth **DISTRESS OF NATIONS,** with **perplexity;** the sea and the waves (the peoples of the earth) roaring; men's hearts **failing them for fear,** and for looking after those things which are coming on the earth: for the 'Powers of Heaven' (the Principalities and Powers of Evil, Eph. 6:11-12), shall be shaken. And **THEN** shall they see the Son of Man coming in a cloud with power and great glory." In the prophecy of Haggai 2:6-7, we read: "Thus saith the Lord of hosts; yet once, it is a **little while,** and I will shake the heavens, and the earth, and the sea, and the dry land; and I will **SHAKE ALL NATIONS,** and the **DESIRE** (Christ) **OF ALL NATIONS WILL COME."** This has never been fulfilled as yet, and the present **"Distress of Nations,"** the uprising of the masses in "National Revolutions," the "Tottering Thrones" and other indications that the nations are **Being Shaken,** is still further proof that we are living in the times just preceding the appearing of the Son of Man, the **"DESIRE OF ALL NATIONS",** who will bring peace to this troubled earth.

10. NOAH DAYS.

The last "sign" that we would mention is the "sign" of the "Noah Days." Luke 17:26-30. As it was in the days of Noah, they did eat, they drank, they married wives, they were given in marriage, they bought, they sold, they planted, they builded, so shall it be in the days of the Son of Man. Where, you say, is the sin in doing these things? They are not only commanded, they are necessary. That is true. The sin was not in "doing" them, but in doing them **"UNTIL the Flood came."** That is, they did nothing else. They forgot to worship their Maker. So today men and women are so busily engaged in doing the good things of life that they have no time to worship God. They are so busy building homes for themselves on earth that they are neglecting to secure a home in heaven. They are more anxious that their children should make a good match on earth, than that they should be united to the Lord. They are so much concerned about their case in Court, that they have forgotten that they must stand at the Judgment Bar of God.

HE SHALL COME

"What I say unto you I say unto all, Watch."
"At even, or at midnight, or at the cock-crowing."

It may be in the evening,
When the work of the day is done,
And you have time to sit in the twilight,
And to watch the sinking sun;
While the long bright day dies slowly
    Over the sea,
And the hour grows quiet and holy
    With thoughts of **Me**;
While you hear the village children
    Passing along the street,
Among these thronging footsteps
May come the sound of **My** feet;
    Therefore I tell you, watch!
By the light of the evening star,
When the room is growing dusky
    As the clouds afar;
Let the door be on the latch
    In your home,
For it may be through the gloaming,
    I will come.

It may be in the midnight
When 'tis heavy upon the land,
And the black waves lying dumbly
    Along the sand;
When the moonless night draws close
And the lights are out in the house,
When the fires burn low and red,
And the watch is ticking loudly
    Beside the bed;
Though you sleep tired on your couch,
Still your heart must wake and watch
    In the dark room;
For it may be that at midnight
    I will come.

It may be at the cock-crow,
When the night is dying slowly
    In the sky,
And the sea looks calm and holy,
Waiting for the dawn of the golden sun
    Which draweth nigh;
When the mists are on the valleys, shading,
    The rivers chill,
And my morning star is fading, fading
    Over the hill;
Behold, I say unto you, watch!

Let the door be on the latch
    In your home,
In the chill before the dawning,
Between the night and morning,
    I may come.

It may be in the morning
When the sun is bright and strong,
And the dew is glittering sharply
    Over the little lawn,
When the waves are laughing loudly
    Along the shore,
And the little birds are singing sweetly
    About the door;
With the long day's work before you
    You are up with the sun,
And the neighbors come to talk a little
    Of all that must be done;
But, remember, that I may be the next
    To come in at the door,
To call you from your busy work,
    For evermore.
As you work, your heart must watch,
For the door is on the latch
    In your room,
And it may be in the morning
    I will come.

So I am watching quietly
    Every day,
Whenever the sun shines brightly
    I rise and say,
Surely it is the shining of His face,
And look unto the gate of His high place
    Beyond the sea,
For I know He is coming shortly
    To summon me;
And when a shadow falls across the window
    Of my room,
Where I am working my appointed task,
I lift my head to watch the door and ask
    If He is come!
And the Spirit answers softly
    In my home,
"Only a few more shadows,
    And He will come."

—Selected.